Rick Steves®

ROME

Rick Steves & Gene Openshaw

2015

CONTENTS

Rick Steves

ROME
2015

VILLA
BORGHESE

VATICAN
MUSEUM

TERMINI TRAIN
STATION

SPANISH
STEPS

ST. PETER'S

PANTHEON

PIAZZA
VENEZIA

TREVI
FOUNTAIN

Tiber

GHETTO

TRAJAN'S
COLUMN

FORUM

TRASTEVERE

COLOSSEUM

SAN GIOVANNI
IN LATERANO

APPIAN
WAY

INTRODUCTION

Rome is magnificent and brutal at the same time. It's a showcase of Western civilization, with astonishingly ancient sights and a modern vibrancy. But if you're careless, you'll be run down or pick-pocketed. And with the wrong attitude, you'll be frustrated by the kind of chaos that only an Italian can understand. On my last visit, a cabbie struggling with the traffic said, *"Roma chaos."* I responded, *"Bella chaos."* He agreed.

While Paris is an urban garden, Rome is a magnificent tangled forest. If your hotel provides a comfortable refuge; if you pace yourself; if you accept—and even partake in—the siesta plan; if you're well-organized for sightseeing; and if you protect yourself and your valuables with extra caution and discretion, you'll love it. (And Rome is much easier to live with if you can avoid the mid-summer heat.)

For me, Rome is in a three-way tie with Paris and London as Europe's greatest city. Two thousand years ago the word "Rome" meant civilization itself. Everything was either civilized (part of the Roman Empire, Latin- or Greek-speaking) or barbarian. Today, Rome is Italy's political capital, the capital of Catholicism, and the center of its ancient empire, littered with evocative remains. As you peel through its fascinating and jumbled layers, you'll find Rome's buildings, cats, laundry, traffic, and 2.7 million people endlessly entertaining. And then, of course, there are its stupendous sights.

Visit St. Peter's, the greatest church on earth, and scale Michelangelo's 448-foot-tall dome, the world's tallest. Learn something about eternity by touring the huge Vatican Museum. You'll find the story of creation—bright as the day it was painted—in the restored Sistine Chapel. Do the "Caesar Shuffle" through ancient Rome's Forum and Colosseum. Savor Europe's most sumptuous building, the Borghese Gallery, and take an early evening Dolce

Map Legend

⅄ Viewpoint	✈ Airport	Tunnel
↟ Entrance	Ⓣ Taxi Stand	Pedestrian Zone
✚ Tourist Info	Ⓣ Tram Stop	Railway
WC Restroom	Ⓑ Bus Stop	Ferry/Boat Route
Castle	Ⓜ Metro Stop	Tram
Church	Ⓟ Parking	Stairs
▪ Statue/Point of Interest	Gelato	Walk/Tour Route
⊠ Elevator	Park	Trail

Use this legend to help you navigate the maps in this book.

Vita Stroll down Via del Corso with Rome's beautiful people. Enjoy an after-dark walk from Campo de' Fiori to the Spanish Steps, lacing together Rome's Baroque and bubbly nightspots. Dine well at least once.

ABOUT THIS BOOK

Rick Steves Rome 2015 is a personal tour guide in your pocket. Better yet, it's actually two tour guides in your pocket: The co-author of this book is Gene Openshaw. Since our first "Europe through the gutter" trip together as high school buddies in the 1970s, Gene and I have been exploring the wonders of the Old World. An inquisitive historian and lover of European culture, Gene wrote most of this book's self-guided museum tours and neighborhood walks. Together, Gene and I keep this book current (though for simplicity, from this point "we" will shed our respective egos and become "I").

In this book, you'll find the following chapters:

Orientation to Rome includes specifics on public transportation, helpful hints, local tour options, easy-to-read maps, and tourist information. The "Planning Your Time" section suggests a schedule for how to best use your limited time.

Sights in Rome describes the top attractions and includes their cost and hours.

The **Self-Guided Walks and Tours** lead you through the heart of Rome, connecting the great monuments and atmospheric squares. You'll tour the Pantheon, Colosseum, Roman Forum, Palatine Hill, and Capitoline Museums. You'll visit the pilgrimage churches, including the grandest of all—St. Peter's. You'll see the Vatican Museum, Borghese Gallery, National Museum of Rome, and St. Peter-in-Chains Church. You'll explore Trastevere, the heart of the crusty, colorful neighborhood across the river; learn

Key to This Book

Updates

This book is updated every year—but once you pin down Italy, it wiggles. For the latest, visit www.ricksteves.com/update.

Abbreviations and Times

I use the following symbols and abbreviations in this book:

Sights are rated:

 Don't miss

▲▲ Try hard to see

▲ Worthwhile if you can make it

No rating   Worth knowing about

Tourist information offices are abbreviated as TIs, and bathrooms are **WC**s. To categorize accommodations, I use a **Sleep Code** (described on page 346).

Like Europe, this book uses the **24-hour clock.** It's the same through 12:00 noon, then keeps going: 13:00, 14:00, and so on. For anything over 12, subtract 12 and add p.m. (14:00 is 2:00 p.m.).

When giving **opening times,** I include both peak season and off-season hours if they differ. So, if a museum is listed as "May-Oct daily 9:00-16:00," it should be open from 9 a.m. until 4 p.m. from the first day of May until the last day of October (but expect exceptions).

If you see a ✪ symbol near a sight listing, it means that sight is described in far greater detail elsewhere—either with its own self-guided tour, or as part of a self-guided walk.

For **transit** or **tour departures,** I first list the frequency, then the duration. So, a train connection listed as "2/hour, 1.5 hours" departs twice each hour and the journey lasts an hour and a half.

about the Jewish Ghetto, the city's medieval Jewish quarter; and take a spin on the ancient Appian Way.

Sleeping in Rome describes my favorite hotels, from good-value deals to cushy splurges, mainly in several convenient (and for Rome, relatively quiet) neighborhoods near the sights.

Eating in Rome serves up a range of options, from inexpensive cafés to fancy restaurants.

Rome with Children includes my top recommendations for keeping your kids (and you) happy.

Shopping in Rome gives you tips for shopping painlessly and enjoyably, without letting it overwhelm your vacation or ruin your budget.

Nightlife in Rome is your guide to fun, including concerts, nightclubs, and my Dolce Vita Stroll.

Rome Connections lays the groundwork for your smooth

arrival and departure, covering transportation by train, bus, car, plane, and cruise ship, with detailed information on Rome's two airports (Fiumicino and Ciampino) and its two train stations (the main Termini Station and smaller Tiburtina).

Day Trips cover nearby sights: Ostia Antica, Tivoli, Naples, and Pompeii.

The **Roman History** chapter takes you on a whirlwind tour through the ages, covering three millennia from ancient Rome to the city today.

Practicalities is a traveler's tool kit, with our best travel tips and advice about money, sightseeing, staying connected, and transportation. There's also a list of recommended books and films.

The **appendix** has nuts-and-bolts information, including useful phone numbers and websites, a festival list, a climate chart, a handy packing checklist, and Italian survival phrases.

Browse through this book and select your favorite sights. Then have a great trip! Traveling like a temporary local, you'll get the absolute most out of every mile, minute, and dollar. As you visit places I know and love, I'm happy that you'll be meeting my favorite Romans.

Planning

This section will help you get started planning your trip—with advice on trip costs, when to go, and what you should know before you take off.

TRAVEL SMART

Many people travel through Italy thinking it's a chaotic mess. They feel that any attempt at efficient travel is futile. This is dead wrong—and expensive. Rome, which seems as orderly as spilled spaghetti, actually functions well. Only those who understand this and travel smart can enjoy Rome on a budget.

This book can save you lots of time and money. But to have an "A" trip, you need to be an "A" student. Read it all before your trip, noting holidays, specific advice on sights, and days when sights are closed. For instance, to see the Borghese Gallery, you must reserve ahead. If you go to the Vatican Museum on a Sunday, you'll run smack into closed doors, or—if it's the last Sunday of the month—huge crowds. You can wait an hour to buy a ticket at the Colosseum, or save time by buying your ticket online or at the nearby Palatine Hill. Day-tripping to Ostia Antica on Monday is bad news. A smart trip is a puzzle—a fun, doable, and worthwhile challenge.

When you're plotting your itinerary, strive for a mix of intense and relaxed stretches. Every trip—and every traveler—needs slack time (laundry, picnics, people-watching, and so on). Pace yourself. Assume you will return.

Update your plans as you travel. You can carry a small mobile device (phone, tablet, laptop) to find out tourist information, learn the latest on sights (special events, tour schedule, etc.), book tickets and tours, make reservations, reconfirm hotels, research transportation connections, and keep in touch with your loved ones. If you don't want to bring a pricey device, you can use guest computers at hotels and make phone calls from landlines.

Enjoy the friendliness of the Roman people. Connect with the culture. Set up your own quest for the best piazza, church facade, or gelato. Slow down and be open to unexpected experiences. Ask questions—most locals are eager to point you in their idea of the right direction. Keep a notepad in your pocket for noting directions, organizing your thoughts, and confirming prices. Wear your money belt, learn the currency, and figure out how to estimate prices in dollars. Those who expect to travel smart, do.

TRIP COSTS

Six components make up your trip costs: airfare, surface transportation, room and board, sightseeing/entertainment, shopping/miscellany, and gelato.

Airfare: A basic round-trip flight from the US to Rome can cost, on average, about $1,000-2,000 total, depending on where you fly from and when (cheaper in winter). If Rome is part of a longer trip, consider saving time and money in Europe by flying into one city and out of another; for instance, into Rome and out of Paris. Overall, Kayak.com is the best place to start searching for flights on a combination of mainstream and budget carriers.

Surface Transportation: For a typical one-week visit, allow $60 to $100 for taxis (which can be shared by up to four people); if you opt for buses and the Metro, figure about $25 per person. The cost of round-trip transportation to day-trip destinations ranges from minimal (a few dollars to get to Tivoli or Ostia Antica) to pricey ($90 for second-class train tickets for a day trip to Naples and Pompeii—book a month in advance for deals). For a one-way trip between Rome's main airport and the city center, allow $20 per person by train or about $60 by taxi (can be shared by up to 4 people). For more on trains, buses, and car rentals, see "Transportation" in the Practicalities chapter.

Room and Board: You can manage comfortably in Rome in 2015 on $145 a day per person for room and board. This allows $15 for lunch, $30 for dinner, and $100 for lodging (based on two people splitting the cost of a $200 double room). Students and tightwads can enjoy Rome for as little as $65 a day ($35 for a hostel bed, $30 for meals and snacks).

Rome Almanac

Population: Approximately 2.7 million people

Currency: Euro (€)

Nickname: The Eternal City

City Layout: Rome, the capital of Italy, is divided into 22 *rioni* (districts). Of the famous seven hills of Rome, you're most likely to see Palatine Hill (birthplace of the legendary founders of the city, Romulus and Remus), Capitoline Hill (topped by museums and a Michelangelo-designed square), and the Quirinale, one of the highest of the hills and the site of many of my recommended hotels.

Best Viewpoints: From the rooftop of the Victor Emmanuel Monument (you can take the Rome from the Sky elevator to the top); from the top of the dome of St. Peter's Basilica; and from the top of Castel Sant'Angelo. The best view of the Roman Forum is from Capitoline Hill—particularly the Tabularium (underground galleries) that are part of the Capitoline Museums.

Best Strolls: Two major thoroughfares are opened to pedestrians and closed to traffic at certain times: the northern part of the Via del Corso in the early evening (Mon-Sat around 17:00-19:00, earlier afternoon on Sun) and the southern part of Via dei Fori Imperiali (daily except for buses and taxis). My two favorite walks in Rome take me through Trastevere, and through the heart of the city at night. The Monti area (near the Roman Forum) is another enjoyable area to wander.

Tourist Tracks: The Colosseum attracts about 4 million visitors every year. About €3,000 is collected from the Trevi Fountain daily.

Culture Count: The vast majority of Romans are indigenous Italians; only about 10 percent of the city's residents are immigrants, mostly from Poland, Romania, Ukraine, and Albania. Rome's population is largely Roman Catholic (90 percent).

Average Roman: The average Roman is 44 years old, has 1.4 children, and will live until the age of 82. Romans consume enough wine to average one bottle per person per day.

Sightseeing and Entertainment: Figure about $17-21 per major sight (Colosseum, Vatican Museum), $2 for minor ones (lights to illuminate art in churches), and $30 for splurge experiences (such as concerts). An overall average of $20 per day works for most people. Don't skimp here. After all, this category is the driving force behind your trip—you came to sightsee, enjoy, and experience Rome.

Shopping and Miscellany: Figure $3 per postcard and $5 per coffee, soft drink, and gelato. Shopping can vary in cost from nearly nothing to a small fortune. Good budget travelers find that this category has little to do with assembling a trip full of lifelong and wonderful memories.

WHEN TO GO

Rome's best travel months (also busiest and most expensive) are April, May, June, September, October, and early November. These months combine the convenience of peak season with pleasant weather.

The most grueling thing about travel in Rome is the summer heat in July and August, when temperatures can soar to the high 90s and pricier hotels discount their rooms. Fortunately air-conditioning is the norm in all but the cheapest hotels (though it's generally available only from June through September).

Spring and fall can be cool, and many hotels do not turn on their heat. Rome is fine in winter—cold and crisp with temperatures in the 40s and 50s (for more information, see the climate chart in the appendix). Off-season has none of the sweat and stress of the tourist season, but sights may have shorter hours, lunchtime breaks, and fewer activities. Confirm your sightseeing plans locally, especially when traveling off-season.

KNOW BEFORE YOU GO

Your trip is more likely to go smoothly if you plan ahead. Check this list of things to arrange while you're still at home.

You need a **passport**—but no visa or shots—to travel in Italy. You may be denied entry into certain European countries if your passport is due to expire within three months of your ticketed date of return. Get it renewed if you'll be cutting it close. It can take up to six weeks to get or renew a passport (for more on passports, see www.travel.state.gov). Pack a photocopy of your passport in your luggage in case the original is lost or stolen.

Book rooms well in advance if you'll be traveling during the peak of summer season and any major **holidays** (see page 566).

While plenty of the city's sights can be nearly empty, the famous ones come with very long lines. These lines are entirely avoidable if you follow the directions in this book to **get tickets or make reservations in advance** (for the Colosseum, the Forum, the Borghese Gallery—where reservations are required—and the Vatican Museum).

Call your **debit and credit card companies** to let them know the countries you'll be visiting, to ask about fees, to request your PIN code (it will be mailed to you), and more. See page 526 for details.

Do your homework if you want to buy **travel insurance.** Compare the cost of the insurance to the likelihood of your using

Rick Steves Audio Europe

If you're bringing a mobile device, be sure to check out **Rick Steves Audio Europe,** where you can download free audio tours and hours of travel interviews (via the Rick Steves Audio Europe app, www.ricksteves.com/audioeurope, Google Play, or iTunes).

My self-guided **audio tours** are user-friendly, easy-to-follow, fun, and informative, covering the major sights and neighborhoods in Rome (Pantheon, St. Peter's Basilica, Roman Forum, Colosseum, Sistine Chapel, Trastevere Walk, Jewish Ghetto Walk, Ostia Antica, Pompeii). Compared to live tours, my audio tours are hard to beat: Nobody will stand you up, the quality is reliable, you can take the tour exactly when you like, and they're free.

Rick Steves Audio Europe also offers a far-reaching library of intriguing **travel interviews** with experts from around the globe. The interviews are organized by destination, including many of the places in this book.

it and your potential loss if something goes wrong. Also, check whether your existing insurance (health, homeowners, or renters) covers you and your possessions overseas. For more information, see www.ricksteves.com/insurance.

If you're taking an **overnight train** (especially between Rome and Paris), and you need a couchette *(cuccetta)* or sleeper—and you *must* leave on a certain day—consider booking it in advance through a US agent (such as www.ricksteves.com/rail), even though it may cost more than buying it in Italy. Other Italian trains, like the high-speed ES trains, require a seat reservation, but it's usually possible to make arrangements in Italy just a few days ahead. (For more on train travel, see the Practicalities chapter.)

If you're planning on **renting a car** in Italy, you'll need your driver's license. (If you plan to drive it around Rome, you'll need your head examined.) An International Driving Permit is required (see page 554). Driving is prohibited in some city centers; obey the signage or risk getting a huge fine (see page 558).

If you plan to hire a **local guide,** reserve ahead by email. Popular guides can get booked up.

If you're bringing a **mobile device,** download any apps you might want to use on the road, such as translators, maps, and transit schedules. Check out **Rick Steves Audio Europe,** featuring audio tours of Rome's major sights, hours of travel interviews on Rome, and more (for details, see sidebar above).

Check the **Rick Steves guidebook updates** page for any recent changes to this book (www.ricksteves.com/update).

Because **airline carry-on restrictions** are always changing,

> ## How Was Your Trip?
>
> Were your travels fun, smooth, and meaningful? If you'd like to share your tips, concerns, and discoveries, please fill out the survey at www.ricksteves.com/feedback. I value your feedback. Thanks in advance—it helps a lot.

visit the Transportation Security Administration's website (www.tsa.gov) for an up-to-date list of what you can bring on the plane with you...and what you must check.

Traveling as a Temporary Local

We travel all the way to Italy to enjoy differences—to become temporary locals. You'll experience frustrations. Certain truths that we find "God-given" or "self-evident," such as cold beer, ice in drinks, bottomless cups of coffee, and bigger being better, are suddenly not so true. One of the benefits of travel is the eye-opening realization that there are logical, civil, and even better alternatives. A willingness to go local ensures that you'll enjoy a full dose of Italian hospitality.

Europeans generally like Americans. But if there is a negative aspect to Italians' image of Americans, it's that we are loud, wasteful, ethnocentric, too informal (which can seem disrespectful), and a bit naive. Think about the rationale behind "crazy" Italian decisions. For instance, many hoteliers turn off the heat in spring and can't turn on air-conditioning until summer. The point is to conserve energy, and it's mandated by the Italian government. You could complain about being cold or hot...or bring a sweater in winter, and in summer, be prepared to sweat a little like everyone else.

While Italians, flabbergasted by our Yankee excesses, say in disbelief, *"Mi sono cadute le braccia!"* ("I throw my arms down!"), they nearly always afford us individual travelers all the warmth we deserve.

Judging from all the happy feedback I receive from travelers who have used this book, it's safe to assume you'll enjoy a great, affordable vacation—with the finesse of an independent, experienced traveler.

Thanks, and *buon viaggio!*

Rick Steves

Back Door Travel Philosophy

From Rick Steves Europe Through the Back Door

Travel is intensified living—maximum thrills per minute and one of the last great sources of legal adventure. Travel is freedom. It's recess, and we need it.

Experiencing the real Europe requires catching it by surprise, going casual..."through the Back Door."

Affording travel is a matter of priorities. (Make do with the old car.) You can eat and sleep—simply, safely, and enjoyably—anywhere in Europe for $125 a day plus transportation costs. In many ways, spending more money only builds a thicker wall between you and what you traveled so far to see. Europe is a cultural carnival, and time after time, you'll find that its best acts are free and the best seats are the cheap ones.

A tight budget forces you to travel close to the ground, meeting and communicating with the people. Never sacrifice sleep, nutrition, safety, or cleanliness to save money. Simply enjoy the local-style alternatives to expensive hotels and restaurants.

Connecting with people carbonates your experience. Extroverts have more fun. If your trip is low on magic moments, kick yourself and make things happen. If you don't enjoy a place, maybe you don't know enough about it. Seek the truth. Recognize tourist traps. Give a culture the benefit of your open mind. See things as different, but not better or worse. Any culture has plenty to share.

Of course, travel, like the world, is a series of hills and valleys. Be fanatically positive and militantly optimistic. If something's not to your liking, change your liking.

Travel can make you a happier American, as well as a citizen of the world. Our Earth is home to seven billion equally precious people. It's humbling to travel and find that other people don't have the "American Dream"—they have their own dreams. Europeans like us, but with all due respect, they wouldn't trade passports.

Thoughtful travel engages us with the world. In tough economic times, it reminds us what is truly important. By broadening perspectives, travel teaches new ways to measure quality of life.

Globetrotting destroys ethnocentricity, helping us understand and appreciate other cultures. Rather than fear the diversity on this planet, celebrate it. Among your most prized souvenirs will be the strands of different cultures you choose to knit into your own character. The world is a cultural yarn shop, and Back Door travelers are weaving the ultimate tapestry. Join in!

ORIENTATION TO ROME

Sprawling Rome actually feels manageable once you get to know it. The old core, with most of the tourist sights, sits in a diamond formed by Termini train station (in the east), the Vatican (west), Villa Borghese Gardens (north), and the Colosseum (south). The Tiber River runs through the diamond from north to south. In the center of the diamond sits Piazza Venezia, a busy square and traffic hub. It takes about an hour to walk from Termini Station to the Vatican.

ROME: A VERBAL MAP

Think of Rome as a series of neighborhoods, huddling around major landmarks.

Ancient Rome: In ancient times, this was home to the grandest buildings of a city of a million people. Today, the best of the classical sights stand in a line from the Colosseum to the Forum to the Pantheon. Just north of this area, between Via Nazionale and Via Cavour, is the atmospheric and trendy Monti district.

Pantheon Neighborhood: The Pantheon anchors the neighborhood I like to call the "Heart of Rome." It stretches eastward from the Tiber River through Campo de' Fiori and Piazza Navona, past the Pantheon to the Trevi Fountain. Between the river and the Pantheon area is the Jewish Ghetto.

Vatican City: Located west of the Tiber, it's a compact world of its own, with two great, huge sights: St. Peter's Basilica and the Vatican Museum.

North Rome: With the Spanish Steps, Villa Borghese Gardens, and trendy shopping streets (Via Veneto and the "shopping triangle"—the area along Via del Corso and between the Spanish Steps, Piazza Venezia, and Piazza del Popolo), this is a more modern, classy area.

East Rome: This includes the area around Termini Station and Piazza della Repubblica, with many recommended hotels and public-transportation connections. Just to the south and east is the neighborhood I call "Pilgrim's Rome," with several prominent churches.

South Rome: South of Vatican City is Trastevere, the colorful, wrong-side-of-the-river neighborhood that provides a look at village Rome. It's the city at its crustiest—and perhaps most "Roman." Farther south are the gritty/colorful Testaccio neighborhood, the 1930s suburb of E.U.R., and the Appian Way, home of the catacombs.

Within each of these neighborhoods, you'll find elements from the many layers of Rome's 2,000-plus-year history: the marble ruins of ancient times; tangled streets of the medieval world; early Christian churches; grand Renaissance buildings and statues; Baroque fountains and church facades; 19th-century apartments; and 20th-century boulevards choked with traffic.

Since no one is allowed to build taller than St. Peter's dome, and virtually no buildings have been constructed in the city center since Mussolini got distracted in 1938, central Rome has no modern skyline. The Tiber River is basically ignored—after the last floods (1870), the banks were built up very high, and Rome turned its back on its naughty river.

PLANNING YOUR TIME

After considering Rome's major tourist sights, I've covered just my favorites. You won't be able to see all of these, so don't try—you'll keep coming back to Rome. After several dozen visits, I still have a healthy list of excuses to return.

Rome in a Day

Some people actually try to "do" Rome in a day. Crazy as that sounds, if all you have is a day, it's one of the most exciting days Europe has to offer. Start at 8:30 at the Colosseum. Then explore the Forum, hike over Capitoline Hill, and cap your "Caesar Shuffle" with a visit to the Pantheon. After a quick lunch, taxi to the Vatican Museum (the lines usually die down mid-afternoon, or you can reserve a visit online in advance). See the Vatican Museum, then St. Peter's Basilica (open until 19:00 April-Sept). Taxi back to Campo de' Fiori to find dinner. Finish your day lacing together all the famous floodlit spots (see my Heart of Rome Walk chapter). Note: This busy plan is possible only if you ace the line-avoidance tricks.

Rome in Two to Three Days

On the first day, do the "Caesar Shuffle" from the Colosseum to the Forum, then over Capitoline Hill to the Pantheon. After a

Overview of Maps

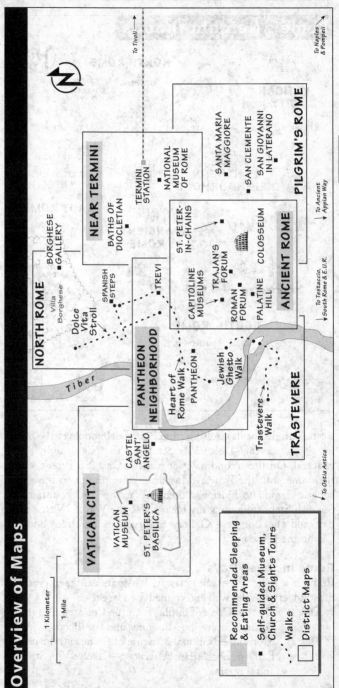

ORIENTATION

1 Kilometer
1 Mile

VATICAN CITY

VATICAN MUSEUM

ST. PETER'S BASILICA

CASTEL SANT'ANGELO

To Ostia Antica

NORTH ROME

Villa Borghese

BORGHESE GALLERY

Dolce Vita Stroll

SPANISH STEPS

Tiber

PANTHEON NEIGHBORHOOD

Heart of Rome Walk

PANTHEON

Jewish Ghetto Walk

Trastevere Walk

TRASTEVERE

TREVI

ANCIENT ROME

CAPITOLINE MUSEUMS

ROMAN FORUM

PALATINE HILL

TRAJAN'S FORUM

ST. PETER-IN-CHAINS

COLOSSEUM

To Testaccio, South Rome & E.U.R.

To Ancient Appian Way

NEAR TERMINI

BATHS OF DIOCLETIAN

TERMINI STATION

NATIONAL MUSEUM OF ROME

To Tivoli

PILGRIM'S ROME

SANTA MARIA MAGGIORE

SAN CLEMENTE

SAN GIOVANNI IN LATERANO

To Naples & Pompeii

Recommended Sleeping & Eating Areas

Self-guided Museum, Church and Sights Tours

Walks

District Maps

ORIENTATION

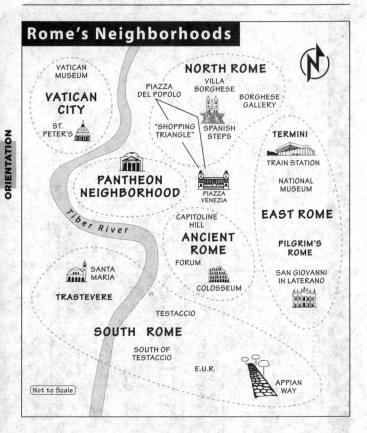

Rome's Neighborhoods

VATICAN MUSEUM

VATICAN CITY

ST. PETER'S

NORTH ROME

PIAZZA DEL POPOLO

VILLA BORGHESE

BORGHESE GALLERY

"SHOPPING TRIANGLE"

SPANISH STEPS

TERMINI

TRAIN STATION

NATIONAL MUSEUM

PANTHEON NEIGHBORHOOD

Tiber River

PIAZZA VENEZIA

CAPITOLINE HILL

ANCIENT ROME

FORUM

COLOSSEUM

EAST ROME

PILGRIM'S ROME

SAN GIOVANNI IN LATERANO

SANTA MARIA

TRASTEVERE

TESTACCIO

SOUTH ROME

SOUTH OF TESTACCIO

E.U.R.

APPIAN WAY

Not to Scale

siesta, join the locals strolling from Piazza del Popolo to the Spanish Steps (see the "Dolce Vita Stroll" in the Nightlife in Rome chapter). On the second day, see Vatican City (St. Peter's, climb the dome, tour the Vatican Museum). Have dinner on the atmospheric Campo de' Fiori, and then walk to the Trevi Fountain and Spanish Steps (following my Heart of Rome Walk). With a third day, add the Borghese Gallery (reservations required) and the Capitoline Museums.

Rome in Seven Days

Rome is a great one-week getaway. Its sights can keep even the most fidgety traveler well entertained for a week.

Day 1: Do the "Caesar Shuffle" from the Colosseum to the Forum, Capitoline Museums, and Pantheon.

Day 2: Morning—National Museum of Rome and the nearby Baths of Diocletian. Afternoon—"Dolce Vita Stroll" and shopping.

Greater Rome

To Florence
To Viterbo & Siena
RING FREEWAY (GRANDE RACCORDO ANULARE)
VIA CASSIA S-2
VIA FLAMINIA
VIA SALARIA
AUDITORIUM CONCERT HALL
CATACOMBS OF PRISCILLA
OLYMPIC STADIUM
MAXXI
To Tivoli
S-5
VATICAN CITY
TERMINI STN.
TIBURTINA TRAIN & BUS STN.
A-24
To L'Aquila
To Civitavecchia
VIA AURELIA S-1
SAN PIETRO STN.
PANTHEON
COLOSSEUM
PORTA PORTESE FLEA MKT.
BATHS OF CARACALLA
HYDROMANIA WATER PARK
TRASTEVERE TRAIN STN.
TESTACCIO
APPIAN WAY & CATACOMBS
A-7
(Note Train to Fiumicino Airport is non-stop)
ST. PAUL'S
OSTIENSE TRAIN STN.
APPIAN WAY
To Naples
To Fiumicino (Da Vinci) Airport
A-12
VIA OSTIENSE
E.U.R.
CIAMPINO AIRPORT
Tiber River
S-8
RING FREEWAY
OSTIA ANTICA
OSTIA STN.
5 Kilometers
5 Miles
☐ = See detail maps
To Ostia Beach

Day 3: Vatican City—St. Peter's Basilica, dome climb, and Vatican Museum (for tips on avoiding lines, see page 230).

Day 4: Side-trip to Ostia Antica (closed Mon). In the evening, take my recommended Heart of Rome Walk from Campo de' Fiori to the Spanish Steps.

Day 5: Borghese Gallery (reservation required) and Pilgrim's Rome: the churches of San Giovanni in Laterano, Santa Maria Maggiore, and San Clemente (see Pilgrim's Rome Tour chapter).

Day 6: Side-trip to Naples and Pompeii.

Day 7: You choose—Hadrian's Villa near Tivoli, Appian Way with catacombs, E.U.R., Castel Sant'Angelo, Testaccio sights, Baths of Caracalla, Capuchin Crypt, a food tour, shopping, or more time at the Vatican.

Overview

ORIENTATION

TOURIST INFORMATION

Rome has two main tourist information offices and several TI kiosks. The TI offices are at the airport (Terminal 3, daily 8:00-19:30) and Termini train station (daily 8:00-19:30, 100 yards down track 24, look for signs). Little kiosks (generally open daily 9:30-19:00) are near the Forum (on Piazza del Tempio della Pace), on Via Nazionale (at Palazzo delle Esposizioni), near Castel Sant'Angelo (at Piazza Pia), near Piazza Navona (at Piazza delle Cinque Lune), and near the Trevi Fountain (at Via del Corso and Via Minghetti). Additionally, an information center is directly across from the Forum entrance, on Via dei Fori Imperiali (see page 152). The TI's website is www.turismoroma.it, but most practical information is found at www.060608.it. That's also the number for Rome's **call center**— the best source of up-to-date tourist information, with English speakers on staff (answered daily 9:00-21:00, just dial 06-0608, and press 2 for English).

At any TI, ask for a free city map (or pay for a better one). Your hotel will have a freebie map and may also have a booklet with up-to-date listings of the city's sights and hours. The best map I found is published by Rough Guide (€9 in bookstores).

Several English-oriented **websites** provide insight into events and daily life in the city: www.inromenow.com (light tourist info on lots of topics), www.wantedinrome.com (events and accommodations), and www.rome.angloinfo.com (on living in and moving to Rome).

ARRIVAL IN ROME

For a rundown of Rome's train stations and airports, see the Rome Connections chapter.

HELPFUL HINTS

Sightseeing Tips: Avid sightseers can save money by buying the Roma Pass (see page 42), available at TIs and participating sights—buy one before visiting the Colosseum or Forum, and you can skip the long lines there. Another way to bypass lines at the Colosseum and Forum is to buy a ticket online in advance (see page 138). If you want to see the Borghese Gallery, remember to reserve ahead (see page 265). To sidestep the long Vatican Museum line, reserve an entry time online (see page 230 for details).

Internet Access: Most hotels have Wi-Fi, but if yours doesn't, your hotelier can point you to the nearest Internet café.

Bookstores: The following stores sell travel guidebooks, including mine (all open daily except Anglo American and Open Door

Daily Reminder

Sunday: These sights are closed: the Vatican Museum (except for last Sun of the month, when it's free and even more crowded), Villa Farnesina (except for second Sun of the month), and the Catacombs of San Sebastiano. In the morning, the Porta Portese flea market hops, and the old center is delightfully quiet. Much of the Appian Way is closed to traffic and fun to stroll.

Monday: Many sights are closed, including the National Museum of Rome, Borghese Gallery, Capitoline Museums, Catacombs of Priscilla, Museum of the Imperial Forums (includes Trajan's Market and Trajan's Forum), Castel Sant'Angelo, Ara Pacis, Montemartini Museum, E.U.R.'s Museum of Roman Civilization, Etruscan Museum, Museum of the Liberation of Rome, MAXXI, some Appian Way sights (Tomb of Cecilia Metella and the Circus and Villa of Maxentius), Ostia Antica, and Villa d'Este (at Tivoli).

Major sights that are open include the Colosseum, Forum, and Vatican Museum, among others. Churches are open as usual. The Baths of Caracalla close early in the afternoon.

Tuesday: All sights are open in Rome. This isn't a good day to side-trip to Naples because its Archaeological Museum is closed.

Wednesday: All sights are open, except the Catacombs of San Callisto. St. Peter's Basilica is typically closed in the morning for a papal audience.

Thursday/Friday: All sights are open.

Saturday: Most sights are open in Rome, except for the Synagogue and Jewish Museum.

closed Sun). The first two are chains, while the others have a more personal touch. **Borri Books** is at Termini Station, and **Feltrinelli** has two branches (at Largo Argentina 11 near the ancient ruins, with a limited English section, and the larger Feltrinelli International, just off Piazza della Repubblica at Via Vittorio Emanuele Orlando 78-81—see map on page 80, tel. 06-487-0171). **Anglo American Bookshop** has great art and history sections (closed all day Sun and Mon morning, a few blocks south of Spanish Steps at Via della Vite 102—see map on page 434, tel. 06-679-5222). **Libreria Fanucci** has a small selection, but is centrally located (a block toward the Pantheon from Piazza Navona at Piazza Madama 8—see map on page 392, tel. 06-686-1141). In Trastevere, Irishman Dermot at the **Almost Corner Bookshop** stocks an Italian-interest section (Via del Moro 45—see map on page 361, tel. 06-583-6942), and the **Open Door Bookshop** carries the only used books in English in town (closed Sun, Via della Lungaretta 23—see map on page 361, tel. 06-589-6478).

Laundry: Your hotelier can direct you to the nearest launderette. The **Ondablu** chain usually comes with Internet access (€2/hour); one of their more central locations is near Termini Station (about €8 to wash and dry a 15-pound load, usually open daily 8:00-22:00, Via Principe Amedeo 70b—see map on page 406, tel. 06-474-4647).

Travel Agencies: You can get train tickets and rail-pass-related reservations and supplements at travel agencies (at little or no additional cost), avoiding a trip to a train station. Your hotelier will know of a convenient agency nearby.

Updates to This Book: For updates to this book, check www.ricksteves.com/update.

DEALING WITH (AND AVOIDING) PROBLEMS

Theft Alert: While violent crime is rare in the city center, petty theft is rampant. With sweet-talking con artists meeting you at the station, well-dressed pickpockets on buses, and thieving gangs of children at the ancient sites, Rome is a gauntlet of rip-offs. Pickpockets don't want to hurt you—they usually just want your money—but green or sloppy tourists will be scammed. Thieves strike when you're distracted. Don't trust kind strangers. Keep nothing important in your pockets. If you must carry a backpack, keep it in front. Always use your money belt.

Be most on guard while boarding and leaving buses and subways. Thieves crowd the door, then stop and turn while others crowd and push from behind. You'll find less crowding and commotion—and less risk—waiting for the end cars of a subway rather than the middle cars. The sneakiest thieves pretend to be well-dressed businessmen (generally with something in their hands) or tourists wearing fanny packs and toting cameras and even Rick Steves guidebooks. Lately a lot of youths and even pregnant mothers are working as pickpockets. Thieves are particularly thick on the Metro and the crowded and made-for-tourists buses #64 and #40.

If you know what to look out for, fast-fingered moms with babies and gangs of children picking the pockets and handbags of naive tourists are not a threat, but an interesting, albeit sad, spectacle. Pickpockets troll through the tourist crowds around the Colosseum, Forum, Vatican, and train and Metro stations. Watch them target tourists who are overloaded with bags or distracted with a camera. The kids look like beggars and hold up newspapers or cardboard signs to confuse their victims. They scram like stray cats if you're on to them.

Scams abound: Always be clear about what paper money you're giving someone, demand clear and itemized bills, and count your change. Don't give your wallet to self-proclaimed "police" who stop you on the street, warn you about counterfeit (or drug) money, and ask to see your cash. If a bank machine eats your ATM card, see if there's a thin plastic insert with a tongue hanging out that thieves use to extract it.

Reporting Losses: To report lost or stolen items, file a police report (at Termini Station, with *polizia* at track 11 or with Carabinieri at track 20; offices are also at Piazza Venezia and at the corner of Via Nazionale and Via Genova). You'll need the report to file an insurance claim for lost gear, and it can help with replacing your passport—first file the police report, then call your embassy to make an appointment (US embassy: tel. 06-46741, www.usembassy.it, Via Vittorio Veneto 121). For information on how to report lost or stolen credit cards, see page 527.

Emergency Numbers: Police—tel. 113. Ambulance—tel. 118.

Pedestrian Safety: Your main safety concern in Rome is crossing streets without incident. Use extreme caution. Some streets have pedestrian-crossing signals (red means stop—or jaywalk carefully; green means go...also carefully; and yellow means go...extremely carefully, as cars may be whipping around the corner). But just as often, multi-lane streets have crosswalks with no signals at all. And even when there are traffic lights, they are provisional: Scooters don't need to stop at red lights, and even cars exercise what drivers call the "logical option" of not stopping if they see no oncoming traffic. Each year, as noisy gasoline-powered scooters are replaced by electric ones, the streets get quieter (hooray) but more dangerous for pedestrians.

Follow locals like a shadow when you cross a street (or spend a good part of your visit stranded on curbs). When you do cross alone, don't be a deer in the headlights. Find a gap in the traffic and walk with confidence while making eye contact with approaching drivers—they won't hit you if they can tell where you intend to go.

Staying/Getting Healthy: The siesta is a key to survival in summertime Rome. Lie down and contemplate the extraordinary power of gravity in the Eternal City. I drink lots of cold, refreshing water from Rome's many drinking fountains (the Forum has three).

Every neighborhood has a pharmacy (marked by a green cross). Pharmacies stay open late in Termini Station (daily 7:30-22:00), at Piazza dei Cinquecento 51 (Mon-Fri 7:00-23:30, Sat-Sun 8:00-23:00, next to Termini Station on the corner of Via Cavour—see map on page 406, tel. 06-488-0019), and in the Pantheon neighborhood (Farmacia Senato, between Piazza Navona and the Pantheon, Mon-Fri 7:30-24:30, Sat 8:30-24:30, Sun 12:00-23:00, Corso del Rinascimento 50—see map on page 392). There's also a 24-hour pharmacy several blocks down from Piazza della Repubblica at Via Nazionale 228 (tel. 06-488-4437).

Embassies and hotels can recommend English-speaking doctors. Consider MEDline, a 24-hour home-medical service; doctors speak English and make calls at hotels for €150 (tel. 06-808-0995). Anyone is entitled to free emergency treatment at public hospitals. The hospital closest to Termini Station is Policlinico Umberto 1 (entrance for emergency treatment on Via Lancisi, translators available, Metro: Policlinico). Readers report that the staff at Santa Susanna Church, home of the American Catholic Church in Rome, offers useful advice and medical referrals (see page 85).

GETTING AROUND ROME

Sightsee on foot, by city bus, by Metro, or by taxi. I've grouped your sightseeing into walkable neighborhoods. Make it a point to visit sights in a logical order. Needless backtracking wastes precious time.

The public transportation system, which is cheap and efficient, consists primarily of buses, a few trams, and the two underground subway (Metro) lines. Consider it part of your Roman experience.

Rome Walks has produced an orientation video to Rome's transportation system; find it on YouTube by searching for "Understanding Rome's Public Transport."

For information, visit www.atac.roma.it, which has a useful route planner in English, or call 06-57003. If you have a smartphone and an international data plan, consider downloading the free app "Roma Bus" by Movenda, which also has a route planner and real-time updates on the bus schedule. The ATAC mobile website has similar info (www.muovi.roma.it).

Buying Tickets

All public transportation uses the same ticket. It costs €1.50 and is valid for one Metro ride—including transfers underground—plus unlimited city buses and trams during a 100-minute period. Passes good on buses and the Metro are sold in increments of one day (€6, good until midnight), three days (€16.50), one week (€24, about the cost of three taxi rides), and one month (€35, valid for a calendar month).

You can purchase tickets and passes at some newsstands, tobacco shops (*tabacchi*, marked by a black-and-white *T* sign), and major Metro stations and bus stops, but not on board. It's smart to stock up on tickets early, or to buy a pass or a Roma Pass (which includes a three-day transit pass—see page 42). That way, you don't have to run around searching for an open tobacco shop when you spot your bus approaching. Metro stations rarely have human ticket sellers, and the machines are unreliable (it helps to insert your smallest coin first).

Validate your ticket by sticking it in the Metro turnstile (magnetic-strip-side up, arrow-side first) or in the machine when you board the bus (magnetic-strip-side down, arrow-side first)—watch others and imitate. It'll return your ticket with your expiration time printed. To get through a Metro turnstile with a transit pass or Roma Pass, use it just like a ticket; on buses and trams, however, you need to validate your pass only if that's your first time using it.

By Metro

The Roman subway system (Metropolitana, or "Metro") is simple, with two clean, cheap, fast lines—A and B—that intersect at Ter-

mini Station. The Metro runs from 5:30 to 23:30 (Fri-Sat until 1:30 in the morning). Remember, the subway's first and last compartments are generally the least crowded, and the least likely to harbor pickpockets.

You'll notice lots of big holes in the city while a new line is being built to run across town, including through the historic heart. It will likely not be completed until 2020.

While much of Rome is not served by its skimpy subway, the following stops are helpful:

Termini (intersection of lines A and B): Termini Station, shuttle train to airport, National Museum of Rome, and recommended hotels

Repubblica (line A): Baths of Diocletian, Via Nazionale, and recommended hotels

Barberini (line A): Capuchin Crypt, Trevi Fountain, and Villa Borghese

Spagna (line A): Spanish Steps and classy shopping area

Flaminio (line A): Piazza del Popolo, start of my "Dolce Vita Stroll" down Via del Corso, easy buses to the Borghese Gallery

ORIENTATION

Ottaviano (line A): St. Peter's Basilica, Vatican Museum, and recommended hotels

Tiburtina (line B): Tiburtina train and bus station (direction: Rebibbia; trains going in the direction of Conca d'Oro/Jonio do not stop at Tiburtina)

Colosseo (line B): Colosseum, Roman Forum, bike rental, and recommended hotels

San Giovanni (line B): Church of San Giovanni in Laterano

Piramide (line B): Protestant Cemetery, Testaccio, and trains to Ostia Antica

San Paolo (line B): Church of St. Paul's Outside the Walls

E.U.R. (line B, three different stops depending on your destination): Mussolini's futuristic suburb

By Bus

The Metro is handy, but it won't get you everywhere—take the bus (or tram). Bus routes are clearly listed at the stops. TIs usually don't have bus maps, but with some

knowledge of major stops, you won't necessarily need one.

Buses—especially the touristy #40 and #64—are havens for thieves and pickpockets. These two lines in particular can be nose-to-armpit crowded during peak times...and while you're sniffing that guy's pit, his other hand could be busily rifling through your pockets. Assume any commotion is a thief-created distraction. If one bus is packed, there's likely a second one on its tail with far fewer crowds and thieves. Or read the signs posted at stops to see if a different, less crowded bus route can get you to or near your destination.

The tram lines are of limited use for most tourists, but a few lines can save some walking. For all intents and purposes, trams function identically to buses. Once you know the bus/tram system, you'll find it's easier than searching for a cab.

Tickets have a barcode and must be stamped on the bus in the yellow box with the digital readout (be sure to retrieve your ticket). Validate your ticket as you board (magnetic-strip-side down, arrow-side first), otherwise you're cheating. While relatively safe, riding without a stamped ticket on the bus is stressful. Inspectors fine even innocent-looking tourists €50. There's no need to validate a transit pass or Roma Pass on the bus, unless your pass is new and hasn't yet been stamped elsewhere in the transit system. Bus etiquette (not always followed) is to board at the front or rear doors and exit at the middle.

Regular bus lines start running at about 5:30, and during the day major routes run every 5-10 minutes. After 23:30, and sometimes earlier (such as on Sundays), buses are less frequent. Night buses are marked with an *N* and an owl symbol on the bus-stop signs. Frustratingly, the exact frequency of various bus routes is difficult to predict (and not printed at bus stops). At major stops, an electronic board shows the number of minutes until the next buses arrive, but at most stops you'll never know how long you have to wait. If your phone has Internet access, you can try checking the schedule with the route planner at www.muovi.roma.it.

These are the major bus routes:

Bus #64: This bus cuts across the city, linking Termini Station with the Vatican, stopping at Piazza della Repubblica (sights), Via Nazionale (recommended hotels), Piazza Venezia (near Forum), Largo Argentina (near Pantheon and Campo de' Fiori), St. Peter's Basilica (get off just past the tunnel), and San Pietro Station. Ride it for a city overview and to watch pickpockets in action. The #64 can get horribly crowded.

Bus #40: This express bus, which mostly follows the #64 route (but ends near the Castel Sant'Angelo on the Vatican side of the river), is especially helpful—fewer stops and (somewhat) fewer crowds.

The following routes conveniently connect Trastevere with other parts of Rome:

Bus #H: This express bus, linking Termini Station and Trastevere, makes a stop near Piazza Repubblica and at the bottom of Via Nazionale (for Trastevere, get off at Piazza Belli/Sonnino, just after crossing the Tiber River).

Tram #2: Leaving from near the Flaminio Metro stop, this route gives easy access to the Etruscan Museum and MAXXI, Rome's contemporary art museum.

Tram #8: This tram connects Piazza Venezia and Largo Argentina with Trastevere (get off at Piazza Belli).

Buses #23 and #280: These link the Vatican with Trastevere and Testaccio, stopping at the Vatican Museum (nearest stop is Via Leone IV), Castel Sant'Angelo, Trastevere (Piazza Belli), Porta Portese (Sunday flea market), and Piramide (Metro and gateway to Testaccio).

Other useful routes include:

Bus #16: Termini Station, Santa Maria Maggiore, and San Giovanni in Laterano.

Bus Bravado

Zip around Rome like a local by using the following tips to read bus signs.

The sign in the photo shows the three buses (#40, #60, and #64) that stop at the "Nazionale" stop. If you're asking yourself the following questions, it's got answers.

❶ **Where am I?** You're at the bus stop *(fermata)* called Nazionale (at the cross-street Torino; the cross-street differentiates this Nazionale stop from others nearby).

❷ **Which buses stop here?** Three do: #40, #60, and #64. Notice the arrow—it shows which direction the bus is headed.

❸ **Where is the bus going?** Bus #64, for example, starts its journey at "Termini" (Termini Station), goes to Repubblica, and then arrives at Nazionale—this stop. (Find "Nazionale," with the box around it.) From here, the #64 continues to "Pza Venezia" (Piazza Venezia), "Argentina" (Largo Argentina), makes several more stops, and ends its journey

at "Pza Stz S. Pietro" (Piazza Stazione San Pietro). Easy.

Scan the list to see if any of these buses stop at your destination. If you don't see a particular street or piazza, look for a major landmark where you can transfer—such as Largo Argentina, Piazza Venezia, or Termini Station. Note that if your destination is listed *above* your current bus stop, you need to cross the street to catch the bus going in the other direction.

❹ **When will my bus come?** The bottom of the sign lists the first and last departure times from the beginning of the route. *"Lun./ven."* means it runs on weekdays, *"sab."* means Saturday, and *"fest."* means Sundays and holidays.

Will pickpockets take my wallet? Probably, if you read this entire sidebar at the bus stop without paying attention to your surroundings.

Bus #49: Piazza Cavour/Castel Sant'Angelo, Piazza Risorgimento (Vatican), and Vatican Museum.

Bus #62: Largo Argentina to St. Peter's Square.

Bus #81: San Giovanni in Laterano, Largo Argentina, and Piazza Risorgimento (Vatican).

Buses #85 and #87: Piazza Venezia, Forum, Colosseum, San Clemente, and San Giovanni in Laterano.

Bus #492: Travels east-west across the city, connecting Tiburtina (train and bus stations), Largo Santa Susanna (near Piazza della Repubblica), Piazza Barberini, Piazza Venezia, Largo Argentina, Piazza Cavour (Castel Sant'Angelo), and Piazza Risorgimento (St. Peter's Basilica and Vatican).

Bus #714: Termini Station, Santa Maria Maggiore, San Giovanni in Laterano, Terme di Caracalla (Baths of Caracalla), and on to E.U.R.

Tram #3: Zips from the Colosseum to San Giovanni in Laterano in one direction, and to Piramide (Testaccio) in the other.

Buses #660, #118, and #218: These run to/from the Appian Way.

Elettrico **Minibuses:** Two cute *elettrico* minibuses that wind through the narrow streets of old and interesting neighborhoods are great for transport or simple joyriding, but due to budget cuts, they may not be operating. *Elettrico* #116 runs through the medieval core of Rome: Ponte Vittorio Emanuele II (near Castel Sant'Angelo) to Campo de' Fiori, Pantheon, Piazza Barberini, and the southern edge of the scenic Villa Borghese Gardens. *Elettrico* #117 connects San Giovanni in Laterano, Colosseo, Via dei Serpenti, Trevi Fountain, Piazza di Spagna, and Piazza del Popolo—and vice versa. Where Via del Corso hits Piazza del Popolo, a #117 is usually parked and ready to go. Riding it from here to the end of the line, San Giovanni in Laterano, makes for a fine joyride that leaves you, conveniently, at a great sight.

By Taxi

I use taxis in Rome more often than in other cities. They're reasonable and useful for efficient sightseeing in this big, hot metropolis.

Taxis start at €3, then charge about €1.50 per kilometer (surcharges: €1.50 on Sun, €3.50 for nighttime hours of 22:00-7:00, one regular suitcase or bag rides free, tip by rounding up to the nearest euro). Sample fares: Termini area to Vatican-€11; Termini area to Colosseum-€7; Termini area to the Borghese Gallery-€8; Colosseum to

ORIENTATION

Trastevere-€8 (or look up your route at www.worldtaximeter.com). Three or four companions with more money than time should taxi almost everywhere.

It's tough to wave down a taxi in Rome, especially at night. Find the nearest taxi stand by asking a passerby or a clerk in a shop, *"Dov'è una fermata dei taxi?"* (doh-VEH OO-nah fehr-MAH-tah DEH-ee TAHK-see). Some taxi stands are listed on my maps. To save time and energy, have your hotel or restaurant call a taxi for you; the meter starts when the call is received (generally adding a euro or two to the bill). To call a cab on your own, dial 06-3570, 06-4994, or 06-6645, or use the official city taxi line, 06-0609; they'll likely ask you for an Italian phone number (if you don't have one, you can give them your hotel's). It's routine for Romans to ask the waiter in a restaurant to call a taxi when they ask for the bill. The waiter will tell you how many minutes you have to enjoy your coffee.

Beware of corrupt taxis. First, make sure the meter *(tassametro)* is turned on. If it isn't, get out and hail another cab. Check that the meter is reset to the basic drop charge (should be around €3, or around €5 if you or your hotelier phoned for the taxi). Some meters show both the fare and the time elapsed during the ride, and some tourists—mistaking the time for the fare—end up paying more than the fair meter rate. Keep an eye on the fare on the meter as you near your destination; some cabbies turn the meter off instantly when they stop and tell you a higher price.

When you arrive at the train station or airport, beware of hustlers conning naive visitors into unmarked, rip-off "express taxis." Only use official taxis, with a *taxi* sign and phone number marked on the door. By law, they must display a multilingual official price chart; point to the chart and ask the cabbie to explain it if the fare doesn't seem right. A common cabbie scam is to take your €20 note, drop it, and pick up a €5 note (similar color), claiming that's what you gave him. To avoid this scam, pay in small bills; if you only have a large bill, show it to the cabbie as you state its face value.

If you encounter any problems with a taxi, making a show of writing down the taxi number (to file a complaint) can motivate a driver to quickly settle the matter.

If you take a Rome city cab from Fiumicino Airport to anywhere in central Rome within the old city walls, the cost should be €48 (covering up to four people and their bags); however, every year some readers report being ripped off. The catch is that cabbies *not* based in Rome or Fiumicino can charge €70. At the airport, look specifically for a Rome city cab—you'll see a maroon logo with the words "Roma Capitale" on the door. By law, they can charge only €48 for the ride (still, be sure to establish the price before you get in). Tired travelers arriving at the airport will likely find it less stressful (and cheaper) to take an airport shuttle van to their hotel, or catch the train to Termini Station and take the Metro or a cheaper taxi from there (see page 440 for details on getting from the airport to downtown Rome via taxi, shuttle, or train).

By Bike

Biking in the big city of Rome can speed up sightseeing or simply be an enjoyable way to explore. Though Roman traffic can be stressful, Roman drivers are respectful of cyclists. Still, use caution and never assume you have the right of way. The best rides are on small streets in the city center. A bike path along the banks of the Tiber River makes a good 20-minute ride (easily accessed from the ramps at Porta Portese and Ponte Regina Margherita near Piazza del Popolo). Get a bike with a well-padded seat—the little stones that pave Roman streets are unforgiving.

Top Bike Rental and Tours is professionally run by Roman bike enthusiasts who want to show off their city. Your rental comes with a helmet, a lock, and a handy map that suggests a route and indicates less-trafficked streets. They also offer English-only guided tours around the city (4 hours) and the Appian Way (6 hours); check their website for itineraries and schedules (rental: €15/day, €25/day for electric bike, 10 percent discount with this book, best to reserve in advance via email, bring ID for deposit; bike tours start at €45, reservations required; daily 10:00-19:00, Via Labicana 49, Metro: Colosseo—exit left and pass the Colosseum, tel. 06-488-2893, www.topbikerental.com, info@topbikerental.com).

Cool Rent, near the Colosseo Metro stop, is cheaper but less helpful and has more basic bikes (€3/hour, €10/day, daily April-Oct 9:30-20:00, Nov-March 9:30-18:00, driver's license or other ID for deposit, 10 yards to the right as you exit the Metro). A second outlet is just off Via del Corso (on Largo di Lombardi, near corner of Via del Corso and Via della Croce, mobile 388-695-9303, Sasin).

You can also rent a bike at the Appian Way (see Ancient Appian Way Tour chapter) and in the Villa Borghese Gardens (see page 67).

Tours in Rome

ON FOOT

Finding the best guided tours in Rome is challenging. Local guides are good but pricey. Tour companies are cheaper, but quality and organization are unreliable. To sightsee on your own, download my series of free audio tours that illuminate some of Rome's top sights and neighborhoods (see sidebar on page 8 for details).

If you do hire a private Italian guide, consider organizing a group of four to six people from your hotel to split the cost (around

€180 for a three-hour tour); this ends up costing about the same per person as going on a scheduled tour from one of the walking-tour companies listed below (about €25, generally expat guides).

Local Guides

I've worked with each of these licensed independent local guides. They're worth every euro. They speak excellent English and enjoy tailoring tours to your interests. Their prices (roughly €55-60/hour) flex with the day, season, and demand. Arrange your date and price by email.

Francesca Caruso loves to teach and share her appreciation of her city, and has contributed generously to this book (www. francescacaruso.com, francescainroma@gmail.com). Popular with my readers, Francesca understandably books up quickly; if she's busy, she'll recommend one of her colleagues. **Carla Zaia** is an engaging expert on all things Roman (carlaromeguide@gmail.com). **Cristina Giannicchi** has an archaeology background (mobile 338-111-4573, www.crisromanguide.com, crisgiannicchi@gmail.com). **Sara Magister,** a Roman with doctorates in art history and archaeology, leads tours throughout the city (a.magister@iol.it). **Giovanna Terzulli** is a personable, knowledgeable art historian (gioterzulli@gmail.com). **Alessandra Mazzoccoli** is experienced, easygoing, and good with all ages (alemazzoccoli@gmail.com). Italian-American **Sean Finelli,** known as "The Roman Guy," offers several walking tours and a trip-planning service (www.theromanguy.com).

Walking-Tour Companies

Rome has many highly competitive tour companies, each offering a series of themed walks through various slices of Rome. Three-hour guided walks generally cost €25-30 per person. Guides are usually native English speakers, often American expats. Tours are limited to small groups, geared to American tourists, and given in English only. I've listed some here, but without a lot of details on their offerings. Before your trip, spend some time on these companies' websites to get to know your options, as each company has a particular teaching and guiding personality. Some are highbrow, and others are less scholarly. It's sometimes required, and always smart, to book a spot in advance (easy online). I must add that we get a lot of negative feedback on some tour companies. Readers report that advertising can be misleading, and scheduling mishaps are common. Make sure you know what you are booking and when.

Context Rome's walking tours are more intellectual than most, designed for travelers with longer-than-average attention spans. They are more expensive than others and are led by "docents" rather than guides (tel. 06-9672-7371, US tel. 800-691-6036, www. contextrome.com). **Enjoy Rome** offers a number of different walks

---

Is the Pope Catholic?

Rome's tour guides, who introduce tourists to the city's great art and Christian history, field a lot of interesting questions and comments from their groups. Here are a few of their favorites:

- Oh, to be here in Rome...where our Lord Jesus walked.
- Is this where Christ fought the lions?
- Who's the guy on the cross?
- This guy who made so many nice things, Rene Sance, who is he? (Say it fast, and you'll get the gist.)
- Was John Paul II the son of John Paul I?
- What's the Sistine Chapel worth in US dollars?
- How did Michelangelo get Moses to pose for him?
- What's Michelangelo doing now?
- (Upon seeing the arrow-pierced St. Sebastian) Oh, you Italians had problems with the Indians, too.

ORIENTATION

---

and a website filled with helpful information (Via Marghera 8a, tel. 06-445-1843, www.enjoyrome.com, info@enjoyrome.com). **Rome Walks** has put together several particularly creative itineraries (mobile 347-795-5175, www.romewalks.com, info@romewalks.com, Annie). **Europe Odyssey** gives readers of this book a 10 percent discount off their walks (tel. 06-8854-2416, mobile 328-912-3720, www.europeodyssey.com, Rahul). **Through Eternity** offers travelers with this book a 10 percent discount off most group tours and a 20 percent discount off its Underground Rome; book through their website (look for "Group Tours Rome") and enter the promotional code "RICKSTEVES" for the best discount (tel. 06-700-9336, mobile 347-336-5298, www.througheternity.com, office@througheternity.com, Rob). **Walks of Italy** has fun guides who lead a variety of good walks for groups of no more than 12 people at a time (10 percent discount for readers of this book— if booking online enter the code "10ricksteves" when ordering, US tel. 202/684-6916, Italian mobile 334-974-4274, tel. 06-9558-3331, www.walksofitaly.com, Jason Spiehler). **ArtViva** also offers a 10 percent discount to my readers (book at www.artviva.com/ricksteves—log in with username "ricksteves" and password "reader"; tel. 055-264-5033 during day or mobile 329-613-2730 from 18:00 to 20:00).

For **food-oriented walking tours,** see page 387.

ORIENTATION

ON WHEELS

Hop-on, Hop-off Bus Tours

Several different agencies, including the ATAC public bus company, run hop-on, hop-off tours around Rome. These tours are constantly evolving and offer varying combinations of sights. You can grab one (and pay as you board) at any stop; Termini Station and Piazza Venezia are handy hubs. Although the city is perfectly walkable and traffic jams can make the bus dreadfully slow, these open-top bus tours remain popular.

The **110open Bus** seems to be the best. Operated by the ATAC city-bus lines, it offers an orientation tour on big red double-decker buses with an open-air upper deck. In less than two hours, you'll have 80 sights pointed out to you, with a next-to-worthless recorded narration. While you can hop on and off, the service can be erratic (mobbed midday, not ideal in bad weather), and it can be very slow

in heavy traffic. It's best to think of this as a 90-minute quickie orientation with scant information and lots of images. Stops include the Colosseum, Circus Maximus, Bocca della Verità (the Mouth of Truth from *Roman Holiday* fame), Piazza Venezia, St. Peter's Square, Via del Tritone (Trevi Fountain), and Piazza Barberini. The 110open Bus departs roughly every 20 minutes (less frequent off-season). You can catch it at any stop, including Termini Station. Buy the ticket as you board (runs daily April-Oct 8:30-20:30, Nov-March 8:30-19:00, single tour-€12, 1-day ticket-€15, 48-hour ticket-€20, family tickets available, kids 9 and under ride free, tel. 800-281-281, www.trambusopen.com).

Archeobus is an open-top bus, also operated by ATAC, that runs twice hourly from Termini Station out to the Appian Way

(with stops at the Colosseum, Baths of Caracalla, San Callisto, San Sebastiano, and the Tomb of Cecilia Metella). This is a handy way to see the sights down this ancient Roman road, but it can be frustrating for various reasons—sparse narration, weekend-only service, and not ideal for hopping on and off (single tour-€10, 48-hour ticket-€12, €25 combo-ticket with 110open Bus valid 72 hours, deals for families and children, 1.5-hour loop, bus runs Fri-Sun only April-mid-Oct 9:00-16:30, from Termini Station and Piazza Venezia, tel. 800-281-281, www.trambusopen. com). A similar bus laces together all the Christian sights.

Car and Minibus Tours

Autoservizi Monti Concezio, run by gentle, capable, and English-speaking Ezio, offers private cars or minibuses with driver/ guides (car-€40/hour, minibus-€45/hour, 3-hour minimum for city sightseeing, long rides outside Rome are more expensive, mobile 335-636-5907 or 349-674-5643, www.tourservicemonti.it, info@tourservicemonti.it).

Miles & Miles Private Tours, a family-run company, offers a number of tours, all with good English-speaking driver/guides (descriptions and pricing on their website, mention Rick Steves when booking direct then show the book on the day of service to get a discount, mobile 331-466-4900, www.milesandmiles.net, info @milesandmiles.net, Italian driver/guides and an American-run office). They also provide walking tours, shore excursions (from Civitavecchia, Livorno, Naples, Venice, and other ports), and unguided long-distance transportation; if traveling with a small group or a family from Rome to Florence, the Amalfi Coast, or elsewhere, consider paying extra to turn the trip into a memorable day tour with door-to-door service.

TOUR PACKAGES FOR STUDENTS

Andy Steves (Rick's son) runs **WSA Europe**, offering three-day and longer guided and unguided packages—including accommodations, sightseeing, and unique local experiences—for budget travelers across 11 top European cities, including Rome (from €99, see www.wsaeurope.com for details).

SIGHTS IN ROME

I've clustered Rome's sights into walkable neighborhoods, some quite close together (see "Rome's Neighborhoods" map on page 14). Save transit time by grouping your sightseeing according to location. For example, the Colosseum and the Forum are a few minutes' walk from Capitoline Hill; a 15-minute walk beyond that is the Pantheon. I like to tour these sights in one great day, starting at the Colosseum, then the Forum, then Capitoline Hill, and from there either to the Pantheon or back to the Colosseum (by way of additional ruins along Via dei Fori Imperiali).

Don't let the length of my descriptions determine your sightseeing priorities. In this chapter, Rome's most important sights have the shortest listings and are marked with a ✪. These sights are covered in much more detail in one of the tours included in this book. Check www.ricksteves.com/update for any significant changes that have occurred since this book was printed.

To connect some of the most central sights, follow my Heart of Rome Walk (see the next chapter), which takes you from Campo de' Fiori to the Trevi Fountain and Spanish Steps. This walk is most enjoyable in the evening—after the churches and museums have closed, when the evening air and lit-up fountains show off Rome at its most magical. To join the parade of people strolling down Via del Corso every evening, take my Dolce Vita Stroll (see the end of the Nightlife in Rome chapter).

Price Hike Alert: As budget cuts have taken their toll on cultural institutions, some of Rome's sights have found another way to make money. They host a special exhibit that few tourists really care to see, and require you to pay extra for your ticket, even if all you want to see is the permanent collection. This means admission fees jump by about €3. Expect this practice at the Capitoline

Museums, Borghese Gallery, National Museum of Rome, Ara Pacis, and others.

The prices I've listed here include these obligatory temporary exhibits. Come expecting this higher price...and consider yourself lucky if you happen to visit on the rare occasion when you can get in for less.

Ancient Rome

The core of ancient Rome, where the grandest monuments were built, is between the Colosseum and Capitoline Hill. Among the ancient forums, a few modern sights have popped up. I've listed these sights from south to north, starting with the biggies—the Colosseum and Forum—and continuing up to Capitoline Hill and Piazza Venezia. Then, as a pleasant conclusion to your busy day, consider my relaxing self-guided walk back south along the broad, parklike main drag—Via dei Fori Imperiali—with some enticing detours to nearby sights.

ANCIENT CORE
▲▲▲Colosseum (Colosseo)
This 2,000-year-old building is the classic example of Roman engineering. Used as a venue for entertaining the masses, this colossal,

functional stadium is one of Europe's most recognizable landmarks. Whether you're playing gladiator or simply marveling at the remarkable ancient design and construction, the Colosseum gets a unanimous thumbs-up.

Cost and Hours: €12 combo-ticket includes Roman Forum and Palatine Hill (see page 42), open daily 8:30 until one hour before sunset (see page 138 for times), last entry one hour before closing, audioguide-€5.50, Metro: Colosseo, tel. 06-3996-7700, www.archeoroma.beniculturali.it/en. For line-avoiding tips, see page 139.

✪ See the Colosseum Tour chapter.

▲Arch of Constatine
This well-preserved arch, which stands between the Colosseum and the Forum, commemorates a military coup and, more important, the acceptance of Christianity by the Roman Empire. When the ambitious Emperor

SIGHTS

Rome

SIGHTS

CIRC. CLODIO

To Foro Italico &
Autostrada

To MAXXI &
Parco della
Musica

VIA FLAMINIA

PONTE
MATTEOTTI

VIALE DELLE MILIZIE

VIA GIULIO CESARE

Lepanto

VIA ANGELICO

VIALE ANGELICO

VIA OTTAVIANO

Flaminio

S. MARIA
DEL POPOLO

Piazza
del Popolo

Piazzale
degli Eroi

VIA ANDREA DORIA

VIA LEONE IV

Cipro

VIA CANDIA

V. VATICANO

Ottaviano

Piazza del
Risorgimento

VIA COLA DI RIENZO

VIA M.A. COLONNA

PONTE
REG. MARG.

MAUSOLEUM
OF AUGUSTUS

VIA CIPRO

PISANI

VIA CRESCENZIO

ARA
PACIS

PONTE
CAVOUR

VATICAN
MUSEUM

Piazza
Cavour

VATICAN
CITY

VIA BORGO PIO

CASTEL
SANT'
ANGELO

PALACE OF
JUSTICE

Piazza
Borg.

SISTINE
CHAPEL

St.
Peter's
Square

Piazza
Pio XII

VIA
CONCILIAZIONE

PONTE
UMBERTO I

ST.
PETER'S

PONTE
S. ANGELO

PONTE
VITTORIO
EMANUELE

CORSO VITTORIO

VIA
CORONARI

PANTHEON

VIA PORTA
CAVALLEGGERI

TUNNEL

PONTE
AMEDEO

V. GIULIA

Piazza
Navona

To
Civitavecchia

EMANUELE

PONTE
MAZZINI

V. MONGERARDO

Campo
de' Fiori

SAN PIETRO
STATION

ANITA
GARIBALDI
STATUE

Tiber River

LUNGOTEVERE

V. MONSERRATO

Largo
Argentina

VILLA
FARNESINA

PALAZZO
FARNESE

To Termini Station
via Trastevere and
Ostiense Stations

Parco
Gianicolense

GHETTO

PONTE
SISTO

Piazza
Trilussa

Isola
Tiburina

Piazzale
Garibaldi

PONTE
GARIBALDI

VIA AURELIA ANTICA

GIUSEPPE
GARIBALDI
STATUE

SAN PIETRO
DI MONTORIO
(TEMPIETTO)

VIA LUNGA

Piazza
Belli

PONTE
CESTIO

ACQUA
PAOLA
FOUNTAIN

SANTA MARIA
IN TRASTEVERE

SAN
PANCRAZIO
GATE

ITALIAN
INDEPENDENCE
WAR
MEMORIAL

TRASTEVERE

VIA DI TRASTEVERE

Villa
Doria
Pamphili

OLD CITY
WALLS

PORTA
PORTESE

PORTA
PORTESE
MARKET

PONTE
SUBLICIO

VIALE DI TRASTEVERE

VIA PORTUENSE

LUNG. TESTACCIO

VIA BRANCA

Piazza
Testaccio

To Trastevere
Train Station

TESTACCIO
MARKET

TESTAC

Monte
Testaccio

ETRUSCAN MUSEUM

NATIONAL GALLERY OF MODERN ART

ZOO

To Catacombs of Priscilla & Autostrada

VIA SALARIA

VIA REINA MARGHERITA

Villa Borghese Gardens

BORGHESE GALLERY

OLD CITY WALLS

Pincio

VIA FLAVIA

Piazza Fiume

PORTA PINCIANA

VIA PIEMONTE

VILLA MEDICI

VIA MARGUTTA

Spagna

VIA DEL CORSO

VIA DEL BABUINO

Piazza di Spagna

V. COND.

Spagna

SPAN. STEPS

PINCIANA

VIA LUDOVISI

U.S. EMBASSY

VIA PALESTRO

Piazza Indipendenza

VIA VENETO

VIA SISTINA

CAPUCHIN CRYPT

SANTA MARIA VITTORIA

VIA CERNAIA

Piazza Barberini

PALAZZO BARBERINI

Barberini

VIA XX SETTEMBRE

BATHS OF DIOCLETIAN

Castro Pretorio

PARLIAMENT

VIA TRITONE

VIA DEL TRITONE

VIA TORINO

Repubblica

Piazza Repubblica

Piazza dei Cinquecento

TERMINI STATION

TREVI FOUNTAIN

PALAZZO DEL QUIRINALE

VIA DEL QUIRINALE

VIA NAZIONALE

SAN CARLO

SANT' ANDREA

VIA DELLE QUATTRO FONTANE

VIA FIRENZE

NAT'L MUSEUM OF ROME

Termini

VIA MARSALA

Piazza Colonna

SAN IGNAZIO

Piazza del Quirinale

VIA NAZIONALE

VIA DEPRETIS

SANTA MARIA MAGGIORE

VIA GIO. GIOLITTI

VIA TURATI

S. MARIA SOPRA MINERVA

GESÙ

VIA IV NOV.

Largo Mag.

VIA BOSCHI

SERPENTI

MILANO

VIA URBANA

VIA CAVOUR

SANTA PRASSEDE

Piazza Vittorio Emanuele II

ESQUILINO MARKET

Piazza Venezia

VICTOR EMMANUEL MONUMENT

IMPERIAL FORUMS

V. PAN.

MONTI

VIA BACCINA

VIA MADONNA

V. LEO.

LANZA

Cavour

Vittorio Emanuele

V. CONTE VERDE

CAPITOLINE HILL

VIA DEI FORI IMPERIALI

VIA CAVOUR

ST. PETER-IN-CHAINS

CAPITOLINE MUSEUMS

TEATRO DI MARCELLO

ROMAN FORUM

Colosseo

Parco del Colle Oppio

VIA LABICANA

SAN CLEMENTE

VIA MERULANA

VIALE MANZONI

Manzoni

PONTE PALATINO

SANTA MARIA IN COSMEDI

PALATINE HILL

COLOSSEUM

ARCH OF CONSTANTINE

VIA DI S. GIOVANNI LAT.

MUSEUM OF THE LIBERATION OF ROME

HOLY STAIRS

VIA DI S. GREG.

Parco del Celio

SANTA SABINA

CIRCUS MAXIMUS

SANT' ALESSIO

Circo Massimo

Parco Celimontana

SAN GIOVANNI IN LATERANO

PORTA SAN GIO.

San Giovanni

VIA SANNIO

Piazza Cav. di Malta

VIALE AVENTINO

Piazza Albania

BATHS OF CARACALLA

OLD CITY WALLS

MAMMORATA

CIO

Piazza di Porta San Paolo

OLD CITY WALLS

500 Meters

500 Yards

PYRAMID

Piramide

To Ostiense Train Station & E.U.R.

To Ancient Appian Way & E.U.R.

Constantine (who had a vision that he'd win under the sign of the cross) defeated his rival Maxentius in A.D. 312, Constantine became sole emperor of the Roman Empire and legalized Christianity. The arch is free to see—always open and viewable.

✪ See page 148 of the Colosseum Tour chapter.

▲▲▲Roman Forum (Foro Romano)

This is ancient Rome's birthplace and civic center, and the common ground between Rome's famous seven hills. As just about anything important that happened in an-

cient Rome happened here, it's arguably the most important piece of real estate in Western civilization. While only a few fragments of that glorious past remain, history seekers find plenty to ignite their imaginations amid the half-broken columns and arches.

Cost and Hours: €12 combo-ticket includes Colosseum and Palatine Hill (see page 42), open daily 8:30 until one hour before sunset (see page 138 for times), last entry one hour before closing, audioguide-€5, Metro: Colosseo, tel. 06-3996-7700, www.archeoroma.beniculturali.it/en.

✪ See the Roman Forum Tour chapter.

▲▲Palatine Hill (Monte Palatino)

The hill overlooking the Forum was the home of the emperors and now contains a museum, scant (but impressive when understood)

remains of imperial palaces, and a view of the Circus Maximus (if it's not blocked by ongoing archaeological work).

Cost and Hours: €12 combo-ticket includes Roman Forum and Colosseum—see page 42, open same hours as Forum and Colosseum, audioguide-€5, Metro: Colosseo.

✪ See the Palatine Hill Tour chapter.

Mamertine Prison

This 2,500-year-old cistern-like prison is where, according to Christian tradition, the Romans imprisoned Saints Peter and Paul. Though it was long a charming and historic sight, its artifacts have been removed, and today it's run by a commercial tour-bus company charging €5 for a cheesy "multimedia" walk-through. Don't go in. Instead, stand outside and imagine how this dank cistern

Ancient Rome

SIGHTS

once housed prisoners of the emperor. Amid fat rats and rotting corpses, unfortunate humans awaited slow deaths. It's said that a miraculous fountain sprang up inside so Peter could convert and baptize his jailers, who were also subsequently martyred.

Bocca della Verità

The legendary "Mouth of Truth" at the Church of Santa Maria in Cosmedin—a few blocks south-west of the other sights listed here—draws a playful crowd. Stick your hand in the mouth of the gaping stone face in the porch wall. As the legend goes (and was popularized by the 1953 film *Roman Holiday*, starring

Gregory Peck and Audrey Hepburn), if you're a liar, your hand will be gobbled up. The mouth is only accessible when the church gate is open, but it's always (partially) visible through the gate, even when closed. If the church itself is open, step inside to see one of the few unaltered medieval church interiors in Rome. Notice the mismatched ancient columns and beautiful cosmatesque floor—a centuries-old example of recycling.

Cost and Hours: €0.50 suggested donation, daily 9:30-17:50, closes earlier off-season, Piazza Bocca della Verità, near the north end of Circus Maximus, tel. 06-678-7759.

CAPITOLINE HILL

Of Rome's famous seven hills, this is the smallest, tallest, and most famous—home of the ancient Temple of Jupiter and the center of city government for 2,500 years. There are several ways to get to

the top of Capitoline Hill. If you're coming from the north (from Piazza Venezia), take Michelangelo's impressive stairway to the right of the big, white Victor Emmanuel Monument. Coming from the southeast (the Forum), take the steep staircase near the Arch of Septimius Severus. From near Trajan's Forum along Via dei Fori Imperiali, take the winding road. All three converge at the top, in the square called Campidoglio (kahm-pee-DOHL-yoh).

▲Piazza del Campidoglio

This square atop the hill, once the religious and political center of ancient Rome, is still the home of the city's government. In the 1530s, the pope called on Michelangelo to re-establish this square as a grand center. Michelangelo placed the ancient equestrian statue of Marcus Aurelius as its focal point. Effective. (The original statue is now in the adjacent museum.) The twin buildings on either side are the Capitoline Museums. Behind the replica of the statue is the mayoral palace (Palazzo Senatorio).

Michelangelo intended that people approach the square from his grand stairway off Piazza Venezia. From the top of

Capitoline Hill & Piazza Venezia

To Piazza del Popolo ↑

GALLERIA DORIA PAMPHILJ

VIA DEL CORSO

VIA BATTISTI
#64,40

VIA 4 NOVEMBRE

VIA 4 NOVEMBRE

VIA DEL PLEBISCITO

Piazza Venezia

PALAZZO VENEZIA ❼ Ⓑ
#64,85

S. MARIA DI LORETO

Largo Magnanapoli

VIA NAZIONALE

Piazza San Marco Ⓣ #8

To Gesù & Pantheon →

VIA SAN MARCO

TRAJAN'S COLUMN

MUSEUM OF IMPERIAL FORUMS & TRAJAN'S MARKET

Ⓣ

VIA PARACOLI

Ⓑ #64

VICTOR EMMANUEL MONUMENT CAFÉ

TRAJAN'S FORUM

ROME FROM THE SKY ELEVATOR

INSULA (APARTMENT) RUINS

STA. MARIA ARACOELI

VIA ALESSANDRINA

CAESAR'S FORUM

MICHELANGELO'S GRAND STAIRCASE

#110 Ⓑ

PALAZZO NUOVO ❻

❺

STATUE ❶ ❸ ❹

VIA DEI FORI IMPERIALI

Piazza Caffarelli

❷

PALAZZO SENATORIO

MAMERTINE PRISON

To Colosseum & Ⓜ →

To Teatro di Marcello ←

VIA TEATRO MARCELLO

PUBLIC CAFÉ ENTRANCE

CAPITOLINE MUSEUMS

PALAZZO DEI CONSERVATORI

CAFÉ

TABULARIUM

FORUM EXIT

SANTI LUCA E MARTINA

ARCH OF SEPTIMIUS SEVERUS

ROMAN FORUM

FORO ROMANO

100 Meters

100 Yards

❶ Piazza del Campidoglio
❷ Capitoline Museums
❸ Copy of She-Wolf Statue
❹ "Il Nasone" Water Fountain
❺ Shortcut to Santa Maria in Aracoeli Church
❻ Shortcut to Victor Emmanuel Monument
❼ Mussolini's Balcony

SIGHTS

the stairway, you see the new Renaissance face of Rome, with its back to the Forum. Michelangelo gave the buildings the "giant order"—huge pilasters make the existing two-story buildings feel one-storied and more harmonious with the new square. Notice how the statues atop these buildings welcome you and then draw you in.

The terraces just downhill (past either side of the mayor's palace) offer grand views of the Forum. To the left of the mayor's palace is a copy of the famous she-wolf statue on a column. Farther down

Tips on Sightseeing in Rome

These tips will help you use your time and money efficiently, making the Eternal City seem less eternal and more entertaining. For general advice on sightseeing, see page 530.

Passes

Roma Pass: Rome offers several sightseeing passes to help you save money. For most visitors, the Roma Pass (www.romapass. it) is the clear winner. The Roma Pass costs €36 and is valid for three days, covering public transportation and free or discounted entry to Roman sights. You get free admission to your first two sights (where you also get to skip the ticket line)

and then a discount on the rest within the three-day window. Sights covered (or discounted) by the pass include the following: Colosseum/Palatine Hill/Roman Forum, Borghese Gallery (though you still must make a reservation), Capitoline Museums, Castel Sant'Angelo, Montemartini Museum, Ara Pacis, Museum of Roman Civilization, Etruscan Museum, Baths of Caracalla, Trajan's Market, and some of the Appian Way sights. The pass also covers four branches of the National Museum of Rome, considered as a single "sight": Palazzo Massimo (the most important of the lot), Crypta Balbi (medieval art), Palazzo Altemps (sculpture collection), and Museum of the Bath (ancient inscriptions). The pass does not cover the Vatican Museum (which contains the Sistine Chapel).

If you'll be using public transportation and visiting any two of the major sights in a three-day period, get the pass. It's sold at participating sights, TIs, and many tobacco shops and newsstands all over town (look for a *Roma Pass* sign; all should offer the same price). Try to buy it at a less crowded TI or sight (you can buy it at a sight even if you don't intend to use it there). Don't bother ordering it online—you have to physically pick up the pass in Rome, which negates any time-saving advantage.

Validate your Roma Pass by writing your name and validation date on the card. Then insert it directly into the turnstile at your first two (free) sights. At other sights, show it at the ticket office to get your reduced (*ridotto*) price—about 30 percent off.

To get the most out of your pass, visit the two most expensive sights first—for example, the Colosseum (€12) and the National Museum of Rome (€10). Definitely use it to bypass the long ticket-buying line at the Colosseum. For sights that normally sell a combined ticket (such as the Colosseum/Palatine Hill/Roman Forum or the National Museum branches), visiting the various sights counts as a single entry.

The Roma Pass comes with a three-day transit pass. Write your name and birthdate on the transit pass, validate it on your first bus or Metro ride by passing it over a sensor at a turnstile or validation machine (look for a yellow circle), and you can take unlimited rides within Rome's city limits until midnight of the third day.

A Roma Pass can work well for families. Children under age 18 get into covered sights for free, and they can skip the lines alongside their pass-holding parents.

Combo-Ticket for Colosseum, Forum, and Palatine Hill: A €12 combo-ticket covers these three adjacent sights (no individual tickets are sold). The combo-ticket allows one entry per sight and is valid for two days. Note that these sights are also covered by the Roma Pass. To avoid ticket-buying lines at the Colosseum and Forum, purchase your combo-ticket or Roma Pass at the lesser-visited Palatine Hill, or buy your combo-ticket online in advance (see page 139).

Top Tips

Museum Reservations: The marvelous Borghese Gallery requires reservations in advance (for specifics, see page 265). You can reserve online to avoid long lines at the Vatican Museum (see page 230).

Opening Hours: Rome's sights have notoriously variable hours from season to season. It's smart to check each sight's website in advance. On holidays, expect shorter hours or closures.

Churches: Many churches, which have divine art and free entry, open early (around 7:00-7:30), close for lunch (roughly 12:00-15:00), and close late (about 19:00). Kamikaze tourists maximize their sightseeing hours by visiting churches before 9:00 or late in the day; during the siesta, they see major sights that stay open all day (St. Peter's, Colosseum, Forum, Capitoline Museums, Pantheon, and National Museum of Rome). Dress modestly for church visits.

Picnic Discreetly: Public drinking and eating is not allowed at major sights, though the ban has proven difficult to enforce. To avoid the risk of being fined, choose an empty piazza for your picnic, or keep a low profile.

Miscellaneous Tips: I carry a water bottle and refill it at Rome's many public drinking spouts. Because public restrooms are scarce, use toilets at museums, restaurants, and bars.

is *il nasone* ("the big nose"), a refreshing water fountain (see photo). Block the spout with your fingers, and water spurts up for drinking. Romans joke that a cheap Roman boy takes his date out for a drink at *il nasone*. Near the she-wolf statue is the staircase leading to a shortcut to the Victor Emmanuel Monument (see sidebar).

▲▲▲Capitoline Museums (Musei Capitolini)

Some of ancient Rome's most famous statues and art are housed in the two palaces that flank the equestrian statue in the Campidoglio. You'll see the Dying Gaul, the original she-wolf, and the original version of the equestrian statue of Marcus Aurelius. Admission includes access to the underground vacant Tabularium, with its panoramic overlook of the Forum.

Cost and Hours: €13, Tue-Sun 9:00-20:00, closed Mon, last entry one hour before closing, audioguide-€5, tel. 06-0608, www.museicapitolini.org.

○ See the Capitoline Museums Tour chapter.

Santa Maria in Aracoeli Church

The church atop Capitoline Hill is old and dear to the hearts of Romans. It stands on the site where Emperor Augustus (supposedly) had a premonition of the coming of Mary and Christ standing on an "altar in the sky" *(ara coeli)*.

Cost and Hours: Free, daily April-Oct 9:00-12:30 & 15:00-18:30, Nov-March 9:00-12:30 & 14:30-17:30, tel. 06-6976-3839.

Visiting the Church: While dedicated pilgrims climb up the long, steep staircase from street level (the right side of Victor Emmanuel Monument as you face it), savvy sightseers prefer to enter through the shortcut atop Capitoline Hill (see sidebar).

The church is Rome in a nutshell, where you can time-travel across 2,000 years by standing in one spot. The building dates from Byzantine times (sixth century) and was expanded in the 1200s. Inside, the mismatched columns (red, yellow, striped, fluted) and marble floor are ancient, plundered from many different monuments. The medieval world is evident in the gravestones beneath your feet. The early Renaissance is featured in beautiful frescoes by Pinturicchio (first chapel on the right from the main entrance), with their 3-D perspective and natural landscapes. The coffered ceiling celebrates the Christian victory over the Ottoman Turks (Battle of Lepanto, 1571), with thanks to Mary (in the center of the ceiling). The chandeliers in the nave hint at the elegance of

Shortcut to the Victor Emmanuel Monument and Aracoeli Church

A clever shortcut lets you go directly from Piazza del Campidoglio, the square atop Capitoline Hill, to Santa Maria in Aracoeli Church and an upper level of the Victor Emmanuel Monument, avoiding long flights of stairs. Facing the square's equestrian statue, head to the left, climbing the wide set of stairs near the she-wolf statue. Midway up the stairs (at the column), turn left to reach the back entrance to the Aracoeli Church. To reach the Victor Emmanuel Monument, pass the column and continue to the top of the steps, pass through the iron gate, and enter the small unmarked door at #13 on the right. You'll soon emerge on a café terrace that leads to the monument and the Rome from the Sky elevator.

SIGHTS

Baroque. Napoleon's occupying troops used the building as a horse stable. But like Rome itself, it survived and retained its splendor.

The church comes alive at Christmastime. Romans hike up to enjoy a manger scene *(presepio)* assembled every year in the second chapel on the left. They stop at the many images of the Virgin (e.g., the statue in the marble gazebo to the left of the altar), who made an appearance to the pagan Augustus so long ago. And, most famously, they venerate a wooden statue of the Baby Jesus (Santo Bambino), displayed in a chapel to the left of the altar (go through the low-profile door and down the hall). Though the origi-nal statue was stolen in 1994, the copy continues this longtime Roman tradition. A clear box filled with handwritten prayers sits nearby.

The daunting 125-step staircase up Capitoline Hill to the entrance was once climbed—on their knees—by Roman women who wished for a child. Today, they don't...and Italy has Europe's lowest birthrate.

Rome at a Glance

▲▲▲ **Colosseum** Huge stadium where gladiators fought. **Hours:** Daily 8:30 until one hour before sunset: April-Aug until 19:15, Sept until 19:00, Oct until 18:30, off-season closes as early as 16:30. See page 35.

▲▲▲**Roman Forum** Ancient Rome's main square, with ruins and grand arches. **Hours:** Same hours as Colosseum. See page 38.

▲▲▲**Pantheon** The defining domed temple. **Hours:** Mon-Sat 8:30-19:30, Sun 9:00-18:00, holidays 9:00-13:00, closed for Mass Sat at 17:00 and Sun at 10:30. See page 59.

▲▲▲**St. Peter's Basilica** Most impressive church on earth, with Michelangelo's *Pietà* and dome. **Hours:** Church—daily April-Sept 7:00-19:00, Oct-March 7:00-18:30, often closed Wed mornings; dome—daily April-Sept 8:00-18:00, Oct-March 8:00-17:00. See page 63.

▲▲▲**Vatican Museum** Four miles of the finest art of Western civilization, culminating in Michelangelo's glorious Sistine Chapel. **Hours:** Mon-Sat 9:00-18:00. Closed on religious holidays and Sun, except last Sun of the month (open 9:00-14:00). May be open some Fri nights by online reservation only. Hours are subject to change. See page 63.

▲▲▲**Borghese Gallery** Bernini sculptures and paintings by Cara-vaggio, Raphael, and Titian in a Baroque palazzo. Reservations mandatory. **Hours:** Tue-Sun 9:00-19:00, closed Mon. See page 68.

▲▲▲**National Museum of Rome** Greatest collection of Roman sculpture anywhere. **Hours:** Tue-Sun 9:00-19:45, closed Mon. See page 78.

▲▲▲**Capitoline Museums** Ancient statues, mosaics, and expan-sive view of Forum. **Hours:** Tue-Sun 9:00-20:00, closed Mon. See page 44.

▲▲**Palatine Hill** Ruins of emperors' palaces, Circus Maximus view, and museum. **Hours:** Same hours as Colosseum. See page 38.

▲▲**Trajan's Column, Market, and Forum** Tall column with narra-tive relief, forum ruins, and museum with entry to Trajan's Market. **Hours:** Forum and column always viewable; museum open Tue-Sun 9:00-19:00, closed Mon. See page 50.

▲▲**Museo dell'Ara Pacis** Shrine marking the beginning of Rome's Golden Age. **Hours:** Tue-Sun 9:00-19:00, closed Mon. See page 75.

▲▲**Dolce Vita Stroll** Evening *passeggiata,* where Romans strut their stuff. **Hours:** Roughly Mon-Sat 17:00-19:00 and Sun afternoons. See page 74.

▲▲**Catacombs** Underground tombs, mainly Christian, some outside the city. **Hours:** Generally open 10:00-12:00 & 14:00-17:00. See pages 77, 108, and 109.

▲▲**Church of San Giovanni in Laterano** Grandiose and historic "home church of the popes," with one-of-a-kind Holy Stairs across the street. **Hours:** Church—daily 7:00-18:30; Holy Stairs—generally same hours but closed for lunch. See page 89.

▲**Arch of Constantine** Honors the emperor who legalized Christianity. **Hours:** Always viewable. See page 35.

▲**St. Peter-in-Chains** Church with Michelangelo's *Moses.* **Hours:** Daily 8:00-12:30 & 15:00-19:00, until 18:00 in winter. See page 59.

▲**Piazza del Campidoglio** Square atop Capitoline Hill, designed by Michelangelo, with a museum, grand stairway, and Forum overlooks. **Hours:** Always open. See page 40.

▲**Victor Emmanuel Monument** Gigantic edifice celebrating Italian unity, with Rome from the Sky elevator ride up to 360-degree city view. **Hours:** Monument open daily 9:30-18:30; elevator open Mon-Thu 9:30-18:30, Fri-Sun 9:30-19:30. See page 48.

▲**Trevi Fountain** Baroque hot spot into which tourists throw coins to ensure a return trip to Rome. **Hours:** Always flowing. See page 62.

▲**Castel Sant'Angelo** Hadrian's Tomb turned castle, prison, papal refuge, now museum. **Hours:** Tue-Sun 9:00-19:30, closed Mon. See page 65.

▲**Capuchin Crypt** Decorated with the bones of 4,000 Franciscan friars. **Hours:** Daily 9:00-19:00. See page 71.

▲**Baths of Diocletian** Once ancient Rome's immense public baths, now a Michelangelo church. **Hours:** Mon-Sat 7:00-18:30, Sun 7:00-19:30. See page 78.

SIGHTS

PIAZZA VENEZIA

This vast square, dominated by the big, white Victor Emmanuel Monument, is a major transportation hub and the focal point of modern Rome. With your back to the monument (you'll get the best views from the terrace by the guards and eternal flame), look down Via del Corso, the city's axis, surrounded by Rome's classiest shopping district. In the 1930s, Benito Mussolini whipped up Italy's nationalistic fervor from a balcony above the square (it's the less-grand building on the left). He gave 64 speeches from this balcony, including the declaration of war in 1940. This Early Renaissance building (with hints of medieval showing with its crenellated roof line) was the seat of Mussolini's fascist government. Fascist masses filled the square screaming, "Four more years!"—or something like that. Mussolini created the boulevard Via dei Fori Imperiali (to your right, capped by Trajan's Column) to open up views of the Colosseum in the distance. Mussolini lied to his people, mixing fear and patriotism to push his country to the right and embroil the Italians in expensive and regrettable wars. In 1945, they shot Mussolini and hung him from a meat hook in Milan. (Former Prime Minister Silvio Berlusconi's headquarters are still located—thought-provokingly—just behind Mussolini's. That explains all the security on Via del Plebiscito.)

With your back still to the monument, circle around the left side. At the back end of the monument, look down into the ditch on your left to see the ruins of an ancient apartment building from the first century A.D.; part of it was transformed into a tiny church (faded frescoes and bell tower). Rome was built in layers—almost everywhere you go, there's an earlier version beneath your feet. (The hop-on, hop-off 110open Bus stops just downhill from here.)

Continuing on, you reach two staircases leading up Capitoline Hill. One is Michelangelo's grand staircase up to the Campidoglio. The steeper of the two leads to Santa Maria in Aracoeli, a good example of the earliest style of Christian church (described earlier). The contrast between this climb-on-your-knees ramp to God's house and Michelangelo's elegant stairs illustrates the changes Renaissance humanism brought civilization.

From the bottom of Michelangelo's stairs, look right several blocks down the street to see a condominium actually built upon the surviving ancient pillars and arches of Teatro di Marcello.

▲Victor Emmanuel Monument

This oversize monument to Italy's first king, built to celebrate the 50th anniversary of the country's unification in 1861, was part of Italy's push to overcome the new country's strong regionalism and create a national identity. The scale of the monument is over-the-top: 200 feet high, 500 feet wide. The 43-foot-long statue of the king on his high horse is one of the biggest equestrian statues in the world. The king's moustache forms an arc five feet long, and a person could sit within the horse's hoof. At the base of this statue, Italy's Tomb of the Unknown

Soldier (flanked by Italian flags and armed guards) is watched over by the goddess Roma (with the gold mosaic background).

Cost and Hours: Monument—free, daily 9:30-18:30, a few WCs scattered throughout, tel. 06-6920-2049. Elevator—€7, Mon-Thu 9:30-18:30, Fri-Sun 9:30-19:30, ticket office closes 45 minutes earlier, WC at entrance, tel. 06-679-3598; follow *ascensori panoramici* signs inside the Victor Emmanuel Monument or take the short-cut from Capitoline Hill (no elevator access from street level).

Background: With its gleaming white sheen (from a recent scrubbing) and enormous scale, the monument provides a vivid sense of what Ancient Rome looked like at its peak—imagine the Forum filled with shiny, grandiose buildings like this one. It's also lathered in symbolism meant to connect the modern city and nation with its grand past: The eternal flames are reminiscent of the Vestal Virgins and the ancient flame of Rome. And it's crowned by glorious chariots like those that topped the ancient Arch of Constantine.

Locals have a love/hate relationship with this "Altar of the Nation." Many Romans say it's a "punch in the eye" and regret its unfortunate, clumsy location atop precious antiquities. Others consider it a reminder of the challenge that followed the creation of the modern nation of Italy: actually creating "Italians."

Visiting the Monument: The "Vittoriano" (as locals call it) is open and free to the public. You can simply climb the front stairs, or go inside from one of several entrances: midway up the monument through doorways flanking the central statue, on either side at street level, and at the base of the colonnade (two-thirds of the way up, near the shortcut from Capitoline Hill). The little-visited **Museum of the Risorgimento** fills several floors with displays (well-described in English) on the movement and war that led to the unification of Italy in 1870. A section on the lower east side hosts temporary exhibits of minor works by major artists (€5 to enter museum, temporary exhibits around €10, tel. 06-322-5380, www.comunicareorganizzando.it). A café is at the base of the top colonnade, on the monument's east side.

Best of all, the monument offers a grand view of the Eternal City. You can climb the stairs to the midway point for a decent view,

keep climbing to the base of
the colonnade for a better view,
or, for the best view, ride the
Rome from the Sky (Roma dal
Cielo) elevator, which zips you
from the top of the stair climb
(at the back of the monument)
to the rooftop for the grandest,
360-degree view of the center of

Rome—even better than from the top of St. Peter's dome. Once on
top, you stand on a terrace between the monument's two chariots.
You can look north up Via del Corso to Piazza del Popolo, west to
the dome of St. Peter's Basilica, and south to the Roman Forum
and Colosseum. Helpful panoramic diagrams describe the skyline,
with powerful binoculars available for zooming in on particular
sights. It's best in late afternoon, when it's beginning to cool off and
Rome glows.

THE IMPERIAL FORUMS AND
VIA DEI FORI IMPERIALI

The original Roman Forum is the main attraction for today's tourists, but several more forums and ruins—the legacy of later emperors (especially Trajan)—line the broad, Mussolini-built Via dei
Fori Imperiali, which runs from Piazza Venezia to the Colosseum.
Today the imperial forums are out in the open, free to view 24/7,
and linked by this self-guided walk. Visiting here is especially nice
now that the once-busy street has been closed to private car traffic—and, on Sundays and holidays, to all vehicles.

    Background: As Rome grew from a village to an empire,
it outgrew the Roman Forum. Several energetic emperors built
their own forums—which stood in a line from the Colosseum to
Trajan's Column—complete with temples, shopping malls, government buildings, statues, monuments, and piazzas. While the
Roman Forum was built with no grand plan over 1,200 years, these
new imperial forums were distinct modules, with a cohesive plan
stamped with the emperor's unique personality. Julius Caesar built
the first one (46 B.C.), and over the next 150 years, it was added
onto by Augustus (2 B.C.), Vespasian (A.D. 75), Nerva (A.D. 97), and
Trajan (A.D. 112). What you see today are mostly the remains of
Trajan's great building campaign.

    ◉ Self-Guided Walk: For an overview of the entire archaeo-
logical area, take this walk from Piazza Venezia to the Colosseum.
After a busy day of sightseeing, this stroll offers a relaxing way to
wind down (while seeing a few more ancient wonders, but without
crowds or turnstiles) on your way to the Colosseum and its handy
Metro stop.

The Imperial Forums

SIGHTS

• *Start in Piazza Venezia.*

Piazza Venezia: Mussolini's office was here, and the Fascist dictator longed to see the Colosseum from his window. So this self-styled modern emperor leveled an entire neighborhood, dug up the forum ruins, and ran a strip of pavement right down the middle, creating this wide, straight boulevard directly to the Colosseum. (For more on Piazza Venezia, see the listing earlier.)

• *Head in the direction of the Colosseum, walking along the left side of Via dei Fori Imperiali. At the start of the boulevard, the big park with umbrella pines stands in front of...*

Trajan's Forum: Rome peaked under Emperor Trajan (ruled A.D. 98-117), when the empire stretched from England to the Sahara, from Spain to the Fertile Crescent. A triumphant Trajan returned to Rome with his booty and shook it all over the city. He extended the Forum by building his own commercial, political, and religious center nearby, complete with temples, law courts, a semicircular shopping mall, and a monumental column covered with detailed carvings that tell the story of one of his most famous conquests.

SIGHTS

Trajan's Forum was a crucial expansion of the old Roman Forum, which was too small and ceremonial to fill the commercial needs of a booming city of more than a million people. To build his forum, Trajan literally moved mountains. He cut away a ridge that once connected the Quirinal and Capitoline hills, creating this valley. This was the largest forum ever, and its opulence astounded even jaded Romans.

In Roman times, you would have entered at the Colosseum end through a triumphal arch and been greeted in the main square by a large statue of the soldier-king on a horse. Continuing on, you'd enter the Basilica Ulpia (the gray granite columns near Trajan's Column), the largest law court of its day. Finally, at the far end, you would have found Trajan's Column, flanked by two libraries that contained the world's knowledge in Greek and Latin. Balconies on the libraries gave close-up looks at the upper reliefs of the column, in case anyone doubted the outcome of Trajan's war.

• *Speaking of which: Rising 140 feet above Trajan's Forum (circle it on the sidewalk above for a complete view) is...*

Trajan's Column: The world's grandest column from antiquity is decorated with a spiral relief of 2,500 figures trumpeting the emperor's exploits. It has stood for centuries as a symbol of a truly cosmopolitan civilization. At one point, the ashes of Trajan and his wife were held in the base, and the sun glinted off a polished bronze statue of Trajan at the top. (Today, St. Peter is on top.) Built as a stack of 17 marble doughnuts, the column is hollow (note the small window slots) with a spiral staircase inside, leading up to the balcony.

The **relief** unfolds like a scroll, telling the story of Rome's last and greatest foreign conquest, Trajan's defeat of Dacia (modern-day

Romania). The staggering haul of gold plundered from the Dacians paid for this forum. The narrative starts at the bottom with a trickle of water that becomes a river and soon picks up boats full of supplies. Then come the soldiers themselves, who spill out from the gates of the city. A river god (bottom band, south side) surfaces to bless the journey. Along the way (second band), they build roads and forts to sustain the vast enterprise, including (third band, south side) Trajan's half-mile-long bridge over the Danube, the longest for a thousand years. (Find the three tiny crisscross rectangles representing the wooden span.) Trajan himself (fourth band, in military skirt with toga over his arm) mounts a podium to fire up the troops. They hop into a Roman galley ship (fifth band) and head off to fight the valiant Dacians in the middle of a forest (eighth band). Finally, at the very top, the Romans hold a sacrifice to give thanks for the victory, while the captured armor is displayed on the pedestal.

Originally, the entire story was painted in bright colors. If you were to unwind the scroll, it would stretch over two football fields—it's far longer than the frieze around the Greek Parthenon. (An unscrolled copy is in E.U.R.'s Museum of Roman Civilization; see page 106.)

• *Continue through the park about 150 yards down Via dei Fori Imperiali. Detour left onto a pedestrian walkway, with good views of Trajan's entire ensemble. Below the bridge are the foundations of the medieval-era neighborhood that was cleared out to build the boulevard. Under these medieval ruins lie ancient ones.*

The big, semicircular structure nestled into the cutaway curve of Quirinal Hill is...

Trajan's Market: This was likely part shopping mall, part warehouse, and part administration building and/or government offices. For now the conventional wisdom holds that at ground level, the 13 tall (shallow) arches housed shops selling fresh fruit,

vegetables, and flowers to people who passed by on the street. The 26 arched windows (above) lit a covered walkway lined with shops that sold wine and olive oil. On the roof (now lined with a metal railing) ran a street that likely held still more shops, making about 150 in all. Shoppers could browse through goods from every corner of Rome's vast empire—exotic fruits from Africa, spices from Asia, and fish-and-chips from Londinium.

Above the semicircle, the upper floors of the complex housed bureaucrats in charge of a crucial element of city life: doling out free grain to unemployed citizens, who lived off the wealth plundered from distant lands. Better to pacify them than risk a riot. Above the offices, at the very top, rises a tower added in the Middle Ages.

The market was beautiful and functional, filling the space of the curved hill perfectly and echoing the curved side of the Forum's main courtyard. (The wall of rough volcanic stones on the ground once extended into a semicircle.) Unlike most Roman buildings, the brick facade wasn't covered with plaster or marble. The architect liked the simple contrast between the warm brick and the white stone lining the arches and windows.

If you'd like to walk around the market complex and see some excavated statues, visit the **Museum of the Imperial Forums** (described later; enter just uphill from Trajan's Column).

• *Returning to the main street, continue toward the Colosseum for about 100 more yards.*

Emperor Statues and More Forums: A bronze statue of **Emperor Trajan** stands beside Trajan's Forum. Notice the date on the pedestal—Anno XI. The statue was erected by Mussolini in "the 11th year of the Fascist Renovation of Italy." Mussolini came to power in 1922, so this would be from 1933. Across the street is a similar statue of **Julius Caesar.** Caesar built the first of the imperial forums in 46 B.C., as an extension of the Roman Forum. Behind him stand the three remaining columns of his forum's Temple of Venus—the patron goddess of the Julian family.

• *Continue along (down the left side).*

You soon come to **Emperor Augustus** in his famous hailing-a-cab pose (a copy of the original, which you can see at the Vatican Museum). This is actually his "commander talking to his people" pose. Behind him was the Forum of Augustus, marked by the four remaining columns of the Temple of Mars. The main thing that survives of the forum is the towering, ugly wall built to protect Augustus' temple from city fires.

Farther along is a statue of **Emperor Nerva,** trying but failing to have the commanding presence of Augustus. Gazing across the boulevard from here to the Roman Forum, you have good views of the back side of the Curia, where the senate met. Beyond that is Palatine Hill, with the foundation of one of its palaces. Behind Nerva, you can look down at an original marble inlaid floor that was once under a grand roof, surrounded by offices and shops within a semicircular mall. Nerva's Forum is also marked by its surviving fire wall.

A few steps beyond the remains of a **medieval tower** are some fine surviving marble reliefs from Nerva's Forum showing religious rituals. The tower was a medieval noble family's fortified residence—a reminder that the fall of Rome left a power vacuum, and with no central authority, it was every big shot for himself.

• *Cross the busy Via Cavour. If you were to head up this street two blocks, then turn left (near the Cavour Metro stop), you'd be immersed in the Monti district, one of Rome's most characteristic neighborhoods (described later). But for now, continue along the main drag.*

Sights in Rome 55

You'll pass by the main entry to the Roman Forum (on the right side of Via dei Fori Imperiali) and the information center (on the left), with a handy café, info desk, and WC. Also on the right side of the street is the back side of the vast Basilica of Constantine (see page 157), with its apse from a time before there were churches.

• *Cross the street (using the handy crosswalk directly in front of the information center), and turn your attention to the wall just below the arches of the basilica. (Note: This area may be torn up due to construction of a new Metro line.)*

Four Black-and-White Maps: These chart the growth of the Roman Empire. As if to validate his greatness, Mussolini made sure to celebrate the greatness of Rome. He posted this handy history lesson, showing the rise (but not the fall) of the greatest civilization in Western history: 509 B.C.—Roman Republic established;

200 B.C.—Rome after the Punic War; A.D. 1—Rome under Augustus, during the time of Christ when St. Peter was here; and A.D. 100—during Trajan's rule, with the empire at its peak. A fifth plaque is missing. It showed Italy in 1936, after Mussolini had made his own mark on history by conquering Ethiopia. Mussolini may have pointed it out to his fellow Fascist, Adolf Hitler, when the two paraded down the street together in 1938. A few years later, Italy had lost World War II, Mussolini was arrested and executed, and the plaque was torn down.

• *Our walk is over. From here, you have several options. The **Colosseum** (and a handy **Metro** stop) are straight ahead. To visit **St. Peter-in-Chains Church**, head up the hill above the Metro stop (see St. Peter-in-Chains Tour chapter). If you haven't yet toured the **Roman Forum**, you can enter either along Via dei Fori Imperiali (just right of the maps), or use the entrance facing the Colosseum.*

SIGHTS

SIGHTS

Rome vs. Milan: A Classic Squabble

In Italy, the North and South bicker about each other, hurling barbs, quips, and generalizations. All the classic North/South traits can be applied to Rome (the government capital) and Milan (the business capital). Although the differences have become less pronounced lately, the sniping continues.

The Milanese say the Romans are lazy. Roman government jobs come with short hours—cut even shorter by too many coffee breaks, three-hour lunches, chats with colleagues, and phone calls to friends and relatives. Milanese contend that *Roma ladrona* (Rome the big thief) is a parasite that lives off the taxes of people up North. Until recently, there was a strong Milan-based movement seriously promoting secession from the South.

Romans, meanwhile, dismiss the Milanese as uptight workaholics with nothing else to live for—gray like their foggy city. Romans do admit that in Milan, job opportunities are better and based on merit. And the Milanese grudgingly concede that the Romans have a gift for enjoying life.

While Rome is more of a family city, Milan is the place for high-powered singles on the career fast track. Milanese yuppies

NORTH OF VIA DEI FORI IMPERIALI

Several worthwhile sights sit across Via dei Fori Imperiali from the Roman Forum—and offer a break from the crowds.

Museum of the Imperial Forums (Museo dei Fori Imperiali)

The museum, housed in buildings from Trajan's Market, features discoveries from the forums built by the different emperors. Though its collection of statues is not impressive compared to Rome's other museums, it's well displayed. And—most importantly—it allows you to walk outside, atop and amidst the ruins, making this the only way you can actually get up close to Trajan's Market and Forum (described earlier). Focus on the big picture to mentally resurrect the fabulous forums.

Cost and Hours: €9.50, Tue-Sun 9:00-19:00, closed Mon, last entry one hour before closing, tel. 06-0608, www. mercatiditraiano.it. Skip the museum's slow, dry €4 audioguide (you'll find some English descriptions within the museum); enter at Via IV Novembre 94 (up the staircase from Trajan's Column).

Visiting the Museum: Start by simply admiring the main hall— three stories with marble framed entries, fine brickwork, and high mix with each other...not the city's long-time residents. Milan is seen as inward-looking and wary of foreigners, and Rome as fun-loving, tolerant, and friendly. In Milan, bureaucracy (like social services) works logically and efficiently, while in Rome, accomplishing even small chores can be exasperating. In Rome, everything—from finding a babysitter to buying a car—is done through friends. In Milan, while people are not as willing to discuss their personal matters, they are generous and active in charity work.

Milanese find Romans vulgar. The Roman dialect is considered one of the coarsest in the country. Much as they try, Milanese just can't say, "Damn your dead relatives" quite as effectively as the Romans. Still, they enjoy Roman comedians and love to imitate the accent.

The Milanese feel that Rome is dirty and Roman driving nerve-wracking. But despite the craziness, Rome maintains a genuine village feel. People share family news with their neighborhood grocer. Milan lacks people-friendly piazzas, and entertainment comes at a high price. But in Rome, *la dolce vita* is as close as the nearest square, and a full moon is enjoyed by all.

windows to allow natural light. (Cheapskates can see this much from outside the entrance without paying admission.) A caryatid (a female statue serving as a column) from the Forum of Augustus stands in the museum's entryway, alongside a bearded mask of Giove (Jupiter). Nearby, a bronze foot is all that's left of a larger-than-life *Winged Victory* that adorned Augustus' Temple of Mars the Avenger. Then explore the statues and broken columns that once decorated the sites.

Upstairs, cross over to the other side of the hall (use the outdoor balcony) to find a section on Julius Caesar's Forum, including baby Cupids (the son of Venus and Mars) carved from the pure white marble that would eventually adorn all of Rome.

The rest of the upstairs is dedicated to the Forum of Augustus. A model of the Temple of Mars and some large column fragments give a sense of the enormous scale. You'll see bits and pieces of the hand of the 40-foot statue of Augustus that once stood in his forum.

From here, you can go outside. Walkways let you descend to stroll along the curved top of Trajan's Market. You get a sense of how inviting the market must have been in its heyday. As you walk around, you'll also enjoy expansive views of Trajan's Forum, his column, other forums in the distance, and the modern Victor Emmanuel Monument.

▲Monti Neighborhood: Village Rome

Tucked behind the imperial forums is a quintessentially Roman district called Monti. Squeezed between Via Nazionale and Via Cavour, this hilly tangle of lanes helps visitors understand why the Romans see their hometown not as a sprawling metropolis, but as a collection of villages. Neighbors hang out on the square and chat, funky boutiques and fashionable shops share narrow streets with hole-in-the-wall hardware shops and *alimentari,* and wisteria-strewn cobbled lanes beckon photographers. How this charming little bit of village Rome survived, largely undisturbed, just a few steps from some of Italy's most trafficked sights, is a miracle worthy of canonization. While not quite "undiscovered" (savvy travelers have been reading about Monti in "hidden Rome" magazine and newspaper articles for years), it's certainly untrampled relative to its ample charms.

From a practical point of view, Monti (with the best assortment of colorful, characteristic, and inexpensive Roman eateries I've found) is a delightful complement to your ancient Roman sightseeing. For a lunch break or cool and relaxing evening wander and dinner, it's made-to-order.

From the Roman Forum's main entrance, cross Via dei Fori Imperiali and angle up Via Cavour two blocks to Via dei Serpenti. Turn left, and in one block, you hit Monti's main square, **Piazza della Madonna dei Monti.** (The Cavour Metro stop also gets you steps away.) To get oriented, face uphill, with the big fountain to your right. That fountain is the neighborhood's meeting point—and after hours, every square inch is thronged with young Romans socializing and drinking. They either buy bottles of wine or beer to go at the little grocery at the top of the square or at a convenience store on nearby Via Cavour. Often they order something more interesting from the adjacent Full Monti bar, which specializes in freshly squeezed fruit-juice drinks (served in plastic cups).

From this hub, interesting streets branch off in every direction. Via dei Serpenti (to your left) and Via del Boschetto (at the top of the square, then left) are both lined with an eclectic array of boutiques, gourmet bakeries and sandwich shops, lively *enoteche* and pubs, and fine restaurants. If you go to the top of the square, jog right, then left, you'll be on Via Leonina, which becomes Via Urbana, with more shops and eateries. And, over your right shoulder is one of Monti's most charming streets, Via Baccina—though the parallel Via della Madonna dei Monti is even cuter (head down Baccina and take the first left, then jog right). Although a bit less developed—with only a few shops and eateries—these streets offer the chance to really immerse yourself in village Rome…all within a few hundred yards of the city's greatest landmarks. In front of Via della Madonna dei Monti 82, look for the bronze cobbles embedded in the street, marking the place where several of the victims of the Fosse Ardeatine massacre lived (see page 521).

Monti is an ideal place for a quick lunch or early dinner, or for a memorable meal; for recommendations, see page 400. It's also a fine place to shop (see page 420) or hang out after dark (see page 429).

▲St. Peter-in-Chains Church (San Pietro in Vincoli)

Built in the fifth century to house the chains that held St. Peter, this church is most famous for its Michelangelo statue of Moses, intended for the tomb of Pope Julius II (which was never built). Check out the much-venerated chains under the high altar, then focus on mighty Moses. (Note that this isn't the famous St. Peter's Basilica, which is at Vatican City.)

Cost and Hours: Free, daily April-Sept 8:00-12:30 & 15:00-19:00, until 18:00 in winter, modest dress required; the church is a 10-minute uphill walk from the Colosseum, or a shorter, simpler walk from the Cavour Metro stop; tel. 06-9784-4950.

⊘ See the St. Peter-in-Chains Tour chapter.

Pantheon Neighborhood

Besides being home to ancient sites and historic churches, the area around the Pantheon gives Rome its urban-village feel. Wander narrow streets, sample the many shops and eateries, and gather with the locals in squares marked by bubbling fountains. Just south of the Pantheon is the Jewish quarter, with remnants of Rome's Jewish history and culture.

PANTHEON AND NEARBY

Exploring this area is especially good in the evening, when the restaurants bustle and streets are jammed with foot traffic. For a self-guided walk of this neighborhood, from Campo de' Fiori to the Trevi Fountain (and ending at the Spanish Steps), ⊘ see the Heart of Rome Walk chapter.

▲▲▲Pantheon

For the greatest look at the splendor of Rome, antiquity's best-preserved interior is a must. Built two millennia ago, this influential domed temple served as the model for Michelangelo's dome of St. Peter's and many others.

Cost and Hours: Free, Mon-Sat 8:30-19:30, Sun 9:00-18:00, holidays 9:00-13:00, closed for Mass Sat at 17:00 and Sun at 10:30, audioguide-€5, tel. 06-6830-0230.

⊘ See the Pantheon Tour chapter.

Pantheon Neighborhood

(Map labels:) To Spanish Steps · To Piazza del Popolo · To M Barberini · PONTE UMBERTO · Piazza Ponte Umberto I · ANCIENT STADIUM ENTRANCE · CORONARI · VIA D. ORSO · BRIANZO · VIA D. SCROFA · VIA D. COPPELLE · PARLIAMENT · UFF. VICARIO · Piazza Montecitorio · Piazza Colonna · VIA TRITONE · DEL · SABINA · CORSO · MURATTE · TREVI FOUNTAIN · SAN LUIGI · SALV. · VIA DELLA SCROFA · GIUST. · Piazza Rotunda · AGUIRO · PASTINI · Piazza di Pietra · Piazza San Ignazio · TRE SCALINI GELATERIA · Piazza Navona · FOUR RIVERS FOUNTAIN · S. EUST. · SEMINARIO · PANTHEON · SAN IGNAZIO · SANT' AGNESE · Piazza S. Eust. · S. IVO · ELEPHANT OBELISK · SANTA MARIA SOPRA MINERVA · Piazza Collegio Rom. · GALLERIA DORIA PAMPHILJ · Piazza Pasquino · CITY MUSEUM · CORSO · VITTORIO · ARGENTINA · CESTARI · EMANUELE II · VIA PLEBISCITO · Piazza Venezia · Campo de' Fiori · Largo Argentina · LARGO ARGENTINA RUINS · GESÙ · VIA DI SAN MARCO · To Colosseum & M · Piazza Farnese · VIA D. FARINA · VIA D. B. OSCURE · ARACOELI · VICTOR EMMANUEL MONUMENT · PALAZZO FARNESE · CHIAVARI · VIA GIUBBONARI · SPECCHI · VIA ARENULA · VIA DEL PORTICO D'OTTAVIA · 200 Meters · 200 Yards · CAPITOLINE HILL · Piazza Campidoglio

(Side tab:) SIGHTS

▲▲Churches near the Pantheon

For more information on the following churches, see the latter half of my Pantheon Tour chapter. Modest dress is recommended.

The **Church of San Luigi dei Francesi** has a magnificent chapel painted by Caravaggio (free, daily 10:00-12:30 & 15:00-19:00 except closed Thu afternoon, between the Pantheon and the north end of Piazza Navona). The only Gothic church in Rome is the **Church of Santa Maria sopra Minerva,** with a little-known Michelangelo statue, *Christ Bearing the Cross* (free, Mon-Fri 7:00-19:00, Sat-Sun 8:00-12:30 & 15:30-19:00, on a little square behind the Pantheon, to the east). The **Church of San Ignazio,** several blocks east of the Pantheon, is a riot of Baroque illusions with a false dome (free, Mon-Sat 7:30-19:00, Sun 9:00-19:00). A few blocks away, across Corso Vittorio Emanuele, is the rich and Baroque **Gesù Church,** headquarters of the Jesuits in Rome (free, daily 7:00-12:30 & 16:00-19:45, interesting daily service at 17:30—see page 130 for details).

Two blocks down Corso Vittorio Emanuele from the Gesù

Church, you'll hit **Largo Argentina,** an excavated square about four blocks south of the Pantheon. Stroll around this square and look into the excavated pit at some of the oldest ruins in Rome. Julius Caesar was assassinated near here. At the far (west) side of the square is a cat refuge where volunteers care for some 250 cats, though there's talk of eviction (www.romancats.com).

▲Galleria Doria Pamphilj

This underappreciated gallery, in the heart of the old city, offers a rare chance to wander through a noble family's lavish rooms with the prince who calls this downtown mansion home. Well, almost.

Through an audioguide, the prince lovingly narrates his family's story as you tour the palace and its world-class art.

Cost and Hours: €11, includes worthwhile 1.5-hour audioguide, daily 9:00-19:00, last entry one hour before closing, elegant café, from Piazza Venezia walk 2 blocks up Via del Corso to #305, tel. 06-679-7323, www.dopart.it/roma.

Visiting the Galleria: The story begins upstairs in the grand entrance hall (Salone del Poussin), wallpapered with French landscapes. In the adjoining throne room, you'll see a portrait of Pope Innocent X (1574-1655), patriarch of the Pamphilj (pahm-FEEL-yee) family. His wealth and power flowed to his nephew, who built the palace—a cozy relationship that inspired the word "nepotism" (*nepotem* is Latin for "nephew"). The family eventually married into English nobility, which is why today's prince speaks the Queen's English. You'll visit the red velvet room, the green living room, and the mirror-lined ballroom that once hosted music by resident composers Scarlatti and Handel. Along the way, the prince tells charming family secrets, like when he and his sister were scolded for roller-skating through the palace.

Past the bookshop is the painting collection. (Major works have a number to dial up audioguide information.) Don't miss Velázquez's intense, majestic, ultra-realistic portrait of the family founder, Innocent X. It stands alongside an equally impressive bust of the pope by Bernini. Stroll through a mini-Versailles-like hall of mirrors to more paintings, including works by Titian and Raphael. Finally, relax along with Mary, Joseph, and Jesus, and let the angel serenade you in Caravaggio's *Rest on the Flight to Egypt*.

Piazza di Pietra (Piazza of Stone)

The square was actually a quarry set up to chew away at the abandoned Temple of Hadrian, dedicated to the emperor responsible for building the Pantheon (look for his bust and a model of the temple in a window on the square). You can still see the holes that hungry medieval scavengers chipped into the columns to steal the metal pins that held the slabs together. Look over the railing to see ground level 1,900 years ago. (The piazza is two blocks toward Via del Corso from the Pantheon.)

▲Trevi Fountain

The bubbly Baroque fountain, worth ▲▲ by night, is a minor sight to art scholars...but a major nighttime gathering spot for teens on the make and tourists tossing coins. Those coins are collected daily to feed Rome's poor.

○ See the Heart of Rome Walk chapter.

JEWISH QUARTER

From the 16th through the 19th centuries, Rome's Jewish population was forced to live in a cramped ghetto at an often-flooded bend of the Tiber River. While the medieval Jewish ghetto is long gone, this area—between Campo de' Fiori and Capitoline Hill—is still home to Rome's synagogue and fragments of its Jewish heritage. For more on this neighborhood, ○ see the Jewish Ghetto Walk chapter.

Synagogue (Sinagoga) and Jewish Museum (Museo Ebraico)

Rome's modern synagogue stands proudly on the spot where the medieval Jewish community was sequestered for more than 300 years. The site of a historic visit by Pope John Paul II, this synagogue features a fine interior and a museum filled with artifacts of Rome's Jewish community. The only way to visit the synagogue—unless you're here for daily prayer service—is with a tour.

Cost and Hours: €11 ticket includes museum, audioguide, and guided tour of synagogue; mid-June-mid-Sept Sun-Thu 10:00-19:00, Fri 10:00-16:00, shorter hours off-season, closed Sat year-round; last entry 45 minutes before closing, English tours usually at :15 past the hour, 30 minutes, check schedule at ticket counter, modest dress required, on Lungotevere dei Cenci, tel. 06-6840-0661, www.museoebraico.roma.it. Walking tours of the ghetto are conducted at least once a day except Saturday.

SIGHTS

Vatican City

Vatican City, the world's smallest country, contains St. Peter's Basilica (with Michelangelo's exquisite *Pietà*) and the Vatican Museum

um (with Michelangelo's Sistine Chapel). A helpful **TI** is just to the left of St. Peter's Basilica as you're facing it (Mon-Sat 8:30-18:15, closed Sun, tel. 06-6988-1662, www.vatican.va). The entrances to St. Peter's and to the Vatican Museum are a 15-minute walk apart (follow the outside of the Vatican wall, which links the two sights). The nearest Metro stop—Ottaviano—still involves a 10-minute walk to either sight. For information on Vatican tours, post offices, and the pope's schedule, see page 206.

Modest dress is required of men, women, and children throughout Vatican City, even outdoors. Otherwise, the Swiss Guard can turn you away. Cover your shoulders; bring a light jacket or cover-up if you're wearing a tank top. Wear long pants instead of shorts. Skirts or dresses should extend below your knee.

▲▲▲St. Peter's Basilica (Basilica San Pietro)
There is no doubt: This is the richest and grandest church on earth. To call it vast is like calling Einstein smart.

Cost and Hours: Free, daily April-Sept 7:00-19:00, Oct-March 7:00-18:30. The church closes on Wednesday mornings during papal audiences. Masses occur daily throughout the day. Audioguides can be rented near the checkroom (€5 plus ID, for church only, daily 9:00-17:00). The view from the dome is worth the climb (€7 for elevator to roof, then take stairs; €5 to climb stairs all the way, cash only, allow an hour to go up and down, daily April-Sept 8:00-18:00, Oct-March 8:00-17:00, last entry one hour before closing if you take the stairs the whole way). Tel. 06-6988-1662, www.vatican.va (select "Basilicas and Papal Chapels" at the bottom of the page).

✪ See the St. Peter's Basilica Tour chapter.

▲▲▲Vatican Museum (Musei Vaticani)
The four miles of displays in this immense museum—from ancient statues to Christian frescoes to modern paintings—culminate in the Raphael Rooms and Michelangelo's glorious Sistine Chapel.

Cost and Hours: €16, €4 online reservation fee, Mon-Sat 9:00-18:00, last entry at 16:00 (though the official closing time is 18:00, the staff starts ushering you out at 17:30), closed on

SIGHTS

Vatican City & Nearby

religious holidays and Sun except last Sun of the month (when it's free, more crowded, and open 9:00-14:00, last entry at 12:30); may be open Fri nights May-July and Sept-Oct 19:00-23:00 (last entry at 21:30) by online reservation only—check the website. Hours are subject to constant change and frequent holidays; look online for current times. Lines are extremely long in the morning—go in the late afternoon, or skip the ticket-buying line altogether by reserving an entry time on their website. A €7 audioguide is available (ID required). Tel. 06-6988-3860 or 06-6988-1662, http://mv.vatican.va.

  ☻ See the Vatican Museum Tour chapter.

NEAR VATICAN CITY
▲Castel Sant'Angelo

Built as a tomb for the emperor, used through the Middle Ages as a castle, prison, and place of last refuge for popes under attack, and today a museum, this giant pile of ancient bricks is packed with history. The structure itself is striking, but the sight feels empty and underexplained—come for the building itself and the views up top, not for the exhibits or artifacts.

Cost and Hours: €10.50, Tue-Sun 9:00-19:30, closed Mon, last entry one hour before closing, audioguide-€5, near Vatican City, Metro: Lepanto or bus #40 or #64, tel. 06-681-9111, www. castelsantangelo.beniculturali.it.

Background: Ancient Rome allowed no tombs—not even the emperor's—within its walls. So Emperor Hadrian grabbed the most commanding position just outside the walls and across the river and built a towering tomb (c. A.D. 139) well within view of the city. His mausoleum was a huge cylinder (210 by 70 feet) topped by a cypress grove and crowned by a huge statue of Hadrian himself riding a chariot. For nearly a hundred years,

Roman emperors (from Hadrian to Caracalla, in A.D. 217) were buried here.

In the year 590, the archangel Michael appeared above the mausoleum to Pope Gregory the Great. Sheathing his sword, the angel signaled the end of a plague. The fortress that was Hadrian's mausoleum eventually became a fortified palace, renamed for the "holy angel."

Castel Sant'Angelo spent centuries of the Dark Ages as a fortress and prison, but was eventually connected to the Vatican via an elevated corridor at the pope's request (1277). Since Rome was repeatedly plundered by invaders, Castel Sant'Angelo was a handy place of last refuge for threatened popes. In anticipation of long sieges, rooms were decorated with papal splendor (you'll see paintings by Carlo Crivelli, Luca Signorelli, and Andrea Mantegna). In 1527, during a sacking of Rome by troops of Charles V of Spain, the pope lived inside the castle for months with his entourage of hundreds (an unimaginable ordeal, considering the food service at the top-floor bar).

Visiting the Castle: Touring the place is a stair-stepping workout. After you walk around the entire base of the castle—buying your ticket en route—take the small staircase down to the original Roman floor (following the route of Hadrian's funeral procession). In the atrium, study the model of the mausoleum as it was in Roman times. Imagine being surrounded by a veneer of marble, and the niche in the wall filled with a towering "welcome to my tomb" statue of Hadrian. From here, a ramp leads to the right, spiraling 400 feet. While some of the fine original brickwork and bits of mosaic survive, the marble veneer is long gone (notice the holes in the wall from the pins that held it in place).

At the end of the ramp, turn left and go up the stairs. A bridge crosses over the room where the ashes of the emperors were kept. From here, more stairs continue out of the ancient section and into the medieval structure (built atop the mausoleum) that housed the papal apartments. Explore the rooms and enjoy the view. Then go through the Sala Paolina and up the stairs; don't miss the Sala del Tesoro (Treasury—likely once Hadrian's tomb, and later a prison), where the wealth of the Vatican was locked up in a huge chest. (*Do* miss the 58 rooms of the military museum.) From the pope's piggy bank, a narrow flight of stairs leads to the rooftop and perhaps the finest view of Rome anywhere (pick out landmarks as you stroll around). From the safety of this dramatic vantage point, the pope surveyed the city in times of siege. Look down at the bend of the Tiber, which for 2,700 years has cradled the Eternal City.

Ponte Sant'Angelo

The bridge leading to Castel Sant'Angelo was built by Hadrian for quick and regal access from downtown to his tomb. The three middle arches are actually Roman originals and a fine example of the empire's engineering expertise. The statues of angels (each bearing a symbol of the passion of Christ—nail, sponge, shroud, and so on) are Bernini-designed and textbook Baroque. In the Middle Ages, this was the only bridge in the area that connected St. Peter's and the Vatican with downtown Rome. Nearly all pilgrims passed this bridge to and from the church. Its shoulder-high banisters recall a tragedy: During a Jubilee Year festival in 1450, the crowd got so huge that the mob pushed out the original banisters, causing nearly 200 to fall to their deaths.

Today, as through the ages, pilgrims cross the bridge, turn left, and set their sights on the Vatican dome. Around the year 1600, they would have also set their sights on a bunch of heads hanging from the crenellations of the castle. Ponte Sant'Angelo was infamous as a place for beheadings (banditry in the countryside was rife). Locals said, "There are more heads at Castel Sant'Angelo than there are melons in the market."

North Rome

BORGHESE GARDENS AND NEARBY
▲Villa Borghese Gardens

Rome's semi-scruffy three-square-mile "Central Park" is great for its shade and for people-watching plenty of modern-day Romeos and Juliets. The best entrance is at the head of Via Veneto

(Metro: Barberini, then 10-minute walk up Via Veneto and through the old Roman wall at Porta Pinciana, or catch a cab to Via Veneto—Porta Pinciana). There you'll find a cluster of buildings with a café, a kiddie arcade, and bike rental (Bici Pincio, €4/hour). Rent a bike or, for romantics, a pedaled rickshaw (*riscio*, €12/hour). Bikes come with locks to allow you to make sightseeing stops. Follow signs to discover the park's cafés, fountains, statues, lake, great viewpoint over Piazza del Popolo, and prime picnic spots. Some sights require paid admission, including the Borghese Gallery (see Borghese Gallery Tour chapter), Rome's zoo (described on page 414), the National Gallery of Modern Art (which holds 19th-century art; not to be confused with MAXXI, described later), and the Etruscan Museum (described below).

▲▲▲Borghese Gallery (Galleria Borghese)

This plush museum, filling a cardinal's mansion in the park, offers one of Europe's most sumptuous art experiences. You'll enjoy a collection of world-class Baroque sculpture, including Bernini's *David* and his excited statue of Apollo chasing Daphne, as well as paintings by Caravaggio, Raphael, Titian, and Rubens. The museum's mandatory reservation system keeps crowds to a manageable size.

Cost and Hours: €16, price includes €2 reservation fee, Tue-Sun 9:00-19:00, closed Mon, ticket office closes 30 minutes before museum. Reservations are mandatory and easy to get in English online (www.galleriaborghese.it) or by calling 06-32810. Reserve a minimum of several days in advance for a weekday visit, or at least a week ahead for weekends. The 1.5-hour audioguide (€5) is excellent.

For more on reservations, as well as a self-guided tour, ✪ see the Borghese Gallery Tour chapter.

Etruscan Museum (Museo Nazionale Etrusco di Villa Giulia)

The fascinating Etruscan civilization thrived in Italy around 600 B.C., when Rome was an Etruscan town. The Villa Giulia (a fine Renaissance palace in the Villa Borghese Gardens) hosts a museum that tells the story. The displays are clean and bright, with good English information.

Cost and Hours: €8, Tue-Sun 8:30-19:30, closed Mon, last entry one hour before closing, good English information, 20-minute walk from Borghese Gallery or from most of the Villa Borghese

Garden's entrances, Metro: Flaminio, then tram #2 to Viale delle Belli Arti and a 5-minute walk (east) to the museum, Piazzale di Villa Giulia 9, tel. 06-322-6571, www.villagiulia.beniculturali.it.

Visiting the Museum: A map of the Etruscan world (in Room I) shows the Etruscans centered from Rome northward (in modern-day Tuscany and Umbria), co-existing with neighboring civilizations like the Greeks and Phoenicians. Find key

Etruscan cities (Vulci, Tarquinia, Cerveteri) where the museum's treasures were unearthed. Farther along, a painted, room-sized tomb from Tarquinia (Room 8, down the spiral staircase) shows how Etruscans buried their dead along with their possessions, thus preserving these objects. Stroll through room after room of cases with vases—pottery painted either red-on-black or black-on-red. The star of the museum is the famous "husband and wife sarcophagus" (Il Sarofago degli Sposi, Room 12)—a dead couple seeming to enjoy an everlasting banquet from atop their tomb (sixth century B.C. from Cerveteri). Room 13b has a few gold sheets from Pyrgi, with inscriptions in two languages—the "Etruscan Rosetta Stone" that has helped scholars decipher their odd language.

Upstairs on the mezzanine, pass through the long hall of small, mostly bronze objects (statuettes and mirrors). Continuing up to the second floor, you can ogle the gold jewelry of the sophisticated, luxury-loving Etruscans (Room 24). Near the exit, Room 40 displays the well-known terra-cotta statue, the Apollo of Veio, which stood atop Apollo's temple. The smiling god welcomes Hercules, while his mother Latona stands nearby cradling baby Apollo.

MAXXI

Rome's "National Museum of Art of the 21st Century" is the big news on the museum scene here—as you can imagine it would be, after the 10 years and €150 million it took to make it happen. This complex, designed by Zaha Hadid and billed as Italy's "first national museum dedicated to contemporary creativity," is a playful concrete and steel structure filled with bizarre installations. Like many contemporary art museums, it's notable more for the building than the art inside. To me, it comes off as a second-rate Pompidou Center. While not to my taste, it's one of the few places in the city where fans of contemporary architecture can see the latest trends.

Since it's away from the center, consider combining it with a walk around fellow "starchitect" Renzo Piano's **Auditorium** to see how the city continues to evolve (15-minute walk to auditorium, from MAXXI follow Via Guido Reni to tram #2 stop and keep going—it's just beyond the elevated road; see page 429).

Cost and Hours: €11, Tue-Sun 11:00-19:00, Sat until 22:00, closed Mon, last entry one hour before closing; no permanent collection, several rotating exhibits throughout the year—preview on their website; tram #2 (direction: Mancini) from Piazza del Popolo to the Apollodoro stop, then walk west 5 minutes to Via Guido Reni 4a; to return (direction: Flaminio), the tram stop is 50 yards closer to MAXXI, tel. 06-322-5178, www.fondazionemaxxi.it.

VIA VENETO

In the 1960s, movie stars from around the world paraded down curvy Via Veneto, one of Rome's glitziest nightspots. Today it's still lined with the city's poshest hotels and the US Embassy, and retains a sort of faded Champs-Elysées elegance—but any hint of local color has turned to bland.

▲Capuchin Crypt

If you want to see artistically arranged bones, this is the place. The crypt is below the Church of Santa Maria della Immacolata Concezione on the tree-lined Via Veneto, just up from Piazza Barberini. The bones of more than 4,000 friars who died between 1528 and 1870 are in the basement, all lined up in a series of six crypts for the delight—or disgust—of the always-wide-eyed visitor.

Cost and Hours: €6, daily 9:00-19:00, last entry 30 minutes before closing, modest dress required, no photos, Via Veneto 27, Metro: Barberini, tel. 06-4201-4995.

Visiting the Crypt: Before the crypt, a high-tech, six-room museum covers the history of the Capuchins, a branch of the Franciscan order. You'll see painting after painting of monks with brown robes and tonsure (ring-cut hair). The exhibits, featuring clothing, books, and other religious artifacts used by members of the order, are explained in English, but the only real artistic highlight is a painting of *St. Francis in Meditation*, once attributed to Caravaggio (but now thought to be a contemporary copy).

For most travelers, however, the main attraction remains the morbid crypt. You'll begin with the Crypt of the Three Skeletons (#1). The ceiling is decorated with a skeleton grasping a grim-reaper scythe and scales weighing the "good deeds and the bad deeds so God can judge the soul"—illustrating the Catholic doctrine of earning salvation through good works. The clock with no hands, on the ceiling above the aisle, is a symbol: It means that life goes on forever, once led into the afterlife by Sister Death. The chapel's bony chandelier and the stars and floral motifs made by ribs and vertebrae are particularly inspired. Finally, look down to read the macabre, monastic, thought-provoking message that serves as the moral of the story: "What you are now, we used to be; what we are now, you will be."

In the large Crypt of the Tibia and Fibia (#2), niches are inhabited by Capuchin friars, whose robes gave the name to the brown coffee drink with the frothy white cowl. (Unlike monks, who live apart from society, the Capuchins are friars, who depend on charity and live among the people, and are part of the Franciscan order.) In this chapel we see the Franciscan symbol: the bare arm of Christ and the robed arm of a Franciscan friar embracing the faithful. Above that is a bony crown. And below, in dirt brought from Jerusalem 400 years ago, are 18 graves with simple crosses.

The Crypt of the Hips (#3) is named for the canopy of wavy hip-bones with vertebrae bangles over its central altar. Between crypts #3 and #4, look up to see the jaunty skull with a shoulder-blade bow-tie.

In the Crypt of the Skulls (#4), look close on the central wall to find the hourglass with wings. Yes, time on earth flies.

The next room (#5) is the boneless chapel. This is part of a church, and the monks sometimes hold somber services here.

In the last room, the Crypt of the Resurrection (#6), with a painting of Jesus bringing Lazarus back to life, sets the theme of your visit: the Christian faith in resurrection.

As you leave (humming "the foot bone's connected to the..."), pick up a few of Rome's most interesting postcards—the proceeds support Capuchin mission work. Head back outside, where it's not just the bright light that provides contrast with the crypt. Within a few steps are the US Embassy, Hard Rock Café, and fancy Via Veneto cafés, filled with the poor and envious keeping an eye out for the rich and famous.

BETWEEN PIAZZA DEL POPOLO AND THE PANTHEON

These sights are on or within a short walk of the bustling Via del Corso thoroughfare, which connects Piazza del Popolo to the heart of town.

▲Piazza del Popolo

This vast oval square marks the traditional north entrance to Rome. From ancient times until the advent of trains and airplanes, this was just about any visitor's first look at Rome. Today the square, known for its symmetrical design and its art-filled churches, is the starting point for the city's evening *passeggiata* (see the Dolce Vita Stroll at the end of the Nightlife in Rome chapter).

In 1480, Pope Sixtus IV recognized that the ramshackle medieval city was making a miserable first impression on pilgrims who walked here from all over Europe (similar to the Muslim pilgrimage to Mecca). He authorized city planners to appropriate property (establishing "eminent domain"), demolish old buildings, and create straight streets to accommodate traffic. This was the first of several papal campaigns to spruce up the square and make it a suitable entrance for the grand city.

From the Flaminio Metro stop, pass through the third-century Aurelian Wall via the Porta del Popolo, and look south. The 10-story **obelisk** in the center of the square once graced the temple of Ramses II in Egypt and the Roman Circus Maximus racetrack. The obelisk was brought here in 1589 as one of the square's beautification projects. (The oval shape dates from the early 19th century.) At the south side of the square, twin **domed churches** mark the spot where three main boulevards exit the square and form a trident. The central boulevard (running between the churches) is Via del Corso, which since ancient times has been the main north-south drag through town, running to Capitoline Hill (the governing center) and the Forum. The road to the right led to the Vatican, and the road to the left led to the big pilgrimage churches of San Giovanni in Laterano and Santa Maria Maggiore. With the help of this *tridente,* pilgrims arriving without a good Rome guidebook knew just where to go. The three churches on Piazza del Popolo are all dedicated to Mary, setting the right tone.

Along the north side of the square (flanking the Porta del Popolo) are two 19th-century buildings that give the square its pleasant symmetry: the Carabinieri station and the Church of Santa Maria del Popolo.

Two large **fountains** grace the sides of the square—Neptune to the west and Roma to the east (marking the base of Pincio Hill; steps lead up to the overlook with fine views to St. Peter's and the rest of the city). Though the name Piazza del Popolo means "Square of the People" (and it is a popular hangout), the word was probably derived from the Latin *populus,* after the poplar trees that once stood here.

Church of Santa Maria del Popolo

One of Rome's most overlooked churches, this features two chapels with top-notch art by Caravaggio and Bernini, and a facade built of travertine scavenged from the Colosseum. The church is brought to you by the Rovere family, which produced two popes, and you'll see their symbol—the oak tree and acorns—throughout.

Cost and Hours: Free but bring coins to illuminate the

SIGHTS

art, Mon-Sat 7:00-12:30 & 16:00-19:00, Sun 8:00-13:30 & 16:30-19:30, often partially closed to accommodate its busy schedule of Masses, on north side of Piazza del Popolo—as you face the gate in the old wall from the square, the church entrance is to your right.

Visiting the Church: Go inside. The **Chigi Chapel** (KEE-gee, second on the left as you face the main altar) was designed by Raphael and inspired (as Raphael was) by the Pantheon. Notice the Pantheon-like dome, pilasters, and capitals. Above in the oculus, God looks in, aided by angels who power the eight known planets. Raphael built the chapel for his wealthy banker friend Agostino Chigi, buried in the pyramid-shaped tomb in the wall to the right of the altar. Later, Chigi's great-grandson hired Bernini to make two of the four statues, and Bernini delivered a theatrical episode. In one corner, Daniel straddles a lion and raises his praying hands to God for help. Kitty-corner across the chapel, an angel grabs the prophet Habakkuk's hair and tells him to go take some food to poor Daniel in the lion's den.

In the **Cerasi Chapel** (left of altar), Caravaggio's *Conversion of St. Paul* shows the future saint sprawled on his back beside his horse while his servant looks on. The startled Paul is blinded by the harsh light as Jesus' voice asks him, "Why do you persecute me?" In the style of the Counter-Reformation, Paul receives his new faith with open arms.

In the same chapel, Caravaggio's *Crucifixion of St. Peter* is shown as a banal chore; the workers toil like faceless animals. The light and dark are in high contrast. Caravaggio liked to say, "Where light falls, I will paint it."

▲▲Dolce Vita Stroll

All over the Mediterranean world, people are out strolling in the early evening. Rome's *passeggiata* is both elegant (with chic people enjoying fancy window shopping in the grid of streets around the Spanish Steps) and a little crude (with young people on the prowl). Watching the spectacle is a key Rome experience; I recommend following the action on Piazza del Popolo and along Via del Corso (roughly Mon-Sat 17:00-19:00 and Sun afternoons; for more, see the Dolce Vita Stroll in the Nightlife in Rome chapter).

▲Spanish Steps

The wide, curving staircase, culminating with an obelisk between two Baroque church towers, makes for one of Rome's iconic sights. Beyond that, it's a people-gathering place. By day, the area hosts shoppers looking for high-end fashions; on warm evenings, it attracts young people in love with the city. For more, ❸ see the Heart of Rome Walk chapter.

Shopping Triangle
The triangular-shaped area between the Spanish Steps, Piazza Venezia, and Piazza del Popolo (along Via del Corso, see map on page 69) contains Rome's highest concentration of upscale boutiques and fashion stores. For more, see the Shopping in Rome chapter.

▲▲Museo dell'Ara Pacis (Museum of the Altar of Peace)
On January 30, 9 B.C., soon-to-be-emperor Augustus led a procession of priests up the steps and into this newly built "Altar of

Peace." They sacrificed an animal on the altar and poured an offering of wine, thanking the gods for helping Augustus pacify barbarians abroad and rivals at home. This marked the dawn of the Pax Romana (c. A.D. 1-200), a Golden Age of good living, stability, dominance, and peace *(pax)*. The Ara Pacis (AH-rah PAH-chees) hosted annual sacrifices by the emperor until the area was flooded by the Tiber River. Buried under silt, it was abandoned and forgotten until the 16th century, when various parts were discovered and excavated. Mussolini gathered the altar's scattered parts and reconstructed them in a building here in 1938. Today, the Altar of Peace stands in a pavilion designed by American architect Richard Meier (opened 2006). If this modern building seems striking, perhaps that's because it's about the only entirely new structure permitted in the old center of Rome since Mussolini's day.

Cost and Hours: €8.50 (more with special exhibits), tightwads can look in through huge windows for free, Tue-Sun 9:00-19:00, closed Mon, last entry one hour before closing, good audioguide-€4, good WC downstairs; a long block west of Via del Corso on Via di Ara Pacis, on the east bank of the Tiber near Ponte Cavour, Metro: Spagna plus a 10-minute walk down Via dei Condotti; tel. 06-0608, www.arapacis.it.

❸ **Self-Guided Tour:** Start with the model in the museum's lobby. The Altar of Peace was originally located east of here, along today's Via del Corso. The model shows where it stood in relation to the Mausoleum of Augustus (now next door) and the Pantheon. (The Ara Pacis originally faced west; now it faces east. Be aware that some art-history books and even the Ara Pacis website may describe it using the original—and opposite—orientation.) Nearby, you'll also see a row of emperors' heads, a good film telling the

SIGHTS

story of the Ara Pacis and its recovery (press the button for English), and other exhibits.

Entrance Side: Approach the Ara Pacis and look through the doorway to see the raised altar. This simple structure has just the basics of a Roman temple: an altar for sacrifices surrounded by cubicle-like walls that enclose a consecrated space. Its well-preserved reliefs celebrate Rome's success. After a sacrifice, the altar was washed, and the blood flowed out drain holes still visible at the base of the walls. Flanking the doorway are (badly damaged) reliefs of Rome's legendary founders—Romulus and Remus (on the left, being suckled by the she-wolf) and bearded Aeneas (right), the mythical hero of Troy and Rome, who's pouring a wine offering and preparing to sacrifice a sow.

Interior: Climb the 10 steps and go inside. From here, the priest would climb the eight altar steps to make sacrifices. The walls of the enclosure are decorated with the kinds of things offered to the gods: animals (see the cow skulls), garlands of fruit, and ceremonial platters to present the offerings. Circle to the left side of the altar to find a relief showing a sacrifice in action. Priests lead the animals to slaughter. They carry swords to do the job, plates and jugs for offering food and wine, and leafy sprigs to dip into the blood and shake around.

Right (North) Side: Head back out and walk around the right side of the structure. This relief probably depicts the parade of dignitaries who consecrated the altar. Just left of center is Augustus, his body sliced in two vertically by a missing stone—he's the one with only half a body. Augustus wears the victor's crown of laurel leaves, having just conquered parts of Spain and Gaul. Augustus is followed by a half-dozen bigwigs and priests (with spiked hats) and the man shouldering the sacrificial ax. Next comes Agrippa (wearing the hood of a priest), Augustus' right-hand man in battles against Mark Antony and Cleopatra. Agrippa married Augustus' daughter, Julia—their little son, Gaius, tugs on his dad's toga while turning to look at Livia, Augustus' wife (a few heads farther back). When Agrippa died, Gaius was adopted and named as successor by Augustus. Gaius also died young, making the next in line Tiberius, Livia's son by a first marriage, shown standing next to his mother. Confused? Find these names and other descendants of Julius Caesar on the genealogical chart and the row of busts in the museum lobby.

Before proceeding farther around the altar, look out the window to see the overgrown Mausoleum of Augustus and his family, once capped with a dome of earth, elegant spruces, and statues of the emperor. To the left is an example of Mussolini's fascist architecture—intended to remind Italians of their imperial Roman roots. Note the travertine, brick, low-relief propaganda, stony inscriptions, Roman numerals, and cold rationality. (Locals don't like it.) This area was the Field of Mars, Rome's only neighborhood continuously inhabited since ancient times.

Back Side: The altar's back door is flanked with reliefs celebrating the two things Augustus brought to Rome: peace (goddess Roma as a conquering Amazon, right side) and prosperity (fertility goddess surrounded by children, plants, and animals, left side). For a closer look at details from the various reliefs, see the model back near the museum entrance.

Left (South) Side: Leading the parade of senators is a *lictor*—a ceremonial bodyguard—carrying the *fasces.* This bundle of sticks symbolized how unity brings strength, and it gave us the modern word "fascism." The reliefs feature the first official portrayal of women and children in a public monument.

Beneath the parade, notice the elaborate floral relief that runs all the way around the Ara Pacis. Acanthus tendrils spiral out, forming decorative garlands, intertwining with ivy, laurel, and more. Swans with outstretched wings hide among the patterns. Some 50 plants are blooming in this display of abundance. Imagine the altar as it once was, standing in an open field, painted in bright colors—a mingling of myth, man, and nature.

BEYOND THE ANCIENT WALLS
▲▲Catacombs of Priscilla (Catacombe di Priscilla)
Of the dozens of catacombs honeycombing the ground just outside the ancient city walls, only five are open to the public. While most tourists and nearly all tour groups go out to the Appian Way to see the famous catacombs of San Sebastiano and San Callisto, the Catacombs of Priscilla (on the other side of town) are less commercialized and less crowded—they just feel more intimate, as catacombs should.

Cost and Hours: €8, Tue-Sun 8:30-12:00 & 14:30-17:00, closed Mon, last entry 30 minutes before closing, closed one random month a year—check website or call first, tel. 06-8620-6272, www.catacombepriscilla.com.

Getting There: The catacombs are northeast of Termini train station (at Via Salaria 430), far from the center (a €15 taxi ride) but well-served by buses (20-30 minutes). From Termini, take bus #86, #92, or #310 from Piazza Cinquecento. From Piazza Venezia, along Via del Corso or Via Barberini, take bus #63. Tell the driver "Piazza Crati" and "kah-tah-KOHM-bay" and he'll let you off near Piazza Crati (at the Nemorense/Crati stop). From there, walk through the little market in Piazza Crati, then down Via di Priscilla (about 5 minutes). The entrance is in the orange building on the left at the top of the hill.

Visiting the Catacombs: The Catacombs of Priscilla likely originated as underground tombs for Christians, who'd meet to worship in the wealthy Christian's home that was on this spot. As poor people couldn't generally afford a nice plot in a cemetery, they would dig graves at a generous person's home...and dig and dig.

At the Catacombs of Priscilla, you enter from a convent and explore the result of 250 years of tunneling that occurred from the second to the fifth century. Visits are by 30-minute guided tour only (English-language tours go whenever a small group gathers—generally every 20 minutes or so). You'll see a few thousand of the 40,000 niches carved here, along with some beautiful frescoes, including what is considered the first depiction of Mary nursing the Baby Jesus.

As in other catacombs, some of the tunnels date from an earlier quarry. Volcanic tuff, the stone ancient Rome was built with, works great for burial niches—it's easy to dig and dries hard when exposed to air.

For more information on catacombs, ✪ see the Ancient Appian Way Tour chapter.

East Rome

NEAR TERMINI TRAIN STATION

Most of these sights are within a 10-minute walk of the train station (except for the Baroque Surprises Stroll and art exhibitions, which are a bit farther).

▲▲▲National Museum of Rome (Museo Nazionale Romano Palazzo Massimo alle Terme)

The National Museum's main branch, at Palazzo Massimo, houses the greatest collection of ancient Roman art anywhere, including busts of emperors and a Roman copy of the Greek Discus Thrower.

Cost and Hours: €10 combo-ticket covers three other branches—all skippable, Tue-Sun 9:00-19:45, closed Mon, last entry 45 minutes before closing, audioguide-€5, about 100 yards from train station, Metro: Repubblica or Termini, tel. 06-3996-7700, www.archeoroma.beniculturali.it/en.

✪ See the National Museum of Rome Tour chapter.

▲Baths of Diocletian (Terme di Diocleziano)

Of all the marvelous structures built by the Romans, their public baths were arguably the grandest, and the Baths of Diocletian were the granddaddy of them all. Built by Emperor Diocletian around A.D. 300 and sprawling over 30 acres—roughly five times the size of

Baths of Diocletian

VIA VOLTURNO

VIA GAETA

MUSEUM OF THE BATH

GREAT CLOISTER

GARDEN

VIA PASTRENGO

FRIGIDARIUM

EXHIBITS

COURTYARD & WC

CENTRAL   HALL

SANTA MARIA DEGLI ANGELI

EXHIBITION HALL

TEPIDARIUM

CALDARIUM

Piazza della Repubblica

FOUNTAIN

VIA ORLANDO

SAN BERNARDO

M Repubblica

Piazza San Bernardo

VIA TORINO

VIA PARIGI

VIA CERNAIA

VIALE ENRIQUE DE NICOLA

Piazza del Cinquecento

To Termini Station
Ⓣ Ⓜ Ⓑ

VIALE EINAUDI

NATIONAL MUSEUM OF ROME

VIA TERME DIOCLEZIANO

VIA D. VIMINALE

VIA NAZIONALE

SIGHTS

100 Meters

100 Yards

To Victor Emanuele Monument

—— Existing Walls
----- Ancient Outline
▓▓ Santa Maria degli Angeli
······· La Meridiana

the Colosseum—these baths could cleanse 3,000 Romans at once. Today, tourists can visit one grand section of the baths, the former main hall. This impressive remnant of the ancient complex was later transformed (with help from Michelangelo) into the Church of Santa Maria degli Angeli.

Cost and Hours: Free, Mon-Sat 7:00-18:30, Sun 7:00-19:30. The entrance is on Piazza della Repubblica (Metro: Repubblica or buses #40 and #64).

Background: Large building projects like the baths were political security: They provided employment and fed the masses.

Diocletian (ruled A.D. 285-305) struggled to find a system to rule his unwieldy empire. He broke it into zones ruled by four "tetrarchs." During Diocletian's "tetrarchs" period, architecture and art were grandiose, but almost a caricature of greatness—

Near Termini Station

US EMBASSY

To Spanish Steps

V.D. ARTISTI

VIA VENETO

V. BISO

CAPUCHIN CRYPT

B

WALK BEGINS

SANTA MARIA VITTORIA

V. EURIFICAZIONE

VIA SISTINA

Barberini

M

T

Piazza Barberini

VIA BARBERINI

SANTA SUSANNA

MOSES FOUNTAIN

PALAZZO BARBERINI

VIA XX SETTEMBRE

SAN BERNARDO

FELTRINELLI BOOKSTORE

VIA DEL TRITONE

V. AVIG.

K. BOCC.

VIA TRAFORO

V. D. QUATTRO FONTANE

V. RASELLA

FOUR FOUNTAINS

VIA FIRENZE

VIA

To Trevi & Pantheon

V. ARCIONE

Quirinal Gardens

VIA QUIRINALE

VIA DEPRETIS

#40 & 64 B

To Trevi & Pantheon

PALAZZO DEL QUIRINALE

SAN CARLO

PHARMACY

VIA NAZIONALE

VIA NAPOLI

VIA FERRARA

SANT' ANDREA

DESPAR GROCERY

VENEZIA VIA

PALERMO.

Piazza del Quirinale

PALAZZO DELLE ESPOSIZIONE

i

T

GENOVA VIA

WALK ENDS

VIA MILANO

SCUDERIE DEL QUIRNALE

To Piazza Venezia

VIA XXIV MAGGIO

VIA NAZIONALE

To Piazza Venezia

Largo Magnanapoli

VIA DEI SERPENTI

VIA PANISPERNA

MONTI

VIA CAVOUR

- - - Baroque Surprises
Self-Guided Walk

SIGHTS

meant to proclaim to Romans that their city was still the power it had once been.

The baths were one of the last great structures built before Rome's 200-year fall. They functioned until A.D. 537, when barbarians attacked and the city's aqueducts fell into disuse, plunging Rome into a thousand years of poverty, darkness, and B.O.

● **Self-Guided Tour:** Start outside the church. The curved brick facade of today's church was once part of the *caldarium,* or steam room, of the ancient baths. Romans loved to sweat out last night's indulgences. After entering the main lobby (located where

Piazza della Repubblica is today), they'd strip in the locker rooms, then enter the steam room. The *caldarium* had wood furnaces under the raised floors. Stoked by slaves, these furnaces were used to heat the floors and hot tubs. The low ceiling helped keep the room steamy.

Entry Hall: Step into the vast and cool church. This round-domed room with an oculus (open skylight, now with modern stained glass) was once the *tepidarium*—the cooling-off room of the baths, where medium, "tepid" temperatures were maintained. This is where masseuses would rub you down and scrape you off with a stick (Romans didn't use soap).

SIGHTS

Large Transept: Step into the biggest part of the church and stand under the towering vault on the inlaid marble cross. In ancient

times, from the *tepidarium,* Romans would have continued on to this space, the **central hall** of the baths. While the decor around you dates from the 18th century, the structure dates from the fourth century.

This hall retains the grandeur of the ancient baths. It's the size of a football field and seven stories high—once even higher, since the original ancient floor was about 15 feet below its present level. The ceiling's crisscross arches were an architectural feat unmatched for a thousand years. The eight red granite columns are original, from ancient Rome—stand next to one and feel its five-foot girth. (Only the eight in the transept proper are original. The others are made of plastered-over brick.) In Roman times, this hall was covered with mosaics, marble, and gold, and lined with statues.

From here, Romans could continue (through what is now the apse, near the altar) into an open-air courtyard to take a dip in the vast 32,000-square-foot swimming pool (in the *frigidarium*) that paralleled this huge hall. Many other rooms, gardens, and courtyards extended beyond what we see here. The huge complex was built in only 10 years (around A.D. 300)—amazing when you think of the centuries it took builders of puny medieval cathedrals, such as Paris' Notre-Dame.

Mentally undress your fellow tourists and churchgoers, and imagine hundreds of naked or toga-clad Romans wrestling, doing jumping jacks, singing in the baths, networking, or just milling about.

The baths were more than washrooms. They were health clubs with exercising areas, equipment, and swimming pools. They had gardens for socializing. Libraries, shops, bars, fast-food vendors, pedicurists, depilatories, and brothels catered to every Roman need. Most important, perhaps, the baths offered a spacious, cool-in-summer/warm-in-winter place for Romans to get out of their stuffy apartments and schmooze or simply hang out.

Admission was virtually free, requiring only the smallest coin. Baths were open to men and women—and during Nero's reign, coed bathing was popular—but generally there were either separate rooms or separate entry times. Most Romans went daily.

Michelangelo's Church: The church we see today was (at least partly) designed by Michelangelo (1561), who used the baths' main hall as the nave. Later, when Piazza della Repubblica became an important Roman intersection, another architect renovated the church. To allow people to enter from the grand new piazza, he spun it 90 degrees, turning Michelangelo's nave into a long transept. The four large paintings flanking the main altar were originally in St. Peter's (they were replaced there with mosaics).

La Meridiana (1702): Embedded in the floor of the right transept (roped off) is a brass rod, pointing due north. It acts as a sun-

dial. As the sun arcs across the southern sky, a ray of light beams into the church through a tiny hole high in the wall and a cut in the cornice of the right transept. (To find the hole, follow the rod to the right to the wall and look up 65 feet.) The sunbeam sweeps across the church floor, crossing the meridian rod at exactly noon (before modern innovations like Daylight Saving Time).

This celestial clock is also a calendar. In summer, when the sun is high overhead, the sunbeam strikes the southern end of the rod. With each passing day, the sun travels up the rod (toward the apse), passing through the signs of the zodiac (the 28-day months of the moon's phases) marked alongside the rod. Many of the meridian's markings were intended for its other use, charting the movement of the stars. However, the tiny window that once let in light from the North Star (originally above the archway of the entrance to the apse) has been filled in.

La Meridiana was Rome's official city timekeeper until 1846, when it was replaced by the cannon atop Gianicolo Hill (which is still fired every day at exactly noon).

Exhibits: The small room to the left of the main altar, the **Sacrestia,** now houses temporary exhibits, often illuminating the church's rich architectural history. Admire both the immensity and height of the ancient Roman brickwork in this room. Step outside into the courtyard and re-create the grand architecture. Notice the *exedra* (semicircular recess in a wall or building)—a motif Romans used for decoration and as a kind of stage for philosophers and orators. See the niches that once housed statues, the rectangular holes that could be used to hold wood-beam scaffolding, and the small pockmarks where iron pegs once secured the marble paneling.

Nearby: Piazza della Repubblica, in front of the baths, was once a garden at the center of the vast, ancient complex. It was called Piazza Esedra until Italian unification (and is still called that by many Romans). The building wrapping around it is a monumental office block, typical of Italian-unification architecture of the late 19th century. The thundering Via Nazionale starts on the far side at what was an ancient door. Look down it (past the erotic nymphs of the Naiad fountain) to the Victor Emmanuel Monument. The Art Nouveau fountain of the four water nymphs created quite a stir when unveiled in 1911. The nymphs were modeled after a set of twins, who kept coming to visit as late as the 1960s to remind themselves of their nubile youth. Here at the site of the ancient Thermae, the statues bathe eternally.

▲Church of Santa Maria della Vittoria

This church houses Bernini's best-known statue, the swooning *St. Teresa in Ecstasy*.

Cost and Hours: Free, pay €0.50 for light, Mon-Sat 8:30-12:00 & 15:30-18:00, Sun 15:30-18:00, about 5 blocks northwest of Termini train station at Via XX Settembre 17, Metro: Repubblica.

Visiting the Church: Inside the church, you'll find St. Teresa to the left of the altar. Teresa has just been stabbed with God's arrow of fire. Now, the angel pulls it out and watches her reaction. Teresa swoons, her eyes roll up, her hand goes limp, she parts her lips...and moans. The smiling, cherubic angel understands just how she feels. Teresa, a 16th-century Spanish nun, later talked of the "sweetness" of "this intense pain," describing her oneness with God in ecstatic, even erotic, terms.

Bernini, the master of multimedia, pulls out all the stops to make this mystical vision real. Actual sunlight pours through the alabaster windows, bronze sunbeams shine on a marble angel holding a golden arrow. Teresa leans back on a cloud and her robe ripples from within, charged with her spiritual arousal. Bernini has created a little stage-setting of heaven. And watching from the "theater boxes" on either side are members of the family who commissioned the work.

The church, originally a poor Carmelite church, was slathered with Baroque richness in the 17th century. (It grew popular in modern times for its part in Dan Brown's *Angels and Demons,* something that serious historians scoff at.) At the altar, in the center of the starburst, is an icon of the Virgin Mary, considered miraculous for the military victories attributed to it during the Thirty Years' War (early 1600s). And, as the 17th century was a time when the Roman Catholic Church was threatened by Protestants, the ceiling shows Mary defeating (Protestant) snakes, who grasp scriptures translated from the pope's Latin into the evil vernacular.

Santa Susanna Church

The home of the American Catholic Church in Rome, Santa Susanna may be closed for renovation during your visit. When open,

they hold Mass in English Monday through
Saturday at 18:00, and on Sunday at 9:00
and 10:30; if they're closed, check their website for the temporary location and time.
They arrange papal audience tickets (see
page 206), and their excellent website contains tips for travelers and a list of convents
that rent out rooms. You'll find a description
of the church's facade next, in my Baroque
Surprises Stroll.

Cost and Hours: Free, Mon-Sat 9:00-
12:00 & 16:00-19:00, open Sun only for
Mass, Via XX Settembre 15, near recommended Via Firenze hotels, Metro: Repubblica, tel. 06-4201-4554, www.santasusanna.org.

SIGHTS

Baroque Surprises Stroll on Via XX Settembre

When Pope Sixtus V developed an ambitious plan to reorganize
Rome around key landmarks (c. 1580s), he transformed this formerly sleepy neighborhood near the Baths of Diocletian. Within
three generations, it was a major traffic hub and the center of a new
city water system. The streets were lined with grand fountains, obelisks, and churches, all decorated in the new style of the 1600s—
Baroque.

 Self-Guided Walk: This half-mile walk starts in Piazza di
San Bernardo (near the Church of Santa Maria della Vittoria, with
Bernini's famous statue of St. Teresa, described earlier), travels
down Via XX Settembre, and ends at the Palazzo del Quirinale,
where you can see a distant obelisk (see map on page 80 for route).
The churches we'll look at are free to enter; the hours are listed for
each one, but keep in mind that they close for an early afternoon
break (from 12:00 or 13:00 until 15:30 or 16:00).

• *Start at the wide square known as...*

Piazza di San Bernardo: At the end of the square is the
imposing **Fountain of Moses.** After a thousand years of living
on well water, the citizens of this neighborhood finally got fresh
running water with the opening of this public fountain (1585-1588).
It was built by Pope Sixtus V as the end point for a newly restored,
15-mile-long ancient aqueduct. From here, water was distributed
to dozens of other nearby fountains. The vast undertaking was
celebrated with statues by Domenico Fontana, starring Moses—
renowned for miraculously bringing forth water in the desert. Take
a look at the fountain's four huge columns, recycled from ancient

ruins. Besides being decorative, the fountain was functional, designed to quench the thirst of visiting pilgrims and their horses.

Also on the square is the **Church of Santa Susanna.** You're looking at what was considered the first Baroque facade—see the date: MDCIII (1603). It was designed by Carlo Maderno at the same time he was working on the facade of St. Peter's. As this is Baroque rather than Renaissance, the columns are in higher relief. The structure seems to pop out at you from the center with an energy that enlivens the entire building. The architect added a new Baroque element—curves—seen in the scrollwork "shoulders." We'll see curves in spades later in this walk. (This church usually offers a daily Mass in English but may be closed for renovation—see page 85, and can also help you get tickets for a papal audience—see page 206).

Turn 180 degrees. Opposite the Church of Santa Susanna is the circular **Church of San Bernardo** (built 1598). Why is the church round? Because it was incorporated into one of the corner towers of the Baths of Diocletian. Think of how far away the baths' central hall is (see map on page 80), and appreciate how vast that ancient health club was.

• *Now, with the Fountain of Moses at your back, walk down...*

Via XX Settembre: This is an ancient road. Pope Sixtus knew it as Via Pia, but its name now memorializes a modern military victory—the capture of Rome by Italian nationalists in 1870 on the "20th of September." As you walk, you'll pass the local "Pentagon" (on the left, with the stony bottom and pink top) and other governmental buildings marked by uniforms, tight security, barriers against car bombs, and Italian and European flags.

• *At a very pedestrian unfriendly spot, you reach...*

Via delle Quattro Fontane: This sooty intersection, named for its four fountains, was a big deal for 16th-century pilgrims, as two main roads crossed here. Imagine poor and haggard wayfarers trudging into town with little money and bereft of a Rick Steves guidebook. They navigated by sighting the obelisks and domes that Sixtus' plan had planted around the city. Entering from the north (as most Northern European visitors did), they'd pause here to drink from their choice of fountains. They could then either continue straight to the famous pilgrimage church of Santa Maria Maggiore—whose spire is visible to the left—or (spotting the obelisk down the road), head for Palazzo del Quirinale, then the residence of the pope. The intersection's fountains depict river gods relaxing in the shade. They were designed by a familiar name—Domenico Fontana, or Signor "Fountain."

• *Just past the fountain on the left side of the street (best viewed from the right side, to take in the full facade) is the...*

Church of San Carlo alla Quattro Fontane: On the facade, the distinct curves of Baroque have now evolved into undulating waves, rippling the surface of this watershed church. And the medallion on top introduces another Baroque element—the oval.

The church was designed by Francesco Borromini (c. 1640), who had served his apprenticeship at St. Peter's, carving putti for his cousin Maderno and building the altar canopy *(baldacchino)* for the famous Bernini. He and Bernini split on bad terms. Now Bernini's competitor, Borromini used this church as a chance to finally go solo and show his stuff.

Step inside (Mon-Fri 10:00-13:00 & 15:00-18:00, Sat 10:00-13:00, Sun 12:00-13:00). The tiny interior is oval-shaped, topped with an oval dome, which is itself topped with a tiny oval lantern. The whole upper story is a riot of wavy lines—ovals, arches, circles—that defy classical notions of symmetry. The dome is coffered with a complex mix of polygons and crosses. The dome seems to float, with no visible support, and is lit by no obvious light source.

The church looks rich. But Borromini's patrons—an order of poor monks—had little money. So the church is small and made of simple materials—brick, concrete, and plaster—but manipulated with lots of 3-D tricks. Borromini's design is brilliant: light, soft, and as if in a cloud. Light, a symbol of God, pours in from the holy dove in the cupola above (which seems higher than it is). Borromini designed everything for the tight space—notice the tidy little confessionals. And the cherubs are ever so huggable.

With this church, Borromini shocked the critics. But over the centuries, it's become classically Roman—locals fondly call it San Carlino. Borromini, who went on to contribute much to Rome's architecture, committed suicide by stabbing himself in the chest.

• *Head one block farther down the street (which is now called Via del Quirinale). On the left is the...*

Church of Sant'Andrea al Quirinale: Often called the "Pearl of the Baroque," this exquisite church sums up the Baroque style (1661). It was designed by the most famous Baroque artist, Gian Lorenzo Bernini, as a chapel for the pope's entourage at the Palazzo del Quirinale. As it was actually used by popes, Bernini had plenty of money for the work—there's lots of marble and gold—but he needed to be pretty conventional. This feels more solid, stable, and classical than the Borromini church.

Inside, the focus is on the altar, dedicated to St. Andrew, or Sant'Andrea (Tue-Sat 8:30-12:00 & 14:30-18:00, Sun 9:00-12:00 & 15:00-18:00, closed Mon). Bernini—the master of multi-media—

uses every artistic device to tell Andrew's story. The apostle (depicted in the altar painting) is being crucified on his X-shaped cross. He gazes up toward the light. His soul seems to follow the bronze angels above him, up through a light-filled shaft. Then he reappears—now as a marble statue—above the altar. He bursts through the pediment, ascending on a cloud, into the golden light where he joins his fellow saints in the dome of heaven.

Bernini makes all these elements come together. The pink marble columns color-coordinate with the pink frame of the painting. A bronze angel rests his hand on the painting's marble frame. The delightfully backlit cherubs at the base of the shaft playfully look down on the action. And the suffused light filtering in from the dome brings all the colors together. Bernini combines sculpture, painting, and architecture into *"un bel composto"*—a beautiful whole.

• *Continue down Via del Quirinale, walking along the loooong extent of Palazzo del Quirinale (on your right). The building looks somewhat bigger than it is, because the side we're walking along is actually just a long, skinny building enclosing the formal Quirinale Gardens (for a glimpse of them, peek past the guards when you get to the square). Keep walking toward the main entrance on Piazza di Quirinale.*

Palazzo del Quirinale: The building (by Maderno and Signor Fountain) dates from 1583, but this site has housed Rome's ruling elite for 2,000 years. Ancient Roman aristocrats, Baroque-era popes, the kings of reunited Italy (after XX Settembre, 1870), and today's presidents of Italy have all resided here—it feels like a combination White House/Palace of Versailles. The current president is Giorgio Napolitano (the president is elected by parliament and serves a seven-year term). While less powerful than the prime minister, Napolitano is very well respected, acting as a stabilizing influence in Italy's chaotic political landscape. Notice the three flags above the entrance: Europe, Italy, and—if he's currently at home in the palace—the personal flag of the president. The palace is occasionally open and tourable—in Italian—on Sunday mornings (see www.quirinale.it for details).

Piazza del Quirinale: The square in front of the palace marks the summit of Quirinal Hill, the highest of Rome's fabled seven hills. The fountain in the middle of the square has colossal statues of horses and men (probably Castor and Pollux, third century); as part of his reordering of the city, Pope Sixtus V had the figures moved here around 1585 from a spot near the Baths of Constantine. The obelisk, which formerly stood in front of the Mausoleum of Augustus, was erected here in the late 1700s. Take in the views—there's a fine vista of St. Peter's Basilica in the distance. From here, a set of stairs (in the direction of the dome) leads down to the Trevi Fountain. The big road continues on to Piazza Venezia.

Art Exhibitions

Two temporary exhibition spaces, near Palazzo del Quirinale and just a few blocks from each another, show top-notch art on a rotating basis. Scuderie del Quirinale typically focuses on the great masters (Titian, Vermeer, Caravaggio), while Palazzo delle Exposizioni favors contemporary artworks and photography.

Cost and Hours: €12 for each, can be more with some exhibits, €20 combo-ticket covers both for three days; both open Sun-Thu 10:00-20:00, Fri-Sat 10:00-22:30 except the Palazzo is closed Mon; both may open—and stay open—much later in summer; last entry one hour before closing; Scuderie—Via XXIV Maggio 16, tel. 06-696-271, www.scuderiequirinale.it; Palazzo—Via Nazionale 194, tel. 06-3996-7500, www.palazzoesposizioni.it.

PILGRIM'S ROME

East of the Colosseum (and south of Termini train station) are several venerable churches that Catholic pilgrims make a point of visiting. Near one of the churches is a small WWII museum. For more on these churches, ✪ see the Pilgrim's Rome Tour chapter.

▲▲Church of San Giovanni in Laterano

Built by Constantine, the first Christian emperor, this was Rome's most important church through medieval times. A building alongside the church houses the Holy Stairs (Scala Santa) said to have been walked up by Jesus, which today are ascended by pilgrims on their knees.

Cost and Hours: Church and Holy Stairs-free, cloister-€5, chapel at Holy Stairs-€3.50 (€8 combo-ticket covers both); church open daily 7:00-18:30, audioguide available; Holy Stairs open April-Sept Mon-Sat 6:00-12:00 & 15:00-19:00, Sun 7:00-12:30 & 15:30-19:00, Oct-March daily 7:00-12:30 & 15:00-18:30, last entry 15 minutes before closing; Piazza di San Giovanni in Laterano, Metro: San Giovanni, or bus #85 or #87; tel. 06-6988-6409, www.scalasanta.net.

Museum of the Liberation of Rome (Museo Storico della Liberazione di Roma)

This small memorial museum, near the Church of San Giovanni in Laterano, is housed in the prison wing of the former Nazi police headquarters of occupied Rome. Other than a single pamphlet,

Pilgrim's Rome

there's little in English. Still, for those interested in resistance movements and the Nazi occupation, it's a stirring visit. You'll see a few artifacts, many photos of heroes, and a couple of cells preserved as they were found on June 4, 1944, when the city was liberated.

Cost and Hours: Free but donations accepted, Tue-Sun 9:30-12:30, Tue and Thu-Fri also 15:30-19:30, closed Mon and Aug, just behind the Holy Stairs, look for the flags at Via Tasso 145; tel. 06-700-3866.

▲Church of Santa Maria Maggiore

Home of Rome's best-surviving mosaics line the nave of this church built as Rome was falling. The nearby Church of Santa Prassede has still more early mosaics (described on page 298 in the Pilgrim's Rome Tour chapter).

Cost and Hours: Free, daily 7:00-19:00, Piazza Santa Maria Maggiore, Metro: Termini or Vittorio Emanuele, tel. 06-6988-6802.

▲Church of San Clemente

Besides visiting the church itself, with frescoes by Masolino, you can also descend into the ruins of an earlier church. Descend yet one more level and enter the eerie remains of a pagan temple to Mithras. It's one of the easiest places to fully appreciate the layers of history that lie underfoot in Rome.

Cost and Hours: Upper church-free, lower church-€5, both open Mon-Sat 9:00-12:30 & 15:00-18:00, Sun 12:00-18:00, last entry to lower church 20 minutes before closing; Via di San Giovanni in Laterano, Metro: Colosseo, or bus #85 or #87; tel. 06-774-0021, www.basilicasanclemente.com.

South Rome

The area south of the center contains some interesting but widely scattered areas, from Trastevere to Testaccio to E.U.R. Many sights appear on the color map of South Rome at the beginning of this book. Note that Metro line B hits several of the outlying sights listed here: Piramide (Testaccio area and trains to Ostia Antica), Garbatella (Montemartini Museum), Basilica San Paolo (St. Paul's Outside the Walls), E.U.R. Magliana (Palace of the Civilization of Labor), and E.U.R. Fermi (Museum of Roman Civilization). For maximum efficiency, use this spine to quickly hop between these sights.

TRASTEVERE AND NEARBY

Trastevere is the colorful neighborhood across *(tras)* the Tiber *(Tevere)* River. Trastevere (trahs-TAY-veh-ray) offers the best look at medieval-village Rome. The action unwinds to the chime of the church bells. Go there and wander. Wonder. Be a poet. This is Rome's Left Bank. For a self-guided tour, ✪ see the Trastevere Walk chapter.

This proud neighborhood was long a working-class area. Now that it's becoming trendy, high rents are driving out the source of so much color. Still, it's a great people scene, especially at night. Stroll the back streets (for restaurant recommendations, see the Eating in Rome chapter).

To reach Trastevere by foot from Capitoline Hill, cross the Tiber on Ponte Fabricio to Isola Tiberina; from there, Ponte Cestio takes you to Trastevere. You can also take tram #8 from Piazza Venezia or Largo Argentina, or bus

#H from Termini or Piazza della Repubblica (get off at Sonnino/ Piazza Belli). From the Vatican (Piazza Risorgimento), it's bus #23 or #271.

Linking Trastevere with the Heart of Rome Walk: You can walk from Trastevere to Campo de' Fiori to link up with the beginning of my Heart of Rome Walk (see next chapter): From Trastevere's church square (Piazza di Santa Maria), take Via del Moro to the river and cross at Ponte Sisto, a pedestrian bridge that has a good view of St. Peter's dome. Continue straight ahead for one block. Take the first left, which leads down Via di Capo di Ferro through the scary and narrow darkness to Piazza Farnese, with the imposing Palazzo Farnese. Michelangelo contributed to the facade of this palace, now the French Embassy. The fountains on the square feature huge one-piece granite hot tubs from the ancient Roman Baths of Caracalla. One block from there (opposite the palace) is the atmospheric square, Campo de' Fiori.

▲Church of Santa Maria in Trastevere

One of Rome's oldest church sites, a basilica was erected here in the fourth century, when Christianity was legalized. It is said to have been the first church in Rome dedicated to the Virgin Mary. The structure you see today dates mainly from the 12th century. Its portico (covered area just outside the door) is decorated with fascinating fragments of stone—many of them lids from catacomb burial niches—and filled with early Christian symbolism. The church is on Piazza di Santa Maria. While today's fountain is from the 17th century, there has been a fountain here since Roman times.

Cost and Hours: Free, daily 8:30-21:00.

▲Villa Farnesina

Here's a unique opportunity to see a sumptuous Renaissance villa in Rome decorated with Raphael paintings. It was built in the early 1500s for the richest man in Renaissance Europe, Sienese banker Agostino Chigi. Kings and popes of the day depended on generous loans from Chigi, whose bank had more than 100 branches in places as far-flung as London and Cairo. His villa was the meeting place of aristocrats, artists, beautiful women, and philosophers.

Architect Baldassare Peruzzi's design—a U-shaped building with wings enfolding what used to be a vast garden—successfully blended architecture and nature in a way that both ancient and

Renaissance Romans loved. Orchards and flower beds flowed down in terraces from the palace to the riverbanks. Later construction of modern embankments and avenues robbed the garden of its grandeur, leaving it with a more melancholy charm. Inside, cavorting gods and goddesses cover the walls and ceilings, most famously Raphael's depiction of the sea nymph Galatea.

Cost and Hours: €6; Mon-Sat 9:00-14:00, closed Sun except open 9:00-17:00 on second Sun of month, last entry 30 minutes before closing; across the river from Campo de' Fiori, a short walk from Ponte Sisto and a block behind the river at 230 Via della Lungara; tel. 06-6802-7268, www.villafarnesina.it.

❷ Self-Guided Tour: Enjoy the best bits of the villa with this commentary.

• *Begin in Room 1.*

Loggia of Galatea: Note the ceiling painted by Peruzzi, showing the position of the signs of the horoscope at the exact moment of Agostino's birth (21:30, November 29, 1466). The room's claim to fame is Raphael's painting of the nymph Galatea (on the wall by the entrance door). She shuns the doting attention of the ungainly one-eyed giant Polyphemus (in the niche to the left, painted by another artist) and speeds away in the company of her rambunctious entourage on a chariot led by dolphins. She turns back and looks up, amused by the cyclops' crude love song (which, I believe, was "I Only Have Eye

for You"). The trigger-happy cupids and lusty, entwined fauns and nymphs announce the pagan spirit revived in Renaissance Rome. All the painting's lines of sight (especially the cupids' arrows) point to the center of the work, Galatea's radiant face. Galatea is considered Raphael's vision of female perfection—not a portrait of an individual woman, but a composite of his many lovers in an idealized vision.

• *Continue into Room 2.*

Loggia of Psyche: This room was painted by Raphael and his assistants. Imagine it without the glass windows, as a continuation of the garden outside, where plays were performed to entertain

SIGHTS

Agostino's guests. Raphael's two ceiling frescoes were painted to look like tapestries (complete with ruffled edges), suspended from the ceiling by garlands, making the room appear to be an open bower. View the frescoes from the top, with your back to the garden. The ceiling shows episodes in the myth of a lovely mortal woman, Psyche, who caught the eye of the winged boy-god Cupid (Eros). See the loving couple at the far left end, at the base of the ceiling. The big ceiling fresco on the left depicts the gods of Olympus gathered to plan a series of ordeals to test whether Psyche is worthy to marry a god. (Find Hercules with white beard and club, and Dionysius pouring the wine.) The other shows the happy ending, as Cupid (boy with wings) and Psyche (to his left, in topless robe) stand before Zeus to celebrate their wedding feast, attended by the pantheon of gods.

The whole setting—the room by the gardens, the subject of the frescoes, the fleshy bodies—has an erotic subtext. At the time, Raphael was having a passionate affair with the celebrated Fornarina (the "baker's daughter," who lived down the street). Agostino, noticing that his painter was constantly interrupting his workday to be with her, had the girl kidnapped so that Raphael would finally concentrate. But production slowed even more, as Raphael was depressed. Agostino gave up and had the Fornarina move in with Raphael to keep him company as he happily resumed work in this cheery room. The room's imagery abounds with images both phallic and yonic (the female counterpart of phallic). Next to the ripe and split-open cantaloupe (right end, base of ceiling), find the gourd wearing a condom.

• Upstairs, accessed from the stairway near the entrance, is the...

Room of the Perspectives: Peruzzi, another trendsetter, painted this room. Walls seem to open onto views and perspectives that actually correspond with what lies outside. The insulting-to-Catholics graffiti (for example, on the wall at the far end) dates from 1527, when Protestant mercenaries sent by Charles V sacked the city.

Agostino had his wedding banquet in this room. His parties were the talk of the town. On one occasion, he invited his guests in the (now lost) dining loggia overlooking the Tiber to toss the gold and silver dishes they had just used into the river. (The banker had nets conveniently placed just below the river's surface.)

The small chamber at the end of the Room of the Perspectives was the **bedroom.** The painting on the wall depicts the wedding of

Alexander the Great and Roxanne. Roxanne has the features of Agostino's bride, and the bed is the jewel-encrusted ebony bed that received Agostino and his bride here in this room. On the entrance wall, find the three-arched ruins of the Basilica of Constantine in the Forum. The room was painted by Il Sodoma, a devoted fan of Michelangelo and one of the artists who was canned when Raphael took over the decoration of the papal apartments at the Vatican. Had that not happened, the Raphael Rooms at the Vatican might have looked like this.

Agostino had famous affairs with the most beautiful courtesans of his day. He eventually settled down, but his wild-living descendants didn't, and—in the space of a couple of generations—the Chigi family lost its fabulous fortune.

Gianicolo Hill Viewpoint Hike

From this park atop a hill, the city views are superb, and the walk to the top holds a treat for architecture buffs. Start at Trastevere's Piazza di San Cosimato, and follow Via Luciano Manara to Via Garibaldi, at the base of the hill. Via Garibaldi winds its way up the side of the hill to the Church of San Pietro in Montorio. To the right of the church, in a small courtyard, is the **Tempietto** by Donato Bramante. This tiny church, built to commemorate the martyrdom of St. Peter, is considered a jewel of Italian Renaissance architecture.

From the Tempietto you have two choices. To return to Trastevere, retrace your steps down Via Garibaldi. But if you are feeling energetic, more sights await up the hill. See the map on page 317. Go right and you'll see immediately across the street on your left the white fascist arches of the **Italian Independence War Memorial,** commemorating the 1849 battle fought here, when Giuseppe Garibaldi's forces valiantly tried to hold back the invading French army. Atop one side is the inscription *Roma o Morte* (Rome or Death), the battle cry of Garibaldi's troops.

Continuing up, as the road curves, you'll see the monumental Baroque **Acqua Paola** fountain, named after Pope Paul V. Views of the Roman skyline start to open up on your right. You can't miss the blocky, gleaming white Victor Emmanuel Monument along with assorted domes that rise above the Roman roofscape. If you were to continue up Via Garibaldi you'd reach the cube-shaped **Porta San Pancrazio,** an opening in the Aurelian Walls that were extended up this hill in the third century to protect Rome's strategic water mills.

But by now your quad muscles are reminding you that you are climbing a hill—the Janiculum (Gianicolo in Italian) Hill, named after the two-faced Roman god Janus. Leaving the fountain, cross the street and take a right through the gate with two urns up the tree-lined Passeggiata del Gianicolo and enter the hill-crowning park. You'll soon reach the large **Piazzale Giuseppe Garibaldi,** dominated by the equestrian statue of the swashbuckling military leader of the Italian unification. He enjoys a *magnifico* view of the Eternal City that you can drink in by standing at the railing on the right. A little farther along, look left to find the baby-carrying, gun-wielding, horse-riding statue of Anita Garibaldi, Giuseppe's Brazilian-born partner in battle (and in life). The nearby **Manfredi Lighthouse** was built as a gift to Rome from Italian immigrants to Argentina.

From here you can follow the road that snakes its way down to the river. Or if your feet are screaming *"Roma o Morte,"* catch any northbound bus (#115 or #870) down to the river. Consider doing this hike in reverse by taking a bus (or taxi) to the top of the hill and then walking steadily downhill to Trastevere.

TESTACCIO

In the gritty Testaccio neighborhood, several fascinating but lesser sights cluster at the Piramide Metro stop. (This is a quick and easy stop as you return from E.U.R., or when changing trains en route to Ostia Antica.)

In ancient times (when Rome's population topped a million), wharves lined the banks of the Tiber River here. Back then, 90 percent of the city's food came through here, and the long tradition of Testaccio feeding Rome continues today.

Long a working-class neighborhood, Testaccio has recently gone trendy-bohemian. Visitors wander through an awkward mix of hipster and proletarian worlds, not noticing—but perhaps sensing—the "Keep Testaccio for the Testaccians" graffiti.

You can pick and choose among the Testaccio sights described here or link them with my walking directions, starting at the Piramide Metro station. Use the map above to follow along.

• *As you exit the Metro station, look straight across the busy (and slightly seedy) square to find the giant pyramid and the adjacent brick fortress. For a closer look at these—and to begin our walk—carefully cross the several busy lanes of traffic and head for the gap between these two landmarks.*

Testaccio

To Tiber & Trastevere

1 Agustarello Restaurante
2 Flavio al Velavevodetto
3 Pizzeria Remo
4 Volpetti Più
5 Perilli
6 L'Oasi della Birra

VIA GIOVANNI BRANCA

To Tiber

VIADUCCO DELLA ROBBIA

VIA MARMORATA

Piazza Testaccio

To Central Rome & Termini Station

S. MARIA LIBERATRICE

VIA GINORI

VIALE MANLIO GELSOMINI

VIALE PIRAMIDE CESTIA

VIA A. VOLTA

Parco della Resistenza dell'8 Sett.

TESTACCIO MARKET

VIA GALVANI

VIA FRANKLIN

WALK ENDS

TESTACCIO

POST

PORTA SAN PAOLO

POTTERY SHARDS VIEWPOINTS

VIA ZABAGLIA

CEMETERY ENTRANCE

KEATS

OLD CITY WALLS

MACRO-FUTURE MUSEUM (FORMER STOCK-YARDS)

Monte Testaccio

VIA CAIO CESTIO

Protestant Cemetery

SHELLEY

PYRAMID

#118

B

WALK BEGINS

V. MARCO POLO

British Military Cemetery

VIALE CAMPO BOARIO

Piazzale Ostiense

#23, 271 & 769

B

Piramide

M

PORTA SAN PAOLO STATION (TRAINS TO OSTIA ANTICA)

V. CAVE ARDEATINE

UNDERGROUND MOVING SIDEWALK

200 Meters
200 Yards

OLD CITY WALLS

VIA OSTIENSE

STAZIONE OSTIENSE

Piazzale dei Partigiani

OSTIENSE TRAIN STATION

To Montemartini Museum & St. Paul's Outside the Walls ▼

SIGHTS

Pyramid of Gaius Cestius

In the first century B.C., the Roman occupation of Egypt brought exotic pharaonic styles into vogue. Stoking the fascination with Egypt even further was the love affair of Mark Antony and Cleopatra; this power couple was the ancient equivalent of Brangelina (Cleopantony?). A rich Roman magistrate, Gaius Cestius, had this pyramid built as his tomb, complete with a burial chamber inside. Made of brick covered in marble, the 90-foot structure was completed in just 330 days (as stated

in its Latin inscription). While smaller than actual Egyptian pyramids, its proportions are correct. It was later incorporated into the Aurelian Wall (explained next), and it now stands as a marker to the entrance of Testaccio. The most dramatic views of the pyramid are from inside the Protestant Cemetery (described later), on the other side of the wall.

• *Across the narrow street from the pyramid is the...*

Porta San Paolo and Museo della Via Ostiense

This formidable gate is from the Aurelian Wall, begun in the third century under Emperor Aurelian. The wall, which encircled the city, was 12 miles long and averaged about 26 feet high, with 14 main gates and 380 72-foot-tall towers. Most of what you'll see today is circa A.D. 400, but the barbarians reconstructed the gate later, in the sixth century.

Inside the gate is a tiny free museum (find entrance near pyramid; open Tue and Thu 9:00-16:30, Wed and Fri-Sat 9:00-13:30, open first and third Sun of month 9:00-13:30, closed Mon and second and fourth Sun of month, tel. 06-574-3193). The museum offers a chance to explore the gate and a few models of Rome's ancient port, Ostia Antica (see the Ostia Antica Day Trip chapter); its neighbor, Porto, with its famed hexagonal harbor; and the Ostian Way, the straight Roman road that paralleled the curvy Tiber for 15 miles from Rome to the sea.

For more on the Aurelian Wall, visit the San Sebastiano Gate and Museum of the Walls (described in my ✪ Ancient Appian Way Tour chapter).

• *Go through the gap between the pyramid and the gate on Via Raffaele Persichetti/Via Marmorata. On your right, notice the beige travertine* **post office** *from 1932. This is textbook Mussolini–era fascist architecture; the huge X design on the exterior celebrates the 10th anniversary of the dictator's reign.*

Take the first left, on sleepy Via Caio Cestio, and walk about 200 yards, looking on the left for the gate of the cemetery.

Protestant Cemetery

Lush and lovingly cared for, the Cemetery for the Burial of Non-Catholic Foreigners (Cimitero Acattolico per gli Stranieri al Testaccio) is a tomb-filled "park," running along the wall just beyond the pyramid. The cemetery is also the only English-style landscape (rolling hills, calculated vistas) in Rome, making it a favorite spot for a quiet stroll.

Cost and Hours: €3 suggested donation—leave in box by entrance, Mon-Sat 9:00-17:00, Sun 9:00-13:00, last entry 30 minutes before closing, nice WC inside, staff at info office can help you find specific graves, tel. 06-574-1900, www.cemeteryrome.it.

Keats and Shelley on Mortality

Ponder mortality along with Keats and Shelley, with these excerpts from their poetry:

From Keats' "Ode to a Nightingale"
Adieu! adieu! thy plaintive anthem fades
Past the near meadows, over the still stream,
Up the hill-side; and now 'tis buried deep
In the next valley-glades:
Was it a vision, or a waking dream?
Fled is that music:—Do I wake or sleep?

From Shelley's "Adonais: An Elegy on the Death of John Keats"
I weep for Adonais—he is dead!
Oh, weep for Adonais! though our tears
Thaw not the frost which binds so dear a head!
...I am borne darkly, fearfully, afar;
Whilst, burning through the inmost veil of Heaven,
The soul of Adonais, like a star,
Beacons from the abode where the Eternal are.

SIGHTS

Visiting the Cemetery: Originally, none of the Protestant epitaphs were allowed to make any mention of heaven. Signs direct visitors to the graves of notable non-Catholics who have died in Rome since 1716. Many of the buried were diplomats. And many, such as the poets Percy Bysshe Shelley (1792-1822) and John Keats (1795-1821), were from the Romantic Age. They came to Italy on the Grand Tour and—"captivated by the fatal charms of Rome," as Shelley wrote—never left.

Shelley's tomb is straight ahead from the entrance, up the hill and a bit to the left, at the base of the stubby tower. It's a big, inscribed, flat slab in the ground. Like so many Romantic age artists and writers, Shelley was enamored with Rome. In 1821 he wrote, "Go thou to Rome,—at once the Paradise, the grave, the city, and the wilderness" (from *Adonais*, his elegy on Keats' death).

Back at the entrance, with your back to the gate, head 90 degrees left to find **Keats' tomb,** near the fence in the far corner of the big park facing the pyramid. Keats died in his twenties, unrecognized. He wanted to be unnamed on a tomb that read, "Young English Poet, 1821.

Here lies one whose name was writ in water." (To see Keats' tomb when the cemetery is closed, look through the tiny peephole on Via Caio Cestio, 10 yards off Via Marmorata.)

There are cats everywhere. At the big park overlooking the pyramid, look down and to the right to find Matilde Talli's cat hospice. Volunteers use donations to care for these "Guardians of the Departed" who "provide loyal companionship to these dead."

• *Exit the cemetery through the main gate and turn left, continuing down Via Caio Cestio. Cross the wide street and head down into the sunken area ringing...*

Monte Testaccio

This "hill," actually a 115-foot-tall ancient trash pile, is made of *testae*—broken shards of earthenware jars mostly used to haul oil 2,000 years ago, when this was a gritty port warehouse district. For 500 years, rancid oil vessels were discarded here. Slowly, Rome's lowly eighth hill was built. Because the caves dug into the hill stay cool (perfect for storing wine), trendy bars, clubs, and restaurants compete with gritty car-repair places for a spot.

The neighborhood was once known for its huge slaughterhouse and a Roma (Gypsy) camp that squatted inside an old military base. Now it's home to the Testaccio Village (a site for summer concerts and techno raves—dead until late at night, when it thrives), a weekend farmers' market, and a branch of Rome's contemporary art museum (MACRO).

Circle this area around to the left, looping to the old slaughterhouse. Linger here to pick out the history of this spot—the ornamentation of the building itself, the *frigorifero* (ice house adjacent), and the fine view of the shard mountain.

Within Rome, Testaccio's restaurants are known for serving menus heavy on offal—innards and other "unwanted" parts of the animals that were processed here (tripe, sweetbreads, oxtail, lungs, and so on). While the "nose to tail" foodie aesthetic has become trendy in recent years, Testaccio embraced that approach long before it was cool.

• *Circling the rest of the way around Monte Testaccio, you'll run right into the very modern-looking...*

Testaccio Market (Mercato di Testaccio)

The covered and colorful market is a focal point of the neighborhood. It recently moved to this more modern and "hygienic" location—many say that it's lost some of its edgy charm. But while the structure may be new, the community ties are still old, as locals nurture close relationships with the merchants who sell them their favorite foods. A stroll through here affords a fine look at a traditional Roman market (open Mon-Sat until 14:00, closed Sun, WC on the north side, near the clothing stalls). Find the center (where the sky opens up) and look down at the ancient Roman road littered with the shards of broken amphorae.

For tips on where to eat within the market and the surrounding neighborhood, see page 409. For a better understanding of what Testaccio is all about, consider **Eating Italy Food Tours.** They lead an interesting, four-hour food-oriented walk that makes 10 tasty stops and packs the time with cultural insights (see page 387 for details).

SOUTH OF TESTACCIO
You can ride the Metro to the Montemartini Museum and St. Paul's Outside the Walls, but if you prefer to stay above ground, buses #23, #271, and #769 run on Via Ostiense from the Piramide Metro stop to the museum (stop: Ostiense/Garbatella) and the church (stop: Viale S. Paolo).

▲Montemartini Museum
(Musei Capitolini Centrale Montemartini)
This museum houses a dreamy collection of 400 ancient statues, set evocatively in a classic 1932 electric power plant, among generators and *Metropolis*-type cast-iron machinery. While the art is not as famous as the collections you'll see downtown, the effect is fun and memorable—and you won't encounter a single tourist. If you're tackling Rome with kids, this museum is ideal: It's uncrowded and cool, immersed in an old power plant, with art placed at kid level.

Cost and Hours: €6.50, Tue-Sun 9:00-19:00, closed Mon, last entry 30 minutes before closing, look for red banner marking Via Ostiense 106, a short walk from Metro: Garbatella, tel. 06-0608, www.centralemontemartini.org.

▲St. Paul's Outside the Walls
(Basilica San Paolo Fuori le Mura)
According to Christian tradition, the body of St. Paul was buried here, where a small shrine once stood. It was replaced by a much bigger church in around A.D. 380—in what was the last major construction project of Imperial Rome and the largest church in Christendom until St. Peter's. That church burned in 1823, and the stately if stark, Neoclassi-cal church you see today was built on its footprint. Pilgrims flock here to venerate the saint, especially since forensic experts concluded in 2009 that the bones interred under the altar date from the first or second century.

Cost and Hours: Free, daily 7:00-18:30, modest dress code enforced, dry audioguide-€5 plus ID, Via Ostiense 186, Metro: Basilica San Paolo, exit the Metro station following *via Ostiense* sign, and look for the church's round tower, the entrance is on the far side, tel. 06-6988-0800, www.basilicasanpaolo.org.

Visiting the Church: The column-lined courtyard leading up to the church is typical of early Christian churches—the first version of St. Peter's Basilica also had this kind of welcoming zone. The facade, while 19th century, is early Christian in its style—with Rome and Jerusalem flanking the Lamb of God. In the courtyard's center is a statue of Paul holding his trademark sword, the instrument of his martyrdom. The palm trees, while not native to Rome, remind pilgrims of what they saw in the Holy Land. The central door of bronze and silver, from the 1930s, is dedicated to Peter (crucified upside-down) and Paul (beheaded).

Step inside and feel as close as you'll get in the 21st century to experiencing a monumental Roman basilica. Marvel at the ceiling, with those massive wood beams.

The marble-inlaid floor is like that of the Pantheon and typically Roman. Alabaster windows light the vast interior. It feels sterile, but in a good way—as if you're already in heaven. Along with St. Peter's Basilica, San Giovanni in Laterano, and Santa Maria Maggiore, this church is, legally speaking, part of the Vatican rather than Italy. The triumphal arch leading to the altar has a fifth-century mosaic of Christ raising his hand in blessing. He's flanked by the four evangelists (in symbolic animal guise) and, in white, the mysterious 24 elders of the Apocalypse. At the bottom of the arch are the two early followers of Jesus who, according to tradition, came to Rome to spread the Gospel and ended up dying for it: St. Peter (right) carries the keys to the kingdom of heaven, and St. Paul holds a sword symbolizing the piercing truth. Over the altar is a multicolored marble canopy (13th century). A 20-foot-tall Easter candlestick (c. 1170) stands to the right.

The fine 13th-century mosaic filling the dome in the apse is Byzantine in style; it was likely done by the same craftsmen who decorated St. Mark's in Venice. Notice the tiny white bug-like creature washing Jesus' toe. It's Honorius III, the 13th-century pope who paid for the apse renovation—reminding people of his humbleness while getting some credit at the same time.

The church is built upon the supposed grave of St. Paul.

South of Testaccio

According to tradition, Paul was decapitated two miles from this spot. His head was preserved at San Giovanni in Laterano, and his body was buried here under the altar. In 2009, archaeologists unearthed a sarcophagus with early inscriptions identifying it as Paul's, and carbon-dating on the bones inside confirmed their ancient origin. Today, you can descend a few steps in front of the altar to see the exposed end of Paul's supposed stone coffin, and look down through the glass floor to see the remains of the much smaller original fourth-century church.

Ringing the upper part of the church are round mosaic portraits of 266 popes, from St. Peter (the first one in the right transept) to the present. Find the recent popes to the right of the altar—not in the nave, but farther to the right, under the arches of the dim right aisle. You'll see globetrotting John Paul II *(Jo Paulus II)* and progressive John XXIII, who oversaw the Vatican II changes of the 1960s. A portrait of Pope #266—Francis—was recently installed, alongside blank medallions for future popes.

The peaceful 13th-century cloister (€4) has elegant Romanesque columns and arches, and fragments of early Christian/Roman sarcophagi, a relic chapel, and a small painting gallery.

E.U.R.

In the late 1930s, Italy's dictator Benito Mussolini planned an international exhibition to show off the wonders of his fascist society. But these wonders brought us World War II, and Il Duce's celebration never happened. The unfinished mega-project was completed in the 1950s, and today it houses government offices and big, obscure museums filled with important, rarely visited relics.

If Hitler and Mussolini had won the war, our world might look like E.U.R. (AY-oor). Hike down E.U.R.'s wide, pedestrian-mean boulevards. Patriotic murals, aren't-you-proud-to-be-an-extreme-right-winger pillars, and stern squares decorate the soulless planned grid and sterile office blocks. Patriotic quotes are chiseled into walls. Boulevards named for Astronomy, Electronics, Social Security, and Beethoven are more exhausting than inspirational. And, not to be outdone by the ancients, Mussolini had a towering fascist-style obelisk erected in the central Piazza Marconi.

Despite its grim past, E.U.R. is now an up-and-coming place with young people and trendy cafés. It's worth a trip for the Museum of Roman Civilization (described later). And because a few landmark buildings of Italian modernism are located here and there, E.U.R. has become an important destination for architecture buffs. The new futuristic convention center nicknamed "The Cloud" (it's meant to look like a cloud suspended in a glass box) promises to bring even more life to the district.

The Metro skirts E.U.R. with three stops (10 minutes from the Colosseum). Use E.U.R. Magliana for the Palace of the Civilization of Labor and E.U.R. Fermi for the Museum of Roman Civilization. Consider walking 20 minutes from the palace to the museum through the center of E.U.R.

Palace of the Civilization of Labor (Palazzo della Civiltà del Lavoro)

From the E.U.R. Magliana Metro stop, stairs lead uphill to this epitome of fascist architecture. With its giant no-questions-asked patriotic statues and its stark simplicity, this is E.U.R.'s tallest building and key landmark. It's understandably nicknamed the "Square Colosseum." Closed to the public while they decide how to use it, it's still interesting to walk around. Downhill, in front of the palace, Caffè Palombini is a popular Roman institution; their buffet line is a hit with local workers for lunch (daily 7:00-22:00; good gelato, pastries, and snacks; Piazzale Adenauer 12—you'll see it towering above as you exit the E.U.R. Magliana Metro station, tel. 06-591-1700).

Mussolini and Imperial Rome

Benito Mussolini incorporated much from ancient Rome during his dictatorship. His military was organized according to Roman terminology (divided into legions and run by centurions and consuls). The salute with the right arm raised, flat palm down (later used by the Nazis), was also Roman. More hygienic and quicker than a handshake, it fit the dynamic character of fascism.

While the classical values of power and discipline were stressed in the rhythmic march of military parades, convincing Italians of the need for order was a challenge even to Mussolini. He claimed it wasn't impossible to govern the Italian people...just useless.

Mussolini's title, Il Duce, was from the Latin *dux*—a generic term for leader. When chanted by crowds and carved onto monuments, it likely fueled Mussolini's belief that he was carrying out extraordinary historical missions like Caesar and Augustus before him.

For his fascist symbol, rather than the she-wolf or eagle, Mussolini used the *lictor's fasces*—an ax belonging to a Roman officer, with rods tied around the handle, carried in front of magistrates as a sign of authority. This was aimed at destroying the popular image of Italy as a joyous, carefree country and for promoting a new image of austerity and order. In ancient times, the ax stood for decapitation, the rods for flogging.

Fascist architecture, like ancient architecture, used a monumental scale, with arches, bold statues, and rhetorical inscriptions—resulting in an austere and impersonal feel that's generally disliked by Romans today.

In spite of his supposed passion for ancient Rome, Mussolini had a dreadful approach to archaeology. He would isolate a major monument and destroy everything around it. Sections of the imperial forums were sacrificed to build the wide street, Via dei Fori Imperiali, from Piazza Venezia to the Colosseum. A famous fountain by the Colosseum that had survived almost 2,000 years was torn down without another thought.

Museum of Roman Civilization
(Museo della Civiltà Romana)

With dozens of rooms of plaster casts and models illustrating the greatness of classical Rome, this vast and dated museum gives a strangely lifeless, close-up look at Rome. It's calm and quiet, and lets you see virtually every ancient site intact. Each room has a theme, from military tricks to musical instruments, and is well described in English. One long hall is filled with casts of the reliefs of Trajan's Column. The highlight is the huge scale model of Constantine's Rome, circa A.D. 300. There are no ancient artifacts, but the various models can teach volumes about life and war in ancient Rome. The Planetarium and Astronomical Museum are mostly of interest to children—so don't bother with the €10.50 combo-ticket unless you have kids. As this museum has recently been renovated, some of the specifics may have changed.

Cost and Hours: €8.50, Tue-Sat 9:00-14:00, Sun 9:00-13:30, closed Mon, last entry one hour before closing, Piazza G. Agnelli, tel. 06-0608, www.museociviltaromana.it.

SIGHTS

Getting There: It's about a 10-minute walk from the E.U.R. Fermi Metro station. Leave the station and head left on Viale America, toward McDonald's and the wide, narrow Eni skyscraper. Just after the McDonald's, at the T-intersection, turn left on Viale dell'Arte and go uphill three blocks. On the right, you'll pass the huge colonnade of the state archive; when you reach a second colonnade, you've arrived at the museum. To return to the city center, access the Metro entrance across the street, on the side closest to the pond.

ANCIENT APPIAN WAY

Southeast of the city center lie several ancient sites that make the trek here worthwhile.

Baths of Caracalla
(Terme di Caracalla)

Inaugurated by Emperor Caracalla in A.D. 216, this massive bath complex could accommodate 1,600 visitors at a time. Today it's just a shell—a huge shell—with all of its sculptures and most of its mosaics moved to museums. You'll see a two-story roofless brick building surrounded by a garden, bordered by ruined walls. The two large rooms at either end of the building were used for exercise. In between the exercise rooms was a pool flanked by two small mosaic-floored dressing rooms. Niches in the walls once held statues. The baths' statues are displayed elsewhere: For example, the immense *Toro Farnese* (a marble sculpture of a bull surrounded by people) snorts in Naples' Archaeological Museum.

In its day, this was a remarkable place to hang out. For ancient Romans, bathing was a social experience. The Baths of Caracalla functioned until Goths severed the aqueducts in the sixth century. In modern times, grand operas are performed here during the summer (www.operaroma.it).

Cost and Hours: €6, includes the Tomb of Cecilia Metella and the Villa dei Quintili on the Appian Way, Mon 9:00-14:00, Tue-Sun 9:00 until one hour before sunset (roughly April-Sept 19:00, Oct 18:30, Nov-mid-Feb 16:30, mid-Feb-March 17:00), last entry one hour before closing, audioguide-€5, good €8 guidebook; Metro: Circo Massimo, then a 5-minute walk south along Via delle Terme di Caracalla; bus #714 from Termini train station or bus #118 from the Appian Way—see the end of my Ancient Appian Way Tour; tel. 06-3996-7700.

▲Appian Way

For a taste of the countryside around Rome and more wonders of Roman engineering, take the four-mile trip from the Colosseum

out past the wall to a stretch of the ancient Appian Way, where the original pavement stones are lined by several interesting sights. Ancient Rome's first and greatest highway, the Appian Way, once ran from Rome to the Adriatic port of Brindisi—the gateway to Greece. Today you can walk (or bike) some stretches of the road, rattling over original paving stones, past crumbling monuments that once edged the sides. The Tomb of Cecilia Metella and the Circus of Maxentius are the two most impressive pagan sights. Just a few hundred yards away are two major Christian catacombs (briefly described next).

For more on all of these sights, ✪ see the Ancient Appian Way Tour chapter.

▲▲Catacombs of San Sebastiano

A guide leads you underground through the tunnels where early Christians were buried. You'll see faded frescoes and graffiti by early-Christian tag artists, as well as some pagan tombs that predate the Christian catacombs. Besides the catacombs themselves, there's a historic fourth-century basilica with the relics of St. Sebastian, the (supposedly) original Quo Vadis footprints of Christ, and an exquisite Bernini statue.

Cost and Hours: €8, includes 35-minute tour, 2/hour, Mon-Sat 10:00-17:00, closed Sun and late-Nov-late-Dec, last entry 30 minutes before closing, Via Appia Antica 136, tel. 06-785-0350, www.catacombe.org.

▲▲Catacombs of San Callisto

The larger of the two sets of catacombs, San Callisto also is the more prestigious, having been the burial site for several early popes.

Cost and Hours: €8, includes 30-minute tour, at least 2/hour, Thu-Tue 9:00-12:00 & 14:00-17:00, closed Wed and Feb, Via Appia Antica 110, tel. 06-513-0151, www.catacombe.roma.it.

HEART OF ROME WALK

From Campo de' Fiori to the Spanish Steps

Rome's most colorful neighborhood features narrow lanes, intimate piazzas, fanciful fountains, and some of Europe's best people-watching. During the day, this walk shows off the colorful Campo de' Fiori market and trendy fashion boutiques as it meanders past major monuments such as the Pantheon and the Spanish Steps.

But when the sun sets, unexpected magic happens. A stroll in the cool of the evening brings out all the romance of the Eternal City. Sit so close to a bubbling fountain that traffic noise evaporates. Jostle with kids to see the gelato flavors. Watch lovers straddling more than the bench. Jaywalk past *polizia* in flak-proof vests. And marvel at the ramshackle elegance that softens this brutal city for those who were born here and can't imagine living anywhere else. These are the flavors of Rome, best tasted after dark.

Orientation

Length of This Walk: Allow anywhere from one to three hours for this mile-long walk, depending on whether you linger (yes, do) and tour the Pantheon (another good idea).

When to Go: This walk works well at any time. By day, you can enjoy Campo de' Fiori's morning market and sightsee the Pantheon and surrounding churches. But it's most engaging after dark, when the fountains are lit and the cool evening air brings locals out for the *passeggiata* (for more on this Italian tradition, see the sidebar on page 430).

Getting There: Campo de' Fiori is a few blocks west of Largo Argentina, a major transportation hub. Buses #40, #64, and #492 stop both at Largo Argentina and along Corso Vittorio Emanuele II (a long block northwest of Campo de' Fiori). A taxi from Termini Station costs about €8.

Pantheon: Free, Mon-Sat 8:30-19:30, Sun 9:00-18:00, holidays
    9:00-13:00, closed for Mass on Sat at 17:00 and Sun at 10:30.

Other Options: This walk is equally pleasant in reverse order. You
    could ride the Metro to the Spanish Steps and finish at Campo
    de' Fiori, near many recommended restaurants. To lengthen
    this walk, you could start in Trastevere; see directions on page
    313.

The Walk Begins

• *Start this walk at Campo de' Fiori, my favorite outdoor dining room
(especially after dark—see page 390 in the Eating in Rome chapter).*

Campo de' Fiori

One of Rome's most colorful spots, this bohemian piazza hosts a
fruit and vegetable **market** in the morning, cafés in the evening,

and pub-crawlers at night. In
ancient times, the "Field of
Flowers" was an open meadow.
Later, Christian pilgrims passed
through on their way to the
Vatican, and a thriving market
developed.

Lording over the center of
the square is a statue of **Gior-
dano Bruno,** an intellectual
heretic who was burned on this
spot in 1600. The pedestal shows
scenes from Bruno's trial and execution, and reads, "And the flames
rose up." When this statue honoring a heretic was erected in 1889,
the Vatican protested, but they were overruled by angry Campo
locals. The neighborhood is still known for its free spirit and anti-
authoritarian demonstrations.

Campo de' Fiori is the product of centuries of unplanned
urban development. At the east end of the square (behind Bruno),
the ramshackle apartments are built right into the old outer wall of
ancient Rome's mammoth Theater of Pompey. This entertainment
complex covered several city blocks, stretching from here to Largo
Argentina. Julius Caesar was assassinated in the Theater of Pompey, where the Senate was renting space.

The square is surrounded by fun eateries, and is great for
people-watching. Bruno faces the bustling **Forno** (in the left
corner of the square, closed Sun), where take-out *pizza bianco* is sold hot out of the oven. On weekend nights, when
the Campo is packed with beer-drinking kids, the medieval square is transformed into one vast Roman street party.

To Piazza del Popolo

Spagna Ⓜ

Piazza di Spagna

TRINITÀ DEI MONTI

WALK ENDS Ⓣ

SPANISH STEPS

CROCE

CAROZZE

VIA DEL CORSO

VIA CONDOTTI

VIA SISTINA

Piazza Mignanelli Ⓣ

◆ MCDONALD'S

VIA BORGOGNONA

VIA F. BORGHESE

VIA FRATTINA

PROPAGANDA

VIA DUE MACELLI

VIA VITE

Piazza S. Lorenzo

POST

V. MERCEDE

SANT' ANDREA DELLE FRATTE

S. ANDREA

To Barberini Ⓜ

V. CONVERTITE

Piazza San Silvestro

NAZARENO

MARZIO

Piazza del Parlamento

VIA DEL TRITONE

Ⓣ

VIA STAMPERIA

TREVI FOUNTAIN

PARLIAMENT

VICARIO

GALLERIA DELL'ALBERTO SORDI

Ⓣ

Piazza Montecitorio

Piazza Colonna

SABINI

CRUCIFERI

V. LAVATORE

Piazza Capranica

AQUIRO

Piazza Pietra

PIETRA

VIA D. MURATTE

PALAZZO DEL QUIRINALE

LUCCHESI

VIA DELLA DATARIA

PASTINI

S. MARIA

VIA DELL'UMILTÀ

Piazza del Quirinale

TAZZA D'ORO

SHORTCUT

Piazza San Ignazio

VIA SEMINARIO

SANTA MARIA SOPRA MINERVA

SAN IGNAZIO

🍦 **Gelateria**

150 Meters

150 Yards

ELEPHANT & OBELISK

MARMO

Piazza Collegio Rom.

GALLERIA DORIA PAMPHILJ

VIA DEL GESÙ

VIA BATTISTI

VIA IV NOVEMBRE

VIA IV NOV.

VIA PLEBISCITO

Piazza Venezia

Ⓑ

Piazza del Gesú

GESÚ

Piazza San Marco

Ⓣ

S. MARCO

VICTOR EMMANUEL MONUMENT

TRAJAN'S COLUMN

VIA MAG. To Termini

ARACOELI

To Capitoline Hill

Ⓣ To Colosseum & Ⓜ

HEART OF ROME

Giordano Bruno (1548-1600)

Lauded as a martyr to free thought and reviled as an intellectual con man and heretic, the philosopher-priest Bruno has a legacy only a Roman could love. Details of his life are sketchy, and his writings range from the sublime to the ridiculous.

The young Dominican priest was nonconformist and outspoken from the start. He had to flee Italy to avoid a charge of heresy and spent most of his adult life wandering Europe's capitals. In Geneva, he joined the Calvinists, until he was driven out for his unorthodox views. In London, he met with Queen Elizabeth, who found him subversive. In Germany, the Lutherans excommunicated him.

In his writings, Bruno claimed to have discovered the "Clavis Magna" (Great Key) to training the human memory. He published satirical plays tweaking Church morals. He advanced the then-heretical (Copernican) notion that the earth revolved around the sun and speculated about other inhabited planets in the universe. All his works show a vast-ranging mind aware of the scientific trends of the day.

In 1593, Bruno was arrested by the Inquisition and sent to Rome, where he languished in prison for six years. (Tortured? Lost in the bureaucracy? No one knows.) The exact charge against him remains debated by historians.

Bruno was sentenced to death by fire. He replied, "Perhaps you who pronounce this sentence are more fearful than I who receive it." On February 17, 1600, the civil authorities led him to the stake on Campo de' Fiori. As they lit the fire, he was offered a crucifix to hold. He pushed it away.

• *If Bruno did a hop, step, and jump forward, then turned right on Via dei Baullari and marched 200 yards, he'd cross the busy Corso Vittorio Emanuele; then, continuing another 150 yards on Via della Cuccagna, he'd find...*

Piazza Navona

This oblong square retains the shape of the original racetrack that was built around A.D. 80 by the emperor Domitian. Since ancient times, the square has been a center of Roman life. In the 1800s, the city would flood the square to cool off the neighborhood. (To see the ruins of the original entrance, exit the square at the far—or north—end, then take an immediate left, and look down to the left 25 feet below the current street level. Continue a bit farther if you want to pay €5 to tour the foundations up close.)

The **Four Rivers Fountain** in the center is the most famous fountain by the man who remade Rome in the Baroque style, Gian

Lorenzo Bernini. Four burly river gods (representing the four continents that were known in 1650) support an Egyptian obelisk. The water of the world gushes everywhere. The Nile has his head covered, since the headwaters were unknown then. The Ganges holds an oar. The Danube turns to admire the obelisk, which Bernini had moved here from a stadium on the Appian Way. And Uruguay's Río de la Plata tumbles backward in shock, wondering how he ever made the top four. Bernini enlivens the fountain with horses plunging through the rocks and exotic flora and fauna from these newly discovered lands. Homesick Texans may want to find the armadillo. (It's the big, weird, armor-plated creature behind the Plata river statue.)

The Plata river god is gazing upward at the **Church of St. Agnes,** worked on by Bernini's former student-turned-rival, Francesco Borromini. Borromini's concave facade helps reveal the dome and epitomizes the curved symmetry of Baroque. Tour guides say that Bernini designed his river god to look horrified at Borromini's work. Or maybe he's shielding his eyes from St. Agnes' nakedness, as she was stripped before being martyred. But either explanation is unlikely, since the fountain was completed two years before Borromini even started work on the church.

Piazza Navona is Rome's most interesting night scene, with street music, artists, fire eaters, local Casanovas, ice cream, and outdoor cafés that are worthy of a splurge if you've got time to sit and enjoy Italy's human river.

• *Leave Piazza Navona directly across from Tre Scalini (famous for its rich chocolate ice cream), and go east down Corsia Agonale, past rose peddlers and palm readers. Jog left around the guarded building (the Palazzo Madama, where Italy's senate meets), and follow the brown sign to the Pantheon, which is straight down Via del Salvatore. After a block, you'll pass (on your left) the **Church of San Luigi dei Francesi**, with its très*

French decor and precious Caravaggio paintings (church described in detail on page 128 in the Pantheon Tour chapter). If you're planning on touring that church, do it now. Otherwise, head for...

The Pantheon

Sit for a while under the portico of the Pantheon (romantically floodlit and moonlit at night).

The 40-foot, single-piece granite columns of the Pantheon's entrance show the scale the ancient Romans built on. The col-

umns support a triangular Greek-style roof with an inscription that says "M. Agrippa" built it. In fact, it was built *(fecit)* by Emperor Hadrian (A.D. 120), who gave credit to the builder of an earlier structure. This impressive entranceway gives no clue that the greatest wonder of the building is inside—a domed room that inspired later domes, including Michelangelo's St. Peter's and Brunelleschi's Duomo (in Florence).

If it's open, pop into the Pantheon for a look around. Also consider detouring to several interesting churches near the Pantheon before continuing on the walk (**Santa Maria sopra Minerva,** with its purely Gothic interior, and **San Ignazio,** with its 3-D Baroque illusions, are just a few steps away). For details on the Pantheon and these other churches, ✪ see the Pantheon Tour chapter.

• With your back to the Pantheon, veer to the right, uphill toward the yellow sign that reads Casa del Caffè at the Tazza d'Oro coffee shop on Via Orfani.

From the Pantheon to the Trevi Fountain

Tazza d'Oro Casa del Caffè, one of Rome's top coffee shops, dates back to the days when this area was licensed to roast coffee beans.

Locals come here for a shot of espresso or, when it's hot, a refreshing *granita di caffè con panna* (coffee slush with cream).

• From here, our walk continues past some interesting landmarks to the Trevi Fountain. But if you'd like to get there a bit more directly, you can bear right past the coffee shop onto Via de'Pastini, which leads through Piazza

di Pietra (with some surviving chunks of the Temple of Hadrian—described on page 61), then across busy Via del Corso, where it becomes the touristy, pedestrianized Via delle Muratte and heads straight for the fountain.

If you'd rather stick with me for the slightly longer version, instead bear left at the coffee shop and continue up Via degli Orfani to a big square.

Piazza Capranica is home to the big, plain Florentine Renaissance-style Palazzo Capranica (directly opposite as you enter the square). Big shots, like the Capranica family, built towers on their palaces—not for any military use, but just to show off.

• *Leave the piazza to the right of the palace, heading down Via in Aquiro.*

The street Via in Aquiro leads to a sixth-century B.C. **Egyptian obelisk** taken as a trophy by Augustus after his victory in Egypt over Mark Antony and Cleopatra. The obelisk was set up as a sundial. Follow the zodiac markings to the well-guarded front door. This is Italy's **parliament building,** where the lower house meets; you may see politicians, political demonstrations, and TV cameras.

• *One block to your right is Piazza Colonna, where we're heading next—unless you like gelato...*

A one-block detour to the left (past Albergo Nazionale) brings you to Rome's most famous *gelateria*. **Giolitti's** is cheap for takeout or elegant and splurge-worthy for a sit among classy locals (open daily until past midnight, Via Uffici del Vicario 40); get your gelato in a cone *(cono)* or cup *(coppetta)*.

Piazza Colonna features a huge second-century column. Its reliefs depict the victories of Emperor Marcus Aurelius over the barbarians. When Marcus died in A.D. 180, the barbarians began to get the upper hand, beginning Rome's long three-century fall. The big, important-looking palace houses the headquarters for the prime minister's cabinet.

Noisy **Via del Corso** is Rome's main north-south boulevard. It's named for the Berber horse races—without riders—that took place here during Carnevale. This wild tradition continued until the late 1800s, when a series of fatal accidents (including, reportedly, one in front of Queen Margherita) led to its cancellation. Historically the street was filled with meat shops. When it became one of Rome's first gas-lit streets in 1854, these butcher shops were banned and replaced by classier boutiques, jewelers, and antique dealers. Nowadays the northern part of Via del Corso is closed to traffic, and for a few hours every evening it becomes a wonderful parade of Romans out for a stroll (see the "Dolce Vita Stroll" in the Nightlife in Rome chapter).

• *Cross Via del Corso to enter a big palatial build-ing with columns, which houses the Galleria Al-berto Sordi shopping mall (with convenient WCs). Inside, take the fork to the right and exit at the back. (If you're here after 22:00, when the mall is closed, circle around the right side of the Galleria on Via dei Sabini.) Once out the back, head up Via de Crociferi, to the roar of the water, lights, and people at the...*

Trevi Fountain

The Trevi Fountain shows how Rome took full advantage of the abundance of water brought into the city by its great aqueducts. This fountain celebrated the reopening of several of ancient Rome's aqueducts in the Renais-sance and Baroque eras. After a thousand years of surviving on poor-quality well water, Romans could once again enjoy pure water brought from the distant hills east of the city.

This watery Baroque avalanche by Nicola Salvi was completed in 1762. Salvi used the palace behind the fountain as a theatri-cal backdrop for the figure of "Ocean," who represents water in every form. The statue surfs through his wet kingdom—with water gushing from 24 spouts and tumbling over 30 different kinds of plants—while Triton blows his conch shell.

The magic of the square is enhanced by the fact that no streets directly approach it. You can hear the excitement as you draw near, and then—*bam!*—you're there. The scene is always lively, with lucky Romeos clutching dates while unlucky ones clutch beers. Ro-mantics toss a coin over their shoulder, thinking it will give them a wish and assure their return to Rome. That may sound silly, but every year I go through this tourist ritual...and it actually seems to work.

Take some time to people-watch (whisper a few breathy *bellos* or *bellas*) before leaving. There's a peaceful zone at water level on the far right.

• *From the Trevi Fountain, we're 10 minutes from our next stop, the*

Egyptian Obelisks

Rome has 13 obelisks, more than any other city in the world. In Egypt, they were connected with the sun god Ra (like stone sun rays) and the power of the pha- raohs. The ancient Romans, keen on exotic novelty and sheer size, brought the obelisks here and set them up in key public places as evidence and celebration of their occupation of Egypt. Starting from the 1580s, Rome's new rulers—the popes—relocated the obelisks, often topping them with Christian crosses so they came to acquire yet another significance that guaranteed their survival: the triumph of Christianity over all other religions.

The tallest (105 feet) and the most ancient (16th century B.C.) is the one by San Giovanni in Laterano. It once stood in the Circus Maximus next to its sister, which now marks the center of Piazza del Popolo.

 The obelisks were carved out of single blocks of granite. Imagine the work, with only man and horsepower, first to quarry them and set them up in Egypt, then—after the Romans came along—to roll them on logs to the river or the coast, sail (or row) them in special barges across the Mediterranean and up the Tiber, and finally hoist them up.

Rome wasn't above cheap imitations, however: A couple of the obelisks are ancient Roman copies. The one at the top of the Spanish Steps has spelling mistakes in the hieroglyphics.

Spanish Steps. Just use a map to get there, or follow these directions: Facing the Trevi Fountain, go forward, walking along the right side of the fountain on Via della Stamperia. Cross busy Via del Tritone. Continue 100 yards and veer right at Via Sant'Andrea delle Fratte, a street that changes its name to Via Propaganda before ending at the...

Spanish Steps

Piazza di Spagna, with the very popular Spanish Steps, is named for the Spanish Embassy to the Vatican, which has been here for 300 years. It's been the hangout of many Romantics over the years (Keats, Wagner, Openshaw, Goethe, and others). In the 1700s, British aristocrats on the Grand Tour of Europe came here to ponder Rome's decay. The British poet John Keats pondered his mortality, then died of tuberculosis at age 25 in the orange building on the right side of the steps. Fellow Romantic Lord Byron lived across the square at #66.

The wide, curving staircase is one of Rome's iconic sights. Its 138 steps lead sharply up from Piazza di Spagna, forming a butterfly shape as they fan out around a central terrace. The design culminates at the top in an obelisk framed between two Baroque church towers.

The **Sinking Boat Fountain** at the foot of the steps, built by Bernini or his father, Pietro, is powered by an aqueduct. Actually, all of Rome's fountains are aqueduct-powered; their spurts are determined by the water pressure provided by the various aqueducts. This one, for instance, is much weaker than Trevi's gush.

The piazza is a thriving scene at night. Window-shop along Via Condotti, which stretches away from the steps. This is where Gucci and other big names cater to the trendsetting jet set. It's clear that the main sight around here is not the famous steps, but the people who sit on them.

• *Our walk is finished. If you'd like to reach the top of the steps sweat-free, take the free elevator just outside the Spagna Metro stop (to the left, as you face the steps; elevator closes at 21:00). A free WC is underground in the piazza near the Metro entrance, by the middle palm tree (10:00–19:30). The nearby McDonald's (as you face the Spanish Steps, go right one block) is big and lavish, with a salad bar and WC. When you're ready to leave, you can zip home on the Metro (usually open until 23:30, Fri–Sat until 1:30 in the morning) or grab a taxi at either the north or south side of the piazza.*

PANTHEON TOUR

*The Roman Temple and
Nearby Churches*

If your imagination is fried from trying to reconstruct ancient buildings out of today's rubble, visit the Pantheon, Rome's best-preserved monument. Engineers still admire how the Romans built such a mathematically precise structure without computers, fossil fuel-run machinery, or electricity. (Having unlimited slave power didn't hurt.) Stand under the Pantheon's solemn dome to gain a new appreciation for the sophistication of these ancient people.

The Pantheon is the centerpiece of this tour, and is a must-see on any visit to Rome. The second part of this tour features several interesting churches that cluster near the Pantheon, with art by Michelangelo and Caravaggio, and connections with Galileo, St. Ignatius, and the Jesuit order.

Orientation

Pantheon: Free, Mon-Sat 8:30-19:30, Sun 9:00-18:00, holidays 9:00-13:00, closed for Mass on Sat at 17:00 and Sun at 10:30. Tel. 06-6830-0230.

Church of San Luigi dei Francesi: Free, daily 10:00-12:30 & 15:00-19:00 except closed Thu afternoon, good €3 booklet, www.saintlouis-rome.net. Bring coins to light the Caravaggios.

Gesù Church: Free, daily 7:00-12:30 & 16:00-19:45, interesting daily service at 17:30.

Church of Santa Maria sopra Minerva: Free, Mon-Fri 7:00-19:00, Sat-Sun 8:00-12:30 & 15:30-19:00.

Church of San Ignazio: Free, Mon-Sat 7:30-19:00, Sun 9:00-19:00.

When to Go: Don't go midday, when the Pantheon is packed and two of the churches are closed. Visit the Pantheon before 9:00, and you'll have it all to yourself. Note that the churches have slightly varying hours—plan carefully to avoid getting shut out.

Dress Code: The Pantheon does not allow visitors with skimpy shorts or bare shoulders. Modest dress is recommended for the churches near the Pantheon.

Getting There: The Pantheon neighborhood is a 15-minute walk from Capitoline Hill. Taxis and buses stop at a chaotic square called Largo Argentina, a few blocks south of the Pantheon—from here you can walk north on either Via dei Cestari or Via di Torre Argentina to the Pantheon. Buses #40 and #64 carry tourists and pickpockets frequently between the Termini train station and Vatican City (#492 serves the same areas via a different route). Bus #87 connects to the Colosseum. The *elettrico* minibus #116 runs between Campo de' Fiori and Piazza Barberini via the Pantheon.

Tours: The Pantheon has a €5 audioguide that lasts 25 minutes (€8/2 people). You can download the Pantheon portion of this chapter as a free Rick Steves **audio tour** (see page 8).

Length of This Tour: Allow a half-hour to see the Pantheon and at least another hour to visit the nearby churches. If you have less time, the essential Pantheon can be seen in a glance. The four nearby churches are far less important.

Services: The nearest WCs are at bars and cafés on the Pantheon's square.

Photography: It's allowed—even with flash—in the Pantheon, but no flash is allowed in the nearby churches.

Eating: Restaurants abound. Several reasonable eateries within a few steps of the Pantheon are listed in the Eating in Rome chapter (see page 396). You can picnic on the steps of the fountain or along the Pantheon's walls. While picnicking is forbidden under the Pantheon's portico, I enjoy discreetly munching a sandwich at the base of a column. Some of Rome's best gelato is nearby.

Drinks: A drinking fountain spurts near the obelisk in Piazza della Rotonda. For those who prefer their liquids caffeinated, two of Rome's most venerable (and busiest) coffee shops are just steps away: **Tazza d'Oro Casa del Caffè** (their icy *granita di caffè con panna* is heaven on a hot day; Via degli Orfani 84) and **Bar Sant'Eustachio** (they add sugar to their coffee drinks unless you request otherwise; Piazza di Sant'Eustachio 82).

The Tour Begins

• *Start the tour at the top of the square called Piazza della Rotonda, with cafés and restaurants around the edges and an obelisk-topped fountain in the center. You're looking at...*

The Pantheon

Exterior

The Pantheon was a Roman temple dedicated to all *(pan)* of the gods *(theos)*. The original temple was built in 27 B.C. by Augustus' son-in-law, Marcus Agrippa. In fact, the inscription below the triangular **pediment** proclaims in Latin, "Marcus Agrippa, son of Lucio, three times consul made this." But after a couple of fires, the structure we see today was completely rebuilt by the emperor Hadrian around A.D. 120. Some say that Hadrian, an amateur architect (and voracious traveler), helped design it.

The Pantheon looks like a pretty typical temple from the outside, but this is perhaps the most influential building in art history. Its dome was the model for the Florence cathedral dome, which launched the Renaissance, and for Michelangelo's dome of St. Peter's, which capped it all off. Even the US Capitol in Washington, DC, was inspired by this dome.

The **portico** is Greek in style, which is logical, because Hadrian was a Grecophile. (He grew a beard to look like a Greek philosopher, bucking the beardless tradition of Rome's 13 previous emperors.) This fine porch is a visual reminder of the great debt Roman culture owed to the Greeks. Fittingly, you cross this Greek space to enter a purely Roman space, the rotunda. The columns are huge and unadorned, made from 40-foot-high single pieces of red-gray granite rather than the standard stacks of cylindrical pieces. They were quarried in Egypt, then shipped down the Nile and across the Mediterranean to Rome. They were then fitted with leafy Corinthian capitals, the Greek order that was most popular among Romans. They are sequoia-huge—it takes the outstretched arms of four large tourists to encircle one column.

• *Before passing through the portico, notice the two huge, empty niches flanking the door—once filled with towering statues of emperors. Look up at the porch roof, and imagine the ceiling covered in its original bronze plating. It was removed in the 17th century by a scavenging pope from*

Pantheon Cross-Section

30 Meters

30 Yards

GRAY CIRCLE INDICATES HOW A
142' DIAMETER BALL FITS PERFECTLY INSIDE

1 Pediment
2 Portico
3 Thickest Part of Dome
4 Thinnest Part of Dome
5 Coffered Ceiling
6 Oculus

the Barberini family, inspiring the well-known quip, "What the barbarians didn't do, the Barberini did." Melted down, some of the bronze was used to build the huge bronze canopy over the altar at St. Peter's. Now pass through the giant **bronze door**—a copy of the original. Take a seat and take it all in.

Inside the Pantheon

The dome, which was the largest made until the Renaissance, is set on a circular base. The mathematical perfection of this dome-on-a-base design is a testament to Roman engineering. The dome is as high as it is wide—142 feet from floor to rooftop and from side to side. To picture it, imagine a basketball wedged inside a wastebasket so that it just touches bottom.

The dome—clean and feeling loftier than ever—is made from concrete (a Roman invention) that gets lighter and thinner as it reaches the top. The base of the dome is 23 feet thick and made from heavy concrete mixed with travertine, while near the top, it's less than five feet thick and made with a lighter volcanic rock (pumice) mixed in. Note the square indentations in the surface of the dome. This **coffered ceiling** reduces the weight of the dome without compromising

Pantheon

To
Santa Maria
sopra Minerva,
Gesù & Largo
Argentina

1. Portico Columns
2. Bronze Door
3. Oculus
4. Main Altar
5. Tomb of Raphael
6. Tomb of Victor Emmanuel II
7. Tomb of Umberto I & Margherita

PORTICO

To
San
Ignazio

Piazza della Rotonda

To
Piazza
Navona

30 Meters
30 Yards

strength. The walls are strengthened by brick relieving arches ("blind" arches)—visible in the exposed brickwork in a few of the interior niches and easy to see from outside.

Both Brunelleschi and Michelangelo studied this dome before building their own (in Florence and the Vatican, respectively). Remember, the grandiose vision for St. Peter's Basilica was to place the dome of the Pantheon atop the Forum's Basilica of Constantine.

At the top, the **oculus,** or eye-in-the-sky, is the building's only light source. It's completely open and almost 30 feet across. The 1,800-year-old floor—with 80 percent of its original stones surviving—has holes in it and slants toward the edges to let the rainwater drain. Though some of the floor's marble has been replaced, the design—alternating circles and squares—is original.

In ancient times, this was a one-stop-shopping temple where you could worship any of the major gods whose statues decorated the niches. Entering the temple, Romans came face-to-face with a larger-than-life statue of Jupiter, the King of the

PANTHEON

Gods, where the **altar** stands today. After the fall of Rome, the Pantheon became a Christian church (from "all the gods" to "all the martyrs"), which saved it from architectural cannibalism and ensured its upkeep through the Dark Ages. (The year 2009 was the building's 1,400th anniversary as a church.) In the seventh century, a Byzantine emperor stripped the dome's interior of its original golden-tile ceiling. The twin grilled windows just right of the altar (at 2 o'clock) are a modern re-creation of the original and, along with the inlaid marble floor, give you a sense of the colorful ancient decor.

Tombs

While its ancient statuary is long gone, the interior holds decorative statues and the tombs of famous people from more recent cen-

turies. The artist Raphael lies to the left of the main altar, which is in the lighted glass niche (pictured here). Above him is a statue of the Madonna and Child that Raphael himself commissioned for his tomb. The Latin inscription on his tomb reads: "In life, Nature feared to be outdone by him. In death, she feared she too would die."

Halfway around the base of the dome, you'll also see the tombs of modern Italy's first two kings. To the right is Victor Emmanuel II (*"Padre della Patria,"* father of his country); to the left is Umberto I (son of the father). These tombs are a hit with royalists. In fact, a guard often stands by a guestbook in which visitors can register their support for these two kings' now-controversial family, the Savoys (see sidebar on opposite page). And finally, under Umberto lies his queen, Margherita...for whom the classic pizza Margherita (mozzarella, tomato sauce, and basil) was named in 1889.

The Pantheon is the only ancient building in Rome continuously used since its construction. When you leave, notice that the building is sunken below current street level, showing how the rest of the city has risen on 20 centuries of rubble.

The Pantheon also contains the world's greatest Roman column. There it is, spanning the entire 142 feet from heaven to earth—the pillar of light from the oculus.

• *Leaving the Pantheon, take a moment to enjoy the square facing it. Piazza della Rotonda has been a gathering place for 2,000 years. Its slope illustrates the literal "rise of Rome." Imagine in past centuries when there was a fish and chicken market in the portico. In an 18th-century*

The Italian Royal Family... in Switzerland

From Italy's unification in 1870 to the end of World War II, the country had four kings, all members of the Savoy family. One

of Europe's oldest royal families (from the 10th century), the Savoia had long ruled the kingdom of Piedmont (in present-day northern Italy).

In 1946, the Italians voted for a republic and sent the Savoia into exile. Until 2002, a law proclaimed that no male Savoia could set foot on Italian soil. That's why only the first two kings are buried in the Pantheon (the last two died in exile).

The Savoia lost favor with their Italian subjects for several good reasons: When Mussolini marched on Rome in 1922, King Victor Emmanuel III actually asked him to form a government. When the Mussolini government issued anti-Semitic laws, the king signed them. And in 1943, instead of standing by his people, the king abandoned Rome to the Germans and fled south to Allied protection.

Even today, the Savoia heir to Italy's throne is considered a jerk with a knack for saying stupid things. When asked to comment on the racist laws signed by his grandfather, he candidly answered that he was too young at the time so he did not need to apologize, and, he said, the laws were not really all that bad. When the Savoia were allowed back into Italy in 2002, their first mistake was to visit the pope rather than the president of the republic. And while they live in stunning wealth in Switzerland, they still complain that Italy owes them more of the family riches. In 2007, their lawyers claimed that the Italian government should pay the family at least €260 million for damages as a result of their exile.

PANTHEON

urban beautification project, the fountain and obelisk were added. Feel the vibrancy of the piazza culture, which goes back to ancient Rome.

Churches near the Pantheon

Many visitors just see the Pantheon and leave. But consider visiting one or more of these four unique churches, all less than 10 minutes' walk from the Pantheon (see map for locations). If you're budgeting your energy, here's a quick rundown on what each has to offer: San Luigi houses several stunning Caravaggio paintings. The Gesù is packed with ornate art and Jesuit history. Santa Maria sopra Minerva, Rome's only Gothic church, has a Michelangelo sculpture and St. Catherine's tomb. Finally, San Ignazio is full of Baroque perspective illusions that will leave your head spinning.

CHURCH OF SAN LUIGI DEI FRANCESI

This is the French *(dei francesi)* national church in Rome. You'll find French motifs throughout. Outside, check out the salamander, symbol of François I, the French king who brought Leonardo (and the Renaissance) north, from Italy to France. Inside, the stylized fleurs-de-lis are emblems of French royalty. On the ceiling of the nave is France's King (a.k.a. Saint) Louis ascending to heaven, and there he is again in a chapel on the left. Joan of Arc takes it all in from the back of the nave.

But the one truly *magnifique* sight is the chapel in the far-left corner, which was decorated by Caravaggio. This church makes a great little detour between the Pantheon and nearby Piazza Navona.

• *In the Caravaggio chapel, first look to the left wall.*

The Calling of St. Matthew

Matthew (old man with beard) and his well-dressed, tax-collecting cronies sit in a dingy Roman tavern and count the money they've

extorted. Suddenly, two men in robes and bare feet enter from the right— Jesus and Peter. Jesus' "Creation-of-Adam" hand emerges from the darkness to point at Matthew. A shaft of light extends the gesture, lighting up the face of Matthew, who points to himself, *Last Supper*-style, to ask, "You talkin' to me?" Jesus came to convince Matthew to leave his sleazy job and preach Love. Matthew did.

In this, his first large-scale work, 29-year-old Caravaggio (1571-1610) shocked critics and clerics by showing a holy scene in a down-to-earth location. Lower-class people in everyday clothes were his models; his setting was a dive bar (which he knew well). Christ's teeny gold halo is the only hint of the supernatural, as Caravaggio makes a bold proclamation—that miracles are natural events experienced in a profound way.

• *Now look to the center wall.*

The Inspiration of St. Matthew

Matthew followed Christ's call, traveled with him, and (supposedly) wrote Jesus' life story

Churches near the Pantheon

(the Gospel according to Matthew). Here, Matthew is hard at work when he's interrupted by an angel with a few suggestions. This sets the scene in motion. Matthew kneels on a stool, which is just about to fall out of the painting and into our zone. Matthew's bald head, wrinkled face, and grizzled beard make him an all-too-human saint. Even the teen angel lacks a holy glow—he just hangs there. Caravaggio paints a dark background, then shines a dramatic spotlight on the few things that tell the story.

• *Finally, check out the right wall.*

The Martyrdom of St. Matthew

Matthew lies prone, while a truly scary man straddles him and brandishes a sword. The bystanders shrink away from this angry executioner. Caravaggio shines his harsh third-degree spotlight on Matthew and the killer, who are the focus of the painting. The other figures swirl around them in a circle (with the executioner's arm as the radius). Matthew, who thought he had already given up everything to follow Christ, now gives up his life as well. He is as open as a crucifix, accepting his fate, and reaching for a palm frond—symbolic of victory over death. The bearded face in the background (to the left of the executioner's shoulder) is a self-portrait of Caravaggio, observing the violence without getting involved.

When the chapel was unveiled in 1600, Caravaggio's ultra-realism shocked Rome. Although he died only 10 years later, his uncompromising details, emotional subjects, odd compositions, and dramatic lighting set the tone for later Baroque painters. (For a bit more on Caravaggio, see page 273.)

GESÙ CHURCH

The center of the Jesuit order (of which Pope Francis is a member) and the best symbol of the Catholic Counter-Reformation, the Gesù (jay-zoo) is packed with overblown art and underappreciated history. Consider seeing this church en route to Capitoline Hill.

Exterior

The facade looks ho-hum, like a thousand no-name Catholic churches scattered from Europe to Southern California...until you

realize that this was the first, the model for all of the others. Its scroll-like shoulders were revolutionary, breaking up the rigid rectangles of Renaissance architecture and signaling the coming of Baroque. The travertine stone facade has been cleaned but—with its sponge-like proper-

ties and Rome's pollution—it will be black again soon enough.

The adjacent building, to the right of the church—called Camere of St. Ignatius—is where Ignatius of Loyola, the founder of the Jesuits, lived, worked, and died (free, Mon-Sat 16:00-18:00, Sun 10:00-12:00).

• *Step inside the Gesù Church, grab a seat, and look up at the huge painting on the ceiling (or take advantage of the neck-saving mirror).*

PANTHEON

APSE

TRANSEPT

NAVE

❶ **Ceiling Fresco & Stucco**
❷ **Nave**
❸ **Tomb & Altarpiece of St. Ignatius of Loyola**
❹ **Religion Overthrowing Heresy**
❺ **Tomb & Altarpiece of St. Francis Xavier**

10 Meters
10 Yards

← To Pantheon

ENTER

Piazza del Gesù

→ To Capitoline Hill

Inside the Church

❶ Ceiling Fresco—*The Triumph of the Name of Jesus*

The church's sunroof opens, and we can see right up to heaven. A glowing cross with the initials "I.H.S." (from the Latinized Greek, "Jesus Savior of Mankind," adopted as the seal of the Society of Jesus) astounds the faithful and sends the infidels plunging downward. The twisted tangle of bodies—the damned—spill over the edge of the painting's frame on their way to hell. The painted bodies mingle with 3-D stucco bodies and a riot of decoration in a classic example of Baroque multimedia (created by one of Bernini's protégés, Giovanni Battista Gaulli, better known as Il Baciccio, in the 1670s).

During the Counter-Reformation, when Catholics fought Protestants for the hearts and minds of the world's Christians, art was a powerful propaganda weapon. The moral here is clear—hell is the fate of Protestant heretics who dared to pervert the true teachings of Jesus.

❷ Nave

When the church was originally built (1568), the walls were white and the decor was simple. It was designed for what the Jesuits did best—teaching. The Jesuits wanted to educate Catholics to prepare

sù Church

e of Baroque

...te service takes place at the
...Church, and all are welcome.
...tius, housed behind the altar-

...orded music—"Kyrie eleison"
...ded voice (in Italian) tells the
...illustrated by spotlighting dif-

The service is squarely in the Baroque tradition—a multi-media extravaganza that combines painting, sculpture, music, words, and lighting effects. (Don't expect Hollywood-quality SFX—this is "spectacle" on a small, semi-cheesy scale.)

The ceremony is meant to tap into the heart, not the head, encouraging an emotional response to the faith. As the service unfolds, look around the church at its glorious art and architecture. Don't reflect. Be awed, amazed, moved.

At 17:45, church attendants turn a crank, and the altarpiece painting slowly lowers, revealing the gleaming statue of Ignatius in his ta-da pose. After a few closing words, the choir finishes with "Gloria in excelsis Deo" (Glory to God in the highest). Amen.

PANTHEON

them for the onslaught of pesky, probing Protestant questions. The church's nave is like one big lecture hall, with no traditional side aisles.

In the 1500s, the best way to keep Protestants from stealing your church members was to reason with them. By the 1600s, it was easier to kill them, and so the Thirty Years' War raged across Europe. The church became crusted over with the colorful, bombastic, jingoistic Baroque we see today.

• *Now look toward the left transept.*

❸ Tomb and Altarpiece of St. Ignatius of Loyola

A big altarpiece with towering columns and topped with statues of the Trinity marks the burial spot of the humble war veteran who

founded the Jesuit order. In the center of this altarpiece, you'll see a painting (by Andrea Pozzo) of Ignatius receiving his call. Behind the painting rests a gleaming statue of the saint, who spreads his arms wide and gazes up, receiving a vision from on high. But you won't be able to see it unless you come after 17:30 (see sidebar).

Ignatius (1491-1556) was a Spanish soldier during the era of conquistadors. Then, at age 30, he was struck down by a cannon-ball. While convalescing, he was seized by the burning desire to change his life. He wandered Europe and traveled to Jerusalem. He meditated with monks. He lived in a cave. At 33, he enrolled in a school for boys to fill in the knowledge he'd missed. He studied in Paris and Rome. Finally, after almost two decades of learning and seeking, he found a way to combine his military training with his spiritual aspirations.

In 1540, the pope gave approval to Ignatius and his small band of followers—the Society of Jesus (Jesuits). These monks, organized like a military company, vowed complete obedience to their "General" and placed themselves at the service of the pope. Their mission: to be intellectual warriors doing battle with heretics. They were in the right place at the right time—Ignatius and Martin Luther were almost exact contemporaries.

Ignatius' body lies in the small coffin beneath the statue (near ground level). This simple, intense man might have been embar-rassed by the lavish memorial to him, with its silver, gold, green marble, and lapis lazuli columns. Above the painting of Ignatius, a statue of God stands near a lapis lazuli globe (under the sunburst, the biggest in the world) and gestures as though to say, "Go and spread the Word to every land"...which the Jesuits tried to do.

· *Look at the marble statue group to the right of Ignatius.*

❹ Religion Overthrowing Heresy

This statue (and a similar one to the left of Ignatius) shows the Church as an angry nun hauling back with a whip and just spank-

ing a bunch of miserable Protestants. The man with the serpent (Luther) is being stepped upon while the angry cherub rips pages out of a heretical book. Not too subtle.

The Jesuits earned a reputation for unfeeling dedication to truth above all else. Their weapons were words, ideas, and critical reasoning. They taught and defended the recently revamped doctrines of the Council of Trent (a reaction against—and a response to—the Reformation, 1545-1563).

· *Now view the right transept.*

The Jesuit Legacy

The Jesuits produced some great, open-minded thinkers, from the poet Gerard Manley Hopkins to modern mystic Pierre Teilhard de Chardin.

The great sculptor Bernini attended this church. He honored the Jesuit Robert Bellarmine (1542-1621) with a bust, which is sometimes on display in the Gesù Church. Bellarmine, a theologian at the height of Catholic-Protestant differences, was a voice of reason in the often bitter controversy. He's best known as the man who ordered Galileo to stop teaching the Copernican theory, although he was actually a moderating influence in the debate.

Because of their spiritual fervor, the Jesuits caught flack for being closed-minded. In the 1700s, several countries expelled them, and finally the pope even banned the Society (1773). Chastened, they were brought back (1814), and today they fill the staff of many a Catholic college.

The rehabilitation of this once-suspect order reached its culmination in 2013 with the ascension of Francesco I (Francis)—the first Jesuit pope.

PANTHEON

❺ Tomb and Altarpiece of St. Francis Xavier

This was also the Age of Discovery, when Spain and Portugal were colonizing and Christianizing the world, using force if necessary. Francis Xavier joined a Portuguese expedition and headed out to convert the heathens. His right hand, with which he baptized and healed, is encased in a glass reliquary above his tomb. Francis touched down in Africa, India, Indonesia, China, and Japan. Along the way, he learned new languages and customs, trying to communicate a strange, monotheistic religion to puzzled polytheists.

He had been on the road for more than a decade (1552) when he died on an island off the coast of China (see the dim painting over the altar). Thanks largely to the tireless evangelizing of zealous Jesuits such as Francis, Catholicism became a truly worldwide religion.

CHURCH OF SANTA MARIA SOPRA MINERVA

From the outside, survey the many layers of Rome: An Egyptian obelisk sits on a Baroque elephant (by Bernini) in front of a Gothic church built over *(sopra)* a pre-Christian, pagan Temple of Minerva.

Before stepping in, notice the high-water-mark plaques *(alluvione)* on the wall to the right of the door. Each time the Tiber River flooded, it left silt, which contributed to the slow and steady geological rise of Rome. Inside, you'll see that the lower parts of some frescoes were lost to floods. After the last great flood, in 1870, Rome built the present embankments along the river, finally breaking the spirit of the mighty Tiber.

Nave
This is the only Gothic church you'll see in Rome. The ceiling has pointed crisscross arches in a starry, luminous blue sky, and the nave is lit by rows of round stained-glass windows. When this Dominican church was built, Gothic was the rage in northern Europe, with large windows to let in the light—though churches in Italy were so colorful there was less emphasis on colored glass. During the Middle Ages, Rome was almost a ghost town, and what little was built during this time was later gussied up in the Baroque style. The lack of Baroque excess in this church (in spite of its over-the-top, 19th-century renovation) is a refreshing exception.

Main Altar
The body of St. Catherine of Siena lies under the altar (her head is in Siena). In the 1300s, this Italian nun was renowned for her

righteousness and her visions of a mystical marriage with Jesus. Her impassioned letters convinced the pope to return from France to Rome, thus saving Italy from untold chaos. Behind her, two Medici popes are buried: Leo X, the son of Lorenzo the Magnificent and the man who excommunicated Martin Luther; and his cousin Clement VII. Both men were good friends with Michelangelo, who was raised alongside them in the Medici household.

In 1634, a frail 70-year-old Galileo knelt at this altar on the way to his trial before the Inquisition in the church's monastery. Facing the fierce Dominican lawyers, he renounced his heretical belief that the earth moved around the sun. (Legend has it that as he walked out, he whispered, "But it *does* move.")

• *Left of the altar stands a little-known Michelangelo statue...*

Christ Bearing the Cross (1519-1520)
Note Jesus' athletic body, a striking contrast to the docile Jesus of medieval art. This sculpture shares the same bulging biceps as the

Christ in Michelangelo's *The Last Judgment* in the Sistine Chapel. Christ's pose is slightly twisted, with one leg forward in typical *contrapposto* style, leaning on a large cross along with the symbols of the Crucifixion. Originally, Christ was buck naked, but later prudish Counter-Reformation censors gave him his bronze girdle.

This statue was Michelangelo's second attempt—he was forced to abandon a first effort due to a flaw in the block of Carrara marble. In this version, he left parts—including the face—to be finished by an apprentice, who took the liberty of working on and botching the feet and hands. This ineptitude led him to be replaced by yet another sculptor who finally finished the job. Michelangelo, disturbed that anyone would mess up his work, offered to redo the sculpture, but apparently the patrons were pleased. One contemporary said, "The knees alone are worth more than all of Rome together."

The tomb of the great early Renaissance painter (and Dominican brother) Fra Angelico ("Beato Angelico 1387-1455") is farther to the left, just up the three stairs.

Over in the right (south) transept, pop in a coin for light, and enjoy a Filippino Lippi fresco showing scenes of the life of the great Dominican scholar St. Thomas Aquinas (big man in blue and white). In the central scene, Thomas—seeming to interrupt the Annunciation—presents the chapel's patron to Mary. Above, circling an ascended Mary, is a frolicking carousel of heavenly musicians—notice the delightful instruments. Meanwhile, on the right wall, Thomas displays a book to show everyone the true dogma, causing a heretic to slump defeated at his feet.

• *Exit the church via its rear door (behind the Michelangelo statue), walk down tiny Fra Angelico lane, turn left, and walk to the next square. On your right, you'll find the last church on our tour.*

CHURCH OF SAN IGNAZIO

This church is a riot of Baroque illusions. Stand in the middle of the nave and look up at the large, colorful ceiling fresco (or use the big mirror). ❶ St. Ignatius, whom we met in the Gesù Church, was the founder of the Jesuits, a disciplined Catholic teaching order charged with spreading the word of God around a world that was rapidly being "discovered." Here you see him (a small figure perched on a cloud in the center) having a ❷ vision of Christ with the Cross. Heavenly light from the vision bounces off his chest, and the rays beam to the four corners of the earth (including ❸ America, to the left, depicted as a bare-breasted Native American maiden spearing naked men). This fresco epitomizes pure Baroque drama, with perspective illusions that fool the eye into thinking the fresco is an extension of the church architecture. Note how the actual columns of the church are extended into the two-dimensional fresco. Now fix your eyes on the ❹ arch at the far end of the painting. Walk up

the nave, and watch the arch grow and tower over you.

Before you reach the center of the church, stop at the small yellow disc (near the last row of pews) on the floor, and look up into the central (black) dome. Keeping your eye on the dome, walk under and past it. Building project runs out of money? Hire an artist to paint a fake, flat dome.

Now take a moment to survey the art in general, appreciating the tricks of the trade. For example, explore deep inside the right transept, where you'll find an explosive scene. The curtain is pulled back for the theatrical tomb of Pope Gregory XV—textbook bombastic Baroque. With trumpet fanfare and the stony curtain flapping in the spiritual wind, the pope springs with jubilation into eternal life.

Back outside, the church faces a headquarters of the Carabinieri police force (this station deals with art theft—a major problem in a country with so much to protect), forming Piazza San Ignazio, a square with several converging streets that has been compared to a stage set. Sit on the church steps, admire the theatrical yellow backdrop, and watch the "actors" enter one way and exit another, in the human opera that is modern Rome.

• *From here it's a short walk to the left down Via del Seminario back to the Pantheon. Or go right, cross busy Via del Corso, and follow the crowds to the Trevi Fountain.*

COLOSSEUM TOUR

Colosseo

Rome has many layers—modern, Baroque, Renaissance, Christian. But let's face it: "Rome" is Caesars, gladiators, chariots, centurions, *"Et tu, Brute,"* trumpet fanfares, and thumbs-up or thumbs-down. That's the Rome we'll look at. Our "Caesar Shuffle" begins with the downtown core of ancient Rome, the Colosseum. This was where Romans—whose taste for violence was the equal of modern America's—enjoyed their *Dirty Harry*s and *Terminator*s. Gladiators, criminals, and wild animals fought to the death in every conceivable scenario. After the Colosseum, a logical next stop is the Roman Forum, just next door (and covered in the following chapter).

Orientation

Cost: €12 combo-ticket covers both the Colosseum and the Roman Forum/Palatine Hill; also covered by the Roma Pass. The combo-ticket is valid for two consecutive days, but once your ticket is scanned for either the Colosseum or the Forum/Palatine Hill (grouped as one sight for the purposes of the ticket), you can't re-enter that sight (even the next day).

Hours: The Colosseum, Roman Forum, and Palatine Hill are all open daily 8:30 until one hour before sunset: April-Aug until 19:15, Sept until 19:00, Oct until 18:30, Nov-mid-Feb until 16:30, mid-Feb-mid-March until 17:00, mid-March-late March until 17:30; last entry one hour before closing.

Restoration: The arena is being cleaned from top to bottom, given permanent lighting, and outfitted with new shops and services. Long-range plans include building a free-standing ticket booth/visitors center outside the Colosseum. These ongoing renovations, scheduled to last several years, may affect your visit.

Avoiding Lines: Crowds tend to be thinner (and lines shorter) in the afternoon (especially after 15:00 in summer); this is also true at the Forum.

You can save lots of time by buying your combo-ticket in advance, having the Roma Pass, booking a guided tour, or renting an audioguide or videoguide. Here are the options:

1. Buy your combo-ticket (or Roma Pass) at one of the less-crowded ancient sites. First check how long the line is at the Forum entrance facing the Colosseum. If that's also crowded, head to the Palatine Hill entrance, 150 yards away on Via di San Gregorio (facing the Forum, with Colosseum at your back, go left down the street). You can also buy a Roma Pass at the tobacco shop in the Colosseo Metro station, the information center on Via dei Fori Imperiali (see page 152), or other sights around town. It should cost the same no matter where you buy it.

2. Buy a combo-ticket online at www.coopculture.it (€2 booking fee, not changeable). The "free tickets" you'll see listed are valid only for EU citizens with ID.

3. Pay to join an official guided tour, or rent an audioguide or videoguide (see "Tours," next page). This lets you march right up to the Colosseum's guided visits *(Visite Guidate)* desk, thus bypassing the ticket lines. Even if you don't use the device or accompany the guided tour, the extra cost might be worth it just to skip the ticket line.

4. Hire a private walking-tour guide. Guides of varying quality linger outside the Colosseum, offering tours that allow you to skip the line. Be aware that these private guides may try to mislead you into thinking the Colosseum lines are longer than they really are. For more on this option, see "Tours" on the next page.

Warning: Beware of the **greedy gladiators.** For a fee, the incredibly crude, modern-day gladiators snuff out their cigarettes and pose for photos. They're officially banned from panhandling in this area, but you may still see them, hoping to intimidate easy-to-swindle tourists into paying too much money for a photo op. (If you go for it, €4-5 for one photo usually keeps them appeased.) Also, look out for **pickpockets** and con artists in this prime tourist spot.

Getting There: The Colosseo Metro stop on line B is just across the street from the monument. Buses #53, #85, #87, and #175 stop along Via dei Fori Imperiali near the Colosseum entrance, the Forum entrance, and Piazza Venezia.

Getting In: If you need to buy a ticket or sign up for a guided tour, follow the signs for the appropriate line. With a combo-ticket or Roma Pass in hand, look for signs for *ticket holders* or *Roma Pass,* allowing you to bypass the long lines.

Information: Tel. 06-3996-7700, www.archeoroma.beniculturali. it/en.

Tours: A dry but fact-filled **audioguide** is available just past the turnstiles (€5.50/2 hours). A handheld **videoguide** senses where you are in the site and plays related clips (€6).

Official **guided tours** in English depart nearly hourly between 10:00 and 17:00, and last 45-60 minutes (€5 plus Colosseum ticket, purchase inside the Colosseum near the ticket booth marked *Visite Guidate;* if you're lost, ask a guard to direct you to the desk).

A 1.5-hour **"Colosseum, Underground and Third Ring" tour** takes you through restricted areas, including the top floor and underground passageways, which are off-limits to regular visitors. While interesting, this tour certainly isn't essential to appreciating the Colosseum. Although it's possible to sign up for the tour at the Colosseum's guided tours window, it's strongly advised you reserve at least a day in advance, either by phone or online. The tour is operated by CoopCulture, a private company (€9 plus Colosseum ticket, www.coopculture. it). Call 06-3996-7700 during business hours: Mon-Fri 9:00-18:00, Sat 9:00-14:00 (closed Sun, no same-day reservations). After dialing, wait for English instructions on how to reach a live operator, then reserve a time and pre-pay with a credit card. Without a reservation, you can try to join the next available tour (may be in Italian): Once you have your Colosseum entrance ticket and are at the turnstiles, look for the tour meeting point just past the ticket desk; pay the guide directly.

Private guides stand outside the Colosseum looking for business (€25-30/2-hour tour of the Colosseum, Forum, and Palatine Hill). If booking a private guide, make sure that your tour will start right away and that the ticket you receive covers all three sights: the Colosseum, Forum, and Palatine Hill.

You can also download this chapter as a free Rick Steves **audio tour** (see page 8).

Length of This Tour: Allow an hour. If you're short on time, you can basically see the entire interior with a single glance. It's not necessary to go upstairs or circle the place.

Services: A WC (often crowded) is inside the Colosseum. For more tips on where to eat, drink, and find a WC in the area, see the sidebar on page 146.

The Tour Begins

EXTERIOR

• *View the Colosseum from the Forum fence, across the street from the Colosseo Metro station.*

Built when the Roman Empire was at its peak in A.D. 80, the Colosseum represents Rome at its grandest. The Flavian Amphitheater (the Colosseum's real name) was an arena for gladiator contests and public spectacles. When killing became a spectator sport, the Romans wanted to share the fun with as many people as possible, so they stuck two semicircular theaters together to create a freestanding amphitheater. The outside (where slender cypress trees stand today) was decorated with a 100-foot-tall bronze statue of Nero that gleamed in the sunlight. In a later age, the colossal structure was nicknamed a "coloss-eum," the wonder of its age. Towering 150 feet high, it could accommodate 50,000 roaring fans (100,000 thumbs).

The Romans pioneered the use of concrete and the rounded arch, which enabled them to build on this tremendous scale. The exterior is a skeleton of 3.5 million cubic feet of travertine stone. (Each of the pillars flanking the ground-level arches weighs five tons.) It took 200 ox-drawn wagons shuttling back and forth every day for four years just to bring the stone here from Tivoli. They stacked stone blocks (without mortar) into the shape of an arch, supported temporarily by wooden scaffolding. Finally, they wedged a keystone into the top of the arch—it not only kept the arch from falling, it could bear even more weight above. Iron pegs held the larger stones together; notice the small holes—the result of medieval peg poachers—that pockmark the sides.

The exterior says a lot about the Romans. They were great engineers, not artists, and the building is more functional than beautiful. (If ancient Romans visited the US today as tourists, they might send home postcards of our greatest works of "art"—freeways.) While the essential structure of the Colosseum is Roman, the four-story facade is decorated with mostly Greek columns—Doric-like Tuscan columns on the ground level, Ionic on the second story, Corinthian on the next level, and at the top, half-columns with a

COLOSSEUM

Colosseum

MONTI

To St. Peter-in-Chains
(Moses Statue)

VIA EUDOSSIANA

VIA ANNIBALDI

CAFFÈ
DELLO
STUDENTE
& HOSTARIA
DA NERONE

VIA TERME DI TITO

Parco
del Colle
Oppio

Not to Scale

VIA NICOLA SALVI

B

← STAIRS

B

To San Clemente &
San Giovanni in Laterano

To Forum
Entrance,
Trajan's
Forum
& Piazza
Venezia

Colosseo
M

BIKE
RENTAL

T   B

VIA DEI FORI IMPERIALI

EXIT
ONLY
FORUM

ENTER

FORMER
100' TALL
"COLOSSAL
STATUE"

BOOK-
STORE

UPPER

TEMP.
EXHIBITS

LEVEL

TICKETS
(BELOW)

EMPEROR'S
BOX   ✝

WC

ARENA
LEVEL

LIFT

WC

TEMPLE OF
VENUS
& ROME

Piazza del
Colosseo

BOOK-
STORE

VESTAL
VIRGINS
BOX

VIA SACRA

← To Forum
Entrance & Exit

VIA DI SAN GREGORIO

EXIT
ONLY

B   T

ARCH OF
CONSTANTINE

VIA CELIO VIBENNA

PALATINE
HILL

Parco del
Celio

To Palatine Hill
Ticket Office/Entrance
& Circus Maximus

mix of all three. Originally, copies of Greek statues stood in the arches of the middle two stories, giving a veneer of sophistication to this arena of death.

Only a third of the original Colosseum remains. Earthquakes destroyed some of it, but most was carted off as easy pre-cut stones for other buildings during the Middle Ages and Renaissance.

• *To enter, line up in the correct queue: the one for ticket buyers, or the one for those who already have a ticket or Roma Pass (plus people looking to take a guided tour or rent an audio or videoguide). The third line is for groups. Once past the turnstiles, there may be signs directing you on a specific visitors' route. Follow the flow of traffic, making your way into the arena.*

INSIDE THE COLOSSEUM

Entrances and Exits

As you walk through passageways and up staircases, admire the ergonomics. Fans could pour in through ground-floor entrances; there were 76 numbered ones in addition to the emperor's private entrance on the north side. Your ticket (likely a piece of pottery) was marked with your entrance, section, row, and seat number. You'd pass by concession stands selling fast food and souvenirs, such as wine glasses with the names of famous gladiators. A hallway leading to the seats was called a *vomitorium*. At exit time, the Colosseum would "vomit" out its contents, giving us the English word. It's estimated that all 50,000 fans could enter and exit in 15 minutes.

• *Soon you'll spill out into the arena. Wherever you end up—upstairs or downstairs, at one side of the arena or the other—just take it all in and get oriented. The tallest side of the Colosseum (with the large Christian cross) is the north side.*

Arena

The games took place in this oval-shaped arena, 280 feet long by 165 feet wide. The ratio of length to width is 5:3, often called the

golden ratio. Since the days of the Greek mathematician Pythagoras, artists considered that proportion to be ideal, with almost mystical properties. The Colosseum's architects apparently wanted their structure to embody the perfect 5-by-3 mathematical order they thought existed in nature.

When you look down into the arena, you're seeing the underground passages beneath the playing surface (which can only be visited on a private tour). The arena was originally covered with a wooden floor, then sprinkled with sand (*arena* in Latin). The bit of reconstructed floor gives you an accurate sense of the original

arena level and the subterranean warren where animals and prisoners were held. As in modern stadiums, the spectators ringed the playing area in bleacher seats that slanted up from the arena floor. Around you are the big brick masses that supported the tiers of seats.

A variety of materials were used to build the stadium. Look around. Big white travertine blocks stacked on top of each

COLOSSEUM

other formed the skeleton. The pillars for the bleachers were made with a shell of brick, filled in with concrete. Originally the bare brick was covered with marble columns or ornamental facing, so the interior was a brilliant white (they used white plaster for the upper-floor cheap seats).

The Colosseum's seating was strictly segregated. At ringside, the emperor, senators, Vestal Virgins, and VIPs occupied marble seats with their names carved on them (a few marble seats have been restored, at the east end). The next level upheld those of noble birth. The level tourists now occupy was for ordinary free Roman citizens, called plebeians. Up at the very top (a hundred yards from the action), there were once wooden bleachers for

the poorest people—foreigners, slaves, and women. While no seats survive and you're likely viewing the arena from what was a passageway that ran under the seats, you can imagine the scene.

The top story of the Colosseum is mostly ruined—only the north side still retains its high wall. This was not part of the original

three-story structure, but was added around A.D. 230 after a fire necessitated repairs. Picture the awning that could be stretched across the top of the stadium by armies of sailors. Strung along horizontal beams that pointed inward to the center, the awning only covered about a third of the arena—so those at the top always enjoyed shade, while many nobles down below roasted in the sun.

Looking into the complex web of passageways beneath the arena, you can imagine how busy the backstage action was. Gladiators strolled down the central passageway, from their warm-up yard on the east end to the arena entrance on the west. Some workers tended wild animals. Others prepared stage sets of trees or fake buildings, allowing the arena to be quickly transformed from an African jungle to a Greek temple. Props and sets were hauled up to arena level on 80 different elevator shafts via a system of ropes and pulleys. (You might be able to make out some small rectangular shafts, especially near the center of the arena.) That means there were 80 different spots from which animals, warriors, and stage sets could pop up and magically appear.

The games began with a few warm-up acts—dogs bloodying themselves attacking porcupines, female gladiators fighting each other, or a one-legged man battling a dwarf. Then came the main event—the gladiators.

"Hail, Caesar! *(Ave, Caesar!)* We who are about to die salute you!" The gladiators would enter the arena from the west end, parade around to the sound of trumpets, acknowledge the Vestal Virgins (on the south side), then stop at the emperor's box (supposedly marked today by the cross that stands at the "50-yard line" on the north side—although no one knows for sure where it was). They would then raise their weapons, shout, and salute—and begin fighting. The fights pitted men against men, men against beasts, and beasts against beasts. Picture 50,000 screaming people around you (did gladiators get stage fright?), and imagine that they want to see you die.

Some gladiators wielded swords, protected only with a shield and a heavy helmet. Others represented fighting fishermen, with a net to snare opponents and a trident to spear them. The gladiators were usually slaves, criminals, or poor people who got their chance for freedom, wealth, and fame in the ring. They learned to fight in training schools, then battled their way up the ranks. The best were rewarded like our

modern sports stars, with fan clubs, great wealth, and, yes, product endorsements.

The animals came from all over the world: lions, tigers, and bears (oh my!), crocodiles, elephants, and hippos (not to mention exotic human "animals" from the "barbarian" lands). They were kept in cages beneath the arena floor, then lifted up in the elevators. Released at floor level, animals would pop out from behind blinds into the arena—the gladiator didn't know where, when, or by what he'd be attacked. Many a hapless warrior met his death here, and never even knew what hit him. (This sometimes brought howls of laughter from the hardened fans in the cheap upper seats, who had a better view of the action.)

Nets ringed the arena to protect the crowd. The stadium was inaugurated with a 100-day festival in which 2,000 men and 9,000 animals were killed. Colosseum employees squirted perfumes around the stadium to mask the stench of blood.

If a gladiator fell helpless to the ground, his opponent would

Modern Amenities in the Ancient World

The area around the Colosseum, Forum, and Palatine Hill is rich in history, but pretty barren when it comes to food, shelter, and WCs. Here are a few options:

The Colosseum has a crowded **WC** inside. A nice, big WC is behind (east of) the structure (facing ticket entrance, go clockwise; WC is under stairway). If you can wait, the best WCs in the area are at Palatine Hill—at the Via di San Gregorio entrance, in the museum, and in the Farnese Gardens. The Forum has WCs at the main entrance, near the Arch of Titus (in the "Soprintendenza" office), and in the middle of the Forum (near #6 on the map on page 154).

Because the area's **eating** options are limited, consider assembling a small picnic. The Colosseo Metro stop has forgettable €5 hot sandwiches. Snack stands on street corners sell overpriced drinks, sandwiches, fruit, and candy. If you prefer to dine in, you'll find a few restaurants behind the Colosseum (with expansive views of the structure), several recommended places within a few blocks (no views but a better value—see page 400), and a cluster of places near the Forum's main entrance (where Via Cavour spills into Via dei Fori Imperiali).

To refill your **water** bottle, stop at one of the water fountains in the area. You'll find them along a few city streets, as well as inside the Forum and Palatine Hill.

A nice oasis is the free **information center** located near the Forum entrance. It's across Via dei Fori Imperiali and a bit east, toward the Colosseum. It has a small café, a WC, and a few exhibits (daily 9:30-19:00).

If your sightseeing takes you as far as **Capitoline Hill,** you'll find services at the Capitoline Museums, including a nice view café (see page 180).

Several **public buses** (#85, #87, etc.) traverse Via dei Fori Imperiali between the Colosseum and Piazza Venezia, making it easy to hop on for a stop or two. If you need a **taxi,** use the stand near the southeast corner of the Colosseum. The taxis parked near the Colosseo Metro stop (on Via dei Fori Imperiali) have a reputation for being sharks.

COLOSSEUM

approach the emperor's box and ask: Should he live or die? Sometimes the emperor left the decision to the crowd, who would judge based on how valiantly the man had fought. They would make their decision: thumbs-up or thumbs-down.

Consider the value of these games in placating and controlling the huge Roman populace. Imagine never having seen an actual lion, and suddenly one jumps out to chase a prisoner in the arena. Seeing the king of beasts slain by a gladiator reminded the masses of man's triumph over nature.

Modern Amenities in the Ancient World

❶ Colosseum Entrance
❷ Palatine Hill Entrance
❸ Forum Entrance
❹ Via Sacra Entrance (to Forum & Palatine Hill)
❺ Visitors Center

🅵 Food
● Water Fountain

COLOSSEUM

In an age without a hint of a newsreel, it was hard for local Romans to visualize and appreciate the faraway conquests their empire was so dedicated to. The Colosseum spectacles were a way to bring home the environments, animals, and people of these conquered lands, parade them before the public, and make them real. And having the thumbs-up or thumbs-down authority over another person's life gave the spectators a real sense of power. Imagine the psychological boost the otherwise downtrodden masses felt when the emperor granted them this thrilling decision.

Did they throw Christians to the lions as in the movies? Christians were definitely thrown to the lions, made to fight gladiators, crucified, and burned alive...but probably not here in this particular stadium. Maybe, but probably not.

Rome was a nation of warriors that built an empire by conquest. The battles fought against Germans and other barbarians, Egyptians, and strange animals were played out daily here in the Colosseum for the benefit of city-slicker bureaucrats, who got vicarious thrills by watching brutes battle to the death. The contests were always free, sponsored by the government to bribe the people's favor or to keep Rome's growing masses of unemployed rabble off the streets.

• *With these scenes in mind, wander around, then check out the upper level. Stairs are on both the east and west sides, with an elevator at the east end (only accessible to those who really need it). The upper deck offers more colossal views of the arena, plus a bookstore and temporary exhibits. Wherever you may Rome, find a spot at the west end of the upper deck, where you can look out over some of the sights nearby.*

Views from the Upper Level

• *Start your visual tour with the big, white, triumphal arch.*

Arch of Constantine

If you are a Christian, were raised a Christian, or simply belong to a so-called "Christian nation," ponder this arch. It marks one of the great turning points in history: the military coup that made Christianity mainstream. In A.D. 312, Emperor Constantine defeated his rival Maxentius in the crucial Battle of the Milvian Bridge. The night before, he had seen a vision of a cross in the sky. Constantine—whose mother and sister had already become Christians—became sole emperor and legalized Christianity. With this one battle, a once-obscure Jewish sect with a handful of followers became the state religion of the entire Western world. In A.D. 300, you could be killed for being a Christian; a century later, you could be killed for not being one. Church enrollment boomed.

The restored arch is like an ancient museum. It's decorated entirely with recycled carvings originally made for other buildings. By covering it with exquisite carvings of high Roman art—works that glorified previous emperors—Constantine put himself in their league. Hadrian is featured in the round reliefs, with Marcus Aurelius in the square reliefs higher up. The big statues on top are of

Trajan and Augustus. Originally, Augustus drove a chariot similar to the one topping the modern Victor Emmanuel II Monument. Fourth-century Rome may have been in decline, but Constantine clung to its glorious past.

Surrounding Hills

Looking southwest, beyond the Arch of Constantine, you see Palatine Hill, dotted with umbrella pines. To the right of the Arch of Constantine is the road called Via Sacra ("Sacred Way"), once Rome's main street. It heads west up an incline toward the Arch of Titus (you can just make out its white top from here). That marks the head of the Forum, the religious, political, and commercial heart of ancient Rome (covered in the next chapter).

The Colosseum was built between three of Rome's legendary seven hills: Palatine (to the southwest), Esquiline (to the north), and Caelian (to the south). The Colosseum stands on land where the notorious Emperor Nero once had his sumptuous Golden House, which stretched from the Arch of Titus, across the valley, and up onto Esquiline Hill. After the house was replaced by the Colosseum, Nero's statue (or colossus) became the Colosseum's 100-foot-tall doorman.

• *Looking west, in the direction of the Forum, you'll see some ruins sitting atop a raised, rectangular-shaped hill. (You can recognize the hill by some door-like openings cut into the hill's support wall.) The ruins—consisting of an arched alcove made of brick and backed by a church bell tower—are all that remain of the once-great...*

Temple of Venus and Rome

At 100 feet tall, this temple atop a pedestal was one of the most prominent temples in Rome—and also its biggest. The size of a football field, it once covered the entire hill. The style of the temple was Greek—surrounded by white columns and topped with a triangular pediment above the entrance. Today, the perimeter of the complex is still visible, marked by a few massive white columns, six feet thick.

The main ruin in the center—the tall brick arch with a cross-hatched ceiling—was once the *cella,* or sacred chamber of the temple. Here sat two monumental statues, back to back. Venus, the goddess of love, faced the Colosseum. The goddess called Roma Aeterna faced the Forum. The pair of statues symbolized the birth and eternal destiny of the race of people meant to endure forever. The goddesses' Latin names were written in the twin *cella*s. On one side it read "Roma" and on the other, "Amor." Roma and Amor—a perfectly symmetrical palindrome, showing how Rome and Love were meant to go together. In ancient times, newlyweds ascended the staircase from the Colosseum (some parts are still visible) to the temple to ask Venus and Roma Aeterna to bring them good luck. These days, Roman couples get married at the church with the bell tower to ensure themselves love and happiness for eternity.

The temple was designed by Hadrian, the second-century emperor and amateur architect who also designed the Pantheon. Hadrian's design was critiqued by Rome's best-known architect, who complained that the huge statues would be so cramped they'd bump their heads if they stood up. Hadrian listened patiently to the criticism...then had the architect killed.

For a closer-up look at the Temple of Venus and Rome, you can access the ruins from within the Roman Forum.

THE COLOSSEUM'S LEGACY

With the coming of Christianity to Rome, the Colosseum and its deadly games slowly became politically incorrect. However, some gladiator contests continued here sporadically until they were completely banned in A.D. 435. Animal hunts continued a few decades longer. As the Roman Empire dwindled and the infrastructure crumbled, the stadium itself was neglected. Finally, around A.D. 523—after nearly 500 years of games—the last animal was killed, and the Colosseum shut its doors.

For the next thousand years, the structure was inhabited by

various squatters. It was used for makeshift apartments or shops, as a church, a cemetery, and as a refuge during invasions and riots. Over time, the Colosseum was eroded by wind, rain, and the strain of gravity. Earthquakes weakened it, and a powerful quake in 1349 toppled the south side.

More than anything, the Colosseum was dismantled by the Roman citizens themselves, who carted off pre-cut stones to be reused for palaces and churches, including St. Peter's. The marble facing was pulverized into mortar, and 300 tons of iron brackets were pried out and melted down, resulting in the pockmarking you see today.

After centuries of neglect, a series of 16th-century popes took pity on the pagan structure. In memory of the Christians who may (or may not) have been martyred here, they shored up the south and west sides with bricks and placed the big cross on the north side of the arena.

Today, the Colosseum links Rome's glorious past with its vital present. Major political demonstrations begin or end here, providing protesters with an iconic backdrop for the TV cameras. On Good Friday, the pope comes here to lead pilgrims as they follow the Stations of the Cross.

The legend goes that as long as the Colosseum shall stand, the city of Rome shall also stand. For nearly 2,000 years, the Colosseum has been the enduring symbol of Rome, the Eternal City.

• *The Roman Forum is 100 yards to the right of the arch. You can go in through the entrance across from the Colosseum, the main entrance on Via dei Fori Imperiali, or from the Palatine Hill entrance along Via di San Gregorio—see the map on page 154. If you're ready for a visit, turn to the next chapter.*

ROMAN FORUM TOUR

Foro Romano

The Forum was the political, religious, and commercial center of the city. Rome's most important temples and halls of justice were here. This was the place for religious processions, political demonstrations, elections, important speeches, and parades by conquering generals. As Rome's empire expanded, these few acres of land became the center of the civilized world.

Orientation

Cost: €12 combo-ticket covers both the Roman Forum/Palatine Hill (grouped as one sight for the purposes of the ticket) and the Colosseum; also covered by the Roma Pass. The combo-ticket is valid two consecutive days, but once your ticket is scanned for either the Forum/Palatine Hill or the Colosseum, you can't re-enter that sight (even the next day).

Hours: The Roman Forum, Palatine Hill, and Colosseum are all open daily 8:30 until one hour before sunset: April-Aug until 19:15, Sept until 19:00, Oct until 18:30, off-season closing time can be as early as 16:30—for specifics, see "Hours" on page 138; last entry one hour before closing.

Avoiding Lines: See "Avoiding Lines" on page 139.

Getting There: The closest Metro stop is Colosseo. Buses #53, #85, #87, and #175 stop along Via dei Fori Imperiali near the Colosseum, the Forum, and Piazza Venezia. The Forum has three entrances: directly across from the **Colosseum;** at the **Palatine Hill** ticket office on Via di San Gregorio (after buying your ticket, take the path to the right—not up the hill—which leads to the Arch of Titus); and the main entrance along **Via dei Fori Imperiali** ("Road of the Imperial Forums"), about halfway between the Colosseum and Piazza Venezia (from the

Colosseo Metro stop, walk away from the Colosseum on Via dei Fori Imperiali to find the low-profile Forum ticket office—look closely—located across the street from the intersection with busy Via Cavour).

Information: The free information center, located across Via dei Fori Imperiali from the Forum's main entrance, has a TI (which sells the Roma Pass), bookshop, small café, and WCs (daily 9:30-19:00). A bookstore is at the Forum entrance. Vendors outside sell a variety of colorful books with plastic overlays that restore the ruins (official price in bookstore for larger version with DVD is €20, and for smaller version is €10—don't pay more than these prices). Info office tel. 06-3996-7700, http://archeoroma.beniculturali.it/en.

Tours: An unexciting yet informative **audioguide** helps decipher the rubble (€5/2 hours, €7 version includes Palatine Hill and lasts 3 hours, must leave ID), but you'll have to return it to where you rented it—meaning you may not be able to exit directly to Capitoline Hill or the Colosseum, for example. Official **guided tours** in English might be available (inquire at ticket office). You can download this chapter as a free Rick Steves **audio tour** (see page 8).

Length of This Tour: Allow 1.5 hours. If you have less time, end the walk at the Arch of Septimius Severus. Don't miss the Basilica of Constantine hiding behind the trees.

Services: WCs are at the main entrance, near the Arch of Titus (in the "Soprintendenza" office), and in the middle of the Forum, near #6 on the map. For information on food and other WCs in the area, see the sidebar on page 146.

Plan Ahead: The ancient paving at the Forum is uneven; wear sturdy shoes. I carry a water bottle and refill it at the Forum's public drinking fountains.

Improvise: Because of ongoing restoration, paths through the Forum are often rerouted. Use this tour as a starting point, but be prepared for a few detours and backtracking.

The Tour Begins

• *Start at the Arch of Titus (Arco di Tito). It's the white triumphal arch that rises above the rubble on the east end of the Forum (closest to the Colosseum). Stand at the viewpoint alongside the arch and gaze over the valley known as the Forum.*

View of the Forum

The Forum is a rectangular valley running roughly east (the Colosseum end) to west (Capitoline Hill, with its bell tower). The rocky path at your feet is Via Sacra. It leads from the Arch of Titus,

Roman Forum

Not to Scale

CAPITOLINE HILL

GRAND STAIRCASE

VICTOR EMMANUEL MONUMENT

To Piazza Venezia

TRAJANS FORUM

VIA CAVOUR

To Gaul

TOUR ENDS

EXIT ONLY

STEPS TO CAPITOLINE HILL

CAESARS FORUM

F Food
● Water Fountain

FORI IMPERIALI

FORUM SQUARE

VIA SACRA

ENTRANCE

ROMAN FORUM

TICKET OFFICE & WC

"WATCH ROME GROW" MAPS

VIA DEI

To Hollywood

CIRCUS MAXIMUS

PALATINE HILL

ACCESS BETWEEN FORUM & PALATINE HILL

TO CLIMB PALATINE HILL

DIRECT TO FORUM

TOUR BEGINS

ENTRANCE

EXIT ONLY

S. FRANCESCA ROMANA

EXIT ONLY

PALATINE/ FORUM ENTRANCE

PALATINE HILL TICKET OFFICE

TEMPLE OF VENUS & ROME

VIA DI SAN GREGORIO

To Carthage

ARCH OF CONSTANTINE

COLOSSEUM

Colosseo

❶ Arch of Titus	❽ The Forum's Main Square
❷ Basilica of Constantine	❾ Temple of Julius Caesar
❸ Temple of Antoninus Pius & Faustina	❿ Basilica Aemilia
❹ Temple of Vesta	⓫ The Curia
❺ House of the Vestal Virgins	⓬ Rostrum
❻ Caligula's Palace	�913 Arch of Septimius Severus
❼ Temple of Castor & Pollux	⓮ Temple of Saturn
	⓯ Column of Phocas

FORUM

through the trees, past the large brick Senate building, through the triumphal arch at the far end, and up Capitoline Hill. The hill to your left (with all the trees) is Palatine Hill.

Picture being here when a conquering general returned to Rome with crates of booty. The valley was full of gleaming white buildings topped with bronze roofs. The Via Sacra—Main Street of the Forum—would be lined with citizens waving branches and carrying torches. The trumpets would sound as the parade began. First came porters, carrying chests full of gold and jewels. Then a parade of exotic animals from the conquered lands—elephants, giraffes, hippopotamuses—for the crowd to "ooh" and "ahh" at. Next came the prisoners in chains, with the captive king on a wheeled platform so the people could jeer and spit at him. Finally, the conquering hero himself would drive down in his four-horse chariot, with rose petals strewn in his path. The whole procession would run the length of the Forum and up the face of Capitoline Hill to the Temple of Saturn (the eight big columns midway up the hill—#14 on the map in this chapter), where they'd place the booty in Rome's coffers. Then they'd continue up to the summit to the Temple of Jupiter (only ruins of its foundation remain today) to dedicate the victory to the King of the Gods.

❶ Arch of Titus (Arco di Tito)

The Arch of Titus commemorated the Roman victory over the province of Judaea (Israel) in A.D. 70. The Romans had a reputa-

tion as benevolent conquerors who tolerated local customs and rulers. All they required was allegiance to the empire, shown by worshipping the emperor as a god. No problem for most conquered people, who already had half a dozen gods on their prayer lists anyway. But Israelites believed in only one god, and it wasn't the emperor. Israel revolted. After a short but bitter war, the Romans defeated the rebels, took Jerusalem, destroyed their temple (leaving only a fragment of one wall's foundation—today's revered "Wailing Wall"), and brought home 50,000 Jewish slaves...who were forced to build this arch (and the Colosseum).

Roman propaganda decorates the inside of the arch, where a relief shows the emperor Titus in a chariot being crowned by the goddess Victory. (Thanks to modern pollution, they both look like

FORUM

Rome: Republic and Empire
(500 B.C.-A.D. 500)

Ancient Rome lasted for a thousand years, from about 500 B.C. to A.D. 500. During that time, Rome expanded from a small tribe of barbarians to a vast empire, then dwindled slowly to city size again. For the first 500 years, when Rome's armies made her ruler of the Italian peninsula and beyond, Rome was a republic governed by elected senators. Over the next 500 years, a time of world conquest and eventual decline, Rome was an empire ruled by a military-backed dictator.

Julius Caesar bridged the gap between republic and empire. This ambitious general and politician, popular with the people because of his military victories and charisma, suspended the Roman constitution and assumed dictatorial powers in about 50 B.C. A few years later, he was assassinated by a conspiracy of senators. His adopted son, Augustus, succeeded him, and soon "Caesar" was not just a name but a title.

Emperor Augustus ushered in the Pax Romana, or Roman peace (A.D. 1-200), a time when Rome reached her peak and controlled an empire that stretched even beyond Eurail—from England to Egypt, Turkey to Morocco.

they've been through the wars.) The other side shows booty from the sacking of the temple in Jerusalem—soldiers carrying a Jewish menorah and other plunder. The two (unfinished) plaques on poles were to have listed the conquered cities. Look at the top of the ceiling. Constructed after Titus' death, the relief shows him riding an eagle to heaven, where he'll become one of the gods.

The brutal crushing of the A.D. 70 rebellion (and another one 60 years later) devastated the nation of Israel. With no temple as a center for their faith, the Jews scattered throughout the world (the Diaspora). There would be no Jewish political entity again for almost 2,000 years, until modern Israel was created after World War II.

As you begin this Forum tour, here's a hint for seeing things with "period eyes." We imagine the structures in ancient Rome as mostly white, but ornate buildings and monuments like the Arch of Titus were originally more colorful. Through the ages, builders scavenged stone from the Forum, and the finest stone—the colored marble—was cannibalized first. If any was left, it was generally the white stone. Statues that filled the niches were vividly painted, but the organic paint rotted away as statues lay buried for centuries. Lettering was inset bronze and eyes were inset ivory. Even seemingly intact structures, like the Arch of Titus, have been reas-

The Roman Empire at Its Peak: Pax Romana A.D. 120

Roman Empire

sembled. Notice the columns are half smooth and half fluted. The fluted halves are original; the smooth parts are reconstructions—intentionally not trying to fake the original.

And speaking of cannibalizing marble, remember that when marble burns it becomes lime, which is used to make cement. In the Middle Ages, before the historic importance of antiquity was appreciated, the Forum was surrounded by kilns used to melt marble. Much of the grandeur of ancient Rome—statues, reliefs, marble slabs—was loaded into these ovens, melted, and re-poured as concrete into the medieval city.

• *Walk down Via Sacra into the Forum. Imagine Roman sandals on these original basalt stones—the oldest street you'll ever walk. Many of the stones under your feet were walked on by Caesar Augustus 2,000 years ago. After about 50 yards, turn right and follow a path uphill to the three huge arches of the...*

❷ Basilica of Constantine (Basilica Maxentius)
Yes, these are big arches. But they represent only one-third of the original Basilica of Constantine, a mammoth hall of justice. The arches were matched by a similar set along the Via Sacra side (only a few squat brick piers remain). Between them ran the central hall, which was spanned by a roof 130 feet high—about 55 feet higher

FORUM

than the side arches you see. (The stub of brick you see sticking up began an arch that once spanned the central hall.) The hall itself was as long as a football field, lavishly furnished with colorful inlaid marble, a gilded bronze ceiling, and statues, and filled with strolling Romans. At the far (west) end was an enormous marble statue of Emperor Constantine on a throne. (Pieces of this statue, including a hand the size of a man, are on display in Rome's Capitoline Museums.)

The basilica was begun by the emperor Maxentius, but after he was trounced in battle (see page 148), the victor Constantine completed the massive building. No doubt about it, the Romans built monuments on a more epic scale than any previous Europeans, wowing their "barbarian" neighbors.

• *Now stroll deeper into the Forum, downhill along Via Sacra, through the trees. Pass by the only original bronze door still swinging on its ancient hinges (the green door at the Tempio di Romolo, the round building on the right—if it happens to be open, peek in). Just past that, 10 columns stand in front of a much newer-looking church. The colonnade was part of the...*

❸ Temple of Antoninus Pius and Faustina

The Senate built this temple to honor Emperor Antoninus Pius (A.D. 138-161) and his deified wife, Faustina. The 50-foot-tall Corinthian (leafy) columns must have been awe-inspiring to out-of-towners who grew up in thatched huts. Although the temple has been inhabited by a church, you can still see the basic layout—a staircase led to a shaded porch (the columns), which admitted you to the main building (now a church), where the statue of the god sat. Originally, these columns supported a triangular pediment decorated with sculptures.

Picture these columns, with gilded capitals, supporting brightly painted statues in the pediment, and the whole building capped with a gleaming bronze roof. The stately gray rubble of today's Forum is a faded black-and-white photograph of a 3-D Technicolor era.

The building is a microcosm of many changes that occurred after Rome fell. In medieval times, the temple was pillaged. Note the diagonal cuts high on the marble columns—a failed attempt by scavengers to cut through the pillars to pull them down for their precious stone. (They used vinegar and rope to cut the marble...but because vinegar also eats through rope, they abandoned the attempt.) In 1550, a church was housed inside the ancient temple. The green door shows the street level at the time of Michelangelo. The long staircase was underground until excavated in the 1800s.

• *With your back to the colonnade, walk straight ahead—jogging a bit to the right to stay on the path—and head for the three short columns, all that's left of the...*

❹ Temple of Vesta

This is perhaps Rome's most sacred spot. Rome considered itself one big family, and this temple represented a circular hut, like the kind that Rome's first families lived in. Inside, a fire burned, just as in a Roman home. And back in the days before lighters and butane, you never wanted your fire to go out. As long as the sacred flame burned, Rome would stand. The flame was tended by priestesses known as Vestal Virgins.

• *Just to the left and up the stairs is a big, enclosed field with two rectangular brick pools (just below the hill). This was the courtyard of the...*

❺ House of the Vestal Virgins

The Vestal Virgins lived in a two-story building surrounding a long central courtyard with two pools at one end. Rows of statues depicting leading Vestal Virgins flanked the courtyard. This place was the model—both architecturally and sexually—for medieval convents and monasteries.

Chosen from noble families before they reached the age of 10, the six Vestal Virgins served a 30-year term. Honored and revered by the Romans, the Vestals even had their own box opposite the emperor in the Colosseum. The statues that line the courtyard honor dutiful Vestals.

As the name implies, a Vestal took a vow of chastity. If she served her term faithfully—abstaining for 30 years—she was given a huge dowry and allowed to marry. But if they found any Virgin who wasn't, she was strapped to a funeral car, paraded through the streets of the Forum, taken to a crypt, given a loaf of bread and a lamp...and buried alive. Many women suffered the latter fate.

• *Looming just beyond this field is Palatine Hill—the corner of which may have been...*

❻ Caligula's Palace (Palace of Tiberius)

Emperor Caligula (ruled A.D. 37-41) had a huge palace on Palatine Hill overlooking the Forum. It actually sprawled down the hill into the Forum (some supporting arches remain in the hillside).

Caligula was not a nice person. He tortured enemies, stole senators' wives, and parked his chariot in handicap spaces. But Rome's luxury-loving emperors only added to the glory of the Forum, with each one trying to make his mark on history.

• *Continue downhill, passing the three short columns of the Temple of Vesta, and head for the three taller columns just beyond it.*

❼ Temple of Castor and Pollux

These three columns—all that remain of a once-prestigious temple—have become the most photographed sight in the Forum. The temple was one of the city's oldest, built in the fifth century B.C. It commemorated the Roman victory over the Tarquin, the notorious Etruscan king who once oppressed them. As a symbol of Rome's self-governing Republic, the temple was often used as a meeting place of senators, and its front steps served as a podium for free speech. The three columns are Corinthian style, featuring leafy capitals and fluting. They date from a later incarnation of the temple (first century).

• *You're now standing at the corner of a flat, grassy area.*

❽ The Forum's Main Square

The original Forum, or main square, was this flat patch about the size of a football field, stretching to the foot of Capitoline Hill. Surrounding it were temples, law courts, government buildings, and triumphal arches.

Rome was born right here. According to legend, twin brothers Romulus (Rome) and Remus were orphaned in infancy and raised by a she-wolf on top of Palatine Hill. Growing up, they found it hard to get dates. So they and their cohorts attacked the nearby Sabine tribe and kidnapped their women. After they made peace, this marshy valley became the meeting place and then the trading center for the scattered tribes on the surrounding hillsides.

The square was the busiest and most crowded—and often the seediest—section of town. Besides the senators, politicians, and currency exchangers, there were even sleazier types—souvenir hawkers, pickpockets, fortune-tellers, gamblers, slave marketers, drunks, hookers, lawyers, and tour guides.

Ancient Rome's population exceeded one million, more than any city until London and Paris in the 19th century. All those Roman masses lived in tiny apartments as we would live in tents at a campsite, basically just to sleep. The public space—their Forum, today's piazza—is where they did their living. Consider how, to this day, the piazza is still a standard part of any Italian town. Since

FORUM

Roman times, the piazza has reflected and accommodated the gregarious and outgoing nature of the Italian people.

The Forum is now rubble, but imagine it in its prime: blindingly brilliant marble buildings with 40-foot-high columns and shining metal roofs; rows of statues painted in realistic colors; processional chariots rattling down Via Sacra. Mentally replace tourists in T-shirts with tribunes in togas. Imagine the buildings towering and the people buzzing around you while an orator gives a rabble-rousing speech from the Rostrum. If things still look like just a pile of rocks, at least tell yourself, "But Julius Caesar once leaned against these rocks."

• *At the near (east) end of the main square (the Colosseum is to the east) are the foundations of a temple now capped with a peaked wood-and-metal roof.*

❾ Temple of Julius Caesar (Tempio del Divo Giulio, or Ara di Cesare)

On March 15, in 44 B.C., Julius Caesar was stabbed 23 times by political conspirators. After his assassination, Caesar's body was cremated on this spot (under the metal roof). Afterward, this temple was built to honor him. Peek behind the wall into the small apse area, where a mound of dirt usually has fresh flowers—given to remember the man who, more than any other, personified the greatness of Rome.

Caesar (100-44 B.C.) changed Rome—and the Forum—dramatically. He cleared out many of the wooden market stalls and began to ring the square with even grander buildings. Caesar's house was located behind the temple, near that clump of trees. He walked right by here on the day he was assassinated ("Beware the Ides of March!" warned a street-corner Etruscan preacher).

Though he was popular with the masses, not everyone liked Caesar's urban design or his politics. When he assumed dictatorial powers, he was ambushed and stabbed to death by a conspiracy of senators, including his adopted son, Brutus *("Et tu, Brute?")*.

The funeral was held here, facing the main square. The citizens gathered, and speeches were made. Mark Antony stood up to say (in Shakespeare's words), "Friends, Romans, countrymen, lend me your ears. I come to bury Caesar, not to praise him." When Caesar's body was burned, his adoring fans threw anything at hand on the fire, requiring the fire department to come put it out. Later, Emperor Augustus dedicated this temple in his name, making Caesar the first Roman to become a god.

Religion in Ancient Rome

Religion in ancient Rome was all about the *pax deorum* (peace, or pact, with the gods) that guaranteed the prosperity of the incredibly superstitious Romans. To appease the fickle gods, they performed elaborate rituals at lavish temples and shrines. Romans had a god for every moment of their days and each important event in their lives. While the Romans adopted the Greek pantheon, they also embraced the gods from many of the people they came into contact with, sometimes using elaborate ceremonies to persuade these new gods to "move" to Rome. Scholars estimate Romans had about 30,000 gods to keep happy. In this high-maintenance religion, there was Cunina, the goddess who protected cradles; Statulinus, to help children stand up; and Fabulina, for their first words. Fornax was the oven god, Pomona the fruit-tree goddess, Sterculinus the manure god, and Venus Cloacina the sewer goddess.

Priests interpreted the will of the gods by studying the internal organs of sacrificed animals, the flight of birds, and prophetic books. A clap of thunder was enough to postpone a battle.

Astrology, magic rites, the cult of deified emperors, house gods, and the near-deification of ancestors permeated Roman life. But all these gods didn't quite do it for the Romans—they were gradually replaced by the rise of monotheistic religions from the East. In A.D. 313, Emperor Constantine legalized and embraced Christianity. By 390, the Christian God was the only legal god in Rome.

• *Continue past the Temple of Julius Caesar, to the open area between the columns of the Temple of Antoninus Pius and Faustina (which we passed earlier) and the boxy brick building (the Curia). You can view these ruins of the Basilica Aemilia from a ramp next to the Temple of Antoninus Pius and Faustina, or find the entrance near the Curia (if it's not closed for archaeological work).*

❿ Basilica Aemilia

A basilica was a covered public forum, often serving as a Roman hall of justice. In a society that was as legal-minded as America is today, you needed a lot of lawyers—and a big place to

FORUM

put them. Citizens came here to work out matters such as inheritances and building permits, or to sue somebody.

Notice the layout. It was a long, rectangular building. The stubby columns all in a row form one long, central hall flanked by two side aisles. Medieval Christians required a larger meeting hall for their worship services than Roman temples provided, so they used the spacious Roman basilica as the model for their churches. Cathedrals from France to Spain to England, from Romanesque to Gothic to Renaissance, all have the same basic floor plan as a Roman basilica.

• *Now head for the big, well-preserved brick building (just beyond the basilica ruins) with the triangular roof—the Curia. (Ongoing archaeological work may restrict access to the Curia, as well as the Arch of Septimius Severus—described later—and the exit to Capitoline Hill.)*

⓫ The Curia (Senate House)

The Curia was the most important political building in the Forum. While the present building dates from A.D. 283, this was the site of Rome's official center of government since the birth of the republic.

Three hundred senators, elected by the citizens of Rome, met here to debate and create the laws of the land. Their wooden seats once circled the building in three tiers; the Senate president's podium sat at the far end. The marble floor is from ancient times. Listen to the echoes in this vast room—the acoustics are great.

Rome prided itself on being a republic. Early in the city's history, its people threw out the king and established rule by elected representatives. Each Roman citizen was free to speak his mind and have a say in public policy. Even when emperors became the supreme authority, the Senate was a power to be reckoned with. The Curia building is well-preserved, having been used as a church since early Christian times. In the 1930s, it was restored and opened to the public as a historic site. (Note: Although Julius Caesar was assassinated in "the Senate," it wasn't here—the Senate was temporarily meeting across town.)

A statue and two reliefs inside the Curia help build our mental image of the Forum. The statue, made of porphyry marble in about A.D. 100 (with its head, arms, and feet now missing), was a tribute to an emperor, probably Hadrian or Trajan. The two relief panels may have decorated the Rostrum. Those on the left show people (with big stone tablets) standing in line to burn their debt records following a government amnesty. The other shows the distribution of grain (Rome's welfare system), some buildings in the background, and the latest fashion in togas.

• *Go back down the Senate steps and find the 10-foot-high wall just to the left of the big arch, marked...*

⓬ Rostrum

Nowhere was Roman freedom more apparent than at this "Speaker's Corner." The Rostrum was a raised platform, 10 feet high and 80 feet long, decorated with statues, columns, and the prows of ships.

On a stage like this, Rome's orators, great and small, tried to draw a crowd and sway public opinion. Mark Antony rose to offer Caesar the laurel-leaf crown of kingship, which Caesar publicly (and hypocritically) refused while privately becoming a dictator. Men such as Cicero railed against the corruption and decadence that came with the city's newfound wealth. In later years, daring citizens even spoke out against the emperors, reminding them that Rome was once free. Picture the backdrop these speakers would have had—a mountain of marble buildings piling up on Capitoline Hill.

In front of the Rostrum are trees bearing fruits that were sacred to the ancient Romans: olives (provided food, light, and preservatives), figs (tasty), and wine grapes (made a popular export product).

• *The big arch to the right of the Rostrum is the...*

⓭ Arch of Septimius Severus

In imperial times, the Rostrum's voices of democracy would have been dwarfed by images of the empire, such as the huge six-story-

high Arch of Septimius Severus (A.D. 203). The reliefs commemorate the African-born emperor's battles in Mesopotamia. Near ground level, see soldiers marching captured barbarians back to Rome for the victory parade. Despite Severus' efficient rule, Rome's empire was crumbling under

the weight of its own corruption, disease, decaying infrastructure, and the constant attacks by foreign "barbarians."

• *Pass underneath the Arch of Septimius Severus and turn left. If the path is blocked, backtrack toward the Temple of Julius Caesar and around the square. On the slope of Capitoline Hill are the eight remaining columns of the...*

FORUM

Rome Falls

Remember that Rome lasted 1,000 years—500 years of growth, 200 years of peak power, and 300 years of gradual decay. The fall had many causes, among them the barbarians who pecked away at Rome's borders. Christians blamed the fall on moral decay. Pagans blamed it on Christians. Socialists blamed it on a shallow economy based on the spoils of war. (Republicans blamed it on Democrats.) Whatever the reasons, the far-flung empire could no longer keep its grip

on conquered lands, and it pulled back. Barbarian tribes from Germany and Asia attacked the Italian peninsula and even looted Rome itself in A.D. 410, leveling many of the buildings in the Forum. In 476, when the last emperor checked out and switched off the lights, Europe plunged into centuries of ignorance, poverty, and weak government—the Dark Ages.

But Rome lived on in the Catholic Church. Christianity was the state religion of Rome's last generations. Emperors became popes (both called themselves "Pontifex Maximus"), senators became bishops, orators became priests, and basilicas became churches. The glory of Rome remains eternal.

⑭ Temple of Saturn

These columns framed the entrance to the Forum's oldest temple (497 B.C.). Inside was a humble, very old wooden statue of the god Saturn. But the statue's pedestal held the gold bars, coins, and jewels of Rome's state treasury, the booty collected by conquering generals.

• *Standing here, at one of the Forum's first buildings, look east at the lone, tall...*

⑮ Column of Phocas

This is the Forum's last monument (A.D. 608), a gift from the powerful Byzantine Empire to a fallen empire—Rome. Given to commemorate the pagan Pantheon's becoming a Christian church, it's like a symbolic last nail in ancient Rome's coffin. After Rome's 1,000-year reign, the city was looted by Vandals, the population of a million-plus shrank to about 10,000, and the once-grand city center—the Forum—was abandoned, slowly covered up by centuries of silt and dirt. In the 1700s, an English historian named Edward Gibbon overlooked this spot from Capitoline Hill. Hearing Christian monks singing at these pagan ruins, he looked out at the few columns poking up from the ground, pondered the decline and fall of the Roman Empire, and thought, "Hmm, that's a catchy title..."

• *Your tour is over. From the Forum, you have several options:*

1. To exit toward the Colosseum, you'll have to jog through the lower part of Palatine Hill: Head a few steps uphill from the Arch of Titus, and look for the tunnel marked uscita/exit on your left. You'll pop out just below the entrance facing the Colosseum (see Colosseum Tour chapter).

2. Exiting past the Arch of Septimius Severus, at the north end of the Forum, leads you to the stairs up to Capitoline Hill (described on page 40).

3. The Forum's main entrance spills you back out onto Via dei Fori Imperiali, from where you can head to Trajan's Column, Trajan's Market, and Museum of the Imperial Forums (described on page 50). Or you can leave via the exit-only next to the Basilica of Constantine, which also leads to Via dei Fori Imperiali.

4. From the Arch of Titus, you can climb Palatine Hill to the top and start the Palatine Hill Tour—see the next chapter.

PALATINE HILL TOUR

Monte Palatino

While many tourists consider Palatine Hill just extra credit after the Forum, it offers an insight into the greatness of Rome that's well worth the effort. (And, if you're visiting the Colosseum or Forum, you've got a ticket whether you like it or not.) Palatine Hill is jam-packed with history—"the huts of Romulus," the huge Imperial Palace, a view of the Circus Maximus—but there's only the barest skeleton of rubble left to tell the story. This tour will enable the thoughtful sightseer to bring those remains to life.

Palatine Hill is ideal for those who want to get away from the crowds and discover the romantic, melancholy essence of ruins. Become a 19th-century poet or a painter on the Grand Tour, meditating on the destiny of once-great civilizations, and wander through the remains of the palaces that Nature seems to have reclaimed for herself.

Orientation

Cost: €12 combo-ticket covers both the Roman Forum/Palatine Hill (grouped as one sight for the purposes of the ticket) and the Colosseum; also covered by the Roma Pass. The combo-ticket is valid two consecutive days, but once your ticket is scanned for either the Forum/Palatine Hill or the Colosseum, you can't re-enter that sight (even the next day).

Hours: The Palatine Hill, Roman Forum, and Colosseum are all open daily 8:30 until one hour before sunset: April-Aug until 19:15, Sept until 19:00, Oct until 18:30, off-season closing time can be as early as 16:30—for specifics, see "Hours" on page 138; last entry one hour before closing. The House of Augustus, a minor stop on this tour, is usually closed Tue and Fri; on other days it has shorter hours than the rest of the site (generally 8:30-13:30, hours vary off-season, last entry 30 minutes before closing).

Getting There: The closest Metro stop is Colosseo. From the Metro, the nearest entrance is the one to the Forum, across from the Colosseum—once inside the Forum, just climb the hill from the Arch of Titus. The main Palatine Hill entrance is on Via di San Gregorio (facing the Forum with the Colosseum at your back, it's down the street to your left).

Information: Tel. 06-3996-7700, www.archeoroma.beniculturali. it/en.

Tours: Audioguides cost €5/2 hours (€7 version includes Roman Forum and lasts 3 hours, must leave ID—so you have to return the audioguide where you rent it). Guided tours in English might be available (inquire at the ticket booth).

Length of This Tour: Allow 1.5 hours. Don't miss the stadium or the view of the Circus Maximus. If lines are long, skip the House of Augustus.

Services: WCs are rare in the Colosseum-Roman Forum-Palatine Hill area. Your best (though still meager) options are here at Palatine Hill, where you'll find WCs at the ticket office when you enter, at the museum in the center of the site, and hiding among the orange trees in the Farnese Gardens. For restaurants in the area, see the sidebar on page 146.

Expect Changes: Large parts of Palatine Hill—including the viewpoints over the site's highlight, the Circus Maximus— have been closed off in recent years due to ongoing archaeological work. Just see what you can, using this chapter's map to navigate.

The Tour Begins

• *Start on top of the hill at the Palatine Museum (Museo Palatino, #6 on the map). To get there from the main entrance, take the stairs on the left and follow the path up, up, and up, winding under the inviting shade of umbrella pines. Eventually you'll hook to the left and pop out in the midst of all those ruins. Walk past the stadium (#2 on the map) to the one modern building on the crest of the hill. It's the big,* *gray, 1930s-style building that houses the museum. (If you're coming up from the Forum, just hike up to the ruins to find this building.)*

We'll visit the museum later. But for now, grab a stone and sit with your back to the museum to orient yourself, facing in the direction of the Forum (roughly north).

THE IMPERIAL PALACE

You're sitting at the center of what was once a huge palace, the residence of emperors for three centuries. Orgies, royal weddings, assassinations, concerts, intrigues, births, funerals, banquets, and the occasional Tupperware party took place within these walls. What walls? The row of umbrella pines about 200 yards to the east (to your right) now marks one edge of the palace. The reconstructed brick tower (at about 11 o'clock) was the northwest corner. The palace also stretched behind you (the area behind the museum) and beneath you, since some parts of the palace had a lower floor. (Right now, you're standing not on the original palace's ground level, but several floors up.)

The area in front was the official wing of the palace; behind were the private quarters. All in all, it made for a cozy little 150,000-square-foot pad.

The palace was built by Emperor Domitian in about A.D. 81. A poet of the day described it as so grand that it "made Jupiter jealous."

• *Now proceed, following the map for this 12-stop tour. As you walk, you'll see colorful marble scraps all over Palatine Hill. Flashy building stone was used to boast of the power and vastness of the empire. Citizens knew that the Numidian yellow marble was from Tunisia, the veined Cipollino marble (with swirling designs like an onion) was from the island of Euboea in Greece, and the pink granite was from Aswan in Egypt. This was all sliced and laid out in fine pavement and wall designs, enjoyed by those who could only be thankful they were on the winning team.*

With your back to the museum, head left to a big rectangular field with an octagonal brick design in the center—the main courtyard of the palace.

❶ Main Courtyard (Peristilio) and Octagonal Fountain (Fontana Ottagona)

The brick octagon was a sunken fountain in the middle of an open-air courtyard. Like many fine Roman homes, this palace was built around an oasis of peace where you could enjoy the sun, catch the precious rain, and listen to the bab-ble of moving water. The courtyard was lined with columns (notice the fragments) supporting an arcade for shade. Originally, the floor and walls of the courtyard were faced with colorful marble.

• *The palace's stadium is 100 yards behind you (to the east), near the long row of pine trees. Belly up to the railing and look down on the elliptical track.*

Palatine Hill

To Tiber River

VIEW OF ST. PETER'S DOME

TOUR ENDS ⑬

Farnese Gardens

FORUM

Cliffs

S. ANASTASIA

WC

⑫

ARCHAEOLOGICAL ZONE & GARDENS

⑨ ⑩ ⑪

STAIRS & GROTTO

ARCH OF TITUS

Umbrella Pines

FOUNTAIN RUINS

⑧ ① ⑦ ORIGINAL ENTRANCE

ACCESS BETWEEN FORUM & PALATINE HILL

EDGE OF PALATINE HILL

MUSEUM

⑥

TOUR BEGINS

FORUM ENTRANCE

To Forum Exit & Colosseum

③

VIEWS ④ DOMUS AUGUSTANA

IMPERIAL PALACE

CIRCUS ⑤ MAXIMUS

② STADIUM

Direct Route to Forum

Cliffs

Umbrella Pines

PALATINE TICKETS & ENTRANCE

Direct Route to Palatine

WC

To Arch of Constantine, Colosseum & Colosseo Ⓜ

VIA DEI CERCHI

VIA DI SAN GREGORIO

Not to Scale

⁝⁝⁝ STANDING RUINS

⌁ ORIGINAL FOOTPRINT

To Testaccio

Circo Ⓜ Massimo

To Baths of Caracalla

① Main Courtyard & Octagonal Fountain
② Stadium
③ Private Wing of the Palace
④ Domus Augustana – Lower Courtyard
⑤ Circus Maximus
⑥ Museum & WC
⑦ Throne Room

⑧ Dining Room & Fountain Room
⑨ House of Augustus
⑩ House of Livia
⑪ Cryptoporticus
⑫ Huts of Romulus
⑬ Farnese Gardens & Forum View

PALATINE HILL

❷ Stadium (Stadio)

This cigar-shaped, sunken stadium (500 feet long) was the palace's rec room. It looks like a racetrack, but it just held gardens with paths for strolling. The oval running track at the south end

was added later. The emperor had a raised box on the 50-yard line, in the curved apse across from you. At the north end were changing rooms, and the marble fragments that litter the ground once held up an arcade.

• *Stretching between the stadium and the museum is a big, brick structure called the Domus Augustana. Depending on the progress of archaeological work, you may be able to actually walk through the big arches, or you may have to walk around the end (using the path alongside the stadium) to reach the back of the structure. As much as is possible, explore the...*

❸ Private Wing of the Palace (Domus Augustana)

The part of the palace you're standing in now held the private rooms of the emperor and his extended family. Today, all that

marks this part of the palace are some brick ruins and a lone umbrella pine on a mound (which was the courtyard of the Domus Augustana). Survey the maze of brick rooms (many of them reconstructed), noticing...

- The typical Roman building method: Build a rectangular shell of brick, fill it with concrete, then finish it with either plaster (you'll see an occasional faded fresco) or slabs of marble. The small, round pockmarks on many walls show where the marble was fastened.
- The square holes in the walls that held wooden beams, used for scaffolding during construction and maintenance, for shelves, and for wooden floors.
- Over the doorways, the bricks in the walls that form the pattern of an arch. These "blind arches" were structural elements that allowed the walls to be built higher. The iron bar clamps are recent additions and hold the crumbling walls together.
- Niches and apses that once held statues. Every family had

their own household gods and displayed small images of these guardian spirits, as well as busts of honored ancestors.

• The fragments of columns, reliefs, and sculpture scattered about that suggest the wealth of this great palace. The floor plan is complex—a fantasyland maze of small, private, sometimes even curved rooms.

• *In the south part of the Domus Augustana (behind the museum), you can look down on the ruins of the lower story.*

❹ Domus Augustana—Lower Courtyard

This open-air courtyard has the concave-convex remains of a large fountain that must have been a marvel. Try to mentally reconstruct

the palace that surrounded this fountain. The emperors could look down on it from the upper story (where you're standing) or view it from the rooms around it on the lower story, where the emperor and his family ate their meals in private.

The lower story was built into the slope of the hill. The southern part of the palace was an extension of the hillside, supported beneath your feet by big arches.

• *Continue to the southern edge of the hill (directly behind the museum), overlooking a long, wide grassy field—what once was the Circus Maximus. Lean over the railing and you might be able to make out the concave shape of the palace's southern facade. (Note that archaeological work may prevent you from reaching these viewpoints.)*

❺ Circus Maximus

If the gladiator show at the Colosseum was sold out, you could always get a seat at Circus Max. In an early version of today's demolition derby, Ben-Hur and his fellow charioteers once raced recklessly around this oblong course.

The chariots circled the cigar-shaped mound in the center (notice the lone cypress tree that now marks one end of the mound). Bleachers (now grassy banks) originally surrounded the track (see artist's reconstruction in photo on next page).

The track was 1,300 feet long, while the whole stadium measured 2,130 feet by 720 feet and seated—get this—250,000 people. The wooden bleachers once collapsed during a race, killing thousands.

The horses began at a starting gate at the west end (to your right), while the public entered at the other end. Races consisted of seven laps (about 3.5 miles total). In such a small space, collisions and overturned chariots were common. The charioteers were usually poor, lowborn people who used this dangerous sport to get rich and famous. Some succeeded. Most died.

The public was crazy about the races. There were 12 per day, 240 days a year. Four teams dominated the competition—Reds, Whites, Blues, and Greens—and every citizen was fanatically devoted to one of them. Obviously, the emperors had the best seats in the house: Built into the palace's curved facade was a box overlooking the track. For their pleasure, emperors occasionally had the circus floor carpeted with designs in colored powders.

Picture the scene: intact palace; emperor watching; a quarter of a million Romans cheering, jeering, and furiously betting. Horses raced here for more than a thousand years. The track dates from 300 b.c., and the spectacles continued into the Christian era, until a.d. 549, despite Church disapproval.

From this viewpoint, looking to the left, you can see the ruins of the Baths of Caracalla (not worth touring if you've seen Palatine) rising above the trees a half-mile away. About a mile beyond that, Appian Way led from a grand gate in the ancient wall, past the catacombs, to Brindisi.

• *Turn around and head back toward the museum.*

❻ Museum (Museo Palatino)

The museum contains statues and frescoes that help you imagine the luxury of the imperial Palatine. As you climb the stairs and enter, turn left and go to the end of the hall to find the statue of "Magna Mater" on her throne. This Great Mother brought life and fertility to the Roman people, who worshipped her at the nearby Temple of Cybele. Her arms and foot were destroyed by time, but there was always a cavity where her head should be— this was a standard Roman device in which interchangeable heads could be inserted. In this case, the Magna Mater's "head" was actually a sacred black cone-shaped meteorite that caused astonishment when it fell from the sky.

Also on this floor, Room V holds frescoes and statues from the time of Augustus and fine decorative terracotta panels. Room VII has a bust of the notorious Emperor Nero ("Nerone") and exquisite marble-inlay work. In Room VIII is a statue fragment of a river god's stomach. And finally, back near the entrance is a large, headless, topless statue of a Muse ("Musa?") that once decorated the Hippodrome.

There's more in the basement (go back outside, down the stairs, and into the doorway directly below the staircase). Room II holds a model of the eighth-century B.C. Iron Age huts of Romulus that we'll see later in the tour. (There's also a 21st-century WC nearby.)

• *From the museum, begin circling the main courtyard (with its octagonal fountain) counterclockwise. Turn left with the path, then turn right into the first opening, marked by the squat brick pillar with a stubby column on top. Step into the...*

❼ Throne Room (Aula Regia)

The nerve center of an empire that controlled some 50 million people from England to Africa, this was the official seat of power. The curved apse of the largest brick stump (there's now a plaque on it) marks the spot where the emperor sat on his throne for official business.

Imagine being a Roman citizen summoned by the emperor. You'd enter the palace through the main doorway (now a gap) at the far (Forum) end of the room, having climbed up three flights of a monumental staircase. The floor and walls dazzled with green, purple, red, white, and yellow marble. Along the walls were 12 colossal statues of Roman gods. The ceiling towered seven stories overhead. On either side were doorways leading to a basilica and the emperor's private temple.

You'd approach the emperor, who sat on a raised throne in the apse, dressed in royal purple, with a crown of laurel leaves on his head and a scepter cradled in his arm. Big braziers burned on either side, throwing off a flickering light. As you approached, you'd raise your arm to greet him, saying, *"Ave, Caesar!"* The words would echo through the great hall.

Now imagine yourself as emperor. Stand on the small white stone marking the location of the throne (a few feet in front of the plaque), and look out over your palace. (The ceiling was a barrel vault sitting upon towers as high as the brick tower in the distance to the left.)

• *Continue circling the main courtyard counterclockwise until it dead-ends at a big field filled with pebbles.*

❽ Dining Room (Triclinium) and Fountain Room (Nymphaeum)

The floor of the dining room had a hollow space beneath it (you can see the two-foot gap between the two original floors). Slaves stoked fires from underground stoves to heat the floor with forced air. At

the far end of the room, the platform and curved apse mark the spot where the emperor ate while looking down on his subjects. Guests could look into the adjoining room, where an elliptical-shaped fountain (see the brick remains) spurted for their amusement.

Here, the wealthiest Romans enjoyed the spoils that poured into Rome from its vast empire. Reclining on a couch, waited on by slaves, you'd order bowls of larks' tongues or a roast pig stuffed with live birds, then wash it down with wine. If you were full but tempted by yet another delicacy, you could call for a feather, vomit, and start all over. Dancing dark-skinned slaves from Egypt or flute players from Greece entertained. If you fancied one, he or she was yours—the bedrooms were just down the hall.

Or so went the stories. In fact, many emperors were just and simple men, continuing the old Roman traditions of hard work and moderate tastes. But just as many were power-mad scoundrels who used their authority to indulge their every desire.

• *From the dining room, backtrack a few steps and work your way west through openings in the low brick wall to exit the palace.*

ARCHAEOLOGICAL ZONE AND GARDENS

• *As you leave the palace, follow signs directing you to the* Casa di Livia *and* Casa di Augusto. *These were the homes (once joined together) of Rome's first emperor and his wife. In the general vicinity, you'll also find the Cryptoporticus and Huts of Romulus.*

Start with the House of Augustus. Because the space is so small, and the frescoes so fragile, only five visitors at a time are allowed to enter—and for just five minutes. Find the queue for the House of Augustus. The wait is usually about 15 to 30 minutes.

❾ House of Augustus (Casa di Augusto)

Augustus, a.k.a. Octavian, the first emperor, lived in this house (and the neighboring House of Livia) with his wife. This relatively modest dwelling, dating from before Octavian became emperor, is a far cry from the later Imperial Palace that was built on top. The three humble rooms with their finely restored frescoes are well worth the wait. See rooms vibrantly painted with fake columns and arches, and with fake windows that once looked out on illusionary landscapes. Climb the steps outside to see a fourth room. You'll see that Livia and Augustus had little of the lavish marble found in most homes of the wealthy.

Augustus was a modest man who believed in traditional Roman values. His wife and daughter wove the clothes he wore. He slept in the same small bedroom for 40 years. He burned the midnight oil in his study, where he read and wrote his memoirs. Augustus set a standard for emperors' conduct that would last... until his death.

Augustus wanted to be the new Romulus, building his house adjacent to the home of the mythological founder of Rome.

• *After exiting the House of Augustus, see if the House of Livia is open (it probably isn't). If it is, you could take a free 20-minute tour, offered alternately in Italian and English—you may want to take whichever tour leaves first, as there's some English info inside. Otherwise, peek inside through the dirty windows.*

⑩ House of Livia (Casa di Livia)

Augustus' wife Livia lived here during her first marriage. After she married Augustus (and after he became Rome's ruler), they merged their two homes into a larger but still modest complex.

Your visit includes the former entrance hall—a high-ceilinged room with a few faded frescoes in purple, yellow, blue, and white. The best-preserved ones are in the central alcove, the room known as the *tablinum*, where guests were received. The *tablinum*'s right wall depicts the god Mercury (on the right side of the scene), arriving to kill the giant Argus (left) and kidnap the nymph Io (center) so Jupiter can ravish her. Frescoes in the alcove to the right of the *tablinum* show a columned portico draped with garlands. The left alcove has delicate Pompeiian-style designs.

Why do scholars think these ruins were Livia's house? Because they found her honorific name, "Julia Augusta," inscribed on the lead pipes now displayed in the *tablinum*.

• *Near the Casa di Livia is the entrance to a tunnel known as the...*

⑪ Cryptoporticus

This covered passageway, 400 feet long, allowed the imperial entourage to travel privately through the palace complex. The tunnel was elaborately decorated with frescoes (little remains). The cryptoporticus may have been built by Emperor Nero to link the Palatine and Forum with his vast mansion, the Domus Aurea, which extended from the edge of the Forum past (what is now) the Colosseum and onto Esquiline Hill. Nero's cryptoporticus may have been an expansion of an earlier passageway built by Tiberius (Livia's son). Here, the notorious emperor Caligula is said to have been assassinated.

• *Make your way to the nearby section of ruins, protected by a large metal roof. Cozy up to the railing to see ruined walls and foundations.*

⑰ Huts of Romulus (Capanne Romulee)

Looking down into this pit filled with big blocks of stone, you can make out some elliptical and rectangular shapes carved into the stony ground. These are the partial outlines of huts from about 850 B.C. Some have holes that once held the wooden posts of round thatched huts.

According to legend, Romulus and Remus (see photo of statue on page 184) were children of the first Vestal Virgin. For complicated family reasons, she was executed and her babies were set adrift on the flooding Tiber River, eventually washing ashore at the foot of Palatine Hill. In a cave just downhill from here, a shepherd discovered them being suckled by a mother wolf. He took them home—maybe right here—and raised them as his own. When Romulus grew up, he killed his brother and built a square wall (Roma Quadrata) on the hilltop, thus founding the city of Rome.

For centuries, the Romans believed this myth. They honored the wolf's cave (called the "Lupercale," where every February 15 men dressed up in animal skins and whipped women), as well as the spot where Romulus was said to have lived. Lo and behold, in the 1940s, these huts were unearthed, and the legend became history. Archaeologists are still at it, and the more they dig, the more they find to confirm the legends. A nearby cave discovered in 2007—ornamented with seashells, colored marble, and a wolf mosaic—may be that original Lupercale. (It's not open to the public, and dissenting archaeologists believe it's a temple to water nymphs.)

Here at Rome's birthplace, reflect on the rise of this great culture—from thatched huts to the modest House of Augustus to the massive Imperial Palace of Domitian, with its stadium and view over the Circus Maximus. It's no wonder that the hill's name gave us our English word "palace."

• *Climb a few steps to the summit of the hill, and walk among the trees of the Farnese Gardens. Start making your way toward the Forum.*

⓮ Farnese Gardens—View of Forum
Fit for an Emperor

Finish your tour with a stroll through the Renaissance gardens of the Farnese family. Walk past the foundations of the House of Tiberius—Livia's son by her first husband—who became emperor after Augustus. Continue on, admiring the exotic plants, fountains, underground grotto, and pavilions. When you see the incredible view of the Forum from the end of the gardens, you'll know why Palatine Hill was Rome's best address.

• *To exit, wind down Palatine Hill to the Forum, ending up at the Arch of Titus.*

CAPITOLINE MUSEUMS TOUR

Musei Capitolini

This enjoyable museum complex claims to be the world's oldest, founded in 1471 when a pope gave ancient statues to the citizens of Rome. Many of the museum's statues have gone on to become instantly recognizable cultural icons. Perched on top of Capitoline Hill, the museum's two buildings (Palazzo dei Conservatori and Palazzo Nuovo) are connected by an underground passage that leads to the Tabularium and panoramic views of the Roman Forum. (For more on Capitoline Hill, see page 40.)

Orientation

Cost: €13, or €9.50 if there are no temporary exhibits.

Hours: Tue-Sun 9:00-20:00, closed Mon, last entry one hour before closing.

Getting There: It sits atop Capitoline Hill (*Campidoglio* in Italian), housed in two buildings that flank the square. Buy tickets and enter at the Palazzo dei Conservatori (on your right as you face the equestrian statue).

Information: You'll find some English descriptions within the museum. Tel. 06-0608, www.museicapitolini.org.

Tours: The €5 audioguide is good.

Length of This Tour: Allow two hours.

Baggage Check: Free (mandatory for bags larger than a purse).

Cuisine Art: A great view café, called **Caffè Capitolino,** is upstairs in Palazzo dei Conservatori (enter from inside museum; also has exterior entrance for the public—facing museum entrance, go to your right around the building to Piazza Caffarelli and through door #4; see map on page 182). The pavilion on the terrace outside offers full service; inside is self-service (pay first, then take receipt to bar; good salads and toasted sandwiches).

Piazza Caffarelli is a fine place for a snooze or a picnic. (Note: While it has great views, it doesn't overlook the Forum.)

Starring: The original she-wolf statue, Marcus Aurelius, the Dying Gaul, the Boy Extracting a Thorn, and Forum views.

OVERVIEW

Capitoline Hill's main square (Piazza del Campidoglio), home to the museum, began in ancient Rome as a religious center, the site

of temples to the gods Jupiter, Juno, and Minerva. In the 16th century, Michelangelo transformed the square from pagan to papal, while adding a harmonious and refined Renaissance touch. (For more on the square, see page 40.)

The museum's layout—with two different buildings connected by an underground passage—can be confusing, but this self-guided tour is easy to follow.

You'll enter at the Palazzo dei Conservatori (on your right as you face the equestrian statue), cross underneath the square (beneath the Palazzo Senatorio, the mayoral palace, not open to public), and exit from the Palazzo Nuovo (on your left).

Expect changes: Because this museum often puts on special exhibits (mostly as an excuse to up the entry price a few euros), some items may be in different rooms than described. Use this chapter's photos to track down highlights.

The Tour Begins

• *Begin at the square on top of Capitoline Hill. After your ticket is checked, enter the courtyard.*

PALAZZO DEI CONSERVATORI

In the courtyard, enjoy the massive chunks of Constantine: his head, hand, feet, bicep, and other bits and pieces. When intact, this giant, 30-foot statue of the emperor sitting on his throne held the place of honor in the Basilica of Constantine in the Forum. Imagine it's A.D. 330 as you stare up at the emperor, an abstract symbol of power. His face is

Capitoline Museums Overview

Piazza San Marco

Piazza Venezia

TRAJAN'S COLUMN

TRAJAN'S

VIA SAN MARCO

VICTOR EMMANUEL MONUMENT

CAFÉ

FORUM

To Gesù & Pantheon

VIA D'ARACOELI

ROME FROM THE SKY ELEVATOR

INSULA (APARTMENT) RUINS

STA. MARIA ARACOELI

VIA DEI FORI IMPERIALI

SHORTCUTS

To Colosseum & M

MICHELANGELO'S GRAND STAIRCASE

#110

PALAZZO NUOVO

EXIT

Piazza del Campidoglio

STATUE

SHE-WOLF (COPY)

WATER FOUNTAIN

CAESAR'S FORUM

MAMERTINE PRISON

To Teatro di Marcello

VIA TEATRO MARCELLO

ENTRANCE & TICKETS

PUBLIC CAFÉ ENTRANCE

Piazza Caffarelli

PALAZZO DEI CONSERVATORI

PALAZZO SENATORIO

TABULARIUM

FORUM EXIT ONLY

SANTI LUCA E MARTINA

ARCH OF SEPTIMIUS SEVERUS

CAFFÈ CAPITOLINO

ROMAN FORUM

100 Meters

100 Yards

FORO ROMANO

----- Underground passages

otherworldly. You can't really connect. You feel like a subject rather than a citizen. You could say the concept of monarchy by divine right starts here.

Only the extremities of the massive statue survive because a statue of this size was not entirely marble. Its core was cheaper and made of more perishable material, like bricks. Appreciate the detail of the vein in his bicep. Notice also the mortise and tenon joint and imagine the engineering necessary to construct this Goliath.

Also in the courtyard are reliefs of conquered peoples—not in chains, but new members of an expansive empire. These represent provinces such as Gaul, Britannia, and Thracia, and date from the reign of Hadrian (second century A.D.), whose passion was running the empire not as something to exploit, but as a commonwealth.

• Go up the staircase (the one near the entrance, not the one in the courtyard). On the landing, find...

Reliefs of Second-Century Imperial Grandeur

These four fine reliefs show great moments in an emperor's daily grind. Rome was a visual culture and used public art for propa-

ganda purposes. Rather than portray moments unique to a particular emperor, common themes and rituals were illustrated. In this case we see heroics on the battlefield, a triumphal entry into Rome, and the emperor as the top religious authority. Study the three panels, which happen to feature Marcus Aurelius (starting on the left, with him mounted on a horse). The emperor, in an equestrian pose (like the bronze statue in Piazza del Campidoglio), has his hand out, offering clemency to his vanquished foes. The detail, with expressive

faces and banners blowing in the wind, is impressive. In the relief showing Marcus Aurelius in his chariot, someone's missing...it's Commodus, his wicked son (Russell Crowe's nemesis in *Gladiator*). After the assassination of Commodus, his memory was damned, so images of him were erased (or, in this case, chiseled out). And in the religious scene, the emperor oversees preparations to sacrifice a bull (with even the bull looking on curiously).

• *Continue up the stairs to the first floor. Go through two large frescoed rooms (Rooms I and II) and through the doorway on the right of the far wall to find Room III, with the...*

Boy Extracting a Thorn *(Spinario)*

He's just a boy, intent only on picking a thorn out of his foot. As he bends over to reach his foot, his body sticks out at all angles,

like a bony chicken wing. He's even scuffed up, the way small boys get. At this moment, nothing matters to him but that splinter. Our lives are filled with these mundane moments (when we'd give anything for tweezers), which are rarely captured in art.

The boy is a bronze cast with eyes once inlaid as in the adjacent bronze cast of Brutus. Take a close look at Brutus (whose descendent took part in the killing of Caesar). This wonderful bust typifies Roman character: determined, thoughtful, no-nonsense, and capable. The ivory eyes are original.

Now, look up, and appreciate the fresco that has lined this room since it was part of a municipal palace in the 16th century.

It's a stirring battle scene that celebrates the power and glory of ancient Rome. Find the wagonload of enemy armor and weapons and sweep 360 degrees as if joining in this triumphal parade. It's another great military victory, and the troops are bringing home precious statues of bronze and marble as plunder. There's the emperor on his four-horse chariot. The enemy prisoners are bound and ready to absorb your disdain. And after the sacrificial bulls is a chorus of trumpets and throngs of your fellow adoring citizens—all thankful to be loyal subjects of the emperor.

• *In the next room (Room IV) is the...*

Capitoline She-Wolf

The original bronze she-wolf suckles the twins Romulus and Remus. This symbol of Rome is ancient, though the wolf statue

itself (long thought to be Etruscan, from the fifth century B.C.) was made in the 13th century, and the boys are an invention of the 15th century. Look into the eyes of the wolf. An animal looks back, with ragged ears, sharp teeth, and staring eyes.

This wild animal, teamed with the wildest creatures of all—hungry babies—makes a powerful symbol for the tenacious city/empire of Rome.

• *Continue to the next room.*

From Michelangelo to Medusa

Along with a bust of Michelangelo made from his death mask, this room contains Bernini's anguished bust of Medusa—with writhing snakes on her head. This goes way beyond a bad hair day. Enjoy the artistry of Bernini as he fashions a marble lock of hair into a writhing snake.

Then appreciate the room you're in as a piece of art in itself: Murano glass chandelier, fine painted coffered ceiling, fabric walls, inlaid marble floor, medallions celebrating papal donations to the collection, and frescoed panels set in fanciful grotesque-style decor. As a bonus, you've got Rome, including St. Peter's dome, out the window.

• *Pass through three small rooms: Room VI has the* Artemis of Efenina, *with her extremely fertile draping of numerous bull testicles, breasts, or perhaps puka shells (no one knows for sure). Room VII features Greek*

red-figured vases (and the elevator up to the café—need a coffee break?).
Continue through Room VIII, straight to a set of seven stairs and follow
them up to the next room to discover the remarkable bust of...

Commodus as Hercules

This arrogant emperor brat used to run around the palace in animal
skins pretending (or believing) he was Hercules. Here, he wears a

lion's head over his own and drapes the lion's
paws over his chest. This lion king made a
bad emperor (ruled A.D. 180-192). Commodus earned a reputation as a good athlete and
warrior, and a rough character. He hung out
with low-class gladiators, and even fought in
the arena himself. The fights were staged—no
one was allowed to hurt the emperor—which
meant that Commodus killed innocent people,
some of them beaten to death with his beloved Hercules club. The people hated Commodus. Commodus-the-jock was also was at
odds with his father, the previous emperor and
noted scholar and philosopher, Marcus Aurelius.

This statue dates from the late second century, a period of debauchery and decline. The emperor is self-indulgent. The gravitas
is gone, and soon the empire will follow. Examine the statue's details—the perfect curls of hair and beard, sheen of the skin, and
manicured nails. Notice also the symbols of astrology, fertility, and
abundance. While Commodus' memory was damned (remember
how he was chiseled out of the panel downstairs), somehow this
masterpiece survived.

• *As you are looking at Commodus, directly behind you is his dad, the*
Emperor...

Marcus Aurelius (c. A.D. 176)

This is the greatest surviving equestrian statue of antiquity. Marcus
Aurelius was a Roman philosopher-
emperor (ruled A.D. 161-180) known
more for his *Meditations* than his
prowess on the battlefield. His gesture is of clemency, pardoning defeated enemies. The patina of time
almost drips off him. While he has
the same fine hair and features of
his son, Commodus (see earlier), the
emperor is still working for the glory
of Rome rather than for the glory of
himself.

Christians in the Dark Ages thought that the statue's hand was raised in blessing, which probably led to their misidentifying him as Constantine, the first Christian emperor. While most pagan statues were destroyed by Christians, "Constantine" was spared. It has graced several prominent locations in medieval Rome, including the papal palace at San Giovanni in Laterano.

In 1538, this gilded bronze statue was placed in the center of the Campidoglio (directly outside the museum), and Michelangelo was hired to design the buildings around it with the statue as the centerpiece. A few years ago, the statue was moved inside and restored, while the copy you see outside today was placed on the square. (Notice that Aurelius doesn't use stirrups—an Asian invention, those newfangled devices wouldn't arrive in Europe for another 500 years.)

Also in the room are more hunks—head, hand, and a globe—of another statue of Constantine. (Or was it the Emperor Sylvestrus Stalloneus?)

• *Descend the ramp to the wall of blocks from the...*

Temple of Jupiter

This is part of the foundation of the ancient Temple of Jupiter (Giove), once the most impressive in Rome. Find the scale model of the temple (1:40) to get a sense of its size and where you stand in relation to the ruins. Imagine you're standing before a wall that has stood here, crowning the capital hill of Rome, for over 2,500 years. It is *in situ;* this part of the museum is built around this wall.

The King of the Gods resided atop Capitoline Hill in this once-classy 10,000-square-foot temple, which was perched on a podium and lined with Greek-style columns, overlooking downtown Rome. The most important rites were performed here, and victory parades through the Forum ended here. Replicas of this building were erected in every Roman city. The temple was begun by Rome's last king (the Tarquin), and its dedication in 509 B.C. marks the start of the Roman Republic.

All that remains of the temple today are these ruined foundation stones, made of volcanic tuff, an easily carved rock commonly

used in Roman construction. Although there are hundreds of these blocks here, they represent only a portion of the immense foundation, which is only a fraction of the temple itself. In its prime, the temple rose two stories above our heads. Inside stood a statue of the god of thunder wielding a lightning bolt. The temple was refurbished a number of times over the centuries, often after damage by…lightning bolts.

• *By the way, a good WC is behind the wall.*

Here's how to get to the next stop, the Tabularium: With your back to the center of the old wall, climb seven steps and go straight to the end of the hall. You'll walk through rooms lined with stone calendar tablets from around 1700, listing dates with the equivalent of city council members in office at the time. This is a good opportunity to practice deciphering Roman numerals: MDCCCVI is 1806. MCDD is 1700.

Go down the stairs you climbed earlier and continue into the basement—the piano sotteraneo. *Then cross underneath the square through the long passageway filled with ancient inscriptions (well-described in English). Near the far end, turn right and climb a set of stairs into the…*

TABULARIUM

Built in the first century B.C., these sturdy vacant rooms once held the archives of ancient Rome. The word Tabularium comes from "tablet," on which Romans wrote their laws.

The rooms offer a stunning head-on view over the Forum, giving you a more complete picture of the sprawl of ancient Rome. Belly up to the overlook. Panning left to right, find the following landmarks: Arch of Septimius Severus, Arch of Titus (in the distance), the lone Column of Phocas, the three columns of the Temple of Castor and Pollux, the three columns (closer to you) of the Temple of Vespasiano, and the eight columns of the Temple of Saturn.

Now do an about-face and look up to see a huge white hunk of carved marble, an overhang from Temple of Vespasiano. Wander around. Appreciate the towering vaulted ceiling and ancient Roman engineering. While some say Rome was built of marble, that's not quite true. The Romans invented concrete. They baked thin bricks to make their giant buildings, then faced them with marble veneer.

• *Leave the Tabularium by going back down the stairs you just climbed. Turn right (passing a low-key WC), and go up three flights of stairs. You're now on the first floor of the…*

PALAZZO NUOVO

• *From the top of the stairs, continue directly into Room VIII—the "Hall of the Gaul"—with one of the museum's most famous pieces.*

Dying Gaul

A first-century B.C. copy of a Greek original, this was sculpted to celebrate the Greeks' victory over the Galatians. Wounded in

battle, the dying Gaul holds himself upright, but barely. Minutes earlier, before he was stabbed in the chest, he'd been in his prime. Now he can only watch helplessly as his life ebbs away. His sword is useless against this last battle. With his messy hair, downcast eyes, and crumpled position, he poignantly reminds us that every victory also means a defeat.

• *The next few rooms are filled with interesting art. As you wander, take a quick look at...*

Ancient Roman Statues and Busts

In the first room, a faun—carved out of red marble—glories in grapes and life, oblivious to the loss of his penis (at least he still has his tail). The statue, found among a couple of dozen pieces in Hadrian's Villa, was skillfully restored. Check out the chandeliered ceilings in this room and elsewhere; this building is truly a *palazzo* (palace).

The next room, the large hall, features more sculpture from Hadrian's Villa (and elsewhere). Notice the Wounded Amazon, near the window, in a classic *contrapposto* pose (weight on one leg), one breast exposed so the fabric wouldn't be in the way of her archery. This is a Roman copy of a fifth-century B.C. Greek original by Polycletus.

Roll through two rooms lined with busts—the Hall of Philosophers (Socrates, Homer, Euripides, Cicero, and many more) and the Hall of Emperors (Con-

stantine's mom Helena sits center stage, resting after her journey to Jerusalem to find Christ's cross). In this 3-D yearbook of ancient history, there are few labels. The only purple-chested bust is Caracalla. Infamous for his fervent brutality, he instructed his portraitists to stress his meanness. Directly across on the lower shelf, the smallest bust—of Emperor Gordiano (ruled A.D. 238-244)—is one of the finest of late antiquity. His expression shows the concern and consternation of a ruler whose empire is in decline. In this room you can find classic expressions of confidence, brutality, and anguish—human drama through the ages. Before leaving, sample the delicate elegance of ancient Roman hairstyles for women.

• *Enter the hallway, turn right, and start down the hall. The small octagonal room on your left contains one of the museum's treasures.*

Capitoline Venus

This is a Roman copy of a fourth-century B.C. Greek original by the master Praxiteles. Venus, leaving the bath, is suddenly aware that someone is watching her. As she turns to look, she reflexively covers up (nearly). Her blank eyes hold no personality or emotion. Her fancy hairstyle is the only complicated thing about her. She is simply beautiful—generically erotic.

• *Head to the last room on the left before the stairs. Displayed on the wall is the...*

Mosaic of Doves

Four doves perch on the rim of a bronze bowl as one drinks water from the bowl. Minute bits make up this small, exquisite work. Found in the center of a floor in one of the rooms in Hadrian's

Villa, this second-century A.D. mosaic was based on an earlier work done, of course, by the Greeks.

We all know that ancient Rome was grand. But the art in this museum tells us that its culture was refined as well. Before leaving, walk slowly around this last room, looking into the eyes of the characters who were the real foundation of ancient Rome.

• *To exit, head down the stairs to the ground floor, and follow signs to the* uscita. *If you checked a bag, cross the courtyard to retrieve it.*

ST. PETER-IN-CHAINS TOUR

San Pietro in Vincoli

Michelangelo—the world's greatest sculptor—died having failed to complete his greatest work, the tomb of Pope Julius II. Today, you can visit the powerful remains of that unfinished masterpiece, including the famous statue of Moses, housed in a historic church that also contains Peter's chains.

Orientation

Cost: Free.

Hours: Daily April-Sept 8:00-12:30 & 15:00-19:00, until 18:00 in winter.

Dress Code: Modest dress is required.

Getting There: The church is a 10-minute uphill walk north of the Colosseum. From the Colosseo Metro stop, take the escalator just inside the station exit (following *S. Pietro in Vincoli* signs), then work your way slowly uphill. There's also a staircase 50 yards east of the station. For a shorter walk, use the Cavour Metro stop; from that station, go downhill on Via Cavour a half-block, then climb the steep pedestrian staircase called Via di San Francesco di Paola, which leads right to the church. If asking for directions, say "San Pietro in Vincoli" (sahn pee-AY-troh een VEEN-koh-lee). From the outside, St. Peter-in-Chains' rounded arches and columns look more like a Renaissance loggia than a church.

Information: Tel. 06-9784-4950.

Length of This Tour: Allow 30 minutes.

Photography: Generally, photos without flash are allowed in Rome's churches. Bring €1 coins to light Moses and the tomb.

Eating: See the recommended eateries listed on page 400. Several simple dining options are also near the Cavour Metro stop, along Via Leonina.

The Tour Begins

• *In the far-right corner of the church, you'll find a wall full of marble statues. In the center sits...*

Michelangelo's *Moses* (1515)

Moses has just returned from meeting face-to-face with God. Now he senses trouble back home. Slowly he turns to see his followers worshipping a golden calf. As his anger builds, he glares at them. His physical strength is symbolic of his moral and spiritual fortitude as a leader of his people. His powerful left leg tucks under and tenses, as he's just about to spring up out of his chair and punish the naughty Children of Israel with the Ten Commandments under his arm. Enjoy the cascading beard, one of the greatest in art history.

And if he did stand up, this statue would be 13 feet tall, nearly the height of Michelangelo's famous *David*. This Charlton Heston-

with-horns is interesting in photographs...and awe-inspiring when confronted in person. His bare, muscular arms exude power. Michelangelo completed the statue after practicing for four years painting the seated prophets on the Sistine ceiling.

Like other Michelangelo statues, *Moses* is both at rest (seated) and in motion (his tensed leg, turning head, and nervous fingers). This restlessness may reflect Michelangelo's Neo-Platonic belief that the soul is the claustrophobic prisoner of the body. Or it's the statue itself fighting to emerge from the stone around it. A fanciful legend says that Michelangelo, frustrated at trying to bring God's statue into existence, hit *Moses* with his hammer (causing the scar on *Moses'* right knee), imploring, "Now, speak!"

The horns are the crowning touch. In medieval times, the Hebrew word for "rays of light" (halo) was mistranslated as "horns." Michelangelo knew better but wanted to give the statue an air of *terribilità*, a kind of scary charisma possessed by Moses, Pope Julius II...and Michelangelo. This Moses radiates the smoldering *terribilità* of a borderline-abusive father.

The Tomb Today

In 1542, remnants of the tomb project were brought to the St. Peter-in-Chains church and pieced together by Michelangelo's assistants.

The Tomb of Pope Julius II

Moses sits on the bottom level of a three-story marble wall filled with statues. This is a puny, cobbled-together version of what was to have been a grand tomb for Pope Julius II.

In 1505, Pope Julius II hired young Michelangelo to build his tomb, a huge monument to be placed in St. Peter's Basilica. An excited Michelangelo sketched designs for a three-story wedding-cake mountain of marble studded with 48 statues and bronze reliefs, and topped with a huge statue of the egomaniacal pope. *Moses* was to have been placed on an upper level on the right-hand corner, looking away from the monument.

Michelangelo traveled to Carrara, selected 100 tons of marble for the project, and started working. Then Julius changed his mind. He ordered Michelangelo to paint the Sistine Chapel instead. Michelangelo knocked it off in a mere four years so that he could return to his true masterwork. Michelangelo would spend 40 years of his life working in fits and starts on the tomb. But when Julius died (1513), the funding for the project petered out, and Michelangelo eventually moved on to other things. Julius was buried in a simple grave in St. Peter's Basilica at the Vatican.

What we see today is a far cry from the original design, which was to have been fully three-dimensional and five times as big. Some of the best statues ended up elsewhere, such as the *Prisoners* in Florence and the *Slaves* in the Louvre. Though the assistants had Michelangelo's original instruction manual, they were trying to assemble it with most of the parts missing.

Moses and the Louvre's *Slaves* are the only statues Michelangelo personally completed for the project. Flanking *Moses* are the Old Testament sister-wives of Jacob, Leah (to our right) and Rachel, both begun by Michelangelo but probably finished by pupils. On the second story, a Madonna and Child stand above a reclining, thoughtful-looking Pope Julius II on a coffin.

The sheer variety of decoration we see here gives us a glimpse of the tomb's original scope—nearly 50 statues laced together with Pompeii-esque garlands and proto-Baroque scrolls.

Michelangelo went to his grave thinking that he'd wasted the best years of his life on the tomb. Today, we can only reconstruct it in our minds, imagining a monument intended to exceed (according to Giorgio Vasari) "every ancient or imperial tomb ever made."

The Church

Founded in 440, it's one of Rome's oldest, built to house Peter's chains. Though the church was greatly changed in 1475, the 20 Doric columns flanking the wide nave are from the original church. The central ceiling painting (c. 1700) shows the chains—with their miraculous curative powers in action—healing someone possessed by demons, on the steps of St. Peter's Basilica at the Vatican.

• *On the altar is a gold-and-glass case, containing what tradition claims to be...*

Peter's Chains

There are actually two different sets of chains, linked together. One set is said to have held Peter when he and Paul were in the Mamertine Prison in Rome (near the Forum). The other dates from when Herod jailed Peter in Jerusalem (Acts 12; see the scene frescoed on the left wall of the apse). During the night, "Peter was sleeping between two soldiers, bound with chains, while sentries were guarding the doors. And behold, an angel of the Lord appeared and a light shone in the cell. The angel struck Peter on the side and woke him, saying, 'Get up quickly.' And the chains fell off his hands." The angel led Peter, who thought he was dreaming, out of the prison to safety. (Raphael's depiction of this is in the Vatican Museum.)

In the waning days of ancient Rome, the Jerusalem chains ended up here as a gift from the Eastern empress to her son-in-law, the Western emperor (as depicted in the fresco on the right wall of the apse).

According to tradition, when the Jerusalem chains arrived and were paired with the Mamertine chains, the two sets—chink!—joined together miraculously.

JEWISH GHETTO WALK

North Bank of the Tiber

For centuries, Rome's Jewish ghetto—even while a site of relentless persecution—has showcased the undying pride and solidarity of a tight-knit community. Built in 1555 on the banks of a frequently flooded bend of the Tiber River, the ghetto was the forced home of the Roman Jewish population for more than 300 years, between the Counter-Reformation (16th century) and Italian unification (1870). Though most of the old ghetto has been torn down, you can still find a few reminders of the Roman Jews' storied past and lively present.

Orientation

Length of This Walk: Allow about 30 minutes, plus an additional hour or more if you tour the synagogue and visit the museum.

When to Go: If you want to visit the synagogue and museum, go any day but Saturday, when they're closed.

Getting There: The Jewish ghetto was—and Rome's main synagogue still is—on the east bank of the Tiber, near the Isola Tiberina ("Island in the Tiber") and the ancient ruins of the Theater of Marcellus (Teatro di Marcello). It's a three-minute walk from Largo Argentina.

Synagogue and Jewish Museum: €11 ticket covers both, includes one-hour audioguide for museum and guided tour of synagogue; mid-June-mid-Sept Sun-Thu 10:00-19:00, Fri 10:00-16:00, shorter hours off-season, closed Sat year-round; last entry 45 minutes before closing, on Lungotevere dei Cenci, tel. 06-6840-0661, www.museoebraico.roma.it. Modest dress is required. The only way to visit the synagogue (if you're not there for a prayer service) is with a **tour** (included in admis-

In the Ghetto

The word "ghetto" is Italian, first used in Venice in the 1600s to describe the part of town where Jews lived—near the copper foundry (*geto* was the word for foundry). Initially the term meant only Jewish neighborhoods, but as the word spread through Europe and beyond, it was used generically to mean any neighborhood where a single ethnic group is segregated.

sion, English tours usually at :15 past the hour, 30 minutes, check schedule at ticket counter).

Tours: The museum conducts walking tours of the Jewish ghetto at least once a day Sun-Fri (€8, usually at 13:15, no tours on Sat). Ask for the schedule at the museum entry and sign up at least 30 minutes before the tour departure time (minimum of three required).

Local guide Micaela Pavoncello is uniquely equipped to guide visitors through the neighborhood her family has lived in for generations (€130/2 hours, occasionally offers group tours—check website for Ghetto Tour, tel. 328-863-8128, www.jewishroma.com, info@jewishroma.com.

You can also download this chapter as a free Rick Steves **audio tour** (see page 8).

Eateries: Near the end of this tour, you'll find a Jewish bakery and the recommended Sora Margherita, offering traditional Roman and Jewish fare. The restaurant hides on a square a block from the end of this tour (Sept-May daily 12:30-15:00, also dinner Mon and Wed-Sat 20:00-23:30; June-mid-Aug Mon-Fri 12:30-15:00 & 20:00-23:30, closed Sat-Sun; closed second half of Aug; Piazza delle Cinque Scole 30; see page 389).

BACKGROUND

Today, of Italy's 35,000 Jews, nearly half call Rome home. Jews here have a uniquely Roman style of worship and even preserve remnants of their own Judaic-Roman dialect. That's because, unlike most of the world's Jewish people, Roman Jews are neither

Sephardic (descended from Spain) nor Ashkenazi (descended from Eastern Europe). Italy's Jews came directly from the Holy Land before the Diaspora, first arriving in Rome in the second century B.C. as esteemed envoys (hoping to establish business ties) and then, after Rome

invaded Judaea in the first century A.D., as POWs sold into slavery. These first Jews lived, like other foreigners, outside the city—across the river, in Trastevere.

The Romans favored the Jews because they were well-networked throughout the empire, they didn't push their religion on others, and most important, they paid their taxes. But with the fall of the Roman Empire, the status of Jews declined. As Christianity enveloped Rome, the state denied Jews their full rights as citizens, and once the pope became literally the king of Rome, the Church enforced laws that limited the spread of the Jewish faith (such as no proselytizing, no new synagogues, no intermarriage). The severity of these laws varied from pope to pope. Through most of the Middle Ages, the standing of Rome's Jews fluctuated, but for the most part they prospered and were often held in high regard as physicians, businessmen, and confidants of popes. The community in Trastevere was even allowed to spill across to the opposite bank of the Tiber.

Then, in 1492, Spain expelled its Jews, with similar removals following in other European countries. Rome's Jewish population doubled, swelling with refugees. By the 1500s, the Catholic Counter-Reformation—begun to combat rising Protestantism—turned its attention to anything deemed a "heresy" or simply not Catholic, including Judaism. In 1555, Pope Paul IV forcibly moved all of Rome's Jews into the undesirable flood zone inside a bend of the Tiber River, creating a ghetto of some 4,000 Jews packed into a miserable seven acres of mucky land. There they lived—in cramped conditions, behind a wall, with a curfew—for three centuries. They could go out by day, but had to return before the gates were locked at night. Jews were forced to wear yellow scarves and caps, and were prohibited from owning property or holding good jobs. During Carnevale (Mardi Gras), they were forced to parade down Via del Corso while Christians lined the streets and shouted insults. Through this long stretch of oppression, the synagogue was the only place Jews could feel respected and dignified. It's no wonder such loving attention was given to the Jewish tools of worship.

Rome's Jews enjoyed a little boost in freedom when Napoleon occupied the city (1805-1814) and after the ghetto walls were torn down in 1848. But it was only after Italian unification in 1870—when a secular government replaced the religious rule of the Vatican—that the ghetto's inhabitants were granted full rights and citizenship. When Rome became the country's capital, the city—ashamed of its shoddy Jewish quarter—destroyed the old ghetto and modernized the district, giving it the street plan we see today.

Then came the rise of fascism. Even though Mussolini wasn't rabidly anti-Semitic, he instituted a slew of anti-Jewish laws as he allied himself more strongly with Hitler. When Mussolini was de-

Jewish Ghetto Walk

SAN CARLO

To Largo Argentina & Pantheon

Piazza Cairoli

VIA ARENULA

S. M. PIANTO

TURTLE FOUNTAIN

Piazza Mattei

Vicolo Costaguti

WALK ENDS

VIA REGINELLA

ERMANNO TEDESCHI GALLERY

PALAZZO MATTEI

VIA M. CAETANI

VIA DEI FUNARI

VIA DI SANT' AMBROGIO

S. ANGELO PESCH.

S. CATERINA FUNARI

To Capitoline Hill & Forum

VIA DEI DELFINI

TRIB. CAMP.

VIA MONTANARA

TEMPIO

CATALANA

SCHOOL

Piazza delle Cinque Scole

GHETTO

VIA DEL PORTICO D'OTTAVIA

SANT' ANGELO

VIA DEL FORO PICARIO

SYNAGOGUE & MUSEUM

RUINS

To Capitoline Hill & Forum

VIA TEATRO MARCELLO

#23 Ⓑ

LUNGOTEVERE DEI CENCI

TEATRO DI MARCELLO

100 Meters

100 Yards

PONTE FABRICIO

LUNG. PIERLEONI

RUINS

Ⓑ #23

SAN NICOLA

HOSPITAL

Isola Tiberina

Piazza San Bart.

SAN BARTOLOMEO

WALK BEGINS

Tiber

PONTE CESTIO

LUNGOTEVERE DELL' ANGUILLARA

River

TRASTEVERE

Ⓑ #23

JEWISH GHETTO

❶ Ponte Fabricio
❷ Synagogue & Jewish Museum
❸ Santa Maria della Pietà
❹ Largo 16 Ottobre 1943
❺ Portico d'Ottavia
❻ Via del Portico d'Ottavia

❼ Turtle Fountain
❽ Sora Margherita Rest.
❾ Jewish Bakery
❿ Carmelite Convent
⓫ Hotel Arenula
⓬ Fast-Food Stands & Fonzie Burgers

posed and the Nazis occupied Rome late in the war, the ghetto community was suddenly in even greater danger. Of the 13,000 ghetto dwellers, 2,000 were sent off to concentration camps. Only a handful came back.

A measure of healing and reconciliation came with Pope John Paul II, who took a special interest in fostering relations with the Jewish community. It was John Paul II who finally acknowledged that the Church should have intervened more forcefully to defend the Jews during the Holocaust. He was also the first pope in history to enter a synagogue (here in this neighborhood in 1986—described later on this walk).

The Walk Begins

• *Start at the north end of Ponte Fabricio, which connects central Rome with the Isola Tiberina and the neighborhood of Trastevere. You'll see the big synagogue with its square dome. The former ghetto consists of the synagogue and the several blocks behind it.*

❶ Ponte Fabricio

Ponte Fabricio is nicknamed Ponte Quattro Capi ("Bridge of the Four Heads") for its statues of the two-faced pagan god Janus.

In ancient times, it was called Pons Judaeorum ("Jews' Bridge") because foreigners, immigrants, and Jews—who weren't allowed to live in central Rome—would commute across this bridge to get into town. Some 30,000 Jews once lived in a thriving community in Trastevere. Look down at the river. The embankment was only built in the late 19th century. Before then, this was the worst flood zone along the Roman riverbank—just right for a ghetto for the politically powerless.

• *With your back to the river, at your left is the...*

❷ Synagogue (Sinagoga) and Jewish Museum (Museo Ebraico)

In the 16th century, when Pope Paul IV forced the Jews to reside within a walled ghetto, the center was this synagogue. When Rome

became the capital of the newly unified Italy in 1870, Jews regained their civil rights and were free to live anywhere in the city. The ghetto was essentially demolished, replaced with the modern blocks you see today.

The Jews were initially offered better real estate for their synagogue, but chose instead to rebuild here, on the original site. This new "Great Synagogue" was built in a remarkable three years (completed 1904) with the enthusiastic support of the entire Roman community. This is where Pope John Paul II made his historic visit in 1986.

Enter the synagogue from the back (the side farthest from the river). The admission price includes the museum entrance and a guided synagogue visit.

Inside the **Great Synagogue,** take in the impressive dome, which is square to distinguish it from a Christian church. Ponder the inside of the dome, painted with the colors of the rainbow—symbolic of God's promise to Noah that there would be no more floods. The stars on the ceiling recall God's pledge that Abraham's descendants would flourish and be as many as the stars in the sky. Architects designed the structure in the Art Nouveau style, with a dash of Tiffany. The sandy color tones are a reminder of the community's desert heritage. You'll also get a brief tour of the older, smaller **Spanish Synagogue**—which once stood on a nearby square but was moved in 1932 to the ground floor of this building.

The **museum** tells the story of Roman Jews and shows off historically significant artifacts described in English. You'll see second-century B.C. reliefs with Jewish symbols, finely worked Judaica (religious items), and other relics of the Jewish past. As the Jews were not allowed to be craftsmen during the ghetto period, they commissioned many of the pieces you'll see from some of the finest artists of that time—the same artists working for the kings and aristocracy of Europe—making these items historically and artistically significant. The museum also shows a film (subtitled in English) about the Nazi occupation of Rome, along with a display of artifacts and documentation from this dark time.

• *Look for the beige church across from the Ponte Fabricio...*

❸ Santa Maria della Pietà (a.k.a. San Gregorio)

When the ghetto was a walled-in town, Catholics built churches at each gate to try and spread their faith to the Jews. Notice the Hebrew script under the crucifix. It quotes the Jewish prophet Isaiah—"All day long, I have stretched out my hands to a disobedient and faithless nation that has lost its way" (Isaiah 65:2)—but misuses the quote to give it an anti-Semitic twist.

• *Walk away from the river behind the synagogue toward the ancient Roman ruins. The small square in front of the ruins is called...*

❹ Largo 16 Ottobre 1943

This square is named for the day when Nazi trucks parked here and threatened to take the Jews to concentration camps unless the community came up with 50 kilos (110 pounds) of gold in 24 hours.

Everyone, including many non-Jewish Romans, tossed in their precious gold, and the demand was met. The Nazis took the gold—and later, they took the Jews as well.

• *The big ancient ruin is the...*

❺ Portico d'Ottavia

This monumental gateway—with columns supporting a triangular pediment—was built by soon-to-be-emperor Augustus. Once

flanked by temples and libraries, the passageway served as a kind of cultural center. After Rome's fall, the portico housed a thriving fish market. In the eighth century, the ruins of the portico were incorporated into the Church of Sant'Angelo in Pescheria. For centuries, this Christian church was packed every Saturday with Jews—forced by decree to listen to Christian sermons. Notice the faded bits of Christian fresco on the arch. Locals love to tell of the poor old woman who refused to sell her land and now owns this priceless bit of real estate that includes the ancient arch (at #25 under the arch).

To the left is the main drag of today's ghetto. We'll head there soon, but first go to the bridge on your right to look down at the level of the street in Roman times. Just past the bridge, the former oratory is now a wedding-registry shop. (If it's open, pop in and see who's getting married when and admire their choice of table setting.)

From the bridge, you get a fine view of Teatro di Marcello, which predates and inspired the design of the Colosseum. It is one of three major theaters in the ancient city, able to accommodate more than 10,000 spectators. In the Middle Ages, it was converted into a fortress, and today those are luxury apartments on the top level. Beyond it is the tree-capped Capitoline Hill. Take a short detour down the ramp into the archaeological area and enjoy the hodgepodge of ancient fragments scattered about.

• *Now walk back around the arch to the ghetto's main street...*

❻ Via del Portico d'Ottavia

This main drag is a fine place to get a taste of yesterday's ghetto and today's Rome. From the start (near the Roman arch), look down the street. On the left is a new building from 1911. On the right, in the distance, is the only surviving line of old ghetto building-fronts. Imagine today's street as it was then: much narrower (as it is at the far end today). Walking down the street, notice kosher restaurants proudly serving *carciofi* (artichokes, which "only Jewish grandmothers can cook properly"; *carciofi alla giudia* are deep-fried) and shops of fine, locally produced Judaica. You might see posters for community events, a few men wearing yarmulkes, and political graffiti, both pro- and anti-Israel. The Palestine Liberation Organization attacked this area in 1982, and a police presence still lingers.

After a block, you reach the center of the district. Look right, down **Via di Sant'Ambrogio,** to see an old surviving street, and

imagine the dense population, flood muck, and squalor of the past.

At #7 on the main drag (first door on the right after Via di Sant'Ambrogio), the **Ermanno Tedeschi Gallery** generally features modern Israeli artists. At its door is a mezuzah (prayer capsule)—residents touch it as they come and go to recall their Jewish creed.

The pedestrianized **square** ahead is where older folks hang out together and shoot the breeze, sometimes even bringing their favorite chairs from home. Though the Jewish community has long since dispersed all over Rome, most Roman Jews continue to spend time in this neighborhood to enjoy the strong feeling of community that survives. The big tan building (on the left) houses the Jewish school.

This neighborhood has become trendy, and apartment prices are now beyond the means of most members of the Jewish community. Ironically, only the richest Jews could afford to relocate after 1870—and because the poor had to stay, their descendants have enjoyed healthy real-estate appreciation.

Opposite the big school, take a one-block detour down **Via della Reginella,** where you'll find some fun shops (see page 420 in the Shopping in Rome chapter) as well as some poignant artifacts. In front of #10 (on the right), you'll see several small bronze plaques in the shape of cobbles, memorials to members of the community arrested in these homes during the Nazi occupation. At #28, notice where the six-floor buildings end and more elegant and spacious (but no taller) three-floor buildings begin...marking the end of the ghetto.

In the square (Piazza Mattei) at the end of the lane is a fun ❼

turtle fountain—an old Mannerist work, later embellished with turtles by Bernini. It's said that Bernini cared about the Jews and honored them with the symbol of a turtle—an ancient creature that carries all its belongings on its back.

Cross the square and jog right down Via de' Funari ("Street of the Ropemakers") to the big brick **Palazzo Mattei** (#31, on the left). Step inside to notice that very often in Rome, austere, uninviting exteriors contain unexpected treasures, like this building's courtyard. Encrusted with the family's collection of ancient Roman sculpture, it was intended to show off their wealth and refined taste. Today, the palazzo is home to the Italian Center for American Studies.

Returning to the main drag (Via del Portico d'Ottavia), continue to Bar Toto (the second café on the right), where you'll see a

slot in the wall—a ghetto-era charity box for orphans that still accepts donations for worthy causes. The ancient relief above the box marks the home of a big shot who, at the start of the Renaissance age (before the ghetto's establishment in 1555), plugged this chunk of ancient Rome into his facade for prestige. A bit farther down, at the kosher gelato shop at #1, another bit of ancient marble depicts a lion attacking a gazelle (at the far-right end of the big building). Up above, notice the big stone inset with a Latin inscription dated

"MMCCXX." Yes, that's 2220, and no, it's not from the future. It marks the years since the birth of Rome in 753 B.C.—meaning it was carved in A.D. 1467.

At the next intersection (Piazza Costaguti), stand in the white decorative square in the cobbles. The recommended restaurant, **❽**

Sora Margherita, is located on the car-filled square—Piazza delle Cinque Scole—30 yards to the left, at #30 (described on page 389). On your right, at the corner, is a traditional **❾ Jewish bakery.** Go inside to check out the braided challah bread, cheesecakes, almond paste-filled macaroons, and "Jewish pizzas" (*pizza Ebraica*)—like little €3 fruitcakes, but better tasting. Just beyond that, the curving, white-columned structure is part of a former **❿ Carmelite convent.** Imagine the outrage of the Jewish community when the Church built a convent and a Catholic school here in the ghetto to preach to their children, and forced locals to attend Mass.

Pop into the tunnel-like alleyway next to it, and—in the evocative little courtyard—imagine the tight conditions of thousands of Jews living in this small seven-acre area. Then head back to the main square and consider how times are much better today.

ST. PETER'S BASILICA TOUR

Basilica San Pietro

St. Peter's is the greatest church in Christendom. It represents the power and splendor of Rome's 2,000-year domination of the Western world. Built on the memory and grave of the first pope, St. Peter, this is where the grandeur of ancient Rome became the grandeur of Christianity.

Orientation

Cost: Free entry to basilica and crypt. Dome climb—€5 if you take the stairs all the way up, or €7 to ride an elevator partway (to the roof), then climb to the top of the dome (cash only; for details, see "Dome Climb," later). Treasury Museum—€7 (€3 audioguide).

Hours: The **church** is open daily April-Sept 7:00-19:00, Oct-March 7:00-18:30. It closes on Wednesday mornings during papal audiences.

The **dome** *(cupola)* is open to climbers daily from 8:00; if you're climbing the stairs all the way up, the last entry time is 17:00 (16:00 Oct-March); if you're riding the elevator partway up, you can enter until 18:00 (17:00 Oct-March).

The **Treasury Museum** is open daily April-Sept 8:00-18:40, Oct-March 8:00-18:10, last entry 30 minutes before closing.

The **crypt** *(grotte)* is open daily 9:00-16:00.

Avoiding Lines: The security-checkpoint lines can get quite long, and there's no surefire way to avoid them. Note that the checkpoint can switch locations; it's typically on the north side of the square, but can be closer to the church or tucked under the south colonnade.

St. Peter's is often accessible directly from the Sistine

Chapel inside the Vatican Museum—a great time-saving trick, but unfortunately not a reliable one (for details, see page 232).

Avoid the worst crowds by visiting before 10:00. If you come after 16:00, crowds are also light, sunbeams can work their magic, and the 17:00 Mass (on Mon-Sat) in the apse fills the place with spiritual music. The downside to visiting late: After about 16:00, the crypt is closed, and the area around the altar is often roped off to prepare for Mass. (For a detailed Mass schedule, see "Church Services," below.)

Dress Code: No shorts, above-the-knee skirts, or bare shoulders (this applies to men, women, and children). Attendants strictly enforce this dress code, even in hot weather. Carry a cover-up, if necessary.

Getting There: Take the Metro to Ottaviano, then walk 10 minutes south on Via Ottaviano. The #40 express bus drops off at Piazza Pio, next to Castel Sant'Angelo—a 10-minute walk from St. Peter's. The more crowded bus #64 is convenient for pickpockets and stops just outside St. Peter's Square to the south (get off the bus after it crosses the Tiber, at the first stop past the tunnel; backtrack toward the tunnel and turn left when you see the rows of columns). Bus #492 heads through the center of town, stopping at Largo Argentina, and gets you near Piazza Risorgimento (get off when you see the Vatican walls). A taxi from Termini train station to St. Peter's costs about €11.

Information: The TI on the left (south) side of the square is excellent (Mon-Sat 8:30-18:15, closed Sun, free Vatican and church map). Tel. 06-6988-1662, www.vatican.va (select "Basilicas and Papal Chapels" at the bottom of the page).

Church Services: Mass is performed daily, generally in Italian and in just a small area of the vast church: usually either in the south (left) transept, the Blessed Sacrament Chapel (on right side of nave), or the apse (where the 17:00 service is held Mon-Sat). Sunday morning Mass tends to take place at the main altar. Typical schedule: Mon-Sat at 8:30, 10:00, 11:00, 12:00, and 17:00 (in Latin, in the apse); and on Sun and holidays at 9:00, 10:30 (in Latin), 11:30, 12:15, 13:00, 16:00, 17:00 (vespers), and 17:45.

Tours: The Vatican TI conducts free 1.5-hour **tours of St. Peter's** (depart from TI Mon-Fri at 14:15, plus Tue and Thu at 9:45, confirm schedule at TI, tel. 06-6988-1662). **Audioguides** can be rented near the checkroom (€5 plus ID, for church only, daily 9:00-17:00). Or you can download this chapter as a free Rick Steves **audio tour** (see page 8).

To see St. Peter's original grave, you can take a *Scavi*

ST. PETER'S

Vatican City

This tiny independent country of little more than 100 acres, contained entirely within Rome, has its own postal system, armed guards, helipad, mini-train station, and radio station (KPOP). It also has two huge sights: St. Peter's Basilica (with Michelangelo's *Pietà*) and the Vatican Museum (with the Sistine Chapel). Politically powerful, the Vatican is the religious capital of 1.2 billion Roman Catholics. If you're not a Catholic, become one for your visit.

The pope is both the religious and secular leader of Vatican City. For centuries, locals referred to him as "King Pope." Italy and the Vatican didn't always have good relations. In fact, after unification (in 1870), when Rome's modern grid plan was built around the minuscule Vatican, it seemed as if the new buildings were designed to be just high enough so no one could see the dome of St. Peter's from street level. Modern Italy was created in 1870, but the Holy See didn't recognize it as a country until 1929, when the pope and Mussolini signed the Lateran Pact, giving sovereignty and a few nearby churches to the Vatican.

Like every European country, Vatican City has its own versions of the euro coin (with a portrait of Pope Francis I and, before him, of Benedict XVI). You're unlikely to find one in your pocket, though, as they're snatched up by collectors before falling into circulation.

Post Offices: The Vatican postal service is famous for its stamps, which you can get from offices on St. Peter's Square (next to TI or between the columns just before the security checkpoint) or in the Vatican Museum (Mon-Sat 9:00-18:00, closed Sun). A "post bus" is often parked somewhere on St. Peter's Square, selling stamps (also open Sun, when the other post offices are closed). Vatican stamps are good throughout Rome, but to use the Vatican's mail service, you need to mail your cards from the Vatican itself; write your postcards ahead of time, or use the conveniently located writing table in the post office near the TI. (Note that the Vatican won't mail cards with Italian stamps.)

Seeing the Pope: Your best chances for a sighting are on Sunday or Wednesday. The pope usually gives a blessing at noon on Sunday from his apartment on St. Peter's Square (except in August, when he speaks at his summer residence at Castel Gandolfo, 25 miles from Rome, reachable by train from Rome's Termini train station; and in July, when he doesn't do it at all). St. Peter's is easiest (just show up) and, for most, enough of a "visit." Those interested in a more formal appearance (though not more intimate) can get a ticket for the Wednesday general audience (at 10:30) when the pope, arriving in his Popemobile, greets and blesses the crowds at St. Peter's from a canopied platform on the square. (While the usual winter location has been the 7,000-seat Paolo VI Auditorium, next to St. Peter's Basilica, that venue has proven too small for Francis' crowds, so he does it in the square, even in cold weather.) If you only want to see St. Peter's—but not the pope—avoid these times (the basilica closes during papal audiences and crowds are substantial).

For the Wednesday audience, while anyone can observe from a distance, you need a (free) ticket to get close to the papal action (and get a seat). To find out the pope's schedule and request a ticket, see www.vatican.va (click on "Prefecture of the Papal Household") or call 06-6988-3114. Since the papal schedule is set only a month or two in advance, you may not be able to request tickets farther out.

The American Catholic Church in Rome, Santa Susanna, lets you order tickets online (free, no booking fee but donations appreciated) for the Wednesday general audience. Pick up your reserved tickets, or check for last-minute availability at the church the Tuesday before the audience between 17:00 and 18:30—consider staying for the 18:00 English Mass (Via XX Settembre 15, near recommended Via Firenze hotels, Metro: Repubblica, tel. 06-4201-4554—charming Rosanna speaks English, details at www.santasusanna.org).

Probably less convenient—unless you're already at the basilica—is getting a ticket at St. Peter's Square from the Vatican guards at their station at the bronze doors (open Tue officially at 15:00—but can open as early as 9:00—and closes when church does; last-minute tickets may be available Wed morning—just join the line). It's under the "elbow" of Bernini's colonnade, on the right side of the square as you face the basilica (see the map on page 212); you can also try the St. Anne's entrance around the right side of the Vatican complex (on the way to the Vatican Museum).

On Wednesday morning, you'll need to clear security (no big bags; lines tend to move more quickly on the side of the square farthest away from the Metro stop), be dressed appropriately (no short shorts or tank tops—long pants or knee-length skirts are safest), and then join the masses eagerly awaiting the pope's appearance. To get a seat, it's smart to be there a couple of hours early (bring reading material). If you just want to see the pope and get a good photo, you can show up later (though still at least 45 minutes early) and take your place in the standing-room section in the back half of the square. At around 10:00, after the names of attending pilgrim groups have been announced, the Popemobile appears, winding through the adoring crowd along the corridors blocked off by cloth-covered wooden fences (position yourself strategically). The multilingual message begins at 10:30 and lasts for about an hour; you're free to go at any time.

While many visitors come hoping for a more intimate audience, private audiences ended with the death of Pope John Paul II.

ST. PETER'S

(excavations) tour into the **Necropolis** (€13, 1.5 hours, ages 15 and older only, no photos). Book at least two months in advance by phone (tel. 06-6988-5318), email (scavi@fsp.va), or fax (06-6987-3017), following the detailed instructions at www.vatican.va (search for "Excavations Office"); no response means they're booked.

To walk through the **Vatican Gardens,** you must book a guided tour at the very least a day in advance at http://biglietteriamusei.vatican.va. No response means they're booked (€32, 2 hours, usually daily except Wed and Sun, includes entry to Vatican Museum; tours start at 9:30 or 10:00 at Vatican Museum tour desk). On rare occasions, same-day tickets are available at the St. Peter's TI.

Dome Climb: You can take the elevator or stairs to the roof (231 steps), then climb another 323 steps to the top of the dome. The entry to the elevator is just outside the basilica, on the north side of St. Peter's (near the secret exit from the Sistine Chapel). Look for signs to the *cupola*. Note that the dome-climb exit may not be located near the entrance—if you're not climbing the dome with your travel partner, ask about the current exit spot before you split up. For more on the dome, see the end of this chapter.

Length of This Tour: Allow one hour, plus another hour if you climb the dome (or a half-hour to the roof). If you have less time, skip the crypt and the dome climb, but at least stroll the nave, glance up at the dome and down at the marker of St. Peter's tomb. Don't miss the *Pietà*.

Baggage Check: The free bag check (mandatory for bags larger than a purse or daypack) is outside the basilica (to the right as you face the entrance) just inside the security checkpoint.

Services: WCs are to the right and left on St. Peter's Square (just outside the security checkpoint and exit), near baggage storage down the steps on the right side of the entrance, and on the roof. **Drinking fountains** are at the obelisk and near the WCs. **Post offices** are next to the TI and just outside the security checkpoint (you can buy stamps and postcards and drop them into a postbox).

Starring: Michelangelo, Bernini, St. Peter, a heavenly host...and, occasionally, the pope.

BACKGROUND

Nearly 2,000 years ago, St. Peter's oval-shaped "square" was the site of Nero's Circus—a huge, cigar-shaped Roman chariot racecourse. The Romans had no marching bands, so for halftime entertainment they killed Christians. This persecuted minority was forced to fight wild animals and gladiators, or they were simply crucified.

Old & New St. Peter's

❶ Current Site of Obelisk
❷ Original Site of Obelisk
❸ Peter's Crucifixion Site
❹ Peter's Tomb (Under Altar)

.... Roman Circus Course
(1st Century A.D.)

- - - - Old St. Peter's
(A.D. 329-1500)

——— New St. Peter's
Bramante & Michelangelo
(1506-1590)

▨ Maderno's Extension
(1607-1614)

▢ Bernini's Colonnade
(1656-1667)

100 Meters
100 Yards

ST. PETER'S

Some were tarred up, tied to posts, and burned—human torches to light up the evening races.

One of those killed here, in about A.D. 65, was Peter, Jesus' right-hand man, who had come to Rome to spread the message of love. At his own request, Peter was crucified upside down, because he felt unworthy to die as his master had. His remains were buried in a cemetery located where the main altar in St. Peter's is today. For 250 years, these relics were quietly and secretly revered.

Peter had been recognized as the first "pope," or bishop of Rome, from whom all later popes claimed their authority as head of the Church. When Christianity was finally legalized in 313, the Christian emperor Constantine built a church on the site of Peter's martyrdom. "Old St. Peter's" lasted 1,200 years (A.D. 329-1500).

By the time of the Renaissance, Old St. Peter's was falling apart and was considered unfit to be the center of the Western

Church. The new, larger church we see today was begun in 1506 by the architect Bramante. He was succeeded by Michelangelo and a number of other architects, each with his own designs. Later, Carlo Maderno took Michelangelo's Greek cross-shaped church and lengthened it, adding a long nave. As the construction proceeded, the new church rose around the old one (see diagram on preceding page). The project was finally finished 120 years later, and Old St. Peter's was dismantled and carried out of the new church. (A few bits survive from the first church: the central door, some columns in the atrium, eight spiral columns around the tomb from the Jerusalem Temple, the venerated statue of Peter, and Michelangelo's *Pietà*.)

Michelangelo designed the magnificent dome. Unfortunately, although it soars above St. Peter's, it's barely visible from the center of the square because of Maderno's extended nave. To see the entire dome, you'll need to step outside the open end of the square, where in the 1930s Benito Mussolini opened up the broad boulevard, finally letting people see the dome that had been hidden for centuries by the facade. Though I don't make a habit of thanking fascist dictators, in this case I'll make an exception: *"Grazie, Benito."*

The Tour Begins

• *Ideally, you should head out to the obelisk at the center of the square and read this. But let me guess—it's 95 degrees outside, right? OK, find a shady spot under one of these stone sequoias. If the pigeons have left a clean spot, sit on it.*

St. Peter's Square

St. Peter's Square, with its ring of columns, symbolizes the arms of the church welcoming everyone—believers and non-believers—with its motherly embrace. It was designed a century after Michelangelo by the Baroque architect Gian Lorenzo Bernini, who did much of the work that we'll see inside. Numbers first: 284 columns, 56 feet high, in stern Doric style. Topping them are Bernini's 140 favorite saints, each 10 feet tall. The "square" itself is actually elliptical, 660 by 500 feet (roughly the same dimensions as the Colosseum). Though large, it's designed like a saucer, a little higher around the edges, so that even when full of crowds (as it often is), it allows those on the periphery to see above the throngs.

The **obelisk** in the center is 90 feet of solid granite weighing

St. Peter's Square

Vatican Gardens

#64 Ⓑ

ELEVATOR TO DOME

ST. PETER'S BASILICA

SISTINE CHAPEL (VATICAN MUSEUM)

SWISS GUARD

ATRIUM

WALL

EXIT

ENTRANCE

EXIT FROM SISTINE (SOMETIMES CLOSED)

BAGGAGE CHECK, AUDIOGUIDES & WC

🛈 WC
VATICAN POST & BOOKSTORE

PAPAL APARTMENTS (TOP STORY, RIGHT)

SWISS GUARD (POPE TICKETS)

OBELISK

VATICAN POST & WC

"CENTRO DEL COLONNATO" ■ PLAQUE

ST. ANNE'S ENTRANCE

St. Peter's Square

VATICAN WALL

VIA DI PTA. ANGELICA

BERNINI'S COLONNADE

To Ottaviano Metro (10 min) & Vatican Museum Entrance (15 min)

Not to Scale

- - - Route to church entrance

CONCILIAZIONE
VIA DELLA

Ⓣ

Piazza Pio XII   Piazza Pio XII

WALL

To Castel Sant'Angelo & Bus #40

ST. PETER'S

more than 300 tons. It once stood about 100 yards from its current location, in the center of the circus course (to the left of where St. Peter's is today). Think for a second about how much history this monument has seen. Originally erected in Egypt more than 2,000 years ago, it witnessed the fall

of the pharaohs to the Greeks and then to the Romans. Then the emperor Caligula moved it to imperial Rome, where it stood impassively watching the slaughter of Christians at the racecourse and the torture of Protestants by the Inquisition (in the yellow-and-rust building just outside the square, to the left of the church). Today, it watches over the church, a reminder that each civilization builds on the previous ones. The puny cross on top reminds us that Christian culture has cast but a thin veneer over our pagan origins.

• *Now venture out across the burning desert to the obelisk, which provides a narrow sliver of shade.*

As you face the church, the gray building to the right at two o'clock, rising up behind Bernini's colonnade, is, at least officially,

the **pope's abode.** The last window on the right of the top floor is the papal bedroom; to the left of that window is the study window, where popes have often appeared to greet the masses. Pope Francis, however, seems to prefer a more modest residence that houses other cardinals, and has so far expressed no interest in moving into these grand apartments (upon first seeing them, he exclaimed, "You could fit 300 people in here!").

On more formal occasions (which you may have seen on TV), the pope appears from the church itself, on the small balcony above the central door.

The Sistine Chapel is just to the right of the facade—the small gray-brown building with the triangular roof, topped by an antenna. The tiny chimney—the pimple along the roofline midway up the left side—is where the famous smoke signals announce the election of each new pope (an extension is added on for the occasion). If the smoke is black, a two-thirds majority hasn't been reached. White smoke means a new pope has been selected.

Walk to the right, five pavement plaques from the obelisk, to one marked *Centro del Colonnato*. From here, all of Bernini's columns on the right side line up. The curved Baroque square still pays its respects to Renaissance mathematical symmetry.

• *Climb the gradually sloping pavement past crowd barriers and the security checkpoint.*

On the square are two entrances to Vatican City: one to the left of the facade, and one to the right in the crook of Bernini's "arm" (the same entrance that hands out pope-viewing tickets). Guarding this small but powerful country's border crossing are the mercenary guards from Switzerland. You have to wonder if they really know how to use those pikes. Their colorful uniforms are said to have been designed by Michelangelo, though he was not known for his sense of humor.

• *Continue up, passing the huge statues of St. Paul (with his two-edged sword) and St. Peter (with his bushy hair and keys). Along the way, you'll pass by the dress-code enforcers and a gaggle of ticked-off tourists in shorts. Enter the atrium (entrance hall) of the church.*

The Basilica

The Atrium

The atrium is itself bigger than most churches. The huge white columns on the portico date from the first church (fourth century). Five famous bronze doors lead into the church.

Made from the melted-down bronze of the original door of Old St. Peter's, the central door was the first Renaissance work in Rome (c. 1450). It's only opened on special occasions. The panels (from the top down) feature Jesus and Mary, Paul and Peter, and (at the bottom) how each was martyred: Paul decapitated, Peter crucified upside down.

The far-right entrance is the **Holy Door,** opened only during Holy Years. On Christmas Eve every 25 years, the pope knocks three times with a silver hammer and the door opens, welcoming pilgrims to pass through. After Pope John Paul II opened the door on Christmas Eve, 1999, he bricked it up again with a ceremonial trowel a year later to wait another 24 years. (A plaque above the door fudges a bit for effect: It says that Pope "IO-ANNES PAULUS II" opened the door in the year "MM"—2000—and closed it in "MMI.") On the door itself, note the crucified Jesus and his shiny knees, polished by pious pilgrims who touch them for a blessing.

• *Now for one of Europe's great "wow" experiences. Enter the church. Gape for a while. But don't gape at Michelangelo's famous Pietà (on the right). I'll cover it later in the tour. I'll wait for you at the round maroon pavement stone on the floor near the central doorway.*

St. Peter's Basilica

Not to Scale

Vatican Gardens

APSE

MAIN ALTAR

DOME ENTRANCE

VATICAN MUSEUM (GRAY AREA)

TREASURY MUSEUM

SISTINE CHAPEL

EXIT FROM SISTINE CHAPEL (SOMETIMES CLOSED)

N A V E

Courtyard

A T R I U M

SWISS GUARDS

EXIT   **ENTRANCE**

STEPS

AUDIOGUIDES, **WC** & BAGGAGE CHECK

PLATFORM

- - Route to church entrance

St. Peter's Square

ST. PETER'S

1 Holy Door
2 Charlemagne's Coronation Site
3 Extent of Original "Greek Cross" Plan
4 St. Andrew Statue; View of Dome; Crypt Entrance
5 St. Peter Statue (with Kissable Toe)
6 Pope John XXIII
7 Main Altar (under Bernini's Canopy & over Peter's Tomb)

8 BERNINI – Dove Window & Throne of St. Peter
9 St. Peter's Crucifixion Site
10 RAPHAEL – Mosaic Copy of The Transfiguration
11 MICHELANGELO – Pietà
12 Tomb of Pope John Paul II
13 Treasury Museum
14 Blessed Sacrament Chapel
15 Dome Entrance

The Church: An Overview

This church is appropriately huge. Size before beauty: The golden window at the far end is two football fields away. The dove in the window has the wingspan of a 747 (OK, maybe not quite, but it *is* big). The church covers six acres. The babies at the base of the pillars along the main hall (the nave) are adult-size. The lettering in the gold band along the top of the pillars is seven feet high. Really.

The church has a capacity of 60,000 standing worshippers (or 1,200 tour groups).

The church is huge and it feels huge, but everything is designed to make it seem smaller and more intimate than it really is. For example, the statue of St. Teresa near the bottom of the first pillar on the right is 15 feet tall. The statue above her near the top looks the same size, but is actually six feet taller, giving the impression that it's not so far away. Similarly, the fancy bronze canopy over the altar at the far end is as tall as a seven-story building. That makes the great height of the dome seem smaller.

Looking down the nave, we get a sense of the splendor of ancient Rome that was carried on by the Catholic Church. The floor plan, with a central aisle (nave) flanked by two side aisles, is based on that of ancient Roman basilicas—large halls built to accommodate business and legal meetings. In fact, many of the stones used to build St. Peter's were scavenged from the ruined law courts of ancient Rome.

On the floor near the central doorway is a round slab of **porphyry stone** in the maroon color of ancient Roman officialdom. This is the spot where, on Christmas night in A.D. 800, the French king Charlemagne was crowned Holy Roman Emperor. Even in the Dark Ages, when Rome was virtually abandoned and visitors reported that the city had more thieves and wolves than decent people, its imperial legacy made it a fitting place to symbolically establish a briefly united Europe.

St. Peter's was very expensive to build and decorate. The popes financed it by selling "indulgences," allowing the rich to buy forgiveness for their sins from the Church. This kind of corruption inspired an obscure German monk named Martin Luther to rebel and start the Protestant Reformation.

The ornate, Baroque-style interior decoration—a riot of marble, gold, stucco, mosaics, columns of stone, and pillars of light—was part of the Church's "Counter" Reformation. Baroque art and architecture served as cheery propaganda, impressing followers with the authority of the Church and giving them a glimpse of the heaven that awaited the faithful.

• *Now, walk straight up the center of the nave toward the altar.*

From Pope to Pope

When a pope dies—or retires—the tiny, peaceful Vatican stirs from its timeless slumber and becomes headline news. Millions of people converge on Vatican City, and hundreds of millions around the world watch anxiously on TV.

JOAN. PAULUS II

A deceased pope's body is displayed in state in front of the main altar in St. Peter's Basilica. Thousands of pilgrims line up down Via della Conciliazione, waiting for one last look at their pope. On the day of the funeral, hundreds of thousands of mourners, dignitaries, and security personnel gather in St. Peter's Square. The pope's coffin is carried out to the square, where a eulogy is given.

Most popes are laid to rest in the crypt below St. Peter's Basilica, near the tomb of St. Peter and among shrines to many other popes. Especially popular popes—such as John Paul II or John XXIII—eventually find a place upstairs, inside St. Peter's itself.

While the previous pope is being laid to rest, cardinals representing Catholics around the globe descend on Rome to elect a new pope. Once they've assembled, the 100-plus cardinals, dressed in crimson, are stripped of their mobile phones, given a vow of secrecy, and locked inside the Sistine Chapel. This begins the "conclave" (from Latin *cum clave,* with key). As they cast votes with paper ballots, the used ballots are burned in a stove temporarily set up inside the Sistine Chapel. The smoke rises up and out the tiny chimney, visible from St. Peter's Square. Black smoke means they haven't yet agreed on a new pope.

Finally, the anxious crowd in St. Peter's Square looks up to see a puff of white smoke emerging from the Sistine Chapel. The bells in St. Peter's clock towers ring out gloriously (a new tradition) confirming that, indeed, a pope has been elected. The crowd erupts in cheers, and Romans watching on their TVs hail taxis to hurry to the square.

On the balcony of St. Peter's facade, the newly elected pope steps up and raises his hands, as thousands chant *"Viva il Papa."* A cardinal introduces him to the crowd, announcing his newly chosen name. "Brothers and sisters," the cardinal says in several languages, *"habemus papam."* "We have a pope."

"Michelangelo's Church"—The Greek Cross

The plaques on the floor show where other, smaller churches of the world would end if they were placed inside St. Peter's: St. Paul's Cathedral in London (Londinense), Florence's Duomo, and so on.

You'll also walk over circular golden grates. Stop at the second one (at the third pillar from the entrance). Look back at the entrance and realize that if Michelangelo had had his way, this whole long section of the church wouldn't exist. The nave was extended after his death.

Michelangelo was 71 years old when the pope persuaded him to take over the church project and cap it with a dome. He agreed, intending to put the dome over Donato Bramante's original "Greek Cross" floor plan, with four equal arms. In optimistic Renaissance times, this symmetrical arrangement symbolized perfection— the orderliness of the created world and the goodness of man (who was created in God's image). But Michelangelo was a Renaissance Man in Counter-Reformation times. The Church, struggling against Protestants and its own corruption, opted for a plan designed to impress the world with its grandeur—the Latin cross of the Crucifixion, with its nave extended to accommodate the grand religious spectacles of the Baroque period.

• Continue toward the altar, entering "Michelangelo's church." Park yourself in front of the statue of St. Andrew to the left of the altar, the guy holding an X-shaped cross. Like Andrew, gaze up into the dome, and also like him, gasp. (Never stifle a gasp.)

Note: The entrance to the crypt is usually down the stairs beside the statue of St. Andrew. Save the crypt for later, though, as it exits outside the basilica (see the end of this tour for more details).

The Dome

The dome soars higher than a football field on end, 448 feet from the floor of the cathedral to the top of the lantern. It glows with light from its windows, the blue and gold mosaics creating a cool, solemn atmosphere. In this majestic vision of heaven (not painted by Michelangelo), we see (above the windows) Jesus, Mary, and a ring of saints, rings of more angels above them, and, way up in the ozone, God the Father (a blur of blue and red, unless you have binoculars).

When Michelangelo died (1564), he'd completed only the drum of the dome—the circular base up as far as the windows—but the next architects were guided by his designs.

Listen to the hum of visitors echoing through St. Peter's and reflect on our place in the cosmos: half animal, half angel, stretched between heaven and earth, born to live only a short while, a bubble of foam on a great cresting wave of humanity.

• *But I digress.*

Peter's Remains

The base of the dome is ringed with a gold banner telling us in massive blue letters why this church is so important. According to Catholics, Peter was selected by Jesus to head the church. The banner in Latin quotes from the Bible where Jesus says to him, "You are Peter *(Tu es Petrus)* and upon this rock I will build my church, and to you I will give the keys of the kingdom of heaven" (Matthew 16:18). (Every quote from Jesus to Peter found in the Bible is written out in seven-foot-tall letters that continue around the entire church.)

Peter was the first bishop of Rome. His prestige and that of the city itself made this bishopric more illustrious than all others, and Peter's authority has supposedly passed in an unbroken chain to each succeeding bishop of Rome—that is, the 250-odd popes that followed.

Under the dome, under the bronze canopy, under the altar, some 23 feet under the marble floor, rest the bones of St. Peter, the "rock" upon which this particular church was built. You can't see the tomb, but go to the railing and look down into the small, lighted niche below the altar with a box containing bishops' shawls—a symbol of how Peter's authority spread to the other churches. Peter's tomb (not visible) is just below this box.

Are they really the bones of Jesus' apostle? According to a papal pronouncement: definitely maybe. The traditional site of his tomb was sealed when Old St. Peter's was built on it in A.D. 326, and it remained sealed until 1940, when it was opened for archaeological study. Bones were found, dated from the first century, of a robust man who died in old age. His body was wrapped in expen-

Peter, the "Fisher of Men"

According to the Bible, Peter was a fisherman who was chosen by Christ to catch sinners instead. This "fisher of men" had human weaknesses that have endeared him to Christians. He was the disciple who tried to walk on water—but failed. In another incident, he impetuously cut off a man's ear when soldiers came to arrest Jesus. And he even denied knowing Christ, to save his own skin. But Jesus chose him anyway and gave him his nickname—Rock (in Latin: *Petrus*).

Legends say that Peter came to the wicked city of Rome after Jesus' death to spread the gospel of love. He may have been imprisoned in the Mamertine Prison near the Roman Forum (see page 38), and other stories claim he had a vision of Christ along the Appian Way (described on page 325). Eventually, Peter's preaching offended the Nero administration. Christ's fisherman was arrested, crucified upside down, and buried here, where St. Peter's now stands.

sive cloth. A third-century tag artist had graffitied a wall near the tomb with "Peter is here," indicating that early visitors thought this was Peter's tomb. Does that mean it's really Peter? Who am I to disagree with the pope? Definitely maybe.

If you line up the cross on the altar with the dove in the window, you'll notice that the niche below the cross is just off-center compared with the rest of the church. Why? Because Michelangelo built the church around the traditional location of the tomb, not the actual location—about two feet away—discovered by modern archaeology.

Back in the nave sits a bronze **statue of Peter** under a canopy. This is one of a handful of pieces of art that were in the earlier church. In one hand he holds the keys, the symbol of the authority given him by Christ, while with the other hand he blesses us. He's wearing the toga of a Roman senator. It may be that the original statue was of a senator and that the bushy head and keys were added later to make it Peter. His big right toe has been worn smooth by the lips of pilgrims and foot-fetishists. Stand in line and kiss it, or, to avoid foot-and-mouth disease, touch your hand to your lips, then rub the toe. This is simply an act of reverence with no legend attached, though you can make one up if you like.

• *Circle to the right around the statue of Peter to find another stop that's*

Pope Francis I

In 2013, Cardinal Jorge Bergoglio of Argentina became Francis I, the Catholic Church's 266th pope. His election represented three "firsts" that signaled a new direction for the Church: As the first pope from the Americas, Francis personifies the 80 percent of Catholics who now live outside Europe. As the first Jesuit pope—from the religious order known for education—he stands for spreading the faith through teaching, not aggression. And as the first Francis—named after St. Francis of Assisi—he calls to mind that medieval friar's efforts to return a corrupt church to simple Christian values of poverty and humility. In addition, Francis is in the unusual position of sharing the world stage with "pope emeritus" Benedict XVI (who, rather than dying in office, decided to retire).

Born in 1936, Francis grew up in Buenos Aires in a family of working-class Italian immigrants. He spent his 20s in various jobs (chemist, high-school teacher) before entering the priesthood. Ordained a Jesuit in 1969, he would rise to become archbishop of Buenos Aires. He first came to the world's attention in 2005, when he was the runner-up in the election of Pope Benedict. While bishop in Argentina, he worked in the worst of slums, and denounced (though some say not loudly enough) Argentina's bloody dictatorship during the Dirty War of the 1970s.

Now a resident of Vatican City, Francis lives simply, staying in a Vatican guesthouse rather than the official papal apartments overlooking St. Peter's Square. He reportedly eats leftovers. When people talk about Francis, the word that comes up time and again is "dialogue." He's known for listening to every point of view, whether mediating between dictators and union lead-

popular among pilgrims: the lighted glass niche with the red-robed body of...

Pope John XXIII

Pope John XXIII, whose papacy lasted from 1958 to 1963, is nicknamed "the good pope." He is best known for initiating the landmark Vatican II Council (1962-1965) that instituted major reforms, bringing the Church into the modern age. The Council allowed Mass to be conducted in the vernacular rather than in Latin. Lay people were invited to participate more in services, Church leadership underwent some healthy self-criticism, and a spirit of ecumenism flourished. Pope John was a populist, referring to people as "brothers and sisters"...a phrase popular today amongst popes. In 2000, during the beatification process (a stop on the way to sainthood), Church authorities checked his body, and it was surprisingly fresh. So they moved it upstairs, put it behind glass, and now old Catholics who remember him fondly enjoy another stop on their St. Peter's visit.

ers, sitting down with the Orthodox Patriarch, celebrating Rosh Hashanah with Jews, visiting a mosque, or speaking well of atheists. In Argentina, he was often seen sharing *mate* (the national tea) with people of every stripe. At the Vatican, his management style stresses the collegiality of the cardinals. He speaks a number of languages, including fluent Italian—the language of his parents and of the Vatican. As Francis himself has pointed out, the original Latin word for pope—*"pontifex"*—literally means "bridge builder."

But Francis is not a liberal. He strongly defends traditional Catholic beliefs. No one expects major changes under Francis in the Church's positions on abortion, gay marriage, contraception, or the celibate, male-only priesthood. He inherited a Catholic Church with many problems: financial shenanigans, charges that they've protected pedophile priests, and alleged blackmailing of gay priests (as exposed in the "Vatileaks" scandal). And though the Catholic religion is growing worldwide, its home base—Europe—is becoming increasingly secular.

As pope, Francis has made it clear that he wants the Church to focus less on money and power, and more on the poor and the outcast. Francis is skeptical of globalization, worldliness, and unchecked capitalism, with the economic inequality they bring. One of his favorite Christian rituals is to literally kneel down before the poor, sick, or imprisoned, and wash their feet. Francis' personal credo, *"Miserando atque elignedo,"* focuses on how God shows "mercy"—*miserando*—and compassion by forgiving sinners and helping the downtrodden.

ST. PETER'S

We'll visit the tomb of another beloved pope—John Paul II—near the end of this tour.

The Main Altar

The main altar beneath the dome and canopy (the white marble slab with cross and candlesticks) is used only when the pope himself says Mass. He sometimes conducts the Sunday morning service when he's in town, a sight worth seeing. I must admit, though, it's a little strange being frisked for weapons at the door to the holiest place in Christendom.

The tiny altar would be lost in this enormous church if it weren't for Gian Lorenzo Bernini's seven-story bronze canopy (God's "four-poster bed"), which "extends" the altar upward and reduces the perceived distance between floor and ceiling. The corkscrew columns echo the marble ones that surrounded the altar/tomb in Old St. Peter's. Some of the bronze used here was taken and melted down from the ancient Pantheon. On the marble base of the columns are three bees on a shield, the symbol of the Barberini family, who commissioned the work and ordered the raid on the Pantheon.

Starting from the column to the left of the altar, walk clockwise around the canopy. Notice the female faces on the marble

bases, about eye level above the bees. Someone in the Barberini family was pregnant during the making of the canopy, so Bernini put the various stages of childbirth on the bases. Continue clockwise to the last base to see how it came out.

Bernini (1598-1680), the Michelangelo of the Baroque era, is the man most responsible for the interior decoration of the church. The altar area was his masterpiece, a "theater" for holy spectacles. Bernini did: 1) the bronze canopy; 2) the dove window in the apse, surrounded by bronze work and statues; 3) the massive statue of lance-bearing St. Longinus ("The hills are alive..."), which became the model for the other three statues in the niches around the main altar; 4) much of the marble floor decoration; and 5) the balconies above the four statues, incorporating some of the actual corkscrew columns from Old St. Peter's, said to have been looted by the Romans from the Temple of Herod (called "Solomon's Temple") in Jerusalem. Bernini, the father of Baroque, gave an impressive unity to an amazing variety of pillars, windows, statues, chapels, and aisles.

• *Approach the apse, the front area with the golden dove window.*

The Apse

Bernini's **dove window** shines above the smaller front altar used for everyday services. The Holy Spirit, in the form of a six-foot-

high dove, pours sunlight onto the faithful through the alabaster windows, turning into artificial rays of gold and reflecting off swirling gold clouds, angels, and winged babies. During a service, real sunlight passes through real clouds of incense, mingling with Bernini's sculpture. This is the epitome of Baroque—an ornate, mixed-media work designed to overwhelm the viewer.

Beneath the dove is the centerpiece of this structure, the so-called Throne of St. Peter, an oak chair built in medieval times for a king. Subsequently, it was encrusted with tradition and encased in bronze by Bernini as a symbol of papal authority. Statues of four early Church Fathers support the chair, a symbol of how bishops should support the pope in troubled times—times like the Counter-Reformation.

Remember that St. Peter's is a church, not a museum. In the apse, Mass is said daily for pilgrims, tourists, and Roman citizens alike (for Mass times, see "Church Services" on page 205). Wooden confessional booths are available in the north transept (to the right of the main altar) for Catholics to tell their sins to a listening ear and receive forgiveness and peace of mind (daily, usually mornings and late afternoons—see website). The faithful renew their faith, and the faithless gain inspiration. Look at the light streaming through the windows, turn and gaze up into the dome, and quietly contemplate your deity (or lack thereof).

• *To the left of the main altar is the south transept. It may be roped off for worship, but anyone can step past the guard if you're there "for prayer." At the far end, left side, find the dark "painting" of St. Peter crucified upside down.*

South Transept—Peter's Crucifixion Site

This marks the exact spot (according to tradition) where Peter was killed 1,900 years ago. Peter had come to the world's greatest city to preach Jesus' message of love to the pagan, often hostile Romans. During the reign of Emperor Nero, he was arrested and brought to Nero's Circus so all of Rome could witness his execution. When the authorities told Peter he was to be crucified just like his Lord, Peter said, essentially, "I'm not worthy" and insisted they nail him on the cross upside down.

The Romans were actually quite tolerant of other religions, but they required their conquered peoples to worship the Roman emperor as a god. For most religions, this was no problem, but monotheistic Christians refused to worship the emperor even when they were burned alive, crucified, or thrown to the lions. Their bravery,

optimism in suffering, and message of love struck a chord among slaves and members of the lower classes. The religion started by a poor carpenter grew, despite occasional pogroms (persecution of minorities) by fanatical emperors. In three short centuries, Christianity went from a small Jewish sect in Jerusalem to the official religion of the world's greatest empire.

This and all the other "paintings" in the church are actually mosaic copies made from thousands of colored chips the size of your little fingernail. Smoke and humidity would

Bernini Blitz

Nowhere is there such a conglomeration of works by the flamboyant genius who remade this church—and the city—in the Baroque style. Here's your scavenger-hunt list. You have 20 minutes. Go!

1. St. Peter's Square: design and statues
2. Constantine equestrian relief (right end of atrium)
3. Decoration (stucco, gold leaf, marble, etc.) of side aisles (flanking nave)
4. Tabernacle (the temple-like receptacle) inside Blessed Sacrament Chapel
5. Much of the marble floor throughout church
6. Bronze canopy (baldacchino) over main altar
7. St. Longinus statue (holding a lance) near main altar
8. Balconies (above each of the four statues ringing main altar) with corkscrew columns
9. Dove window, bronze sunburst, angels, "Throne," and Church Fathers (in apse)
10. Tomb of Pope Urban VIII (far end of apse, right side)
11. Tomb of Pope Alexander VII (between apse and left transept, over a doorway, with the gold skeleton smothered in jasper poured like maple syrup)

Bizarre...Baroque...Bernini.

damage real paintings. Around the corner on the right (heading back toward the central nave), pause at the copy of Raphael's huge "painting" (mosaic) of *The Transfiguration*, especially if you won't be seeing the original in the Vatican Museum.

• *Back near the entrance of the church, in the far corner, behind bulletproof glass, is the sculpture everyone has come to see, the...*

Pietà

Michelangelo was 24 years old when he completed this *pietà* (pee-ay-TAH) of Mary with the body of Christ taken from the cross. It was Michelangelo's first major commission (by the French ambassador to the Vatican), done for Holy Year 1500.

Pietà means "pity." Michelangelo, with his total mastery of the real world, captures the sadness of the moment. Mary cradles her crucified son in her lap. Christ's lifeless right arm drooping down lets us know how heavy this corpse is. His smooth skin is accented by the rough folds of Mary's robe. Mary tilts her head down, looking at her dead son with sad tenderness. Her left hand turns upward, asking, "How could they do this to you?"

Michelangelo didn't think of sculpting as creating a figure, but as simply freeing the God-made figure from the prison of marble around it. He'd attack a project like this with an inspired passion, chipping away to find what God had placed inside.

The bunched-up shoulder and rigor-mortis legs show that Michelangelo learned well from his studies of cadavers. But realistic as this work is, its true power lies in the subtle "unreal" features. Life-size Christ looks childlike compared with larger-than-life Mary. Unnoticed at first, this accentuates the subconscious impression of Mary enfolding Jesus in her maternal love.

Mary—the mother of a 33-year-old man—looks like a teenager, emphasizing how she was the eternally youthful "handmaiden" of the Lord, always serving him, even at this moment of supreme sacrifice. She accepts God's will, even if it means giving up her son.

The statue is a solid pyramid of maternal tenderness. Yet within this, Christ's body tilts diagonally down to the right and Mary's hem flows with it. Subconsciously, we feel the weight of this dead God sliding from her lap to the ground.

At 11:30 on May 23, 1972, a madman with a hammer entered St. Peter's and began hacking away at the *Pietà*. The damage was repaired, but that's why there's now a shield of bulletproof glass in front of the sculpture.

This is Michelangelo's only signed work. The story goes that he overheard some pilgrims praising his finished *Pietà,* but attributing it to a second-rate sculptor from a lesser city. He was so enraged that he grabbed his chisel and chipped "Michelangelo Buonarroti of Florence did this" in the ribbon running down Mary's chest.

On your right (covered in gray concrete with a gold cross) is the inside of the Holy Door. It won't be opened until Christmas Eve, 2024, the dawn of the next Jubilee Year. If there's a prayer inside you, ask that St. Peter's will no longer need security checks or bulletproof glass when this door is next opened.

• *In the chapel to the left is the...*

Tomb of Pope John Paul II

John Paul II (1920-2005) was one of the most beloved popes of recent times. During his papacy (1978-2005), he was the highly visible face of the Catholic Church as it labored to stay relevant in an increasingly secular world. The first non-Italian pope in four centuries, he traveled widely. He was the first pope to visit a mosque and a synagogue. He oversaw the fall of communism in his native Poland. He survived an assassination attempt, and he publicly endured his slow decline from Parkinson's disease with great stoicism.

When John Paul II died in 2005, hundreds of thousands lined up outside the church, waiting up to 24 hours to pay their respects. At his funeral in St. Peter's Square, the crowd began chanting "*Santo subito, santo subito!*" insisting he be made a saint *(santo)* right now *(subito)*. They didn't have to wait long—he was sainted in April 2014, just nine years after his death...light speed by Vatican standards.

The tomb has no monument—just a simple stone slab with the inscription *Ioannes Paulus PP. II (1920-2005)*. John Paul II lies beneath a painting of the steadfast St. Sebastian—the martyr who calmly suffered the slings and arrows of outrageous Romans. Sebastian was John Paul's favorite saint. There's also a plaque in the floor on the opposite side of the church honoring the man. Of 250-plus popes, two have been given the title "Great." That elite group may soon grow by 50 percent, as there's talk of calling him "John Paul the Great."

Other Sights at the Church
Crypt (Grotte or Tombe)
Visitors can go down to the foundations of Old St. Peter's, containing tombs of popes and memorial chapels. The crypt entrance is usually beside the statue of St. Andrew, to the left of the main altar. Stairs lead you down to the floor level of the previous church, where you'll pass the sepulcher of Peter. This lighted niche with an icon is not Peter's actual tomb, but part of a shrine that stands atop Peter's tomb. Nearby is the chapel where Pope John Paul II was buried before being moved upstairs in 2011. Next are the tombs of past popes, including the traditionalist Paul VI (1897-1978), who suffered reluctantly through the church's modernization. Finally, you can see a few column fragments from Old St. Peter's (a.k.a. "Basilica Costantiniana"). Continue your one-way visit until it spills you out, usually near the checkroom.

The walk through the crypt is free and quick (15 minutes)—but you won't see St. Peter's original grave unless you take a *Scavi* (excavations) tour (see "Tours" on page 205).

Treasury Museum (Museo-Tesoro)
The museum, located on the left side of the nave near the altar, contains the room-size tomb of Sixtus IV by Antonio Pollaiuolo, a big pair of Roman pincers used to torture Christians, an original

corkscrew column from Old St. Peter's, and assorted jewels, papal robes, and golden reliquaries—a marked contrast to the poverty of early Christians.

Blessed Sacrament Chapel (Capella di Santissimo Sacramento)

You're welcome to step through the metalwork gates into this oasis of peace reserved for prayer and meditation. It's located on the right-hand side of the church, about midway to the altar.

Up to the Dome (Cupola)

A good way to finish a visit to St. Peter's is to go up to the dome for the best view of Rome anywhere. The entrance to the dome is along the right side of the church, but the line begins to form out front, at the church's right door (as you face the church).

There are two levels: the rooftop of the church and the very top of the dome. Climb (for €5) or take an elevator (€7) to the first level, on the church roof just above the facade. From the roof, you have a commanding view of St. Peter's Square, the statues on the colonnade, Rome across the Tiber in front of you, and the dome itself—almost terrifying in its nearness—looming behind you. (This view from the roof may only be accessible after you've descended from the dome—the route changes.)

From here, you can also go inside to the gallery ringing the interior of the dome, where you can look down inside the church. Notice the dusty top of Bernini's seven-story-tall canopy far below. Study the mosaics up close—and those huge letters! It's worth the elevator ride for this view alone.

From this level, if you're energetic, continue all the way up to the top of the dome. The staircase actually winds between the outer shell and the inner one. It's a sweaty, crowded, claustrophobic 15-minute, 323-step climb, but worth it. The view from the summit is great, the fresh air even better. Admire the arms of Bernini's colonnade encircling St. Peter's Square. Find the big, white Victor Emmanuel Monument, with the two statues on top; and the Pantheon, with its large, light, shallow dome. The large rectangular building to the left of the obelisk is the Vatican Museum, stuffed with art. Survey the Vatican grounds, with its mini-train system and lush gardens. Look down into the square at the tiny pilgrims buzzing like electrons around the nucleus of Catholicism.

VATICAN MUSEUM TOUR

Musei Vaticani

The glories of the ancient world displayed in a lavish papal palace, decorated by the likes of Michelangelo and Raphael...the Musei Vaticani. A conglomerate of many submuseums, the Vatican Museum holds some of the greatest art anywhere. Unfortunately, many tourists see these collections only as an obstacle between them and the grand finale, the Sistine Chapel. True, this huge, confusing, and crowded megamuseum can be a jungle—but with this book as your vine, you should swing through with ease, enjoying the highlights and getting to the Sistine just before you collapse.

With the Fall of Rome (A.D. 476), the Catholic ("universal") Church became the great preserver of civilization, collecting artifacts from cultures dead and dying. Renaissance popes (15th and 16th centuries) collected most of what we'll see, using it as furniture to decorate their palace (today's museum). Combining the classical and Christian worlds, they found the divine in the creations of man.

We'll concentrate on classical sculpture and Renaissance painting. But along the way (and there's a lot of along-the-way here), we'll stop to leaf through a few yellowed pages from this 5,000-year-old scrapbook of humankind.

The always crowded museum has an online reservation system and a website with up-to-date hours and information. Plan ahead for your visit at http://mv.vatican.va. For more on Vatican City, the small, independent country where this museum is located, see page 206.

Orientation

Cost: €16, €4 online reservation fee, free on the last Sun of each month (when it's very crowded).

Hours: Mon-Sat 9:00-18:00, last entry at 16:00 (though the official closing time is 18:00, the staff starts ushering you out at 17:30). Closed Sun, except last Sun of the month, when it's open 9:00-14:00, last entry at 12:30. May be open Fri nights May-July and Sept-Oct 19:00-23:00 (last entry at 21:30) by online reservation only—check the website; note that during evening visits, parts of the museum—including the Pinacoteca—are often closed.

The museum is closed on many holidays (mainly religious ones), including, for 2015: Jan 1 (New Year's), Jan 6 (Epiphany), Feb 11 (Vatican City established), March 19 (St. Joseph's Day), April 6 (Easter Monday), May 1 (Labor Day), June 29 (Sts. Peter and Paul), Aug 15 plus either Aug 14 or 16—it varies year to year (Assumption of the Virgin), Nov 1 (All Saints' Day), Dec 8 (Immaculate Conception), and Dec 25 and 26 (Christmas). Because changes in hours (which are notoriously irregular) and other holiday closures may occur, always check the current hours and calendar at http://mv.vatican.va.

Individual rooms may close at odd hours, especially in the afternoon. The rooms described here are usually open.

Reservations: Bypass the long ticket lines by reserving an entry time online at http://mv.vatican.va. It costs €20 (€16 ticket plus €4 booking fee, pay with credit card). It's easy. You choose your day and time, they email you a confirmation immediately, and you print out the voucher. At the Vatican Museum, bypass the ticket-buying line and queue up at the "Visitors Entrance with Online Reservations" line (to the right). Show your voucher to the guard and go in. Once inside the museum, present your voucher at a ticket window *(cassa),* either in the lobby or upstairs, and they'll issue your ticket.

When to Go: The museum is generally hot and crowded, with shoulder-to-shoulder sightseeing through much of it. There can be waits of up to two hours to buy tickets (figure about a 10-minute wait for every 100 yards in line). The best (or least-worst) time to visit is a weekday late-afternoon. The worst days are Saturdays, the last Sunday of the month (when it's free), Mondays, rainy days, and any day before or after a holiday closure. Mornings are most crowded.

More Line-Beating Tips: If you've booked a **guided tour** (see next page), you can show the guard your voucher and go right in.

You can often buy **same-day, skip-the-line tickets** (for the same €20 online price) through the TI in St. Peter's Square (to the left, as you face the basilica). Also, the Roma Cristiana tour company sells same-day tickets for a pricey €27.50 (entrances almost hourly, Opera Romana Pellegrinaggi office in front of St. Peter's Square, Piazza Pio XII 9, tel. 06-6980-6380, www.operaromanapellegrinaggi.org). If their kiosk is closed, try the nearby storefront labeled *Opera Romana Pellegrini*, just in front of the square, which also sometimes sells these tickets.

If you don't have a reservation, **try arriving after 14:00,** when crowds subside somewhat. Another good time is during the papal audience, on Wednesday at 10:30, when many tourists are at St. Peter's Square.

Make sure you get in the right line. Generally, individuals without tickets line up against the Vatican City wall (to the left of the entrance as you face it), and reservation holders (both individuals and groups) enter on the right.

Dress Code: Modest dress is required (no shorts, above-knee skirts, or bare shoulders). This dress code is strictly enforced here, at St. Peter's Basilica, and throughout Vatican City.

Getting There: The Ottaviano Metro stop is a 10-minute walk from the entrance. Bus #49 from Piazza Cavour/Castel Sant'Angelo stops at Piazza Risorgimento and continues right to the entrance. Bus #23 from Trastevere hugs the west bank of the Tiber and stops on Via Leone IV, just downhill from the entrance. Bus #492 heads from the city center past Piazza Risorgimento and the Vatican walls, and also stops on Via Leone IV. Bus #64 stops on the other side of St. Peter's Square, a 15- to 20-minute walk (facing the church from the obelisk, take a right through the colonnade and follow the Vatican Wall). Taxis are reasonable (hop in and say, "moo-ZAY-ee vah-tee-KAH-nee").

Information: At http://mv.vatican.va, you can reserve an entry time, sign up for a tour, get general info, and see which days the museum is closed. You can virtually tour the Sistine Chapel ceiling at www.vatican.va (click on "Basilicas and Papal Chapels"). Tel. 06-6988-3860 or 06-6988-1662.

As you enter the main lobby of the museum, an info desk is to your left, and TV screens list which rooms are open or closed. Bookstores are scattered throughout the museum, and many exhibits have English explanations.

Tours: A €7 **audioguide** is available at the top of the spiral ramp/ escalator (ID required). If you rent an audioguide, you lose the option of taking the shortcut from the Sistine Chapel to

St. Peter's (described later, under "Museum Strategies"), since audioguides must be returned to the museum entrance/exit.

You can download the Sistine Chapel portion of this chapter as a free Rick Steves **audio tour** (see page 8).

The Vatican offers **English tours** that are easy to book online (€32, includes admission, http://mv.vatican.va). As with individual ticket reservations, present your confirmation voucher to a guard to the right of the entrance; then, once inside, go to the Guided Tours desk (in the lobby, up a few stairs).

For a list of **private tour** companies and guides, see page 30.

Length of This Tour: Until you expire, the museum closes, or 2.5 hours pass, whichever comes first. If you're short on time, see the octagonal courtyard *(Laocoön)*, then follow the crowd flow directly to the Sistine Chapel, sightseeing along the way; skip the Etruscan Wing and the Pinacoteca. From the Sistine Chapel, head straight to St. Peter's via the shortcut, if open (see "Museum Strategies," below).

Security and Baggage Check: To enter the museum, you pass through a metal detector (no pocket knives allowed). The baggage check (to the right after security) takes only bigger bags, not day bags.

Services: The post office, with stamps that make collectors drool, is upstairs. WCs are mainly at the entrance/exit, plus a few scattered within the collection.

Museum Strategies: The museum has two exits, and you'll want to decide which you'll take before you enter. The **main exit** is right near the entrance. Use this one if you want to rent an audioguide (which you must return at the entrance) or if you plan on following this self-guided tour exactly as laid out, visiting the Pinacoteca at the end.

The other exit is a handy (but sometimes closed) **shortcut** that leads from the Sistine Chapel directly to St. Peter's Basilica (spilling out alongside the church; see map on page 234). This route saves you a 30-minute walk (15 minutes back to the Vatican Museum entry/exit, then 15 minutes to St. Peter's) and lets you avoid the often-long security line at the basilica's main entrance. If you take this route, you'll have to forgo an audioguide and skip the Pinacoteca (or tour it earlier). Officially, this exit is for Vatican guides and their groups only. However, it's often open to anyone (depending on how crowded the chapel is and how the guards feel). It's worth a shot (try blending in with a group that's leaving), but be prepared for the possibility that you won't get through.

Photography: No photos allowed in the Sistine Chapel, but photos without flash are permitted elsewhere.

Cuisine Art: A self-service cafeteria is inside, near the Pinacoteca. Smaller cafés are in the outdoor Cortile della Pigna and near the Sistine Chapel. All offer mediocre food at high prices. Cheaper choices outside the museum include the great Mercato Trionfale produce market on Via Andrea Doria, three blocks north of the entrance (head across the street, down the stairs, and continue straight). Inexpensive *pizza rustica* shops selling pizza by the slice line Viale Giulio Cesare and Via Candia, and good restaurants are nearby (see page 408).

Starring: World history, a pope's palace, Michelangelo, Raphael, *Laocoön*, the Greek masters, and their Roman copyists.

The Tour Begins

This heavyweight museum is shaped like a barbell—two buildings connected by a long hall. The entrance building covers the ancient world (Egypt, Greece, Rome). The one at the far end covers its "rebirth" in the Renaissance (including the Sistine Chapel). The halls there and back are a mix of old and new. Move quickly—don't burn out before the Sistine Chapel, near the end of this tour—and see how each civilization borrows from and builds on the previous one.

• *Leave Italy by entering the doors.*

Once you clear the security checkpoint, exchange your printed voucher (on the ground floor) or buy your ticket (upstairs). Scan your ticket at the turnstiles, then take the long escalator or spiral ramp up, up, up to a glass-covered courtyard with a view of St. Peter's dome.

Pause at the courtyard: To your right are the cafeteria and the Pinacoteca painting gallery (consider touring the Pinacoteca now if you plan to take the Sistine-to-St. Peter's shortcut at the end; for a description of the Pinacoteca, see page 261). To your left is the beginning of our tour.

• *To start our tour, go left, then take another left up a flight of stairs to reach the first-floor Egyptian rooms (Museo Gregoriano Egizio) on your right. Don't stop until you find your mummy.*

Vatican Museum Schematic

ENTRANCE & MAIN EXIT

STATUES   MAPS

EXIT TO ST. PETER'S (SOMETIMES CLOSED)

ANCIENT
EGYPT
GREECE
ROME
ETRURIA

RENAISSANCE
RAPHAEL ROOMS
SISTINE CHAPEL

ST. PETER'S

TAPESTRIES

VATICAN MUSEUM

Vatican Museum Overview

To Cipro
M

To Ottaviano
M

VIA SEBASTIANO VENIERO

VIALE VATICANO

VIA LEONE IV

VIA OTTAVIANO

B #23 & #492

Piazza del Risorgimento

VIA DI PORTA ANGELICA

B T #49

MUSEUM ENTRANCE & EXIT

WALL

ITALIAN POST

BORGO VITTORIO

VATICAN

CITY

BORGO PIO

VATICAN MUSEUM

Gardens

VIA DI PORTA ANGELICA

PAPAL APARTMENTS

To Castel Sant'Angelo

T

SISTINE CHAPEL

CAFETERIA

ELEVATOR TO DOME

CAFÉ

EXIT

ATRIUM

PAPAL TICKET PICKUP

OBELISK

Piazza Pio XII

T

VIA DELLA CONCILIAZIONE

ST. PETER'S BASILICA

St. Peter's Square

i

TREASURY MUSEUM

AUDIENCE HALL

WALL

B #64

TUNNEL

VIA PORTA CAVALLEGGERI

VIA D. FORNACI

To Civitavecchia

VIA INNOCENZO III

VIA D. STAZIONE DI SAN PIETRO

VIA D. ALCIDE DE GASPERI

- - - From obelisk to museum
entry via road is a
15-minute walk

1 Main Entrance & Exit
2 Egyptian Rooms
3 Cortile della Pigna
4 Octagonal Courtyard
5 Etruscan Wing
6 Tapestries
7 Map Gallery & View of Vatican City
8 Raphael Rooms
9 Sistine Chapel & Exit to St. Peter's (can be closed)
10 Pinacoteca

SAN PIETRO TRAIN STATION

100 Meters
100 Yards

To Termini Station

VATICAN MUSEUM

Note: Occasionally, the stairs up to Egypt are closed off, and crowds are routed through a spacious open-air courtyard, the Cortile della Pigna (see map on next page). Just keep following the masses until you reach the Apollo Belvedere *and* Laocoön *figures. Tour the museum from there to the "Sarcophagi," where you'll find the entrance to the Egyptian rooms.*

Ancient Wing

EGYPT (3000-1000 B.C.)

Egyptian art was religious, not decorative. A statue or painting preserved the likeness of someone, giving him or her a form of eternal life. Most of the art was for tombs, where they put the mummies.
• *Pass beyond the imitation Egyptian pillars to the left of the case in the center of the room, and you'll find...*

Mummies

This woman died three millennia ago. Her corpse was disembow-eled, and her organs were placed in a jar like those you see near-

by. Then the body was refilled with pitch, dried with natron (a natural sodium carbonate), wrapped in linen, and placed in a wood coffin, which went inside a stone coffin, which was placed in a tomb. (Remember that the pyramids were just big tombs.) Notice the henna job on her hair—in the next life, your spirit needed a body to be rooted to...and you wanted to look your best.

Painted inside the coffin lid is a list of what the deceased "packed" for the journey to eternity. The coffins were decorated with magical spells to protect the body from evil and to act as crib notes for the confused soul in the netherworld. In nearby cases are *shabtis*, small figurines of the deceased placed inside the tomb.
• *In the next room are...*

Egyptian Statues

Egyptian statues walk awkwardly, as if they're carrying heavy buckets, with arms straight down at their sides. Even these Roman reproductions (made for Hadrian's Villa) are stiff, two-dimensional, and schematic—the art is only realistic enough to get the job done. In Egyptian belief, a

The Ancient World

Not to Scale

BALCONY
WITH VIEW
OF ROME

WC

OCTAGONAL COURTYARD ⑤

⑥

HALL OF ANIMALS

ANIMALS

ROMAN
PINE
CONE

Cortile della Pigna

① MUMMIES

🔊 **TOUR BEGINS**

② ③

EGYPTIAN ROOMS

⑦

ROUND ROOM ⑧ ⑨

END ⑩

UP

To →
the "Long March"

AUDIO-
GUIDES

SPIRAL RAMP

GLASS-COVERED COURTYARD

From
Entrance

ESCALATOR

BOOKSTORE

To ↓
Pinacoteca &
Cafeteria

VATICAN MUSEUM

① Mummies
② Egyptian Statues
③ Gods as Animals
④ Sumerian Writing
⑤ Apollo Belvedere

⑥ Laocoön
⑦ Belvedere Torso
⑧ Hercules
⑨ Porphyry Basin
⑩ Sarcophagi

statue like this could be a stable refuge for the wandering soul of a dead person. Each was made according to an established set of proportions. Little changed over the centuries—these statues had a function, and they worked.

• *Walk through the next small room and into the curved hallway, and look for...*

Various Egyptian Gods as Animals

Before technology made humans top dogs on earth, it was easier to appreciate our fellow creatures. Egyptians saw the superiority of animals and worshipped them as incarnations of the gods. Wander through a pet store of Egyptian animal gods. In the small room, by the big window, find Anubis, a jackal in a toga. In the curved room, find the lioness, the fierce goddess Sekhmet. The clever baboon is the god of wisdom, Thoth. At the end of the curved hall on your right is Bes (the small white marble statue), the patron of pregnant women (and beer-bellied men).

• *Continue into the darkened wing and proceed to the third room (Room VIII), pausing at the glass case, which contains small, brown clay tablets.*

Sumerian Writing

Even before Egypt, civilizations flourished in the Middle East. The Sumerian culture in Mesopotamia (the ancestors of the ancient Babylonians and of today's Iraqis) invented writing in about 3000 B.C. People wrote on clay tablets by pressing into the wet clay with a wedge-shaped (cuneiform) pen. The Sumerians also rolled cylindrical seals into soft clay to make an impression that authenticated documents and marked property.

• *Pass through the next room, and then turn left, to a balcony with a view of Rome through the window. Then enter the octagonal courtyard. Find the statue of* Apollo Belvedere, *on your left as you enter.*

SCULPTURE—GREECE AND ROME (500 B.C.-A.D. 500)

This palace wouldn't be here, this sculpture wouldn't be here, and our lives would likely be quite different if it weren't for a few thousand Greeks in a small city about 450 years before Christ. Athens set the tone for the rest of the West. Democracy, theater, economics, literature, and art all flourished in Athens during a 50-year "Golden Age." Greek culture was then appropriated by Rome, and revived again 1,500 years later, during the Renaissance. The Renaissance popes built and decorated these papal palaces, re-creating the glory of the classical world.

Apollo Belvedere

Apollo, the god of the sun and of music, is hunting. He's been running through the woods, and now he spots his prey. Keeping his eye on the animal, he slows down and prepares to put a (missing)

VATICAN MUSEUM

arrow into his (missing) bow. The optimistic Greeks conceived of their gods in human form...and buck naked.

This Apollo is a Roman copy (2nd century A.D.) of a Hellenistic original that followed the style of the great Greek sculptor Praxiteles. It fully captures the beauty of the human form. The anatomy is perfect, his pose is natural. Instead of standing at attention, face-forward with his arms at his sides (Egyptian-style), Apollo is on the move, coming to rest with his weight on one leg.

The Greeks loved balance. A well-rounded man was both a thinker and an athlete, a poet and a warrior. In art, the *Apollo Belvedere* balances several opposites. He's moving, but not out of control. Apollo eyes his target, but hasn't attacked yet. He's realistic, but with idealized, godlike features. And the smoothness of his muscles is balanced by the rough folds of his cloak. The only sour note: his left hand, added in modern times. Could we try a size smaller?

During the Renaissance, when this Roman copy was discovered, it was considered the most perfect work of art in the world. The handsome face, eternal youth, and body that seems to float just above the pedestal made *Apollo Belvedere* seem superhuman, divine, and godlike, even for devout Christians.

• *In the neighboring niche to the right, a bearded old* **Roman river god** *lounges in the shade. This pose inspired Michelangelo's* Adam, *in the Sistine Chapel (coming soon). While there are a few fancy bathtubs in this courtyard, most of the carved boxes you see are sarcophagi—Roman coffins and relic holders, carved with the deceased's epitaph in picture form.*

In the next niche is...

Laocoön

Laocoön (lay-AWK-oh-wahn), the high priest of Troy, warned his fellow Trojans: "Beware of Greeks bearing gifts." The attacking Greeks had brought the Trojan Horse to the gates as a ploy to get inside the city walls, and Laocoön tried to warn his people not to bring it inside. But the gods wanted the Greeks to win, so they sent huge snakes to crush Laocoön and his two sons to death. We see them at the height of their terror, when they realize that, no matter how hard they struggle, they—and their entire race—are doomed. Laocoön's agonized face says it all: "Snakes...why'd it have to be snakes?"

The figures (carved from four blocks of marble pieced together seamlessly) are powerful, not light and graceful. The poses are as twisted as possible, accentuating every rippling muscle and bulging vein. Follow the line of motion from Laocoön's left foot, up his leg, through his body, and out his right arm (which some historians used to think extended straight out—until the elbow was dug up in the early 1900s). Goethe would stand here and blink his eyes rapidly, watching the statue flicker to life.

Laocoön was sculpted some four centuries after the Golden Age (5th-4th century B.C.), after the scales of "balance" had been tipped. Whereas *Apollo* is a balance between stillness and motion, this is unbridled motion. *Apollo* is serene, graceful, and godlike, while *Laocoön* is powerful, emotional, and gritty.

Laocoön—the most famous Greek statue in ancient Rome and considered "superior to all other sculpture or painting"—was lost for more than a thousand years. Then, in 1506, it was unexpectedly unearthed in the ruins of Nero's Golden House near the Colosseum. The discovery caused a sensation. It was cleaned off and paraded through the streets before an awestruck populace. No one had ever seen anything like its motion and emotion, having been raised on a white-bread diet of pretty-boy *Apollo*s. One of those who saw it was the young Michelangelo, and it was a revelation to him. Two years later, he started work on the Sistine Chapel, and the Renaissance was about to take another turn.

• *Leave the courtyard to the right of* Laocoön *and pause in the Hall of Animals, a jungle of beasts real and surreal. Then continue to the limbless torso in the middle of the next large hall.*

Belvedere Torso

My experience with sculpting statues ends with snowmen. But standing face-to-face with this hunk of shaped rock makes you ap-

preciate the sheer physical labor involved in chipping a figure out of solid stone. It takes great strength but, at the same time, great delicacy.

This is all that remains of an ancient statue of Hercules seated on a lion skin. Michelangelo loved this old rock. He knew that he was the best sculptor of his day. The ancients were his only peers—and his rivals. He'd caress this statue lovingly and tell people, "I am the pupil of the Torso." To him, it contained all the beauty of classical sculpture. But it's not beautiful. Compared with the pure grace of the *Apollo,* it's downright ugly.

But Michelangelo, an ugly man himself, was looking for a new kind of beauty—not the beauty of idealized gods, but the innate beauty of every person, even so-called ugly ones. With its knotty lumps of muscle, the Torso has a brute power and a distinct personality despite—or because of—its rough edges. Remember this Torso, because we'll see it again later on.

• *Enter the next, domed room.*

Round Room

This room, modeled on the Pantheon interior, gives some idea of Roman grandeur. Romans took Greek ideas and made them big-

ger, like the big bronze statue of Hercules with his club, found near the Theater of Pompey (by modern-day Campo de' Fiori). The mosaic floor once decorated the bottom of a pool in an ancient Roman bath. The enormous Roman basin/hot tub/birdbath/vase decorated Nero's place. It was made of a single block of purple porphyry marble stone imported from Egypt. Purple was a rare, royal, expensive, and prestigious color in pre-Crayola days. This particular variety, called "imperial porphyry," came from a single mountain in Egypt, and was the stone of emperors...and then of popes. Now that source is quarried out, and the only "imperial porphyry" available to anyone has been recycled.

• *Enter the next room.*

Sarcophagi

These two large porphyry marble coffins were made (though not used) for the Roman emperor Constantine's mother (Helena, on

left) and daughter (Constanza, on right). Helena's coffin depicts a battle game showing dying victims in their barbarian dress. Constanza's is decorated with a mix of Christian and pagan themes. Helena and Constanza were Christians—and therefore outlaws—until Constantine made Christianity legal in A.D. 313, and they became saints. Both sarcophagi were quarried and worked in Egypt. The technique for working this extremely hard stone (a special tempering of metal was required) was lost after this, and porphyry marble was not chiseled again until Renaissance times in Florence.

• *See how we've come full circle in this building—the Egyptian Rooms are ahead on your left. Go upstairs and prepare for the Long March down the hall lined with statues, toward the Sistine Chapel and Raphael Rooms.*

Overachievers may first choose to pop into the Etruscan wing— labeled Museo Gregoriano Etrusco—*located a few steps up from the Long March level. (Others have permission to save their aesthetic energy for the Sistine.)*

THE ETRUSCANS (800-300 B.C.)

Room I

The chariot is from 550 B.C., when the crude Romans were ruled by their more civilized neighbors to the north—the Etruscans. (The wooden portions are a reconstruction.) Imagine the chariot racing around the dirt track of the Circus Maximus, through the marshy valley of the newly drained Forum, or up Capitoline Hill to the Temple of Jupiter—all originally built by Rome's Etruscan kings.

Room II

The golden breastplate (*Pectoral,* 650 B.C., immediately to the right), decorated with tiny winged figures and animals, shows off the sophistication of the Etruscans. Though unwarlike and politically decentralized, these people were able to "conquer" all of central Italy around 650 B.C. through trade, offering tempting metalwork goods like this.

The Etruscan vases done in the Greek style remind us of the other great pre-Roman power—the Greek colonists who settled in southern Italy (Magna Graecia). The Etruscans traded with the Greeks, adopting their fashions. Rome, cradled between the two, grew up learning from both cultures.

A Greek-style bowl (far corner of the room) depicting a man and woman in bed together would have scandalized early Roman farmers. He's peeing in a chamber pot, she's blowing a flute. Etruscan art often showed husbands and wives at ease together, giving them a reputation among the Romans as immoral, flute-playing degenerates.

Room III

This bronze warrior (late 5th century B.C.), whose helmet was sawed off by lightning, has a rare inscription that's readable (on armor below the navel). It probably refers to the statue's former owner: "Aha! Trutitis gave [this] as [a] gift." Archaeologists understand the Etruscans' Greek-style alphabet and some individual words, but they've yet to fully crack the code. As you look around at beautiful bronze pitchers, candlesticks, shields, and urns, ponder yet another of Etruria's unsolved mysteries—no one is sure where these sophisticated people came from.

Room IV

Most of our knowledge of the Etruscans is from sarcophagi and art in Etruscan tombs. Their funeral art is solemn, but hardly morbid—check out the sarcopha-guy with the bulging belly, enjoying a banquet for all eternity.

The Etruscans' origins are obscure, but their legacy is clear. In 509 B.C., the Etruscan king's son raped a Roman noblewoman.

The king was thrown out, the republic was declared, Etruscan cities were conquered by Rome's legions, and their culture was swallowed up in Roman expansion. By Julius Caesar's time, the few remaining ethnic Etruscans were reduced to serving their masters as flute players, goldsmiths, surgeons, and street-corner preachers, like the one that Caesar brushed aside when he called out, "Beware the Ides of March..."

• *Browse the remaining dozen rooms of the Etruscan Wing, or backtrack to the long hall (the Gallery of the Candelabra) leading to the Sistine Chapel and Raphael Rooms.*

The Long March

1 Diana the Huntress
2 Artemis
3 Bacchus
4 3-D Illusion on Ceiling

ETRUSCAN WING

Not to Scale

ANCIENT WORLD

1 3 CANDELABRA **2**

TAPESTRIES **4**

MAPS

RAPHAEL ROOMS & SISTINE CHAPEL

VIEW OF ST. PETER'S DOME

← ABOUT 1/4 MILE →

THE LONG MARCH—SCULPTURE, TAPESTRIES, MAPS, AND VIEWS

This quarter-mile walk gives you a sense of the scale that Renaissance popes built on. Remember, this building was originally a series of papal palaces. The popes loved beautiful things—statues, urns, marble floors, friezes, stuccoed ceilings—and, as heirs of imperial Rome, they felt they deserved such luxury. The palaces and art represent both the peak and the decline of the Catholic Church in Europe. It was extravagant spending like this that inspired Martin Luther to rebel, starting the Protestant Reformation.

Gallery of the Candelabra (Galleria dei Candelabri): Classical Sculpture

In the second "room" of the long hall, stop at the statue of Diana the Huntress on the left. Here, the virgin goddess goes hunting. Roman hunters would pray and give offerings to statues like this to get divine help in their search for food.

Farmers might pray to another version of the same goddess, in her guise as Artemis, on the opposite wall. This billion-breasted beauty stood for fertility. "Boobs or bulls' balls?" Some historians say that bulls were sacrificed and castrated, with the testicles draped over the statues as symbols of fertility.

VATICAN MUSEUM

• *Shuffle along to the next "room." On the left is Bacchus, with a baby on his shoulders.*

Fig Leaves

Why do the statues have fig leaves? Like Bacchus, many of these statues originally looked much different than they do now. First off, they were painted, often in gaudy colors. Bacchus may have had brown hair, rosy cheeks, purple grapes, and a leopard-skin sidekick at his feet. Even the *Apollo Belvedere*, whose cool gray tones we now admire as "classic Greek austerity," may have had a paisley pink cloak for all we know. Also, many statues had glass eyes like Bacchus'.

And the fig leaves? Those came from the years 1550 to 1800, when the Church decided that certain parts of the human anatomy

were obscene. (Why not the feet?) Perhaps Church leaders associated these full-frontal statues with the outbreak of Renaissance humanism that reduced their power in Europe. Whatever the cause, they reacted by covering classical crotches with plaster fig leaves, the same leaves Adam and Eve had used when the concept of "privates" was invented.

Note: The leaves could be removed at any time if the museum officials were so motivated. There are suggestion boxes around the museum. Whenever I see a fig leaf, I get the urge to pick-it. We could start an organ-ized campaign...

• *Cover your eyes in case they forgot a fig leaf or two, and continue to the...*

Tapestries

Along the left wall are tapestries designed by Raphael's workshop and made in Brussels. They show scenes from the life of Christ: Baby Jesus in the manger, being adored by shepherds, and presented in the temple. Farther along, the Resurrection tapestry, with Jesus striding out of the tomb, is curiously interactive...as you walk, Jesus' eyes, feet, knee, and even the stone slab follow you across the room. Next to it, *The Supper at Emmaus* (with Jesus sitting at a table) seems equally flexible.

Check out the beautiful sculpted reliefs on the ceiling. Admire the workmanship of this relief, then realize that it's not a relief at all—it's painted on a flat surface! Illusions like this were proof that painters had mastered the 3-D realism of ancient statues.

Map Gallery and View of Vatican City

This gallery still feels like a pope's palace. The crusted ceiling of colorful stucco and paint is pure papal splendor. The 16th-century maps on the walls show the regions of Italy. Popes could take visitors on a tour of Italy, from the toe (entrance end) to the Alps (far

end), with east Italy on the right wall, west on the left. The scenes on the ceiling portray exciting moments in Church history in each of those regions.

The windows give you your best look at the tiny country of Vatican City, officially established as an independent nation in 1929. It has its own radio station, as you see from the tower on the hill. What you see here is pretty much all there is—these gardens, the palaces you're in, and St. Peter's (for more on Vatican City, see sidebar on page 206).

If you have the chance to lean out and look left, you'll see the dome of St. Peter's the way Michelangelo would have liked you to see it—without the bulky Baroque facade.

At the far end, maps show Italy's four ports of entry (including Venice). Also look for maps of Antique Italy (names in Latin, Roman political boundaries in gold) and New Italy.

• *Exit the map room, and take a breather in the next small tapestry hall. Then turn left into the crowded rooms that lead to the Raphael Rooms. (From here, tired visitors sometimes have the option of skipping the Raphael Rooms and making a beeline to the Sistine Chapel. But our tour turns left into the Raphael Rooms.)*

Renaissance Wing

Papal Wallpaper

We've seen art from the ancient world; now we'll see its rebirth in the Renaissance. We're entering the living quarters of the great Renaissance popes—where they slept, worked, and worshipped. The rooms reflect the grandeur of their position. They hired the best artists—mostly from Florence—to paint the walls and ceilings, combining classical and Christian motifs.

Entering, you'll immediately see a huge 19th-century painting that depicts the Polish King Jan III Sobieski liberating Vienna from the Ottomans in 1683, finally tipping the tide in favor of a Christian Europe. See the Ottoman tents on the left and the spires of Christian Vienna on the right. This is not by Raphael, but by Jan Matejko, a Polish painter who specialized in grand-scale historical epics like this one.

The second room's paintings celebrate the doctrine of the Immaculate Conception, establishing that Mary herself was conceived free from original sin. This medieval idea wasn't actually made dogma until a century ago. The largest fresco shows how the inspiration came straight from heaven (upper left) in a thin ray of light directly to the pope.

• *Next, you'll pass along an outside walkway that overlooks a courtyard (is that the pope's Fiat?), finally ending up in the first of the Raphael Rooms, the Constantine Room.*

Raphael Rooms
Constantine Room

These frescoes, painted between 1517 and 1524 (finished after Raphael's death by his assistants, notably Giulio Romano), celebrate the passing of the baton from one culture to the next. Remember, Rome was a pagan empire persecuting a new cult from the East—Christianity.

Then, on the night of October 27, A.D. 312 (left wall), as General Constantine (in gold, with crown) was preparing his troops for a coup d'état, he looked up and saw something strange. A cross appeared in the sky with the words, "You will conquer in this sign."

The next day (long wall), his troops raged victoriously into battle with the Christian cross atop their Roman eagle banners. There's Constantine in the center with a smile on his face, slashing through the enemy, while God's warrior angels ride shotgun overhead.

Constantine even stripped (right wall) and knelt before the pope to be baptized a Christian (some say). As emperor, he legalized Christianity and worked hand in hand with the pope, although the document in which he supposedly "gave" Rome to the pope (window wall) was later shown to be

Raphael Rooms

1. MATEJKO – Sobieski Liberating Vienna
2. Immaculate Conception Room
3. Constantine Room
4. RAPHAEL – The Liberation of St. Peter (with Julius II portraits)
5. RAPHAEL – The School of Athens; La Disputa
6. "Fire in the Borgo" Room

Not to Scale

a forgery. When Rome fell, its glory lived on through the Dark Ages in the pomp, pageantry, and learning of the Catholic Church.

Look at the ceiling painting. A classical statue is knocked backward, crumbling before the overpowering force of the cross. Whoa! Christianity triumphs over pagan Rome. (This was painted, I believe, by Raphael's surrealist colleague, Salvadorus Dalio.)

• *Continue on. In the next room you'll reach a room with frescoes arching over the windows (Room of Heliodorus, 1512–1514). Block the sunlight with your hand to see...*

The Liberation of St. Peter

Peter, Jesus' right-hand man, was thrown into prison in Jerusalem for his beliefs. In the middle of the night, an angel appeared and rescued him from the sleeping guards (Acts 12:5-12). The chains miraculously fell away (and were later brought to

the St. Peter-in-Chains Church in Rome), and the angel led him to safety (right), while the guards took hell from their captain (left).

Raphael (1483-1520)

Raphael was only 25 when Pope Julius II invited him, in 1508, to paint the walls of his personal living quarters. Julius was so impressed by Raphael's talent that he had the work of earlier masters scraped off and gave Raphael free rein to paint what he wanted.

Raphael lived a charmed life. He was handsome and sophisticated, and soon became Julius' favorite. He painted masterpieces effortlessly. In a different decade, he might have been thrown out of the Church as a great sinner, but his love affairs and devil-may-care personality seemed to epitomize the optimistic pagan spirit of the Renaissance.

Raphael's paintings are bathed in an even light, with few shadows; his brushwork is smooth and blended, and colors are restrained. In group scenes, Raphael wants you to follow his subjects' gazes as they exchange glances or look off in different directions. This adds a sense of motion and psychological tension to otherwise well-balanced scenes.

Raphael's compositions always have a strong geometric template. Figures are arranged into a pyramid or a circle. Human bodies are composed of oval faces, cylindrical arms, and arched shoulders. Subconsciously, this creates the feeling that God's created world is geometrically perfect. But Raphael always lets a bit of messy reality spill over the lines so his scenes don't appear static. While always graceful, his works are never lightweight or frilly—they're strong, balanced, and harmonious in the best Renaissance tradition. When he died, at just 38 years old, the High Renaissance died with him.

This little "play" is neatly divided into three separate acts that make a balanced composition.

Raphael makes the miraculous event even more dramatic with the use of four kinds of light illuminating the dark cell—half-moonlight, the captain's torch, the radiant angel, and the natural light spilling through the museum's window. Raphael's mastery of realism, rich colors, and sense of drama made him understandably famous.

Find portraits of Pope Julius II in several paintings in this room. Julius was the man who commissioned Raphael to paint these rooms, who browbeat Michelangelo into doing the Sistine ceiling, and who started construction of St. Peter's. You can make out bearded Julius in the role of Peter in *The Liberation*, seated on the left in *The Expulsion of Heliodorus* (on the wall to the right), and as the kneeling pope in *The Mass of Bolsena* (opposite the *Liberation*).

• *Enter the next room (Room of the Segnatura, 1508-1511). Here in the pope's private study, Raphael painted...*

The School of Athens

In both style and subject matter, this fresco sums up the spirit of the Renaissance, which was not only the rebirth of classical art, but a rebirth of learning, discovery, and the optimistic spirit that man is a rational creature. Raphael pays respect to the great thinkers and scientists of ancient Greece, gathering them together at one time in a mythical school setting.

VATICAN MUSEUM

In the center are Plato and Aristotle, the two greatest Greeks. Plato points up, indicating his philosophy that mathematics and

pure ideas are the source of truth, while Aristotle gestures down, showing preference for hands-on study of the material world. There's their master, Socrates (midway to the left, in green), ticking off arguments on his fingers. And in the foreground at right, bald Euclid bends over a slate to demonstrate a geometrical formula.

Raphael shows that Renaissance thinkers were as good as the ancients. There's Leonardo da Vinci, whom Raphael worshipped, in the role of Plato. Euclid is the architect Donato Bramante, who designed St. Peter's. Raphael himself (next to last on the far right, with the black beret) looks out at us. And the "school" building is actually an early version of St. Peter's Basilica (under construction at the time).

Raphael balances everything symmetrically—thinkers to the left, scientists to the right, with Plato and Aristotle dead center—showing the geometrical order found in the world. Look at the square floor tiles in the foreground. If you laid a ruler over them and extended the line upward, it would run right to the center of the picture. Similarly, the tops of the columns all point down to the middle. All the lines of sight draw our attention to Plato and Aristotle, and to the small arch over their heads—a halo over these two secular saints in the divine pursuit of knowledge.

While Raphael was painting this room, Michelangelo was at work down the hall in the Sistine Chapel. Raphael had just fin-

ished *The School of Athens* when he got a look at Michelangelo's powerful figures and dramatic scenes. He was astonished. From this point on, Raphael began to beef up his delicate, graceful style to a more heroic level. He returned to *The School of Athens* and added one more figure to the scene—Michelangelo, the brooding, melancholy figure in front, leaning on a block of marble.

• *On the opposite wall is...*

La Disputa

As if to underline the new attitude that pre-Christian philosophy and Church thinking could coexist, Raphael painted *La Dis-*

puta facing *The School of Athens*. Christ and the saints in heaven are overseeing a discussion of the Eucharist (the communion wafer) by mortals below. The classical-looking character in blue and gold looks out as if to say, "The pagans had their *School of Athens*, but we Christians (pointing up) have the School of Heaven." These rooms were the papal library, so themes featuring learning, knowledge, and debate were appropriate.

In Catholic terms, the communion wafer miraculously becomes the body of Christ when it's consecrated by a priest, bringing a little bit of heaven into the material world. Raphael's painting also connects heaven and earth, with descending circles: Jesus in a halo floats above a circle surrounding the dove of the Holy Spirit, which radiates down toward the round communion wafer on the altar. Balance and symmetry reign, from the angel trios in the upper corners to the books littering the floor. Find Dante wearing his poet's laureate in the lower right. (Hint: He's the guy on your €2 coin, modeled after this detail of *La Disputa*.)

Moving along, the last Raphael Room (called the "Fire in the Borgo" Room, 1514-1517) shows work done mostly by Raphael's students, who were influenced by the bulging muscles and body-builder poses of Michelangelo.

• *Pause here—WCs are nearby. Next stop: the Sistine Chapel, just a five-minute walk away. Exit the final Raphael Room through a passageway, bear right, and go down the stairs. At the foot of the stairs you'll find several quiet rooms with benches. Have a seat and read ahead before entering the hectic Sistine Chapel.*

When you're ready to tackle the Sistine, stroll through the impressive Modern Religious Art collection, following signs to the chapel. Near the end of the modern collection (Room XXXVII and on), you'll pass religious paintings by modern masters—Chagall, Dalí, Bacon, and others.

The Sistine Chapel

The Sistine Chapel contains Michelangelo's ceiling and his huge *Last Judgment.* The Sistine is the personal chapel of the pope and the place where new popes are elected. (The small, old-fashioned stove that burns pope-vote ballots—which sends out puffs of tell-tale smoke—is placed near today's shortcut exit.)

When Pope Julius II asked Michelangelo to take on this important project, he said, "No, *grazie.*" Michelangelo insisted he

was a sculptor, not a painter. The Sistine ceiling was a vast undertaking, and he didn't want to do a half-vast job. But the pope pleaded, bribed, and threatened until Michelangelo finally consented, on the condition that he be able to do it all his own way.

Julius had asked for only 12 apostles along the sides of the ceiling, but Michelangelo had a grander vision—the entire history of the world until Jesus. He spent the next four years (1508-1512) craning his neck on scaffolding six stories up, covering the ceiling with frescoes of biblical scenes.

In sheer physical terms, it's an astonishing achievement: 5,900 square feet, with the vast majority done by his own hand. (Raphael

Sistine Chapel

EXIT DOOR
FOR SHORTCUT
TO ST. PETER'S
(SOMETIMES CLOSED)

MICHELANGELO'S
CEILING
FRESCOES
(ABOVE)

EXIT DOOR
FOR LONG MARCH
BACK TO
PINACOTECA &
MUSEUM ENTRANCE –
A 15-MINUTE WALK

SCREEN

BALCONY

WALL
FRESCOES
(BY BOTTICELLI,
PERUGINO
& OTHERS)

BENCHES

BENCHES

Not to Scale

MICHELANGELO'S
LAST JUDGMENT WALL

ALTAR

ENTRY DOOR
FROM RAPHAEL ROOMS &
MODERN RELIGIOUS ART COLLECTION

VATICAN MUSEUM

only designed most of his rooms, letting assistants do the grunt work.)

First, he had to design and erect the scaffolding. Any materials had to be hauled up on pulleys. Then, a section of ceiling would be plastered. With fresco—painting on wet plaster—if you don't get it right the first time, you have to scrape the whole thing off and start over. And if you've ever struggled with a ceiling light fixture or worked underneath a car for even five minutes, you know how heavy your arms get. The physical effort, the paint dripping in his eyes, the creative drain, and the mental stress from a pushy pope combined to almost kill Michelangelo.

But when the ceiling was finished and revealed to the public, it simply blew 'em away. Like the *Laocoön* statue discovered six years earlier, it was unlike anything seen before. It both caps the Renaissance and turns it in a new direction. In perfect Renaissance spirit, it mixes Old Testament prophets with classical figures. But the style is more dramatic, shocking, and emotional than the balanced Renaissance works before it. This is a very personal work—the Gospel according to Michelangelo—but its themes and subject matter are universal. Many art scholars contend that the Sistine ceiling is the single greatest work of art by any one human being.

The Sistine Schematic

GENESIS
SCENES + PROPHETS + ANCESTORS = THE
SISTINE
CEILING

The Sistine Ceiling:
Understanding What You're Standing Under

The ceiling shows the history of the world before the birth of Jesus. We see God creating the world, creating man and woman, destroying the earth by flood, and so on. God himself, in his purple robe, actually appears in the first five scenes. Along the sides (where the ceiling starts to curve), we see the Old Testament prophets and pagan Greek prophetesses who foretold the coming of Christ. Dividing these scenes and figures are fake niches (a painted 3-D illusion) decorated with nude statue-like figures with symbolic meaning.

The key is to see three simple divisions in the tangle of bodies:
1. The central spine of nine rectangular biblical scenes;
2. The line of prophets on either side; and
3. The triangles between the prophets showing the ancestors of Christ.

• *Ready? Within the chapel, grab a seat along the side (when there's room—people come and go). Face the altar with the big* Last Judgment *on the wall (more on that later). Now look up to the ceiling and find the central panel of...*

The Creation of Adam

God and man take center stage in this Renaissance version of creation. Adam, newly formed in the image of God, lounges dreamily in perfect naked innocence. God, with his entourage, swoops in with a swirl of activity (which—with a little imagination—looks like a cross-section of a human brain...quite a strong humanist statement). Their reaching hands are the center of this work. Adam's is

The Sistine Ceiling

VATICAN MUSEUM

WALL

DAVID & GOLIATH

JUDITH & HOLOFERNES

ZACHA-RIAH

JOEL

DRUNKENNESS OF NOAH

DELPHICA

ZORO-BABEL

THE FLOOD

JOSIAH

ERYTH-RAEA

SACRIFICE OF NOAH

ISAIAH

WALL

OZIAS

TEMPTATION AND EXPULSION

EZEKIAS

EZEKIEL

CREATION OF EVE

CUMAEA

ROBOAM

CREATION OF ADAM

ASA

WALL

PERSICA

SEPARATION OF LAND FROM WATER

DANIEL

See photo on facing page →

SALMON

CREATION OF SUN, MOON & PLANETS

JESSE

JEREMIAH

SEPARATION OF LIGHT FROM DARKNESS

LIBICA

DEATH OF HAMAN

JONAH

BRAZEN SERPENT

LAST JUDGMENT WALL

ENTRY DOOR →
FROM RAPHAEL ROOMS &
MODERN RELIGIOUS ART...

☆ TO USE THIS DIAGRAM:
FACE THE LAST JUDGMENT &
HOLD THE BOOK UP TO THE CEILING.

limp and passive; God's is strong and forceful, his finger twitching upward with energy. Here is the very moment of creation, as God passes the spark of life to man, the crowning work of his creation.

This is the spirit of the Renaissance. God is not a terrifying giant reaching down to puny and helpless man from way on high. Here they are on an equal plane, divided only by the diagonal bit of sky. God's billowing robe and the patch of green upon which Adam is lying balance each other. They are like two pieces of a jigsaw puzzle, or two long-separated continents, or like the yin and yang symbols finally coming together—uniting, complementing each other, creating wholeness. God and man work together in the divine process of creation.

• *This celebration of man permeates the ceiling. Notice the Adonises-come-to-life on the pedestals that divide the central panels. And then came woman.*

The Garden of Eden

In one panel, we see two scenes from the Garden of Eden: *Temptation* and *Expulsion*. On the left is the leafy garden of paradise where Adam and Eve lie around blissfully. But the devil comes along—a serpent with a woman's torso—and winds around the forbidden Tree of Knowledge. The temptation to gain new knowledge is too great for these Renaissance people. They eat the forbidden fruit.

At right, a sword-wielding angel drives them from Paradise into the barren plains. They're grieving, but they're far from helpless. Adam's body is thick and sturdy, and we know they'll survive in the cruel world. Adam firmly gestures to the angel, like he's saying, "All right, already! We're going!"

The Nine Scenes from Genesis

Take some time with these central scenes to understand the story that the ceiling tells. They run in sequence, starting at the front:

1. God, in purple, divides the light from darkness.
2. God creates the sun (burning orange) and the moon (pale white, to the right). Oops, I guess there's another moon.
3. God bursts toward us to separate the land and water.
4. God creates Adam.
5. God creates Eve, who dives into existence out of Adam's side.
6. Adam and Eve are tempted, then expelled, from the Garden of Eden.

7. Noah kills a ram and stokes the altar fires to make a sacrifice to God.

8. The great flood, sent by God, destroys the wicked, who desperately head for higher ground. In the distance, the ark carries Noah's family to safety. (The blank spot dates to 1793, when a nearby gunpowder depot exploded, shaking the building.)

9. Noah's sons see their drunken father. (Perhaps Michelangelo chose to end his work with this scene as a reminder that even the best of men are fallible.)

Prophets

You'll notice that the figures at the far end of the chapel are a bit smaller than those over *The Last Judgment*.

Michelangelo started at the far end, with the Noah scenes. By 1510, he'd finished the first half of the ceiling. When they took the scaffolding down and could finally see what he'd been working on for two years, everyone was awestruck—except Michelangelo. As powerful as his figures are, from the floor they didn't look dramatic enough for Michelangelo. For the other half, he pulled out all the stops.

Compare the Noah scenes (far end), with their many small figures, to the huge images of God at the other end. Similarly,

Isaiah (near the lattice screen, marked "Esaias") is stately and balanced, while Jeremiah ("Hieremias," in the corner by *The Last Judgment*) is a dark, brooding figure. This prophet who witnessed the destruction of Israel slumps his chin in his hand and ponders the fate of his people. Like the difference between the stately *Apollo Belvedere* and the excited *Laocoön*, Michelangelo added a new emotional dimension to Renaissance painting.

The Last Judgment

When Michelangelo returned to paint the altar wall 23 years later (1535), the mood of Europe—and of the artist—was completely different. The Protestant Reformation had forced the Catholic Church to clamp down on free thought, and religious wars raged. Rome had recently been pillaged by roving bands of mercenaries. The Renaissance spirit of optimism was fading. Michelangelo himself had begun to question the innate goodness of mankind.

It's Judgment Day, and Christ—the powerful figure in the center, raising his arm to spank the wicked—has come to find out who's naughty and who's nice. Beneath him, a band of angels blows its trumpets Dizzy Gillespie-style, giving a wake-up call to the sleeping dead. The dead at lower left leave their graves and prepare to be judged. The righteous, on Christ's right hand (the left side of the picture), are carried up to the glories of heaven. The wicked on the other side are hurled down to hell, where demons wait to torture them. Charon, from the underworld of Greek mythology, waits below to ferry the souls of the damned to hell.

It's a grim picture. No one, but no one, is smiling. Even many of the righteous being resurrected (lower left) are either skeletons or cadavers with ghastly skin. The angels have to play tug-of-war with subterranean monsters to drag them from their graves.

The Last Judgment

HEAVEN

THE **GOOD,**

THE **BAD,**

& THE **UGLY**

HELL

ENTRY DOOR
TO SISTINE →

1 Christ with Mary
2 Trumpeting Angels
3 Righteous Dead Ascending
4 Damned Man

5 Charon the Ferryman
6 Demon/Critic Wrapped in Snake
7 St. Bartholomew Holding Flayed
Skin (Michelangelo's Face)

Over in hell, the wicked are tortured by gleeful demons. One of the damned (to the right of the trumpeting angels) has an utterly lost expression, as if saying, "Why did I cheat on my wife?!" Two demons grab him around the ankles to pull him down to the bowels of hell, condemned to an eternity of constipation.

But it's the terrifying figure of Christ that dominates this scene. He raises his arm to smite the wicked, sending a ripple of fear through everyone. Even the saints around him—even Mary beneath his arm (whose interceding days are clearly over)—shrink back in terror from this uncharacteristic outburst from loving Jesus.

The Cleaning Project

The ceiling and *The Last Judgment* were cleaned in the 1980s and 1990s, removing centuries of preservatives, dirt, and soot from candles, oil lamps, and the annual Papal Barbecue (just kidding). The bright, bright colors that emerged are a bit shocking, and have forced many art experts to reevaluate Michelangelo's style. Notice the very dark patches left in the corner above *The Last Judgment,* and imagine how dreary and dark it was before the cleaning.

His expression is completely closed, and he turns his head, refusing to even listen to the whining alibis of the damned. Look at Christ's twisting upper body. If this muscular figure looks familiar to you, it's because you've seen it before—the Belvedere Torso.

When *The Last Judgment* was unveiled to the public in 1541, it caused a sensation. The pope is said to have dropped to his knees and cried, "Lord, charge me not with my sins when thou shalt come on the Day of Judgment."

And it changed the course of art. The complex composition, with more than 300 figures swirling around the figure of Christ, went far beyond traditional Renaissance balance. The twisted figures shown from every imaginable angle challenged other painters to try and top this master of 3-D illusion. And the sheer terror and drama of the scene was a striking contrast to the placid optimism of, say, Raphael's *School of Athens*. Michelangelo had Baroque-en all the rules of the Renaissance, signaling a new era of art.

With the Renaissance fading, the fleshy figures in *The Last Judgment* aroused murmurs of discontent from Church authorities. Michelangelo rebelled by painting his chief critic into the scene—in hell. He's the jackassed demon in the bottom-right corner, wrapped in a snake. Look at how Michelangelo covered his privates. Sweet revenge. (After Michelangelo's death, prudish Church authorities painted the wisps of clothing that we see today.)

Now move in close. Study the details of the lower part of the painting from right to left. Charon, with Dr. Spock ears and a Dalí moustache, paddles the damned in a boat full of human turbulence. Look more closely at the J-Day band. Are they reading music, or is it the Judgment Day tally? Before the piece was cleaned, these details were lost in murk.

The Last Judgment marks the end of Renaissance optimism epitomized in *The Creation of Adam*, with its innocence and exaltation of man. There, he was the wakening man-child of a fatherly God. Here, man cowers in fear and unworthiness before a terrifying, wrathful deity.

VATICAN MUSEUM

Michelangelo himself must have wondered how he would be judged—had he used his God-given talents wisely? Look at St. Bartholomew, the bald, bearded guy at Christ's left foot (our right). In the flayed skin he's holding is a barely recognizable face—the twisted self-portrait of a self-questioning Michelangelo.

• *There are two exits from the Sistine Chapel.*

*1. To return to the main entrance/ exit, leave the Sistine through the side door next to the screen (on the left, with your back to the altar). You'll soon find yourself facing the **Long March back to the museum's entrance** (about 15 minutes away) and the Pinacoteca. Along this corridor (located one floor below the long corridor that you walked to get here), you'll see some of the wealth amassed by the popes, mostly gifts from royalty. Find your hometown on the 1529 map of the world—look in the land labeled "Terra Incognita." The elaborately decorated library that branches off to the right contains rare manuscripts. The corridor eventually spills back outside. Follow signs to the Pinacoteca, where our tour picks up below.*

*2. To take the **shortcut directly to St. Peter's Basilica** (see "Museum Strategies," page 232), you'll exit at the far-right corner of the Sistine Chapel (with your back to the altar). This route saves you a 30-minute walk and the wait in the St. Peter's security line, but you can't get back to the main entrance/exit or the Pinacoteca. Though this corner door is likely labeled "Exit for private tour groups only," you can probably just slide through with the crowds (or protest that your group has left you behind). If this exit is closed (which can happen without notice), hang out in the Sistine Chapel for a few more minutes—it'll likely reopen shortly.*

Pinacoteca

Like Lou Gehrig batting behind Babe Ruth, the Pinacoteca (Painting Gallery) has to follow the mighty Sistine & Co. But after the Vatican's artistic feast, this little collection of paintings is a delicious 15-minute after-dinner mint.

See this gallery of paintings as you'd view the time-lapse blossoming of a flower, walking through the evolution of painting from medieval to Baroque with just a few stops.

• *Enter, passing a plaster cast of Michelangelo's* Pietà *(offering a handy close-up look), and stroll up to Room IV.*

Melozzo da Forlì—*Musician Angels* (1470s)

Removed from the apse of a Roman church, this playful series of frescoes shows the delicate grace and nobility of Italy during the time known fondly as the Quattrocento (1400s). Notice the detail in the serene faces; the soothing primary colors; the bright and even light; and the classical purity given to these religious figures. Rock on.

• *Walk on to the end room (Room VIII), where precious Raphael-designed tapestries that once hung in the Sistine Chapel now surround the highlight of this collection. They've turned on the dark to let Raphael's* Transfiguration *shine. Take a seat.*

Raphael—*The Transfiguration* (1516-1520)

Christ floats above a stumpy mountaintop, visited in a vision by the prophets Moses and Elijah. Peter, James, and John, who wanted vi-

sual proof that Jesus was Lord, cower in awe under their savior, "transfigured before them, his face shining as the sun, his raiment white as light" (as described by the evangelist Matthew—who can be seen taking notes in the painting's lower left).

Raphael composes the scene in three descending tiers: Christ, the holiest, is on top, then Peter-James-John, and finally, the nine remaining apostles surround a boy possessed by demons. They direct him and his mother to Jesus for healing.

Raphael died in 1520, leaving this final work to be finished by his pupils. The last thing Raphael painted was the beatific face of Jesus, perhaps the most beautiful Christ in existence. When Raphael was buried (in the Pantheon, at age 37), this work accompanied the funeral.

• *Heading back down the parallel corridor, stop in Room IX at the brown, unfinished work by Leonardo.*

Pinacoteca

ROOM VIII

IX
VII

X
VI

XI
V

ROOM XII

IV

XIII
III

XIV
II

XV
I

XVII XVI

PIETÀ CAST

Not to Scale

To Cafeteria

To Exit

Courtyard

To Entrance

❶ MELOZZO DA FORLI –
Musician Angels

❷ RAPHAEL –
The Transfiguration

❸ LEONARDO DA VINCI –
St. Jerome

❹ CARAVAGGIO –
Deposition

❺ View of the Dome

Leonardo da Vinci—*St. Jerome* (c. 1482)

Jerome squats in the rocky desert. He's spent too much time alone, fasting and meditating on his sins. His soulful face is echoed by his friend, the roaring lion.

This unfinished work gives us a glimpse behind the scenes at Leonardo's technique. Even in the brown undercoating, we see the psychological power of Leonardo's genius. Jerome's emaciated body on the rocks expresses his intense penitence, while his pleading eyes hold a glimmer of hope for divine forgiveness. Leonardo wrote that a good painter must paint two things: "man and the movements of his spirit." (The patchwork effect is due to Jerome's head having been cut out and used as the seat of a stool in a shoemaker's shop.)

• *Roll on through the sappy sweetness of the Mannerist rooms into the gritty realism of Caravaggio (Room XII).*

Caravaggio—*Deposition* (c. 1600-1604)

Christ is being buried. In the dark tomb, the faces of his followers emerge, lit by a harsh light. Christ's body has a deathlike color. We see Christ's dirty toes and Nicodemus' wrinkled, sunburned face.

Caravaggio was the first painter to intentionally shock his viewers. By exaggerating the contrast between light and dark, shining a brutal third-degree-interrogation light on his subjects, and using everyday models in sacred scenes, he takes a huge leap away from the Raphael-pretty past and into the "expressive realism" of the modern world.

A tangle of grief looms in the darkness as Christ's heavy, dead body nearly pulls the whole group with him from the cross into the tomb. After this museum, I know how he feels.

• *Walk through the rest of the gallery's canvas history of art, enjoy one last view of the Vatican grounds and Michelangelo's dome, then follow the grand spiral staircase down. Go in peace.*

BORGHESE GALLERY TOUR

Museo e Galleria Borghese

More than just a great museum, the Borghese Gallery is a beautiful villa set in the greenery of surrounding gardens. You get to see art commissioned by the luxury-loving Borghese family displayed in the very rooms for which it was created. Frescoes, marble, stucco, and interior design enhance the masterpieces. This is a place where—regardless of whether you learn a darn thing—you can sit back and enjoy the sheer beauty of the palace and its art.

It's hard to believe that a family of cardinals and popes would display so many works with secular and sensual—even erotic—themes. But the Borgheses felt that all forms of human expression, including pagan myths and physical passion, glorified God.

Orientation

Cost: €16, drops to €13 when there's no temporary exhibit, both prices include €2 reservation fee (see "Reservations" below).

Hours: Tue-Sun 9:00-19:00, closed Mon, ticket office closes 30 minutes before museum.

Reservations: Reservations are mandatory and simple to get. It's easiest to book online on their user-friendly website (www.galleriaborghese.it). You can also reserve by telephone (tel. 06-32810, press 2 for English, pay for tickets on arrival). Call during Italian office hours: Mon-Fri 9:00-18:00, Sat 9:00-13:00, office closed Sat in Aug and Sun year-round.

Every two hours, 360 people are allowed to enter the museum. Entry times are 9:00, 11:00, 13:00, 15:00, and 17:00. Reserve a *minimum* of several days in advance for a weekday visit, and at least a week ahead for weekends. Reservations are tightest at 11:00 and 17:00, on Tuesdays, and on weekends. For off-season weekdays (but not weekends), your chances of getting a same-day reservation are fairly high if you're flexible about the entry time—just call and ask.

After you reserve a day and time, you'll get a claim number. They recommend that you arrive at the Borghese Gallery 30 minutes before your appointed time to pick up your ticket in the lobby on the lower level. Don't cut it close—arriving late can mean forfeiting your reservation.

You can use a Roma Pass for entry, but you're still required to make a reservation (by phone only—not online; specify that you have the Roma Pass). If you don't have a reservation, try arriving near the top of the hour, when the museum sells unclaimed tickets to those standing by. Generally, out of 360 reservations, a few will fail to show (but more than a few may be waiting to grab them). You're most likely to land a standby ticket at 9:00.

Getting There: The museum is set idyllically but inconveniently in the vast Villa Borghese Gardens (see page 67). To avoid missing your appointment, allow yourself plenty of time to find the place. A taxi drops you 100 yards from the museum. Your destination is the Galleria Borghese (gah-leh-REE-ah bor-GAY-zay). Don't tell the cabbie "Villa Borghese," which is the park, not the museum.

Bus #910 goes from Termini train station (and Piazza Repubblica) to the Via Pinciana stop, 100 yards from the museum. Coming from Campo de' Fiori or Via del Corso (at Via Minghetti), bus #116 drops you off inside the park, at the Cavalli Marini stop, 200 yards from the museum. From Largo Argentina, bus #63 takes you to the US Embassy on Via Veneto; walk uphill on Via Veneto to the southern edge of the park.

By Metro, from the Barberini Metro stop, walk 10 minutes up Via Veneto, enter the park, and turn right, following signs another 10 minutes to the Borghese Gallery. From the Flaminio Metro stop (specifically from the traffic island just outside the wall), you can catch bus #61, #89, #160, #490, #491, or #495, any of which will take you up the street between the twin columned temples and on a short ride through the Villa Borghese Gardens to Piazzale Brasile (the last stop in the park, just before the city wall); from there it's a 10-minute walk up to the museum. The Spagna Metro stop is equally close, but involves a circuitous walk through underground passageways—a less-than-idyllic approach.

Information: Tel. 06-32810 or 06-841-3979, www.galleriaborghese. it. For info on the park or Rome sights in general, try the nearby park TI (sporadically open; facing Borghese Gallery, turn left, walk 30 yards down, turn right toward the gate and find the poorly signed TI immediately on the left).

Tours: Guided English tours are offered at 9:10 and 11:10 (€6.50; may also be offered on busy weekends at 13:10 and 15:10). You can't book a tour when you make your museum reservation—sign up as soon as you arrive. Or consider the excellent 1.5-hour audioguide tour (€5).

Length of This Tour: Two hours is all you get...and you'll want every minute. But if you have less time, focus on the ground-floor sculptures, especially Bernini. If you're speedy, you could squeeze in all of this tour's highlights (including the Pinacoteca) in about an hour.

Museum Strategy: Visits are strictly limited to two hours. Budget most of your time for the more interesting ground floor, but set aside 30 minutes for the paintings of the Pinacoteca upstairs (highlights are marked by the audioguide icons). Though my tour starts on the ground floor, you can avoid the crowds by seeing the Pinacoteca first (enter through the basement, pass the info desk and café at the far end, and climb the stairs to visit the second-floor Pinacoteca, then descend to see the first-floor main gallery). The fine bookshop is best visited outside your two-hour entry window (it closes 30 minutes before the gallery).

Cloakroom: Baggage check is free, mandatory, and strictly enforced. Even small purses must be checked. The checkroom does not take coats.

Photography: No photos allowed; you must check your camera.

Cuisine Art: A café is on-site. A picnic-friendly park with benches is just in front of the museum (you can check your picnic with your bags, and feast after your visit). CineCaffè, located within the park, has a café and a buffet-lunch restaurant (a pleasant 10-minute walk directly downhill from the museum, near the bike-rental stand).

Starring: Sculptures by Bernini and Canova; paintings by Caravaggio, Raphael, and Titian; and the elegant villa itself.

OVERVIEW

As you visit this palace-in-a-garden, consider its purpose. Cardinal Scipione Borghese (1576-1633) wanted to create a place just outside the city where he could showcase his fine art while wining and dining the VIPs of his age. He had the villa built, collected ancient works, and hired the best artists of his day. In pursuing the optimistic spirit of the Renaissance, they invented Baroque.

The cardinal was controversial because he was not religious. But as nepotism was routine in the 17th century, just being a nephew of the pope was justification enough to be made a cardinal. And the power of a cardinal could be parlayed into great wealth, still on incredible display here in the gallery.

The Tour Begins

• *Go downstairs (into the basement) to pick up your ticket. Head back outside and up the stairs to begin the tour on the ground floor, in the main entry hall. If you want to start in the Pinacoteca, find the entrance at the far end of the basement and go upstairs to the second floor.*

GROUND FLOOR (SCULPTURE)

Main Entry Hall

The first room that guests saw upon entry was a "theater of the arts"—a multimedia and multi-era extravaganza of art treasures. Baroque frescoes on the ceiling, Greek statues along the walls, and ancient Roman mosaics on the floor capture the essence of the collection—a gathering of beautiful objects from every age and culture inside a lavish 17th-century villa.

Five second- and third-century mosaics from a private Roman villa adorn the floor with colorful, festive scenes of slaughter. Gladiators—as famous in their day as the sports heroes of our age—fight animals and each other with swords, whips, and tridents. The Greek letter Θ marks the dead. Notice some of the gladiators' prowrestler nicknames: "Cupid(-o)," "Serpent(-ius)," "Licentious(-us)." On the far left a scene shows how "Alumnusvic" killed "Mazicinus" and left him lying upside down in a pool of blood.

High up on the wall is a thrilling first-century Greek sculpture of a horse falling. The Renaissance-era rider was added by Pietro Bernini, father of the famous Gian Lorenzo Bernini.

• *We'll tour this floor counterclockwise. From the entrance, turn right and head into...*

Room I
Antonio Canova—*Pauline Borghese as Venus* (*Paolina Borghese come Venere*, 1808)

Napoleon's sister went the full monty for the sculptor Canova, scandalizing Europe. ("How could you have done such a

Borghese Gallery—Ground Floor

Stairs up to Pinacoteca

ROOM VI   ROOM V   ROOM IV   ⑨ ROOM III

❻   ❹   CHAPEL   ❸

⑤

ROOM II

ROOM VII   MAIN ENTRY HALL   ❷

❼

ROOM VIII   ROOM I

❽   START   ❶

PORTICO

Not to Scale

To Basement (Tickets, Info, Shop, WC)

❶ CANOVA – Pauline Borghese as Venus
❷ BERNINI – David
❸ BERNINI – Apollo and Daphne
❹ BERNINI – The Rape of Proserpina
⑤ UNKNOWN – Diana the Hunter; other marbles
❻ BERNINI – Aeneas, Anchises, and Ascanius
❼ "Theater of the Universe"
❽ CARAVAGGIO – Various
⑨ Stairs up to Pinacoteca

thing?!" she was asked. She replied, "The room wasn't cold.") With the famous nose of her conqueror brother, she strikes the pose of Venus as conqueror of men's hearts. Her relaxed afterglow and slight smirk say she's already had her man. The light dent she puts in the mattress makes this goddess human.

Notice the contrasting textures that Canova (1757-1822) gets out of the pure white marble: the rumpled sheet versus her smooth skin, the satiny-smooth pillows and mattress versus the creases in them, her porcelain skin versus the hint of a love handle. Canova polished and waxed the marble until it looked as soft and pliable as cloth.

The mythological pose, the Roman couch, the ancient hairdo, and the calm harmony make Pauline the epitome of the Neoclassical style.

Room II
Gian Lorenzo Bernini—*David* (1624)
Duck! David twists around to put a big rock in his sling. He purses his lips, knits his brow, and winds his body like a spring as his

eyes lock onto the target: Goliath, who's somewhere behind us, putting us right in the line of fire.

The face of David is a self-portrait of the 25-year-old Bernini (1598-1680). Looking ready to take on the world, David is charged with the same fighting energy that fueled the missionaries and conquistadors of the Counter-Reformation.

Compared with Michelangelo's *David*, this is unvarnished realism—an unbalanced pose, bulging veins, unflattering face, and armpit hair. Michelangelo's *David* thinks, whereas Bernini's acts—with lips pursed, eyes concentrating, and sling stretched. Bernini slays the pretty-boy *David*s of the Renaissance and prepares to invent Baroque.

Flanking David are two ancient sarcophagi carved with scenes from the *Labors of Hercules* (A.D. 160). The twisting bodybuilders' poses were the Hellenistic inspiration for Bernini's Baroque. The painting high on the wall between them, by a follower of Caravaggio, shows a triumphant David with the giant's head.

Room III
Bernini—*Apollo and Daphne* (*Apollo e Dafne*, 1625)

Apollo—made stupid by Cupid's arrow of love—chases after Daphne, who has been turned off by the "arrow of disgust." Just

as he's about to catch her, she calls to her father to save her. Magically, her fingers begin to sprout leaves, her toes become roots, her skin turns to bark, and she transforms into a tree. Frustrated Apollo will end up with a handful of leaves. (Notice the same scene, colorized, painted on the ceiling above.)

Stand behind the statue to experience it as Bernini originally intended. It's only when you circle around to the front that he reveals the story's surprise ending.

Walk slowly around the statue. Apollo's back leg defies gravity. Bernini chipped away more than half of the block of marble, leaving airy, open spaces. The marble leaves at the top ring like crystal when struck (but don't try it). The statue is now in particularly fine form, having spent two years in restoration (described to me as being similar to dental work). It's virtually flawless—yet Bernini couldn't entirely overcome Nature's imperfections. At the last minute, the sculptor discovered a flaw in the marble that now forms a scar across Daphne's nose.

Bernini carves out some of the chief features of Baroque art. He makes a supernatural event seem realistic. He freezes the scene at its most dramatic, emotional moment. The figures move and twist in unusual poses. He turns the wind machine on, sending Apollo's cape billowing behind him. It's a sculpture group of two, forming a scene, rather than a stand-alone portrait. And the subject is classical. Even in strict Counter-Reformation times, there was always a place for groping, if the subject matter had a moral—this one taught you not to pursue fleeting earthly pleasures. And, besides, Bernini tends to show a lot of skin, but no genitals.

The cardinal's private **chapel** (between Rooms III and IV) is the only even vaguely religious room in the palace. It's relatively humble, a reminder that the cardinal probably didn't stop in here for much longer than tourists do today.

Room IV
Bernini—*The Rape of Proserpina*
(*Il Ratto di Proserpina,* 1622)

Pluto, King of the Underworld, strides into his realm and shows off his catch—the beautiful daughter of the earth goddess Ceres.

His three-headed guard dog, Cerberus (who guards the gates of hell), barks triumphantly. Pluto is squat, thick, and uncouth, with knotted muscles and untrimmed beard. He's trying not to hurt Proserpina, but she pushes her divine molester away and twists to call out for help. Tears roll down her cheeks. She wishes she could turn into a tree.

Bernini was the master of marble. With this work, at the age of 24, he had discovered his Baroque niche. While Renaissance works were designed to be seen from the front, Baroque is theater-in-the-round—full of action, designed to be experienced as you walk around it. Look how Pluto's fingers dig into her frantic body as if it were real flesh. Bernini picked out this Carrara marble, knowing that its relative suppleness and ivory hue would lend itself to a fleshy statue.

• *In a niche over Pluto's right shoulder, find...*

Artist Unknown—*Diana the Hunter (Artemide)*

The goddess has been running through the forest. Now she's spotted her prey, and slows down, preparing to string her (missing) bow with an arrow. Or is she smoking a (missing) cigarette? Scholars debate it.

The statues in the niches are classical originals. Diana the Hunter is a rare Greek original, with every limb and finger intact, from the second century B.C. The traditional *contrapposto* pose (weight on one leg) and idealized grace were an inspiration for artists such as Canova, who grew tired of Bernini's Baroque bombast.

The Marbles in Room IV

The many ancient Roman statues and portrait busts of Roman emperors in this room were intended as a reminder that the pope was essentially a king, the successor to ancient Roman rulers of the past. (Until around 1800, popes held vast political—and even military—power.)

Appreciate the beauty of the different types of marble in the room: Bernini's ivory Carrara, Diana's translucent white, purple porphyry emperors and the granite-like columns supporting them, wood-grained pilasters on the walls, and the various colors on the floor—green, red, gray, lavender, and yellow, some grainy, some "marbled" like a steak. Some of the world's most beautiful and durable things have been made from the shells of sea creatures layered in sediment, fossilized into limestone, then baked and crystallized by the pressure of the earth—marble.

• *Before leaving this room, notice the staircase in the corner. You'll later return here in order to reach the Pinacoteca upstairs. But for now, continue through Room V and into...*

Room VI
Bernini—*Aeneas, Anchises, and Ascanius* (1618-1619)

Aeneas' home in Troy is in flames, and he escapes with the three most important things: his family (elderly father Anchises on his shoulder, baby boy Ascanius at his leg), his household gods (the statues in Dad's hands), and the Eternal Flame (carried by son). They're all in shock, lost in thought, facing an uncertain future. Aeneas isn't even looking where he's going; he just puts one foot in front of the other. Little do they know that eventually they'll wind up in Italy, where—according to legend—Aeneas will house the flame in the Temple of Vesta, and found the city of Rome (and the Borghese dynasty).

Bernini was just 20 when he started this, his first major work for Cardinal Borghese. Bernini was probably helped by his dad, who nurtured the child prodigy much like Leopold mentored Mozart, but without the rivalry. Bernini's portrayal of human flesh—

from baby fat to middle-aged muscle to sagging decrepitude—is astonishing. Still, the flat-footed statue just stands there—it lacks the Baroque energy of his more mature work. More lively are the reliefs up at the ceiling, with their dancing, light-footed soldiers with do-si-do shields.

Room VII
The "Theater of the Universe"

The room's decor sums up the eclectic nature of the villa. You've got everything here—your Greek statues, your Roman mosaics, even your fake "Egyptian" sphinxes and hieroglyphs (perfectly symmetrical, in good Neoclassical style). Look out the window past the sculpted gardens at the mesh domes of the aviary, once filled with exotic birds. Cardinal Borghese's vision was to make a place where art, history, music, nature, and science from every place and time would come together in "a theater of the universe."

Room VIII
Caravaggio

This room holds the greatest collection of Caravaggio paintings anywhere. Michelangelo Merisi (1571-1610), nicknamed "Cara-

vaggio" after his hometown (near Milan), brought Christian saints down to earth with gritty realism. Caravaggio's straightforwardness can be a refreshing change in a museum full of (sometimes overly) refined beauty.

Trace the course of his brief, dramatic, and sometimes messy life. *Self-Portrait as Bacchus* shows twentysomething Caravaggio as he first arrived in Rome, a poor bohemian enjoying the wild life.

On the facing wall, *Boy with a Fruit Basket* dates from when he eked out a living painting minor figures in other artists' paintings. His specialty? Fruit. Ultrarealistic fruit.

In 1600, Caravaggio completed his first major commission, a painting of St. Matthew for San Luigi dei Francesi, a church across town (see page 128). Overnight, Caravaggio was famous.

In the next 10 years, Caravaggio pioneered Baroque painting, much as Bernini soon would in sculpture. Caravaggio's unique style combined two striking elements: uncompromising realism and strong light-dark contrasts. His saints (e.g., *St. Jerome*) are balding and wrinkled. His models were ordinary people—*St. John the*

Gian Lorenzo Bernini (1598-1680)

A Renaissance Man in Counter-Reformation times, Bernini almost personally invented the Baroque style, transforming the city of Rome. If you're visiting Rome, you will see Bernini's work, guaranteed.

Bernini was a child prodigy in his father's sculpting studio, growing up among Europe's rich and powerful. His flamboyant personality endeared him to his cultured employers—the popes in Rome, Louis XIV in France, and Charles I in England. He was extremely prolific, working fast and utilizing an army of assistants.

Despite the fleshiness and sensuality of his works, Bernini was a religious man, seeing his creativity as an extension of God's. In stark contrast to the Protestant world's sobriety, Bernini shamelessly embraced pagan myths and nude goddesses, declaring them all part of the "catholic"—that is, universal—church.

Bernini, a master of multimedia, was a...
- Sculptor (Borghese Gallery and *St. Teresa in Ecstasy,* pictured above and described on page 84)
- Architect (elements of St. Peter's—see "Bernini Blitz," page 224, and the Church of Sant'Andrea al Quirinale)
- Painter (Borghese Gallery)
- Interior decorator (the *baldacchino* canopy and other works in St. Peter's)
- Civic engineer (he laid out St. Peter's Square, and he designed and renovated Rome's fountains in Piazza Navona, Piazza Barberini, Piazza di Spagna, and more).

Even works done by other artists a century later (such as the Trevi Fountain) can be traced indirectly to Bernini, the man who invented Baroque, the "look" of Rome for the next two centuries.

Baptist is a nude teenager with dirty feet, whose belly fat wrinkles up as he turns. The *Madonna of Palafrenieri* was forbidden to hang in St. Peter's because the boy Jesus was buck naked, and because the Madonna's likeness had been inspired by Rome's best-known prostitute. Caravaggio's figures emerge from a dark background, lit by a harsh, unflattering light, which highlights part of the figure, leaving the rest in deep shadows.

Now rich and famous, Caravaggio led a reckless, rock-star existence—trashing hotel rooms and picking fights. In 1606, he killed a man (the details are sketchy), and had to flee Rome to escape prosecution. In one of Caravaggio's last paintings, David sticks Goliath's severed head right in our face—and "Goliath" is the artist himself. From exile, Caravaggio appealed to Cardinal Borghese (one of his biggest fans) to get him a pardon. But while returning to Rome, Caravaggio died under mysterious circumstances. Though he only lived to 38, in his short life he'd rocked the world of art.

• *Caravaggio is the perfect transition between the elegant sculpture rooms and the paintings upstairs, in the other half of the museum. To reach the Pinacoteca, head through the main entry hall back to Room IV, find the entry to the staircase in the far-right corner, and spiral up to the...*

PINACOTECA (PAINTING GALLERY)

You must visit the Pinacoteca within the two-hour window of time printed on your Borghese Gallery ticket. Most visitors wait until the last half-hour to see the Pinacoteca, so that's when it's most crowded (and the ground floor is less crowded). If you see the paintings first, remember to save most of your two-hour visit for the ground-floor sculptures.

• *From the top of the stairs or elevator, step into the large Room XIV. Along the long wall, you'll find the following statues and paintings by Bernini. First, look for the two identical white busts set on columns.*

Room XIV
Two Bernini Busts of Cardinal Borghese (1632)

Say *grazie* to the man who built this villa, assembled the collection, and hired Bernini to sculpt masterpieces. The cardinal is caught turning as though to greet someone at a party. There's a twinkle in his eye, and he opens his mouth to make a witty comment. This man of the cloth was, in fact, a sophisticated hedonist.

Notice that there are two identical versions of this bust. The first one started cracking along the forehead (visible) just as Bernini was finishing it. *No problema*—Bernini whipped out a replacement in just three days.

• *Between the busts, find these paintings...*

Two Bernini Self-Portraits (*Autoritratto Giovanile,* 1623, and *Autoritratto in età Matura,* 1630-1635)

Bernini was a master of many media, including painting. The younger Bernini (age 25) looks out a bit hesitantly, as if he's still finding his way in high-class society. His jet-black eyes came from his southern Italian mother who, it's said, also gave him his passionate personality.

In his next self-portrait (roughly age 35), with a few masterpieces under his belt, Bernini shows himself with more confidence and facial hair—the dashing, vibrant man who would rebuild

Borghese Gallery—Pinacoteca

❶ BERNINI – Two Busts of Cardinal Borghese; Two Self-Portraits; Bust of Pope Paul V

❷ BERNINI – The Goat Amalthea with the Child Jupiter and a Faun

❸ RAPHAEL – Deposition; Young Woman with Unicorn

❹ CORREGGIO – Danae

❺ DOMENICHINO – The Hunt of Diana

❻ TITIAN – Sacred and Profane Love

Rome in Baroque style, from St. Peter's Square to the fountains that dot the piazzas.

• *On the table below, find the smaller...*

Bust of Pope Paul V (1618)

The cardinal's uncle was a more sober man. As pope, Paul V ruled over the artistic era of Caravaggio and Bernini. He reopened an ancient aqueduct, helped steer St. Peter's toward completion, and personally met with Galileo to discuss the heliocentrism controversy.

He was also a patron of the arts with a good eye for talent, who hired Bernini's father. When Paul saw sketches made by little Gian Lorenzo, he announced, "This boy will be the Michelangelo of his age."

• *To the right of the Borghese busts, find a small statue of...*

The Goat Amalthea with the Child Jupiter and a Faun (La Capra Amaltea con Giove Bambino e un Faunetto, 1609/1615)

Bernini was barely entering puberty when he made this. (That's about the age when I mastered how to make a Play-Doh snake.) But already its arrangement takes what would become one of Bernini's trademark forms: the sculptural ensemble. The two kids are milking a goat and drinking it. The kids lean one way, the goat the other, with the whole composition contained neatly in a circle of good fun.

• *Backtrack to the staircase/elevator and turn right to find...*

Room IX
Raphael (Raffaello Sanzio)—*Deposition* (*Deposizione*, 1507)

Jesus is being taken from the cross. The men struggle heroically to support him while the women support Mary (in purple), who has fainted. Mary Magdalene rushes up to take Christ's hand. The woman who commissioned the painting had recently lost her son. She wanted to show the death of a son and the grief of a mother. We see two different faces of grief—mother Mary faints at the horror, while Mary Magdalene still can't quite believe he's gone.

Enjoy the rich colors—solid reds, green, blue, and yellow—that set off Christ's porcelain-skin body. In true Renaissance style, Raphael (1483-1520) orders the scene with geometrical perfection. The curve of Jesus' body is echoed by the swirl of Mary Magdalene's hair, and then by the curve of Calvary Hill, where Christ met his fate.

• *Also in Room IX, to your left as you face the* Deposition, *is...*

Raphael—*Portrait of Young Woman with Unicorn* (*Ritratto di Giovane Donna con un Unicorno*, c. 1506)

Raphael's genius as a portrait painter was his ability to simultaneously portray his subjects with masterful photorealism, yet also show them in their best light.

This is likely a wedding portrait. The blonde teenager poses, cradling her little dog (transformed later into a unicorn). Her body faces formally in one direction. Meanwhile, her eyes turn the other way, as if someone had just interrupted the sitting, capturing an unplanned moment. And the colors! Her rich red clothes, accented by the ruby pendant; the pellucid skin; and her delicate face, framed perfectly by the window behind, with its pale blue atmosphere. It's little wonder that Raphael's sweet style dominated painting for a century, until the coming of Caravaggio.

• *Continue into...*

Room X
Correggio—*Danae* (c. 1531)

Cupid strips Danae as she spreads her legs, most unladylike, to receive a trickle of gold from the smudgy cloud over-head—this was Zeus' idea of intercourse with a human. The sheets are rumpled, and Danae looks right where the action is with a smile on her face.

• *Backtrack through the room with the two cardinal busts, continue through Room XV, then turn left in the small room to get to...*

Room XIX
Domenichino—*The Hunt of Diana* (*La Caccia di Diana,* 1616-1617)

Half-naked Greek nymphs are frolicking under the watchful eye of the goddess of the hunt, Diana (with her crescent-moon diadem). All eyes turn to see that one of the nymphs has successfully shot a bird. The playful scene is epitomized by the girl sprawled back-ward with abandon in the pond. (Psst—you see those two Peeping Toms?)

• *Continue into the next room.*

Room XX
Titian (Tiziano Vecellio)—*Sacred and Profane Love* (*Amor Sacro e Amor Profano,* c. 1515)

While you might guess that the naked woman on the right embod-ies profane love, that's actually represented by the material girl on

the left—with her box of treasures, fortified castle, and dark, claustrophobic landscape. Sacred love is represented by the naked woman who has nothing to hide and enjoys open spaces filled with light, life, a church in the distance, and even a couple of lovers in the field.

The clothed woman at left has recently married, and she cradles a vase filled with jewels representing the riches of earthly love. Her naked twin on the right holds the burning flame of eternal, heavenly love. Baby Cupid, between them, playfully stirs the waters.

Symbolically, the steeple on the right points up to the love of heaven, while on the left, soldiers prepare to "storm the castle" of the new bride. Miss Heavenly Love looks jealous.

This exquisite painting expresses the spirit of the Renaissance—that earth and heaven are two sides of the same coin. And here in the Borghese Gallery, that love of earthly beauty can be spiritually uplifting—as long as you feel it within two hours.

NATIONAL MUSEUM OF ROME

*Museo Nazionale Romano •
Palazzo Massimo*

Rome lasted a thousand years...and so do most Roman history courses. But if you want a breezy overview of this fascinating society, there's no better place than the National Museum of Rome.

Rome took Greek culture and wrote it in capital letters. Thanks to this lack of originality, ancient Greek statues were preserved for our enjoyment today. But the Romans also pioneered a totally new form of art—sculpting painfully realistic portraits of emperors and important citizens.

Think of this museum as a walk back in time. As you gaze at the same statues that the Romans swooned over, the history of Rome comes alive—from Julius Caesar's murder to Caligula's incest to Vespasian's Colosseum to the coming of Christianity.

Orientation

Cost: €10 combo-ticket valid for three days, includes entry into three lesser National Museum branches: the nearby Museum of the Bath (lackluster ancient inscriptions), Palazzo Altemps (so-so sculptures), and Crypta Balbi (medieval art). The price drops to €7 without mandatory special exhibits.

Hours: Tue-Sun 9:00-19:45, closed Mon, last entry 45 minutes before closing.

When to Go: The museum is never crowded. Since it has a convenient and free bag check (even for backpacks and suitcases), consider a visit en route from the train station.

Getting There: The museum is in Palazzo Massimo, situated between Piazza della Repubblica (Metro: Repubblica) and Termini Station (Metro: Termini). It's a few minutes' walk from either Metro stop. As you leave Termini, it's the sandstonebrick building on your left. Enter at the far end, at Largo di Villa Peretti.

Information: Tel. 06-3996-7700, www.archeoroma.beniculturali. it/en.

Tours: Audioguides cost €5 and last three hours.

Length of This Tour: Allow two hours. If you have less time, at least do the ground floor and the first floor as far as the Discus Thrower.

Photography: Photos allowed without flash.

Starring: Roman emperor busts, the Discus Thrower, original Greek statues, and fine Roman copies.

OVERVIEW

The Palazzo Massimo is the permanent home of major Greek and Roman statues that were formerly scattered in other national museums around town.

The museum is rectangular, with rooms and hallways built around a central courtyard. The ground-floor displays follow Rome's history as it changes from a democratic republic to a dictatorial empire. The first-floor exhibits take Rome from its peak through its slow decline. The second floor houses rare frescoes and fine mosaics, and the basement presents coins and everyday objects. As you tour this museum, note that in Italian, "room" is *sala* and "hall" is *galleria*.

The Tour Begins

GROUND FLOOR—FROM SENATORS TO CAESARS

• *Buy your ticket and pass through the turnstile, where you'll find...*

Minerva

It's big, it's gaudy, it's a weird goddess from a pagan cult. Welcome to the Roman world. The statue is also a good reminder that all the statues in this museum—now missing limbs, scarred by erosion, or weathered down to bare stone—were once whole, and painted to look as lifelike as possible.

• *Continue straight ahead into the courtyard. The first corridor—called Gallery I—is lined with portrait busts.*

Gallery I
Portrait Heads from the Republic (500-1 B.C.)

Stare into the eyes of these stern, hardy, no-nonsense farmer-stock people who founded Rome. The wrinkles and crags of these origi-

National Museum—Ground Floor

ROOM III

ROOM II

ROOM I
3

STAIRS ELEV.

BAGGAGE CHECK

6 **7**

GALLERY I

2

1

WC

TICKETS

5

STEPS

ROOM IV

ROOM V

Open-air Courtyard

ENTRY

GALLERY II

4

8 GALLERY III **9**

ROOM VI
10

ROOM VII
11

ROOM VIII

STAIRS UP TO FIRST FLOOR

VIA

VIMINALE

To Termini Train Station

Not to Scale

To Piazza Repubblica

1 Minerva
2 Portrait Heads
3 Julius Caesar (?)
4 Augustus as Pontifex Maximus

5 Livia
6 Tiberius
7 Caligula
8 Alexander the Great

9 Socrates
10 Dying Niobid
11 The Boxer at Rest & Hellenistic Prince

nal "ugly republicans" tell the story of Rome's roots as a small agricultural tribe, fighting for survival with neighboring bands.

These faces are brutally realistic, unlike more idealized Greek statues. Romans honored their ancestors and worthy citizens in the "family" *(gens)* of Rome. They wanted lifelike statues to remember them by, and to instruct the young with their air of moral rectitude.

In its first 500 years, Rome was a republic ruled by a Senate of wealthy landowners. But as Rome expanded throughout Italy, and the economy shifted from farming to booty, changes became necessary.

• *Enter Room I (Sala I). Along the left wall, find the portrait bust that may (or may not) be Julius Caesar.*

Room I
Julius Caesar? (labeled *Rilievo con ritratto di uomo anziano*)

Some scholars have identified this bust as representing Rome's most famous citizen (while others disagree).

Julius Caesar (c. 100-44 B.C.)—with his prominent brow, high cheekbones, and male-pattern baldness with the forward comb-over—changed Rome forever.

When this charismatic general swept onto the scene, Rome was in chaos. Rich landowners were fighting middle-class plebs, who wanted their slice of the plunder. Slaves such as Spartacus were picking up hoes and hacking up masters. And renegade generals—the new providers of wealth and security in an economy of plunder—were becoming dictators. (Notice the **life-size statue** with a shaved-off head, of an unknown but obviously once-renowned general.)

Caesar was a people's favorite. He conquered Gaul (France), then sacked Egypt, then impregnated Cleopatra. He defeated rivals and made them his allies. He gave great speeches. Chicks dug him.

With the army at his back and the people in awe, he took the reins of government, instituted sweeping changes, made himself the center of power...and antagonized the Senate.

A band of republican assassins surrounded him in a Senate meeting. He called out for help as one by one they stepped up to take turns stabbing him. The senators sat and watched in silence. One of the killers was his adopted son, Brutus, and Caesar—astonished that even he joined in—died saying, *"Et tu, Brute?"*

• *At the end of Gallery I, turn left and enter the large glassed-in Room V, with a life-size statue of Augustus.*

Room V
Augustus as Pontifex Maximus *(Augusto Pontefice Massimo)*
Julius Caesar died, but his family name, his politics, and his flamboyance lived on. Julius had adopted his grandnephew, Octavian,

who united Rome's warring factions and took the name and title "Augustus," meaning "venerable" or "protected by the gods."

Here, Emperor Augustus has taken off his armor and laurel-leaf crown, donning the simple hooded robes of a priest. He's retiring to a desk job after a lifetime of fighting to reunite Rome. He killed Brutus and eliminated his rivals, Mark Antony and Cleopatra. For the first time in almost a century of fighting, one general reigned supreme. Augustus became the first of the emperors who would rule Rome for the next 500 years.

In fact, Augustus was a down-to-earth man who lived simply, worked hard, read books, listened to underlings, and tried to restore traditional Roman values after the turbulence of Julius Caesar's time. He outwardly praised the Senate, while actually reducing it to a rubber-stamp body. Augustus' reign marked the start of 200 years of peace and prosperity, the Pax Romana.

See if the statue matches this description of Augustus by a contemporary, the historian Suetonius: "He was unusually handsome. His expression was calm and mild. He had clear, bright eyes, in which was a kind of divine power. His hair was slightly curly and somewhat golden." Any variations were made by sculptors who idealized his features to make him almost godlike.

Augustus proclaimed himself a god—not arrogantly or blasphemously, as Caligula later did, but as the honored "father" of the "family" of Rome. As the empire expanded, the vanquished had to worship statues like this one as a show of loyalty.

• *Nearby—here in Room V, in the hallway, and in Room IV—you'll find busts of other members of his powerful family. Start with his wife, Livia, over in Room IV.*

Room IV—Rome's First Emperors (c. 50 B.C.-A.D. 68)

Julius Caesar's descendants—the Julio-Claudian family—ruled Rome for a century after his death, turning the family surname "Caesar" into a title.

Livia

Augustus' wife, Livia, was a major power behind the throne. Her stern, thin-lipped gaze withered rivals at court. Her hairstyle—bunched up in a peak, braided down the center, and tied in back—

became the rage throughout the empire, as her face appeared everywhere, from statues to coins. Notice that by the next generation, a simpler bun was chic (Antonia Minore, Livia's daughter-in-law, next to Livia). And by the following generation, the trend was tight curls. Empresses dictated fashion the way emperors dictated policy.

Livia bore Augustus no sons. She lobbied hard for Tiberius, her own son by a first marriage, to succeed as emperor. Augustus didn't like him, but Livia was persuasive. He relented, ate some bad figs, and died—the gossip was that Livia poisoned him to seal the bargain. The pattern of succession was established—adopt a son from within the extended family—and Tiberius was proclaimed emperor. (The fine frescoed walls of Livia's Anzio villa are upstairs on the second floor.)

• *In the corner of the room, find the well-worn bust of...*

Tiberius (*Tiberio,* ruled A.D. 14-37)

Scholars speculate that acne may have soured Tiberius to the world (but this statue is pocked by erosion). Shy and sullen but diligent, he worked hard to be the easygoing leader that Augustus had been. Early on, he was wise and patient, but he suffered personal setbacks. Politics forced him to divorce his only beloved and marry a tramp. His favorite brother died, then his son. Embittered, he let subordinates run things and retired to Capri, where he built a villa with underground dungeons. There he hosted orgies of sex, drugs, torture, really loud music, and execution. At his side was his young grandnephew, whom he adopted as the next emperor.

• *To your right, in the glass case, is the small bust of...*

Caligula (*Caligola,* ruled A.D. 37-41)

This emperor had sex with his sisters, tortured his enemies, made off with friends' wives during dinner parties and then returned to rate their performance in bed, crucified Christians, took cuts in line at the Vatican Museum, and ordered men to kneel before him as a god. Caligula has become the archetype of a man with enough power to act out his basest fantasies.

    Politically, he squandered Rome's money, then taxed and extorted from the citizens. Perhaps he was made mad by illness, perhaps he was the victim of vindictive historians, but still, no one mourned when assassins ambushed him and ran a sword through his privates. Rome was tiring of this family dynasty's dysfunction.

• *Continue down Gallery II and turn left. Busts line Gallery III. Find Alexander the Great ("Alessandro Magno," outside Room VI) and Socrates ("Socrate," farther down the hall, outside Room VIII).*

Gallery III—Rome's Greek Mentors

Rome's legions easily conquered the less-organized but more-cultured Greek civilization that had dominated the Mediterranean for centuries. Romans adopted Greek gods, art styles, and fashions, and sophisticates sprinkled their conversation with Greek phrases.

Alexander the Great *(Alessandro Magno)*

Alexander the Great (356-323 B.C.) single-handedly created a Greek-speaking empire by conquering, in just a few short years,

lands from Greece to Egypt to Persia. Later, when the Romans conquered Greece (c. 200 B.C.), they inherited this pre-existing collection of cultured Greek cities ringing the Mediterranean.

Alexander's handsome statues set the standard for those of later Roman emperors. His features were chiseled and youthful, and this statue was adorned with pompous decorations, like a golden sunburst aura (fitted into the holes). The greatest man of his day, he ruled the known world by the age of 30.

Alexander's teacher was none other than the philosopher Aristotle. Aristotle's teacher was Plato, whose mentor was...

Socrates *(Socrate)*

This nonconformist critic of complacent thinking is the father of philosophy. The Greeks were an intellectual, introspective, sensitive, and artistic people. The Romans were practical, no-nonsense soldiers, salesmen, and bureaucrats. Many a Greek slave was more cultured than his master, reduced to the role of warning his boss not to wear a plaid toga with a polka-dot robe.

• *Backtrack and enter Room VI.*

Room VI—Greek Beauty in Originals and Copies
Dying Niobid *(Niobide Morente, 440 B.C.)*

The Romans were astonished by the beauty of Greek statues. The smooth skin of this Niobid (the term for any child of the goddess Niobe) contrasts with the rough folds of her clothing. She twists naturally around an axis running straight up and down. This woman looks like a classical goddess awakening from a beautiful dream, but...

Circle around back. The hole bored in her back, right in that itchy place you can't quite reach, once held a golden arrow. The woman has been shot by Artemis, goddess of hunting, because her mother dared to boast to the gods about her kids. The Niobid reaches back in vain, trying to remove the arrow before it drains her of life.

Romans ate this stuff up: the sensual beauty, the underplayed pathos, the very Greekness of it. They crated up centuries-old statues like this and brought them home to their gardens and palaces. Soon there weren't enough old statues to meet the demand. Crafty Greeks began cranking out knockoffs of Greek originals for mass consumption. Rooms VII and VIII contain both originals (like the Niobid) and copies—some of extremely high quality, others resembling cheesy fake *David*s in a garden store. Appreciate the beauty of the world's rare, surviving Greek originals.

Rome conquered Greece, but culturally the Greeks conquered the Romans.

• *Move next door to see...*

Room VII—Hellenistic and Classical Bronzes
The Boxer at Rest (*Pugilatore,* first century B.C.)

An exhausted boxer sits between rounds and gasps for air. Check out the brass knuckles-type Roman boxing gloves. Textbook Hellenistic, this pugilist is realistic and full of emotion. His face is scarred, his back muscles are knotted, and he's got cauliflower ears. He's losing.

Slumped over, he turns with a questioning look ("Why am I losing again?"), and eyes that once held glass now make him look empty indeed. "I coulda been a contender."

Hellenistic Prince (*Principe Elenistico*)

Back then, everyone wanted to be like Alexander the Great. This restored bronze statue—naked and leaning on a spear—shows a prince (probably Attalus II of Pergamon) in the style of a famous statue of his hero from the second century B.C.

• *We've covered Rome's first 500 years. At the end of the hall are the stairs up to the first floor.*

National Museum—First Floor

ROOM VIII
ROOM IX
ROOM X
ROOM XI
ROOM XII
ROOM VII
ROOM VI
ROOM V
ROOM XIII

Open Courtyard Below

GALLERY II

ROOM I
ROOM II
ROOM XIV

STAIRS FROM GROUND FLOOR

Not to Scale

❶ Vespasian
❷ Domitian
❸ Domitia
❹ Nerva
❺ Trajan
❻ Hadrian
❼ Aphrodite Crouching
❽ The Discus Thrower
❾ Hermaphrodite Sleeping
❿ Apollo
⓫ Septimius Severus
⓬ Caracalla
⓭ Sarcophagus with Processional Scene
⓮ Christ Teaching

FIRST FLOOR—ROME'S PEAK AND SLOW FALL

As we saw, Augustus' family did not always rule wisely. Under Nero (ruled A.D. 54-68), the debauchery, violence, and paranoia typical of the Julio-Claudians festered to a head. When the city burned in the great fire of 64, the Romans suspected Nero of torching it himself to clear land for his enormous luxury palace.

Enough. Facing a death sentence, Nero committed suicide with the help of a servant. An outsider was brought in to rule—Vespasian, from the Flavian family.

• *At the top of the stairs, enter Room I and then move into the hallway on the left. To your left is the...*

Flavian Family
Vespasian (*Vespasianus,* ruled A.D. 69-79)

Balding and wrinkled, with a big head, a double chin, and a shy smile, Vespasian was a common man. The son of a tax collector, he rose through the military ranks with a reputation as a competent drudge. As emperor, he restored integrity, raised taxes, started the Colosseum, and suppressed the Jewish rebellion in Palestine.

NATIONAL MUSEUM

Domitian (*Domitianus*, ruled A.D. 81-96)

Vespasian's son, Domitian, used his father's tax revenues to construct the massive Imperial Palace on Palatine Hill, home to emperors for the next three centuries. Shown with his lips curled in a sneer, he was a moralistic prude who executed several Vestal ex-Virgins, while in private he took one mistress after another. Until...

Domitia

...his stern wife found out and hired a servant to stab him in the groin. Domitia's hairstyle is a far cry from the "Livia" cut, with a high crown of tight curls.

Nerva (ruled A.D. 96-98)

Nerva realized that the Flavian dynasty was no better than its predecessors. Old and childless, he made a bold, far-sighted move—he adopted a son from outside of Rome's corrupting influence.

• *Go back to Room I and head straight to Room II, where you'll find Trajan on the left wall.*

Room II—A Cosmopolitan Culture
Trajan (*Traianus-Hercules,* ruled A.D. 98-117)

Born in Spain, this conquering hero pushed Rome's borders to their greatest extent, creating a truly worldwide empire. The spoils of three continents funneled into a city of a million-plus people. Trajan could dress up in a lion's skin, presenting himself as a "new Hercules," and no one found it funny. Romans, in the words of Livy the historian, felt a spirit of Manifest Destiny: "The gods desire that the City of Rome shall be the capital of all the countries of the world"—the Caput Mundi.

• *On the opposite wall is...*

Hadrian (*Hadrianus*, ruled A.D. 117-138)

Hadrian was a fully cosmopolitan man. His beard—the first we've seen—shows his taste for foreign things; he poses like the Greek philosopher he imagined himself to be.

Hadrian was a voracious tourist, personally visiting almost every cor-

NATIONAL MUSEUM

ner of the vast empire, from Britain (where he built Hadrian's Wall) to Egypt (where he sailed the Nile), from Jerusalem (where he suppressed another Jewish revolt) to Athens (where he soaked up classical culture). He scaled Sicily's Mount Etna just to see what made a volcano tick. Back home, he beautified Rome with the Pantheon and his villa at Tivoli, a microcosm of places he'd visited.

Hadrian is flanked here by the two loves of his life. His wife, **Sabina** (left), with modest hairstyle and scarf, kept the home fires burning for her traveling husband. Hadrian was 50 years old when he became captivated by a teenage boy named **Antinous** (right), with his curly hair and full, sensual lips. Together they traveled the Nile, where Antinous drowned. Hadrian wept. Statues of Antinous subsequently went up throughout the Empire, much to the embarrassment of the stoic Romans.

Hadrian spent his last years at his lavish villa outside Rome, surrounded by buildings and souvenirs that reminded him of his traveling days (see Tivoli Day Trip chapter).

• *Backtrack through Room I and into the gallery, then turn right, down the hall that leads into the large Room V.*

Rooms V and VI—Rome's Grandeur

Pause at Rome's peak to admire the things the Romans found beautiful. Imagine these statues as they originally stood—in the pleasure gardens of the Roman rich, surrounded by greenery with the splashing sound of fountains, all painted in bright, lifelike colors. Though executed by Romans, the themes are mostly Greek, with godlike humans and human-looking gods.

• *At the beginning of Room V is...*

Aphrodite Crouching *(Afrodite al Bagno Accovacciata)*

The goddess of beauty crouches while bathing, then turns to admire herself. This sets her whole body in motion—one thigh goes down, the other up; her head turns clockwise while her body goes in reverse—yet she's perfectly still. The crouch creates a series of symmetrical love handles, molded by the sculptor into the marble-like wax. Hadrian had good taste—he ordered a copy of this Greek classic for his bathroom.

• *At the far end of the room, pass into Room VI, with...*

The Discus Thrower *(Discobolo)*

An athlete winds up, about to unleash his pent-up energy and hurl the discus. The sculptor has frozen the moment for us so that we can examine the inner workings of the wonder called Man. The perfect pecs and washboard abs make this human god-like. Geometrically, you could draw a perfect circle around him, with his hipbone at the center. He's natural yet ideal, twisting yet balanced, moving while at rest. For the Greeks, the universe was a rational place, and the human body was the perfect embodiment of the order found in nature.

This statue is the best-preserved Roman copy (not one member is missing—I checked) of the original Greek work by Myron (450 B.C.). (The subtle nubs on his head were aids for a measuring device used when making copies.) Statues of athletes like this commonly stood in the baths, where Romans cultivated healthy bodies, minds, and social skills, hoping to lead well-rounded lives. The Discus Thrower, with his geometrical perfection and godlike air, sums up all that is best in the classical world.

• *Continue into...*

Room VII
Hermaphrodite Sleeping *(Ermafrodito Dormiente)*
After leaving the baths, a well-rounded Roman may head posthaste to an orgy, where he might see a reclining nude like this, be titillated, circle around for a closer look, and say, "Hey! *(Insert your own reaction here)*!"

This nude lying on his/her stomach possesses the perfect, lithe female form. But as you can see, she/he is equipped with both breasts and a penis. It's the Greek/Roman god Hermaphroditus—the child of Hermes and Aphrodite, and protector of bisexuals.

Apollo *(Apollo del Tevere)*
The god of light appears as a slender youth, not as some burly, powerful, autocratic deity. He stands *contrapposto*—originally he was leaning against the tree—in a relaxed and very human way. His curled hair is tied with a headband, strands tumbling down his neck. His muscles and skin are smooth. (The rusty stains come from the centuries the statue spent submerged in the Tiber.) Apollo is in a reflective mood, and the serenity and intelligence in his face show off classical Greece as a nation of thinkers.

• Exit Room VII at the far end, cut through Gallery II, and make your way to Room XIII, where you'll find the bust of Septimius Severus.

Room XIII—Beginning of the End
Septimius Severus (ruled A.D. 193-211)

Rome's sprawling empire was starting to un-ravel, and it took a disciplined emperor-warrior like this African to keep it together. Severus' victories on the frontier earned him a grand tri-umphal arch in the Forum, but here he seems to be rolling his eyes at the chaos growing around him.

• Near Severus is his son...

Caracalla (ruled A.D. 211-217)

The stubbly beard, cruel frown, and glaring eyes tell us that Severus' son was bad news. He mur-dered his little brother to seize power, then pro-ceeded to massacre thousands of loyal citizens on a whim. The army came to distrust rulers whose personal agenda got in their way, and Caracalla was stabbed in the back by a man whose brother had just been executed. Rome's long slide had begun.

• Move next door into...

Room XIV—The Fall

There are a lot of serious faces in this room. People who grew up in the lap of luxury and security were witnessing the unthinkable—the disintegration of a thousand years of tradition. Rome never re-covered from the chaos of the third century. Disease, corruption, revolts from within, and "barbarians" pecking away at the borders were body blows that sapped Rome's strength.

Sarcophagus with Processional Scene
(*Sarcofago con Corteo,* A.D. 270)

A parade of dignitaries, accompanying a new Roman leader, marches up Capitoline Hill. They huddle together, their backs to

the wall, looking around suspiciously for assassins. Their faces reflect the fear of the age.

By the third century, the Roman army could virtually hand-pick an em-peror to be their front man. At one point, the office of emperor was literally auctioned to the highest bidder. In the space of 40 years, 15 different emperors were saluted, then murdered, at the whims of soldiers of fortune.

Rome would stagger on for another 200 years, but the glory of old Rome was gone. The city was becoming a den of thugs, thieves, prostitutes, barbarians...and Christians.

• *Farther along, on the right-hand wall, find the small...*

Christ Teaching (*Cristo Docente,* A.D. 350)

Christ sits like a Roman senator—in a toga, holding a scroll, dispensing wisdom like the law of the land. The statuette comes from

those delirious days when formerly persecuted Christians could now "come out" and worship in public. Emperor Constantine (ruled A.D. 306-337) legalized Christianity, and within two generations it was Rome's official religion.

Whether Christianity invigorated or ruined Rome is debated, but the fall was inevitable. Rome's once-great legions backpedaled, until even the city itself was raped and plundered by foreigners (410). In 476, the last emperor sold his title for a comfy pension plan, "Rome" became just another dirty city with a big history, and the artistic masterpieces now in this museum were buried under rubble.

THE REST OF THE MUSEUM

• *For extra credit, consider exploring two more parts of the National Museum.*

Second Floor

This floor contains frescoes and mosaics that once decorated the walls and floors of Roman villas. They're remarkably realistic and

unstuffy, featuring everyday people, animals, flowery patterns, and geometrical designs. The **Villa Farnesina frescoes**—in black, red, yellow, and blue—are mostly architectural designs, with fake columns, friezes, and garlands. The **Villa di Livia**

frescoes, owned by the wily wife of Augustus, immerse you in a leafy green garden full of birds and fruit trees, symbolizing the gods.

Basement (Floor -2)

The **"Luxury in Rome"** rooms give a peek into the lives of Rome's well-to-do citizens, featuring fine jewelry, common everyday objects, and an eight-year-old girl's mummy.

Next, enter the **coin collection.** Find your favorite emperor or empress on the coins: Julius Caesar (case 8, #41-44), Augustus (case 8, #65-69, and case 9, #1-38), Augustus' system of denars (case 10), Tiberius (case 10, #1-16), Caligula (case 10, #17-28), and Nero (case 11, #2-33). Evaluate Roman life by studying how Diocletian tweaked the gold standard (glass case 21). In A.D. 300, one denar bought one egg. The rest of the displays trace Europe's money from denars to euros. Exhibit 59 features a more recent monetary unit that is, nevertheless, now history: the Italian lira. And finally, case 62 brings us up-to-date with Rome's latest coinage, the euro.

PILGRIM'S ROME TOUR

Pilgrimage Churches

Rome is the "capital" of the world's 1.2 billion Catholics. In Rome, you'll rub elbows with religious pilgrims from around the world—Nigerian nuns, Bulgarian theology students, extended Mexican families, and everyday Catholics returning to their religious roots.

The pilgrim industry helped shape Rome after the fall of the empire. Ancient Rome's population peaked at about 1.2 million. After Rome fell in A.D. 476, barbarians cut off the water supply by breaking the aqueducts, Romans fled the city, and the mouth of the Tiber River filled with silt and became a swamp.

During the Dark Ages, mosquitoes ruled over a pathetic village of 20,000...bad news for pilgrims, bad news for the papacy. Back then, the Catholic Church was the Christian Church. Centuries later, during the Renaissance, popes sought to project an image of prestige and authority. The Church revitalized the city, creating a place fit for pilgrimages. Owners of hotels and restaurants cheered.

In 1587, Pope Sixtus V reconnected aqueducts and built long, straight boulevards connecting the great churches and pilgrimage sites. Obelisks were moved to serve as markers. As you explore the city, think like a pilgrim. Look down long roads and you'll see either a grand church or an obelisk (from which you'll see a grand church).

Pilgrims to Rome try to visit four great basilicas: St. Peter's Basilica, of course (✪ see tour in this book), St. Paul's Outside the Walls (see page 101), Santa Maria Maggiore, and San Giovanni in Latera-

Pilgrim's Rome

no. The last two are covered in this chapter, as well as two other "honorable mentions": The Church of Santa Prassede (Rome's best Byzantine-style mosaics) is near Santa Maria Maggiore, and the fascinating and central San Clemente is between San Giovanni in Laterano and the Colosseum.

Orientation

Planning Your Time: Depending on your time and interest level, you may want to hit every sight described in this chapter—or maybe just visit one or two of the churches. **Santa Maria Maggiore** (and nearby **Santa Prassede**) have mosaics that date back to the first days of Christian Rome. **San Giovanni in Laterano** is grandiose and historic, and its Holy Stairs are a one-of-a-kind experience. **San Clemente**'s church-beneath-church layout leads you down—layer by mysterious layer—to a pagan Mithraic temple. To link all of this chapter's sights efficiently, check their opening hours (Santa Prassede, San Clemente, and San Giovanni in Laterano's Holy Stairs all close for several hours at midday) and decide whether you want to travel on foot, by taxi, or on public transit.

Getting to the Churches: Santa Maria Maggiore and San Giovanni in Laterano, this chapter's two biggies, are both just a few minutes' walk from Metro stops and both on line A. Santa Maria Maggiore is at Piazza Santa Maria Maggiore (Metro: Termini or Vittorio Emanuele), and San Giovanni in Laterano is located on Piazza di San Giovanni in Laterano (Metro: San Giovanni).

Santa Maria Maggiore is a couple-minute walk from Santa Prassede (see page 302 for walking directions), a 15-minute walk (or €6 taxi ride) to San Clemente, and a 15-20-minute walk to San Giovanni in Laterano. If you don't want to walk from Santa Maria Maggiore to San Giovanni in Laterano, either catch bus #16 (runs along Via Merulana) or bus #714, or hop into a taxi.

San Clemente (Metro: Colosseo) is an easy 15-minute walk from San Giovanni in Laterano, but connected by bus as well (the #87 runs from Largo Argentina to Piazza Venezia to the Colosseo Metro stop to the Church of San Clemente to the Church of San Giovanni in Laterano; bus #85 does the same route but skips Largo Argentina).

Church of Santa Maria Maggiore: Free, daily 7:00-19:00, skip the €3 museum and the €5 "archaeological zone."

Church of Santa Prassede: Free, bring €0.50 and €1 coins for lights, daily 7:00-12:00 & 16:00-18:30.

Church of San Clemente: Upper church-free, lower church-€5, both open Mon-Sat 9:00-12:30 & 15:00-18:00, Sun 12:00-18:00, last entry for lower church 20 minutes before closing.

Church of San Giovanni in Laterano: Church-free, daily 7:00-18:30; cloister-€5, €8 combo-ticket also covers chapel at Holy Stairs, daily 9:00-18:00, last entry 30 minutes before closing; church audioguide available (donation requested unless you're paying for cloister entry, ID required as deposit; pick up at info desk near the main door, either inside or outside).

The **Holy Stairs** (Scala Santa), in a building across the street from the church, are free (April-Sept Mon-Sat 6:00-12:00 & 15:00-19:00, Sun 7:00-12:30 & 15:30-19:00, Oct-March daily 7:00-12:30 & 15:00-18:30, last entry 15 minutes before closing, www.scalasanta.net). The chapel at the Holy Stairs costs €3.50 (€8 combo-ticket also covers San Giovanni in Laterano cloister, Mon-Sat 9:30-12:00 & 15:00-17:10, closed Sun).

Dress Code: Modest dress is recommended (knees and shoulders covered).

Photography: Generally, photos without flash are allowed in Rome's churches. On this tour, however, no photos are allowed in San Clemente.

The Tour Begins

Four churches are covered in this tour. You can visit all four, or pick and choose the ones that interest you most. See "Getting to the Churches," earlier, for details on linking these sights.

CHURCH OF SANTA MARIA MAGGIORE

The basilica of Santa Maria celebrates Holy Mary, the mother of Jesus. One of Rome's oldest and best-preserved churches, it was built (A.D. 432) while Rome was falling around it. The city had been sacked by Visigoths (410), and the emperors were about to check out (476). Increasingly, popes stepped in to fill the vacuum of leadership. The fifth-century mosaics give the church the feel of the early-Christian community. The general ambience of the church really takes you back to ancient times.

Exterior

Mary's column originally stood in the Forum's Basilica of Constantine. The fifth-century church built in her honor proclaims she was

indeed the Mother of God—a point disputed by hair-splitting theologians of the day. When you step inside the church, you'll be exiting Italy and entering the Vatican—the "Maggiore" in the church's name indicates that this church, a Vatican possession, was much more important than other churches dedicated to the Virgin Mary.

Inside the Church

Despite the Renaissance ceiling and Baroque crusting, you still feel like you're walking into an early Christian church. The stately rows of columns, the simple basilica layout (nave flanked by side aisles), the cheery colors, the spacious nave—it's easy to imagine worshippers finding an oasis of peace here as the Roman Empire crashed around them. (The 15th-century coffered ceiling is gilded with gold—perhaps brought back from America by Columbus.)

• *In the center of the church is the main altar, under a purple and gold canopy. Underneath the altar, in a lighted niche, are...*

Santa Maria Maggiore

Piazza dell'Esquilino

APSE

2

3

1 **7**

4 PAULINE CHAPEL

5

SIXTUS V CHAPEL

6

N
A
V
E

GIFT SHOP, MUSEUM & **WC**

20 Meters
20 Yards

P O R C H

↑ ENTER

To Santa Prassede (100 Yards)

Piazza Santa Maria Maggiore

1 Manger Fragments
2 Apse Mosaic
3 Mosaics in Chancel Arch
4 Madonna Painting & Miracle Relief

5 Nave Mosaics
6 Tomb of Sixtus V
7 Bernini's Tomb

1 Manger Fragments

A kneeling Pope Pius IX (who established the dogma of the Immaculate Conception in the 19th century) prays before a glass case with an urn that contains several pieces of wood, bound by iron— these pieces are said to be from Jesus' crib. The church, dedicated to

Mary's motherhood, displays these relics as physical evidence that Mary was indeed the mother of Christ. (The church is also built on the site of a former pagan temple dedicated to Rome's mother goddess, Juno.) Is the manger the real thing? Look into the eyes of pilgrims who visit.

• *In the apse, topped with a semicircular dome, find the...*

❷ Apse Mosaic

This 13th-century mosaic shows Mary being crowned by Jesus, both on the same throne. They float in a bubble representing heaven, borne aloft by angels. By the Middle Ages, Mary's cult status was secure.

• *Up in the arch that frames the outside of the apse, you'll find some of the church's oldest mosaics.*

❸ Mosaics in Chancel Arch

Colorful panels tell Mary's story in fifth-century Roman terms. Haloed senator-saints in white togas (top panel on left side) attend to Mary, who sits on a throne, dressed in gold and crowned like an empress. The angel Gabriel swoops down to announce to Mary that she'll conceive Jesus, and the Dove of the Holy Spirit follows. Below (the panel in the bottom-left corner) are sheep representing the apostles, entering the city of Jerusalem ("HIERVSALEM").

• *In the transept to your left, over the altar, you'll see a...*

❹ Madonna Painting and Miracle Relief

The altar, a geologist's delight, is adorned with jasper, agate, amethyst, lapis lazuli, and gold angels. Amid it all is a simple icon of the lady this church is dedicated to: Mary.

Above the painting is a bronze relief panel showing a pope, with amazed bystanders, shoveling snow. One hot August night in the year 432, Mary appeared to Pope Liberius in a dream, telling him: "Build me a church where the snow falls." The next morning, they discovered a small patch of snow here on Esquiline Hill—on August 5—and this church, dedicated to Santa Maria, was begun.

• *Back out in the nave, on the other side of the altar, take a look at the...*

❺ Nave Mosaics

The church contains some of the world's oldest and best-preserved mosaics from Christian Rome. If the floodlights are on (it doesn't hurt to ask someone), those with good eyesight or binoculars will enjoy watching the story of Moses unfold in a series of surprisingly colorful and realistic scenes—more sophisticated than anything that would be seen for a thousand years.

The small, square mosaic panels are above all the columns, on the right side of the nave. Start at the altar and work back toward the entry.

1. This is a later painting—skip it.
2. Pharaoh's daughter (upper left) and her maids take baby Moses from the Nile.
3. Moses (lower half of panel) sees a burning bush that reconnects him with his Hebrew origins.
4. A parade of Israelites (left side) flees Egypt through a path in the Red Sea, while Pharaoh's troops drown.
5. Moses leads them across the Sinai desert (upper half), and God provides for them with a flock of quail (lower half).
6. Moses (upper half) sticks his magic rod in a river to desalinate it.
7. The Israelites battle their enemies while Moses commands from a hillside.
8. Skip it.
9. Moses (upper left) brings the Ten Commandments, then goes with Joshua (upper right) to lie down and die.
10. Joshua crosses the (rather puny) Jordan River...
11. ...and attacks Jericho...
12. ...and then the walls come a-tumblin' down.

• *Head back toward the altar to see if the gate to the right transept is open. If so, enter the chapel (otherwise skip ahead to Bernini's Tomb). On the right wall of the chapel is a statue of a praying pope, atop the...*

❻ Tomb of Sixtus V

The Rome we see today is due largely to Pope Sixtus V (or was it Fiftus VI?). This energetic pope (1585-1590) leveled shoddy medieval Rome and erected grand churches connected by long, broad boulevards spiked with obelisks as focal points (such as the obelisk in Piazza dell'Esquilino behind Santa Maria Maggiore). Today the city of Rome has 13 Egyptian obelisks (and the ancient city had many more)—whereas all of Egypt has only five. The white carved-marble relief panels (especially the one in the upper right) show some of the obelisks and buildings he commissioned.

• *Walk down the right aisle; on your left, look for an inscription on the first step between two pillars. This marks...*

❼ Bernini's Tomb

The plaque reads, *"Ioannes Laurentivs Bernini"*—Gian Lorenzo Bernini (1598-1680)—"who brought honor to art and the city, here humbly rests." Next to it is another plaque to the *"Familia Bernini."* It's certainly humble...a simple memorial for the man who grew up in this neighborhood, then went on to remake Rome in the ornate Baroque style. (For more on Bernini, see page 274.)

• *After looking around Santa Maria Maggiore, fans of mosaics, Byz-*

*antines, and the offbeat should consider a visit to the nearby Church of
Santa Prassede, about 100 yards away.*

*Exiting Santa Maria Maggiore, walk away from the church and
cross the street to the right of Mary on her column; Santa Prassede is just
behind the building with the cafés.*

CHURCH OF SANTA PRASSEDE

The mosaics at the Church of Santa Prassede, from A.D. 822, are
the best Byzantine-style mosaics in Rome. The Byzantine Empire,
with its capital in Constantinople (ancient Istanbul), was the eastern half of the Roman Empire. Unlike the western half, it didn't
"fall," and its inhabitants remained Christian, Greek-speaking, and
cultured for a thousand years while their distant cousins in Italy
were fumbling for the light switch in the Dark Ages. Byzantine
craftsmen preserved the techniques of ancient Roman mosaicists
(who decorated floors and walls of villas and public buildings), then
re-infused this learning into Rome during the city's darkest era.
Take the time to let your eyes adjust, and appreciate the Byzantine
glory glowing out of the dark church.

Bring €0.50 and €1 coins to buy floodlighting. (While €1 feels
like a lot for five minutes of light, consider it a donation to maintain the church and treat all those visiting to the full sparkle of the
mosaics.) Popping a coin into the box in the Chapel of St. Zeno
(described later) saves you a trip to Ravenna.

• *The best mosaics are in the apse (behind the main altar) and in the small
Chapel of St. Zeno along the right (north) side of the nave.*

Apse Mosaics

On a blue background is Christ, standing in a rainbow-colored
river, flanked by saints. Christ has commanded Peter (to our right
of Christ, with white hair and beard) to spread
the Good News to all the world. Beneath
Christ, 12 symbolic sheep leave Jerusalem's
city gates to preach to the world. Peter came
here to the world's biggest city to preach love...
and was met with a hostile environment. He
turns his palm up in a plea for help. Persecuted Peter was taken in by a hospitable woman
named Pudentia (next to him) and her sister,
Praxedes (to the left of Christ, between two
other saints), whose house was located on this
spot. (The church is named for Praxedes.)

The saint on the far left (with the square halo, indicating he
was alive at the time this was made) is Pope Paschal I, who built
the church in the 800s in memory of these early sisters, hiring the
best craftsmen in the known world to do the mosaics.

Chapel of St. Zeno

The ceiling is gold, representing the Byzantine heaven. An icon-like Christ emerges from the background, supported by winged angels in white. On the walls are saints walking among patches of flowers. In the altar niche, Mary and the child Jesus are flanked by the sisters Praxedes and Pudentia. On the side wall, the woman with the square blue halo is Theodora, the mom of the pope who built this.

The chapel, covered completely with mosaics, may be underwhelming to our modern eyes, but in the darkness of Rome's medieval era, it was known as the "Garden of Paradise."

CHURCH OF SAN GIOVANNI IN LATERANO

Imagine the jubilation when this church—the first Christian church in the city of Rome—was opened in about A.D. 318. Christians could finally "come out" and worship openly without fear of reprisal. (Still, most Romans were pagan, so this first great church was tucked away from the center of things, near the city wall.) After that glorious beginning, the church served as the center of Catholicism and the home of the popes until the Renaissance renovation of St. Peter's and the expansion of the Vatican. Until 1870, all popes were "crowned" here. Even today, it's the home church of the Bishop of Rome—the pope.

• *To reach the church from the San Giovanni Metro station, exit to the right onto Via Magna Grecia, then head toward the old city walls. Before you leave the square, look left to find the* **Via Sannio market,** *which sells clothing and some handicrafts every morning except Sunday. Then pass through the archways, hugging the left side of the street, to approach San Giovanni's white, statue-topped facade.*

Exterior

The massive facade is 18th-century, with Christ triumphant on

the top. The blocky peach-colored building adjacent on the right is the Lateran Palace, standing on the site of the old Papal Palace—residence of popes until about 1300. Across the street to your right are the pope's private chapel and the Holy Stairs (Scala Santa), popular with pilgrims (we'll see the stairs later). To the left is a well-preserved chunk of the ancient

San Giovanni in Laterano

8 APSE
7 CHANCEL

APSE

Piazza di San Giovanni in Laterano

6 TRANSEPT

5

To Cloister Mosaics

N A V E

LATERAN PALACE

WC

4

3

2

1 PORCH

ENTER CHURCH HERE

ENTRANCE

To Holy Stairs

Piazza di Porta San Giovanni

POSTS MARKING WHERE VATICAN CITY CONTROL BEGINS

20 Meters
20 Yards

1 Statue of Constantine
2 Central Doorway
3 Baroque Nave
4 Basilica Floor Plan
5 Baldacchino
6 Golden Columns from Temple of Jupiter
7 Bishop's Chair
8 Mosaic

Roman wall. Pass the three-foot-high granite posts surrounding the church to leave Italy and enter the Vatican State—*carabinieri* must leave their guns at the door.
• *Step inside the portico and look left.*

Inside the Portico and Church
❶ Statue of Constantine

It's October 28, A.D. 312, and Constantine—sword tucked under his arm and leaning confidently on a (missing) spear—has conquered Maxentius and liberated Rome. Constantine marched to this spot where his enemy's personal bodyguards lived, trashed their pagan idols, and dedicated the place to the god who gave him his victory—Christ. The holes in Constantine's head once held a golden, halo-like crown for the emperor who legalized Christianity. In the relief above the statue, you'll see a beheaded John the Baptist.

At the other end of the portico is the Vatican History Museum (€5, Mon-Sat 9:00-13:00, closed Sun). It's worthwhile only if it's the top of the hour (when visitors are admitted), and you like old paintings by no-name artists.

• *In the portico, take a look at the...*

❷ Central Doorway

These tall green bronze doors, with their floral designs and acorn studs, are the original doors from ancient Rome's Senate House (Curia) in the Forum. The Church moved these here in the 1650s to remind people that, from now on, the Church was Europe's lawmaker. The star borders were added to make these big doors bigger. Imagine, those cool little acorns date to the third century.

• *Now go inside the main part of the church. Stand in the back of the nave.*

❸ Baroque Nave

Very little survives from the original church—most of what you see was built after 1600. In preparation for the 1650 Jubilee, Pope Innocent X commissioned architect Francesco Borromini (rival to Bernini) to remake the interior. He redesigned the basilica in the Baroque style, reorganizing the nave, and adding the huge statues of the apostles (stepping out of niches to symbolically bring celestial Jerusalem to our world). The relief panels above the statues depict parallel events from the Old Testament (on the left) and New Testament (on the right). For instance, in the very back you'll see two resurrections: Jonah escaping the whale and Jesus escaping death. Only the ceiling (which should have been a white vault) breaks from the Baroque style—it's Renaissance, and the pope wanted it to stay.

❹ Basilica Floor Plan

San Giovanni was the first public church in Rome and the model for all later churches, including St. Peter's. The floor plan—a large central hall (nave) flanked by two side aisles—was based on the ancient Roman basilica floor plan. These buildings, built to hold law courts and meeting halls, were big enough to accommodate the large Christian congregations. Note that Roman basilicas came with two apses. You came in through the main entrance, which was designed to stress the authority of the place by slightly overwhelming and intimidating those who entered. When the design was adapted for use as a church, a grand and welcoming entry (the west portal) replaced one of the apses. Upon entering, the worshipper could take in the entire space instantly, and the rows of columns welcomed him to proceed to the altar.

• *The canopy over the altar is called the...*

❺ Baldacchino

In the upper cage are two silver statues of Sts. Peter (with keys) and Paul (sword), which contain pieces of their heads. The gossip buzzing among Rome's amateur archaeologists is that the Vatican tested DNA from Peter's head (located here) and from his body (located at St. Peter's)...and they didn't match.

• *Standing in the left transept are the...*

❻ Golden Columns from Temple of Jupiter

Tradition says that these gilded bronze columns once stood in pagan Rome's holiest spot—the Temple of Jupiter, which was dedicated to the king of all gods, on the summit of Capitoline Hill (c. 50 B.C.). Now they support a triangular pediment inhabited by a bearded, Jupiter-like God the Father.

• *In the apse, you'll find the...*

❼ Bishop's Chair

The chair (called a "cathedra") reminds visitors that this is the cathedral of Rome...and the pope himself is the bishop who sits here. Once elected, the new pope must actually sit in this chair to officially become the pope. The ceremonial sitting usually happens within one month of election—Pope Francis took his seat on April 7, 2013.

• *Under the semicircular dome of the apse, take a close look at the...*

❽ Mosaic

The original design dates from about 450 (although it was made in the 13th century and heavily restored in the 19th century). You'll see a cross, animals, plants, and the River Jordan running along the base. Mosaic, of course, was an ancient Roman specialty adapted by medieval Christians. The head of Christ (above the cross) must have been a glorious sight to early worshippers. It was one of the first legal images of Christ ever seen in formerly pagan Rome.

• *Fans of cosmatesque marble-inlay floor (c. 1100-1300) may want to buy a ticket to visit the cloister (enter near left transept).*

   The Holy Stairs are outside the church in a building across the street.

To get there, exit the church, turn left, and cross the street to the nonde-script building.

Holy Stairs (Scala Santa)

In 326, Emperor Constantine's mother (Sta. Helena) brought home the 28 marble steps of Pontius Pilate's residence in Jerusalem. Jesus

climbed these steps on the day he was sentenced to death. Each day, hundreds of faithful penitents climb these steps on their knees reciting a litany of prayers.

Covered with walnut wood spotted with small glass-covered holes showing stains from Jesus' blood, the steps lead to the "Holy of Holies" (Sancta Sanctorum), the private chapel

of the popes in the Middle Ages. With its world-class relics, this chapel was considered the holiest place on earth. The relics were moved to the Vatican in 1905.

You can climb the tourist staircases along the sides; look inside the "Holy of Holies" through the grated windows (you can see essentially the entire chapel through the grates, but if you'd like to go inside, you'll have to buy a ticket at the ticket desk downstairs, near the entrance); and buy a souvenir at the gift shop (at the top floor, on the left). Or you're welcome to actually climb the stairs on your knees (pick up the €2 booklet at the gift shop that gives the proper prayer for each of the 28 steps). If you've done a lot of praying in your life, but never accompanied your prayers with a little pain—actually a lot of pain—give this a try.

On September 20, 1870, as nationalist forces unifying Italy took Rome and ended the pope's temporal power, Pope Pius IX left his Quirinal Palace home for the last time. He stopped here to climb the steps, pray in his chapel, and bless his supporters from the top of the steps. Then he fled to the Vatican, where he spent the rest of his days.

Nearby: After exiting the steps, look right and notice the broken arch of the **Claudian Aqueduct** (1st century A.D.), which once carried water to the city from more than 40 miles away. The **Museum of the Liberation of Rome** isn't far behind it, just a few blocks down Via Tasso (see page 89). Then head toward the center of Piazza San Giovanni in Laterano—straight ahead with your back to the Holy Stairs—for a look at the world's tallest obelisk, dating from the 15th century B.C. (This is also the departure point for bus #16, which runs up Via Merulana to the Church of Santa Maria Maggiore.)

CHURCH OF SAN CLEMENTE

Here, like nowhere else, you'll enjoy the layers of Rome—a 12th-century basilica sits atop a fourth-century Christian basilica, which sits atop a second-century Mithraic temple and some even earlier Roman buildings.

Upper Church—12th Century

The church (at today's ground level) is dedicated to the fourth pope, Clement, who shepherded the small Christian community when

the religion was, at best, tolerated, and at worst, a capital offense. Clement himself was martyred by drowning in about A.D. 100—tied to an anchor by angry Romans and tossed overboard. You'll see his symbol, the anchor, around the church. The painting on the ceiling shows Clement being carried aloft to heaven.

While today's main entry is on the side, the original entry was through the **courtyard** in back, a kind of defensive atrium common in medieval times. To reach the original entry, enter the church through today's main entrance, walk diagonally toward the right, and exit again into this courtyard. Turn around and face the original entry. (This courtyard is inviting for a cool quiet break, as I imagine it was for a visiting medieval pilgrim.)

Back inside the church, step up to the carved marble **choir**—an enclosure in the middle of the church (Schola Cantorum) where the cantors sat. About 1,200 years ago, it stood in the old church beneath us, before that church was looted and destroyed by invading Normans.

In the apse (behind the altar), study the fine 12th-century mosaics. The delicate Crucifixion—with Christ sharing the cross with a dozen apostles as doves—is engulfed by a Tree of Life richly inhabited by deer, birds, and saints. The message is clear: All life springs from God in Christ. Above it all, a triumphant Christ, one hand on the Bible, blesses the congregation.

St. Catherine Chapel

The chapel in the back corner near the side (tourist) entrance—considered one of the first great Renaissance masterpieces—is dedicated to St. Catherine of Alexandria, a noblewoman martyred for her defense of persecuted Christians. The fresco on the left wall—which shows an early Renaissance three-dimensional representation of space—is by the Florentine master Masolino (1428), perhaps aided by his young assistant, Masaccio. Studying the left wall, working from left to right, you can follow her story:

1. Catherine (lower-left panel), in black, confronts an assembly of the pagan Emperor Maxentius and his counselors. She bravely ticks off arguments on her fingers why Christianity should be legalized. Her powerful delivery silences the crowd.

2. Under the rotunda of a pagan temple (above, on the upper-left panel), Catherine, in blue, points up at a statue and tells a crowd of pagans, "Your gods are puny compared to mine."

3. Catherine, in blue (upper-right panel, left side), is thrown in prison, where she's visited by the emperor's wife (in green). Catherine converts her.

4. Emperor Maxentius, enraged, orders his own wife killed. The executioner (upper panel, right side), standing next to the empress' decapitated corpse, impassively sheathes his sword.

5. In the best-known scene (the middle panel on the bottom), Maxentius, in black, looks down from a balcony and condemns Catherine (in black) to be torn apart between two large, spiked wheels turned by executioners. But suddenly, an angel swoops in with a sword to cut her loose.

6. Catherine is eventually martyred (lower-right panel). Now dressed in green, she kneels before the executioner, who raises his sword to finish the job.

7. Finally, on the top of holy Mount Sinai (same panel, upper-right corner), two angels bear Catherine's body to its final resting place.

Taking a few steps back, look up at the arch that frames the chapel, topped by the delightful Annunciation fresco (top of the arch) by Masolino. Also notice the big St. Christopher, patron saint of travelers (left pillar), with 500-year-old graffiti scratched in by pilgrims—now covered with glass.

Lower Church—Fourth Century

Buy a €5 ticket in the bookshop, and descend 1,700 years to the time when Christians were razzed on their way to church by pagan neighbors. The first room you enter was the original atrium (entry hall)—the nave extends to the right. (Everything you'll visit from here on was buried until the 19th century.)

• *Most of the way down the atrium, look for the "reversible" stone set into a metal rack that you can rotate.*

Pagan Inscription

This two-sided recycled marble burial slab—one side (with leafy decorations) for a Christian, the other for a pagan—shows how the two Romes lived side by side in the fourth century.

• *Go through the nearby door into the nave, and walk to the far end. Five yards before the altar, on the left wall, look for the...*

Fresco of St. Clement and Sisinnius

Clement (center) holds a secret Mass for early Christians back when it was a capital crime. Theodora, a prominent Roman (in yellow, to the right), is one of the undercover faithful. Her pagan husband, Sisinnius, has come to retrieve and punish her when—zap!—he's struck blind and has to be led away (right side).

But Sisinnius is still unconvinced. When Clement cures his blindness, Sisinnius (very faded, lower panel, far right) orders two servants to drag Clement off to the authorities. But through a miraculous intervention, the servants mistake a column for Clement (see the shadowy black log) and drag that out of the house instead. The inscription (crossword-style on right, waist-high, very faded) is famous among Italians because it's one of the earliest examples of the transition from Latin to Italian. Sisinnius encourages his servants by yelling *"Fili dele pute, traite!"* ("You sons of bitches, pull!")

• *In the far-left corner of the lower church (in the room behind the fresco you just saw), near the staircase leading down, is the...*

Presumed Burial Place of St. Cyril

Cyril, who died in A.D. 869 (see the modern, icon-like mosaic of him), was an inveterate traveler who spread Christianity to the Slavic lands and Russia—today's Russian Orthodox faithful. Along the way, he introduced the Cyrillic alphabet still used by Russians and many other Slavs. Thanks to their tireless missionary work, Cyril and his brother Methodius are considered the most important figures in Slavic Christianity.

• *Now descend farther to the dark, dank Mithraic temple (Mithreum; through a door immediately to the right of the altar and down steps). Nowhere in Rome is there a better place to experience this weird cult.*

Temple of Mithras (Mithreum)—Second Century

• *The barred room to the left is the...*

Worship Hall

Worshippers of Mithras—men only—reclined on the benches on either side of the room. At the far end is a small statue of the god Mithras, in a billowing cape. In the center sits an altar carved with a relief showing Mithras fighting with a bull that contains all life. A scorpion, a dog, and a snake try to stop Mithras, but he wins, running his sword through the bull. The blood spills out, bringing life to the world.

Mithras' fans gathered here, in this tiny microcosm of the universe (the ceiling was decorated with stars), to celebrate the victory with a ritual meal. Every spring, Mithras brought new life again, and so they ritually kept track of the seasons—the four square shafts in the corners of the ceiling represent the seasons, the seven round ones were the great constellations. Initiates went through hazing rituals representing the darkness of this world, then emerged into the light-filled world brought by Mithras.

Rome's official pagan religion had no real spiritual content and did not offer any concept of salvation. As the empire slowly crumbled, people turned more and more to Eastern religions (including Christianity), in search of answers and comfort. The cult of Mithras, stressing loyalty and based on the tenuousness of life, was popular among soldiers. Part of its uniqueness and popularity (in this very class-conscious society) was due to its belief that all were equal before God. It dates back to the time of Alexander the Great, who brought it from Persia. In 67 B.C., soldiers who had survived the bloody conquest of Asia Minor returned to Rome swearing by Mithras. When Christians gained power, they banished the worship of Mithras.

Facing the barred room are two rectangular Corinthian columns supporting three arches of the temple's entryway, decorated with a fine stucco coffered ceiling.

At the far end of the hallway, another barred door marks the equivalent of a Mithraic Sunday school room. Peek inside to see a faded fresco of bearded Mithras (right wall) and seven niches carved into the walls representing the seven stages a novice had to go through.

Head back the way you came. On your right, watch for a very narrow ancient alleyway separating Roman walls barely three feet across. If it's open, step in and imagine the first Western city to reach one million residents. Forget the two churches above you, and imagine standing on this exact spot and looking up at the sky 2,000 years ago. Now climb back through the centuries to today's street level.

TRASTEVERE WALK

*From the Tiber to the Church of
Santa Maria in Trastevere*

Trastevere—the colorful neighborhood across the river from down-town—is *the* place to immerse yourself in the crustier side of Rome. This half-mile walk is designed to train your eye to see Rome more intimately. In Trastevere (trahs-TAY-veh-ray), you'll discover a se-cret, hidden city of heroic young martyrs, lovers kissing on Vespas, party-loving Renaissance bankers, and feisty "Trasteverini"—old-timers who pride themselves on never setting foot on the opposite bank of the Tiber River.

Orientation

Length of This Walk: Allow 1.5 hours. With limited time, taxi directly to Santa Maria in Trastevere. You'll still capture plenty
of ambience.

When to Go: This walk can work well at any time of day. Mornings are cool and relatively quiet. Note that many churches are
closed at midday, and Villa Farnesina closes at 14:00 Mon-
Sat (and is closed Sun—except on second Sun of the month).
Strolling through Trastevere at dusk is especially atmospheric.
Consider combining this walk with a meal or as a prelude to
my Heart of Rome Walk (see page 110).

Getting There: Trastevere is on the west side of the Tiber River,
south of Vatican City and across the river from the Forum
and Capitoline Hill area. To get there by foot from Capitoline
Hill, cross the Tiber using the bridges linked to Isola Tiberina: the Ponte Fabricio and Ponte Cestio. You can also reach
Trastevere on tram #8 from Piazza Venezia or Largo Argentina, or on express bus #H from Termini train station or Piazza
della Repubblica (on the northeast side of the square, near the
entrance to the Baths of Diocletian); if taking either of these,

get off at Sonnino/Piazza Belli, just after crossing the Tiber. From the Vatican (Piazza Risorgimento), take bus #23 or #271 to the Lungotevere Alberteschi stop (a short walk from Isola Tiberina).

Church of Santa Cecilia: Free, Mon-Sat 9:30-12:30 & 16:00-18:30, Sun 16:00-18:30; crypt-€2.50, opens 30 minutes after church; loft with frescoes-€2.50, same hours as crypt but sometimes closed in the afternoon, closed Sun; tel. 06-4549-2739.

Church of Santa Maria in Trastevere: Free, daily 8:30-21:00.

Villa Farnesina: €6, Mon-Sat 9:00-14:00, closed Sun (except open 9:00-17:00 on second Sun of the month), last entry 30 minutes before closing.

Tour: You can download this chapter as a free Rick Steves audio tour (see page 8).

Eateries: Several recommended restaurants are on the map and described in the Eating in Rome chapter (see page 386).

The Walk Begins

• *Start halfway across the Ponte Cestio (Cestius Bridge)—called the "Ponte Fabricio" on the east side of the river—which connects Isola Tiberina ("Island in the Tiber") to Trastevere.*

❶ Isola Tiberina and the Tiber River

Rome got its start 3,000 years ago along the Tiber River at this point. This was as far upstream as big boats could sail and the first

place the river could be crossed by bridge. As a center of river trade, Rome connected the interior of the Italian peninsula with the Mediterranean. The area below you would have been bustling in ancient times. Look down and imagine small ports, water mills, ramshackle boats, and platforms for fishing.

The **island** itself was once the site of a temple dedicated to Asclepius, the god of medicine. Ancient Romans who were ill spent the night here and left little statues of their healed body parts (feet, livers, hearts...) as thank-you notes. This tradition survives: Today, throughout Italy, Catholic altars are often encrusted with votive offerings, symbolizing gratitude for answered prayers. During plagues and epidemics, the sick were isolated on the island. These days, the island's largest building is the Fatebenefratelli, the public hospital favored by

Roman women for childbirth. The island's reputation for medical care lives on.

The high point of the **bridge** (upon which you're probably leaning) is an ancient stone with a faded inscription dating from about A.D. 370, when this then-400-year-old bridge was rebuilt. The eroding plaque is stapled into the balustrade like a piece of recycled scrap. Run your fingers over the word "Caesar" (top line, just right of center). This part of the Tiber River flooded frequently, which devalued the land on the north bank; in time it would become the site of the Jewish ghetto (started in the 16th century, but now long gone, though Rome's synagogue remains—✪ see the Jewish Ghetto Walk chapter).

In the 1870s, the Romans removed the threat of flooding by practically walling off the Tiber, building the tall, anonymous embankments that continue to isolate the river from the city today.

• *Head south to leave the bridge. If open, the green riverside Sora Mirella kiosk on the right (run by Mirella's son, Stefano) is the most famous vendor of Rome's summer refresher called a* grattachecca *(pronounced grah-tah-kek-kah, €4), a concoction of shaved ice with fruit-flavored syrup and chopped fruit (similar to a granita). Cross the street and go down the steps into the car-filled piazza.*

❷ Piazza in Piscinula

This square is famous for its church bell tower (the cute little thing directly across from the bridge); dating from 1069, it's the oldest working one in the city. Study the brown building on the riverside and spot faint traces of Renaissance decoration. Today's earth-tone shades of the city echo this original Roman brown.

• *Facing the tower, exit the square from the far-right corner, opposite where you entered, going uphill on Via dell'Arco de' Tolomei.*

Trastevere Back Lanes

Look up and directly ahead to the top of the hill to see the elegantly restored, freshly painted **tower** sandwiched between apartments. In medieval times, the city skyline had 300 of these towers (about 50 survive). Each noble family competed for the tallest one until, in about 1250, city authorities got fed up and had them all lopped off. Later (mainly Baroque) construction incorporated most of the remaining "stumps," and you can still see these remnants of medieval Rome all over the old center. Incorporating old structures into new ones was always considered more economical and practical than demolishing and starting again from scratch. In the Middle Ages, Rome had regressed to being a big village; any idea of town planning was lost until the Renaissance.

Notice the plants spilling over the many rooftop terraces—the

To Vatican

VILLA FARNESINA

L. FARNESIO

PALAZZO CORSINI

#115 & 870 Ⓑ
ANITA GARIBALDI MONUMENT

VILLA LANTE

100 Meters
100 Yards

VIA CORSINI

LUNGARA

#115 & 870 Ⓑ

G I A N I C O L O

BOTANICAL GARDENS

S. MARIA DELLA SCALA

Piazza Garibaldi

GIUSEPPE GARIBALDI MONUMENT

Parco Gianicolo

VIA GARIBALDI

V. D. SCALA

V. D. BOLOGNA

V. D. MATTONATO

VIC. SCALA

VIC. LEO

PASSAGIATA DEL GIANICOLO

PASSAGIATA DEL GIANICOLO

V. D. PANIERI

VIC. CEDRO

S. EGIDIO

PAGLIA

#115 & 870 Ⓑ

VIA PORTA SAN PANCRAZIO

PORTA SAN PANCRAZIO & ITALIAN UNIFICATION MUSEUM

VIA GARIBALDI

FONTANA DELL' ACQUA PAOLO

SAN PIETRO IN MONTORIO (BRAMANTE'S TEMPIETTO)

#115 Ⓑ

T R A

#870 Ⓑ

CITY WALLS

ITALIAN INDEPENDENCE WAR MEMORIAL

VIA GARIBALDI

Ⓑ

#115 Ⓑ

VIA LUCIANO

VIALE GLORIOSO

❶ Isola Tiberina & Tiber River
❷ Piazza in Piscinula
❸ Church of Santa Cecilia
❹ Biscottificio Artigiano Innocenti
❺ Church of Santa Maria in Trastevere

Roman equivalent of a leafy backyard. An *attico con terrazzo* (penthouse with a terrace) is every Roman's dream.

Continue on, walking under the low arch. Lots of aristocratic buildings were connected by these elevated passages. Imagine herds of sheep shuffling through here in medieval times while smoke billowed from the windows and doors of homes that lacked chimneys.

• *Turn left and walk along Via dei Salumi ("Cold Cuts Street").*

Because of its vicinity to the river, Trastevere was always a commercial neighborhood, and many of its alleys were named after businesses based here. The streets—rarely paved—were clogged by shop stalls.

The red-brown building on your right (pretty ugly unless

you're a fascist) is a **school from the Mussolini era.** The fascist leader believed in the classical motto *mens sana in corpore sano* ("a healthy mind in a healthy body"), and loved being seen fencing, boxing, swimming, and riding. He endowed school buildings with lots of gyms.

• *After passing the school, turn right again, heading up Vicolo dell'Atleta ("Alley of the Athlete").*

Check out the latest fashions in underwear hanging out to dry. Apartments in Rome tend to be quite small, and electricity is more expensive than in the US, so few have clothes dryers.

Strolling here, you'll understand why the Italian language has no word for "privacy" (they use our word and roll the *r*). Reading a letter on the Metro attracts a crowd. If someone has a fight (or a particularly good orgasm), the entire neighborhood knows. Young lovers with no place to go are adept at riding *motorini*...while parked.

All around, ancient fragments are recycled ingloriously into medieval buildings. Halfway down the alley on the right (at #14) is a restaurant that, a thousand years ago, was a **synagogue.** Find the Hebrew faintly inscribed on the base of the columns of the exposed brick structure (on the upper floor). A large part of Rome's Jewish community, the most ancient outside Palestine, lived in Trastevere until the popes moved them into the ghetto on the other side of the river in the 1500s.

• *Continue, turning left on Via dei Genovesi, then right on Via di S. Cecilia to reach Piazza di Santa Cecilia. Enter the convent courtyard of the church, sit by the fountain, and take a moment to enjoy the peace and quiet.*

❸ Church of Santa Cecilia

Trastevere had early Christian churches like Santa Cecilia because, in the second and third centuries, a large community of foreigners lived here.

Early Christians from Greece and Judaea introduced their cultures and religions to the neighborhood.

Notice the church's eclectic exterior. Its mismatched columns were recycled from pagan temples. The typical medieval bell tower sports an 18th-century facade. This church, dedicated to Cecilia, patron saint of musicians and singers, is popular for weddings. Of Rome's 40 medieval churches, many have two-year waiting lists for weekend weddings. While most young Roman couples favor the more sober elegance of medieval churches over Baroque (usually dismissed as *troppo pesante*—"too heavy"), typical Italian wedding gowns are far from understated.

A Christian convert from a wealthy family in a time of persecution, Cecilia revealed her faith to her pagan husband on their wedding night and told him of her aspiration to remain chaste (uh-oh...). An angel appeared to reason with the frustrated groom. Once converted, he devoted himself to carrying out Christian burials in the catacombs, until he himself was killed. Cecilia was soon condemned as well. The Romans, who tried unsuccessfully for three days to suffocate her with steam in her bath to make it appear accidental, finally lost patience and beheaded her. Cecilia bequeathed her house to the neighborhood community, and this spot has been a place of worship ever since.

In the days when Christianity was illegal, wealthy converts hosted Mass for the local community in their homes. When Christians were finally allowed to build churches, they often did so on the sites of these homes for the sake of continuity. While this site was a place of worship during and after Cecilia's lifetime, what we see today was built in the early ninth century and extensively restored in the eighteenth century.

Enter the church. Find the **statue of St. Cecilia** by Stefano Maderno (in the case below the altar). During the Catholic Counter-Reformation, art charged with great emotional impact was used to enhance faith. The new appetite for relics led to a search for Cecilia's remains. When her tomb was opened, Maderno was present and claimed, along with other bystanders, to have seen her body perfectly preserved for an unforgettable instant before it turned to dust. He created this touching statue from his memory of that scene. Cecilia lies with her face turned and hidden, the violence of her death suggested only by the gash in her neck, the position of her fingers indicating the oneness of the Trinity. (Like Italians today, she counted starting with her thumb.)

The **canopy** above the altar, dating from the 1200s, represents an innovative fusion of Roman and French Gothic architecture and sculpture, showing that the artist (Arnolfo di Cambio) knew his classics and had also been to Paris.

The **mosaic** in the apse dates from the ninth century. Pope Paschal (on the left), who built the church, holds a little model of it in his hands. His square halo (the "halo of the living") signifies that he was alive when the mosaic was made.

If you visit mid-morning, you have two options before leaving: You can go downstairs to see the crypt or head upstairs to the loft to view some fancy frescoes.

The **crypt** contains the scant ancient remains of a complex of ancient buildings, including Cecilia's house. The house is pretty bare, but it does have some early Christian iconography, original mosaic floors, and grain storage bins (€2.50, to the left as you enter the church).

The **loft,** where cloistered nuns would view the Mass while hidden behind a screen, contains a fragmentary but extraordinary Last Judgment fresco painted by Pietro Cavallini, a contemporary of Giotto (c. 1300). Scholars debate who influenced whom: Giotto or Cavallini. But there's no debate that the art here shows cutting-edge realism in the expressive faces of the apostles who sit believably in their chairs (€2.50, ring the bell on the left side of the façade). If you're here at 18:00 on a Saturday, you're welcome to read the Lectio Divina with the nuns.

• *Leaving the church, backtrack left, and take the first left onto Via de Genovesi. To pop into the last traditional cookie bakery in the area, detour right at Via della Luce and walk a half-block to #21 (on the right), where you'll find* ❹ *Biscottificio Artigiano Innocenti. Here, in the face of modern efficiency, humble Stefania Innocenti, who was "artisanal" long before it was cool, keeps the tradition of seasonal cookies alive in Rome.*

Return to Via de Genovesi, and hike straight ahead to where it meets a busy street.

Viale di Trastevere to Piazza di Santa Maria

The wide, modern boulevard called Viale di Trastevere bisects Trastevere, which was otherwise spared most of the demolishing and rebuilding suffered by other traditional neighborhoods when Rome became the capital of a united Italy in 1871. Cross to the other side of Viale di Trastevere and turn right, then left into the square called Largo San Giovanni de Matha. Pass by the textbook Baroque facade of the faded yellow church and continue along the Via della Lungaretta. You'll notice a change in atmosphere—the quiet, mystical charm of the first part of your walk has given way to livelier, more colorful, more touristy (and higher-rent) surroundings. Look up. Now, along with underwear...you see art. Walk several blocks to the big square and sit down on the fountain steps.

Piazza di Santa Maria in Trastevere

You're in the heart of the neighborhood. Piazza di Santa Maria is the district's most important meeting place. With its broad and inviting steps, the 17th-century fountain was actually designed to be the "sofa" of the neighborhood. During major soccer games, a large screen is set up here so that everybody can share in the tension and excitement. At other times, children gather here with a ball and improvise matches of their own. For more on soccer, see the sidebar.

• *Dominating the square is the...*

❺ Church of Santa Maria in Trastevere

One of Rome's oldest church sites, this building stands where early Christians worshipped illegally in a home until the year 313. It was made a basilica—probably the first church in Rome dedicated to the Virgin Mary—in the fourth century, when Christianity was legalized. The tower survives from the 12th century, when the entire church was rebuilt. The portico (covered area just outside the door) is decorated with ancient fragments (some from the earlier church). Filled with early Christian symbolism such as the dove and olive branch, many of these stones were lids to burial niches from catacombs. In the fragment at the far-left end of the portico (left of the door), notice how early Christians prayed as evangelical Christians do today.

Step inside. Face the main door and look left to see a **plaque** on the wall dedicated to "Olea Sancta." The "holy oil" was actually a small petroleum deposit discovered here in 30 B.C. This black liquid was almost magical in its ability to power lamps and was incorporated into the lore of this church.

Grab a pew. Most of what you see dates from around the 12th century, although the granite columns are from ancient Roman buildings. Later architects tried hard to match them, but notice how the shorter columns have taller bases and how the capitals are mismatched. (Some have tiny pagan heads of Egyptian gods.) The ancient basilica floor plan (and ambience) survives. The intricate coffered ceiling has an unusual image of Mary painted on copper at the center.

Step up behind the main **altar** (left side) for a closer look at the fine mosaic work. Pop a coin in the box for light. The central scene

is one of the few surviving examples of an early medieval mosaic (8th-10th century) in Rome. It's rich in symbolism. Christ is flanked by the first two popes. Notice the stature Mary is given. Tour guides claim this is the first mosaic to show her at the throne with Jesus in heaven. He has his arm around his mother as if introducing her to us. The flock of sheep is not just any flock—it represents Jesus in the middle (marked by a halo with a cross in it) and the 12 apostles. Sitting on the ground below all of these mosaics is the throne-like chair of the bishop, giving legitimacy to the Church leadership.

The more "modern" mosaic panels, below the sheep, show scenes from the life of Mary. These mosaics from the late 1300s (by Cavallini) are impressively realistic and expressive, yet predate the Renaissance by a hundred years. The first of six panels (to the left of the curved apse) shows the birth of Mary. A servant in the cor-

Soccer: The National Obsession

One of Rome's most local "sights" is a soccer match. Winston Churchill said that Italians lose wars like soccer matches and soccer matches like wars. Soccer *(calcio)* is the national obsession: Everyone, regardless of age or social class, is an expert, quick

with an opinion on a coach's lousy decision or a referee's unprofessional conduct. Fans love to insult officials: A favorite is *"arbitro cornuto!"*—the referee is a cuckold (i.e., his wife sleeps around). The country's obsession turned into jubilation on July 9, 2006, when Italy won the World Cup, and Rome—along with every other city, town, and village in Italy—went crazy with joy.

Rome has a special passion for soccer. It has two teams, Roma (representing the city) and Lazio (the region), and the rivalry is fanatic. When Romans are introduced, they ask each other, *"Laziale o romanista?"* The answer can compromise a relationship. Both Roma (jersey: yellow and red; symbol: she-wolf) and Lazio (jersey: light blue and white; symbol: imperial eagle) claim to be truly Roman. Lazio is older (founded in 1900), but Roma has more supporters. Lazio is supposed to be more upper-class, Roma more popular, but the social division is blurred.

The most eagerly awaited sporting event of the year is the derby, when the two teams fight it out at the Olympic Stadium

ner checks the temperature of the water with her hand before she bathes the baby, introducing an element of tenderness that breaks the abstract rigidity of medieval art. Next comes the angel announcing Jesus' coming to Mary, Jesus' birth, the adoration of the Magi, the presentation of Jesus in the temple, and Mary's eternal sleep (not "death"). The gold mosaic backgrounds show buildings that, while still unrealistic, are a good step toward accurate 3-D representation.

The incredibly expensive 13th-century **floor** is a fine example of Cosmati mosaic work—a style of mosaic featuring intricate geometric shapes (in this case, made with marble scavenged from Roman ruins).

As you leave, spend a moment with **St. Anthony** (in the back corner, opposite the entry). He was a favorite of the poor and is inundated with prayer requests on scraps of paper. The Community of St. Egidio operates from this church. They feed the local poor and care for young drug addicts. Each Christmas they take out all

(Stadio Olimpico). All of Italy acknowledges that team spirit is most fervent in Rome. Fans prepare months in advance, and on the day of the match they fill the entire stadium with team colors, flags, banners, and smoke candles.

Witty slogans on banners work like dialogues: A Roma banner proclaimed, "Roma: Only the sky is higher than you." The Lazio banner replied, "In fact, the sky is blue and white" (like its team colors). The exchange revealed that there had been a Lazio informer on the Roma side, which traumatized Roma fans for weeks. Tourists go to a match more for the action in the stands than the action on the field—for

some, it's the most Roman of all experiences.

Both teams call the Olympic Stadium home, so you can catch a game most weekends from September to May (Metro line A to Flaminio, then catch tram #2 to the end of the line, Piazza Mancini, and cross the bridge to the stadium). If you're coming from Termini train station, take bus #910; from the Vatican, take bus #32 from Piazza Risorgimento. It's best to buy tickets in advance (which is often the only way to get them) at www.listicket.it or in town at a team store (bring ID).

the pews, move in tables and chairs, and put on a huge dinner for those in need.

• *From here, enjoy simply exploring Rome's most colorful district. Saunter around the streets to the left of the church as you leave. The farther you venture from the square, the less touristy and more rustic the neighborhood becomes. Wandering the back lanes and pondering the earthy enthusiasm people seem to have for life here, I can imagine that bygone day when proud Trastevere locals would brag that they never crossed the river.*

To cap off your Trastevere stroll with one more sight, consider visiting **Villa Farnesina,** *a Renaissance villa decorated by Raphael (see page 93 for a self-guided tour). To get there, face the Church of Santa Maria in Trastevere and leave the piazza by walking along the right side of the church, following Via della Paglia to Piazza di S. Egidio. Turn right and exit the piazza near the church—you'll be on Via della Scala. Follow through the Porta Settimiana, where the street changes names to Via della Lungara. On your right, you'll pass John Cabot University. Look* for a white arch that reads Accademia dei Lincei (#230). The villa is through this gate.

If you're in the mood to extend this walk, head to the river, cross the pedestrian bridge, Ponte Sisto, and make your way to Campo de' Fiori, where my **Heart of Rome Walk** begins (see that chapter for details).

ANCIENT APPIAN WAY TOUR

Via Appia Antica

The wonder of its day, the Appian Way was the largest, widest, fastest road ever, called the "Queen of Roads." Begun in 312 B.C. and named after Appius Claudius Caecus (a Roman official), it connected Rome with Capua (near Naples), running in a straight line for much of the way, ignoring the natural contour of the land. Eventually, this most important of Roman roads stretched 430 miles to the port of Brindisi—the gateway to the East—where boats sailed for Greece and Egypt. Twenty-nine such roads fanned out from Rome. Just as Hitler built the Autobahn system in anticipation of empire maintenance, the expansion-minded Roman government realized the military and political value of a good road system.

The Hollywood-created image of the Appian Way as lined with the crucified bodies of Spartacus and his slave rebels is only partially accurate—Spartacus was killed in battle after a two-year conflict. But historians do believe that after his defeat in 71 B.C., 6,000 slaves were crucified on crosses spaced about 30 yards apart along the length of the Appian Way—a distance of over 100 miles. As a warning to other slaves, their bodies were left to hang for several months. Imagine the eerie welcome this provided visitors arriving in Rome.

When the Christian faith permeated Rome, the Appian Way became a popular underground burial place for Christians. Though untrue, it later entered Romantic lore as a place where Christians hid from persecution. Today the road and the landscape around it are preserved as a cultural park.

For the tourist, the ancient Appian Way offers three attractions: the road itself, with its ruined monuments; the two major Christian catacombs open to visitors; and the peaceful atmosphere, which provides a respite from the city. Be aware, however, that the road today is very narrow (with high walls on both sides), busy with traffic, and actually quite treacherous in spots. I recommend following this tour's route, which avoids the worst of the traffic, making the area a pleasant place for strolling or biking.

Orientation

Length of This Tour: Budget five hours to get to and from the Appian Way, to walk or bike the stretch of sights, and to visit one of the catacombs.

When to Go: Visit in the morning or mid-afternoon (note that the Catacombs of San Callisto shut down from 12:00 to 14:00), but don't go too late; the last tours at both catacombs depart at 16:30 (and other sights close as early as 16:00). All the recommended sights are open on Tuesday, Thursday, Friday, and Saturday. On Monday, several sights are closed, including the Tomb of Cecilia Metella and the Circus and Villa of Maxentius. On Wednesday, the Catacombs of San Callisto and the pedestrian path through the park are closed. On Sunday, the Catacombs of San Sebastiano are closed; however, the Appian Way is closed to most car traffic, making it a great day for walking or biking (see "Bike Rental," later).

Getting There: Several buses run from Rome to the Appian Way, and some can also be used for connecting the dots along this tour—though there are some challenges. Stops are squeezed onto the very narrow (sometimes nonexistent) shoulder of the road, and the specific locations of the stops can change. Use this chapter's map as a guideline, but be flexible, and ask around to find the current locations. There are only a few places to buy bus tickets on the Appian Way (including the TI and the shop at the Catacombs of San Sebastiano)—have one in hand for your return trip.

Bus #660 is the best way to reach the Appian Way, since it drops you off right where our tour starts, at the Tomb of Cecilia Metella. In Rome, take Metro line A to the Colli Albani stop, where you catch bus #660 (2/hour) and ride 15 minutes to the last stop—Cecilia Metella/Via Appia Antica (at the intersection of Via Cecilia Metella and Via Appia Antica).

Bus #118 runs partway down the Appian Way, linking the major stops at the northern part (as far as the Catacombs of San Sebastiano). In Rome, catch #118 from either one of two Metro stops: Piramide (look for the bus-stop island right in front of the Metro station) or Circo Massimo; going away from the city center, it stops at the Baths of Caracalla, San Sebastiano Gate, Domine Quo Vadis Church, Catacombs of San Callisto, and Catacombs of San Sebastiano. In a pinch,

Sebastiano vs. Callisto

Which of the two catacombs is the best? They're actually quite similar. Both include a half-hour tour, where you go underground to see the niches where early Christians were buried (but no bones). Both have some faded frescoes and graffiti with Christian symbols. Both have small chapels and a few memorial statues. Most people pick one catacomb to visit, and either will fit the bill.

I lean slightly in favor of San Callisto, but only because of its historical importance, not because it's inherently more interesting. San Sebastiano tends to be slightly less crowded, is historic in its own right (as the relics of Sts. Peter and Paul and St. Sebastian were kept here), and—most significantly—offers an experience with a bit more variety, since it also includes several remarkably well-preserved pagan Roman tombs and a Baroque church with a bust by Gian Lorenzo Bernini.

(Note that the **Catacombs of Priscilla**—more intimate and less crowded than these two more famous ones—can be found at the other end of town, northeast of the Villa Borghese Gardens; see page 77.)

APPIAN WAY

you could use this bus to get to the starting point of our walk: Ride bus #118 to the San Sebastiano stop, then walk 500 yards (less than 10 minutes) to the Tomb of Cecilia Metella. Going back to Rome, bus #118 takes a somewhat different route (skipping the Catacombs of San Sebastiano); catch this northbound bus just up the road at the Catacombs of San Callisto or near Domine Quo Vadis.

Bus #218 goes from San Giovanni in Laterano to Domine Quo Vadis Church and the west entrance of the Catacombs of San Callisto, but isn't useful for reaching Appian Way sights farther south.

The handy, but much more expensive, **Archeobus** runs from Termini train station to the major Appian Way sights (see page 32, under "Tours in Rome"). It stops at all the key attractions—you can hop off, tour the sights, and pick up a later bus (officially runs twice hourly Fri-Sun during summer, but service can be spotty).

A **taxi** will get you from Rome to the Tomb of Cecilia Metella for about €20. However, to return by taxi, you'll have to phone for one; there are no taxi stands on the Appian Way.

Getting Back: No matter how you arrive at the Appian Way, the bus is the easiest and cheapest way to return to Rome. Bus **#118** has more stops along the Way, and takes you quickly to the Piramide Metro stop in Testaccio (end of the line). Bus **#218** is handy to the northern part of the Way (including a stop near Domine Quo Vadis Church, where this tour ends), and brings you to the San Giovanni in Laterano Church, where you can hop on the Metro (San Giovanni stop, line A) or transfer to another bus (#85 or #87 to the Colosseum and Piazza Venezia; #81 to Largo Argentina and the Vatican).

Information: The **Via Appia Antica TI** near Domine Quo Vadis Church gives out maps and information on the entire park, which stretches east and south of the visit outlined here (daily April-Oct 9:30-17:30, Nov-March 9:30-16:30, rents bikes, good €1 map, Via Appia Antica 58/60, tel. 06-513-5316, www.parcoappiaantica.it, general info at www.archeoroma. beniculturali.it/e). The Archeobus map shows everything clearly.

The archaeological site of **Capo di Bove** has a small info center that sits deep in a tranquil, inviting garden surrounding active excavations (Mon-Sat 10:00-16:00, Sun 10:00-18:00, closes earlier in winter, good place for discreet picnic, clean WCs, Via Appia Antica 222, tel. 06-3996-7700); it's 100 yards beyond (south of) **Appia Antica Caffè,** which also sells maps (described later, under "Bike Rental").

Tomb of Cecilia Metella: €6, includes entry to the Baths of Caracalla and Villa dei Quintili, April-Sept Tue-Sun 9:00-19:00, closes earlier Oct-March, closed Mon year-round, last entry 30 minutes before closing, tel. 06-3996-7700, www. archeoroma.beniculturali.it/en.

Circus and Villa of Maxentius: €5, Tue-Sun 10:00-16:00, closed Mon, last entry 30 minutes before closing, tel. 06-780-1324.

Catacombs of San Sebastiano: €8, includes 35-minute tour, 2/hour; Mon-Sat 10:00-17:00, closed Sun and late-Nov-late-Dec, last entry 30 minutes before closing, handy café and WCs, tel. 06-785-0350, www.catacombe.org.

Catacombs of San Callisto: €8, includes 30-minute tour, at least 2/hour; Thu-Tue 9:00-12:00 & 14:00-17:00, closed Wed and Feb, tel. 06-513-0151, www.catacombe.roma.it.

Domine Quo Vadis Church: Free, daily 8:00-19:00 (until 18:00 off-season), tel. 06-512-0441.

Bike Rental: Some may find the old paving stones too bumpy for biking. But if you'd like to try it, the best day for biking is Sunday, when the Appian Way is closed to traffic (though a few cars with special permission can still sneak through). Take bus #660 to the last stop (Cecilia Metella/Via Appia Antica), and you'll find **Appia Antica Caffè,** where you can rent a bike (€4/hour, €10/3 hours, 10 percent discount off bikes and food with this book, handy €3.50 map, daily 9:00-sunset, at corner of Appian Way and Via Cecilia Metella, near Tomb of Cecilia Metella at Via Appia Antica 175, mobile 338-3465-440, www.appiaanticacaffe.it). You can also rent a bike from the

Via Appia Antica TI (€3/hour, €15/day; see "Information," earlier). If you don't mind heavy traffic, you could even bike from the Colosseum or Santa Maria Maggiore out past the wall and down the Appian Way. For bike rental in the city center, see "By Bike," on page 29.

Services: Free WCs are at the San Sebastiano and San Callisto catacombs and at Capo di Bove, and WCs for paying customers are at the Tomb of Cecilia Metella and the Appia Antica Caffè. There are several fountains along the way for refilling water bottles.

Eating: Appia Antica Caffè (see "Bike Rental," earlier) makes big salads and abundant sandwiches and has a shaded, restful seating area in back; tucked even farther back in their garden is a fine little *gelateria*. Or, to buy picnic fixings, go 50 yards farther south to **Tabernae Appia Antica,** a hole-in-the-wall *alimentari* (Mon-Sat 7:00-14:00 & 15:00-20:00, Sun 9:00-15:00, at #210, tel. 06-780-3746). Great picnic spots are just a half-mile farther south from here. Several pricey restaurants are along the stretch between the Tomb of Cecilia Metella and the Catacombs of San Sebastiano (which normally has a sandwich-and-drinks cart).

Starring: An old road, crumbling tombs, and underground Christian cemeteries.

OVERVIEW

Our tour begins near the Tomb of Cecilia Metella, at the far (southern) end of the sightseeing highlights, and works northward for a mile-and-a-half to Domine Quo Vadis Church, toward the center of Rome. Sightseers share the road with speeding drivers talking on mobile phones (except on Sundays, when it's off limits to most cars), but there's really only one bad stretch—between the Catacombs of San Sebastiano and Domine Quo Vadis Church. We'll avoid that traffic by taking a pedestrian path through a quiet park that parallels the busy road (except on Wednesdays, when the path is closed).

The Tour Begins

• *From the café near the Tomb of Cecilia Metella, head south (away from downtown) 100 yards, where you walk (or rattle your bike) over a stretch of the...*

Original Paved Road

Huge basalt stones formed the sturdy base of a road 14 feet across. In its heyday, a central strip accommodated animal-powered vehicles, and elevated sidewalks served pedestrians. The first section (near Rome) was perfectly straight and lined with tombs and funerary monuments.

Back near where you started (to the right of the entrance to the Tomb of Cecilia Metella) is the original **mile marker III,** one of more than 400 such stones that counted the distance from Rome to Brindisi. Emperors knew that a fine network of roads was key to expanding and administering the empire. This road, from c. 312 B.C., kicks off the expansion period.

• *You can't miss (on the right side) the...*

Tomb of Cecilia Metella (Mausoleo di Cecilia Metella)

This massive cylindrical tomb, one of the best preserved of the many tombs of prominent Romans that line the road, was built in the time of Augustus (c. 30 B.C.) for the daughter-in-law of Crassus, Rome's richest man. Faced with white travertine and situated on the crest of a hill, the tomb was an imposing sight. This grand tomb in the suburbs rivaled Augustus' own round mausoleum in the city center (see page 76).

Since no one was allowed to be buried inside the city walls, the Appian Way was a popular place to have a tomb where everyone could see and admire it. Later, Christians were buried here, though not in tombs (they preferred to be buried underground). Picture a funeral procession passing under the pines and cypresses, past a long line of pyramids, private mini-temples, altars, and tombs.

In the 1300s, the area was turned into a fortified compound for an aristocratic family. The circular tomb was used as a tower (notice the crenellation on top) and a wall continued across the street, enclosing the newly built church and other structures (since destroyed).

If you pay to go inside, you'll see the tomb's eerily hollow interior *(il sepolcro);* a few statues of deceased Romans that once adorned tombs; and, in the cellar, a former paving-stone quarry with a preserved wagon-wheel groove.

• *About 200 yards farther along (north) from the tomb, on the right, are the ruins of the...*

Circus and Villa of Maxentius (Circo e Villa di Massenzio)

This was the suburban home of the emperor who was eventually defeated by Constantine in A.D. 312. The main sight to see here is a whole lot of nothing—that is, the expansive stretch of open

Ancient Appian Way

To San Sebastiano Gate, Museum of the Walls & Central Rome

(B) #118, 218 & Archeobus

(B) #118, 218 & Archeobus

DOMINE QUO VADIS CHURCH

VIA ARDEATINA

VIA LATINA

VIA DELLA CAFFARELLA

(B) #118 (B) #118 & Archeobus

(B) #118

COLUMBARIUM

(B) #218

PEDESTRIAN WALKWAY (CLOSED WED.)

SECOND MILESTONE

(B) #118 & Archeobus (B) (B) #118 & Archeobus

VIA APPIA

CATACOMBS OF SAN CALLISTO (CLOSED WED.)

(B) #118

(B) #218

V. D. SETTE CHIESE

FOSSE ARDEATINE

VIA APPIA PIGNATELLI

Archeobus

CATACOMBS OF SAN SEBASTIANO (CLOSED SUN.) & WC

(B) **VILLA OF MAXENTIUS**

BASILICA

CIRCUS OF MAXENTIUS

VIA APPIA ANTICA

(B) #118 & Archeobus

VIA ARDEATINA

VIA SAN SEB.

Archeobus

#118 (B)

TOMB OF CECILIA METELLA

Note: Bus stops on east side of road are northbound; bus stops on west side of road are southbound

ENTRANCE/TICKETS FOR CIRCUS/VILLA OF MAXENTIUS

Archeobus (B)

THIRD MILESTONE

V. CECILIA METELLA

To Aqueduct Park

#218 (B)

APPIA ANTICA CAFFÈ & BIKE RENTAL

(B) #660 & Archeobus

ALIMENTARI (GROCERIES)

CAPO DI BOVE

TORRE DI CAPO DI BOVE

Park (i) & WC

SCENIC SECTION

500 Meters

500 Yards

To 4th through 11th Milestones & Brindisi

APPIAN WAY

space contained by this huge former chariot racetrack. You can see essentially all of it for free from the road. If you pay the admission, you can walk between the entrance towers to the long central spine, and imagine chariots racing around it while 10,000 fans cheered. Maxentius watched from the building rising up above the bleachers, where the chariots made their hairiest turn. At the far end of the 260-yard track is the triumphal arch under which the winner rode to receive his reward.

Also, just down the Appian Way from this circus is a square wall of ruins enclosing a modern building. Behind that modern building, you can glimpse the circular mausoleum of Maxentius' son, Romulus.

• *About 300 yards farther down the road (on the left) are the...*

▲▲Catacombs of San Sebastiano

This underground cemetery is named for the Christian soldier who was tied to a column and shot through with arrows because of his faith—a subject depicted by many artists throughout history. A guide takes you below ground to see burial niches, frescoes, and graffiti. It's said that the bodies of Peter and Paul were kept here for several decades in the third century. You'll also see the underground chapel (in its original location, but spiffed up in the 17th century) where the relics of St. Sebastian were originally kept. But what distinguishes this from other catacombs experiences is the chance to also see some pagan Roman tombs, which provide an interesting contrast and a fascinating finale to the tour.

Besides the catacombs, the site also has a basilica (free) containing various relics. In the first chapel to the left are St. Sebastian's supposed remains, marked with a statue of an arrow-pierced corpse. On the opposite side of the nave, a chapel displays an arrow he was shot with, a section of the column he was tied to, and the (supposedly) original footprints from the Domine Quo Vadis legend (see next page). Nearby stands a curly-haired bust of *The Savior (Il Salvatore)* by Bernini—his final creation, carved when he was in his eighties.

• *The stretch of the Appian Way beyond the Catacombs of San Sebastiano is the least interesting and most crowded (and dangerous). Avoid it by taking the pedestrian and bike path (open daily except Wed), which begins just past the Catacombs of San Sebastiano, at the intersection with Via delle Sette Chiese. To reach the path, go through the arch at #126. The quiet path parallels the Appian Way and takes you directly to the Catacombs of San Callisto. On Wednesdays, when the gate is closed, you'll have to stay straight on Via Appia Antica, being careful of traffic.*

▲▲Catacombs of San Callisto

Because of their historical significance, I tend to favor these catacombs, named for the cemetery's first caretaker, St. Callixtus. This was the official cemetery for Rome's early Christians and the burial place of nine third-century popes, other bishops of Rome, and various martyrs. The most famous martyr was St. Cecilia, patron saint of music, a Roman noble who was killed for converting to Christianity. Her tomb is marked with a copy of a famous Maderno statue. (For more on Cecilia and the statue, ✪ see the Trastevere Walk chapter.)

Buy your ticket and wait for your language to be called. They move lots of people quickly. If one group seems ridiculously large (more than 50 people), wait for the next tour in English.

• *After you visit the catacombs, an optional detour (about 10 minutes each way) brings you to the evocative mausoleum of* **Fosse Ardeatine**, *a memorial to 335 Italians gunned down by Nazis during World War II to avenge a bomb attack in Rome that killed 32 German soldiers. With your back to the San Callisto ticket booth, go right, walk through the gate (where you can also catch bus #218 back to San Giovanni), cross the busy street, turn left, and follow signs downhill to* Fosse Ardeatine *(Mon–Fri 8:15–15:00, Sat–Sun 8:15–16:30, tel. 06-513-6742).*

Back at the catacombs, continue along the pedestrian path another three-quarters of a mile, where you'll spill out at a busy three-way intersection. There you'll find the small...

Domine Quo Vadis Church

The tiny ninth-century church (redone in the 17th) was built on the spot where Peter, while fleeing the city to escape Nero's per-secution, saw a vision of Christ. Peter asked Jesus, "Lord, where are you going?" (*"Domine quo vadis?"* in Latin), to which Christ replied, "I am going to Rome to be crucified again." This miraculous sign gave Peter faith and courage and caused him to return to Rome. Inside the nave of the church, stumble over the stone marked with the supposed footprints of Jesus. You'll see a fresco of Peter with keys on the left wall and one of Jesus on the right. A bust depicts Nobel Prize-winning Polish author Henryk Sienkiewicz, who wrote a historical novel that was the basis for the 1951 Hollywood movie *Quo Vadis*.

• *The tour is over.* "Quo vadis, *pilgrim?*"

To return to central Rome, it's another two miles north along a busy stretch of road, not recommended on foot or bike. Instead, catch bus #118 from the bus stop about 75 yards past Domine Quo Vadis Church (beyond the TI and across the street). Bus #118 makes several interesting stops (see page 336) on its way to the Piramide Metro stop. (Note that another bus, #218, also goes from here to San Giovanni in Laterano.)

Catacombs

The catacombs are burial places for (mostly) Christians who died in ancient Roman times. By law, no one was allowed to be buried within the walls of Rome. While pagan Romans were into cremation, Christians preferred to be buried (so that they could be resurrected when the time came). But land was expensive, and most Christians were poor. A few wealthy, landowning Christians allowed their properties to be used as burial places.

The 40 or so known catacombs are scattered outside the ancient walls of Rome. *Catacombe* means, literally, "near the quarry"—as some of these were dug into the exposed walls of existing quarries. From the first through the fifth centuries, Christians dug an estimated 375 miles of tomb-lined tunnels, with networks of galleries as many as five layers deep. The volcanic tuff that Rome sits atop—which is soft and easy to cut, but hardens when exposed to air—was perfect for the job. The Christians burrowed many layers deep for two reasons: to get more mileage out of the donated land, and to be near martyrs and saints already buried there. Bodies were wrapped in linen (like Christ's). Since they figured the Second Coming was imminent, there was no interest in embalming the body. They called this place a *dormitorio*—a "place to sleep" while awaiting the rapture. After each corpse was laid to rest, it was covered with a stone slab—though most of these are now long-gone, shattered by looters and vandals.

When Emperor Constantine legalized Christianity in A.D. 313, Christians had a new, interesting problem: There would be no more recently persecuted martyrs to bind them together and inspire them. Instead, the early martyrs and popes assumed more importance, and Christians began making pilgrimages to their burial places in the catacombs.

In the 800s, when barbarian invaders started ransacking the tombs, Christians moved the relics of saints and martyrs to the safety of churches in the city center. For a thousand years, the catacombs were forgotten. In early modern times, they were

For those with more energy, there's more to see, especially if you're renting a bike and want to just get away from it all.

Other Sights on or near Appian Way

Consider these diversions if you have the time and interest.

More of the Appian Way: Heading south (away from downtown Rome), past the Tomb of Cecilia Metella, you'll find the best-preserved part of the Appian Way—quieter, less touristed, and lined with cypresses, pines, and crumbling tombs. It's all downhill after the first few hundred yards. On a bike, you'll travel over lots of rough paving stones (or dirt sidewalks) for about 30 minutes to reach a big pyramid-shaped ruin on its tiny base, and then five excavated and became part of the Romantic Age's Grand Tour of Europe.

When abandoned plates and utensils from ritual meals were found, 18th- and 19th-century Romantics guessed that persecut-

ed Christians hid out in these candlelit galleries. The popularity of this legend grew, even though it was untrue: By the second century, more than a million people lived in Rome, and the 10,000 early Christians didn't need to camp out in the catacombs. They hid in plain view, melting into obscurity within the city itself.

The underground tunnels, while empty of bones, are rich in early Christian symbolism, which functioned as a secret language. The dove represented the soul. You'll see it quenching its thirst (worshipping), with an olive branch (at rest), or happily perched (in paradise). Peacocks, known for their purportedly "incorruptible flesh," embodied immortality. The shepherd with a lamb on his shoulders was the "good shepherd," the first portrayal of Christ as a kindly leader of his flock. The fish was used because the first letters of these words—"Jesus Christ, Son of God, Savior"—spelled "fish" in Greek. The combination of an X and a P was actually a chi and a rho—the first two letters of CHRist's name in the Greek alphabet. And the anchor, a cross in disguise, symbolized how true believers felt anchored by their faith. Some fragments were stamped with the hallmark of the mason who created it. A second-century bishop had written on his tomb, "All who understand these things, pray for me." You'll see pictures of people praying with their hands raised—the custom at the time.

minutes more to the back side of Villa dei Quintili. Usually, you can't enter the villa from here, but you can admire the semicircular

nymphaeum, or fake grotto. Enjoy a picnic, then turn around and pedal up that long hill to return your bike.

Aqueduct Park (Parco degli Acquedotti): Rome's mighty aqueducts kept water flowing into the thriving and thirsty ancient city of one million. (They also eventually provided a handy

Achilles' heel for invading barbarians: Simply break an arch in the aqueduct, and life becomes very tough within the city walls.) This sprawling, evocative park is a favorite these days with Roman joggers, picnickers, and anyone looking for a break from the big city. From the Appian Way, start at Appia Antica Caffè (near the Tomb of Cecilia Metella), take bus #660 to the Colli Albani Metro station, and catch the Metro to Giulio Agricola. (If you're coming straight from Rome, take Metro line A to Giulio Agricola.)

As you exit the Giulio Agricola Metro stop, follow signs for *Viale Giulio Agricola*. This street has trees in its median strip and ends at a modern church several blocks away. Head for the church, passing a number of cafés and grocery stores (good for picnic fare). To the right of the church, enter the park and pass through the squat brick arches of the first aqueduct (actually two aqueducts— the 16th-century Acqua Felice piggybacked on top of the Acqua Marcia, which dates from the second century B.C.). Continue across the field and up the small hill where you'll see fragments of the more impressive Acqua Claudia (first century A.D.). Follow the path to the left for about 10 minutes; you'll come to the best-preserved section, which stretches into the distance and makes for an easy walk. Loop back to the church and Metro when you're done. If you're not afraid of traffic, you could bike from the Appian Way to Aqueduct Park (takes about an hour; get directions when you rent your bike).

Sights on Bus #118 Route Back to Rome: On the way back, about a half-mile from Domine Quo Vadis Church, the bus stops alongside Rome's ancient city wall. The **San Sebastiano Gate and Museum of the Walls** (Porta San Sebastiano; €5, Tue-Sun 9:00-14:00, closed Mon) offers an interesting look at Roman defenses and a chance to scramble along a stretch of the ramparts. The Aurelian Wall (c. A.D. 270) was built in five years because of the threat of invasions. At 12 miles around, it was the biggest building project ever undertaken within the city of Rome.

A few minutes farther on, bus #118 stops near the **Baths of Caracalla** (described on page 107). Next, it makes a stop at the east end of the **Circus Maximus** (the Circo Massimo Metro stop is nearby). The bus terminates at **Piramide,** which has several interesting sights clustered around the Metro station (see page 96). From Piramide, catch the Metro home.

SLEEPING IN ROME

Contents

For hassle-free efficiency, I favor accommodations and restaurants that are handy to your sightseeing activities. Rather than list hotels scattered throughout Rome, I describe my favorite neighborhoods and recommend the best accommodation values in each, from hotels with all of the comforts to less-expensive hostels and convents.

A major feature of this book is its extensive listing of good-value rooms—especially in Rome, where hotels are generally pricey, the cheaper hotels can be depressing, and the TI isn't allowed to give opinions on quality. I like places that are clean, central, relatively quiet at night, reasonably priced, friendly, small enough to have a hands-on owner and stable staff, run with a respect for Italian traditions, and not listed in other guidebooks. (In Rome, for me, meeting six out of these eight criteria means it's a keeper.) I'm more impressed by a convenient location and a fun-loving philosophy than flat-screen TVs and a pricey laundry service.

Book your accommodations well in advance, especially if you'll be traveling during busy times. See page 566 for a list of major holidays and festivals in Rome; for tips on making reservations, see page 342.

RATES AND DEALS

I've described my recommended accommodations using a Sleep Code (see sidebar). Prices listed are for one-night stays in peak season, and assume you're booking directly with the hotel (not through a TI or online hotel-booking engine). Booking services extract a commission from the hotel, which logically closes the door on special deals. Book direct.

While most taxes are included in the price, a city tax of €2-3/person per night (and possibly more in 2015) is added to all hotel bills, and must be paid in cash. The only exemptions are for hostelers and children under the age of two.

For most of the hotels I list, I provide a website (which often has a built-in booking form) and an email address; you can expect a response in English within a day (and often sooner).

If you're on a budget, it's smart to email several hotels to ask for their best price. Comparison-shop and make your choice. This is especially helpful when dealing with the larger hotels that use "dynamic pricing," a computer-generated system that predicts the demand for particular days and sets prices accordingly: High-demand days will often be more than double the price of low-demand days. This makes it impossible for a guidebook to list anything more accurate than a wide range of prices. I regret this trend. While you can assume that hotels listed in this book are good, it's very difficult to say which ones are the better value unless you email to confirm the price.

As you look over the listings, you'll notice that some accommodations promise special prices to Rick Steves readers. To get these rates, you must book directly with the hotel (that is, not through a booking site like TripAdvisor or Booking.com), mention this book when you reserve, and then show the book upon arrival. Rick Steves discounts apply to readers with ebooks as well as printed books. Because I trust hotels to honor this, please let me know if you don't receive a listed discount. Note, though, that discounts understandably may not be applied to promotional rates.

In general, prices can soften if you do any of the following: offer to pay cash, stay at least three nights, or mention this book. You can also try asking for a cheaper room or a discount, or offer to skip breakfast.

Haggle if you arrive late in the day during off-season (roughly mid-July through August and November through mid-March). It's common for hotels in Rome to lower their prices 10-50 percent in the off-season, although prices at hostels and the cheaper hotels won't fluctuate much. Room rates are lowest in sweltering August.

SLEEPING

The Good and Bad of Online Reviews

User-generated travel review websites—such as TripAdvisor, Booking.com, and Yelp—have quickly become a huge player in the travel industry. These sites give you access to actual reports—good and bad—from travelers who have experienced the hotel, restaurant, tour, or attraction.

My hotelier friends in Europe are in awe of these sites' influence. Small hoteliers who want to stay in business have no choice but to work with review sites—which often charge fees for good placement or photos, and tack on commissions if users book through the site instead of directly with the hotel.

While these sites work hard to weed out bogus users, my hunch is that a significant percentage of reviews are posted by friends or enemies of the business being reviewed. I've even seen hotels "bribe" guests (for example, offer a free breakfast) in exchange for a positive review. Also, review sites can become an echo chamber, with one or two flashy businesses camped out atop the ratings, while better, more affordable, and more authentic alternatives sit ignored farther down the list. (For example, I find review sites' restaurant recommendations skew to very touristy, obvious options.)

Remember that a user-generated review is based on the experience of one person. That person likely stayed at one hotel and ate at a few restaurants, and doesn't have much of a basis for comparison. A guidebook is the work of a trained researcher who has exhaustively visited many alternatives to assess their relative value. I recently checked out some top-rated TripAdvisor listings in various towns; when stacked up against their competitors, some are gems, while just as many are duds.

Both types of information have their place, and in many ways, they're complementary. If a hotel or restaurant is well-reviewed in a guidebook or two, and also gets good ratings on one of these sites, it's likely a winner.

Types of Accommodations

HOTELS

Double rooms listed in this book range from about €65 (very simple, toilet and shower down the hall) to €530 (maximum plumbing and more), with most clustering around €150 (with private bathrooms). I've favored these pricier options, because intense Rome is easier to enjoy with a welcoming oasis to call home.

Solo travelers find that the cost of a *camera singola* is often only 25 percent less than a *camera doppia*. Three or four people can save money by requesting one big room. (If a Db is €110, a Qb would be about €150.) Most listed hotels have rooms for anywhere from

Chill Out

All but the cheapest hotels have air-conditioning. Because Europeans are generally careful with energy use, you'll find government-enforced limits on air-conditioning and heating. There's a one-month period each spring and fall when neither is allowed. Air-conditioning sometimes costs an extra per-day charge, is worth seeking out in summer (though it may be on only at certain times of the day), and is rarely available from fall through spring. Conveniently, many business-class hotels drop their prices in July and August, just when the air-conditioned comfort they offer is most important.

Most hotel rooms with air-conditioners come with a control stick (like a TV remote) that generally has the same symbols and features: fan icon (click to toggle through wind power, from light to gale-force); louver icon (choose steady airflow or waves); snowflake and sunshine icons (cold air or heat, depending on season); clock ("O" setting: run x hours before turning off; "I" setting: wait x hours to start); and the temperature control (21 degrees Celsius is comfortable).

one to five people. If there's room for an extra cot, they'll cram it in for you (charging you around €25). English works in all but the cheapest places.

Traffic in Rome roars. Thanks to double-paned windows and air-conditioning, night noise is not the problem it once was. Even so, light sleepers who ask for a *tranquillo* room will likely get a room in the back...and sleep better. Once you actually see your room, consider the potential problem of night noise. If necessary, don't hesitate to ask for a quieter room.

Nearly all places offer private bathrooms. Generally rooms with a bath or shower also have a toilet and a bidet (which Italians use for quick sponge baths). The cord over the tub or shower is not a clothesline. You pull it when you've fallen and can't get up.

Double beds are called *matrimoniale*, even though hotels aren't interested in your marital status. Twins are *due letti singoli*. Convents offer cheap accommodation but only *letti singoli*.

When you check in, the receptionist will normally ask for your passport and keep it for anywhere from a couple of minutes to a couple of hours. Hotels are legally required to register each guest with the police. Relax. Americans are notorious for making this chore more difficult than it needs to be.

Hotels and B&Bs are sometimes located on the higher floors of a multipurpose building with a secured door. In that case, look for your hotel's name on the buttons by the main entrance. When you ring the bell, you'll be buzzed in. Hotel elevators, while becoming more common, are often very small—pack light, or you may need to take your bags up one at a time.

Assume that breakfast is included in the prices I've listed, unless otherwise noted. If breakfast is included but optional, you may want to skip it. While convenient, it's usually expensive—€8-10 for a simple continental buffet with (at its most generous) bread, ham, cheese, yogurt, and unlimited *caffè latte*. A picnic in your room followed by a coffee at the corner café can be lots cheaper.

More pillows and blankets are usually in the closet or available on request. Towels and linens aren't always replaced every day. Hang your towel up to dry. Some hotels use lightweight "waffle" or very thin tablecloth-type towels; these take less water and electricity to launder and are preferred by many Italians.

Most hotel rooms have a TV, telephone, and free Wi-Fi (although in old buildings with thick walls, the Wi-Fi signal doesn't always make it to the rooms; sometimes it's only available in the lobby). Sometimes there's a guest computer with Internet access in the lobby. Simpler places rarely have a room phone, but often have free Wi-Fi. Pricier hotels usually come with a small fridge stocked with beverages called a *frigo bar* (FREE-goh bar; pay for what you use).

Almost no hotels have parking, but nearly all have a line on spots in a nearby garage (about €24/day).

If you're arriving early in the morning, your room probably won't be ready. You can drop your bag safely at the hotel and dive right into sightseeing.

Hoteliers can be a great help and source of advice. Most know their city well, and can assist you with everything from public transit and airport connections to finding a good restaurant, the nearest launderette, or a Wi-Fi hotspot.

Even at the best places, mechanical breakdowns occur: Air-conditioning malfunctions, sinks leak, hot water turns cold, and toilets gurgle and smell. Report your concerns clearly and calmly at the front desk. For more complicated problems, don't expect instant results.

To guard against theft in your room, keep valuables out of sight. Some rooms come with a safe, and other hotels have safes at the front desk. I've never bothered using one.

Checkout can pose problems if surprise charges pop up on your bill. If you settle your bill the afternoon before you leave, you'll have time to discuss and address any points of contention (before 19:00, when the night shift usually arrives).

Above all, keep a positive attitude. Remember, you're on vacation. If your hotel is a disappointment, spend more time out enjoying the city you came to see.

SLEEPING

Making Hotel Reservations

Reserve your rooms several weeks in advance—or as soon as you've pinned down your travel dates. Note that some national holidays jam things up and merit your making reservations far in advance (see "Holidays and Festivals" on page 566).

Requesting a Reservation: It's easiest to book your room through the hotel's website. (For the best rates, always use the hotel's official site and not a booking agency's site.) If there's no reservation form, or for complicated requests, send an email (see below for a sample request). Most recommended hotels take reservations in English.

The hotelier wants to know:

- the number and type of rooms you need
- the number of nights you'll stay
- your date of arrival (use the European style for writing dates: day/month/year)
- your date of departure
- any special needs (such as bathroom in the room or down the hall, cheapest room, twin beds vs. double bed, and so on)

Mention any discounts—for Rick Steves readers or otherwise—when you make the reservation.

Confirming a Reservation: Most places will request a credit-card number to hold your room. If they don't have a secure online reservation form—look for the *https*—you can email it (I do), but it's safer to share that confidential info via a phone call or two emails (splitting your number between them).

Canceling a Reservation: If you must cancel, it's courteous—and smart—to do so with as much notice as possible (at least

BED-AND-BREAKFASTS (B&BS)

B&Bs offer double the cultural intimacy for a good deal less than most hotel rooms. Roman B&Bs are small—most have no more than three rooms, and the owner generally lives on-site. (Be aware that small hotels sometimes erroneously use the term "B&B.") You'll pay in cash rather than by credit card. Expect few services and no amenities such as public lounges, in-room phones, private bathrooms, and daily bed-sheet changes (though the basics, such as sheets and towels, are provided). After picking up your keys, you can come and go as you wish. When reserving, confirm what kind of breakfast is included—some less-expensive B&Bs simply give you a voucher for a pastry and coffee at a nearby bar.

Doubles with breakfast start at around €65, with prices increasing along with the number of amenities. Because of my large volume of readers and the small size of Roman B&Bs, it isn't practical to include many B&B listings here. To find a B&B in Rome,

From:	rick@ricksteves.com
Sent:	Today
To:	info@hotelcentral.com
Subject:	Reservation request for 19-22 July

Dear Hotel Central,

I would like to reserve a double room for 2 people for 3 nights, arriving 19 July and departing 22 July. If possible, I would like a quiet room with a bathroom inside the room.

Please let me know if you have a room available and the price.

Thank you!
Rick Steves

three days) especially for smaller family-run places. Be warned that cancellation policies can be strict; read the fine print or ask about these before you book. Internet deals may require prepayment, with no refunds for cancellations.

Reconfirming a Reservation: Always call to reconfirm your room reservation a few days in advance. For smaller hotels and B&Bs, I call again on my day of arrival to tell my host what time I expect to get there (especially important if arriving late—after 17:00).

Phoning: For tips on how to call hotels overseas, see page 532.

start your search with a website such as www.bedandbreakfast.com or www.b-b.rm.it. You'll get better prices, however, by booking directly with the B&B. Some websites connect you directly with the B&B owner, including www.wheninromebandb.com and www.gulliverslodge.com (see listing on page 351).

Many B&Bs come with thin walls and doors that can make for a noisy night. If you're a light sleeper, bring earplugs. And please be quiet in the halls and in your rooms at night (talk softly, and keep the TV volume low)...those of us getting up early will thank you for it.

CONVENTS

Although I list just a few, Rome has many convents that rent out rooms. See the Church of Santa Susanna's website for a list (www.santasusanna.org, select "Coming to Rome"). At convents, the beds are twins and English is often in short supply, but the price is right.

Consider these nun-run places, all listed in this chapter: the expensive but divine **Casa di Santa Brigida** (near Campo de' Fiori), **Suore di Santa Elisabetta** (near Santa Maria Maggiore), **Casa Il Rosario** (near Piazza Venezia), and **Casa per Ferie Santa Maria alle Fornaci** (near the Vatican).

HOSTELS

You'll pay about €30 per bed to stay at a hostel. Travelers of any age are welcome if they don't mind dorm-style accommodations and meeting other travelers. Most hostels offer kitchen facilities, guest computers, Wi-Fi, and a self-service laundry. Nowadays, concerned about bedbugs, hostels are likely to provide all bedding, including sheets. Family and private rooms may be available on request.

Independent hostels tend to be easygoing, colorful, and informal (no membership required); www.hostelworld.com is the standard way backpackers search and book hostels, but also try www.hostelz.com and www.hostels.com.

Official hostels are part of Hostelling International (HI) and share an online booking site (www.hihostels.com). HI hostels typically require that you either have a membership card or pay extra per night.

If going the hostel route, consider the ones I list in this chapter (within a 10-minute walk of Termini train station), or check www.backpackers.it for more listings.

APARTMENTS

Many locals rent out their apartments in downtown Rome, a great value for families or multiple couples traveling together. Rentals are generally by the week, with prices around €120 per day. Apartments typically offer a couple of bedrooms, a sitting area, and a teensy *cucinetta* (kitchenette), usually stocked with dishes and flatware. After you check in, you're basically on your own. While you won't have a doorman to carry your bags or a maid to clean your room each day, you will get an inside peek at a Roman home, and you can save lots of money—especially if you take advantage of the cooking facilities—with no loss of comfort. Most places are rented through booking agencies, the TI, or websites.

Whether you're in a city or the countryside, renting an apartment, house, or villa can be a fun and cost-effective way to delve into Europe. Websites such as HomeAway and its sister sites VRBO and GreatRentals let you correspond directly with European property owners or managers. Also browse through www.wantedinrome.com.

Steve and Linda of **The Beehive** run a booking service for private rooms and apartments in the old centers of Rome, Florence, and Venice; rates start at €30 per person (see listing on page 351, www.cross-pollinate.com). Frederick of **Tournights** runs a similar apartment-finding service in Rome and Florence (www.tournights. com).

OTHER OPTIONS

Airbnb and Roomorama make it reasonably easy to find a place to sleep in someone's home. Beds range from air-mattress-in-living-room basic to plush-B&B-suite posh. If you want a place to sleep that's free, www.couchsurfing.org is a vagabond's alternative to Airbnb. It lists millions of outgoing members, who host fellow "surfers" in their homes.

Accommodations

NEAR TERMINI TRAIN STATION

While not as atmospheric as other areas of Rome, the hotels near Termini train station are less expensive, and public-transportation options link these places easily with the entire city. The city's two Metro lines intersect at the station, and most buses leave from here. Piazza Venezia is a 20-minute walk down Via Nazionale.

West of the Station

Most of these hotels are on or near Via Firenze, a safe, handy, central, and relatively quiet street that's a 10-minute walk from Termini train station and the airport train, and two blocks beyond Piazza della Repubblica. The Defense Ministry is nearby, so you've got heavily armed guards watching over you all night.

The neighborhood is well-connected by public transportation (with the Repubblica Metro stop nearby). Virtually all the city buses that rumble down Via Nazionale (#60, #64, #70, and the #40 express) take you to Piazza Venezia (Forum). From Piazza Venezia, bus #64 (jammed with people and thieves) and the #40 express bus continue to Largo Argentina (Pantheon, Campo de' Fiori) and the Vatican area. Or, at Piazza Venezia, you can transfer to tram #8 to Trastevere (get off at first stop after crossing the river). Bus #H also makes the journey to Trastevere, leaving from Piazza della Repubblica (on the northeast side of the square, near the entrance to Baths of Diocletian). If you are staying near the Santa Susanna and Santa Maria della Vittoria churches, buses from nearby Largo Santa Susanna (#62, #85, #116, #175, and #492) wind through the city center (leaving from the Bissolati stop; returning the stop name is Largo S. Susanna).

To stock your closet pantry, pop over to **Despar Supermarket** (daily 8:00-21:00, Via Nazionale 213, at the corner of Via Venezia). A 24-hour **pharmacy** near the recommended hotels is Farmacia Piram (Via Nazionale 228, tel. 06-488-4437).

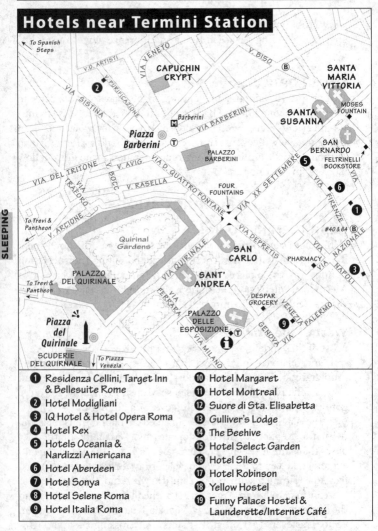

Hotels near Termini Station

1. Residenza Cellini, Target Inn & Bellesuite Rome
2. Hotel Modigliani
3. IQ Hotel & Hotel Opera Roma
4. Hotel Rex
5. Hotels Oceania & Nardizzi Americana
6. Hotel Aberdeen
7. Hotel Sonya
8. Hotel Selene Roma
9. Hotel Italia Roma
10. Hotel Margaret
11. Hotel Montreal
12. Suore di Sta. Elisabetta
13. Gulliver's Lodge
14. The Beehive
15. Hotel Select Garden
16. Hotel Sileo
17. Hotel Robinson
18. Yellow Hostel
19. Funny Palace Hostel & Launderette/Internet Café

$$$ Residenza Cellini feels like the guest wing of a gorgeous Neoclassical palace. It offers 11 rooms, "ortho/anti-allergy beds," four-star comforts and service, and a breezy breakfast terrace (Db-€190, larger Db-€210, extra bed-€25, prices good through 2015 with this book and cash, air-con, elevator, guest computer, Wi-Fi, Via Modena 5, reception on third floor, tel. 06-4782-5204, www.residenzacellini.it, residenzacellini@tin.it, Barbara, Gaetano, and Donato). They hope to open a seven-room annex in the same building in 2015.

$$$ Hotel Modigliani, a delightful 23-room place, is energetically run in a clean, bright, minimalist yet in-love-with-life style that its artist namesake would appreciate. It has a vast and plush lounge, a garden, and a newsletter introducing you to each of the staff (Db-€202, check website for deals and ask for a 10 percent Rick Steves discount when you book directly with the hotel through 2015, air-con, elevator, Wi-Fi; northwest of Via Firenze—from Tritone Fountain on Piazza Barberini, go 2 blocks up Via della Purificazione to #42; tel. 06-4281-5226, www.hotelmodigliani.com, info@hotelmodigliani.com, Giulia and Marco).

$$$ IQ Hotel, facing the Opera House, feels almost Scandinavian in its efficiency, without a hint of the Old World. It lacks charm, but more than compensates with modern amenities. Its 88

Sleep Code

(€1 = about $1.40)

Price Rankings

To help you easily sort through my listings, I've divided the accommodations into three categories based on the highest price for a standard double room with bath during high season:

$$$ **Higher Priced**—Most rooms €180 or more.

  $$ **Moderately Priced**—Most rooms between €125-180.

    $ **Lower Priced**—Most rooms €125 or less.

I always rate hostels as $, whether or not they have double rooms, because they have the cheapest beds in town. Prices can change without notice; verify the hotel's current rates online or by email. For the best prices, always book directly with the hotel.

Abbreviations

To pack maximum information into minimum space, I use the following code to describe accommodations in this book. Prices listed are per room, not per person. When a price range is given for a type of room (such as double rooms listing for €100-150), it means the price fluctuates with the season, size of room, or length of stay; expect to pay the upper end for peak-season stays.

  S = Single room (or price for one person in a double).

  D = Double or Twin room. "Double beds" can be two twins sheeted together and are usually big enough for nonromantic couples.

  T = Triple (generally a double bed with a single).

  Q = Quad (usually two double beds; adding an extra child's bed to a T is usually cheaper).

  b = Private bathroom with toilet and shower or tub.

  s = Private shower or tub only (the toilet is down the hall).

According to this code, a couple staying at a "Db-€140" hotel would pay a total of €140 (about $182) per night for a double room with a private bathroom. Unless otherwise noted, breakfast is included, hotel staff speak basic English, and credit cards are accepted.

Rome charges a hotel tax of €2-3 per person, per night (though this may increase in 2015). This tax is typically not included in the prices I've listed here.

If I've listed Wi-Fi or a guest computer, it's free.

rooms are fresh and spacious, the roof garden comes with a play area and foosball, and vending machines dispense bottles of wine (Db-€100-230 depending on room size and season—likely €200 in peak season, €40 extra for third and fourth person, 10 percent discount off best Web price for Rick Steves readers through 2015— must book direct and request at time of booking, breakfast-€10, air-con, elevator, guest computer, Wi-Fi, cheap self-service laundry, gym, Via Firenze 8, tel. 06-488-0465, www.iqhotelroma.it, info@iqhotelroma.it, manager Diego).

$$$ Hotel Rex is modern, cool, and sleek, but also family-friendly, with an engaging lounge and a rooftop breakfast terrace (Db-€197, air-con, elevator, guest computer, Wi-Fi, Via Torino 149, tel. 06-482-4828, www.hotelrex.net, rex@hotelrex.net).

$$ Hotel Oceania is a peaceful slice of air-conditioned heaven. This 24-room manor house-type hotel is spacious and quiet, with tastefully decorated rooms. Stefano runs a fine staff, serves wonderful coffee, provides lots of thoughtful extra touches, and works hard to maintain a caring family atmosphere (Sb-€135, Db-€168, Tb-€198, Qb-€220, these prices good through 2015 with this book, 5 percent discount if you pay cash, deep discounts summer and winter, family suite, elevator, guest computer, Wi-Fi, videos in the TV lounge, Via Firenze 38, third floor, tel. 06-482-4696, www.hoteloceania.it, info@hoteloceania.it; Anna and Radu round out the staff).

$$ Hotel Aberdeen, which perfectly combines quality and friendliness, is warmly run by Annamaria, with support from sister Laura and cousin Cinzia, and staff members Mariano and Costel. The 37 comfy, modern rooms are a fine value (Sb-€102, Db-€170, Tb-€180, Qb-€200, for these rates—or better—book direct via email or use the "Rick Steves reader reservations" link on their website, air-con, guest computer, Wi-Fi, Via Firenze 48, tel. 06-482-3920, www.hotelaberdeen.it, info@hotelaberdeen.it).

$$ Hotel Opera Roma, with contemporary furnishings and marble accents, boasts 15 spacious, modern, and thoughtfully appointed rooms. It's quiet and just a stone's throw from the Opera House (Db-€150, Tb-€165, for these rates book direct and mention Rick Steves, 5 percent discount if you pay cash, air-con, elevator, guest computer, Wi-Fi, Via Firenze 11, tel. 06-487-1787, www.hoteloperaroma.com, info@hoteloperaroma.com, Reza, Litu, and Federica).

$$ Hotel Sonya offers 40 well-equipped if small rooms, a hearty breakfast, and decent prices (Sb-€90, Db-€150, Tb-€165, Qb-€185, Quint/b-€200, 5 percent discount with this book if you pay cash through 2015, air-con, elevator, guest computer, Wi-Fi, faces the Opera House at Via Viminale 58, Metro: Repubblica or

Termini, tel. 06-481-9911, www.hotelsonya.it, info@hotelsonya.it, Francesca and Ivan).

$$ Hotel Selene Roma spreads its 40 stylish rooms out on a few floors of a big palazzo. With elegant furnishings and room to breathe, it's a fine value (Db-€160, Tb-€190, email direct for 10 percent discount, additional 5 percent discount if you pay cash upon arrival, air-con, elevator, Wi-Fi, family rooms, Via del Viminale 8, tel. 06-474-4781, www.hotelseleneroma.it, reception@hotelseleneroma.it).

$$ Target Inn is a sleek, practical six-room place next to Residenza Cellini (listed earlier). It's owned by the same people who run the recommended Target Restaurant nearby (Db-€150, this special price for Rick Steves readers through 2015, air-con, elevator, Wi-Fi, Via Modena 5, third floor, tel. 06-474-5399, www.targetinn.com, info@targetinn.com).

$$ Bellesuite Rome offers six rooms that feel dated for the price, but are worth considering for the location—in the same fine building as Residenza Cellini and Target Inn (Db-€160, Tb-€199, Qb-€240, 5 percent discount through 2015 if you show this book and pay cash, air-con, elevator, Wi-Fi, Via Modena 5, third floor, tel. 06-9521-3049, www.bellesuiterome.com, mail@bellesuiterome.com).

$ Hotel Nardizzi Americana, with a small rooftop terrace and 40 standard rooms spread throughout the building, is another decent value (Sb-€95, Db-€125, Tb-€155, Qb-€175; to get the best rates, check their "Rick Steves readers reservations" link along with the rest of their website; additional 10 percent off any price if you pay cash, air-con, elevator, Wi-Fi, Via Firenze 38, reception on fourth floor, tel. 06-488-0035, www.hotelnardizzi.it, info@hotelnardizzi.it; friendly Stefano, Fabrizio, Mario, and Giancarlo).

$ Hotel Italia Roma, in a busy and handy locale, is located safely on a quiet street next to the Ministry of the Interior. Thoughtfully run by Andrea, Sabrina, Abdul, and Gabriel, it has 35 modest but comfortable rooms (Sb-€80, Db-€120, Tb-€150, Qb-€180, book direct via email for these rates, air-con, elevator, guest computer, Wi-Fi, Via Venezia 18, just off Via Nazionale, tel. 06-482-8355, www.hotelitaliaroma.it, info@hotelitaliaroma.it). The four "residenza" rooms upstairs on the third floor are newer and about €10 more expensive. They also have eight similar annex rooms across the street for the same price as the main hotel.

$ Hotel Margaret offers few frills and 12 simple rooms at a fair price (Db-€110, Tb-€140, Qb-€155, mention this book and pay cash for best rates, air-con, elevator, Wi-Fi, north of Piazza Repubblica at Via Antonio Salandra 6, fourth floor, tel. 06-482-4285, www.hotelmargaret.net, info@hotelmargaret.net, Emanuela).

Southwest of the Station

These good-value places cluster around the basilica of Santa Maria Maggiore, on the edge of Rome's international district.

$ Hotel Montreal is a basic three-star place with 27 small rooms on a big street a block southeast of Santa Maria Maggiore (Sb-€90, Db-€110, Tb-€135, email direct and ask for a Rick Steves discount, air-con, elevator, guest computer, Wi-Fi, small garden terrace, good security, Via Carlo Alberto 4, 1 block from Metro: Vittorio Emanuele, 3 blocks from Termini train station, tel. 06-445-7797, www.hotelmontrealroma.it, info@hotelmontrealroma.it, Pasquale).

$ Suore di Santa Elisabetta is a heavenly Polish-run convent with a serene garden and 70 beds in tidy twin-bedded (only) rooms. Often booked long in advance, with such tranquility it's a super value (S-€40, Sb-€48, D-€66, Db-€85, Tb-€106, Qb-€128, Quint/b-€142, fans but no air-con, elevator serves top floors only, fine view roof terrace and breakfast hall, 23:00 curfew, a block southwest of Santa Maria Maggiore at Via dell'Olmata 9, Metro: Termini or Vittorio Emanuele, tel. 06-488-8271, www.csse-roma.eu, ist.it.s.elisabetta@libero.it).

$ Gulliver's Lodge has four colorful rooms on the ground floor of a large, secure building. While on a busy street, the rooms are quiet. Although the public spaces are few, in-room extras like DVD players (and DVDs, including my Italy shows) make it a fine home base (Db-€120, Tb-€145, includes small breakfast at nearby bar, mention this book for these prices through 2015, cash only, air-con, guest computer, Wi-Fi, a 15-minute walk southwest of Termini train station at Via Cavour 101, Metro: Cavour, tel. 06-9727-3787, www.gulliverslodge.com, info@gulliverslodge.com, Sara and Mary).

Sleeping Cheaply, Northeast of Termini Train Station

The cheapest beds in town are northeast of Termini train station (Metro: Termini). Some travelers feel this area is weird and spooky after dark, but these hotels feel plenty safe. With your back to the train tracks, turn right and walk two blocks out of the station. **Splashnet** launderette/Internet café is handy (€8 full-serve wash and dry, guest computer-€1.50/hour, €2 luggage storage per day—or free if you wash and go online, daily 8:30-23:00, just off Via Milazzo at Via Varese 33, tel. 06-4470-3523).

$ The Beehive gives vagabonds—old and young—a cheap, clean, and comfy home in Rome. Thoughtfully and creatively run by Steve and Linda, a friendly American couple, and their hard-working staff, the place offers six great-value artsy-mod double rooms (D-€80, T-€120) and an eight-bed dorm (€35 bunks) in the main building (with no air-con, only fans). Their nearby annex,

The Sweets, has similar style and several rooms with private baths (Sb-€70, D-€90, Db-€100, air-con-€10; breakfast extra, guest computer, Wi-Fi, private garden terrace, dinner available some nights, 2 blocks from Termini train station at Via Marghera 8, tel. 06-4470-4553, www.the-beehive.com, info@the-beehive.com). They're also a good resource for apartments across the city (www.cross-pollinate.com).

$ Hotel Select Garden, a modern and comfortable 21-room hotel run by the cheery Picca family, boasts lively modern art adorning the walls and a beautiful lemon-tree garden. It's a safe, tranquil, and welcoming refuge just a couple of blocks from the train station (Sb-€95, Db-€125, Tb-€145, book direct and mention Rick Steves for these prices through 2015, air-con, Wi-Fi, Via V. Bachelet 6, tel. 06-445-6383, www.hotelselectgarden.com, info@hotelselectgarden.com, Cristina and Maurizia).

$ Hotel Sileo, with shiny chandeliers in dim rooms, is a homey little place renting 10 basic rooms. It's worn, but run with warmth by friendly Alessandro and Maria Savioli (who don't speak English) and their daughter Anna (who does); their other daughter, Stefania, painted the wall murals (Db-€70, Tb-€85, mention Rick Steves to get these prices through 2015, discount if you pay cash, air-con, elevator, Wi-Fi, Via Magenta 39, fourth floor, tel. 06-445-0246, www.hotelsileo.com, info@hotelsileo.com).

$ Hotel Robinson is just a few steps from the station, but tucked away from the commotion. Set on an interior courtyard, it has 20 small and simple rooms, handsomely decorated with dark-wood accents, that are a good value (Sb-€65, Db-€85, Tb-€120, mention this book for these rates and a small breakfast plus free air-con, Wi-Fi, Via Milazzo 3, tel. 06-491-423, www.hotelrobinsonrome.com, info@hotelrobinsonrome.com).

$ Yellow Hostel rents 220 beds in 4-, 6-, and 10-bed dorms to 18- through 40-year-olds only (I'd skip their 16 private rooms, which are basic and overpriced). Hip yet sane, it's well-run with fine facilities, including lockers and a café/late-night bar (€18-40/bed depending on plumbing, size, and season, Db-€140; reserve online—no telephone reservations accepted, breakfast extra, loaner towels, elevator, Wi-Fi, loaner iPads, no curfew, 6 blocks from station, just past Via Vicenza at Via Palestro 40/44, tel. 06-4938-2682, www.yellowhostel.com, questions@the-yellow.com).

$ Funny Palace Hostel, adjacent to Splashnet and run by the same entrepreneurial owner, Mabri, rents dorm beds in quiet four-person rooms and 18 stark-but-clean private rooms. It's far less convivial than Yellow Hostel, but suitable for introverts (dorm beds-€30, Db-€100, cash only, includes breakfast in café, elevator, lockers, guest kitchen, Wi-Fi, reception in the launderette—

described earlier, Via Varese 33/31, tel. 06-4470-3523, www. hostelfunny.com, info@hostelfunny.com).

NEAR ANCIENT ROME

Stretching from the Colosseum to Piazza Venezia, this area is central. Sightseers are a short walk from the Colosseum, Roman Forum, and Trajan's Column—and all of these listings (except Hotel Lancelot) are close to or in the charming Monti district, with good restaurants and shopping (see pages 400 and 420). While buses are your best bet here, I list a Metro stop if it's convenient.

$$$ Hotel Lancelot is a comfortable refuge—a 60-room hotel with the ambience of a B&B. Located in a pleasant, low-key residential neighborhood a 10-minute stroll or easy tram or bus ride beyond the Colosseum, it's quiet and safe, with a shady courtyard, restaurant, bar, and tiny communal sixth-floor terrace. It's well-run by Faris and Lubna Khan, who serve a good €25 dinner—a tasty way to connect with your hotel neighbors and the friendly staff. No wonder it's popular with returning guests (Sb-€130, Db-€200, Tb-€230, Qb-€270, €20 extra for sixth-floor terrace room with a Colosseum view, 5 percent off these rates in 2015 if you book direct and mention Rick Steves, air-con, elevator, wheelchair-accessible, Wi-Fi, parking-€10/day, 10-minute walk behind Colosseum near San Clemente Church at Via Capo d'Africa 47, tel. 06-7045-0615, www.lancelothotel.com, info@lancelothotel.com). Faris and Lubna speak the Queen's English.

$$$ Hotel Nerva is a boutiquey, snazzy slice of tranquility with 19 small, overpriced (but often discounted) rooms. It sits on a quiet, ideally located side street that faces the Roman Forum and has the lovable Monti neighborhood in its backyard (Sb-€160, Db-€230, extra bed-€50, book direct and use promo code "RICK-STEVES" for an additional discount through 2015, air-con, elevator, Wi-Fi, Via Tor de' Conti 3, tel. 06-678-1835, www.hotelnerva. com, info@hotelnerva.com, Antonio and Paolo).

$$ Hotel Paba is a cozy throwback, with seven fresh rooms, chocolate-box-tidy and lovingly cared for by Alberta Castelli. It's just two blocks from the Forum. Although it overlooks busy Via Cavour, it's quiet enough (Db-€135, extra bed-€40, 5 percent discount if you pay cash, big beds, breakfast served in room, air-con, elevator, Wi-Fi, Via Cavour 266, Metro: Cavour, tel. 06-4782-4902, www.hotelpaba.com, info@hotelpaba.com).

$$ Nicolas Inn Bed & Breakfast, a delightful little four-room place with thoughtful touches, is spacious and bright. While on a busy street, it's just steps from the lively Monti district. It's run by François and American expat Melissa, who make you feel like you have caring friends in Rome (Db-€150-170, 10 percent Rick Steves discount with this book through 2015, cash only, includes

Hotels & Restaurants near Ancient Rome

To Pantheon
PLEBISCITO
BATT.
VIA NAZIONALE

Piazza Venezia

GESÙ
S. MARCO
VIA D'ARACOELI

Piazza Madonna di Loreto

TRAJAN'S COLUMN

Largo Magnanapoli

TRAJAN'S MARKET

VICTOR EMMANUEL MONUMENT

TRAJAN'S FORUM

VIA ALESSANDRINA

VIA TOR DI CONTE

VIA BACCINA

VIA MADONNA

To Ghetto
VIA TEATRO DI MARCELLO

Piazza Campidoglio

CAPITOLINE HILL

VIA DEI

CAPITOLINE MUSEUMS

EXIT ONLY

1 Hotel Lancelot
2 Hotel Nerva
3 Hotel Paba
4 Nicolas Inn B&B & Hotel Rosetta
5 Hotel Raffaello
6 Hotel Antica Locanda
7 Domus Nova Bethlem
8 Casa Il Rosario
9 L'Asino d'Oro
10 To La Taverna dei Monti
11 La Carbonara
12 Enoteca Cavour 313
13 Taverna Romana
14 La Vacca M'Briaca
15 La Cicala e La Formica
16 Taverna dei Fori Imperiali & dall'Antò

17 Trattoria da Valentino
18 Enoteca Nel Cuore di Roma
19 Ai Tre Scalini
20 Pizzeria Chicco di Grano
21 Fafiuché Vineria
22 Zia Rosetta
23 Pizzeria la Boccaccia
24 Gaudeo
25 Antico Forno ai Serpenti
26 Fatamorgana Gelateri
27 Il Gelatone Gelateria
28 Trattoria Luzzi
29 Rist. Pizzeria Naumachie
30 Li Rioni Pizzeria
31 La Taverna dei Quaranta
32 Hostaria da Nerone Rest. & Caffè dello Studente

breakfast served at neighboring bar, air-con, Wi-Fi, Via Cavour 295, tel. 06-9761-8483, www.nicolasinn.com, info@nicolasinn.com).

$$ Hotel Raffaello, with its courteous and professional staff, offers 41 rooms in a grand 19th-century building in Monti. This formal hotel comes with generous public spaces and a breakfast room fit for aristocrats (Sb-€80-100, Db-€120-180, Tb-€168-228, family room-€210-270, save by booking direct, includes breakfast, air-con, Wi-Fi, Via Urbana 3, Metro: Cavour, tel. 06-488-4342, www.hotelraffaello.it, info@hotelraffaello.it, helpful Elena).

$ Hotel Antica Locanda is a quiet gem in the heart of Monti. While the entrance is nothing special and stairs are plentiful, the seven rooms—each named for a composer or artist—come with stylish furnishings that are romantically rustic. The rooftop terrace is great for sunbathing or relaxing with a sunset drink (Db-€90-140, Tb-€120-170, includes breakfast, air-con, no elevator,

Via del Boschetto 84, Metro: Cavour, tel. 06-484-894, www.
anticalocandaroma.it, anticalocandaroma@gmail.com).

$ Domus Nova Bethlem, run by the Oblate Sisters of Baby
Jesus, is a spacious, pristine, and institutional-feeling hotel in the
Monti district. The 24 high-ceilinged rooms are modest yet classy,
and guests have access to a peaceful and leafy courtyard garden
(Sb-€88, Db-€110-135, Tb-€140-175, family rooms, includes
breakfast, air-con, Wi-Fi, 1:00 in the morning curfew, Via Cavour
85A, Metro: Cavour, tel. 06-4782-4414, www.domusnovabethlem.
it, info@domusnovabethlem.it).

$ Hotel Rosetta, a homey and family-run *pensione* in the
same building as Nicolas Inn, rents 15 simple rooms. It's pretty
minimal, with no lounge and no breakfast, but its great location
makes it a fine budget option (Sb-€70, Db-€95, Tb-€110, air-con,
Wi-Fi, Via Cavour 295, tel. 06-4782-3069, www.rosettahotel.com,
info@rosettahotel.com, Antonietta and Francesca).

$ Casa Il Rosario is a peaceful, well-run Dominican convent
renting 40 rooms with monastic simplicity to both pilgrims and
tourists in a steep but pleasant corner of the Monti neighborhood
(reserve several months in advance, S-€42, Sb-€56, Db-€94, Tb-
€120, single beds only but can be pushed together, some rooms
with air-con and others with fans, elevator, guest computer, Wi-
Fi, picnics welcome in small garden or on rooftop terrace, 23:00
curfew, midway between Quirinale and Colosseum near bottom of
Via Nazionale at Via Sant'Agata dei Goti 10, bus #40 or #170 from
Termini, tel. 06-679-2346, irodopre@tin.it).

IN THE PANTHEON NEIGHBORHOOD

Winding, narrow lanes filled with foot traffic and lined with boutique shops and tiny trattorias...this is village Rome at its best. And
like a real village, buses are the only practical way to connect with
other destinations. The atmosphere doesn't come cheap, but this
is where you want to be—especially at night, when Romans and
tourists gather in the floodlit piazzas for the evening stroll, the
passeggiata.

Near Campo de' Fiori

You'll pay a premium (and endure a little extra night noise) to stay
in the old center. But each of these places is romantically set deep
in the tangled back streets near the idyllic Campo de' Fiori and, for
many, worth the extra money.

$$$ Casa di Santa Brigida overlooks the elegant Piazza
Farnese. With soft-spoken sisters gliding down polished hall-
ways and pearly gates instead of doors, this lavish 20-room con-
vent makes exhaust-stained Roman tourists feel like they've died
and gone to heaven. If you don't need a double bed or a TV in

Hotels in the Pantheon Neighborhood

Tiber River
PONTE UMBERTO
Piazza Ponte Umberto I
VIA D. BRIANZO
Piazza Nicosia
VIA CLEMENTINO
To Piazza del Popolo
To Spanish Steps
VIA SAN ANDREA
VIA D'ORSO
VIA D. SCROFA
To Barberini
ANCIENT STADIUM ENTRANCE
CORONARI
UFF. VICARIO
PARLIAMENT
VIA DEL TRITONE
TREVI FOUNTAIN
SAN LUIGI
VIA D. COPPELLE
Piazza di Montecitorio
Piazza Colonna
SABINA
MURATTE
TRE SCALINI
SALV.
GIUST.
VIA DELLA SCROFA
SAL. CRESC.
AQUIRO
Piazza Rotonda
PASTINI
Piazza di Pietra
DEL CORSO
Piazza Navona
SEMINARIO
PANTHEON
SAN IGNAZIO
S. APOST.
Piazza Pasquino
Piazza Sant' Eust.
S. CHIARA
Piazza Collegio Rom.
GALLERIA DORIA PAMPHILJ
CITY MUSEUM
CORSO VITTORIO EMANUELE II
SANTA MARIA SOPRA MINERVA
ARGENTINA
CESTARI
To Colosseum & M
Campo de' Fiori
Piazza Farnese
PALAZZO FARNESE
V. M. D. FARINA
CHIAVARI
GIUBBONARI
LARGO ARGENTINA RUINS
GESÙ
VIA PLEBISCITO
Piazza Venezia
VIA DI SAN MARCO
Piazza del Campidoglio
200 Meters
200 Yards
SPECCHI
VIA ARENULA
VIA D. BOTT. OSCURE
ARACOELI
VIA DEL PORTICO D'OTTAVIA
GHETTO
CAPITOLINE HILL
VICTOR EMMANUEL MONUMENT

1 Casa di Santa Brigida
2 Relais Teatro Argentina
3 Hotel Smeraldo
4 Dipendenza Smeraldo
5 Hotel Arenula
6 Hotel Nazionale
7 Albergo Santa Chiara
8 Hotel Portoghesi
9 Hotel Due Torri

your room, it's worth the splurge—especially if you luxuriate in its ample public spaces or on its lovely roof terrace (Sb-€120, twin Db-€200, book well in advance, air-con, elevator, guest computer, Wi-Fi, tasty €25 dinners, roof garden, plush library, Monserrato 54, tel. 06-6889-2596, www.brigidine.org, piazzafarnese@brigidine.org, many of the sisters are from India and speak English—pray you get to work with wonderful sister Gertrude).

$$$ Relais Teatro Argentina, a six-room gem, is steeped in tasteful old-Rome elegance, but has all the modern comforts. It's cozy and quiet like a B&B and couldn't be more centrally located (Db-€210, Tb-€255, discounts if you pay cash and stay 3 nights or more, air-con, no elevator, 3 flights of stairs, guest computer, Wi-

Fi, Via del Sudario 35, tel. 06-9893-1617, mobile 331-198-4708, www.relaisteatroargentina.com, info@relaisteatroargentina.com, Carlotta).

$$ Hotel Smeraldo, with 50 rooms, is strictly run by an impersonal staff, but it's clean and a reasonable deal (Sb-€110, Db-€140, Tb-€170, buffet breakfast free in 2015 if you show this book, air-con, elevator, guest computer, Wi-Fi, flowery roof terrace, midway between Campo de' Fiori and Largo Argentina at Vicolo dei Chiodaroli 9, tel. 06-687-5929, www.smeraldoroma. com, info@smeraldoroma.com; Massimo, Walter, and Eugenio). Their **Dipendenza Smeraldo,** 10 yards around the corner at Via dei Chiavari 32, has 16 similar rooms (same price and free breakfast, same reception and contact info).

In the Jewish Ghetto
$$ Hotel Arenula, with 50 decent rooms, is the only hotel in Rome's old Jewish ghetto. Though it has the ambience of a gym and attracts lots of students, it is in the thick of old Rome (Sb-€100, Db-€140, 5 percent off with this book in 2015, extra bed-€21, air-con, no elevator, Wi-Fi, opposite the fountain in the park on Via Arenula at Via Santa Maria de' Calderari 47, tel. 06-687-9454, www.hotelarenula.com, info@hotelarenula.com).

Close to the Pantheon
These places are buried in the pedestrian-friendly heart of ancient Rome, each within about a five-minute walk of the Pantheon. You'll pay more here—but you'll save time and money by being exactly where you want to be for your early and late wandering.

$$$ Hotel Nazionale, a four-star landmark, is a 16th-century palace that shares a well-policed square with the Parliament building. Its 100 rooms are accentuated by lush public spaces, fancy bars, a uniformed staff, and a marble-floored restaurant. It's a big, stuffy hotel but it's a worthy splurge if you want security, comfort, and the heart of Rome at your doorstep (Sb-€220, Db-€390, giant deluxe Db-€530, extra person-€70, check online for summer and weekend discounts—you'll typically save 30 percent off their sky-high rack rates, air-con, elevator, Wi-Fi, Piazza Montecitorio 131, tel. 06-695-001, www.hotelnazionale.it, info@hotelnazionale.it).

$$$ Albergo Santa Chiara, in the old center, is big, solid, and hotelesque. Flavia, Silvio, and their fine staff offer marbled elegance (but basic furniture) and all the hotel services. Its ample public lounges are dressy and professional, and its 99 rooms are quiet and spacious (Sb-€138, Db-€215, Tb-€260, check website for discounts, book online direct and request special Rick Steves rates, elevator, air-con, Wi-Fi, behind Pantheon at Via di Santa

Chiara 21, tel. 06-687-2979, www.albergosantachiara.com, info@albergosantachiara.com).

$$$ Hotel Portoghesi is a classic hotel with 27 colorful rooms in the medieval heart of Rome. It's peaceful, quiet, and calmly run, and comes with a delightful roof terrace—though you pay for the location (Sb-€160, Db-€200, Tb-€260, Qb suite-€300, €30 extra for bigger deluxe room, breakfast on roof, air-con, elevator, Wi-Fi, Via dei Portoghesi 1, tel. 06-686-4231, www.hotelportoghesiroma.it, info@hotelportoghesiroma.it).

$$$ Hotel Due Torri, hiding out on a tiny quiet street, is beautifully located. It feels professional yet homey, with an accommodating staff, generous public spaces, and 26 rooms (the ones on upper floors are smaller but have views). While the location and lounge are great, the rooms are overpriced unless you score a discount (Sb-€125, Db-€200, family apartment-€240 for 3 and €265 for 4, check website for frequent discounts, air-con, elevator, Wi-Fi, a block off Via della Scrofa at Vicolo del Leonetto 23, tel. 06-6880-6956, www.hotelduetorriroma.com, info@hotelduetorriroma.com, Cinzia).

Near the Spanish Steps

$$$ Hotel San Carlo is buried in the thick of Rome's bustling "shopping triangle," which also has many restaurants. Its 50 rooms, connected by a treehouse floor plan, provide a tranquil haven (Sb-€125, standard Db-€195, superior Db-€224, 10 percent discount with this book through 2015, air-con, elevator, guest computer, Wi-Fi, Via delle Carrozze 92—see map on page 434, tel. 06-678-4548, www.hotelsancarloroma.com, info@hotelsancarloroma.com).

IN TRASTEVERE

Colorful and genuine in a gritty sort of way, Trastevere is a treat for travelers looking for a less touristy and more bohemian atmosphere. Choices are few here, and public transit is limited to a few buses and trams. But by trekking across the Tiber, you can have the experience of being comfortably immersed in old Rome.

$$$ Residenza Arco dei Tolomei is your most poetic Trastevere experience imaginable, with six small, unique, antique-filled rooms, some boasting fragrant balconies. With its quiet and elegant setting, you can pretend you're visiting aristocratic relatives (Db-€205, discounts if you pay cash and stay more than 3 nights, reserve well in advance, guest computer, Wi-Fi, from Piazza Piscinula a block up Via dell'Arco de' Tolomei at #27, tel. 06-5832-0819, www.bbarcodeitolomei.com, info@bbarcodeitolomei.com; Marco and Gianna Paola).

$$$ Hotel Santa Maria sits like a lazy hacienda in the midst

SLEEPING

100 Meters
100 Yards

1. Residenza Arco dei Tolomei & Arco del Lauro B&B
2. Hotel Santa Maria
3. Casa San Giuseppe
4. To Hotel San Francesco
5. Taverna Trilussa
6. La Gensola Restaurante
7. Trattoria da Lucia
8. Trattoria da Olindo
9. Osteria Ponte Sisto
10. Pizzeria "Ai Marmi"
11. Pizzeria Dar Poeta
12. Cantina Paradiso Wine & Cocktail Bar
13. Gelateria Checco er Carettiere
14. Grattachecca Stand
15. Almost Corner Bookshop
16. Open Door Bookshop

of Trastevere. Surrounded by a medieval skyline, you'll feel as if you're on some romantic stage set. Its 20 small but well-equipped, air-conditioned rooms—former cells in a cloister—are all on the ground floor, as are a few suites for up to six people. The rooms circle a gravelly courtyard of orange trees and stay-awhile patio furniture (Db-€190, Tb-€230; prices good through 2015 with this book, cash, and minimum stay of three nights; family rooms, free loaner bikes, guest computer, Wi-Fi, face church on Piazza Maria Trastevere and go right down Via della Fonte d'Olio 50 yards to Vicolo del Piede 2, tel. 06-589-4626, www.hotelsantamariatrastevere. it, info@hotelsantamaria.info). Some rooms come with family-friendly fold-down bunks for €30 extra per person. Their freshly

Hotels & Restaurants in Trastevere

To Campo de' Fiori • *To Largo Argentina & Pantheon*

Tiber

#23 & 271

9

PONTE SISTO

Piazza Trilussa

#23

PONTE SISTO

13

V. BENE

VIC. CINQUE

15

2

VIA PELLICCIA

VIA

SANTA MARIA IN TRASTEVERE

Piazza San Calisto

LUNGO. RAPHAEL SANZIO

River

5

VIA D. RENELLA

VIA D. ZOCCO

LUNGOTEVERE VALLATI

#8

#8 & 271

#23

GHETTO

SCHOOL

SYNAGOGUE & MUSEUM

LUNGOTEVERE DEI CENCI

PONTE GARIBALDI

Isola Tiberina

HOSPITAL

PONTE FABRICIO

#23

VIA MODENA

#H

S. AGATA

Piazza Belli

#8

LUNGO. DELL' ANGUILLARA

PONTE CESTIO

SAN BART.

14

VIA DELLA LUNGARETTA

Largo S. Giovanni

VIA LUNGARETTA

6

16

#23 & 271

ARCO S. CALISTO

SAN CRISOGONO

Piazza Sonnino

Piazza in Piscinula

1

S T E V E R E

Piazza di San Cosimato

MANARA

10

V. CARD.

Piazza Mastai

#8

STA. CECILIA

GENOVESI

12

Tiny arrows (↗) indicate one-way streets. Not all shown.

To Trastevere Station

To Porta Portese Flea Market

SLEEPING

renovated six-room **Residenza Santa Maria** is a couple of blocks away (same prices, www.residenzasantamaria.com).

$$ Casa San Giuseppe is down a characteristic laundry-strewn lane with a sunny roof terrace and views of Aurelian Walls. While convent-owned, it's a secular place renting 29 plain but peaceful, spacious rooms that are getting a bit long in the tooth (Sb-€115, Db-€155, Tb-€190, Qb-€220, garden-facing rooms are quiet, air-con, elevator, guest computer, Wi-Fi in lobby, parking-€15/day, just north of Piazza Trilussa at Vicolo Moroni 22, tel. 06-5833-3490, www.casasangiuseppe.it, info@casasangiuseppe.it, Matteo).

$$ Arco del Lauro B&B rents six white, minimalist rooms

Hotels & Restaurants near Vatican City

in a good location. Facing a courtyard (no views but little noise), the friendly welcome and good value make up for the lack of public spaces (Db-€135, Qb-€185, prices good if booked direct, cash only, 3-4 night minimum stay over weekends in high season, includes breakfast served in a café, air-con, guest computer, Wi-Fi, from Piazza Piscinula a block up Via dell'Arco de' Tolomei at #29, tel. 06-9784-0350, mobile 346-244-3212, www.arcodellauro.it, info@arcodellauro.it, Lorenza and Daniela).

$$ Hotel San Francesco, big and blocky yet welcoming, stands like a practical and efficient oasis at the edge of all the Trastevere action. Renting 24 trim rooms in this authentic district, it comes with an inviting roof terrace and a helpful staff. Handy trams to Piazza Venezia are just a couple of blocks away (Db-€90-180, prices vary

1. Hotel Alimandi Vaticano
2. Hotel Alimandi Tunisi
3. Hotel Gerber
4. Hotel dei Consoli
5. Hearth Hotel
6. Excel Rome St. Peter
7. Casa Valdese
8. To Casa per Ferie Rooms
9. Hostaria dei Bastioni Rest.
10. L'Insalata Ricca & Duecento Gradi
11. Gelateria Old Bridge
12. Ristorante La Rustichella & Gelateria Millennium
13. Forno Feliziani
14. Tre Pupazzi Restaurant
15. Vecchio Borgo Restaurant
16. Mercato Trionfale
17. Supermarket

wildly, email direct and mention this book for best rates, air-con, elevator, Wi-Fi, Via Jacopa de' Settesoli 7, tel. 06-5830-0051, www. hotelsanfrancesco.net, hotelsanfrancesco@gmail.com).

NEAR VATICAN CITY

Sleeping near the Vatican is expensive, but some enjoy calling this more relaxed, residential neighborhood home. While jammed with tourists, the tree-lined streets are wider than in the historical center, and it feels less claustrophobic. Even though it's handy to the Vatican (when the rapture hits, you're right there), everything else is a long way away. Fortunately, it's well-served by public transit—use the Metro (line A) and bus (ask your hotel for the most convenient routes) to easily connect with the center.

$$$ Hotel Alimandi Vaticano, facing the Vatican Museum, is beautifully designed. Run by the Alimandi family (Enrico, Irene, and Germano), it features four stars, 24 spacious rooms, and all the modern comforts you can imagine (Sb-€170, standard Db-€200, big Db with 2 double beds-€260, Tb-€260, 5 percent discount if you pay cash, air-con, elevator, guest computer, Wi-Fi, Viale Vaticano 99, Metro: Ottaviano, tel. 06-3974-5562, www.alimandi. com, alimandivaticano@alimandi.com).

$$$ Hotel Alimandi Tunisi is a good value, run by other members of the friendly and entrepreneurial Alimandi family— Paolo, Luigi, Marta, and Barbara. They have 27 modest but comfortable rooms and vast public spaces, including a piano lounge, pool table, and rooftop terrace where the grand buffet breakfast is served (Sb-€90, Db-€180, 5 percent discount if you pay cash, elevator, air-con, guest computer, Wi-Fi, down the stairs directly in front of Vatican Museum, Via Tunisi 8, Metro: Ottaviano, tel. 06-3972-3941, www.alimandi.it, alimandi@tin.it).

$$$ Hotel Gerber, set in a quiet residential area, is family-run with 27 thoughtfully decorated rooms—some chic and modern, others polished and businesslike (Sb-€140, Db-€180, Tb-€200, Qb-€220, 10 percent high-season discount and 15 percent low-season discount off these prices with this book in 2015 when you book direct, air-con, elevator, Wi-Fi, small leafy terrace; from Lepanto Metro station, go one block down Via M. Colonna and turn right to Via degli Scipioni 241; tel. 06-321-6485, http:// hotelgerberrome.com, info@hotelgerber.it; Peter, Simonetta, and nice dog Kira).

$$$ Hotel dei Consoli, with 26 rooms tucked down a side street near Piazza del Risorgimento, feels stately and old-fashioned (Db-€180, air-con, elevator, Wi-Fi, Via Varrone 2D, tel. 06-6889-2972, www.hoteldeiconsoli.com, info@hoteldeiconsoli.com).

$$$ Hearth Hotel, a block from the Vatican wall, has 20 small, modern, efficient, and characterless rooms (Db-€180, air-con, elevator, Wi-Fi, Via Santamaura 2, tel. 06-3903-8383, www. hearthhotel.com, info@hearthhotel.com).

$$$ Excel Rome St. Peter is all glassy modernity, with 24 rooms and an impersonal feel (Db-€180, air-con, elevator, Wi-Fi, Via Catone 34, tel. 06-3973-5082, www.excelstpeter.it, booking@ excelstpeter.it).

$$ Casa Valdese is an efficient, well-managed, church-run hotel that's popular with Germans. Its 33 big, quiet rooms feel older and a bit institutional, with the bonus of two breezy, communal roof terraces with incredible views (two external Sb-€63, Sb-€100, Db-€133, Tb-€183, Qb-€213, discounts for 3-night stays, air-con, elevator, guest computer, Wi-Fi; from Lepanto Metro station, go one block down Via M. Colonna, turn left on Via degli Scipioni, then continue for a block to the intersection with Via Alessandro Farnese 18; tel. 06-321-5362, www.casavaldeseroma.it, reception@casavaldeseroma.it, Matteo).

$ Casa per Ferie Santa Maria alle Fornaci is simple and efficient, housing pilgrims and secular tourists just a short walk south of the Vatican in a dull, high-rise residential zone. Its 54 identical, stark, utilitarian rooms are mostly twin-bedded. Reserve at least three months in advance (Sb-€70, Db-€100, Tb-€135, air-con, elevator, guest computer, Wi-Fi; take bus #64 from Termini train station to San Pietro train station, then walk 100 yards north along Via della Stazione di San Pietro to Piazza Santa Maria alle Fornaci 27; or from the airport, take the train to Trastevere Station, then transfer to San Pietro Station; tel. 06-3936-7632, www.trinitaridematha.it, cffornaci@tin.it, Carmine).

SLEEPING

EATING IN ROME

Contents

The Italians are masters of the art of fine living. That means eating long and well. Lengthy, multi-course meals and endless hours sitting in outdoor cafés are the norm. Americans eat on their way to an evening event and complain if the check is slow in coming. For Italians, the meal is an end in itself, and only rude waiters rush you. When you want the bill, mime-scribble on your raised palm or request it: *"Il conto, per favore."* You may have to ask for it more than once. If you're in a hurry, request the check when you receive the last item you order.

A highlight of your Italian adventure will be this country's cafés, cuisine, and wines. Trust me: This is sightseeing for your palate. Even if you liked dorm food and are sleeping in cheap hotels, your taste buds will relish an occasional first-class splurge. You can eat well without going broke. But be careful: You're just as likely to blow a small fortune on a disappointing meal as you are to dine wonderfully for €25.

In general, Italians eat meals a bit later than we do. Eating like a Roman means stopping at the neighborhood bar each morning for a light breakfast (coffee—usually cappuccino or espresso—and a pastry, often standing up at a café). Lunch (between 13:00 and 15:00) is traditionally the largest meal of the day, eaten at home, although work habits have changed this for many people who don't want to spend time commuting. Instead, they grab a quick meal in a *tavola calda* bar (cafeteria) or buy a *panino* or *tramezzino* (sandwich). They eat a late, light dinner (around 20:00-21:30, or maybe earlier in winter). To bridge the gap, people drop into a bar in the late afternoon for a *spuntino* (snack) and aperitif.

Most restaurant kitchens close between their lunch and dinner service. Good restaurants don't reopen for dinner before 19:00. Small restaurants with a full slate of reservations for 20:30 or 21:00 often will accommodate walk-in diners willing to eat a quick, early meal, but you aren't expected to linger.

What's Cooking

BREAKFAST

Italian breakfasts, like Italian bath towels, are small: The basic, traditional version is coffee and a roll with butter and marmalade. These days, many places also have juice, yogurt, maybe cereal, possibly cold cuts and sliced cheese, and sometimes eggs (typically hard-boiled; scrambled or fried eggs are rare). Small budget hotels may leave a basic breakfast in a fridge in your room (stale croissant, roll, jam, yogurt). In general, the pricier the hotel, the bigger the breakfast.

The strong coffee at breakfast is often mixed about half-and-half with heated milk. At your hotel, refills are usually free. The delicious blood orange juice *(spremuta di arance rosse)* is made from Sicilian oranges.

If you want to skip your hotel breakfast, consider browsing for a morning picnic at a local open-air market. Or do as the Italians do: Stop into a bar or café to drink a cappuccino and munch a *cornetto* (croissant) while standing at the bar. While the *cornetto* is the most common pastry, you'll find a range of *pasticcini* (pastries, sometimes called *dolci*—"sweets"). Look for *otto* (an "8"-shaped pastry, often filled with custard, jam, or chocolate), *sfoglia* (can be fruit-filled, like a turnover), or *ciambella* (doughnut filled with custard or chocolate)—or ask about local specialties.

ITALIAN RESTAURANTS

While *ristorante* is self-explanatory, you'll also see other types of Italian eateries: A *trattoria* or an *osteria* (which can be more casual) is generally a family-owned place serving home-cooked meals, often at moderate prices. A *locanda* is an inn, a *cantina* is a wine cellar, and a *birreria* is a brewpub. *Pizzerie, rosticcerie* (delis), *tavola calda* ("hot table") bars, *enoteche* (wine bars), and other alternatives are explained later.

When restaurant hunting, choose a spot filled with locals, not the place with the big neon signs boasting, "We speak English and accept credit cards." Restaurants parked on famous squares generally serve bad food at high prices to tourists. Locals eat better at lower-rent locales. Family-run places operate without hired help and can offer cheaper meals. Venturing even a block or two off the main drag leads to higher-quality food for less than half the price of the tourist-oriented places.

Cover and Tipping

Before you sit down, look at a menu to see what extra charges a restaurant tacks on. Two different items are routinely factored into your bill: the *coperto* and the *servizio*.

The **coperto** (cover charge), sometimes called *pane e coperto* (bread and cover), offsets the restaurant's overhead expenses—from the basket of bread on your table to the electricity running the dishwasher. It's not negotiable, even if you don't eat the bread. Think of it as covering the cost of using the table for as long as you like. (Italians like to linger.) Most restaurants add the *coperto* onto your bill as a flat fee (€1-3.50 per person; the amount should be clearly noted on the menu).

The **servizio** (service charge) of about 10 percent pays for the waitstaff. At most legitimate eateries, the words *servizio incluso* are written on the menu and/or the receipt—indicating that the listed prices already include the fee. You can add on a tip, if you choose, by including a euro or two for each person in your party. While Italians don't think about tips in terms of percentages—and many don't tip at all—this extra amount usually comes out to about 5 percent (10 percent is excessive for all but the very best service).

A few trendy restaurants don't include the service in the menu prices—but will automatically tack on a 10 percent *servizio* charge to your bill. If a menu reads *servizio 10%*, the listed prices don't include the fee; it will be added onto your bill for you (so you don't need to calculate it yourself and pay it separately). Rarely, you'll

Eating with the Seasons

Italian cooks love to serve you fresh produce and sea-food at its tastiest. If you must have porcini mush-rooms outside of fall, they'll be dried. To get a plate of the freshest veggies at a fine restaurant, request *"Un piatto di verdure della stagioni, per favore"* ("A plate of veggies in season, please").

Here are a few examples of what's fresh when:

April-May:	Calamari, green beans, fava beans, romanesco (similar to cauliflower), asparagus, artichokes, and zucchini flowers
April-May and Sept-Oct:	Black truffles
May-June:	Mussels, asparagus, zucchini, cantaloupe, and strawberries
May-Aug:	Eggplant
Oct-Nov:	Mushrooms, white truffles, and chestnuts
Fresh year-round:	Clams, meats, and cheese

EATING

see the words *servizio non incluso* on the menu or bill; here you are expected to add a tip of about 10 percent.

Most Italian restaurants have a cover charge and include service in the menu prices (i.e., *servizio incluso*). A few have just a service charge. Places with *both* a cover and a tacked-on service charge are best avoided—that's a clue that a restaurant is counting on a nonlocal clientele who can't gauge value. Self-service restaurants never have a cover or service charge, and in recent years some (especially less formal) cafés and restaurants with table service have stopped charging these fees as well.

Courses: Antipasto, *Primo,* and *Secondo*

A full Italian meal consists of several courses:

Antipasto (usually €5-10): An appetizer such as bruschetta, grilled veggies, deep-fried tasties, thin-sliced meat (such as prosciutto or *carpaccio*), or a plate of olives, cold cuts, and cheeses. A plate of *antipasti misti* ("mixed"—an assortment) could make a light meal in itself.

Primo piatto (usually €7-15): A "first dish" generally consisting of pasta, rice, or soup. If you think of pasta when you think of Italy, you can dine well here without ever going beyond the *primo*.

Secondo piatto (usually €10-25): A "second dish," equivalent to our main course, of meat or fish/seafood. Italians freely admit the *secondo* is the least interesting part of their cuisine.

A vegetable side dish *(contorno)* may come with the *secondo* but more often must be ordered separately (€5-6).

For most travelers, a complete meal with all three courses (plus *contorni,* dessert, and wine) is simply too much food—and euros can add up in a hurry. To avoid overeating (and to stretch your budget), share dishes. A good rule of thumb is for each person to order any two courses. For example, a couple can order and share one antipasto, one *primo,* one *secondo,* and one dessert; or two *antipasti* and two *primi;* or whatever combination appeals. Some restaurants serve a *piatta unica,* with smaller portions of each course on one dish (for instance, a meat, starch, and vegetable).

Another good option is sharing an array of *antipasti*—either by ordering several specific dishes or, at restaurants that offer self-serve buffets, by choosing a variety of cold and cooked appetizers from an *antipasti* buffet spread out like a salad bar. At buffets, you pay per plate; a typical serving costs about €8 (generally Italians don't treat buffets as all-you-can-eat, but take a one-time moderate serving; watch others and imitate).

To maximize the experience and flavors, small groups can mix *antipasti* and *primi* family-style (skipping *secondi*). If you do this right, you can eat well in better places for less than the cost of a tourist *menù* in a cheap place.

Ordering

Seafood and steak may be sold by weight (priced by the kilo—1,000 grams, or just over two pounds; or by the *etto*—100 grams). The abbreviation *s.q. (secondo quantità)* means an item is priced "according to quantity." Unless the menu indicates a fillet *(filetto),* fish is usually served whole with the head and tail. However, you can always ask your waiter to select a small fish for you. Sometimes, especially for steak, restaurants require a minimum order of four or five *etti* (which diners can share). Make sure you're really clear on the price before ordering.

Some special dishes come in larger quantities meant to be shared by two people. The shorthand way of showing this on a menu is "X2" (for two), but the price listed generally indicates the cost per person.

In a traditional restaurant, if you order a pasta dish and a side salad—but no main course—the waiter will bring the salad after the pasta (Italians prefer it this way, believing that it enhances digestion). If you want the salad with your pasta, specify *insieme* (een-see-YEH-meh; together). At eateries more accustomed to tourists, you may be asked when you want the salad.

Because pasta and bread are both starches, Italians consider them redundant. If you order only a pasta dish, bread may not come with it; you can request it, but you may be charged extra. On the other hand, if you order a vegetable antipasto or a meat *secondo*, bread is provided to balance the ingredients.

At places with counter service—such as at a bar or a freeway rest-stop diner—you'll order and pay at the *cassa* (cashier). Take your receipt over to the counter to claim your food.

Fixed-Price Meals

You can save by getting a fixed-priced meal, which is normally exempt from cover and service charges. Avoid the cheapest ones (often called a *menù turistico*), which tend to be bland and heavy, pairing a very basic pasta with reheated schnitzel and roast meats. Look instead for a genuine *menù del giorno* (menu of the day), which offers diners a choice of appetizer, main course, and dessert. It's

MENU € 19,00
TURISTICO
ANTIPASTO di MARE
PRIMI PIATTI
RISOTTO alla PESCATORA
SPAGHETTI alla MARINARA
SPAGHETTI allo SCOGLIO
TRENETTE al PESTO
SECONDI PIATTI
PESCE ai FERRI
FRITTO MISTO
GRIGLIATA di CARNE
CONTORNI
PATATE FRITTE o INSALATA

worth paying a little more for an inventive fixed-price meal that shows off the chef's creativity.

While fixed-price meals can be easy and convenient, galloping gourmets order à la carte with the help of a menu translator. (The *Rick Steves Italian Phrase Book & Dictionary* has a menu decoder and plenty of useful phrases for intermediate eaters.) When going to an especially good restaurant with an approachable staff, I like to find out what they're eager to serve, or I'll simply say, *"Mi faccia felice"* (Make me happy) and set a price limit.

BUDGET EATING

Rome offers many budget options for hungry travelers, but beware of cheap eateries that sport big color photos of pizza and piles of different pastas. They have no kitchens and simply microwave disgusting prepackaged food.

Self-service cafeterias offer the basics without add-on charges. Travelers on a hard-core budget equip their room with a pantry stocked at the market (fruits and veggies are remarkably cheap) or pick up a kebab (or the equivalent), then dine in at picnic prices. Bars and cafés, described later, are also good places to grab a meal on the go.

Pizzerias

Pizza is cheap and readily available. Stop by a pizza shop for stand-up or takeout (*pizza al taglio* means "by the slice"). Some shops sell individual slices of round, Naples-style pizza, while others feature *pizza rustica*—thick pizza baked in a large rectangular pan and sold by weight. If you simply ask for a piece, you may wind up with a gigantic slab and be charged top euro. Instead, clearly indicate how much you want: 100 grams, or *un etto*, is a hot and cheap snack; 200 grams, or *due etti*, makes a light meal. Or show the size with your hands—*tanto così* (TAHN-toh koh-ZEE; this much).

In sit-down pizza restaurants, the local specialty is Roman-style pizza, made with a very thin and crispy dough *(scrocchiarella)* that's even thinner and less chewy than Neapolitan-style pizza. In Rome, *pizza bianco* (white pizza) can mean a pizza made without tomato sauce, but can also simply mean a chunk of flat, crispy bread, or a sandwich made with that bread (similar to what's called a *panino* in other parts of Italy).

Key pizza vocabulary: *capricciosa* (prosciutto, mushrooms, olives, and artichokes—literally the chef's "caprice"), *funghi* (mushrooms), *marinara* (tomato sauce, oregano, garlic, no cheese), *napoletana* (mozzarella, anchovies, and tomato sauce), *vegetariana* or *ortolana* ("greengrocer-style," with vegetables), *quattro formaggi* (four different cheeses), and *quattro stagioni* (different toppings on each of the four quarters, for those who can't choose just one menu item). If you ask for pepperoni on your pizza, you'll get *peperoni* (green or red peppers, not sausage); request *diavola* or *salsiccia piccante* instead (the closest thing in Italy to American pepperoni). Kids like the bland *margherita* (tomato sauce, mozzarella, and basil—the red, white, and green of the Italian flag).

Bars/Cafés

Italian "bars" are not taverns, but inexpensive cafés. These neighborhood hangouts serve coffee, mini-pizzas, sandwiches, and drinks from the cooler. Many dish up plates of fried cheese and vegetables from under the glass counter, ready to reheat. This budget choice is the Italian equivalent of English pub grub.

Food: For quick meals, bars usually have trays of cheap, premade sandwiches (*panini*, made with a baguette; *piadini*, made with flatbread; or *tramezzini*, made with crustless white bread)—some are delightful grilled. (Others have too much mayo.) To save time for sightseeing and room for dinner, stop by a bar for a light lunch, such as a ham-and-cheese sandwich (called *toast*); have it grilled twice if you want it really hot. To get food "to go," say, *"da portar via"* (for the road). Many bars are small—if you can't find a table, you'll need to stand up or find a ledge to sit on outside. Most charge extra for table service (see next). All bars have a WC *(toilette, bagno)* in the back, and customers—and the discreet public—can use it.

Prices and Paying: You'll notice a two- or three-tiered pricing system. Drinking a cup of coffee while standing at the bar is cheaper than drinking it at an indoor table (you'll pay still more at an outdoor table). Many places have a *lista dei prezzi* (price list) with two columns—*al bar* and *al tavolo* (table)—posted somewhere by the bar or cash register. If you're on a budget, don't sit down without first checking out the financial consequences. Ask, "Same price if I sit or stand?" by saying, *"Costa uguale al tavolo o al banco?"* (KOH-stah oo-GWAH-lay ahl TAH-voh-loh oh ahl BAHN-koh). Throughout Italy, you can get cheap coffee at the bar of any establishment, no matter how fancy, and pay the same low, government-regulated price (generally less than a euro if you stand).

If the bar isn't busy, you can probably just order and pay when you leave. Otherwise: 1) Decide what you want; 2) find out the price by checking the price list on the wall, the prices posted near the food, or by asking the barista; 3) pay the cashier; and 4) give the receipt to the barista (whose clean fingers don't handle dirty euros) and tell him or her what you want.

For more on drinking, see "Beverages," later.

Ethnic Food

A good bet for a cheap, hot meal is a *döner kebab.* Look for little hole-in-the-wall kebab shops (especially around Termini Station and Santa Maria Maggiore), where you can get a hearty takeout dinner wrapped in pita bread for €3.50. Pay an extra euro to super-size it, and it'll feed two. Asian restaurants, although not as common as in northern Europe, usually serve only Chinese dishes and can also be a good value.

Tavola Calda Bars and *Rosticcerie*

For a fast and cheap lunch, find an Italian variation on the corner deli: a *rosticceria* (specializing in roasted meats and accompanying *antipasti*) or a *tavola calda* bar ("hot table," a point-and-shoot cafeteria with a buffet spread of meat and vegetables). For a healthy light meal, ask for a mixed plate of vegetables with a hunk of mozzarella (*piatto misto di verdure con mozzarella;* pee-AH-toh MEE-stoh dee vehr-DOO-ray). Don't be limited by what's displayed. If you'd like a salad with a slice of cantaloupe and a hunk of cheese, they'll whip that up for you in a snap. Belly up to the bar and, with a pointing finger, you can assemble a fine meal. If something's a mystery, ask for *un assaggio* (oon ah-SAH-joh) to get a little taste. To

EATING

Pasta, Pasta!

Italy is famous for its cuisine, but above all, it's known for pasta. Each of the more than 600 varieties of Italian pasta has a reason for being—usually as the perfect platform for highlighting the sauce, meat, or regional ingredients of a particular dish. While we think of pasta as a main dish, in Italy it's considered a *primo piatto*—first course. Italian pasta falls into two broad categories: long and short.

Long pasta *(pasta lunga)* is long enough to twist around a fork. Aside from the universally familiar spaghetti, you'll find *capellini* (thin "little hairs"); *vermicelli* (slightly thicker "little worms"); and long, hollow *bucatini*. Flattened versions of *pasta lunga* include *linguine* (narrow "little tongues"), *fettuccine* (wider "small ribbons"), *tagliatelle* (even wider), and *pappardelle* (very wide, best with meat sauces).

Short pasta *(pasta corta)* can be speared or scooped with a fork. The most common *pasta corta* are short tubes, such as *penne, rigatoni, ziti, manicotti,* and *cannelloni;* they come either *lisce* (smooth) or *rigate* (grooved—better to catch and cling to sauce). Many short pastas are named for their unique shapes: *conchiglie* (shells), *farfalle* (butterflies), *cavatappi* (corkscrews), *ditali* (thimbles), *gomiti* ("elbow" macaroni), *lumache* (snails), *marziani* (spirals resembling "Martian" antennae), and even *strozzapreti* (priest stranglers)...to name just a few.

Short pastas are almost always made fresh and often are designed to be filled *(ripieni).* Aside from the familiar ravioli and tortellini, this category includes *gnocchi* (shell-shaped, hand-rolled dumplings usually made from potatoes), *tortelli* (C-shaped, stuffed ravioli), and *angolotti* or *mezzelune* (stuffed pasta shaped like "priest's hats" or "half-moons").

Most types of pasta can come in slight variations: If it's a bit thicker, *-one* is added to the end; if it's a bit thinner, *-ine, -ette,* or *-elle* is added. For example, *tortellini* are smaller *tortelli,* while *tortelloni* are bigger.

have your choices warmed up, ask for them to be heated (*scaldare;* skahl-DAH-ray).

Wine Bars

Wine bars *(enoteche)* are a popular, fast, and inexpensive option for lunch. Surrounded by the office crowd, you can get a salad, a plate of meats (cold cuts) and cheeses, and a glass of good wine (see blackboards for the day's selection and price per glass). A good *enoteca* aims to impress visitors with its wine, and will generally choose excellent-quality ingredients for the simple dishes it offers with the wine (though the prices add up—be careful with your ordering to keep this a budget choice). The area around the Pantheon and Piazza del Parlamento (popular with politicians and bureaucrats) has

As for what to put on that pasta, the options are almost as endless as the shapes. The following terms are usually preceded by *alla* (in the style of) or *in* (in):

aglio e olio: garlic and olive oil

alfredo: butter, cream, and parmesan

amatriciana: pork cheek, pecorino cheese, and tomato

arrabbiata: "angry," spicy tomato sauce with chili peppers

bolognese: meat and tomato sauce

boscaiola: mushrooms and sausage

burro e salvia: butter and sage

cacio e pepe: *parmigiano* cheese and ground pepper

carbonara: bacon, egg, cheese, and pepper

carrettiera: spicy and garlicky, with olive oil and little tomatoes

diavola: "devil-style," spicy hot

funghi: mushrooms

frutti di mare: seafood

genovese: pesto (basil ground with *parmigiano* cheese, garlic, pine nuts, and olive oil)

gricia: cured pork and pecorino romano cheese

marinara: usually tomato, often with garlic and onions, but can also be a seafood sauce ("sailor's style")

norma: tomato, eggplant, and ricotta cheese

pajata (or **pagliata**): calf intestines

pescatora: seafood ("fisherman style")

pomodoro: tomato only

puttanesca: "harlot-style" tomato sauce with anchovies, olives, and capers

ragù: meaty tomato sauce

scoglio: mussels, clams, and tomatoes

sorrentina: "Sorrento-style," with tomatoes, basil, and mozzarella (usually over gnocchi)

sugo di lepre: rich sauce made of wild hare

tartufi (or **tartufate**): truffles

umbria: sauce of anchovies, garlic, tomatoes, and truffles

vongole: clams and spices

plenty of *enoteche* handy for a sightseeing lunch break or evening destination.

Aperitivo Buffets

The Italian term *aperitivo* means a pre-dinner drink (specific drinks described later), but it's also used to describe their version of what we might call "happy hour": a light buffet that many bars serve to customers during the pre-dinner hours (typically around 19:00-21:00). The drink itself may not be cheap (typically €8-15), but they lay out an enticing array of meats, cheeses, grilled vegetables, and other *antipasti*-type dishes, and you're welcome to nibble to your heart's content while you nurse your drink. While it's intended as an appetizer course before heading out for a full dinner, light eaters could discreetly turn this into a small meal. If this interests you, drop by a few bars around this time to scope out their buffets before choosing.

Groceries and Delis

Another budget option is to drop by a supermarket, *alimentari* (neighborhood grocery), or *salumeria* (delicatessen) to pick up some cold cuts, cheeses, and other supplies for a picnic. Some *salumerie*, and any *paninoteca* or *foccaceria* (sandwich shop), can make you a sandwich to order. Just point to what you want, and they'll stuff it into a *panino;* if you want it heated, say, *"Scaldare, per favore"* (skahl-DAH-ray pehr fah-VOH-ray).

To get a sampler plate of cold cuts and cheeses in a restaurant, ask for *affettato misto* (mixed cold cuts) or *antipasto misto* (cold cuts, cheeses, and marinated vegetables). If ordering an assortment, some unscrupulous shops may try to pad the bill by pushing their most expensive ingredients. Be clear on what you want: *un tagliere da ___ euro, per favore* ("a sampler board—tah-lee-eh-ray—of ___ euros, please").

Salumi ("salted" meats), also called *affettati* ("cut" meats), are an Italian staple. While most American cold cuts are cooked, in Italy they're far more commonly cured by air-drying, salting, and smoking. (Don't worry; these so-called "raw" meats are safe to eat, and you can really taste the difference.)

The two most familiar types of *salumi* are *salame* and prosciutto. **Salame** is an air-dried, sometimes spicy sausage that comes in many varieties, including *finocchiona* (with fennel seeds), *salame piccante* (spicy hot, similar to pepperoni), and *salame di Sant'Olcese* (what we'd call "Genoa salami"). When Italians say *"prosciutto,"* they usually mean *prosciutto crudo*—the "raw" ham that air-cures on the hock and is then thinly sliced. Produced mainly in the north of Italy, prosciutto can be either *dolce* (sweet) or *salato* (salty). Purists say the best is *prosciutto di Parma*.

Other *salumi* may be less familiar. Air-cured pork variations include *culatello* (prosciutto made with only the finest cuts of meat), *capocollo* (or *coppa;* peppery pork shoulder), *speck* (smoked pork shoulder), *guanciale* (tender pork cheek), and *lonzino* (cured pork loin). *Pancetta*—which can be eaten raw or added to cooked dishes—is salt-cured, peppery pork belly meat (similar to bacon). *Mortadella*, a finely ground pork loaf, is similar to our baloney, and *bresaola* is air-cured beef. But look out for *testa in cassetta* (head-cheese—organs in aspic) and *lampredotto*—cow stomach that resembles a lamprey (eel).

As for **formaggio** (cheese), you're probably already familiar with several Italian favorites: *asiago* (hard cow cheese that comes either *mezzano*—young, firm, and creamy; or *stravecchio*—aged, pungent, and granular); *fontina* (semi-hard, nutty, Gruyère-style mountain cheese); *gorgonzola* (pungent, blue-veined cheese, either *dolce*—creamy, or *stagionato*—aged and hard); *mascarpone* (sweet, buttery, spreadable dessert cheese); *parmigiano-reggiano* (hard, crumbly, sharp, aged cow cheese with more nuanced flavor than American "parmesan"; *grana padano* is a less expensive variation); *pecorino* (either *fresco*—fresh, soft, and mild; or *stagionato*—aged and sharp, sometimes called *pecorino romano*); *provolone* (rich, firm, aged cow cheese), *ricotta* (soft, airy cheese made by "recooking" leftover whey), and, of course, mozzarella. The best mozzarella is *mozzarella di bufala*, made from the milk of water buffaloes; other variations include *burrata* (a creamy mozzarella) and *scamorza* (similar to mozzarella, but often smoked).

Picnic Tips

Picnicking saves lots of euros and is a great way to sample regional special-ties. A typical picnic for two might be fresh rolls, 100 grams (*un etto*, EH-toh, plural *etti*, EH-tee—about a quarter pound) of cheese, and 100 grams of meat (sometimes ordered by the slice—*fetta*—or piece—*pezzi*; for two people, I might get *cinque pezzi*—five pieces—of prosciutto). Add two tomatoes, three carrots, two apples, yogurt, and a liter box of juice. Total cost: about €10.

In the process of assembling your meal, you get to deal with the Romans in the market scene. For a colorful experience, gather your ingredients in the morning at one of Rome's open-air produce markets (see the Shopping in Rome chapter); you'll probably need to hit several market stalls to put together a complete meal (note that many stalls close in the early afternoon).

While it's fun to visit small specialty shops, an *alimentari* is your one-stop corner grocery store (most will slice and stuff your sandwich for you if you buy the ingredients there). The rare *supermercato* (look for the Conad, Despar, and Co-op chains) gives you more efficiency with less color for less cost. At busier supermarkets, you'll need to take a number for deli service. You'll find handy late-night supermarkets near the Pantheon (Via Giustiniani), Spanish Steps (Via Vittoria), Trevi Fountain (Via del Bufalo), and Campo de' Fiori (Via di Monte della Farina). And *rosticcerie* sell cheap food to go—you'll find options such as lasagna, rotisserie chicken, and sides like roasted potatoes and spinach.

Juice lovers can get a liter of O.J. for the price of a Coke or cof-

EATING

fee. Look for *100% succo* (juice) or *senza zucchero* (without sugar) on the label—or be surprised by something diluted and sugary sweet. Hang on to the half-liter mineral-water bottles (sold everywhere for about €1). Buy juice in cheap liter boxes, then drink some and store the extra in your water bottle. (I refill my water bottle with tap water—*acqua del rubinetto*.)

Picnics can be an adventure in high cuisine. Be daring. Try the fresh mozzarella, *presto* pesto, shriveled olives, and any regional specialties the locals are excited about. If ordering *antipasti* (such as grilled or marinated veggies) at a deli counter, you can ask for *una porzione* in a plastic take-away container *(contenitore)*. Use gestures to show exactly how much you want. The word *basta* (BAH-stah; enough) works as a question or as a statement.

Shopkeepers are happy to sell small quantities of produce, but it's customary to let the merchant choose for you. Say *"per oggi"* (pehr OH-jee; for today) and he or she will grab you something ready to eat. To avoid being overcharged, know the cost per kilo and study the weighing procedure as if you're doing the arithmetic.

Rome discourages people from picnicking or drinking at historic monuments (such as on the Spanish Steps) in the old center. Technically violators can be fined, though it rarely happens. You'll be fine if you eat *with* a view rather than *on* the view.

GELATO

Gelato is an edible art form—and it's one souvenir that can't break and won't clutter your luggage. While American ice cream is made with cream and has a high butterfat content, Italian gelato is made with milk. It's also churned more slowly, making it denser. Connoisseurs believe that because gelato has less air and less fat (which coats the mouth and blocks the taste buds), it's more flavorful than American-style ice cream.

Stop by a *gelateria* and survey your options. A key to gelato appreciation is sampling liberally and choosing flavors that go well together. Ask, as Italians do, for *"Un assaggio, per favore?"* (oon ah-SAH-joh pehr fah-VOH-ray; A taste, please?) and *"Quali gusti stanno bene insieme?"* (KWAH-lee GOO-stee STAH-noh BEH-nay een-see-EH-may; What flavors go well together?).

Most *gelaterie* clearly display prices and sizes. But in the textbook *gelateria* scam, the tourist orders two or three flavors—and the clerk selects a fancy, expensive chocolate-coated waffle cone, piles it high with huge scoops, and cheerfully charges the tourist

€10. To avoid rip-offs, point to the price or say what you want, "*Una coppetta da tre euro*" (OO-nah koh-PEH-tah dah tray eh-oo-roh; a €3 cup).

Not all *gelaterie* are created equal. The best ones display signs reading *artiginale, nostra produzione,* or *produzione propia,* indicating that the gelato is made on the premises. Seasonal flavors are also a good sign. Gelato stored in covered metal tins (rather than white plastic) is more likely to be homemade. Gelato aficionados avoid colors that don't appear in nature; for fewer chemicals and real flavor, go for mellow hues. In recent years gourmet gelato shops have popped up all over Italy, selling more expensive, exotic flavors. A chain called Grom is comparable to Ben & Jerry's in the US.

As far as flavors, the sky's the limit. Most *gelaterie* label each tub with the flavor (in Italian and, often, in English) and, sometimes, a little picture to help identify it. Aside from the typical *crema* (vanilla), *cioccolato* (chocolate), and *fragola* (strawberry), here are a few flavors worth trying: After Eight (chocolate and mint), *bacio* (chocolate hazelnut, named for Italy's popular "kiss" candies), *croccantino* ("crunchy," with toasted peanut bits), *cassata* (with dried fruits), *fior di latte* (sweet milk), *macedonia* (mixed fruits), *riso* (with actual bits of rice mixed in), *malaga* (similar to rum raisin), *tartufo* (super chocolate), *zabaione* (named for the egg yolk and Marsala wine dessert), *zuppa inglese* (sponge cake, custard, chocolate, and cream), and the popular *stracciatella* (vanilla with chocolate chips). Flavors named Snickers, Lion, and Bounty resemble their namesake candy bars.

Gelato variations or alternatives include *sorbetto* (sorbet—made with fruit, but no milk or eggs); *granita* or *grattachecca* (a cup of slushy ice with flavored syrup); and *cremolata* (a gelato-*granita* float).

BEVERAGES

Italian bars serve great drinks—hot, cold, sweet, caffeinated, or alcoholic. Chilled bottled water, still *(naturale)* or carbonated *(frizzante),* is sold cheap in stores. Coffee and wine—two Italian specialties—are covered in greater depth later.

Juice: *Spremuta* means freshly squeezed, as far as *succo* (fruit juice) is concerned (order *una spremuta*—don't confuse it with *spumante,* sparkling wine). It's usually orange juice *(arancia),* and from February through April it's almost always made from blood oranges *(arance rosse).*

Beer: While Italy is traditionally considered wine country, in recent years there's been a huge and passionate growth in the production of craft beer *(birra artigianale).* Even in small towns, you'll see microbreweries slinging their own brews. Beer on tap is *alla spina.* Get it *piccola* (33 cl, 11 oz), *media* (50 cl, about a pint), or *grande* (a liter). Italians drink mainly lager beers. You'll also find local brews (Peroni and Moretti), as well as imports such as Heineken. A *lattina* (lah-TEE-nah) is a can and a *bottiglia* (boh-TEEL-yah) is a bottle.

Cocktails and Spirits: Italians appreciate both *aperitivi* (palate-stimulating cocktails) and *digestivi* (after-dinner drinks designed to aid digestion). Popular *aperitivo* options include Campari (dark-colored bitters with herbs and orange peel), Americano (vermouth with bitters, brandy, and lemon peel), Cynar (bitters flavored with artichoke), and Punt e Mes (sweet red vermouth and red wine). Widely used vermouth brands include Cinzano and Martini. *Digestivo* choices are usually either a strong herbal bitters or something sweet. Many restaurants have their own secret recipe for a bittersweet herbal brew called *amaro;* popular commercial brands are Fernet Branca and Montenegro. If your tastes run sweeter, try *amaretto* (almond-flavored liqueur), Frangelico (hazelnut liqueur), *limoncello* (lemon liqueur), *nocino* (dark, sweet walnut liqueur), and *sambuca* (syrupy, anise-flavored liqueur; *con moscha* adds "flies"—three coffee beans). *Grappa* is a brandy distilled from grape skins and stems; *stravecchio* is an aged, mellower variation.

Coffee and Other Hot Drinks

The espresso-based style of coffee so popular in the US was born in Italy. If you ask for *"un caffè,"* you'll get a shot of espresso in a little cup—the closest thing to American-style drip coffee is a *caffè americano.* Most Italian coffee drinks begin with espresso, to which is added varying amounts of hot water and/or steamed or foamed milk. Milky drinks, like cappuccino or *caffè latte,* are served to locals before noon and to tourists any time of day (to an Italian, cappuccino is a morning drink; they believe having milk after a big meal impairs digestion). If they add any milk after lunch, it's just a splash, in a *macchiato* (mah-kee-AH-toh). Italians like their coffee only warm—to get it very hot, request *"Molto caldo, per favore"* (MOHL-toh KAHL-doh pehr fah-VOH-ray). Any coffee drink is available decaffeinated—ask for it *decaffeinato* (deh-kah-feh-ee-NAH-toh).

Experiment with a few of the options:
- **Cappuccino:** Espresso with foamed milk on top
- ***Caffè latte:*** Espresso mixed with hot milk, no foam, in a tall glass (ordering just a "latte" gets you only milk)
- ***Caffè macchiato:*** Espresso "marked" with just a splash of milk, in a small cup
- ***Latte macchiato:*** Layers of hot milk and foam, "marked" by an espresso shot, in a tall glass
- ***Caffè corto/lungo:*** Concentrated espresso diluted with a tiny bit of hot water, in a small cup

EATING

- *Caffè americano:* Espresso diluted with even more hot water, in a larger cup
- *Caffè corretto:* Espresso "corrected" with a shot of liqueur (normally *grappa, amaro,* or *sambuca*)
- *Marocchino:* "Moroccan" coffee with espresso, foamed milk, and cocoa powder; the similar *mocaccino* has chocolate instead of cocoa
- *Caffè freddo:* Sweet and iced espresso
- *Cappuccino freddo:* Iced cappuccino
- *Caffè hag:* Instant decaf

Notice that there's a big difference between *caffè macchiato* and *latte macchiato.* If you order simply a *"macchiato,"* you'll probably get the coffee version...and have to get your milk fix elsewhere.

More Hot Drinks: *Cioccolato* is hot chocolate. *Tè* is hot tea. *Tè freddo* (iced tea) is usually from a can—sweetened and flavored with lemon or peach.

Wine

The ancient Greeks who colonized Italy more than 2,000 years ago called it Oenotria—land of the grape. Centuries later, Galileo wrote, "Wine is light held together by water." Wine *(vino)* is certainly a part of the Italian culinary trinity—grape, olive, and wheat. (I'd add gelato.) Ideal conditions for grapes (warm climate, well-draining soil, and an abundance of hillsides) make the Italian peninsula a paradise for grape growers, winemakers, and wine drinkers. Italy makes and consumes more wine per capita than any other country.

To order a glass *(bicchiere;* bee-kee-EH-ree) of red *(rosso)* or white *(bianco)* wine, say, *"Un bicchiere di vino rosso/bianco." Corposo* means full-bodied. House wine *(vino della casa)* comes in a carafe; choose from a quarter-liter pitcher (8.5 oz, *un quarto*), half-liter pitcher (17 oz, *un mezzo*), or one-liter pitcher (34 oz, *un litro*).

Wine Labels and Lingo: Even if you're clueless about wine, the information on an Italian wine label can help you choose something decent. Terms you may see on the bottle include *classico* (from a defined, select area), *annata* (year of harvest), *vendemmia* (harvest), and *imbottigliato dal produttore all'origine* (bottled by producers). To figure out what you like—and what suits your pocketbook—visit an *enoteca* (wine bar) and sample wines side-by-side.

Describing Wine in Italian

As you can see from many of the words listed below, adding a vowel to the English word often gets you close to the Italian one. Have some fun, gesture like a local, and you'll have no problems speaking the language of the *enoteca. Salute!*

dry	*secco*	SEH-koh
sweet	*dolce*	DOHL-chay
earthy	*terroso*	teh-ROH-zoh
tannic	*tannico*	TAH-nee-koh
young	*giovane*	JOH-vah-nay
mature	*mature*	mah-TOO-roh
sparkling	*spumante, frizzante*	spoo-MAHN-tay, freed-ZAHN-tay
fruity	*fruttato*	froo-TAH-toh
full-bodied	*corposo, pieno*	kor-POH-zoh, pee-EH-noh
elegant	*elegante*	eh-leh-GAHN-tay

In general, Italy designates its wines by one of four official categories:

Vino da Tavola (VDT) is table wine, the lowest grade, made from grapes grown anywhere in Italy. It's inexpensive, but Italy's wines are so good that, for many people, a basic *vino da tavola* is just fine with a meal. Many restaurants, even modest ones, take pride in their house wine *(vino della casa),* bottling their own or working with wineries.

Denominazione di Origine Controllata (DOC) meets national standards for high-quality wine. Made from grapes grown in a defined area, it's usually quite affordable and can be surprisingly good. Hundreds of wines have earned the DOC designation. In Tuscany, for example, many such wines come from the Chianti region, located between Florence and Siena.

Denominazione di Origine Controllata e Guarantita (DOCG), the highest grade, meets national standards for the highest-quality wine (made with grapes from a defined area whose quality is "guaranteed"). These wines can be identified by the pink or green label on the neck...and the scary price tag on the shelf. Only a limited number of wines in Italy can be called DOCG. They're generally a good bet if you want a quality wine, but you don't know anything else about the winemaker. (*Riserva* indicates a DOC or DOCG wine matured for a longer, more specific time.)

Indicazione Geographica Tipica (IGT) is a broad group of wines that range from basic to some of Italy's best. These wines don't follow the strict "recipe" required for DOC or DOCG status, but give local vintners creative license. This category includes the Super Tuscans—wines made from a mix of international grapes (such as cabernet sauvignon) grown in Tuscany and aged in small oak barrels for only two years. The result is a lively full-bodied wine that dances all over your head...and is worth the steep price for aficionados.

Roman Cuisine

In ancient times, the dinner party was the center of Roman social life. It was a luxurious affair, set in the *triclinium* (formal dining room). Guest lists were small (3-9 people), and the select few reclined on couches during the exotic multi-course meal. Today the couches are gone, and the fare may not include jellyfish, boiled tree fungi, or flamingo, but the *cucina Romana* influence remains. It's fair to say that while French cuisine makes an art of the preparation, Italian (and Roman) cuisine is simpler and all about the ingredients.

Roman meals are still lengthy social occasions. Simple, fresh, seasonal ingredients dominate the dishes. The *cucina* is robust, strongly flavored, and unpretentious—much like the people who've created it over the centuries. It is said that Roman cooking didn't come out of emperors' or popes' kitchens, but from the *cucina povera*—the home cooking of the common people. This may explain the Romans' fondness for meats known as the *quinto quarto* ("fifth quarter"), such as tripe, tail, brain, and pigs' feet, as well as their interest in natural preservatives like chili peppers and garlic.

Rome belongs to the warm, southern region of Lazio, which produces a rich variety of flavorful vegetables and fruit that are the envy of American supermarkets. Rome's proximity to the Mediterranean also allows for a great variety of seafood (especially on Fridays), which can be pricey if you're dining out.

Specialties you may find on a menu include the following:

Antipasto

Antipasto misto: A plate of marinated or grilled vegetables (eggplant, artichokes, peppers, mushrooms), cured meats, cheeses, or seafood (anchovies, octopus).

Bruschetta: Toasted bread brushed with olive oil and garlic, topped with chopped tomatoes, mushrooms, or whatever else sounds good.

Fritti: Little fried snacks that have been either battered or breaded—often olives stuffed with meat, potato croquettes, and mozzarella cheese. Other classic *fritti* are *suppli* (oval-shaped rice balls with tomato sauce and mozzarella) and *fiori di zucca* (squash blossoms filled with mozzarella and anchovies).

Prosciutto e melone: Thin slices of ham wrapped around pieces of cantaloupe.

Salumi: Cured meat, usually pork, such as salami, prosciutto, and *mortadella*.

Primo Piatto

Spaghetti alla carbonara: Any type of pasta with a sauce made from beaten eggs, *pancetta* or *guaniciale* (cured pork cheek), cheese (*pecorino romano* or *parmigiano reggiano*), and black pepper.

Bucatini all'amatriciana: Thin pasta tubes with a sauce of tomatoes, onion, pancetta, and pecorino cheese on top.

Gnocchi alla romana: Small flattened dumplings made from semolina (not potatoes) and baked with butter and cheese.

Penne all'arrabbiata: Tube pasta topped with a spicy tomato sauce of chili peppers *(pepperoncini)* and garlic.

Rigatoni con la pajata: Medium-size wide pasta tubes topped with a stew of milk-fed calf intestines.

Stracciatella alla romana: Meat broth with whipped eggs, topped with parmesan cheese.

Spaghetti alle vongole veraci: Small clams in the shell sautéed with white wine and herbs, served over pasta.

Secondo Piatto

Saltimbocca alla romana: "Jump-in-the-mouth"—thinly sliced veal layered with prosciutto and sage, then lightly fried.

Abbacchio alla scottadito: Baby lamb chops grilled and eaten as finger food.

Trippa alla romana: Tripe braised with onions, carrots, and mint.

Coda alla vaccinara: Oxtail braised with garlic, wine, tomato, and celery.

Involtini di vitello al sugo: Veal cutlets rolled with prosciutto, celery, and cheese in a tomato sauce.

Anguillette in umido: Stewed baby eels from nearby Lake Bracciano.

Filetti di baccalà: Salt cod fried in a batter (like "fish and chips" minus the chips).

Contorno

Sometimes the second course is not served with a vegetable, and you may want to order a side dish *(contorno)* separately. If you get a salad, note that olive oil and wine vinegar are the only dressings.

Carciofi alla romana: Artichokes simmered with garlic and mint.

Carciofi alla giudia: Artichokes flattened and fried.

The *Aperitivo* Tradition

Milan and northern Italian cities have long enjoyed the *aperitivo* tradition: Bars serve up an enticing buffet of small dishes, and anyone buying a drink (at an inflated price) gets to eat "for free." Now, competition for customers in the early evening hours has driven bars in Rome to embrace the same practice. All over town, bars—from humble to chic and trendy—are offering a light meal with a cocktail during happy hour. Drinks generally cost €8-10, and the food's out from 18:00 to 21:00. Some places limit you to one plate; others allow refills. Either way, if you want a quick, light dinner with a drink, it's a great deal. You'll notice happy crowds all over town.

Fave al guanciale: Fava beans simmered with cured pork cheek and onion.

Misticanza: Mixed green salad of arugula *(rucola)* and curly endive *(puntarelle)* with anchovies.

Dolci

Dessert can be a seasonal fruit, such as *fragole* (strawberries) or *pesche* (peaches), or even cheese, such as *pecorino romano* (made from ewe's milk) or *caciotta romana* (made from a combination of ewe's and cow's milk).

Crostata di ricotta: A cheesecake-like dessert with ricotta, sweet Marsala wine, cinnamon, and bits of chocolate.

Bignè: Cream puff-like pastries filled with *zabaione* (egg yolks, sugar, and Marsala wine).

Tartufo: Rich dark-chocolate gelato ball with a cherry inside. **Con panna** gets you whipped cream on top.

Gelato: Rather than order dessert in a restaurant, I like to stroll with a cup or cone of gelato picked up at one of Rome's popular *gelaterie* (for more, see "Gelato," earlier).

Grattachecca: Shaved ice flavored with syrups—perfect for when it's hot outside. Try the combo-flavors such as *limoncocco*—lemon and coconut syrups with fresh chunks of coconut.

Top Local Wines

Although Lazio is not the most notable wine region in Italy, it produces several pleasant white wines and a few reds.

Frascati: An inexpensive dry white made from trebbiano and malvasia grapes. This is probably the best-known wine of the region.

EATING

Castelli Romani: Also made from trebbiano grapes, from the hills just south of Rome. This wine is similar to **Marino, Colli Albani,** and **Velletri,** which are all light and fairly dry.

Torre Ercolana: Known as Lazio's best-quality red. This dense, balanced, medium-bodied wine is made from the regional cesanese grape, as well as cabernet and merlot. Produced in small quantities, it must be aged for at least five years.

Restaurants

I've listed a number of restaurants I enjoy. While many are in quaint and therefore pricey and touristy areas (Trastevere and the Pantheon neighborhood, including Piazza Navona and Campo de' Fiori), others are tucked away just off the tourist crush.

I'm impressed by how small the price difference can be between a mediocre Roman restaurant and a fine one. You can pay about 20 percent more for double the quality. If I had $100 for three meals in Rome, I'd spend $50 for one and $25 each for the other two, rather than $33 on all three. For splurge meals, I'd consider Gabriello, Fortunato, and Taverna Trilussa (in that order).

Rome's fabled nightspots (most notably Piazza Navona, near the Pantheon, and Campo de' Fiori) are lined with the outdoor tables of touristy restaurants with enticing menus and formal-vested waiters. The atmosphere is super-romantic: I, too, like the idea of dining under floodlit monuments, amid a constantly flowing parade of people. But you'll likely be surrounded by tourists, and noisy English-speakers can kill the ambience of the spot...leaving you with just a forgettable and overpriced meal. Restaurants in these areas are notorious for surprise charges, forgettable food, microwaved ravioli, and bad service.

I enjoy the view by savoring just a drink or dessert on a famous square, but I dine with locals on nearby low-rent streets, where the proprietor needs to serve a good-value meal and nurture a local following to stay in business. If you're set on eating—or just drinking and snacking—on a famous piazza, you don't need a guidebook listing to choose a spot; enjoy the ritual of slowly circling the square, observing both the food and the people eating it, and sit where the view and menu appeal to you. (And pizza is probably your best value and least risky bet.)

IN TRASTEVERE

Colorful Trastevere is now pretty touristy. Still, Romans join the tourists to eat on the rustic side of the Tiber River. Start at the central square, Piazza di Santa Maria. This is where the tourists dine, while others wander the back streets in search of mom-and-

Resources for Foodies

For those looking to take their Roman culinary endeavors seriously, there's no shortage of in-depth advice. Books and blogs on Roman cuisine abound, and several local companies run food- and wine-themed tours. Here is a sampling:

- **Parlafood.com,** Katie Parla's website, has all the latest on the Roman food scene. She also offers private food-oriented tours and tastings.
- **Rome for Foodies,** Parla's app, transfers her highly selective, top-notch recommendations into an easy-to-use, searchable format (and once it's on your device, it doesn't require an Internet connection).
- **Eat Rome,** an excellent app by food writer Elizabeth Minchilli, takes a more all-encompassing approach, listing a wider range of good eateries and food-oriented shops throughout Rome (works without Internet connection). Her website also features recipes and eating info for other Italian cities (www.elizabethminchilliinrome.com).
- **Eating Italy Food Tours** leads fun and insightful walks almost daily through Rome's colorful Testaccio and Trastevere neighborhoods, interspersing history, tradition, and local food culture while giving you a great glimpse into daily life in less-seen parts of the city (€65-85, 4 hours, several morning and evening departures Mon-Sat, www.eatingitalyfoodtours.com). They also offer cooking classes with a real Italian grandma and pizza-making classes for kids. Rick Steves readers get a 10 percent discount (use promo code: ricksteves).
- **Vino Roma** is a small wine "school" run by several sommeliers who offer evening tasting classes designed to help you understand and enjoy Italian wine. They also offer several neighborhood walks (www.vinoroma.com). *Buon appetito, e salute!*

EATING

pop places with barely a menu. My recommendations are within a few minutes' walk of each other (between Piazza di Santa Maria in Trastevere and Ponte Sisto; see map on page 361).

Taverna Trilussa is your best bet for dining well in Trastevere. Brothers Massimo and Maurizio offer quality at high prices, but without pretense. With a proud 100-year-old tradition, this place has the right mix of style and informality. The service is fun-loving (they're happy to let you split plates into smaller portions to enjoy a family-style meal), yet professional. The menu celebrates local classics and seasonal specials, and comes with a big wine selection. The spacious dining hall is strewn with eclectic Roman souvenirs. For those who'd rather eat outdoors, Trilussa has an actual terrace rather than just tables jumbled together on the sidewalk (€15 pastas, €20-28 *secondi*, Mon-Sat from 19:30 for dinner, closed Sun, reservations very smart, Via del Politeama 23, tel. 06-581-8918, www.tavernatrilussa.it).

La Gensola is one of the best places in town to splurge on seafood (though they also have Roman classics on the menu). The interior, which feels like a rustic yet sophisticated living room, is pleasantly homey. Warmly and unpretentiously run by Irene and Claudio, this place is justifiably popular—reserve ahead for dinner (€14-20 seafood pastas, €15-25 *secondi*, daily 12:00-15:00 & 19:30-24:00, Piazza della Gensola 15, tel. 06-581-6312, www.osterialagensola.it).

Trattoria da Lucia lets you enjoy simple, traditional food at a good price. It's your basic old-school, Trastevere dining experience, and has been family-run since World War II. You'll meet four generations of the family, including Giuliano and Renato, their uncle Ennio, and Ennio's mom—pictured on the menu in the 1950s. The family specialty is *spaghetti alla Gricia*, with *pancetta* (€9-10 pastas, €11-14 *secondi*, Tue-Sun 12:30-15:30 & 19:30-24:00, closed Mon and several weeks in Aug, cash only, evocative outdoor or comfy indoor seating—but avoid back room, just off Via del Mattonato at Vicolo del Mattonato 2, tel. 06-580-3601).

Trattoria da Olindo takes homey to extremes. You really feel like you dropped in on a family that cooks for the neighborhood to supplement their income (€8 pastas, €10 *secondi*, Mon-Sat dinner served 19:30-22:30, closed Sun—also closed Mon off-season, cash only, indoor and funky outdoor seating, on the corner of Vicolo della Scala and Via del Mattonato at #8, tel. 06-581-8835).

Osteria Ponte Sisto, small and Mediterranean, specializes in traditional Roman cuisine, but has frequent Neapolitan specials as well. Just outside the tourist zone, it caters mostly to Romans and offers beautiful desserts and a fine value. Reservations for dinner are smart (€8-12 pastas, €12-18 *secondi*, March-Oct Thu-Tue 12:30-23:30, closes between lunch and dinner off-season, closed Wed, Via Ponte Sisto 80, tel. 06-588-3411, www.osteriapontesisto.com, Oliviero). If you're coming from the city center, cross Ponte Sisto (pedestrian bridge), and continue across the little square (Piazza Trilussa). It's on the right.

Pizzeria "Ai Marmi" is a bright and noisy festival of pizza, where the oven and pizza-assembly line are surrounded by marble-slab tables (hence the nickname "the Morgue"). It's a classic Roman scene, whether you enjoy the chaos inside or sit at a sidewalk table, with famously good €8 Roman-style pizza (thin and crispy) and very tight seating. Expect a long line between 20:00 and 22:00 (Thu-Tue 18:30-24:00, closed Wed, cash only, tram #8 from Piazza Venezia to first stop over bridge, just beyond Piazza Sonnino at Viale di Trastevere 53, tel. 06-580-0919).

Pizzeria Dar Poeta, tucked in a back alley and a hit with local students, cranks out less traditional, thick-crust, wood-fired pizza—some of the best I've had in Rome. It's run by three friends—Marco, Paolo, and another Marco—who welcome you into the informal restaurant beneath exposed brick arches. If you're in a spicy mood, order *lingua di fuoco* (tongue of fire). If you're extra hungry, pay an extra euro for *pizza alto* (even thicker crust). Choose between their classic, cramped interior and lively tables outside on the cobblestones. Their chocolate dessert calzone is a favorite (€5-10 pizza and salads, daily 12:00-24:00, Vicolo del Bologna 45, tel. 06-588-0516).

Cantina Paradiso Wine and Cocktail Bar, a block over Viale di Trastevere from the touristy action, has a funky romantic charm. During happy hour (18:00-21:00), the €8 drinks come with a well-made little buffet that can turn into a cheap, light dinner (€8 pastas, daily 18:00-24:00, Via San Francesco a Ripa 73, tel. 06-589-9799, Weronika).

Gelato: **Gelateria alla Checco er Carettiere,** run by and next door to the famous restaurant of the same name, is many locals' favorite spot for gelato in Trastevere (Via Benedetta 7). **Fatamorgana** offers innovative flavors of organic gelato (Via Roma Libera 11).

IN THE JEWISH GHETTO

The Jewish Ghetto sits just across the river from Trastevere (see map on page 197).

Sora Margherita, hiding on a cluttered square, has been a rustic neighborhood favorite since 1927. Amid a picturesque commotion, families chow down on old-time Roman and Jewish dishes. It's technically not a real restaurant (it avoids red tape by officially registering itself an *associazione culturale*)—you can even sign a card to join the "cultural association" (don't worry; membership has no obligations except that you enjoy your meal). The menu's crude term for the fettuccini gives you some idea of the mood of this place: *nazzica culo* ("shaky ass"—what happens while it's made). Reservations are almost always necessary (€11-12 pastas, €13-15 *secondi;* Sept-May daily 12:30-15:00, also dinner Mon and Wed-Sat 20:00-23:30—no dinner Tue or Sun; June-mid-Aug Mon-Fri 12:30-15:00 & 20:00-23:30, closed Sat-Sun; closed second half of Aug; just south of Via del Portico d'Ottavia at Piazza delle Cinque Scole 30—look for the red curtain, tel. 06-687-4216).

A Fast Lunch in the Ghetto: The ghetto's main drag, Via del Portico d'Ottavia, is an ideal place for a quick lunch. Several kosher delis and other food stands line the broad street—particularly at the far (west) end. Walk the full length of the street before choosing. In addition to kosher hot dogs, you'll find falafel and *carciofi alla giudia*—"Jewish-style" artichokes that are deep-fried. Near the end of this drag—just after the gourmet cheese shop—is **Fonzie,** a good "kosher burger house" (Santa Maria del Pianto 13/14).

IN THE PANTHEON NEIGHBORHOOD

For the restaurants in this central area, I've listed them based on which landmark they're closest to: Campo de' Fiori, Piazza Navona, the Trevi Fountain, or the Pantheon itself.

On and near Campo de' Fiori

By day, Campo de' Fiori hosts one of the few markets in downtown Rome, selling fruit and veggies (and an increasing number of tourist knickknacks; Mon-Sat closes around 13:30, closed Sun). Combined with a sandwich and a sweet from the **Forno** (bakery) in the west corner of the square (behind the fountain), you can assemble a nice picnic.

By night, while it is touristy, Campo de' Fiori offers a sublimely romantic setting. And, since it's so close to the heart of the Roman people, it remains popular with locals, even though its restaurants offer greater atmosphere than food value. The square is lined with popular and interesting bars, pizzerias, and small restaurants—all great for people-watching over a glass of wine. Later at night it's taken over by a younger clubbing crowd.

Ristorante ar Galletto is nearby, on the more elegant and peaceful Piazza Farnese. Angelo entertains the upscale Roman clientele enjoying the magical outdoor seating or trendy interior. Regrettably, service can be brusque, you need to double-check the bill, and single diners aren't treated very well. Still, if you're in no hurry and ready to savor my favorite al fresco setting in Rome (while humoring the waiters), this can be a good bet (€10-13 pastas, €19-22 *secondi,* daily 12:15-15:00 & 19:30-23:00, reservations smart for outdoor seating, Piazza Farnese 104, tel. 06-686-1714, www.ristoranteargallettoroma.com).

Vineria Salumeria Roscioli is an elegant *enoteca* that's a hit with local foodies, so reservations are a must. While it's just a salami toss away from touristy Campo de' Fiori, you'll dine with classy locals, and feel like you're sitting in a romantic (and expensive) deli after hours. They have a good selection of fine cheeses, meats, local dishes, and top-end wines by the glass (€12-16 pastas, €18-25 *secondi,* Mon-Sat 12:30-16:00 & 19:00-24:00, closed Sun, 3 blocks east of Campo de' Fiori at Via dei Giubbonari 21, tel. 06-687-5287, www.salumeriaroscioli.com). Their nearby **Forno Roscioli** is a favorite for a quick slice of pizza or pastry to go (Mon-Sat 6:00-20:00, closed Sun, Via dei Chiavari 34, tel. 06-686-4045).

Trattoria der Pallaro, an eccentric and well-worn eatery that has no menu, has a slogan: "Here, you'll eat what we want to feed you." Paola Fazi—with a towel wrapped around her head turban-style—and her gang dish up a five-course meal of homey Roman food. You have three menu choices: €25 for the works; €20 for appetizers, *secondi,* and dessert; or €16 for appetizers and pasta. Any option is filling, includes wine and coffee, and is capped with a thimble of mandarin juice. While the service can be odd and the food is rustic, the experience is fun (daily 12:00-16:00 & 19:00-24:00, reserve if dining after 20:00, cash only, indoor/outdoor seating on quiet square, a block south of Corso Vittorio Emanuele, down Largo del Chiavari to Largo del Pallaro 15, tel. 06-6880-1488).

Filetti di Baccalà is a cheap and basic Roman classic, where nostalgic regulars cram in at wooden tables and savor their old-school favorites—fried cod finger-food fillets (€5 each) and raw, slightly bitter *puntarelle* greens (slathered with anchovy sauce, available in spring and winter). Study what others are eating, and order from your grease-stained server by pointing at what you want. Sit in the fluorescently lit interior or try to grab a seat out on the little square, a quiet haven a block east of Campo de' Fiori (Mon-Sat 17:00-23:00, closed Sun, cash only, Largo dei Librari 88, tel. 06-686-4018). If you're not into greasy spoons, avoid this place.

Open Baladin is a busy, modern pub featuring a few dozen Italian craft beers on tap and menu of burgers, salads, and freshly cooked potato chips. As this is a relatively new concept in Italy, prices are somewhat high—and the food can be hit or miss—but it's a nice break if you're parched and ready for pub grub (€7-12 sandwiches and plates, daily 12:00-24:00, Via degli Specchi 5, tel. 06-683-8989).

Near Piazza Navona

Piazza Navona is the quintessential setting for dining on a Roman square. Whether you eat here or not, you'll want to stroll the piazza before or after your evening meal. This is where many people fall in love with Rome. The tangled streets just to the west are lined with popular eateries of many stripes.

Ciccia Bomba (a.k.a. Bomba Ciccia) is a traditional and touristy trattoria where Gianpaolo, Gianluca, and their crew serve up tasty homemade pasta, wood-fired pizza, and other Roman specialties (consider their daily-special sheet)—all at a good price. While downstairs you can sit at a table on ancient pavement next to your own column, I like the ambience on the main level. Reserve at least a week in advance for their 45-minute pizza-making "lesson" that costs €25 (€7-10 pastas and pizzas, €10-18 *secondi*, daily 7:00-24:00, Via del Governo Vecchio 76, a block west of Piazza Navona, just north of Piazza Pasquino, tel. 06-6880-2108).

Cul de Sac, a corridor-wide trattoria lined with wine bottles, is packed with an enthusiastic crowd enjoying a wide-ranging menu,

Restaurants in the Pantheon Neighborhood

Tiber River

Piazza Nicosia

Piazza Cardelli

21

PREFETTI

UFF

VIA DELLA SCROFA

CAMPANA

LUNGOTEVERE MARZIO

VIA DEI CORONARI

To Ponte Sant'Angelo

13

12

VOLPE

VIA DELLA PACE

ANCIENT STADIUM ENTRANCE

T

Piazza delle Coppelle

VIA D. COPPELLE

POZZO D. CORN.

SAN LUIGI

26

29

18

VIA GIUSTINIANI

23

Piazza Rotonda

9

Piazza Fico

10

CHIESA NUOVA

VIA DI PARIONE

SANT' AGNESE

PHARMACY

SALVATORE LIBRERIA FANUCCI (BOOKSTORE)

FOUR RIVERS FOUNTAIN

Piazza Navona

CRESCENZI

28

PANTHEON

11

VIA GOV. VECCHIO

BORA

7

8

Piazza Pasquino

CITY MUSEUM

Piazza della Chiesa Nuova

CORSO VITTORIO

VIA DEL PELLEGRINO

VIA DEI CAPPELLARI

VIA MONSERRATO

CANCELLERIA

VIA DEL BAULLARI

BOVARI

BRUNO STATUE

Campo de' Fiori

1

Piazza Farnese

PALAZZO FARNESE

VIA GIULIA

CAPO DE FERRO

14

SANT' ANDREA DELLA VALLE

EMANUELE II

30

4

Largo Pallaro

VIA GIUBBONARI

5

VIA CHIAVARI

3

VIA SPECCHI

2

6

To Trastevere

Piazza Cairoli

Piazza S. Eustachio

22

ARGENTINA

24

Largo Argentina

B

T

LARGO ARGENTINA RUINS

FLORIDA

Largo Arenula

Tiber River

GHETTO

EATING

1	Ristorante ar Galletto	9	Baguetteria del Fico
2	Vineria Salumeria Roscioli	10	Rist. Pizzeria "da Francesco"
3	Forno Roscioli	11	Pizzeria da Baffetto
4	Trattoria der Pallaro	12	Chiostro del Bramante
5	Filetti di Baccalà	13	No.Au
6	Open Baladin Pub	14	L'Insalata Ricca
7	Ciccia Bomba	15	To Hostaria Romana
8	Cul de Sac & L'Insalata Ricca	16	L'Antica Birreria Peroni

EATING

⑰ Rist. Pizzeria Sacro e Profano	㉔ Frullati Pascucci
⑱ Ristorante da Fortunato	㉕ Super Market Carrefour Express
⑲ Enoteca Corsi	㉖ Supermercato Despar (2)
⑳ Trattoria dal Cav. Gino	㉗ Gelateria Giolitti
㉑ Ristorante la Campana	㉘ Crèmeria Monteforte
㉒ Miscellanea	㉙ San Crispino Gelateria
㉓ Antica Salumeria	㉚ Gelateria Vice

from pasta to homemade pâté. They have fun tasting-plates of *salumi* and cheese, more than a thousand different wines, and fine outdoor seating. It's small, and they don't take reservations—come early to avoid a wait (€9-10 pastas, €8-11 *secondi*, daily 12:00-24:00, a block off Piazza Navona on Piazza Pasquino, tel. 06-6880-1094).

Baguetteria del Fico is a very cramped, trendy microbrew pub (with 150 different craft beers lining the walls) and a baguette-sandwich counter. With a sophisticated wine-bar ambience and a dedication to quality ingredients, this place is handy for a quick, light, and tasty lunch just west of Piazza Navona. Think of it as a notch above the interchangeable *paninoteche* scattered around the neighborhood (€5-7 sandwiches, well-described English menu, daily 10:00-late, Via della Fossa 12, tel. 06-9604-5541).

Ristorante Pizzeria "da Francesco," bustling and authentic, has a 50-year-old tradition, a hardworking young waitstaff, great indoor seating, and classic outdoor seating on a cluttered little square that makes you want to break out a sketchpad. Their blackboard explains the daily specials (€9-11 pizzas and pastas, €15-20 *secondi,* daily 12:00-15:30 & 19:00-24:00, 3 blocks west of Piazza Navona at Piazza del Fico 29, tel. 06-686-4009).

Pizzeria da Baffetto, buried deep in the old quarter behind Piazza Navona, is a Roman favorite, offering tasty pizza and surly service. Its tables are tightly arranged amid the mishmash of photos and sketches littering the walls. The pizza-assembly kitchen keeps things energetic, and the pizza oven keeps the main room warm (you can opt for a table on the cobbled street). Come early or late, or be prepared to wait (€6-12 pizzas, daily from 18:30, cash only; order "P," "M," or "D"—small, medium, or large; west of Piazza Navona on the corner of Via Sora at Via del Governo Vecchio 114, tel. 06-686-1617).

Chiostro del Bramante offers drinks and light lunches in a unique setting—overlooking the tranquil open-air *chiostro* (cloister) of the San Bramante church, just west of Piazza Navona. Find the entrance just to the left of the church entrance, climb upstairs, order at the counter, and choose a stony bench—so close to all the tourists, yet so far away. Or sit in the mod lounge, with a window view of the church interior and its original Raphael fresco. Though food prices are high and portions small, the setting is unique and relaxing (€8-12 plates, Mon-Fri 10:00-20:00, Sat-Sun 10:00-21:00, lunch served until 15:00—only drinks after that, Arco della Pace 5, tel. 06-6880-9035).

No.Au (as in "Know-How") is a hip bar with light food in the heart of old Rome. The lively, cluttered interior breeds conviviality, and patrons enjoy organic craft beers on tap, along with wine and other drinks. Red tape prevents staff from operating a real kitchen ("no fire"), so they prepare creative and pricey dishes *dalla cucina di MacGyver* ("from MacGyver's kitchen"). Come here not for a filling, traditional meal, but for a chance to sample a local beer, make some Roman friends, and nibble jury-rigged cuisine in a fresh locale tucked among all the touristy *trattorias* (€6-12 small plates, Tue-Fri 18:00-late, Sat-Sun 12:00-late, closed Mon, Piazza di Montevecchio 16A, tel. 06-4565-2770).

L'Insalata Ricca is a popular local chain that specializes in healthy, filling €6-9 salads and less-healthy pastas and main courses (daily 12:00-24:00). They have a handy branch on Piazza Pasquino (next to the recommended Cul de Sac, tel. 06-6830-7881) and a more spacious and enjoyable location a few blocks away, on a bigger square next to busy Corso Vittorio Emanuele (near Campo de' Fiori at Largo dei Chiavari 85, tel. 06-6880-3656).

Near the Trevi Fountain

The streets surrounding the Trevi Fountain are littered with mediocre restaurants catering exclusively to tourists—try one of these instead.

Hostaria Romana is a busy bistro with a hustling and fun-loving gang of waiters. The upstairs is a tight, tidy, glassed-in terrace, while the cellar has noisy walls graffitied by happy eaters. As its menu specializes in traditional Roman dishes, it's a good place to try *saltimbocca alla romana* or *bucatini all'amatriciana* (see "Roman Cuisine," earlier in this chapter). Their €12 *antipasti della casa* plate, with a variety of vegetables and cheeses, makes a hearty start to your meal (€11 pastas, €15 *secondi*, Mon-Sat 12:30-15:00 & 19:15-23:00, closed Sun and Aug, reservations smart, a block up the lane just past the entrance to the big tunnel near the Trevi Fountain, corner of Via Rasella and Via del Boccaccio—see map on page 392, tel. 06-474-5284, www.hostariaromana.it).

L'Antica Birreria Peroni is Rome's answer to a German beer hall. Serving hearty mugs of the local Peroni beer and lots of just plain fun beer-hall food and Italian classics, the place is a hit with Romans for a cheap night out (€7 pastas, €4-12 *secondi*, Mon-Sat 12:00-24:00, closed Sun, midway between Trevi Fountain and Capitoline Hill, a block off Via del Corso at Via di San Marcello 19, tel. 06-679-5310).

Ristorante Pizzeria Sacro e Profano fills an old church with spicy southern Italian (Calabrian) cuisine and satisfied tourists. Run with enthusiasm, this is just far enough away from the Trevi mobs. Their pizza oven is wood-fired, and their hearty €15 *golosità calabresi* appetizer plate is a filling montage of Calabrian taste treats (€7-9 pizzas, €10-12 pastas, €15-18 *secondi*, Tue-Sun 12:00-15:00 & 18:00-23:00, closed Mon, a block off Via del Tritone and Via della Panetteria at Via dei Maroniti 29, tel. 06-679-1836).

Close to the Pantheon

Eating on the square facing the Pantheon is a temptation, and I'd consider it just to relax and enjoy the Roman scene. But if you walk a block or two away, you'll get less view and better value. Here are some suggestions.

Ristorante da Fortunato is an Italian classic, with fresh flowers on the tables and white-coated, black-tie career waiters politely serving good meat and fish to politicians, foreign dignitaries, and tourists with good taste. Don't leave without perusing the photos of their famous visitors—everyone from former Iraqi Foreign Minister Tariq Aziz to Bill Clinton seems to have eaten here. All are pictured with the boss, Fortunato, who started this restaurant in 1975 and was a master of simple edible elegance. (His son Jason now runs the show.) The outdoor seating is fine for watching the river of Roman street life flow by, but the real atmosphere is inside. For a dressy night out, this is a reliable and surprisingly reasonable choice—but be sure to reserve ahead (plan to spend €45 per person, daily 12:30-15:30 & 19:30-23:30, a block in front of the Pantheon at Via del Pantheon 55, tel. 06-679-2788, www.ristorantefortunato.it).

Enoteca Corsi is a wine shop that grew into a thriving lunch-only restaurant. The Paiella family serves straightforward, traditional cuisine to an appreciative crowd of office workers. Check the board for daily specials (gnocchi on Thursday, fish on Friday, and so on). Friendly Giuliana, Claudia, Sara, and Manuela welcome eaters to step into their wine shop and pick out a bottle. For the cheap takeaway price, plus €4-8 (depending on the wine), they'll uncork it at your table. With €9 pastas, €13 main dishes, and fine wine at a third of the price you'd pay in normal restaurants, this can be a good value. And guests with this book finish their meal with a free glass of homemade *limoncello* (Mon-Sat 12:00-15:30, closed Sun, no reservations possible, a block toward the Pantheon from the Gesù Church at Via del Gesù 87, tel. 06-679-0821).

Trattoria dal Cavalier Gino, tucked away on a tiny street behind the Parliament, has been a favorite since 1963. Photos on the wall recall the days when it was the haunt of big-time politicians. Grandpa Gino shuffles around grating the parmesan cheese while his English-speaking children Carla and Fabrizio serve up traditional Roman favorites and make sure things run smoothly. Reserve ahead, even for lunch, as you'll be packed in with savvy locals (€8-12 pastas, €11-15 *secondi*, cash only, Mon-Sat 13:00-14:45 & 20:00-22:30, closed Sun, behind Piazza del Parlamento and just off Via di Campo Marzio at Vicolo Rosini 4, tel. 06-687-3434).

Ristorante la Campana is a classic—an authentic slice of Rome with a local following. Claiming a history dating to 1518, it boasts a clientele of mostly well-dressed Romans. This place feels unchanged over the years...probably because it doesn't have to. It serves typical Roman dishes and daily specials, plus it has a good self-service *antipasti* buffet (€10-12 pastas, €11-18 *secondi,* Tue-Sun 12:30-15:00 & 19:30-23:00, closed Mon, inside seating only, reserve for dinner, just off Via della Scrofa and Piazza Nicosia at Vicolo della Campana 18, tel. 06-687-5273, www.ristorantelacampana.com).

Miscellanea is run by much-loved Mikki, who's on a mission to keep foreign students well-fed. Welcoming travelers as well as locals, he offers hearty €4 sandwiches and a long list of €7 salads, along with pasta and other staples. This is a great value for a cheap and hearty dinner featuring typical rustic Roman cuisine. Mikki (and his son Romeo) often tosses in a fun little extra, including—if you have this book on the table—a free glass of Mikki's "sexy wine" (from *fragoline*—strawberry-flavored grapes). While basic, it's convenient (€7-8 pastas, €10-15 *secondi,* daily 11:00-24:00, indoor/outdoor seating, facing the rear of the Pantheon at Via della Palombella 34, tel. 06-6813-5318).

Picnicking Close to the Pantheon

It's fun to munch a picnic with a view of the Pantheon. (Remember to be discreet.) Here are some options.

Antica Salumeria is an old-time *alimentari* (grocery store) on the Pantheon square. While they hustle most tourists into premade €5 sandwiches, you can make your own picnic. Find your way to the back to buy artichokes, mixed olives, bread, cheese, and meat (daily 8:00-21:00, mobile 334-340-9014).

Frullati Pascucci, a hole-in-the-wall convenient for takeaway, has been making refreshing fruit *frullati* and frappés (like smoothies and shakes) for more than 75 years. Add a sandwich or fruit salad to make a healthy light meal (Mon-Sat 6:00-23:00, closed Sun, north of Largo Argentina at Via di Torre Argentina 20, tel. 06-686-4816).

Supermarkets near the Pantheon: Food is relatively cheap at Italian supermarkets. **Super Market Carrefour Express** is a convenient place for groceries a block from the Gesù Church (Mon-Sat 8:00-20:30, Sun 9:00-19:30, 50 yards off Via del Plebiscito at Via del Gesù 59). Nearby, just across the busy road, is a **Despar** (Mon-Sat 8:00-21:00, Sun 9:00-21:00, Corso Vittorio Emanuele II 42). Another **Despar** is half a block from the Pantheon toward Piazza Navona (daily 8:30-22:00, Via Giustiniani 18).

Gelato Close to the Pantheon

Several fine *gelaterie* are within a five-minute walk of the Pantheon.

Giolitti is Rome's most famous and venerable ice-cream joint (although few would say it has the best gelato). Takeaway prices are reasonable, and it has elegant Old World seating (just off Piazza Col-

EATING

onna and Piazza Montecitorio at Via Uffici del Vicario 40, tel. 06-699-1243).

Crèmeria Monteforte is known for its traditional gelato and super-creamy sorbets *(cremolati).* The fruit flavors are especially refreshing—think gourmet slushies (closed Mon and Dec-Jan, faces the west side of the Pantheon at Via della Rotonda 22, tel. 06-686-7720).

San Crispino serves small portions of particularly tasty gourmet gelato. Because of their commitment to natural ingredients, the colors are muted; gelato purists consider bright colors a sign of unnatural chemicals, used to attract children (a block in front of the Pantheon on Piazza della Maddalena, tel. 06-6889-1310).

Gelateria Vice is a relative newcomer but might be the best of all. Using top-quality ingredients in innovative ways, the flavors change with the seasons (around the northwest corner of Largo Argentina at Corso Vittorio Emanuele II 96, tel. 06-8117-3023).

IN NORTH ROME: NEAR THE SPANISH STEPS AND ARA PACIS

To locate these restaurants, see the "Dolce Vita Stroll" map on page 434.

Ristorante il Gabriello is inviting and small—modern under medieval arches—and provides a peaceful and local-feeling respite from all the top-end fashion shops in the area. Claudio serves with charisma, while his brother Gabriello cooks creative Roman cuisine using fresh, organic products from his wife's farm. Italians normally just trust their waiter and say, "Bring it on." Tourists are understandably more cautious, but you can be trusting here. Simply close your eyes and point to anything on the menu. Or invest €45 (not including wine) in "Claudio's Extravaganza." Specify whether you'd prefer fish, meat, or both. (Romans think raw shellfish is the ultimate in fine dining. If you differ, make

that clear.) When finished, I stand up, hold my belly, and say, *"Ahhh, la vita è bella."* While you're likely to dine surrounded by my readers here (especially if eating before 21:00), the atmosphere is fun and convivial (€11-18 pastas, €14-20 *secondi,* dinner only, Mon-Sat 19:00-23:00, closed Sun, reservations smart, air-con, dress respectfully—no shorts, 3 blocks from Spanish Steps at Via Vittoria 51, tel. 06-6994-0810, www.ilgabriello.it).

Antica Enoteca, an upbeat, atmospheric 200-plus-year-old *enoteca,* has around 60 Italian-only wines by the glass (€6-10, listed on a big blackboard) and a full menu of eating options, from €6-12 salads to a €14 *antipasti* plate of veggies, *salumi,* and cheese. Very crowded on summer evenings, it comes with wonderful ambience both inside and out; its outside tables are set on a quiet cobbled street (€10-12 pastas, €12-18 *secondi*, daily 11:00-24:00, best to reserve for outdoor seating, Via della Croce 76b, tel. 06-679-0896, www.anticaenoteca.com).

Palatium Enoteca Regionale is a crisp, modern restaurant funded by the region of Lazio (home to Rome) to show off its finest agricultural fare. Surrounded by locals, you'll enjoy generous, shareable plates of cheeses and *salumi* (€12-15), a limited menu of pasta and meat (€11-13 pastas, €12-16 *secondi*), and a huge selection of local wine (Mon-Sat 12:30-15:30 & 19:30-22:30, closed Sun and one week in Aug, 5 blocks in front of the Spanish Steps at Via Frattina 94, tel. 06-6920-2132).

Gusto Wine Bar is a convenient choice for a glass of wine or a light meal. Popular with trendy locals, it gives a glimpse of today's Roman scene, though some of the decor has a 1930s ambience. While much of the food at their other nearby venues is pricey (and mediocre), the weekday €11 lunch buffet (12:30-15:30) is a good value. During happy hour (18:00-21:00) you get a light, self-service meal with your drink for €10-12 (daily 11:00-late, kitchen closes at 24:00; just behind the Ara Pacis at Via della Frezza 23, tel. 06-322-6273). Their *osteria,* next door, has a similar atmosphere (€12 pastas, €15-22 *secondi*).

Caffè Ciampini is delightfully set on one of my favorite traffic-free squares in the center of town. The food is quite pricey and won't win any awards—and you pay for the location—so I'd only stop here to sit outside and people-watch. This is a good place to make the scene with trendy and professional Romans. The cocktails come with a little tray of finger sandwiches and nuts; for some it's a light and inexpensive meal (€10-16 pizzas, salads, pastas, sandwiches; Mon-Fri 7:30-20:30, Sat 7:30-24:00, closed Sun, Piazza San Lorenzo in Lucina 29, tel. 06-687-6606, www.ciampini.com).

Eating Light on the Via della Croce: Two blocks north of the Spanish Steps, the Via della Croce offers a few simple options for a light meal or snack. As you walk down this street from Via del Corso, you'll reach the following places (listed in order). Several takeout shops for pizza and sandwiches cluster near the start of this street, including **Grano, Frutta e Farina** (#49A). The **Despar** minisupermarket at #48 fits the bill for budget picnickers, or you can try a sandwich-on-request from the intriguing **Foccaci** shop (at #43, end of first block), with a long, enticing counter of meats and cheeses. Farther down is the more formal, sit-down **Antica Enoteca** (#76b, described earlier). Tucked away in a quiet, vine-covered courtyard, **Trattoria Otello alla Concordia** (#81) is a decent choice for traditional food served in a slightly faded old-time atmosphere (€11-13 pastas, €13-16 *secondi*, Mon-Sat 12:30-15:00 & 19:30-23:00, Sun 12:30-15:00 only, tel. 06-679-1178). Then comes another classic *alimentari* (grocery), **Salsamenteria F.lli Fabi** at #28. **Venchi** (#25-26) has chocolate in every form—good for their rich gelato and edible souvenirs. **Pompi** (#82), the self-proclaimed "kingdom of tiramisu," features several flavors (classic, strawberry, pistachio) in €4 portions. And finally, **Pastificio** (#8) is a pasta shop that serves up two types of fresh pasta each day at 13:00. There are only a few stools so you might be eating in the street (off a plastic plate), but for €4 you also get water and a "drop of wine for the most deserving"—be nice and say "*per favore*" (daily 13:00-16:00 or when the pasta is gone).

Gelato: For organic gelato with some unusual flavors, head a few blocks north of Via della Croce to **Fatamorgana** (Via Laurina 10—see map on page 354).

IN ANCIENT ROME: NEAR THE COLOSSEUM AND FORUM

Within a block of the Colosseum and Forum, you'll find convenient eateries catering to weary sightseers, offering neither memorable food nor good value. To get your money's worth, stick with one of my recommendations or head to the Monti neighborhood. Note that some of these are ideal for lunch, while others are dinner-only—worth considering after a long day of sightseeing, or as an excuse to stroll the floodlit ruins after dark. For locations, see the map on page 354.

In Monti

Tucked behind Trajan's Forum, in the tight and cobbled lanes between Via Nazionale and Via Cavour, is the characteristic Monti neighborhood. It's just a few steps farther from the ancient sites than the battery of forgettable touristy restaurants, but that extra effort opens up a world of inexpensive and characteristic dining experiences. From the Forum, head up Via Cavour and then left on Via dei Serpenti; the action centers on Piazza della Madonna dei Monti and unfolds along Via dei Serpenti, Via del Boschetto, and Via Leonina/Urbana. For more on this area, see page 58.

L'Asino d'Oro ("The Golden Donkey") is a top choice for foodies in this neighborhood (so reserve ahead). Chef Lucio Sforza, who previously ran restaurants in Orvieto, serves Umbrian cuisine with a creative twist—and mingles savory and sweet flavors to create a memorable meal. The service is crisp, the pasta is homemade, and the simple, modern space is filled with savvy diners (€11-13 pastas, €14-17 main dishes, €13 fixed-price lunch is a great value, Tue-Sat 12:30-15:00 & 19:30-23:00, closed Sun-Mon, some delightful outdoor seating, Via del Boschetto 73, tel. 06-4891-3832).

La Taverna dei Monti is frequented by locals and in-the-know tourists who want great, old-fashioned Roman cooking and the Italian standards. Perhaps the dressiest of my Monti recommendations, it has good seating inside and out. Baked lamb is a favorite (dinner only, €8 pastas, €12-18 main dishes, just off of Via Nazionale at Via del Boschetto 41, tel. 06-481-7724).

La Carbonara has been serving locals since 1906 with food that makes up for the lack of smiles. Under walls scribbled with notes from happy diners, you'll enjoy tasty dishes and great prices (€7-9 pastas, €9-15 *secondi*, Mon-Sat 12:30-14:30 & 19:00-23:00, closed Sun, reserve for dinner, Via Panisperna 214, tel. 06-482-5176, www.lacarbonara.it).

Enoteca Cavour 313 is a wine bar with a mission: to offer good wine and food with an old-fashioned commitment to value and friendly service. Its slightly unconventional menu, ranging from couscous and salads to high-quality *affettati* (cold cuts) and cheese, makes a nice alternative to the usual pasta/pizza choices. You'll be served with a mellow ambience under lofts of wine bottles (€9-14 plates, daily 12:30-14:45 & 18:30-24:00, 100 yards off Via dei Fori Imperiali at Via Cavour 313, tel. 06-678-5496).

Taverna Romana is small and simple—with an open kitchen and hams and garlic hanging from the ceiling. Their *cacio e pepe* (cheese and pepper pasta) is the hands-down favorite at this family-run eatery. It's popular so arrive early or call to reserve (€9-10 pastas, €9-14 *secondi*, Mon-Sat 12:30-14:45 & 19:00-23:00, closed Sun, Via Madonna dei Monti 79, tel. 06-474-5325).

La Vacca M'Briaca ("The Drunk Cow") has a casual and fun vibe with its open kitchen, indoor and outdoor tables, and good mix of hearty Roman and Italian fare. The *bucatini all'Amatriciana* and *saltimbocca* are favorites. Avoid the back room if possible (daily, Via Urbana 29, tel. 06-4890-7118).

La Cicala e La Formica has its own little nook on Via Leonina. The terrace dining is good for people-watching, while the homey interior is livelier. The cuisine is more Italian than Roman, and the €10 two-course lunch special—offered weekdays only—is a good value (€10 pastas, €10 *secondi*, daily 12:00-15:30 & 19:00-23:00, Via Leonina 17, tel. 06-481-7490).

Taverna dei Fori Imperiali is a favorite with Monti locals and understandably popular with tourists. You'll enjoy typical Roman cuisine served in a snug interior that bustles with energy (€9 *antipasti*, €9-12 pastas, €12-16 *secondi*, Wed-Mon 12:30-15:00 & 19:30-23:00, closed Tue, Via della Madonna dei Monti 9, reserve for dinner, tel. 06-679-8643, www.latavernadeiforiimperiali.com).

Trattoria da Valentino is a classic time-warp hiding behind its historic (and therefore protected) Birra Peroni signs. Serving simple plates, pastas, and salads—but no *secondi*—to a smart local clientele, it's a hit with government ministry workers (closed Sun, Via del Boschetto 37, tel. 06-488-0643).

Closer to Piazza Venezia and Trajan's Column: Enoteca Nel Cuore di Roma, while not strictly in Monti, is nearby and even more convenient to Piazza Venezia and Capitoline Hill. Overlooking Trajan's Column, this modern little place has a cool, peaceful, and well-lit dining room and a few outside tables. It celebrates Roman cuisine with fresh local produce; the prices are quite high (€12-14 pastas, €15-22 *secondi*), but the daily €13 specials including wine are a good value (Tue-Sat 11:00-16:00 & 18:00-23:30, Sun-Mon 11:00-17:00, Foro Traiano 82, tel. 06-6994-0273).

Fast, Simple Meals and Takeaway in Monti

The streets of Monti are crowded with fun and creative places offering inexpensive quality snacks and light meals to eat on tiny informal tables or to take away. Here are my favorites:

Ai Tre Scalini feels like the youthful meeting point of the entire community. The cobbles out in front of this bar are jammed with hipsters enjoying drinks al fresco (it's tough to get a seat unless you arrive early). While the focus here is on drinking and socializing more than dining, they do have a chalkboard menu of €5-10 plates (daily 12:30-24:00, Via Panisperna 251, tel. 06-4890-7495).

Pizzeria Chicco di Grano is a big, sloppy pizzeria with a large outdoor terrace serving tasty, wood-fired pizzas. It has plenty of red-and-white-checkered tables and is ideal for families (€2-4 bruschetta with a wide array of toppings, €8-11 pizzas, daily 12:00-24:00, Via degli Zingari 6 at the corner of Via del Boschetto, tel. 06-4782-5033).

Fafiuché Vineria is an intimate yet vibrant family-run wine bar with a fun-loving vibe and no pretense. They serve a broad selection of wines and beers inside or at tables on the cobblestones outside. Each evening from 18:30 to 21:00 Andrea and Mario offer a popular *aperitivo* special: €8 covers a glass of wine and one trip to the buffet—making it a cheap, light meal. Or, for more money, you can order serious regional specialties from Apulia and Piedmont (Mon-Sat 18:00 until late, closed Sun, Via della Madonna dei Monti 28, tel. 06-699-0968).

Zia Rosetta is a tiny eatery specializing in gourmet-like *rosette*, sandwiches on rose-shaped buns. At €3 for the tiny ones or €6 for the standard size, they're perfect for a light bite—either to take away or eat in. Their fun, healthy, and creative menu includes salads and fresh-squeezed, vitamin-bomb fruit and veggie juices (Tue-Sun 11:00-22:00, closed Mon, Via Urbana 54, tel. 06-3310-2516).

Pizzeria la Boccaccia serves eye-catching pizza-to-go by the gram. Point at what you like and mime how big of a rectangle you want. I recommend sampling several small slices, or go for a stuffed one—*pizza farcita*. They also have vegan and vegetarian options (Via Leonina 73, mobile 340-455-1968).

At **dall'Antò**, it's all about traditional Italian bread hot out of the wood-fired oven. While you'll find inexpensive standards such as bruschetta and focaccia, the owners (Antonio and Antonio) encourage you to branch out with chickpea flatbread, chestnut crêpe, or crispy Sardinian flatbread. They serve €4 wine in paper cups (Tue-Thu 12:00-20:00, Fri-Sat 12:00-15:00 & 19:00-23:00, Sun 12:00-15:00, closed Mon, Via della Madonna dei Monti 16, tel. 06-678-0712).

Gaudeo ("I'm Happy" in Latin) prides itself on assembling sandwiches from seasonal ingredients, either to go or eaten in their small, modern interior (€3-4 small sandwiches, €5-7 big sandwiches, €6-9 salads, €10 *tagliere* cheese-and-meat sampler platter, daily 10:00-21:00, Via del Boschetto 112, tel. 06-9818-3689).

Antico Forno ai Serpenti ("Old Bakery on Serpenti Street") feels anything but old. This hip bakery—where you can watch the bakers through the *laboratorio* window—serves good bread, pastries, and other foods to go (daily 8:00-20:00, Via dei Serpenti 122, tel. 06-4542-7920).

Gelato: **Fatamorgana,** hiding on a welcoming little square a long block off of Monti's main drag, features some of the most creative gelato flavor combinations I've seen in Italy—along with more conventional ones. Portions are small but good quality—everything is organic and gluten-free (Piazza degli Zingari 5, tel. 06-4890-6955).

Il Gelatone is another neighborhood favorite, with a crowd-pleasing array of flavors including soy options (a block from main square at Via dei Serpenti 28, tel. 06-482-0187).

Behind the Colosseum

A pleasant little residential zone just up the street from the Colosseum (opposite direction from the Forum) features a real neighborhood feel and a variety of restaurants that capably serve tired and hungry sightseers.

Trattoria Luzzi is a well-worn, no-frills eatery serving simple food in a high-energy environment (as they've done since 1945). With good prices, big portions, and proximity to the Colosseum, it draws a crowd—reserve or expect a short wait at lunch and after 19:30 (€5-7 pizzas and pastas, €7-12 *secondi,* Thu-Tue 12:00-24:00, closed Wed, Via San Giovanni in Laterano 88, tel. 06-709-6332). If Luzzi is jam-packed, as it often is, **Ristorante Pizzeria Naumachia** (next door at Via Celimontana 7, tel. 06-700-2764) is a bit more upscale and serves good-quality pizza and pastas at decent prices (€6-8 pizzas, €8-10 pastas, €14-24 *secondi*).

EATING

Li Rioni is open only for dinner, when its over-the-rooftops interior and terrace out front are jammed with Romans watching the busy chef plunge dough into its wood-fired oven, then pull out crispy-crust Roman-style pizzas (€7-8 pizzas, Thu-Tue 19:30-24:00, closed Wed, Via S.S. Quattro 24, tel. 06-7045-0605).

La Taverna dei Quaranta, a casual neighborhood favorite, has a humble, red-checkered tablecloth ambience. In the evening, they fire up the wood oven for pizza, to go along with a basic menu of Roman classics and seasonal specialties. As the place caters mostly to locals, service can be a bit slow and straightforward—but it's a good bet in this touristy area (€9-10 pastas, €10-14 *secondi,* daily 12:00-15:30 & 19:00-23:30, Via Claudia 24, tel. 06-700-0550).

Between the Colosseum and
St. Peter-in-Chains Church

You'll find these places across the street and up the hill from the Colosseum. They're more convenient than high cuisine, though they work fine in a pinch.

Hostaria da Nerone is a traditional place serving hearty classics, including tasty homemade pasta dishes. Their *antipasti* plate—with a variety of veggies, fish, and meat—is a good value for a quick lunch. While the *antipasti* menu indicates specifics, you can have a plate of whatever's out—just direct the waiter to assemble the €10 *antipasti* plate of your lunchtime dreams (€11 pastas, €13-15 *secondi,* Mon-Sat 12:00-15:00 & 19:00-23:00, closed Sun, indoor/outdoor seating, Via delle Terme di Tito 96, tel. 06-481-7952, Teo and Eugenio).

Caffè dello Studente, next door to Hostaria da Nerone, is popular with engineering students attending the nearby University of Rome. The owners—Pina, Mauro, their perky daughter Simona, and their son-in-law Emiliano (the last two speak English)—give my readers a friendly welcome. They serve average, microwaved *bar gastronomia* fare—toasted sandwiches, salads, and mixed bruschetta. If it's not busy, show this book when you order at the bar and sit at a table without paying extra (€9 pastas, €10 fixed-price meal, Mon-Sat 7:30-21:00, Sun 8:30-19:00 in April-Oct, closed Sun in Nov-March, Via delle Terme di Tito, mobile 328-362-2186).

NEAR TERMINI STATION

These restaurants are near my recommended hotels on Via Firenze. Several are clustered on Via Flavia, others are nearby (Target, etc.), and a few, such as Caffè Torino, are good options for quick meals.

On (or near) Via Flavia

To easily check out a fun and varied selection of eateries within a block of each other, walk to Via Flavia (a block behind the Church of Santa Maria della Vittoria of *St. Teresa in Ecstasy* fame) and survey these choices—an old-time restaurant, a good pizzeria, a small romantic place, and a friendly wine bar.

Ristorante da Giovanni, well-worn and old-fashioned, makes no concessions to tourism or the modern world—just hardworking cooks and waiters serving standard dishes at great prices to a committed clientele. It's simply fun to eat in the middle of this high-energy, Roman time warp (€6-14 pastas and *secondi,* daily specials, Mon-Sat 12:00-15:00 & 19:00-22:00, closed Sun and Aug, corner of Via XX Settembre at Via Antonio Salandra 1, tel. 06-485-950).

Ristorante la Pentolaccia, pricier and more romantic than the nearby Da Giovanni, is a dressy, more upscale, but still tourist-friendly place with tight seating and traditional Roman cooking—consider their daily specials. This is a local hangout, and reservations are smart (€8-14 pastas, €10-18 *secondi,* daily 12:00-15:00 & 17:30-23:00, a block off Via XX Settembre at Via Flavia 38, tel. 06-483-477, www.lapentolaccia.eu). To start things off with a free bruschetta, leave this book on the table.

Pizzeria Annicinquanta, big and classic, serves the neighborhood's favorite pizzas in a calm ambience with outdoor seating (€6-8 Neapolitan-style pizzas, €9-18 pastas and *secondi,* daily 12:30-15:30 & 19:30-24:00 except no lunch on Sat, Via Flavia 3, tel. 06-4201-0460).

I Colori del Vino Enoteca is a modern wine bar that feels like a laboratory of wine appreciation. It has woody walls of bottles, a creative menu of *affettati* (cold cuts) and cheeses with different regional themes, and a great list of fine wines by the glass. Helpful, English-speaking Marco carries on a long family tradition of celebrating the fundamentals of good nutrition: fine wine, cheese, meat, and bread. Remember Shakespeare's sage warning about drinking: "It provokes the desire, but it takes away the performance" (also €10-18 hot plates including pastas, Mon-Fri 10:30-15:00 & 17:30-23:00, closed Sat-Sun—except open Sat evenings in April-June and Sept-Nov, corner of Via Flavia and Via Aureliana, tel. 06-474-1745).

More Eateries near the Station

Target Restaurant seems to be the favorite recommendation of every hotel receptionist and tour guide for this neighborhood. It has a sleek and dressy ambience, capable service, and food that's reliably good, but pricey (€9-14 salads, pastas, and pizzas; €17-22 *secondi,* free *aperitivo* with this book, daily 12:00-15:30 & 19:00-24:00 except no lunch on Sun, reserve to specify seating outside or inside—avoid getting seated in basement, Via Torino 33, tel. 06-474-0066, www.targetrestaurant.it).

Restaurants near Termini Station

To Spanish Steps

V.D. ARTISTI

VIA VENETO

V. BISO

CAPUCHIN CRYPT

SANTA MARIA VITTORIA

VIA SISTINA

V. FURIFICAZIONE

Barberini

VIA BARBERINI

MOSES FOUNTAIN

Piazza Barberini

SANTA SUSANNA

VIA DEL TRITONE

VIA D. QUATTRO FONTANE

PALAZZO BARBERINI

SAN BERNARDO

FELTRINELLI BOOKSTORE

V. AVIG.

V. BOCC.

V. RASELLA

FOUR FOUNTAINS

VIA FIRENZE

❹

❺

To Trevi & Pantheon

V. ARCIONE

V. TRAFORO

VIA DEPRETIS

#40 & 64 ⒷⒷ

❼

Quirinal Gardens

SAN CARLO

❻

PHARMACY

VIA NAZIONALE

VIA NAPOLI

PALAZZO DEL QUIRINALE

SANT' ANDREA

❽

To Trevi & Pantheon

VIA FERRARA

DESPAR GROCERY

VENEZIA

PALERMO

Piazza del Quirinale

PALAZZO DELLE ESPOSIZIONE

GENOVA

VIA

SCUDERIE DEL QUIRINALE

VIA MILANO

VIA XXIV MAGGIO

VIA NAZIONALE

To Piazza Venezia

❶ Ristorante da Giovanni

❷ Ristorante la Pentolaccia
Pizzeria Annicinquanta
& I Colori del Vino Enoteca

❸ Pizzeria Annicinquanta

❹ Target Restaurant

❺ Caffè Torino

❻ Snack Bar

❼ Forno Firenze &
Bufala e Pachino Pizza

❽ Flann O'Brien Irish Pub

❾ Hostaria Romana

Fast, Simple Meals near the Station

Caffè Torino is a workers' favorite for a quick, cheap lunch. They have good, fresh, hot dishes ready to go for a fine price. Head back past the bar to peruse their enticing display, point at what you want, then grab a seat and the young waitstaff will serve you (Mon-Fri 6:00-18:00, closed Sat-Sun, Via Torino 40, tel. 06-474-2767).

Snack Bar puts out a lunchtime display of inexpensive pastas, colorful sandwiches, fresh fruit, and salad. Their loyal customers appreciate the fruit salad with yogurt (€3-5 sandwiches and pasta dishes, daily 6:00-24:00, Via Firenze 33, tel. 06-9784-3866, Enrica).

EATING

Forno Firenze makes simple sandwiches and mini-pizzas, has a selection of well-priced wine, and stocks a few other goodies for a picnic to go (€2-4 sandwiches priced by weight, Mon-Fri 7:00-19:00, Sat 8:00-14:00, closed Sun, Via Firenze 51-52, tel. 06-488-5035, Giovanni).

Bufala e Pachino Pizza is a convenient place for pizza by the slice *(al taglio)* and priced by weight—just point and tell them how much you'd like. Their *supplì* (fried rice balls filled with mozzarella), at just €1 each, make for cheap, filling snacks (daily 8:00-23:00, Via Firenze 54).

Flann O'Brien Irish Pub is an entertaining place for a light meal of pasta...or something *other* than pasta, such as grilled meats and giant salads, served early and late, when other places are closed. They have Irish beer, live sporting events on TV, and perhaps the most Italian crowd of all. Walk way back before choosing a table. Live bands play about once per week (€11-16 pub grub, daily 7:00-24:00, Via Nazionale 17, at intersection with Via Napoli, tel. 06-488-0418).

NEAR VATICAN CITY

As in the Colosseum area, eateries near the Vatican cater to exhausted tourists. Avoid the restaurant pushers handing out fliers: They're usually hawking places with bad food and expensive menu tricks. Instead, tide yourself over with a slice of pizza or at any of these eateries (see map on page 362) and save your splurges for elsewhere.

Handy Lunch Places near Piazza Risorgimento

These are a stone's throw from the Vatican wall, located halfway between St. Peter's Basilica and the Vatican Museum. They're all fast and cheap, with a good *gelateria* next door.

Hostaria dei Bastioni, run by Antonio while Emilio cooks, has noisy streetside seating and a quiet interior (€8-10 pastas, €8-13 *secondi,* Mon-Sat 12:00-15:30 & 18:30-23:00, closed Sun, at corner of Vatican wall at Via Leone IV 29, tel. 06-3972-3034).

L'Insalata Ricca is another branch of the popular chain that serves hearty salads and pastas (€6-10 meals, daily 12:30-23:30, across from Vatican walls at Piazza Risorgimento 5, tel. 06-3973-0387).

Duecento Gradi is a good bet for fresh and creative €5-7 sandwiches. Munch your lunch on a stool or take it away (daily 11:00-24:00, Piazza Risorgimento 3, tel. 06-3975-4239).

Gelato: **Gelateria Old Bridge** scoops up hearty portions of fresh gelato for tourists and nuns alike—join the line (just off Piazza Risorgimento across from Vatican walls at Via Bastioni 3).

Other Options in the Vatican Area

The first three listings—the restaurant, the streets with pizza shops, and the covered market—are near the Vatican Museum. The Borgo Pio eateries are near St. Peter's Basilica.

Ristorante La Rustichella serves tasty wood-fired pizzas (€6-9) and the usual pastas (€7-10) in addition to their *antipasti* buffet (€8 for a single plate) in a no-frills, neighborhood setting. Do like the Romans do—take a moderate amount of *antipasti* and make one trip only (Tue-Sun 12:00-15:00 & 19:00-24:00, closed Mon, near Metro: Cipro, opposite church at end of Via Candia, Via

Angelo Emo 1, tel. 06-3972-0649). Consider the fun and fruity **Gelateria Millennium** next door.

Viale Giulio Cesare and *Via Candia:* These streets are lined with cheap *pizza rustica* shops, self-serve places, and basic eateries. **Forno Feliziani** (closed Sun, Via Candia 61, tel. 06-3973-7362) is a good bet for pizza by the slice and simple cafeteria-style dishes.

Covered Market: As you collect picnic supplies, turn your nose loose in the wonderful **Mercato Trionfale** covered market. Almost completely untouristy (with lots of vendors, but no real prepared-food stands), it's one of the best in the city, located three blocks north of the Vatican Museum (Mon-Sat roughly 7:00-14:00, Tue and Fri some stalls stay open until 19:00, closed Sun, corner of Via Tunisi and Via Andrea Doria). If the market is closed, try several nearby supermarkets; the most convenient is **Carrefour Express** (Mon-Sat 8:00-20:00, Sun 9:00-20:30, Via Sebastiano Veniero 16).

Along Borgo Pio: The pedestrians-only Borgo Pio—a block from Piazza San Pietro—has restaurants worth a look, such as **Tre Pupazzi** (Mon-Sat 12:00-15:00 & 19:00-23:00, closed Sun, at corner of Via Tre Pupazzi and Borgo Pio, tel. 06-686-8371). At **Vecchio Borgo,** across the street, you can get pasta, pizza slices, and veggies to go (Mon-Sat 9:00-21:00, closed Sun, Borgo Pio 27a, tel. 06-8117-3585).

IN TESTACCIO

Once a slaughterhouse district, working-class Testaccio is now going upscale. In recent years, particularly with the renovation of their bustling market hall, Testaccio has increasingly become a destination for local chefs and international foodies. While this zone is a bit more run-down, and feels slightly sketchy after dark, adventurous diners find it worth exploring.

Thanks to its history as the neighborhood of slaughterhouses, Testaccio (more so than elsewhere in Rome) is home to restaurants that are renowned for their ability to cook up the least palatable part of the animals...the *quinto quarto* ("fifth quarter"): tripe (stomach), lungs, brains, sweetbreads (organs), tail, and so on. While trendsetting foodies (who call this "nose-to-tail" eating) seek out these dishes—and you'll find them at most restaurants here—every place also has plenty of non-offal offerings.

For more information on this district—including a self-guided walk to the market and a map showing the locations of the restaurants listed here—see page 97.

Testaccio Market is the place to head at lunchtime (open Mon-Sat until 14:00—though some food stalls stay open a bit later, closed Sun). Head toward the left side of the market (closest to Via Beniamino Franklin) to search out a few favorites for a light lunch.

EATING

At **Mordi & Vai** (stall 15), Sergio makes tasty €3-4 sandwiches; locals love the *trippa* (tripe), but I prefer the *panino con allesso* (boiled beef with the bread dipped in broth) and *picchiapò* (stewed beef in a mildly spicy tomato sauce). As this is a popular place, you'll need to take a number. Nearby, **Dess'art** (stall 66) will satisfy your sweet tooth with their creative pastries. For olives, cheese, and cold cuts, try **Ferraro's** (stall 2-3, around the corner from Mordi & Vai). They're also a good bet for edible souvenirs—dried porcini mushrooms and sun-dried tomatoes, as well as other specialties, many from Calabria (think spicy).

Agustarello has been serving Roman specialties since 1957, but their restaurant feels up-to-date and without pretense—the emphasis is on the food. As this family-run place is quite small and very lively, reservations are smart (€10 pastas, €12-18 *secondi*, Mon-Sat 12:30-15:00 & 19:30-24:00, closed Sun, Via Giovanni Branca 98, tel. 06-574-6585 or mobile 345-066-5646).

Flavio al Velavevodetto, partially set inside Monte Testaccio (windows reveal the ancient stacked pottery shards), is a good place to try traditional Roman classics like *coda alla vaccinara* (oxtail) or less adventurous options (€8-10 pastas, €12-18 *secondi*, daily 12:30-15:00 & 19:30-23:00, reservations smart for dinner, Via di Monte Testaccio 97, tel. 06-574-4194, www.flavioalvelavevodetto.it).

Pizzeria Remo—the humble pizza joint with the huge mob of locals out front late into the evening—is a favorite for Roman-style (thin, crispy-crust) pizza and deep-fried appetizers. If people are jamming the entrance, muscle your way inside and put your name on the list; there's ample seating, and table turnover is brisk (€6-8 pizzas, Mon-Sat 19:00-24:00, closed Sun, Piazza Santa Maria Liberatrice 44, tel. 06-574-6270).

Volpetti Più is a fixture in this neighborhood of foodies for its great pizza and *tavola calda*. If you need a cheap, quick, and tasty lunch or early dinner, drop by, pick up a tray, and point to what looks (and is) good (€5-8 meals, Mon-Sat 10:30-15:30 & 17:30-21:30, closed Sun, just off Via Marmorata at Via Alessandro Volta 8, tel. 06-574-2352). Their deli (similar hours) at Via Marmorata 47 is a sensory extravaganza for anyone enthusiastic about gourmet Italian cheeses, meats, and olive oils.

Perilli is the neighborhood's classic, old-school eating house—rollicking with tight tables of local families since 1911 (€11-13 pastas, €11-14 daily specials, Thu-Tue 12:30-15:00 & 19:30-23:15, closed Wed, Via Marmorata 39, tel. 06-5710-2846).

L'Oasi della Birra ("Beer Oasis") is well-known among Roman beer lovers, as it stocks more than 500 Italian and international brews. The main floor is a bottle shop and classy grocery, while the nondescript cellar and the terrace out front serve as a popular bar for locals to hang out and dine on pub grub. This is not a place for a fine meal or special ambience, but rather, to enjoy a beer and the lively local scene (€8 bruschetta and salads, €9-12 daily specials; during happy hour from 17:30 to 20:30—except on Sun—€10 buys you a beer and access to their light dinner spread; open Mon-Sat 8:00-13:30 & 16:00-24:00, Sun 19:00-24:00 only, Piazza Testaccio 38/41, tel. 06-574-6122).

EATING

ROME WITH CHILDREN

Sorry, but Rome is not a great place for little kids. Parks are rare. Kid-friendly parks are rarer. Most of the museums are low-tech and lack hands-on fun.

But there is some good news. Rome's many squares are traffic-free, with plenty of space to run and pigeons to feed while Mom and Dad enjoy coffee at an outdoor table. Italians are openly fond of kids, so you'll probably get lots of friendly attention from locals. Rome's huge ancient sites (I'm thinking the Colosseum and Pantheon) instill awe in travelers of any age—especially if they can conceive of just how old they are. And you won't get many complaints about the cuisine: pizza and gelato. *Buona fortuna!*

Sights and Activities

ANCIENT SITES, CHURCHES, AND MUSEUMS

While some ancient sites, such as the **Colosseum,** are naturally captivating for kids, others, like the Roman Forum, may be a snooze. To keep them engaged, consider picking up a copy of *Rome: Past and Present,* a book with plastic overlays showing how the ruins used to look. It's available at stalls near the entrance of ancient sites (prices are soft, so negotiate).

For a fun overview of the city, the topless double-decker **110open Bus tour** offers a 1.5-hour swing past all of the major sights—and kids nine and under ride free (see page 32).

The spooky tunnels of the **catacombs** are goblin-pleasers (the Catacombs of Priscilla offer half-off entry for kids 15 and under; for catacombs, see pages 77 and 108). The macabre **Capuchin Crypt,** decorated with bones, fascinates children and adults alike (see page 71).

Family Travel Tips

- Ask at Rome's TIs about kid-friendly activities. TIs often have a helpful "kid's pack."
- Don't overdo it. Tackle only one or two key sights a day (Vatican Museum, or Colosseum and Forum), and mix in a healthy dose of fun activities, like exploring Rome's great public sights (Piazza Navona, Trevi Fountain, and Villa Borghese Gardens).
- Italy's national museums generally offer free admission to children under 18—always ask before buying tickets for your kids.
- Rome's hotels often give price breaks for kids. (Air-conditioning can be worth the splurge.)
- Eat dinner early (around 19:00), and you'll miss the romantic crowd. While kids may do best in self-serve cafeterias or even fast-food places, if you eat early you'll find that children are comfortable and welcome in better restaurants. Eating *al fresco* is great with kids. For ready-made picnics that can please adults and kids, try the *rosticcerie* (delis). *Pizza rustica* shops sell cheap take-out pizza; kids like *margherita* (tomato and cheese) and *diavola* (similar to pepperoni).
- Public WCs are hard to find: Try museums, bars, gelato shops, and fast-food restaurants.
- Follow this book's crowd-beating tips. Kids don't want to stand in a long line for a museum (which they might not even want to see). Consider getting a Roma Pass for yourself, as kids get to skip the line with parents who have the pass (see page 42 for details on the pass).
- Give your kids a business card from your hotel, along with your contact information, just in case you get separated.
- Any person under 39 inches tall travels free on Rome's public transit.
- If you're taking the train to another city, check for family discounts; see page 547 for information.

In Vatican City, the climb to the top of **St. Peter's** is great for its dizzy railing view into the church from halfway up the dome—plus the hike will tire out young tots (see page 227). The **Vatican Museum** comes with mummies, cool statues, and has an audioguide designed for families. Nearby, **Castel Sant'Angelo**—with Vatican views and weapon displays—appeals to young knights (see page 65).

The **Church of San Ignazio,** with its false dome, intrigues kids and adults (see page 136). Your children can get a whiff of Egypt by visiting Rome's funky little **pyramid** (free and always viewable, Metro: Piramide—see page 97). Check out the cat hospice in the adjacent park and climb on the chunk of old Roman wall across the street.

Bocca della Verità, the legendary "Mouth of Truth" at the Church of Santa Maria in Cosmedin, is fun for kids and parents with cameras (see page 39). Liars beware.

Several museums are particularly enjoyable for kids. The **Montemartini Museum,** in an old power plant, features ancient statuary, with art at kids' level and no crowds (see page 101). The **Planetarium** and **Astronomical Museum** at the Museum of Roman Civilization in E.U.R. also appeal to kids (see page 106).

Explora, a children's museum, is a hands-on wonderland for kids 12 and under. Descriptions are in Italian (with some English), but younger kids probably won't care (€5 for kids 1-2, €8 for kids 3-99, parent must accompany child; four 2-hour self-guided sessions/day: Tue-Sun at 10:00, 12:00, 15:00, and 17:00; closed Mon, confirm session times in advance by checking website—www.mdbr.it—or calling 06-361-3776, helpful English-speaking staff; 10-minute walk from Piazza del Popolo at Via Flaminia 82, Metro: Flaminio).

OUTDOOR FUN

The sprawling **Villa Borghese Gardens** are Rome's version of New York City's Central Park. The best kids' zones are near Porta Pinciana, where you'll find rental bikes, pony rides, and other amusements (Metro: Barberini, Spagna, or Flaminio). Summer weekends at the gardens, sure to be a hit with kids, include classic Roman puppet shows at Teatro dei Burattini. Rome's **zoo,** Bioparco, in the northeast section of the park, houses about 900 animals—including the endangered black lemur, pygmy hippopotamus, Gila monster, and painted hunting dog (free for kids "under 1 meter tall," €12 for kids over 1 meter and under age 12, €15 for adults, daily April-Oct 9:30-18:00, Nov-March 9:30-17:00, last entry one hour before closing, café and picnic areas, Piazzale del Giardino Zoologico 1, Metro: Spagna or Flaminio, then a 20-minute walk through the park, tel. 06-360-8211, www.bioparco.it).

Rome feels safe at night, and you can easily take your kids on the **walks** suggested in this book, such as the "Dolce Vita Stroll" on page 433. On the Heart of Rome Walk, children like slurping up chocolate gelato at the Tre Scalini *gelateria* on Piazza Navona and tossing coins in the Trevi Fountain. Consider letting your child act as tour guide for an hour by leading one of the walks.

Older children may want to **rent a bike** at the Appian Way (❂ see Ancient Appian Way Tour chapter); use the bike/pedestrian path to avoid the traffic.

BEACHES

Beyond the ruins of Ostia Antica, the sandy beaches of modern Ostia are easily accessible via a combination Metro/train ride. As elsewhere in Italy, most of the shoreline is occupied by private "clubs" that charge a fee to use their facilities. Clubs lay out rows of beach chairs and umbrellas (expect to pay around €10 for each chair and another €10 for an umbrella) and most have cafés, WCs, changing rooms, lockers, and lifeguards on duty. Some even have full-service restaurants and swimming pools (usually costs extra). Most are open roughly May through September—the rest of the year, the beaches are free to access and uncrowded.

Bring your own towel and picnic, and expect to be surrounded by a thoroughly local scene.

The journey to Ostia is covered by a normal Metro ticket (passes valid) and takes about an hour from central Rome. Take Metro line B to the Piramide stop, which is linked to the Roma Porta San Paolo train station. Follow signs to *Lido*—go up the escalator, turn left, and go down the steps into the Roma-Lido station. From here, it's easy since all trains depart in the direction of Lido, leaving every 15 minutes. Look for the information board that reads something like, *"Prossima partenza alle ore 13.25, bin 3,"* meaning, "Next departure at 13:25 from track 3." Hop on and ride for about 40 minutes (no need to validate your Metro ticket again).

From the Lido Centro stop, it's about a 15-minute walk through town (and past stores selling food and beach gear), to the Pontile di Ostia, the public pier, and surrounding clubs (not well marked; don't hesitate to ask). The subsequent stops, Stella Polare, Castel Fusano, and Cristoforo Colombo, leave you in more residential areas but closer to the beach and a variety of clubs.

Any club will work (look around for one that looks appealing). Families may prefer Belsito (www.belsitoostia.com) and its neighbor to the north, Il Capanno (www.ilcapanno.net), which are decent, unpretentious choices. They are a 15-minute walk south from the pier (or slightly closer to the Stella Polare stop—head straight for the water and turn right). Next to Il Capanno, there's a small, free public beach that's usually packed, especially on weekends. Other public beaches are few and far between.

WATER PARKS

Rome has a big water park called **Hydromania** (€19, cheaper for kids 12 and under and anyone arriving after 14:00; open daily June-

Aug 9:30-18:30, Sat-Sun until 19:00, closed Sept-May; Vicolo del Casale Lumbroso 200, exit 33 off ring freeway west of the city, tel. 06-6618-3183, www.hydromania.it).

Aquapiper, another water park, is near Tivoli (€10, daily June-Aug 9:00-19:30, closed Sept-May, Via Maremmana Inferiore, in Guidonia, 15-minute drive east of Rome, tel. 0774-326-538, www.aquapiper.it); occasionally a free shuttle bus leaves from the center of Rome (Piazza della Repubblica).

SHOPPING IN ROME

Rome is a wonderful city to shop in. Even if you're not aiming to buy anything, exploring popular shopping areas can provide a respite from the stressful, clogged tourist sights and an excuse to lose yourself on a charming street. Sometimes window-shopping, rather than museum-going, is the best way to connect with the contemporary life of a city. And that's certainly true in Rome.

Traditionally, shops are open from 9:00 to 13:00 and from 15:30 or 16:30 to 19:00 or 19:30. They're often closed on Sundays, summer Saturday afternoons, and winter Monday mornings. But in the city center, you'll find that many are now staying open through lunch (generally 10:00-19:00). Shop early if you intend to hit Rome's produce or flea markets (described at the end of this chapter)—with the exception of the weekend MercatoMonti market in the Monti neighborhood, they typically close by 13:30.

For information on VAT refunds and customs regulations, see page 528.

Shopping Neighborhoods

I've described four of Rome's most engaging and easy-to-reach shopping zones: in the heart of Rome near Piazza Navona and Campo de' Fiori; the Jewish Ghetto; the Monti district, convenient to the ancient sites; and Rome's most famous (and, arguably, least characteristic) shopping zone, the "shopping triangle" along Via del Corso and near the Spanish Steps. For each one, I've outlined a spine to help you find the highest concentration of interesting shops, highlighting a few that caught my eye (though turnover is rampant, so some of the shops I mention may be closed by the time you visit). Be sure to venture off this framework to make discoveries of your own.

A few other areas are worth exploring. **Via Nazionale** features a range of reasonably priced shops, especially for clothes and shoes. The back lanes of **Trastevere** have a similar feel to Monti, with offbeat boutiques. **Via Cola di Rienzo,** near the Vatican, is good for mid-range clothes. Cheapskates scrounge through the junky but dirt-cheap shops in the gritty area around **Piazza Vittorio Emanuele II,** just south of Termini Station.

HEART OF ROME

Although right in the tourist-clogged center, the streets near Piazza Navona and Campo de' Fiori are surprisingly less crowded—and the shops less tacky—than along the main thoroughfares connecting Rome's top squares (outlined in my ♥ Heart of Rome Walk). Heavy on antiques and home furnishings, this area may be better for window-shopping than buying, but I've noted some shops with take-home souvenirs as well. Everything mentioned here is within about a 15-minute walk of each other.

Near Piazza Navona

The tangle of lanes just west of Piazza Navona can be fun to explore. But the main shopping street here—and one of the most charming streets in all of Rome, with cobblestones, leafy planters, and little to no traffic—is the straight-shot **Via dei Coronari,** between Piazza Navona and the bend in the river. To find it, pop out the north end of Piazza Navona and turn left. This is the place to browse antiques and daydream about furnishing a Roman apartment. Stampe Antiche "Trincia" Restauro (#15) is a fascinating shop that specializes in painstaking restoration of works of art, with antique prints that will fit in your suitcase. This street also boasts several fine clothing and shoe stores, such as Superga (#18), the classic Italian athletic shoe brand (which also makes designer heels). Made (#25) is a "creative bakery" with bagel sandwiches and delicate cupcakes.

After Piazzetta di San Simeone, there are fewer antiques and more clothes—stylish yet accessible. For example, tucked in the little square on the left, Spazio IF (#44a) features eye-catching Sicilian style—mostly women's fashion, including handbags and scarves. Dimorae Design (#57) sells trendy Italian home furnishings. If you need a snack, Gelateria del Teatro (#65) is a good choice. At Pastori Antichi (#110), an army of military miniatures from around the world stands watch. Lisa Corti Home Textile Emporium (#197, part of a small Italian chain) fills its showroom with colorful fabrics, while Le Tele di Carlotta (#228) is a charming spot with hand-embroidered towels and handkerchiefs.

At the end of Via dei Coronari, you could angle right one block to Castel Sant'Angelo (described on page 65). Or, to make your

SHOPPING

walk a loop, hook left at the big square and Alimentari Coronari (gourmet sandwiches) onto **Via di Panico.** You'll pass a few more shops along here—including Kromatika Lab (#14), with striking design.

From here, turn right on Via degli Orisni; one block later, turn left onto **Via del Governo Vecchio,** another top shopping street. Passing the Penny Lane shop (#4, with youthful vintage wear), you'll be greeted by a street with fashion, home decor, textiles, and plenty of cute boutiques (casual wear and accessories—mostly women's, but some men's as well). The closer you get to Piazza Navona, the more crowded the street becomes, with souvenir stands and tourist-trap restaurants mixed in with boutiques. When the street opens up into a square, bear left up the narrow Via di Pasquino to reach Piazza Navona.

Near Campo de' Fiori

Two worthwhile parallel shopping streets run northwest (toward the river) from Piazza Farnese, just a block south of Campo de' Fiori: Via Monserrato/Via dei Banchi Vecchi and Via Giulia. (Streets in the opposite direction—to the southeast—are sleepier, with fewer shops.) While I've arranged these as a loop, you can pick and choose as you go.

Heading away from Piazza Farnese on low-key **Via Monserrato,** you'll see several antique, furniture, and home-decorating shops. But there are also some interesting clothing boutiques, as well as some unique shops. Hollywood (#107) is a cinephile's dream, with movie posters and rare DVDs; their sister store, at #110, sells movie-themed embroidered T-shirts. Between these two, at #108, is a fascinating old-time cobbler, with a crowded workbench crammed into a tiny shop. Estremi (#101) has some inspiring retro furniture, while Antichi Kimono (#43b-44) features Asian-themed dresses and fabrics.

Farther along, Via Monserrato becomes **Via dei Banchi Vecchi,** with even more antiques of varying aesthetics—from mothballed grannies to hipster vintage. Small and tasteful, Macoco (#138) sells colorful, artisanal toys for kids. Banchievecchi Pellami (#40) is an old-school leather shop, with belts and wallets. And Restore (#51) is packed with housewares, home furnishings, and kitchen gadgets.

When Via dei Banchi Vecchi dead-ends at the big cross street, loop left around the block to stroll more atmospheric **Via Giulia**—narrower, cobbled, and mostly traffic-free. Here you'll find fewer shops and more real-estate offices and architecture firms. House Kitchen & Design, near the start of the street at #101, is a cramped hole-in-the-wall with cooking gadgets; farther down, Magie di Casa (#140c) has a nice selection of linens, from tea towels to aprons.

One more street near Campo de' Fiori may be worth exploring: **Via Giubbonari,** which stretches southeast from the square. More heavily trafficked (and more touristy), it has dozens of stores selling affordable apparel aimed mainly at a younger crowd.

JEWISH GHETTO

In addition to its gorgeous synagogue, evocative history, and bustling Jewish restaurants, Rome's ghetto is also a great place to browse. My ✪ Jewish Ghetto Walk provides a natural spine for shopping explorations.

Near the start of that walk, just around the corner from the synagogue, the Leone Limentani housewares and dishware shop feels like a well-stocked mini-warehouse—this is where Roman couples register for wedding gifts (walk away from the river, and turn left at the ruins onto Via del Portico d'Ottavia; it's at the corner on the left). If you head across the street to the ruins and cross the little bridge, you'll find the showroom where customers' chosen place settings are laid out to review (shop and showroom both open Mon-Fri 9:00-13:00 & 15:30-19:30, Sat 10:00-19:30, closed Sun, Via del Portico d'Ottavia 47).

Farther along Via del Portico d'Ottavia, turn right up **Via della Reginella,** lined with cute boutiques: L'Officinaturale (at #3), a natural-products shop with oils, soaps, perfumes, and health foods; takeawaygallery, which is a mod art boutique (#10-11); Giuseppe Casetti's funky shops (#25-28)—one branch with vintage black-and-white photos, and the other with stacks of antique, yellowing books; and, at the end of the street (#30), Peperita, run by sisters—one of whom makes olive oil, and the other, all manner of hot peppers. Their products—powders, pastes, and infused oils—are ranked on a spiciness scale of 1 to 16; generous samples let you test your limits.

Back on the main drag, Mondo di Laura (#6) sells artisan cookies. And beyond that is a long row of Judaica shops, as well as kosher butchers and food stands. Less than a 10-minute walk straight ahead is the Campo de' Fiori shopping zone described earlier.

MONTI, NEAR THE ROMAN FORUM

Located between Via Cavour and Via Nazionale, across the street from the Roman Forum, the Monti neighborhood is a delight for exploring, dining, and shopping. Rather than designer fashions, Monti has Rome's closest thing to a hipster aesthetic: gourmet foodie shops and funky boutiques alongside very traditional neighborhood stores. Get oriented from the main square, Piazza della Madonna dei Monti (see page 58 for an orientation to this neighborhood). Then take off, strolling each of these areas.

Via del Boschetto and Via dei Serpenti

This little loop takes you up and down the parallel main drags of Monti. First, from the top of the square, head left down **Via del Boschetto.** You'll pass several little boutiques and jewelry shops. Along the way, watch for the recommended Gaudeo sandwich shop (#112); the fragrant Il Giardino di Tè tea house (#107); King Size vintage shop (#94); a cute kids' clothing store (#96); Gallina Smilza, selling colorful plastic dishes and housewares (#129); and Pulp, featuring women's casual fashion (#140).

Soon you'll reach the intersection with **Via Panisperna;** several pioneers in the early study of radiation, including Enrico Fermi, lived or worked along here, earning them the nickname "the Panisperna boys." From this intersection, you can turn right up Panisperna for more shopping (boutiques, antiques, and the Monti Bio organic shop at #225), or continue straight ahead for a few more shops (and the highly recommended L'Asino d'Oro restaurant, with a great lunch special—see page 400). Otherwise, loop left (downhill on Panisperna), noticing—on the corner—Macelleria Stecchiotti, a classic Roman butcher (where, reportedly, VIPs from the prime minister to the pope get their meat). Continuing downhill on Panisperna, you'll spot the neighborhood's favorite hangout—the recommended Ai Tre Scalini bar—and (at the corner) the recommended Antico Forno ai Serpenti bakery.

Turning left on **Via dei Serpenti,** on the left just past the bakery entrance, peek in the window to see the bakers at work. Continuing down Serpenti, watch for a funky collection of shops, including Podere Vecciano (at #33)—"a farm in the city" selling enticing Tuscan (not Roman) goods, including wines, olive oils, other gifty edibles, and wood-carved items. Then you'll reach Oic-FiFna Gioielli jewelry store (#25); a tempting *alimentari* (grocery); Faces, a boutique selling T-shirts with...faces (#138); the Pifebo vintage shop next door (#141); and on the right, at #4, a neighborhood fixture dating to the days when vintage wasn't yet vintage: the aptly named Di Tutto di Più ("Everything and More"), a general store stuffed to the gills with everything you could possibly need. Near the end of the street is American Apparel—which incited minor outrage in this extremely provincial and proud corner of Rome when it opened a few years back. And just beyond that, you've circled back to the main square.

Via Leonina/Via Urbana

To explore another set of streets with similar shops, leave the top of the main square and jog right (on Via dell'Angeletto, passing some fun little galleries), then left at the T-intersection (where you'll find a local chocolatier, La Bottega del Cioccolato). This puts you on **Via Leonina,** the first few blocks of which are a bit more crowded and

Shopping in Rome

1. Via dei Coronari
2. Via del Governo Vecchio
3. Via Monserrato
4. Via dei Banchi Vecchi
5. Via Giulia
6. Via Giubbonari
7. Via della Reginella
8. Via del Boschetto & Via dei Serpenti
9. Via Leonina/Via Urbana
10. Via Baccina & Via delle Madonna dei Monti
11. Shopping Triangle: Via del Corso to Via del Babuino
12. Piazza Borghese
13. Via Margutta
14. La Rinascente
15. Galleria Alberto Sordi
16. UPIM (3)
17. Oviesse/OVS (2)
18. Piazza Pio XII
19. Porta Portese Flea Market
20. Via Sannio Flea Market
21. Mercato Trionfale
22. Mercato Esquilino
23. Piazza delle Coppelle
24. Via Balbo
25. Via della Pace
26. Mercato di Testaccio

SHOPPING

urban, with lots of little hole-in-the-wall eateries. The big garage on the right opens its doors on weekends to host the lively Merca-toMonti (see "Department Stores, Souvenirs, and Markets" near the end of this chapter).

After passing the entrance to Cavour Metro station, the street swings left, becomes **Via Urbana,** and gets a bit more charming, as it runs through the bottom of a narrow valley between Via Cavour and Santa Maria Maggiore. At the gap with the parking lot, look high on the left to spot the recommended Fatamorgana *gelateria* (see page 400). Farther along, watch on the left for the Studio Cassio mosaics workshop (#98), then a fascinating *orologiaio* (clock shop, #103a). Continuing along Via Urbana, window-shop local designers' boutiques. Aromaticus, at #134, sells nothing but fresh herbs, as if to emphasize the Italian obsession with seasonal cooking. As the street climbs uphill, you can either go back the way you came, or turn left at Via Panisperna to return to Via del Boschetto, Via dei Serpenti, and the heart of Monti.

Via Baccina and Via della Madonna dei Monti
Via Baccina and Via della Madonna dei Monti have a lower concentration of shops, but they're even more atmospheric than the main drags. From the main square, head down **Via Baccina,** noticing Sotto Bosco at #40, selling colorful, minimalist jewelry and hats. Farther along, this street has a range of art galleries, boutiques, and jewelry shops. Better yet, turn left down vine-strewn Via dei Neofiti (across from Sotto Bosco), then right on **Via della Madonna dei Monti.** While there are more bars and restaurants than shops along here, it's worth a browse.

THE SHOPPING TRIANGLE, NEAR VIA DEL CORSO AND THE SPANISH STEPS
Via del Corso runs south, from Piazza del Popolo to the heart of Rome, and the little streets that poke east off the main drag—toward the Spanish Steps—form an area nicknamed the "shopping triangle." This zone has big international chains to suit every budget—from Dolce & Gabbana to the Gap—along with some very famous designers...all of which makes it less funky and colorful than the neighborhoods described previously. Nevertheless, a few quirky shops hide out here as well.

Streets Between Via del Corso and Via del Babuino
I've described the streets branching off of Via del Corso from north to south, starting at Piazza del Popolo. These are to the left as you walk; the streets to the right have fewer shops. Also note that **Via del Babuino** angles off parallel to Via del Corso, with mostly pricey international chains (Tiffany, Chanel, Dolce & Gabbana, and

so on). See the "Dolce Vita Stroll" map in the Nightlife in Rome chapter for specific locations of these streets.

Via Fontanella isn't interesting in its own right, but it does lead to the very chichi Via Margutta—described later.

Via Laurina has some funkier shops, including several with youth fashions; halfway down at #10 is the recommended Fatamorgana *gelateria,* and classier galleries and antiques sit at the far end.

Via di Gesù e Maria, running along its namesake church, has fewer stores. Discount dell'Alta Moda (at #16a, literally "Discount on Old Fashion," where last year's big-name designer duds are marked down by half) is a hit with bargain shoppers, while sports fans peruse the store with merchandise promoting the local Lazio soccer team. **Via di San Giacomo,** on the other side of the church, is also fairly sleepy—though it's fun to peek in the windows of the art school to see the artisans and craftspeople of the 21st century hard at work.

Via del Greci has a sheet music store, antiques, fashion boutiques, and a fragrant flower stall.

Via Vittoria and **Via della Croce** are major thoroughfares for reaching the Spanish Steps, so they have less interesting shops and more touristy crowds; however, Via della Croce is a great place to browse for a meal (see suggestions on page 398). The recommended Pastificio (near the end of the street, at #8) is, true to its name, a pasta factory, where you can buy dry pasta as an edible souvenir.

Some of the streets that run parallel to Via del Corso along here are also fun to wander. For example, **Via Mario de' Fiori** is crammed with upscale boutiques, but tucked amidst the glitz is the appealing c.u.c.i.n.a. shop (at #65), where you can stock up on Italian-style kitchen gadgets, utensils, and crockery.

Via delle Carrozze is fun to browse, with shops carrying specialties from other parts of Italy (handy if Rome is your only destination): The Santa Maria Novella perfume shop (#87) stocks scents from that famous church-run perfume works in Florence; Il Cerichio dei Goloso (#19) serves delicate pastries—and sells colorful plates—from Sicily; and La Peonia (#85) specializes in products from Sardinia. Also along this stretch, look in the window of the old-time tailor, Attilio Roncaccia (#12), and pick up some stylish fashions for Junior at Gocco (#18).

From **Via dei Condotti,** you can see the Spanish Steps hovering in the distance. This busy, glamorous strip has the same type of high-roller international shops found on Via del Babuino.

For one more taste of a simpler side of this area, find your way a few blocks west (on Via dei Condotti *away* from the Spanish Steps—toward the river, just south of Ara Pacis) to **Piazza Borghese.** This sleepy little square is filled with green kiosks selling prints, antique books, and curios. Shops in the surrounding streets have a similar flavor.

Via Margutta

Hiding parallel to Via del Corso and Via del Babuino is one of the most chic addresses in town, **Via Margutta.** (To find it, go down Via della Fontanella, near the top of Via del Corso; or head up from the Spanish Steps.) Here you'll find exclusive-feeling designer boutiques, big-ticket antique shops, home-decorating galleries, day spas, fashion eyewear shops, jewelers, wedding planners, and other places where you have to ring the bell to be let inside (assuming your hem meets their standards). One shop—called Flair—sums up this whole street. Lelli (at #5) has colorful home furnishings and textiles; Saddlers Union (#11) has very expensive leather goods; and Grossi Maurizio (across the street at #109) has marble sculptures and mosaics. Artemide (#107) is one of this street's many intriguing suppliers of mod, upscale home furnishings. Tucked along here, however, is one holdover from simpler times: La Bottega del Marmoraro (#153), where Sandro busily carves marble in a cramped hole-in-the-wall slathered with carved marble signs.

Department Stores, Souvenirs, and Markets

If all you need are souvenirs, a surgical strike at any gift shop will do. Otherwise, stop at a department store, scout near the Vatican or in the Jewish Ghetto for religious items, hit the flea market and produce markets, or—if you're in a pinch—pick up some mementos at the airport on your way out of town.

DEPARTMENT STORES

To conveniently peruse clothes, bags, shoes, and perfume at several major Italian chain stores, wander the shopping complex under Termini train station (most stores open daily 8:00-22:00).

Large department stores offer relatively painless one-stop shopping. A good upscale department store is **La Rinascente** (like Nordstrom or Macy's). Its main branch is on Piazza Fiume (east of Borghese Gallery near the old city walls), and a smaller store is on Via del Corso in the **Galleria Alberto Sordi,** an elegant 19th-century "mall" (across from Piazza Colonna). **UPIM** is a popular mid-range department store (many branches, including inside Termini train station, Via Nazionale 111, and Piazza Santa Maria Maggiore). **Oviesse/OVS,** a cheap clothing outlet, is near the Vatican Museum (on the corner of Via Candia and Via Mocenigo, Metro: Cipro) and also near Piazza Barberini (Via del Tritone 172, Metro: Barberini).

RELIGIOUS SOUVENIRS

Rome is a magnet for pilgrims, who find no shortage of shops near the Vatican—in the area directly in front of St. Peter's Square (on and around Piazza Pio XII), or along nearby Via Borgo Pio. Several shops in the Jewish Ghetto sell Judaica, Jewish-themed art and other souvenirs.

FLEA MARKETS

For antiques and fleas, the granddaddy of markets is the **Porta Portese** *mercato delle pulci* (flea market). This Sunday-morning market

 is long and spindly, running between the actual Porta Portese (a gate in the old town wall) and the Trastevere train station. Starting at Porta Portese, walk through the long, tacky parade of stalls selling cheap bras and shoes. Along the way, check out the con artists with the shell games. Each has shills in the crowd "winning big money" to get suckers involved. Hang on to your wallet—literally, in your front pocket, or better yet, use a money belt and make sure it's safely tucked under your clothes. This is a den of thieves. The heart of the market for real flea-market junk (hiding a few little antique treasures) is the square in the center near Via Cesare Pascarella. I find that a slow stroll through the entire market and back to the Porta Portese takes about an hour and a half. While the shopping gets old (and the vendor food will make you sick), the people-watching is endlessly entertaining (6:30-13:00 Sun only, on Via Portuense and Via Ippolito Nievo; to get to the market, catch bus #75 from Termini train station or tram #8 from Piazza Venezia, get off the bus or tram on Viale di Trastevere, and walk toward the river—and the noise).

At the **Via Sannio** market, you'll find new and used clothing and leather goods, some handicrafts, and random items that were probably stolen. You won't find antiques (Mon-Sat 9:00-13:30, closed Sun, behind Coin department store, just outside the walls of San Giovanni in Laterano, Metro: San Giovanni).

For something a bit hipper, don't miss the weekend **MercatoMonti** in the Monti district. This flea market has an emphasis on vintage clothes and housewares and up-and-coming designers (Sat-Sun only, 10:00-20:00, Hotel Palatino, Via Leonina 46, Metro: Cavour, www.mercatomonti.com).

OPEN-AIR PRODUCE MARKETS

Rome's outdoor markets provide a fun and colorful dimension of the city that even the most avid museumgoer should not miss. Wander through the easygoing neighborhood produce markets that clog certain streets and squares every morning (7:00-13:30) except Sunday. Consider the huge **Mercato Trionfale** (three blocks north of Vatican Museum at Via Andrea Doria). Another great food market is the **Mercato Esquilino** (Via Turati near Piazza Vittorio). Smaller but equally charming slices of everyday Roman life are at markets on these streets and squares: **Piazza delle Coppelle** (near the Pantheon), **Via Balbo** (near Termini train station and recommended hotels off Via Nazionale), and **Via della Pace** (near Piazza Navona). The covered **Mercato di Testaccio** sells produce and housewares and is a hit with photographers and people-watchers (Metro: Piramide). And **Campo de' Fiori,** despite having become quite touristy, is still a fun scene.

SHOPPING AT FIUMINCINO AIRPORT

Rome's main airport (a.k.a. Leonardo da Vinci Airport) sells Italian specialty foods vacuum-packed to clear US customs. Most shops are near the departure gates (after you check your bags and pass through security). Try *parmigiano reggiano* cheese, dried porcini mushrooms or peppers, and better olive oil than you can buy at home. Don't bother buying any salami or prosciutto unless it's canned; you're not allowed to bring fresh meat into the US (and even canned beef products are prohibited). Remember, if you're flying to the US and transferring before your final destination, you'll likely be required to pack purchased liquids in your checked luggage after clearing customs (a potential recipe for disaster).

NIGHTLIFE IN ROME

Romans get dressed up and eat out in casual surroundings for their evening entertainment. For most visitors, the best after-dark activity is simply to grab a gelato and stroll the medieval lanes that connect the romantic, floodlit squares and fountains. Head for Piazza Navona, the Pantheon, Campo de' Fiori, Trevi Fountain, the Spanish Steps, Via del Corso, Trastevere (around the Santa Maria in Trastevere Church), or Monte Testaccio.

For a great evening stroll, ✪ see my Heart of Rome Walk chapter and "Dolce Vita Stroll" (at the end of this chapter).

PERFORMANCES AND FILM

Check out the current listings of concerts, operas, dance, and films. Posters around town also advertise upcoming events. For the most up-to-date events calendar, check these English-language websites: www.inromenow.com, www.wantedinrome.com, and www. rome.angloinfo.com.

Music

Music lovers will seek out the mega-music complex of the Rome **Auditorium** (Auditorium Parco della Musica), designed by contemporary architect Renzo Piano (€20-60 tickets, check availability in advance—concerts often sell out, Viale Pietro de Coubertin 30, take Metro to Flaminio and then catch tram #2 to Apollodoro, from there it's a 5-minute walk east, just beyond the elevated road, tram/metro runs until 23:30, box office tel. 06-892-982, www.auditorium.com). Also called the "Park of Music," it's a place where many Romans go just for the scene—music store, restaurants, cafés, and fresh modern architecture with three state-of-the-art auditoriums (known as "the beetles" for their

The *Passeggiata*

Throughout Italy, early evening is time to stroll. While elsewhere in Italy this is called the *passeggiata*, in Rome it's a cruder, big-city version called the *struscio* (meaning "to rub").

Unemployment among Italy's youth is very high; many stay with their parents even into their 30s. They spend a lot of time being trendy and hanging out. Like American kids gathering at the mall, working-class suburban youth *(coatto)* converge on the old center, as there's little to keep them occupied in Rome's dreary outskirts (which lack public spaces). The hot *vroom-vroom* motor scooter is their symbol; haircuts and fashion are follow-the-leader.

In a more genteel small town, the *passeggiata* comes with sweet whispers of *"bella"* and *"bello"* ("pretty" and "handsome"). In Rome, the admiration is stronger, oriented toward consumption—they say *"buona"* and *"buono"*—meaning roughly "tasty." But despite how lusty this all sounds, you'll see just as many chunky, middle-aged Italians out and about as hormone-charged youth.

appearance). If you want to see today's Rome enjoying today's culture, an evening here is the best you'll do.

Classical Music and Opera

The **Teatro dell'Opera** has an active schedule of opera and classical concerts. In the summer, the productions move to the Baths of Caracalla, where ancient ruins make an evocative backdrop. You'll see locals in all their finery, so pull your fanciest outfit from your backpack (near Via Firenze/Via Nazionale hotels at Via Firenze 72, tel. 06-4816-0255, www.operaroma.it).

Musical events at the Episcopal **Church of St. Paul's Within the Walls** range from orchestral concerts (usually Tue and Fri) to full operatic performances, which are usually on Saturdays (€15-20, performances at 20:30, tickets usually available on day of show, arrive 30-45 minutes early for a good seat, lasts 1.5-2.5 hours, corner of Via Nazionale at Via Napoli 58, near Termini train station and recommended hotels, tel. 06-482-6296, www.musicaemusicasrl.com). On Sunday evenings at 18:30, the church occasionally hosts hour-long candlelit *Luminaria* concerts (€10-20, buy tickets at the church on Sunday, www.stpaulsrome.it).

Jazz

Rome has a relatively small but vibrant jazz scene. **Alexanderplatz** is the venerable club in town, with performances most evenings (Sun-Thu concerts at 21:45, Fri-Sat at 22:30, closed in summer,

NIGHTLIFE

Via Ostia 9, Ottaviano Metro stop, tel. 06-3972-1867, www. alexanderplatz.it).

Il Pentagrappolo is an intimate *enoteca*, serving light meals (proudly, no pasta) to go with their selection of quality wines, many organic. Thursday through Saturday, they host live music (often jazz) starting around 22:00 (open Tue-Sun 18:00-24:00, closed Mon, music Sept-June, best to reserve on weekends, three blocks east of the Colosseum at Via Celimontana 21—see map on page 354, www.ilpentagrappolo.com, tel. 06-709-6301, Simone).

TramJazz, a creative venture by the public transit company, combines dinner, music, and a journey through the city in a vintage cable car for a mostly local crowd (€59, daily at 21:00, 3 hours, leaves from Piazza di Porta Maggiore, book at least a week in advance, www.tramjazz.com).

Movies
Movies in their original language are hard to come by in Rome (look for v.o.—*versione originale*). The one reliable cinema is the **Nuovo Olimpia** (3 blocks north of Piazza Colonna, just off Via del Corso at Via in Lucina 16, tel. 06-686-1068). **Multisala Barberini** occasionally has v.o. screenings as well (Piazza Barberini, www.multisalabarberini.it). For movie listings, check www. inromenow.com (includes English-language film showings) and www.romereview.com.

EVENING SIGHTSEEING
Some **museums** have later opening hours (especially on Sat in summer), offering a good chance to see art in a cooler, less-crowded environment. See the "Rome at a Glance" sidebar on page 46, and ask the TI if any museums are currently open late.

Both the **Scuderie del Quirinale** and the nearby **Palazzo delle Esposizioni** stay open late when they're hosting major art exhibitions (€12 for each, can be more with some exhibits, €20 combo-ticket covers both for three days; both open Sun-Thu 10:00-20:00, Fri-Sat 10:00-22:30 except the Palazzo is closed Mon; may open—and stay open—much later in summer; last entry one hour before closing; Scuderie—Via XXIV Maggio 16, tel. 06-696-271, www.scuderiequirinale.it; Palazzo—Via Nazionale 194, tel. 06-3996-7500, www.palazzoesposizioni.it).

BARS AND NIGHTSPOTS
I've listed some fun neighborhoods worth exploring after dark, along with a few bars and *enoteche* (wine bars) in each. All of these places are recommended in the Eating in Rome chapter, where you'll find more details on each.

NIGHTLIFE

Heart of Rome, near the Pantheon

This is a touristy but delightful scene. The monuments—especially the Pantheon and Trevi Fountain—are magically floodlit at night. Not far from the Trevi Fountain, **L'Antica Birreria Peroni** is a big, boisterous beer hall. Farther west, the hip hangout **No.Au** hides on a little square just off Piazza Navona. Farther south, Campo de' Fiori and the surrounding streets become one big, rude street party around 22:00. One good place to sample the youthful energy, as well as some craft beers, is the rollicking **Open Baladin** pub. (For more on these places, see their listings under "In the Pantheon Neighborhood," page 390 of the Eating in Rome chapter.)

North Rome, near the Spanish Steps and Via del Corso

A babel of international tourists, this glitzy zone is bustling after dark. For many, just hanging out on and around the Spanish Steps is enough to fill an evening. Or, for a wine bar that matches the neighborhood ambience—with an upscale, almost snooty yuppie atmosphere—consider **Gusto** (see listing on page 399).

Near the Colosseum and Forum, in Monti

The best plan in this lively village Rome zone is to pop the top off a brew and hang out at the fountain on Piazza della Madonna dei Monti. To join the after-dark scene, buy a drink at the shop on the uphill side of the square (cheap bottles of wine with plastic glasses, beer, fruit, and munchies) and be part of what becomes the hottest bar in the area. There are plenty of makeshift benches around the fountain (this scene is described on page 58). For something a bit less casual, head for the neighborhood hangout, **Ai Tre Scalini,** where there's often a Roman mob out front, so engrossed in conversation they've forgotten they're waiting for a table. For more refined locales, see **Enoteca Cavour 313** or **Enoteca Nel Cuore di Roma.** (For details, see the "In Monti" section, page 400 of the Eating in Rome chapter.)

Trastevere

This youthful district crawls with students and young tourists after hours, drinking beer, consuming late-night pizza-by-the-slice, and licking gelato as they prowl the cobbles. For a more upscale atmosphere, head for **Cantina Paradiso Wine and Cocktail Bar** (see listing on page 389).

Near Termini Station

This is a pretty sleepy area at night, though there's often some activity around Piazza della Repubblica. To sip wine in a sophisticated setting, stroll over to **I Colori del Vino Enoteca. Flann O'Brien,** a sprawling Irish pub, occasionally has live music. (For more on these places, see the "Near Termini Station" section, page 404 of the Eating in Rome chapter.)

Testaccio

Some find this district a bit seedy after dark, but young Romans don't seem to mind. Beer pilgrims flock to **L'Oasi della Birra,** with hundreds of microbrews (see listing on page 410). **Monte Testaccio,** once an ancient trash heap, is now a small hill whose cool caves house funky restaurants and trendy clubs. And the area around Monte Testaccio is a hotspot for club-hopping—after 21:00, just follow the noise.

Pub Crawls

Offered year-round by several companies, these attract a boisterous crowd. I tried one and had never seen 50 young, drunk people having so much fun (or seen so many locals roll their eyes). Look for fliers locally. Late on Friday and Saturday evenings, entire quarters of old Rome seem to be overtaken by young beer-drinking revelers.

▲▲DOLCE VITA STROLL

This is the city's chic stroll, from Piazza del Popolo (Metro: Flaminio) down a wonderfully traffic-free section of Via del Corso, and up Via Condotti to the Spanish Steps. It takes place from around 17:00 to 19:00 each evening (Fri and Sat are best), except on Sunday, when it occurs earlier in the afternoon. Leave before 18:00 if you plan to visit the Ara Pacis (Altar of Peace), which closes at 19:00 and is closed Monday.

As you stroll, you'll see shoppers, people watchers, and flirts on the prowl filling this neighborhood of some of Rome's most fashionable stores (some open after siesta 16:30-19:30). While both the crowds and the shops along Via del Corso have gone downhill recently, elegance survives in the grid of streets between here and the Spanish Steps. For a detailed description of several streets and shops in this area, see page 424 of the Shopping in Rome chapter. If you get hungry during your stroll, see page 398 for descriptions of neighborhood wine bars and restaurants.

To reach **Piazza del Popolo,** where the stroll starts, take Metro line A to Flaminio and walk south to the square. Delightfully car-free, Piazza del Popolo is marked by an obelisk that was brought to Rome by Augustus after he conquered Egypt. (It used to stand in the Circus Maximus.) In medieval times, this area was just inside Rome's main entry (for more background on the square, see page 72).

If starting your stroll early enough, the Baroque church of **Santa Maria del Popolo** is worth popping into (Mon-Sat until

Dolce Vita Stroll

1 Hotel San Carlo

2 Ristorante il Gabriello

3 Antica Enoteca & other Via della Croce Eateries

4 Palatium Enoteca Regionale

5 Gusto Wine Bar

6 Caffè Ciampini

7 Fatamorgana Gelato

8 Anglo American Bookshop

19:00, Sun until 19:30, next to gate in old wall on north side of square). Inside, look for Raphael's Chigi Chapel (second on left as you face the main altar) and two paintings by Caravaggio (in the Cerasi Chapel, left of altar; see church listing on page 74).

From Piazza del Popolo, shop your way down **Via del Corso.** With the proliferation of shopping malls, many chain stores lining Via del Corso are losing customers and facing hard times. Still, this remains a fine place to feel the pulse of Rome at twilight.

Historians side-trip right down Via Pontefici past the fascist architecture to see the massive, rotting, round-brick **Mausoleum of Augustus,** topped with overgrown cypress trees. Beyond it, next to the river, is Augustus' **Ara Pacis,** enclosed within a protective glass-walled museum (see the self-guided tour on page 75). From the mausoleum, walk down Via Tomacelli to return to Via del Corso and the 21st century.

From Via del Corso, window shoppers should take a left down **Via Condotti** to join the parade to the **Spanish Steps,** passing big-name boutiques. The streets that parallel Via Condotti to the south (Borgognona and Frattina) are also elegant and filled with high-end shops. A few streets to the north hides the narrow Via Margutta. This is where Gregory Peck's *Roman Holiday* character lived (at #51); today it has a leafy tranquility and is filled with pricey artisan and antique shops.

Historians: Ignore Via Condotti and forget the Spanish Steps. Stay on Via del Corso, which has been straight since Roman times, and walk a half-mile down to the Victor Emmanuel Monument. Climb Michelangelo's stairway to his glorious (especially when floodlit) square atop Capitoline Hill. Stand on the balcony (just past the mayor's palace on the right), which overlooks the Forum. As the horizon reddens and cats prowl the unclaimed rubble of ancient Rome, it's one of the finest views in the city.

ROME CONNECTIONS

Rome is well-connected with the rest of the planet: by train, bus, plane, car, and cruise ship. This chapter addresses your arrival and departure from the city. It explains the various options and gives a rundown on their points of departure.

By Train

Rome's main train station is the centrally located **Termini** train station, which has connections to the airport. Rome's other major station is the **Tiburtina** bus/train station, which is starting to get some high-speed rail connections, including privately run Italo trains (see page 543).

Minimize your time in a station—the banks of Trenitalia's user-friendly automated ticket machines (marked *Biglietto Veloce/ Fast Ticket*) are handy but cover Italian destinations only. They take euros and credit cards, display schedules, issue tickets, and even make reservations for rail pass holders (found under the "Global Pass" ticket type). Still, if you're not near a station, it can be quicker to get tickets and train info from travel agencies in town or online. For more on train travel in Italy—including your ticket-buying options—see page 543.

TERMINI TRAIN STATION

Termini, Rome's main train station, is a buffet of tourist services. However, it's undergoing renovation, so services might have moved by the time you visit. The customer service and ticket windows in the main hall (out in the big atrium, beyond the head of the tracks) can be jammed with travelers—take a number and wait. For simple questions, several handy red info kiosks are located near the head of the tracks. The ticket machines can also be helpful for checking schedules. Most trains departing from Termini are operated by Italy's state rail company, Trenitalia; however, privately run Italo will likely begin using the station soon as well (for more on Italo, see "Tiburtina Train and Bus Station," later).

Along track 24, about 100 yards down, you'll find the **TI** (daily 8:00-19:30), a **hotel booking** office, and **car rental** desks. The **baggage storage** *(deposito bagagli)* is downstairs, hiding down the long corridor past the bathrooms, under track 24 and the TI (€6/5 hours, then cheaper, daily 6:00-23:00). The **Leonardo Express train** to Fiumicino Airport runs from track 24 (see "By Plane," later).

In general, the best places in the station to sit are in one of its eateries. A snack bar and a good self-service **cafeteria** (Ciao) are perched above the ticket windows, accessible from the side closest to track 24 (daily 11:00-22:30). For good-quality **sandwiches** to go, try VyTA in the atrium across from track 1.

Near track 1, you'll find a **pharmacy** (daily 7:30-22:00); along the same track is an often cramped **waiting room** and **Despar Express,** selling groceries and toiletries (daily 7:00-21:30). If you can't find what you're looking for there, downstairs is a larger shopping complex that includes the **Conad** supermarket (daily 6:00-24:00; closest to track 1). Pricey **WCs** (€1) are also downstairs, just below the main exits on the north or south side.

Elsewhere in the station are **ATMs,** late-hours banks, and 24-hour thievery. Opposite the ticket windows in the station's main entrance lobby, **Borri Books** sells books in English, including popular fiction, Italian history and culture, and kids' books, plus maps (daily 7:00-23:00).

Termini is also a local transportation hub. Metro lines A and B intersect downstairs at Termini Metro station. Buses (including Rome's hop-on, hop-off bus tours—see page 32) leave across the square directly in front of the main station hall. The Metro and bus areas are a work in progress and change frequently—look for signs directing you to the Metro platform or bus stop, or ask at the transit information kiosk just out front (to the right as you leave the main hall). Taxis queue in front and outside exits on both the north and south sides; if there's a long taxi line in front, try a side exit instead. Avoid con men hawking "express taxi" services in unmarked cars (only use cars marked with the word *taxi* and a phone number).

From Termini, many of my recommended hotels are easily accessible by foot (for those near this train station) or by Metro (for those in the Colosseum and Vatican neighborhoods).

The station has some sleazy sharks with official-looking business cards; avoid anybody selling anything unless they're in a legitimate shop at the station. Other shady characters linger around the ticket machines—offers to help usually come with the expectation of a "tip."

Since the most convenient connections for travelers nearly all depart from Termini, I've listed those next. But as a precaution, it's always smart to confirm whether your train departs from Termini or Tiburtina. Note that the following connections are for Trenitalia; for Italo connections, see www.italotreno.it.

From Rome's Termini Station by Train to: Venice (roughly hourly, 3.5 hours, overnight possible), **Florence** (at least hourly, 1.5 hours, some stop at Orvieto en route), **Siena** (1-2/hour, 1 change, 3-4 hours), **Orvieto** (roughly hourly, 1-1.5 hours), **Assisi** (nearly hourly, 2-3.5 hours, 5 direct, most others change in Foligno), **Pisa** (2/hour, 3-4 hours, many change in Florence), **La Spezia** (4/day direct, more with transfers in Pisa, 3-4.5 hours), **Milan** (hourly, 3-8 hours, overnight possible), **Milan's Malpensa Airport** (hourly, 5 hours, change in Milan), **Naples** (at least hourly, 1.25 hours on Frecciarossa or Italo trains, otherwise 2 hours), **Civitavecchia** cruise-ship port (2-3/hour, 40-80 minutes), **Brindisi** (6/day, 3 direct, 5-9 hours, overnight possible), **Amsterdam** (6/day, 20 hours), **Interlaken** (5/day, 6.5-8 hours), **Frankfurt** (6/day, 11-12 hours), **Munich** (5/day, 9-10 hours, 1 direct night train, 11.5 hours), **Nice** (1/day, 13 hours), **Paris** (3/day, 11-12 hours, 1-2 changes), **Vienna** (2/day, 11.75 hours, 1 direct night train, 12 hours).

TIBURTINA TRAIN AND BUS STATION

Tiburtina, Rome's second-largest train station, is located in the city's northeast corner. Recently rebuilt, it's a sleek and modern complex but still a work in progress. In general, slower trains (from Milan, Bolzano, Bologna, Udine, and Reggio di Calabria) and some night trains (from Munich, Milan, Venice, Innsbruck, and Udine) use Tiburtina, as does the night bus to Fiumicino Airport. Direct night trains from Vienna use Termini train station instead.

Tiburtina has been redeveloped for high-speed rail, including some Frecce trains and the newer Italo service. This competitor to Trenitalia connects major Italian cities and is comparable to the high-speed Frecce trains in comfort, speed, and price (though it's often cheaper, if you book well in advance). It doesn't accept rail passes, but it's a worthy alternative if you want to buy a point-to-point ticket. Italo serves Tiburtina and Ostiense stations, which are farther away from the center than Termini and have relatively few services (though Italo will likely start using Termini Station as well in the near future). Tiburtina is a better choice than Ostiense, as it has more amenities and provides an interesting look at contemporary Italian architecture. A separate "Casa Italo" area has dedicated service counters, red ticket machines, and a small waiting area (in the upper part of the station, across from track 23). You can also book Italo tickets by phone (tel. 06-0708) or from their user-friendly website (www.italotreno.it). For more on Italo, see page 545.

Tiburtina is also known as a hub for bus service to destinations all across Italy. Buses depart from the piazza in front of the station. Ticket offices are located in the piazza and around the corner on Circonvallazione Nomentana (just beyond the elevated freeway).

Getting Between Tiburtina and Downtown Rome: Tiburtina is on Metro line B, with easy connections to Termini (a straight shot, four stops away) and the entire Metro system (note that when going to Tiburtina, Metro line B splits—you want a train signed *Rebibbia*). Or take bus #492 from Tiburtina to various city-center stops (such as Piazza Barberini, Piazza Venezia, and Piazza Cavour) and the Vatican neighborhood (as you emerge from the station, the bus stop is to the left).

From Rome's Tiburtina Station by Train to: Florence (2-4/hour, 1.5 hours), **Milan** (almost hourly, 3-3.5 hours), **Naples** (almost hourly, 1.5 hours), **Venice** (almost hourly, 3.5 hours).

SMALLER STATIONS

Ostiense has some high-speed rail service, mostly Italo (that company's office is near track 15a, next to the Eataly gourmet supermarket). Ostiense's neighbor, **Porta San Paolo,** has connections to Ostia Antica. If you're staying near the Vatican and taking a regional train, it saves time to get off at the **San Pietro** train station rather than at Termini; from this station, bus #64 connects you to the Vatican area and to other major landmarks around Rome. Cruise-ship passengers coming from Civitavecchia on a day trip usually use Ostiense or San Pietro.

By Bus

Long-distance buses (such as from Siena and Assisi) arrive at Rome's **Tiburtina Station** (described earlier).

From Rome by Bus to: Assisi (2/day, 3 hours—the train makes much more sense), **Siena** (6/day, 3 hours), **Sorrento** (1-2/day, 4 hours; this is a cheap and easy way to go straight to Sorrento, buy tickets at Ticket Bus at Tiburtina, other travel agencies, or on board for a €3 surcharge; tel. 080-579-0111, www.marozzivt.it—in Italian only).

By Plane

Rome's two airports—**Fiumicino** (a.k.a. Leonardo da Vinci, airport code: FCO) and the small **Ciampino** (airport code: CIA)—share the same website (www.adr.it).

FIUMICINO AIRPORT

Rome's major airport has a TI (in Terminal 3, daily 8:00-19:30), ATMs, banks, luggage storage, shops, and bars. The Rome Walks website (www.romewalks.com) has a useful video on options for getting into the city from the airport. For airport information, call 06-65951. To inquire about flights, call 06-6595-3640.

Getting Between Fiumicino Airport and Downtown Rome

The slick, direct **Leonardo Express train** connects the airport and Rome's central Termini train station in 30 minutes for €14. Trains run twice hourly in both directions from roughly 6:00 to 23:00 (leaving the airport usually at :06 and :36). From the airport's arrival gate, follow signs to the train icon or *Stazione/Railway Station*. Buy your ticket from a machine, the Biglietteria office, or a newsstand near the platform; then validate it in a yellow machine near the track. Make sure the train you board is going to the central "Roma Termini" station, not "Roma Orte" or others.

Going from Termini train station to the airport, trains depart at about :20 and :50 past each hour, usually from track 24. Check the departure boards for "Fiumicino Aeroporto"—the local name for the airport—and confirm with an official or a local on the platform that the train is indeed going to the airport (€14, buy ticket from any tobacco shop or a newsstand in the station, or at the self-service machines, Termini-Fiumicino trains run 5:50-22:50). Read your ticket: If it requires validation, stamp it in the green or yellow machines near the platform before boarding. From the train station at the airport, you can access most of the terminals. American air carriers flying direct to the US depart from Terminal 5, which is a separate building not connected to the rest of the terminals. If you arrive by train, catch the T5 shuttle bus *(navetta)* on the sidewalk in front of Terminal 3—it's too far to walk with luggage.

Allow lots of time going in either direction; there's a fair amount of transportation involved (e.g., getting from your hotel to Termini, the ride to the airport, the walk from the airport train station to check-in, etc.). Flying to the US involves an extra level of security—plan on getting to the airport even earlier than normal (flying transatlantic, I like to arrive 2.5 hours ahead of my flight; within Europe, 2 hours is usually sufficient).

CONNECTIONS

Various **bus** companies, including Terravision (www.terravision.eu), SIT (www.sitbusshuttle.com), and Atral (www.atral-lazio.com) connect Fiumicino and Termini train station, departing roughly every 40 minutes. While cheaper than the train (about €5 one-way), buses take twice as long (about an hour, depending on traffic) and can potentially fill up (allow plenty of extra time; leaves the airport from Terminal 3, leaves Termini Station from Via Marsala—just outside the exit closest to track 1). The Terravision bus also stops near the Vatican. At the airport, the companies' desks line up in Terminal 3, near the entrance to the train station; I'd just compare my options and hop on whichever one is departing first.

Shuttle van services run to and from the airport and can be economical for one or two people. It's cheaper from the airport to downtown, as several companies compete for this route; by surveying the latest deals, you should be able to snare a ride into town for around €10-15. To get from your hotel to the airport, consider Rome Airport Shuttle (€25/1 person, extra people-€6 each, by reservation only, tel. 06-4201-4507 or 06-4201-3469, www.airportshuttle.it).

A **taxi** between Fiumicino and downtown Rome takes 45 minutes in normal traffic (for tips on taxis, see page 27). If you're catching a taxi at the airport, be sure to wait at the taxi stand. Avoid unmarked, unmetered taxis; these guys will try to tempt you away from the taxi-stand lineup by offering an immediate (rip-off) ride. Rome's and Fiumicino's official taxis have a fixed rate to and from the airport (€48 for up to four people with normal-size bags).

Cabbies not based in Rome or Fiumicino are allowed to charge €70 for the ride. That sign is posted next to the €48-fare sign—confusing many tourists and allowing dishonest cabbies to overcharge. It's best to use Rome city cabs, which have a maroon logo with the words *"Roma Capitale"* on the door. They can only charge €48 for the ride to anywhere in the historic center (within the old city walls, where most of my recommended hotels are located).

If your cab driver tries to charge you more than €48 from the airport into town, say, *"Quarant'otto euro—è la legge"* (kwah-RAHNTOH-toe AY-oo-roh—ay lah LEJ-jay; which means, "Forty-eight euros—it's the law"), and they should back off.

To get from the airport into town cheaply by taxi, try teaming up with any tourist also just arriving (most are heading for hotels near yours in the center). When you're departing Rome, your hotel can arrange a taxi to the airport at any hour.

CIAMPINO AIRPORT
Rome's smaller airport (tel. 06-6595-9515) handles charter flights and some budget airlines (including most Ryanair flights).

Getting Between Ciampino Airport and Downtown Rome

Various **bus** companies—including Cotral, Terravision, and SIT—will take you to Rome's Termini train station (about €5 and 2/hour for each company, 45 minutes). Cotral also runs a quicker route (25 minutes) to the Anagnina Metro stop, where you can connect by Metro to the stop nearest your hotel (departs every 40 minutes). At Termini Station, buses pick up on Via Marsala (closest to track 1).

The fixed price for any official **taxi** (with the maroon "*Roma Capitale*" logo on the door) is €30 to downtown (within the old city walls, including most of my recommended hotels).

Rome Airport Shuttle also offers service to and from Ciampino (€25/1 person, listed earlier).

By Car

DRIVING AND PARKING IN ROME

The Grande Raccordo Anulare circles greater Rome. This ring road has spokes that lead you into the center. Entering from the north, leave the autostrada at the Settebagni exit. Following the ancient Via Salaria (and the black-and-white *Centro* signs), work your way doggedly into the Roman thick of things. This will take you along the Villa Borghese Gardens and dump you right on Via Veneto in downtown Rome. Avoid rush hour and drive defensively: Roman cars stay in their lanes like rocks in an avalanche.

Parking in Rome is dangerous. Park near a police station or get advice at your hotel. The Villa Borghese underground garage is handy (Metro: Spagna). Garages charge about €24 per day.

Consider this: Your car is a worthless headache in Rome. Avoid a pile of stress and save money by parking at the huge, easy, and relatively safe lot behind the train station in the hill town of Orvieto (follow *P* signs from autostrada) and catching the train to Rome (hourly, 1-1.5 hours).

If you absolutely must drive and park a car in Rome, try to avoid commuter traffic by arriving Friday evening, or anytime during the weekend, and by leaving town during the weekend. Park your car at Tiburtina Station (€1/hour, www.atac.roma.it) and take a 10-minute ride on the Metro line B into the center.

For more information on car rental and driving in Italy, see page 554.

By Cruise Ship

PORT OF CIVITAVECCHIA

Hundreds of cruise ships—including Carnival, Royal Caribbean, Princess, and Celebrity lines—dock each year at the port of Civitavecchia, about 45 miles northwest of Rome. If your trip includes cruising beyond Rome, consider my guidebook, *Rick Steves Mediterranean Cruise Ports*. Port facilities include a TI (tel. 0766-679-619), ATMs, Internet access, bag storage, and cafés.

To get from your ship to Civitavecchia's train station, take the free shuttle bus to the port entrance (some shuttles may take you all the way to the station—ask). From the shuttle-bus stop, walk through the security checkpoint at the port gate, and then walk about 10 minutes straight ahead up the main road with the sea on your right-hand side. After about three blocks, at Hotel de La Ville, bear left and uphill through a long parking lot to the pale-orange train station (marked *Civitavecchia*); if you get turned around, look for signs to *Stazione FF. SS.*

Taxis also wait at the port gate, attempting to extort €15 for the very short ride to the train station (tel. 076-626-121). A local bus to the train station only saves you a few minutes of walking; take one only if you're carrying heavy bags or have limited mobility. **Buses** #B, #C, and #D go from just above the port gate on Largo Plebiscito (Viale Garibaldi stop) one stop to the train station (Stazione FF. SS. stop; €1, 3-4/hour, 5 minutes, buy ticket at a tobacco shop before you board).

Getting Between Civitavecchia and Downtown Rome

The traffic between Civitavecchia and Rome is terrible, making trains faster and more economical than a **taxi** (which can run €110-150 one-way). Recommended driver Ezio of Autoservizi Monti Concezio takes cruise travelers to Rome in a private car (€130/2 people, €20 for each additional person) and offers full-day tours of the city (€400 for up to 6 people, €450 for up to 8; see "Car and Minibus Tours" on page 33). Beware of unlicensed taxis offering a huge price break; local police sometimes follow these "gypsy" cabs in a scam that imposes hefty fines on both the driver and the passengers (the driver later gets a kickback from the cop).

Keep in mind that it takes approximately 1.5 hours each way to get between your ship and downtown Rome—so you'll need to mentally subtract at least three hours from the time you have in port.

Frequent **trains** (2-3/hour) connect Civitavecchia with several stations in Rome. Depending on your sightseeing plans, you'll likely be best off heading either to **Ostiense Station** (with a handy Metro station, just two stops from the Colosseum) or **San Pietro Station** (10-minute walk or a couple of stops on bus #64 to get to St. Peter's Basilica). Termini Station, the main hub for the city's transit and for shuttle trains to the airport, overshoots the key sights a bit.

Regional trains (marked *REG*) head into Rome roughly twice

an hour, stopping at San Pietro and Ostiense stations on their way to Termini (40-55 minutes to San Pietro, 55-70 minutes to Ostiense, 65-80 minutes to Termini). The Intercity train (marked *IC*) is somewhat faster (40-50 minutes to Ostiense, 50 minutes to Termini), but doesn't stop at San Pietro, and isn't covered by the good-value BIRG ticket (described next). When there are enough ships in port to justify it, there's also a special express "Vatican train non-stop" to San Pietro, offering one daily round-trip designed for cruise travelers.

If you're taking a regional train, save money by getting the wonderful BIRG ticket: a €12 day pass covering second-class, round-trip train travel between Civitavecchia and Rome as well as unlimited travel on Rome's buses, Metro, and trams—a great convenience (not valid on fast Intercity trains or the express train to San Pietro). Otherwise, expect to pay about €5 each way for regional trains or €10 on the Intercity. All train tickets must be validated in the green or yellow box before getting on the train.

The Civitavecchia train station has five main platforms (*binario,* or *bin;* numbered 1 through 5), connected by an underground tunnel. There are also two "short" *(tronco)* platforms, 1T and 2T, at the far-right end of the station as you face the tracks; these are *not* the same as tracks 1 and 2. Be sure you're waiting at the correct platform. For a useful video on taking the train from the port into the city, check out the Rome Walks website (www.romewalks.com).

Getting Between Civitavecchia and Fiumicino Airport

You'll need to take two **trains** to link Civitavecchia and Fiumicino Airport: one between Civitavecchia and Rome's Termini train station, and another between Termini and the airport. See "By Plane," earlier.

Shuttle van services run between the port and Rome's Fiumicino Airport. Try Rome Airport Shuttle (€90/1-2 people, €15 each additional person up to 8, share with others and save, much more for pickup between 21:00 and 7:00, tel. 06-4201-4507 or 06-4201-3469, www.airportshuttle.it). A **taxi** costs about €120 one-way between Civitavecchia and Fiumicino Airport.

Rome Tours from Civitavecchia

A small company called **Can't Be Missed Tours** offers Rome tours from the port (€65 plus €21.50 for Vatican Museum admission and €13.50 for optional Colosseum/Forum admission, 10 percent discount when you book using promo code "RICKSTEVES" and then show this book, small groups, mobile 329-129-8182, www.cantbemissedtours.com, info@cantbemissedtours.com). Your guide first meets you at the Civitavecchia train station, leads you on a tour through Rome's ancient city center, the Vatican Museum, and St. Peter'sBasilica before accompanying you on a train all the way back to the port (on-time return is guaranteed).

Many of Civitavecchia's private limousine companies and the Rome Airport Shuttle also offer Rome tours. Look for a tour that is a minimum of eight hours in length: six hours for sightseeing and two-plus hours of travel time. On shorter tours you'll see most of Rome from the bus window. Plan to spend about €300 for three or four people.

DAY TRIPS

Ostia Antica • Tivoli
• Naples and Pompeii

There's so much to see and do in Rome that you could easily fill a vacation without ever leaving the city limits. But here are several nearby sights that might match your particular interests.

Ostia Antica is similar to Pompeii, but without the crowds. This excavated ancient Roman city is located an easy 45 minutes by Metro and train from Rome. Or stay on the train another 15 minutes and enjoy Ostia's beaches (see page 415).

Tivoli is less accessible (consider seeing it via private tour, or

Day Trips from Rome map:

- To Pisa & Cinque Terre
- To Florence
- To Assisi
- Orvieto
- Orte
- **Tivoli** — ■ VILLA D'ESTE, ■ HADRIAN'S VILLA
- Civitavecchia
- **Rome**
- Fiumicino (da Vinci) ✈
- Ciampino ✈
- Ostia Beach
- **OSTIA ANTICA**
- **ITALY**
- Adriatic Sea
- Mt. Vesuvius
- **Naples** •
- **POMPEII RUINS**
- Salerno
- Sorrento
- Capri
- Paestum
- PAESTUM RUINS
- To Palermo
- Mediterranean Sea
- 50 Kilometers
- 50 Miles
- ----- Train
- ---- Bus

hire your own driver for the day), but you're rewarded with the evocative ruins of Hadrian's Villa and with the lush gardens and restored fountains of a Renaissance mansion, the Villa d'Este.

Thanks to Italy's excellent train system, it's 1.25 hours to **Naples** on a direct high-speed train (or 2 hours on cheaper trains) that lands you right in the middle of town. Visit Roman statues and mosaics at the wonderful Archaeological Museum, stroll colorful Spaccanapoli street, and have lunch in the city where pizza was born, sampling the exotic chaos of southern Italy.

History hounds can venture an hour farther south of Naples to see the ultimate in ruined Roman cities—**Pompeii**—frozen in time by the eruption of Mt. Vesuvius.

Arrive back in Rome for a late dinner at a sidewalk café to recount your busy day over a glass of wine.

Italy's fast trains put other cities within day-trip range, including **Orvieto** (1-1.5 hours by train), **Assisi** (2-3.5 hours), and **Florence** (1.5 hours). For in-depth information on Orvieto and Assisi, see *Rick Steves Italy*, and for Florence, see *Rick Steves Florence & Tuscany*.

OSTIA ANTICA DAY TRIP

For an exciting day trip, pop down to the Roman port of Ostia, which is similar to Pompeii but a lot closer and, in some ways, more interesting. Because Ostia was a working port town, it offers a more complete and gritty look at Roman life than wealthier Pompeii. Wandering around today, you'll see warehouses, apartment flats, mansions, shopping arcades, and baths that served a once-thriving port of 60,000 people. With over 70 peaceful park-like acres to explore and relatively few crowds, it's a welcome break from the bustle of Rome.

Orientation

Cost: €8 for the site and museum, €10 with special exhibits.

Hours: April-Aug Tue-Sun 8:30-19:15, Sept Tue-Sun 8:30-19:00, Oct Tue-Sun 8:30-18:30, Nov-mid-Feb Tue-Sun 8:30-16:30, mid-Feb-March Tue-Sun 8:30-17:00, late March Tue-Sun 8:30-17:30, closed Mon year-round, last entry one hour before closing. The museum sometimes closes from 13:30 to 14:30 for lunch.

Getting There: Getting to Ostia Antica from downtown Rome is a snap—it's a 45-minute combination Metro/train ride. (Since the train is part of the Metro system, it only costs one Metro ticket each way—€3 total round-trip.)

From Rome, take Metro line B to the Piramide stop, which is attached to the Roma Porta San Paolo train station. The train tracks are just a few steps from the Metro tracks: Follow signs to *Lido*—go up the escalator, turn left, and go down the steps into the Roma-Lido station. All trains depart in the direction of Lido, leave every 15 minutes, and stop at Ostia Antica along the way. The lighted schedule reads something like, *"Prossima partenza alle ore 13.25, bin 3,"* meaning, "Next departure at 13:25 from track 3." Look for the next train, hop on, ride for about 30 minutes (no need to stamp your Metro ticket again, but keep it handy in case they decide to check), and get off at the Ostia Antica stop.

Leaving the train station in Ostia Antica, cross the road via the blue skybridge and walk straight down Via della Stazione di Ostia Antica, continuing straight until you reach the parking lot. The entrance is to your left. (If you don't have a ticket to get back, purchase one at the ticket window at the station, or from the nearby snack bar.)

Information: A map of the site with suggested itineraries is available for €2 from the ticket office. Tel. 06-5635-0215. Helpful websites include www.ostiaantica.beniculturali.it and www. ostia-antica.org.

Tours: Although you'll see little audioguide markers throughout the site, there may not be audioguides for rent. But you can download this chapter as a free Rick Steves **audio tour** (see page 8).

Length of This Tour: Allow two hours inside the site. Add in your round-trip train rides, and it's at least a four-hour excursion from Rome.

Services: There are WCs at the entrance, near the cafeteria, and (often the cleanest of all) in the modern building behind the marble chunks, east of the cafeteria.

Eating: A small cafeteria with sandwiches, veggies, pasta, and more is next to Ostia's museum. It's also a great place for a discreet picnic.

Sightseeing Tip: If you're using the Metro and want to maximize sightseeing efficiency on your Ostia day trip, consider visiting the sights in south Rome on your return. The Piramide Metro stop—where you'll change trains—really *is* next to a pyramid, and is on the edge of the Testaccio neighborhood, which has several interesting sights. Other south Rome sights include St. Paul's Outside the Walls, E.U.R., and the Montemartini Museum (for more on all of these, see page 101).

Beach Time: The train line that leads to Ostia also connects Romans to their beaches. To combine some fun with your sightseeing, read up on these beaches on page 415.

BACKGROUND

Located at (and named for) the mouth *(ostium)* of the Tiber, Ostia was founded in the fourth century B.C. Gobbled up early by Rome, its main industry was the salt—precious preserver of meat in ancient times—gleaned from nearby salt flats. Often called Rome's first colony, Ostia served as a naval base, protecting Rome from any

Ostia Antica

OSTIA ANTICA

❶ Necropolis
❷ Porta Romana
❸ Republican Warehouses
❹ Baths of Neptune
❺ Theater
❻ Square of the Guilds
❼ Mill
❽ Via Casa di Diana
❾ Forum
❿ Forum Baths
⓫ Ostia Museum

invasion by river. By 150 B.C., when Rome controlled the Mediterranean, Ostia's importance became commercial rather than military. Rome eventually outgrew the port of Ostia, and a vast new port was dug nearby (where Rome's airport now stands). But Ostia remained a key administrative and warehousing center, busy with the big business of keeping more than a million Romans fed and in sandals.

Eventually things really soured for Ostia. Rome fell. The river changed course. The port was abandoned, silted up, became a malaria-infested swamp, and was eventually forgotten. The mud that buried Ostia actually protected it from the ravages of time—and from stone-scavenging medieval peasants.

The Tour Begins

Consider your visit a three-part affair:

1. Follow this tour, which leads you straight down Decumanus Maximus (the town's main drag), with a couple of slight detours, finishing at the forum (the main square).

2. Pop into the museum, and consider getting a bite to eat at the cafeteria.

3. Explore the back lanes—going on a visual scavenger hunt— as you wander your way back to the entry point.

• *Find the map (30 yards inside the gate, on the right) for an orientation. The pale green shows the ancient coast and course of the river—which eventually abandoned its city. Notice how the core of Ostia is a rectangular Roman military camp, with two major roads crossing at the forum. One of four city gates lies ahead, and on your left is the...*

❶ Necropolis

Ancient Romans buried their dead outside the city walls. Ostia was a famously pagan town, slow to become Christian. To a pagan,

the closest thing to an afterlife was to be remembered. If their families could afford it, they'd place the tomb on the roadside with a thumbnail bio carved into the stone that all could read as they came and went (for example, "My name was Caius. I was a baker."). This area was called a ne- cropolis (city of the dead); Christians preferred the term cemetery (from the

Greek for resting place). Detour to find family sepulchers (marked by arches)—private open-air rooms lined with niches for ash-filled urns. Until the first century A.D., cremation was common. In the second and third centuries A.D., the Romans here buried their dead in marble and terra-cotta sarcophagi in tombs.

• *Ahead (where the road narrows) you enter the ancient city of Ostia through the scant remains of the gate called...*

❷ Porta Romana

Just as Rome's Porta San Paolo faced Ostia, Ostia's Porta Romana faced Rome. Inside the gate (which was locked at night) you'd find

a place to leave your animal (on the left) and a warehouse (on the right). To the left (under the big tree), you can see on the gate the bits of the Latin inscription that pro- claimed to all who entered: "The Senate and the people of the colony of Ostia con-

structed the walls." The "colony" reference is a reminder that Ostia was the first bit of the Roman Empire. The big basin, once fed by a fountain, was where animals could be watered. Information panels like the one here are generally helpful only for the artist's reconstruction of the sight. The verbiage is what locals refer to as *aria fritta* (fried air—greasy and heavy but containing nothing of value).

From the gate, Ostia's main street (named Decumanus Maximus) leads straight to the forum, where this walk ends. Note that this road was elevated above some buildings' foundations. Over the centuries, Ostia's ground level rose. You can actually identify buildings from the republic (centuries before Christ) and the empire (centuries after Christ) by their level. Anything you walk down into is from the earlier period.

• *Just inside the gate and to the right are the...*

❸ Republican Warehouses (Magazzini Repubblicani)

The first century B.C. was busy with activities relating to the river port. Walking along the main street, you pass vast warehouses on

the right. The goods of the port, such as grain from Sicily, Egypt, and all of North Africa, were processed and stored in warehouses here (which had elevated floors to keep things dry) before being consumed by Rome.

Ahead, a series of stubby brick columns are the remains of a roofed portico that once provided a shaded walkway into town. Notice the bricks—generally, rough bricks are original, while smooth bricks are part of the reconstruction. Ostia has been picked clean since ancient times. The port's treasures ended up gracing buildings as far away as Constantinople.

• *Continue straight ahead about 100 yards. The little well in the road is medieval—a remnant from Middle Age squatters who found shelter in these ruins. From here, you'll see a viewpoint (with railings, above on the right). Climb up for a view of the...*

❹ Baths of Neptune (Terme di Nettuno)

Examine the fine mosaic depicting Neptune riding four horses through the sea. Apart from the cupid riding the dolphin, the sea looks frightening—which it was. The large square to the left of the mosaic would have been busy with people wrestling, stretching, doing jumping jacks, and getting rubdowns. The niches that ring the square housed small businesses. The row of umbrella pines in the distance marks the original channel of the river before it changed course, abandoning the town.

• *Climb back down to the main drag, and continue to the right until you reach the theater on your right. Enter the theater through its main central gate.*

❺ Theater (Teatro)

The scant remains of the stucco decor under the entry arch hint at the elegance of this place 2,000 years ago. At the end of the tun-

nel, men would bid farewell to their women (before the women went to sit in the higher seats—typical of the gender division in public Rome).

Before you is a typically Roman complex mixing religion, business, and entertainment: a grand theater facing a temple surrounded by a commercial square. Up to 4,000 residents could gather in this theater. Plays were rowdy daytime events—like going to a day game at the ballpark—with lots of audience participation. And heaven help a bad actor. The three rows of marble steps near the orchestra were reserved for the chairs of big shots. In its day, a wall rose behind the stage, enclosing the theater. Even today, this place—one of the oldest brick theaters anywhere—is used for concerts. Climb to the top of the theater for a fine view.

• *From the theater, continue (farther away from the main street) behind the stage into the big square. Head to the right and walk counterclockwise around the square, ending up back at the theater.*

Most of the notable mosaics line the right side of the square.

❻ Square of the Guilds (Piazzale delle Corporazioni)

This grand square evolved from a simple place where businessmen would stroll and powwow together to a monumental square lined with more than 60 offices of ship owners and traders. This was the bustling center of Rome's import-export industry. Along the sidewalk, second-century A.D. mosaics advertise the services offered by the various shops. Walking counterclockwise, circle the square to "read" the mosaics that advertised in Latin and in pictograms for illiterate or non-Latin-reading sailors. The most common symbol—the lighthouse—was the sign of the port of Ostia. Grain containers are reminders that grain was its major import. The elephant marking the office of the Sabratans (a place in present-day Libya) symbolized the sale of ivory or perhaps of exotic animals (great for parties and private spectacles and Colosseum events). The fine mosaic in the corner shows the innovative Roman ships. When ship technology enabled boats to tack and sail against the wind, commerce moved more readily, making the Mediterranean a thriving Roman free-trade zone.

Statues of notable local guild members and business leaders decorated the courtyard. The temple in the center was likely related to Ceres, the goddess of harvest and abundance (prosperity from good business).

At the end of the square, as you leave, notice the small white altar on the right. This would have been used to sacrifice animals—such as the rams carved into the corners—to ask for favor from the gods. The entrails would be read to divine the future and to determine whether the gods were for or against a particular business venture. This altar is a copy; the original is in Rome. (Consider the burden on Italy of protecting and preserving what is actually the cultural heritage of all of Europe against illegal digging, exportation, vandalism, weather, and pollution. There's a special branch of the Carabinieri dedicated to art theft.)

• *Continue down the main street. About two blocks down (look for Tempio Repubblicano on the corner to the right), Via dei Molini marks the wall of the original military* castrum *(rectangular camp). Before continuing straight into that oldest part of Ostia, turn right, down Via dei Molini. Walk about a block and a half until you see Molino del Silvano on the left. (Don't take the left onto Via Casa di Diana—we'll get to that next.)*

❼ Mill (Molino)

This mill and bakery building *(panificio)* dates from A.D. 120. The lava millstones in front of you were used to grind grain. Study the workings: A bowl-like lower structure carefully cupped a moving upper section. Grain would be sprinkled in from a sack hanging from the ceiling. Mules or workers would power the grinding by walking in circles, pushing inserted wood poles. Powdery flour (with not much grit) would eventually tumble out of the bottom of the mill, ready to be made into bread.

• *Now, backtrack half a block down Via dei Molini in the direction of the main street. At the big tree, take the first right onto...*

❽ Via Casa di Diana

There are two places of interest along this street: a tavern (just over halfway down on the left) and a typical apartment building

with stairs leading to a commanding rooftop view (across the street from the tavern, on the right).

At the **Insula of the Thermopolium,** step past the grooved threshold—which once held a sliding wooden door—and belly up to the tavern's bar. You'll see display shelves with food and drinks for sale, a small sink, and a cute fresco advertising food, drink, and music. Too smoky and noisy? Step out back and enjoy the quiet courtyard with the fountain.

The **Insula of the Paintings** is across the street. Climb all the way to the open rooftop for a good view and a chance to imagine life as an apartment dweller in ancient Rome. An *insula* was a multistoried tenement complex where the lower-middle class lived. In ancient times, the lower classes lived in miserable, cramped apartment buildings up to 10 floors high (the average was 5 floors). To reach their rooms on the higher floors, people climbed treehouse-type stairs. Plumbing didn't exist. It was stinky. "Windows" covered with shutters or cloth curtains dipped in grease did little to cut the street din.

Buildings were made cheaply of wood, with weak foundations, so many burned or collapsed. The apartments had no heat and no kitchen, so residents cooked or purchased food elsewhere. They tossed garbage out the windows. Because chariot and cart traffic was allowed only after dark, there was lots of night noise.

The wealthier classes, on the other hand, lived in sprawling and luxurious homes. These were generally built on one floor, with a series of rooms facing a central open courtyard. Decorative pools collected rainwater. Statues, mosaics, and frescoes were everywhere. Rome's wealthy were as comfortable as the poor were wretched.

From this rooftop perch, find the museum (the modern building). Behind the museum, see modern pleasure boats where today's

Tiber leaves Ostia. The temporary arched roofing protects rooms warehousing lots of ancient bits and pieces (worth a look).

• *Now, walk (from street level, of course) to the end of the street, toward the high brick wall and then left into Ostia's...*

❾ Forum

Whenever possible, Rome imposed a grid road plan on its conquered cities. After Rome conquered Ostia in about 400 B.C., it built a military camp, or *castrum*—a rectangular fort with east, west, north, and south gates and two main roads converging on the forum. Throughout the empire, Romans found comfort in this familiar city plan. While people found it no fun to be conquered, the empire brought order and stability to their lives through laws and the creation of grid-planned cities and grand squares such as this one.

Ostia's main square became a monumental forum in the imperial period. And dominating this square, as in most Roman towns, was the **grand temple** (from A.D. 120). The marble veneer was scavenged in the Middle Ages, leaving only the core brickwork. Note the reinforcement arches in the brick. The temple, called the Capitolium (after the original atop Capitoline Hill in Rome), was dedicated to the pagan trinity of Jupiter, Juno, and Minerva. A forum dominated by a Capitolium temple was a standard feature of colonies throughout the empire. The purpose: to transport the Roman cult of Jupiter, Juno, and Minerva to the newly conquered population.

On the opposite side of the square, distinguished by its sawed-off column, is the Temple of Roma and Augustus. Its position is powerfully symbolic. The power of the emperor stands equal, facing the power of the Capitolium Triad.

The basilica also faces the forum square. Dating from about A.D. 100, this was where legal activities and commercial business took place. (With your back to the Capitolium temple, it's to your right and consists of little more than the footprint of the building.) Its central nave and two side aisles lead to the "high altar," where the judge sat.

Behind the Capitolium temple—and a little to the right—the pink modern building houses the fine little Ostia Museum. Behind that is a shop and a modern cafeteria. From the forum, the Decumanus Maximus continues into a vast urban expanse, great for simply wandering (see "Archaeological Scavenger Hunt" at the end of this chapter).

• *But first, make one more stop. Walk to the front left corner of the Temple of Roma and Augustus. As you're facing it, look left for a street marked by a grand arch. This leads to Ostia's best and largest baths (entrance on right).*

⓾ Forum Baths (Terme del Foro)

As you wander around this huge complex, try to imagine it peopled, steaming, and busy. Government-subsidized baths were a popular social and business meeting place in any Roman city. Roman engineers were experts at radiant heat. A huge furnace heated both the water and air that flowed through pipes under the floors and in the walls (you can see the hollow bricks in the walls). Notice the fine marble steps—great for lounging—that led into the pools. Bathers used olive oil rather than soap to wash, so the water needed to be periodically skimmed by servants. Like a high-end spa, there was a *laconicum* (sweating room), two *tepidariae* (where Romans were rubbed down by masseuses), and the once-steamy *caldarium* with three pools.

From the baths (across the street and a bit to the right from the entry), find the 20-hole latrine. You can still see the pivot hole in the floor that once supported its revolving door. The cutout below each seat was to accommodate the washable sponge on a stick, which was used rather than toilet paper. Rushing water below each seat (brought in by aqueduct) did the flushing. So much for privacy—even today, there's no word in Italian for it.

⓫ Ostia Museum

This small museum offers a delightful look at some of Ostia's finest statuary. Without worrying too much about exactly what's what, just wander and imagine these fine figures—tangled wrestlers,

kissing cupids, playful gods—adorning the courtyards of wealthy Ostian families. Most of the statues are second- and third-century A.D. Roman pieces inspired by rare and famous Greek originals. The portrait busts are of real people—the kind you'd sit next to in the baths (or on the toilets).

Roman sculptors excelled at realistic busts. Roman religion revered the man of the house (and his father and grandfather). Statues of daddy and grandpa were common in the corner of any proper house. And with the emperor considered a god, you'd find his bust in classrooms, at the post office, and so on. The sarcophagi (marble coffins) generally show mythological scenes.

Perhaps the most interesting room (to the left as you enter, just before the steps) features statuary from religions of foreign lands. Being a port town, Ostia accommodated people (and their worship needs) from all over the known world. The large statue of a man sacrificing a bull is a Mithraic altarpiece (see page 311).

The **cafeteria, WC,** and **shop** are in a modern building just behind the museum.

ARCHAEOLOGICAL SCAVENGER HUNT

As you return to the entry gate, get off the main drag and explore Ostia's back streets. Wandering beyond the forum and then taking the back lanes as you return to the entry, see if you can find:

- Tarp- and sand-protected mosaic flooring.
- White cornerstones put into buildings to fend off wild carts and reflect corners in the dark.
- Fast-food fish joint (on Decumanus Maximus, just beyond the forum).
- Hidden bits of fresco (clue: under hot tin roofs).
- Republican buildings and buildings dating from the empire.
- Stucco roughed up for fresco work (before applying the wet plaster of a fresco, the surface needs to be systematically gouged so the plaster can grip the wall).
- Millstones for grinding grain (Ostia's big industry).
- Floor patterns made colorful with inlaid marble.
- A *domus*—a single-family dwelling facing a fancy, central open-air courtyard.

TIVOLI
DAY TRIP

At the edge of the Sabine Hills, 18 miles east of Rome, sits the medieval hill town of Tivoli, a popular retreat since ancient times. Today, it's famous for two very different villas: Hadrian's Villa, a Versailles-like seat of government from which the emperor ruled (outside but still near the capital), and the restored Villa d'Este, the lush and watery 16th-century residence of a cardinal in exile. These two sights complement each other well: While Hadrian's Villa is about evocative ruins that ache with an untold history, Villa d'Este is simply beautiful, carefree, and relaxing—a pure confection.

Getting to Tivoli, you'll likely travel along the Via Tiburtina. The road was initially built by the ancient Romans; today it takes you through areas of ugly concrete sprawl. Famous for its thermal baths (smell the sulfur?), the area also contains the travertine quarries that supplied Rome with material for many of its buildings, including the Colosseum. While you're out in the countryside, also keep an eye out for the many olive groves (this area bottles up the prized Sabina olive oil), as well as flocks of sheep that produce the local *pecorino romano* cheese.

PLANNING YOUR TIME

Because public-transportation connections are a bit complicated and time-consuming, give yourself the better part of a day for the trip to Tivoli, and to see both of the villas. Note that Hadrian's Villa is open daily, Villa d'Este is closed on Monday, and fewer buses run on Sunday.

If visiting both villas, see Villa d'Este first, then head straight back to Rome after Hadrian's Villa.

GETTING TO TIVOLI

With a Tour or Driver: Several Rome tour companies—including Context Rome, Rome Walks, and Through Eternity—offer private tours of the villas (see their respective websites for specifics; tour companies listed on page 30). You can also hire a driver for the day to make the trip there and back faster and easier (drivers are recommended on page 33).

On Your Own: Reaching the town of Tivoli and Villa d'Este is easy. Getting to Hadrian's Villa is more of a challenge and requires patience, but many find it well worth the trouble.

From Rome, take a Metro/bus combination. Ride Metro line B to Ponte Mammolo (direction: Rebibbia), and then catch the local blue Cotral bus to Tivoli (€2.20, 3/hour, 50 minutes; at Ponte Mammolo, check the monitor for departure schedule, then buy bus tickets at the bar or newsstand downstairs, easiest to buy return ticket at the same time, buses leave upstairs—and can be crowded, be prepared to stand, validate ticket on board, direction: Tivoli, www.cotralspa.it/TrovaPercorso.asp).

If you're only going to **Hadrian's Villa** and not all the way to Tivoli, hop off the Cotral bus shortly after passing the quarries and walk approximately 20 minutes through a residential area (ask the driver or fellow passengers which stop you need for "Villa Adriana"; it's roughly 35 minutes from Ponte Mammolo). The way is not well-signed, so don't be shy about asking locals for directions.

For **Villa d'Este,** get off in downtown Tivoli, near the central square and the big park with the playground (start paying attention as the bus winds up the hill—your stop is shortly after it levels out; ask the driver, "Villa d'Este?"). The round TI kiosk is just uphill to the right. The entrance to the villa is across the square, past the modern-art arch—follow the signs (for about a block downhill).

To get to **Hadrian's Villa** from downtown Tivoli, catch orange "CAT" city bus #4X. Buy your ticket at a tobacco shop (there's one right where you got off the Cotral bus) or newsstand (€1, bus stop is near the playground, every 40 minutes, 10-minute ride, infrequent on Sun, www.cattivoli.com). Bus #4X takes you very close to the villa entrance; #4 works in a pinch, but leaves you a 20-minute walk from the villa. A taxi is €10-15 (look for one near the arch in the main square under the pine trees; confirm the price before getting in).

When you're ready to leave Hadrian's Villa, catch bus #4X in the direction of Tivoli (sporadically passes right in front of the site, ask for schedule and directions when you buy entrance ticket, bus tickets also available). To continue on to Rome, get off at the main road, Via Tiburtina, and change to a Cotral bus (confirm destination with bus driver—you want *"per Roma";* have your Cotral ticket in advance). Note that some buses go to the train station in Tivoli, where departures are sporadic but will eventually get you back to Rome (usually Tiburtina station)—the bus is better.

Orientation to Tivoli

The town of Tivoli, with Villa d'Este in its center, is about 2.5 miles from Hadrian's Villa ("Villa Adriana" in Italian). Pick up a map and bus schedule at the **TI** on Largo Garibaldi, near the bus stop (TI open Tue-Sun 9:30-17:30, closed Mon, tel. 0774-313-536).

Sights in Tivoli

▲VILLA D'ESTE

Clinging to a steep hillside just below Tivoli's main square, this Renaissance-era palace has a dull interior but a spectacularly en-

tertaining garden, divinely landscaped and punctuated by pools, streams, waterfalls, and thundering fountains that harness the natural hydro power of the Aniene River. If you can handle the many stairs (it's more vertical than horizontal), exploring these gardens is a peaceful and picturesque experience.

Cost and Hours: €8, €11 with special exhibits, May-Aug Tue-Sun 8:30-19:45, April until 19:30, Sept until 19:15, Oct

until 18:30, closes earlier Nov-March, closed Mon year-round, last entry one hour before closing, audioguide-€4, tel. 0774-335-850 or 0774-332-920, www. villadestetivoli.info.

Background: Ippolito d'Este's grandfather, Alexander VI, was the pope. Ippolito was fast-tracked for church service from birth and became a cardinal. His claim to fame: his pleasure palace at Tivoli. In the 1550s, he destroyed a Benedictine monastery to

build this fanciful late-Renaissance palace. Like Hadrian's Villa, the Villa d'Este is a large residential estate. But this one features hundreds of Baroque fountains, all gravity-powered. The Aniene River, frazzled into countless threads, weaves its way entertainingly through the villa. At the bottom of the garden, the exhausted little streams once again team up to make a sizable river. Pirro Ligorio, Tivoli's architect, was also the archaeologist in charge of excavat-

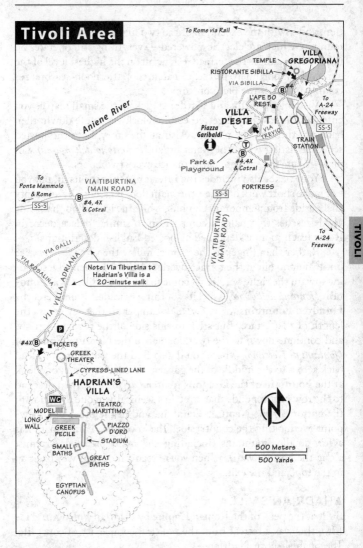

Tivoli Area

To Rome via Rail

Aniene River

VILLA GREGORIANA

TEMPLE

RISTORANTE SIBILLA

VIA SIBILLA

L'APE 50 REST.

VILLA D'ESTE

Piazza Garibaldi

TIVOLI

VIA TREVIO

To A-24 Freeway

SS-5

TRAIN STATION

Park & Playground

#4,4X & Cotral

FORTRESS

To Ponte Mammolo & Rome

SS-5

VIA TIBURTINA (MAIN ROAD)

#4, 4X & Cotral

SS-5

VIA TIBURTINA (MAIN ROAD)

To A-24 Freeway

VIA GALLI

VIA ROSALINA

VIA VILLA ADRIANA

Note: Via Tiburtina to Hadrian's Villa is a 20-minute walk

TICKETS

#4X

GREEK THEATER

CYPRESS-LINED LANE

HADRIAN'S VILLA

WC

MODEL

LONG WALL

GREEK PECILE

TEATRO MARITTIMO

PIAZZO D'ORO

STADIUM

SMALL BATHS

GREAT BATHS

EGYPTIAN CANOPUS

500 Meters

500 Yards

TIVOLI

ing Hadrian's Villa, and that site provided much in both inspiration and raw material for the fancy fountains of Villa d'Este. Ligorio could basically use Hadrian's Villa as a quarry to provide statuary and decorative stonework for his vision here.

The cardinal had a political falling-out with Rome, and he was exiled. With this watery wonderland on a cool hillside with fine views, he made sure Romans would come to visit. It's symbolic of the luxurious tastes and secular interests of the cardinal.

After years of neglect, the villa has been completely restored. All the most eye-popping fountains have been put back in opera-tion, and—with the exception of the two highest jets of the central fountain, which are electric-powered—everything still operates on natural hydraulics. The terrace restaurant on the highest level of the garden is opportunely placed to catch cool afternoon sea breezes coming in across the plain of Rome.

Visiting the Villa and Gardens: Pick up the small map as you enter, and follow its suggested counterclockwise route down, then back up, through the garden. Also at the entry, note the posted schedule listing when the water organ *(la fontana dell'organa)* will play—a cute five-minute performance every two hours.

Your ticket also includes the **interior** of the villa itself, but you can make short work of that—the main floor is essentially an empty shell, aside from temporary exhibits, while the lower floor has some vivid frescoes that pale in comparison to similar palace decor in Rome (each room is described by posted English descriptions).

Rather than linger in the rooms, follow the signs for *giardino* until you pop out at the terrace overlooking the gardens. Descending toward the right, you'll first come to the grotto-like **Oval Fountain** *(fontana dell'ovato),* with its soothing cascades. From here, the **Hundred Fountains** *(cento fontane)* scamper all the way across the length of the terrace. But stick to this side of the garden for now, and continue down to the overlook above the **Neptune Fountain** *(fontana di Nettuno),* where you'll also find the water organ. Head back across to the middle of the garden, descending for a good look at the **Fountain of the Dragons** *(fontana dei draghi).* Then descend to the row of fish ponds that stretches scenically in one direction to the bottom of the Neptune Fountain, and in the other to a viewpoint overlooking the countryside. The lowest level of the park has a few smaller fountains (including the many-breasted Artemis, along the bottom wall). When you're ready, huff your way back up to the top...and the exit.

▲HADRIAN'S VILLA

Built at the peak of the Roman Empire by Hadrian (ruled A.D. 117-138), this was a retreat from the political complexity of court life. The Spanish-born Hadrian—an architect, lover of Greek culture (nicknamed "The Little Greek"), and great traveler—envisioned the site as a microcosm of the lands he ruled as emperor, which at that point stretched from England to the Euphrates and encompassed countless diverse cultures. In the spirit of Legoland, Epcot, and Las Vegas, he

TIVOLI

re-created famous structures from around the world, producing a kind of diorama of his empire in the form of the largest and richest Roman villa anywhere. Just as Louis XIV governed France from Versailles rather than Paris, Hadrian ruled Rome from this villa of more than 300 evocative acres. He basically spent his last decade here. Regrettably, this "Versailles of Ancient Rome" was plundered by barbarians and Renaissance big shots who all wanted something classical in their courtyards. They even burned the marble to make lime for cement. The scavenged art wound up in the Vatican Museum, the Louvre, and other museums throughout Europe. Today, Hadrian's Villa is a harmonious blend of nature and ruins—ideal for wandering while pondering the legacy of a great civilization.

Cost and Hours: €8, €11 with special exhibits, cash only, daily May-Aug 9:00-19:30, April and Sept 9:00-19:00, closes as early as 17:00 off-season, last entry 1.5 hours before closing, audioguide-€5, tel. 0774-382-733.

Visiting the Ruins: Information at the site is sparse, but occasional posted maps and English descriptions do help keep you on track.

From the ticket booth, hike about 10 minutes up the main path through olive groves. You'll reach a field with a WC (hidden underground); beyond that, inside the modern beige building, is a **model** of the reconstructed site that's helpful for getting oriented.

Just beyond that, go through the high brick wall to pop out at the Athenian-style **Greek Pecile,** a long, enclosed courtyard with a tranquil, fish-stocked pond. This wall—and the pond—are all that remain of the original structure.

Beyond the left end of the pond is a cluster of other ruins, including the long stadium and the **Teatro Marittimo** (a circular palace, Hadrian's favorite retreat on an island, where he did his serious thinking). Continuing up through the ruins and to the left, you'll reach what's left of the palace itself; at the far corner is the vast **Piazza d'Oro,** which was once filled with fountains and flowing water.

Looping back around, you'll come to a dramatic overview of the gigantic (and aptly named) **Great Baths** complex. Descending to explore this area, continue to the left to find the villa's highlight, the **Egyptian Canopus** (sanctuary of the god Serapi), a canal lined with statues.

Backtrack a bit to complete your loop, passing the **Small Baths** on your way to the Pecile. When you get back to the long wall, walk through it and continue straight ahead, down the cypress-lined lane, to reach the circular temple; stairs on the left lead down to the **Greek Theater,** and then back to the entrance.

TIVOLI

Modern Tivoli was heavily reconstructed after being bombed during World War II, when it was a Nazi stronghold. While most of Tivoli blankets the hilltop in less-than-charming concrete, a more rustic and picturesque quarter clings to the cliffs above a gorge on the back side of town. This area, anchored by the sleepy Piazza Rivarola, has a few evocative ancient ruins of its own. Strolling the main pedestrian drag gives you a glimpse of a small, unembellished Italian town.

Eateries catering to tourists cluster around the main square, Largo Garibaldi—but for more choices and a better look at this tidy, no-frills town, head up Via del Trevio (which eventually curves and becomes Via Palatina then Via Ponte Gregoriano). This also takes you to the more scenic, older part of Tivoli—well-worth exploring.

About a 10-minute walk from Largo Garibaldi, you'll arrive at l'Ape 50 (on the left), a classy but unpretentious place serving gourmet sandwiches and other foods at a reasonable price (big €5 sandwiches, daily 12:00-15:00 & 18:00-24:00, may close Sun-Tue in winter, seating inside or out, Via di Ponte Gregoriano 5, tel. 0774-556-471).

Farther on, angling left at Piazza Rivarola, you'll find the gourmet's choice for a splurge, **Ristorante Sibilla.** It's been open since 1720 but boasts a trendy, modern ambience. The restaurant neighbors two ancient temples, provides a glimpse of the waterfalls from its spectacularly set terrace, and offers pricey but tasty traditional cuisine (€9-12 pastas, €18-22 *secondi*, Tue-Sun 12:30-15:30 & 19:30-22:30, closed Mon, reserve for outdoor seating, Via della Sibilla 50, tel. 0774-335-281).

Adjacent to the restaurant is the back entrance to the steep park called **Villa Gregoriana,** which incorporates a landscape enjoyed from antiquity to the Romantic Age and today. Over a 1.5-mile network of trails, you'll descend into the Aniene River valley, passing views of waterfalls, trees, and raw wilderness. For those with more interest in nature than antiquity—although bits of the ancient villa remain—it offers a convenient alternative to Hadrian's Villa (€6, April-Oct Tue-Sun 10:00-18:30, shorter hours off-season, closed Jan-Feb and Mon year-round, last entry one hour before closing, several hundred feet of elevation change over uneven steps—good shoes and knees helpful, tel. 0774-332-650). From the exit/main entrance (on the other side of the ravine from where you entered), it's a 15-minute walk back to the center of town. Or bus #4 leaves sporadically from the piazza out front (Largo San Angelo) and goes through the center of town on its way to Hadrian's Villa and beyond (tickets at green newspaper kiosk or Flo's Bar, but better to buy ahead).

NAPLES AND POMPEII DAY TRIP

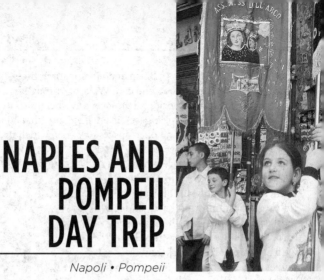

Napoli • Pompeii

While the Eternal City can keep you busy for ages, here are two excuses to leave Rome for a day. The trip south to Naples and Pompeii is demanding (four to five hours of train travel round-trip). But you'll be rewarded for your time with a chance to wander ancient Rome's most evocative ruins and go on an urban safari in what is perhaps Europe's most intense city.

If you have a week in Rome and are interested in maximum travel thrills, take a day trip to Naples and Pompeii. (See map on page 447.) Note that Naples' Archaeological Museum is closed on Tuesday. Pompeii is open daily.

Naples (Napoli)

If you like Italy as far south as Rome, go farther south—it gets better. If Italy is getting on your nerves, don't go farther. Italy intensifies as you plunge deeper. Naples is Italy in the extreme—its best (birthplace of pizza and Sophia Loren) and its worst (home of the Camorra, Naples' "family" of organized crime).

Neapolis ("new city") was a thriving Greek commercial center 2,500 years ago. Today, it remains southern Italy's leading city. Naples impresses visitors with one of Europe's top archaeological museums (holding the artistic treasures of Pompeii), fascinating churches that convey the city's unique personality and powerful devotion, an underground warren of Greek and Roman ruins, fine works of art (including pieces by Caravaggio, who lived here for a time), and evocative nativity scenes (called *presepi*). Naples, of course, makes the best pizza you'll find anywhere, and tasty pastries as well (try the crispy, ricotta-stuffed *sfogliatella*). But more than anything, Naples has a brash and vibrant street life—"Italy in your face" in ways both good and bad. Walking through its colorful old town is one of my favorite experiences anywhere in Europe.

Naples—Italy's third-largest city, with more than one million people—has almost no open spaces or parks, which makes its position as Europe's most densely populated city plenty evident. Watching the police try to enforce traffic sanity is almost comical in Italy's grittiest, most polluted, and most crime-ridden city. But Naples surprises the observant traveler with its impressive knack for living, eating, and raising children in the streets with good humor and

decency. Overcome your fear of being run down or ripped off long enough to talk with people. Enjoy a few smiles and jokes with the man running the neighborhood tripe shop, or the woman taking her day-care class on a walk through the traffic.

The pulse of Italy throbs in Naples. Like Cairo or Mumbai, it's appalling and captivating at the same time, the closest thing to "reality travel" that you'll find in Western Europe. But this tangled mess still somehow manages to breathe, laugh, and sing—with a joyful Italian accent. Thanks to its reputation as a crime-ridden and dangerous place, Naples doesn't get nearly as many tourists as it deserves. While the city has its problems, it has improved a lot in recent years. And even though it's a bit edgy, I feel comfortable here. Naples richly rewards those who venture in.

PLANNING YOUR TIME

A blitz visit to Naples and Pompeii looks something like this:

7:35	Catch the express train from Rome to Naples Centrale train station, where you'll head downstairs to transfer to the commuter train to Pompeii.
10:00	Tour Pompeii, grab a quick lunch (it's best to bring a picnic), then catch the commuter train back to Naples.
14:30	Visit Naples' Archaeological Museum during the heat of the day (closed Tue).
15:30	Take my self-guided "Slice of Neapolitan Life" walk.
18:30	Finish with a pizza dinner as the city comes to life in the early evening.
20:30	Hop on the train back to Rome.
22:30	Arrive in Rome.

Orientation to Naples

Naples is set deep inside the large and curving Bay of Naples, with Mount Vesuvius looming just five miles away. Although Naples is a sprawling city, its fairly compact core contains the most interesting sights. The tourist's Naples is a triangle, with its points at the Centrale train station in the east, the Archaeological Museum to the west, and the Piazza del Plebiscito (with the Royal Palace) and the port to the south. Steep hills rise above this historic core, including San Martino, capped with a mighty fortress.

TOURIST INFORMATION

Central Naples has six TIs (run variously by the city, the region, and a local business association), all of which are equally incapable

of dispensing reliable advice. All are understaffed and have little to offer besides free maps. The most convenient—but perhaps least helpful—is in the **Centrale train station** (daily 9:00-18:00, near track 23, operated by a private agency, tel. 081-268-779).

Other TIs are scattered around town: There are two near **Piazza del Plebiscito,** near the port: one right on the piazza at #14, under the arches to the right of church entrance (Mon-Fri 9:00-19:00, closed Sat-Sun, tel. 081-795-6162); and another by the entrance to the Galleria Umberto I shopping mall, across from Teatro di San Carlo (Mon-Sat 9:00-17:00, Sun 9:00-13:00, tel. 081-402-394). Along Spaccanapoli, there's an office across from the **Church of Gesù Nuovo** (Mon-Sat 9:00-17:00, Sun 9:00-13:00, tel. 081-551-2701). By the Museo Metro stop, in the park next to the **Archaeological Museum,** is a tiny information kiosk (Mon-Fri 10:00-17:00, Sat 10:00-14:00, closed Sun). And cruise-ship passengers exiting the **cruise terminal** complex through a little checkpoint (marked *Molo Angioino*) will find a small TI.

For information online, the best overall website is www.inaples.it. At www.inaples.it/eng/quinapoli.htm, you can download the PDF version of the *Qui Napoli* booklet, which lists museum hours, events, and transportation info. A print version is occasionally available at the TI.

ARRIVAL IN NAPLES
By Train
Express trains from Rome arrive at the main station, **Napoli Centrale.**

Naples

To Museo di Capodimonte
Piazza Cavour
To Museo Cavour
VIA FORIA   CARBONARA
Piazza Capuana
CASANOVA   NOV.
Alibus (to Airport)
FIRENZE
#1
ARCHAEO-LOGICAL MUSEUM
PESSINA
Museo
S. APOST
S. PAOLO
VIA DUOMO
DUOMO
S. POERIO
B
Piazza Garibaldi
CENTRALE STN.(F.S.)
CAPPELLA SANSEVERO
VIA S. BIAGIO
PIO MONTE MISERICORDIA
FORCELLA
FISH MKT.
CORSO GARIBALDI
Piazza Dante
Dante
SAN DOM.
VIA B. CROCE
"SPACCANAPOLI"
Porta Nolana
To Pompeii (Ruins) & Sorrento
Monte-santo Metro & Funicular
TARSIA
GESÙ NUOVO
CORSO UMBERTO
PORTA NOLANA CIRCUMVESUVIANA TERMINUS STN.
SANTA CHIARA & CLOISTER
VIA P. SCURA
Piazza Carità
VIA ROMA
VIA DIAZ
Piazza Bovio
Università
NUOVA MARINA
Toledo
#R4 (to Arch. Mus.)
DEPRETIS
VIA C. COLOMBO
Port
SPANISH QUARTER
CORSO VIT. EMAN.
Centrale Funicular
GALLERIA UMBERTO I
Municipio
Piazza Municipio
Alibus (to Airport)
#1 (to Train Stn.)
STAZIONE MARITTIMA
Car Ferries to Sicily & Sardinia
TEATRO DI SANCARLO
CASTEL NUOVO
MOLO BEVERELLO DOCK
ROYAL PALACE
Piazza del Plebiscito
S. FRAN. DI PAOLA
To Sorrento, Capri, Ischia & Procida
See "Slice of Neapolitan Life Walk" detail map
VITTORIO TUNNEL
VIA NAZARIO SAURO
Bay of Naples
N
VIA PARTENOPE
To Lungomare
CASTEL DELL'OVO
BORGO MARINARO
500 Meters
500 Yards

It's been spruced up in the past few years and has lots of facilities, including a small TI (near track 23), an ATM (at Banco di Napoli near track 24), a bookstore (*La Feltrinelli*, daily 7:00-21:00, near track 24), a baggage check (€6/5 hours, then €0.90/hour, daily 8:00-20:00, marked *deposito bagagli*, near track 5), and a ticket office (daily 5:50-21:10). WCs (€1) are down the stairs across from track 13. Immediately downstairs is the **Garibaldi** train station, which you'll use if you ride to Pompeii (see next).

CONTINUING TO POMPEII ON THE CIRCUMVESUVIANA

Naples and Pompeii are connected by a **commuter train**—the Ferrovia Circumvesuviana—handy for tourists, commuters...and pickpockets (www.vesuviana.it). Note: When coming from Rome, don't be tempted to take a Trenitalia connection to the stop called "Pompei," which leaves you at a station in the ugly, modern city center—a long walk to the actual site. It's better to simply get off at Naples' Centrale Station and transfer to the Circumvesuviana.

At Naples' Centrale Station, follow Circumvesuviana signs downstairs and down the corridor to the Circumvesuviana ticket windows and turnstiles. There are two trains per hour to Pompeii—just take any train marked for Sorrento, and get off at the stop called Pompei Scavi-Villa Misteri (about 40 minutes, €2.90 one-way, not covered by rail passes, skip the day pass except on weekends when it's half-price). When you buy your ticket, ask which track your train will depart from ("Quale binario?"; KWAH-lay bee-NAH-ree-oh). Insert your ticket at the turnstiles and find your platform (down another level). As you board, double-check with a local that the train goes to your destination, as the Circumvesuviana has several lines that branch out.

The Circumvesuviana also has another station in central Naples (called Napoli Porta Nolana, across from the Porta Nolana fish market), but there's no reason to use it unless you happen to be nearby.

When returning to Naples on the Circumvesuviana, remember that the name of the Circumvesuviana stop at Centrale Station is "Garibaldi."

HELPFUL HINTS

Theft Alert: While most travelers visit Naples completely safely, err on the side of caution. Don't venture into neighborhoods that make you uncomfortable. The areas close to the train station are especially seedy. Walk with confidence, as if you know where you're going and what you're doing. Touristy Spaccanapoli and the posh Via Toledo shopping boulevard are more upscale, but you'll still see rowdy kids and panhandlers. Assume able-bodied beggars are thieves.

Stick to busy streets and beware of gangs of hoodlums. A third of the city is unemployed, and past local governments have set an example that the Mafia would be proud of. Assume con artists are more clever than you. Any jostle or commotion is probably a thief-team smokescreen. To keep bags safe, it's probably best to leave them back in Rome or at the left-luggage office in Centrale Station.

Always walk on the sidewalk (even if the locals don't) and carry your bag on the side away from the street—thieves on scooters have been known to snatch bags as they swoop by. The less you have dangling from you (including cameras and necklaces), the better.

Perhaps your biggest risk of theft is while catching or riding the Circumvesuviana commuter train. If you're connecting from a long-distance express, you'll be stepping from a relatively secure compartment into an often crowded and dingy train, where disoriented tourists with luggage delicately mix with the residents of Naples' most down-at-heel districts. It's prime hunting ground for thieves. While I ride the Circumvesuviana comfortably and safely, each year I hear of many travelers who get ripped off on this ride. You won't be mugged—but you may be conned or pickpocketed. Especially late at night, the Circumvesuviana train is plagued by intimidating ruffians. For maximum safety and peace of mind, sit in the front car, where the driver will double as your protector, and avoid riding it after dark.

Con artists may say you need to "transfer" by taxi to catch the Circumvesuviana; you don't. Carry your own bags and keep valuables buttoned up.

Traffic Safety: In Naples, red lights are discretionary, and pedestrians need to be wary, particularly of motor scooters. Even on "pedestrian" streets, stay alert to avoid being sideswiped by scooters that nudge their way through the crowds. Keep children close. Smart tourists jaywalk in the shadow of bold and confident locals, who generally ignore crosswalks. Wait for a break in traffic, cross with confidence, and make eye contact with approaching drivers. The traffic will stop.

Supermarket: Superò is a block off Piazza Dante, close to Via Toledo and Spaccanapoli (Mon-Sat 8:30-20:30, Sun 8:30-14:00, Via San Domenico Soriano 20e).

GETTING AROUND NAPLES

Naples' entire public transportation system—Metro, buses, funicular railways, and the single tram line—uses the same tickets, which must be stamped as you enter (in the yellow machines). A €1.30 single transit ticket gives you the run of the system for 1.5 hours, with unlimited changes. Tickets are sold at *tabacchi* stores, some newsstands, and occasionally at station windows; the few ticket machines you'll see are usually out of order. A *giornaliero* day pass costs €3.70 (€3.10 on weekends) and pays for itself with three rides, but can be hard to find; many *tabacchi* stores don't sell them. For general information, maps, and fares in English, visit www.unicocampania.it. For schedules, your only option is the Italian-only site www.anm.it.

By Subway: Naples' subway, the *Metropolitana,* has three main lines.

Line 1 is currently being extended, adding several new stations that will eventually make it very useful for tourists. The completion dates given here are subject to change: From the Museo stop

(Archaeological Museum), line 1 heads to Dante (at Piazza Dante, between the museum and Spaccanapoli), Toledo (south end of Via Toledo, near Piazza del Plebiscito), Municipio (may open in 2015; at Piazza Municipio, just above the harbor and cruise terminal), Università (the university), Duomo (scheduled to open in 2016; near the cathedral and the end of my self-guided walk), and Garibaldi (on Piazza Garibaldi in front of Centrale Station).

Line 2 (technically part of the Italian rail system) is most useful for getting from the train station to the Archaeological Museum quickly: It runs from Centrale Station (catch it downstairs—the stop is called Garibaldi; usually leaves from *binario* 4) to Piazza Cavour (by the Archaeological Museum) to Montesanto (top of Spanish Quarter and Spaccanapoli street, and base of funicular up to San Martino). The new line 6 is not yet complete; it will begin at Municipio and head west—unlikely to be of much use to tourists.

Station entrances and signs to the Metro are marked by a red square with a white *M*.

By Funicular: Central Naples' three funiculars *(funicolare)* carry commuters and sightseers into the hilly San Martino neighborhood just west of downtown. All three converge near Piazza Fuga, a short walk from the hilltop fortress and monastery/museum. The Centrale line runs from the Spanish Quarter, just near Piazza del Plebiscito and the Toledo Metro stop; the Montesanto line from the Montesanto Metro stop and Via Pignasecca market zone; and the Chiaia line from near the Piazza Amadeo Metro stop.

By Bus: Buses can be handy for certain trips, such as getting from the port to the Archaeological Museum (bus #R4), or if you curtail my self-guided walk from Via Toledo back to the station. But buses are crowded and poorly signed, and aren't a user-friendly option for uninitiated newcomers.

By Tram: Tram line #1 runs along Corso Garibaldi (at the other end of the big square from Centrale Station) and down to the waterfront, terminating by the ferry and cruise terminals (direction: *Stazione Marittima;* with your back to the station, the tram heads toward the left). It's useful if you're connecting from boat to train, or returning to the port after finishing my self-guided walk.

By Taxi: Taxi drivers in Naples are notorious for overcharging. A short ride in town should cost €10-12. Ask for the *tariffa predeterminata* (a fixed rate). There are some legitimate extra charges (baggage fees, €2.50 supplement after 22:00 or all day Sun and holidays). Radio Taxi 8888 is one reputable company (tel. 081-8888).

Tours in Naples

Local Guides

Pina Esposito knows her ancient archaeology and art and does fine private walking and driving tours of Naples and the region (Pompeii, Capri, the Amalfi Coast, etc.), including Naples' Archaeological Museum (€60/hour, 2-hour minimum, 10 percent off with this book, lower rates for full-day tours, mobile 366-622-8217, giuseppina.esposito20@istruzione.it). The team at **Mondo Guide** also offers private tours of the museum (€120/2 hours), city (€240/4 hours), and region, along with a special deal for my readers—see sidebar (tel. 081-751-3290, www.mondoguide.it, info@mondoguide.it).

Hop-On, Hop-Off Bus Tours

CitySightseeing Napoli tour buses make three different loops through the city, allowing riders to get on and off to explore. While the city's most engaging charms are buried in the tight tangle of lanes near Spaccanapoli, a bus tour does give you a better sense of

Mondo Tours Offers Shared Tours for Rick Steves Readers

Mondo Tours, a big Naples-based company, offers co-op tours for my readers. These include a private, professional guide at a fraction of the usual cost, because you're sharing the expense with other travelers using this book. Their tours, which run from April through October, include **Pompeii** (€15; the €11 Pompeii entry is extra; daily at 10:30, 1.5 hours, meet in Pompeii at Ristorante Suisse on Piazza Esedra) and a walking tour of **Naples** (€25, daily at 15:00, 3 hours, meet at steps of Archaeological Museum—not included in walk). They also offer an **Amalfi Coast** minibus tour from Sorrento for €50. For specifics and to sign up, see their website, www.mondoguide.it, and select the Rick Steves tab (Mondo tel. 081-751-3290, mobile 340-460-5254, info@mondoguide.it). *You'll need to book in advance* using your credit-card number to hold a spot, then pay cash for the tour. If you must cancel, email them more than three days in advance or you'll be billed. You'll be sent an email confirmation when your tour reaches the required minimum of participants to make it run (6 people for Pompeii and Naples, 8 people for Amalfi Coast).

the greater Naples that this chapter largely ignores (€22, ticket valid 24 hours, sparse frequency—4-11/day depending on route, buy from driver or from kiosk at Piazza Municipio in front of Castel Nuovo near the port, scant recorded narration; for details, see the brochure at the TI, tel. 081-551-7279, www.napoli.city-sightseeing. it). The same company offers another route, traversing the historical center in an open-top minibus, but it's of marginal value as it misses the city's best parts: the pedestrian areas (€7, €25 combo-ticket with the main route, 40-minute loop, departs in front of the Church of Gesù Nuovo).

Self-Guided Tour

▲▲▲ARCHAEOLOGICAL MUSEUM (MUSEO ARCHEOLOGICO)

This museum offers the best possible peek at the art and decorations of Pompeii and Herculaneum, the two ancient burgs that were buried in ash by the eruption of Mount Vesuvius in A.D. 79. For lovers of antiquity, this museum alone makes Naples a worthwhile stop. When Pompeii was excavated in the late 1700s, Naples'

Bourbon king bellowed, "Bring me the best of what you find!"
The finest art and artifacts ended up here, and today, the ancient
sites themselves are impressive but barren. (Pompeii is described in
detail later in this chapter.)

Orientation

Cost and Hours: €8, sometimes more for temporary exhibits, cash
only, Wed-Mon 9:00-19:30, closed Tue, last entry 30 minutes
before closing. Early and temporary closures are noted on a
board near the ticket office. In July and August, expect many
rooms to be closed due to lack of staff.

Getting There: To take the **subway** *(Metropolitana)* from Centrale
Station, follow the signs to the Garibaldi subway station (down
the stairs in front of track 13). Buy a single transit ticket at the
newsstand or a tobacco shop (unless you're getting a pass), and
validate it in the small yellow boxes near the escalator going
down to the tracks. You're looking for trains on line 2 *(Linea
2)*, heading in the direction of Pozzuoli (generally depart from
track 4). Hop on any train that comes through (confirm by
its sign or with a local that it's going to Pozzuoli), and ride
the subway one stop to Cavour. As you leave the Metro, exit
and hike five minutes uphill through the park along the busy
street. Look for a grand old red building located up a flight of
stairs at the top of the block.

If taking the Metro back to Centrale Station, make sure
to catch your train in the Cavour subway station, rather than
at the connected Museo stop (which is on a different line that
takes longer to get back to Garibaldi).

Figure on €12 for a **taxi** from the train station to the
museum.

Information: The shop sells a worthwhile *National Archaeological
Museum of Naples* guidebook for €12. Tel. 081-442-2149.

Tours: My self-guided tour (below) covers all the basics. For more
detail, the decent **audioguide** costs €5 (at ticket desk). For a
guided tour, book Pina Esposito (see "Tours in Naples," earlier).

Baggage Check: Bag check is obligatory and free.

Photography: Photos are allowed without a flash.

Eating: The museum has no café, but vending machines sell drinks
and snacks at reasonable prices. There are several good places
to grab a meal within a few blocks; see page 496.

Overview

Entering the museum, stand at the base of the grand staircase. To
your right, on the ground floor, are the larger-than-life statues of
the Farnese Collection, starring the *Toro Farnese* and the *Farnese*

Hercules. Up the stairs on the mezzanine level (turn left at the lion) are mosaics and frescoes from Pompeii, including the *Battle of Alexander* and the Secret Room of erotic art. On the top floor are more frescoes, a scale model of Pompeii, and bronze statues from Herculaneum. WCs are behind the staircase.

• *From the base of the grand staircase, turn right through the door marked* Collezione Farnese *and head to the far end—walking through a rich collection of idealistic and realistic ancient portrait busts—to reach the farthest room (Sala XIII).*

Ground Floor: The Farnese Collection

The museum's ground floor alone has enough Greek and Roman art to put any museum on the map. This floor has nothing from Pompeii; its highlight is the Farnese Collection, a grand hall of huge, bright, and wonderfully restored statues excavated from Rome's Baths of Caracalla. Peruse the larger-than-life statues filling the hall. They were dug up in the 1540s at the behest of Alessandro Farnese (by then Pope Paul III) while he was building the family palace on the Campo dei Fiori in Rome. His main purpose in excavating the baths was to scavenge quality building stone. The sculptures were a nice extra and helped the palace come in under budget on decorations. In the 1700s, the collection ended up in the hands of Charles, the Bourbon king of Naples (whose mother was a Farnese). His son, the next king, had it brought to Naples.

• *Quick—look down to the left end of the hall. There's a woman being tied to a snorting bull.*

The tangled *Toro Farnese* tells a thrilling Greek myth. At 13 feet, it's the tallest ancient marble group ever found, and the largest intact statue from antiquity. A

third-century A.D. copy of a lost bronze Hellenistic original, it was carved out of one piece of marble. Michelangelo and others "restored" it at the pope's request—meaning that they integrated surviving bits into a new work. Panels on the wall show which pieces were actually carved by Michelangelo (in blue on the chart): the head of the woman in back, the torso of the aunt under the bull, and the dog. (Imagine how the statue would stand out if it were thoughtfully lit and not surrounded by white walls.)

Here's the tragic story behind the statue: Once upon an ancient Greek time, King Lycus was bewitched by Dirce. He abandoned his pregnant wife, Antiope (standing regally in the background). The single mom gave birth to twin boys (shown here). When they grew up, they killed their deadbeat dad and tied Dirce to the horns of a bull to be bashed against a mountain. Captured in marble, the action is thrilling: cape flailing, dog snarling, hooves in the air. You can almost hear the bull snorting. And in the back, Antiope oversees this harsh ancient justice with satisfaction.

At the opposite end of the hall stands the *Farnese Hercules*. The great Greek hero is exhausted. He leans wearily on his club (draped with his lion skin) and bows his head. He's just finished the daunting Eleventh Labor, having traveled the world, fought men and gods, freed Prometheus from his rock, and carried Atlas' weight of the world on his shoulders. Now he's returned with the prize: the golden apples of the gods, which he cups behind his back. But, after all that, he's just been told he has to return the apples and do one final labor: descend into Hell itself. Oh, man.

The 10-foot colossus is a third-century A.D. Roman marble copy (signed by "Glykon") of a fourth-century B.C. Greek bronze original (probably by Lysippos). The statue was enormously famous in its day. Dozens of copies—some marble, some bronze—have been found in Roman villas and baths. This version was unearthed in Rome's Baths of Caracalla in 1546, along with the *Toro Farnese*.

The *Farnese Hercules* was equally famous in the 16th-18th centuries. Tourists flocked to Rome to admire it, art students studied it from afar in prints, Louis XIV made a copy for Versailles, and petty nobles everywhere put small-scale knock-offs in their gardens. This curly-haired version of Hercules became the modern world's image of the Greek hero.

• Backtrack to the main entry hall, then head up to the mezzanine level (turning left at the lion).

Mezzanine: Pompeiian Mosaics and the Secret Room

Most of these mosaics—of animals, musicians, and geometric designs—were taken from Pompeii's House of the Faun (see page 509). Walk into the third room and look for the 20-inch-high statue in a freestanding glass case: the house's delightful centerpiece, the *Dancing Faun.* This rare surviving Greek bronze statue (from the fourth century B.C.) is surrounded by some of the best mosaics of that age.

A museum highlight, just beyond the statue, is the grand *Battle of Alexander,* a second-century B.C. copy of the original Greek fresco, done a century earlier. It decorated a floor in the House of the Faun and was found intact; the damage you see occurred as this trea-

sure was moved from Pompeii to the king's collection here. Alexander (left side of the scene, with curly hair and sideburns) is about to defeat the Persians under Darius (central figure, in chariot with turban and beard). This pivotal victory allowed Alexander to quickly overrun much of Asia (331 B.C.). Alexander is the only one without a helmet...a confident master of the battlefield while everyone else is fighting for their lives, eyes bulg-

ing with fear. Notice how the horses, already in retreat, add to the scene's propaganda value. Notice also the shading and perspective, which Renaissance artists would later work so hard to accomplish. (A modern reproduction of the mosaic is now back in Pompeii, at the House of the Faun.)

Farther on, the **Secret Room** *(Gabinetto Segreto)* contains a sizable assortment of erotic frescoes, well-hung pottery, and perky statues that once decorated bedrooms, meeting rooms, brothels, and even shops at Pompeii and Herculaneum. These bawdy statues and frescoes—many of them once displayed in Pompeii's grandest houses—were entertainment for guests. (By the time they made it to this museum, in 1819, the frescoes could be viewed only with permission from the king—see the letters in the glass case just outside the door.) The Roman nobles commissioned the wildest scenes imaginable. Think of them as ancient dirty jokes.

At the entrance, you're enthusiastically greeted by big stone penises that once projected over Pompeii's doorways. A massive phallus was not necessarily a sexual symbol, but a magical amulet used against the "evil eye." It symbolized fertility, happiness, good luck, riches, straight A's, and general well-being.

Circulating counterclockwise through this section, look for the following: a faun playfully pulling the sheet off a beautiful woman, only to be grossed out by a hermaphrodite's plumbing (perhaps the original *"Mamma mia!"*; #12); horny pygmies from Africa in action (#27); a toga with an embarrassing bulge (#34); a particularly high-quality statue of a goat and a satyr illustrating an act of sodomy (#36); and, watching over it all with remarkable aplomb, Venus, the patron goddess of Pompeii (#39).

The back room is furnished and decorated the way an ancient brothel might have been. The 10 frescoes on the wall functioned as both a menu of services offered and as a kind of *Kama Sutra* of sex positions. The glass cases contain more phallic art.

• *So, now that your travel buddy is finally showing a little interest in art...finish up your visit by climbing the stairs to the top floor.*

Top Floor: Frescoes, Statues, Artifacts, and a Model of Pompeii

At the top of the stairs, go through the center door to enter a grand, empty hall. This was the **great hall** of the university (17th and 18th centuries) until the building became the royal museum in 1777. Walk to the center. The sundial (from 1791) still works. Look up to the far-right corner of the hall and find the tiny pinhole. At noon (13:00 in summer), a ray of sun enters the hall and strikes the sundial, showing the time of the year...if you know your zodiac.

To your left, you'll see a door marked *affreschi*. This leads to eight rooms showing off the museum's impressive and well-described collection of (non-erotic) **frescoes** taken from the walls of Pompeii villas. Pompeiians loved to decorate their homes with scenes from mythology (Hercules' labors, Venus and Mars in love), landscapes, everyday market scenes, and faux architecture. Continue around this wing counterclockwise (with the courtyard on your left) through rooms of artifacts found at Pompeii. At the far end is a scale model of Pompeii as excavated in 1879 *(plastic di Pompeii)*. Another model (on the wall) shows the site in 2004, after more excavations.

• *Eventually you'll end up back in the great hall.*

Step out to the top landing of the staircase you climbed earlier. Turn left and go down, then up, 16 steps and into the wing labeled *La Villa dei Papiri*. This ex-hibition shows off artifacts (particularly bronze statues) from the Herculaneum holiday home of Julius Caesar's father-in-law. In the second room (numbered CXVI), look into the lifelike blue eyes of the intense *Corri-*

dore (athletes), bent on doing their best. The *Five Dancers,* with their inlaid-ivory eyes and graceful poses, decorated a portico. The next room (CXVII) has more fine works: *Resting Hermes* (with his tired little heel wings) is taking a break. Nearby, the *Drunken Faun* (singing and snapping his fingers to the beat, a wineskin at his side) is clearly living for today—true to the *carpe diem* preaching of the Epicurean philosophy. Caesar's father-in-law was a fan of Epicurean philosophy, and his library—containing 2,000 papyrus scrolls—supported his outlook. Back by the entrance, check out the plans of the villa, and in the side room, see how the half-burned scrolls were unrolled and (with luck) read after excavation in the 1750s.

• *Return to the ground floor. The exit hall (right) leads around the museum courtyard and to the gift shop.*

Doriforo

For extra credit on your way out, find **Doriforo.** He was last spotted on the right as you walk down the exit hall. (If he's been moved, ask a guard, *"Dov'è il Doriforo?"*) This seven-foot-tall "spear-carrier" (the literal translation of *dori-foro*) just stands there, as if holding a spear. What's the big deal about this statue, which looks like so many others? It's a marble replica made by the Ro-mans of one of the most-copied statues of antiquity, a fifth-century B.C. bronze Greek original by Polyclitus. This copy once stood in a Pompeii gym, where it inspired ancient athletes by showing the ideal proportions of Greek beauty. So full of motion, and so realistic in its *con-trapposto* pose (weight on one foot), the *Doriforo* would later inspire Donatello and Michelangelo, helping to trigger the Renaissance. And so the glories of ancient Pompeii, once buried and forgotten, live on today.

Naples Walk

▲▲▲A SLICE OF NEAPOLITAN LIFE

This walk takes you from the Archaeological Museum through the heart of town and back to Centrale Station. Allow at least three hours, plus time for pizza and sightseeing stops. If you're in a rush, do it in half the time by walking briskly and skipping Part 2.

Naples, a living medieval city, is its own best sight. Couples

A Slice of Neapolitan Life Walk

To Museo di Capodimonte

VIA STA. TERESA

VIA TERESA

Cavour

VIA FORIA

VIA DUOMO

Piazza Cavour

UNDERGROUND PASSAGE

One stop on Metro to Piazza Garibaldi & Centrale Station

ARCHAEOLOGICAL MUSEUM

Museo

WALK BEGINS

GALLERIA PRINCIPE

V. PESSINA

BELLINI THEATER

V. BELLINI

V. SAPIENZA

PORTA D'ALBA

V. PORT' ALBA

Piazza Bellini

NAPOLI SOTTERRANEA

VIA DEI TRIBUNALI

VIA GREG. ARMENO

S. PAOLO

S. LORENZO MAGGIORE

VIA S. BIAGIO

DUOMO

PIO MONTE MISERICORDIA

VIA VICARIA VECCHIA

FORCELLA

COLLETTA

POLO NORD GELATERIA

PIZZA

PIZZA

CAFFÈ MEXICO

Piazza Dante

Danse

SUPER-MARKET

VIA TARSIA

To Montesanto (& funicular)

Piazza Sette Settembre

V. PIGNASECCA

SPANISH QUARTER

GESÙ NUOVO

Piazza Gesù Nuovo

VIA MADDALONI

SANTA CHIARA

CALATA TRINITÀ MAGGIORE

VIA B. CROCE

SAN SEB.

SAN DOM.

CAPPELLA SANSEVERO

CHAPEL OF MARADONA

SCATURCHIO PASTICCERIA

CLOISTER

DOLL HOSPITAL

"SPACCANAPOLI"

VIA MEZZOCANNONE

VIA

VIA DUOMO

WALK ENDS

To Piazza Garibaldi & Centrale Station (10 min. walk)

CORSO UMBERTO I

VIA NUOVA MARINA

FASCIST BLDG.

VIA TOLEDO

VIA BATT.

MONTEOLIVETO

V. DONNALBINA

POST

Piazza Matteotti

VIA A. DIAZ

BNL BANK

Toledo

Piazza Bovio

Università

VIA S. FELICE

VIA AGOSTINO DEPRETIS

VIA ALCIDE D. GASPERI

VIA CRISTOFORO COLOMBO

Port

VIA PORTA DI TAPPIA

BANCO DI NAPOLI

Municipio

Piazza Municipio

BANCA INTESA SANPAOLO

GALLERIA UMBERTO I

Alibus Bus To Airport

Tram #1 to Train Station

Centrale Funicular

Piazza Carità

TEATRO DI SAN CARLO

CASTEL NUOVO

MOLO BEVERELLO DOCK

STAZIONE MARITTIMA (CRUISE TERMINAL)

GRAN CAFFÈ GAMBRINUS

ROYAL PALACE

V. AM. FERDINANDO ACTON

Piazza del Plebiscito

SAN FRANCESCO DI PAOLA

CONSOLE

To Sorrento & Capri

TUNNEL

VIA NAZARIO SAURO

To Castel dell'Ovo

Bay of Naples

300 Meters

300 Yards

artfully make love on Vespas surrounded by more fights and smiles per cobblestone than anywhere else in Italy. Rather than seeing Naples as a list of sights, visit its one great museum and then capture its essence by taking this walk through the core of the city.

Part 1: From the Archaeological Museum to Piazza Bellini and Piazza Dante

The first two parts of this walk are a mostly straight one-mile ramble down a fine boulevard (with a few colorful detours) to the waterfront at Piazza del Plebiscito. Your starting point is the Archaeological Museum (at the top of Piazza Cavour, Metro: Cavour or Museo; for a self-guided tour of the museum, see earlier). As you stroll, remember that here in Naples, red traffic lights are considered "decorations." When crossing a street, try to tag along with a native.

• *From the door of the Archaeological Museum, cross the street, veer right, and pass through the fancy mall.*

Galleria Principe di Napoli: This was named for the first male child of the royal Savoy family, the Prince of Naples. Walk di-

rectly through it, enjoying this fine shopping gallery from the late 19th century, similar to those popular in Paris and London. This is "Liberty Style," Italy's version of Art Nouveau (named for a British department store), which was in vogue at a time when Naples was nicknamed the "Paris of the South." Parisian artist Edgar Degas left Paris to adopt Naples—which he actually considered more cosmopolitan and sophisticated—as his hometown.

• *Leaving the gallery through the opposite end, walk one block downhill. At Via Conte di Ruvo, head left, passing the fine Bellini Theater (also in the Liberty Style). After one block, turn right on Via Costantinopoli, continuing directly downhill to Piazza Bellini. As you walk, look up to enjoy architecture built in the late 19th century, when Naples was the last stop on Romantic Age travelers' Grand Tour of Europe. (From a tourism perspective, Sorrento only rose with the cultural and economic fall of Naples in the decades following Italian independence, around the early 20th century.)*

Soon you'll run into the ragtag urban park called...

Piazza Bellini: Walking between columns of two grand churches, suddenly you're in neighborhood Napoli. A statue of Vincenzo Bellini marks the center of Piazza Bellini. It's dedicated to the Sicilian opera composer who worked here in the early 1800s. Survey the many balconies—and the people who use them as a "backyard" in this densely packed city. The apartment flats were originally palaces of noble families, as indicated by the stately family crests above grand doorways. Look down below the square to see the ruined Greek walls: tuff blocks without mortar. This was the wall, and you're standing on land that was outside of the town. You can see the street level from the fifth century B.C., when Neapolis—literally, "the new city"—was founded. For 2,500 years, laundry has blown in the breeze right here.

• *Walk 30 yards downhill. Stop at the horseshoe-shaped Port'Alba gate (on the right). Spin slowly 360 degrees and take in the scene. The proud tile across the street shows Piazza Bellini circa 1890. Learn to ignore graffiti (as the locals do). Pass through the gate, and stroll past the book stalls down Via Port'Alba to the next big square...*

Piazza Dante: This square is marked by a statue of Dante, the medieval poet. Fittingly, half the square is devoted to bookstores.

Old Dante looks out over an urban area that was once grand, then chaotic, and is now slowly becoming grand again.

While this square feels perfectly Italian to me, for many Neapolitans it represents the repression of the central Italian state. When Napoleon was defeated, Naples briefly became its own independent kingdom. But within a few decades of Italian unification, in 1861, Naples went from being a thriving cultural and political capital to a provincial town, its money used to help establish the industrial strength of the north, its dialect considered backward, and its bureaucrats transferred to Rome.

Originally, a statue of a Spanish Bourbon king stood in the square. (The grand orange-and-gray building is typical of Bourbon structures from that period.) But with the unification of Italy, the king, who was symbolic of Naples' colonial subjugation, was replaced by Dante, the father of the unified Italian language—a strong symbol of nationalism (and yet another form of subjugation).

The Neapolitan people are survivors. A long history of corrupt and greedy colonial overlords (German, Norman, French, Austrian, and Spanish) has taught Neapolitans to deal creatively with authority. Many credit this aspect of Naples' past for the strength of organized crime here.

Across the street, **Caffè Mexico** (at #86) is an institution known for its espresso, which is served already sweetened—ask for *senza zucchero* if you don't want sugar (pay first, then take receipt to the counter and hand it over). Most Italians agree that Neapolitan coffee is the best anywhere.

• *Walk downhill on...*

Via Toledo: The long, straight street heading downhill from Piazza Dante is Naples' principal shopping drag. It originated as a military road built under Spanish rule (hence the name) in the 16th century. Via Toledo skirted the old town wall to connect the Spanish military headquarters (now the museum where you started this walk) with the Royal Palace (down by the bay, where you're heading). As you stroll, peek into lovely atriums, an ancient urban design feature providing a break from the big street.

After a couple of hundred yards, you'll reach Piazza Sette Settembre. In 1860, from the white marble balcony of the Neoclassical building overlooking the square, the famous revolutionary Giuseppe Garibaldi declared Italy united and Victor Emmanuel II its first king. Only in 1870, a decade later, was the dream of Italian unity fully realized when Rome fell to unification forces.

• *Continue straight on Via Toledo. About three blocks below Piazza Dante and a block past Piazza Sette Settembre, you'll come to Via Maddaloni, which marks the start of the long, straight, narrow street nicknamed...*

Spaccanapoli: Before crossing the street—whose name translates as "split Naples"—look left (toward the train station).

Then look right (to see San Martino hill rising steeply above the center). Since ancient times, this thin street has bisected the city. It changes names several times: Via Maddaloni (as it's called here), Via B. Croce, Via S. Biagio dei Librai, and Via Vicaria Vecchia. We'll return to this intersection later.

• *If you want to abbreviate this walk, turn left here and skip ahead to Part 3. Part 2, described next, is a bit of a detour, and requires backtracking uphill (or a short taxi ride) later. But if you have time, it's worth the effort.*

Part 2: Monumental Naples (Via Toledo, the Spanish Quarter, and Piazza del Plebiscito)

• *We'll detour off of Via Toledo for just a couple of blocks (rejoining it later). At the Spaccanapoli intersection, go right (toward the church facade on the hill, up Via Pasquale Scura). After about 100 yards, you hit a busy intersection. Stop. You're on one of Naples' most colorful open-air market streets...*

Via Pignasecca Market: Snoop around from here if you are so inclined. Then, turn left down Via Pignasecca and stroll this colorful strip. You'll pass meat and fish stalls, produce stands, street-

food vendors, and much more. This is a taste of Naples' famous Spanish Quarter, which we'll experience more of later in this walk.
• *Via Pignasecca meets back up with Via Toledo at the square called...*

Piazza Carità: This square, built for an official visit by Hitler to Mussolini in 1938, is full of stern, straight, obedient lines. The big building belonged to an insurance company. (For the best example of fascist architecture in town, take a slight detour from here: With your back to Via Toledo, leave Piazza Carità downhill on the right-hand corner and walk a block to the Poste e Telegrafi building. There you'll see several government buildings with stirring reliefs singing the praises of lobotomized workers and a totalitarian society.)

In Naples—long a poor and rough city—rather than being heroic, people learn from the cradle the art of survival. The modern memorial statue in the center of the square celebrates Salvo d'Acquisto, a rare hometown hero. In 1943, he was executed after falsely confessing to sabotage...in order to save 22 fellow Italian soldiers from a Nazi revenge massacre.
• *From Piazza Carità, continue south down Via Toledo for a few blocks, looking to your left for more...*

Fascist Architecture (Banks): You can't miss the two big, blocky bank buildings. First comes the chalky-white BNL Bank.

A bit farther down, past the Metro, imagine trying to rob the even more imposing Banco di Napoli (Via Toledo 178). Step across the street and check out its architecture: typical fascist arches and reliefs, built to celebrate the bank's 400th anniversary (est. 1539—how old is *your* bank?).

The street here was pedestrianized after the Toledo Metro stop opened in 2012. Now the street is even more popular for strolling, property values have risen, and international brands such as H&M and the Disney Store have moved in.
• *On the next block (at #184) is the...*

Banca Intesa Sanpaolo: This fills an older palace—take a free peek at the opulent atrium. In the entry hall, you can buy a ticket for the **Galleria d'Italia Palazzo Zevallos Stigliano,** a small collection located in the upper two floors. The gallery's only piece worth seeing—on the second floor—is a great late Caravaggio painting. *The Martyrdom of Saint Ursula* shows a terrible scene: His marriage proposal rejected, the king of the Huns shoots an arrow into Ursula's chest. Blood spurts, Ursula is stunned but accepts her destiny sweetly, and Caravaggio himself—far right, his last self-portrait—screams to symbolize the rejection of evil. The rest of the second floor holds opulent chandeliered apartments, a few Neapolitan landscapes, and little else. The first floor has temporary exhibits (€4, Tue-Sun 10:00-18:00, closed Mon; entry includes audioguide, a look at old Naples paintings, and a fine WC; Via Toledo 185, tel. 800-454-229, www.palazzozevallos.com).

• *Feeling bold? From here, side-trip uphill a couple of blocks into the...*

Spanish Quarter: This is a classic world of *basso* (low) living. The streets—which were laid out in the 16th century for the

Spanish military barracks outside the city walls—are unbelievably narrow (and cool in summer), and the buildings rise five stories high. In such tight quarters, life—flirting, fighting, playing, and loving—happens in the road. This is *the* cliché of life in Naples, as shown in so many movies. The Spanish Quarter is Naples at its most characteristic. The shopkeepers are friendly, and the mopeds are bold (watch out). Concerned locals will tug on their lower eyelids, warning you to be wary. Hungry? Pop into a grocery shop and ask the clerk to make you his best prosciutto-and-mozzarella sandwich (the price should be about €4).

• *Return to Via Toledo and work your way down. Near the bottom of the street, on the right at #275, is **Pintauro**, a takeaway bakery famous for its* sfogliatelle. *These classic, ricotta-filled Neapolitan pastries are often served warm from the oven and make a tasty €2 treat.*

*Just beyond, on the right, notice the station for the **Centrale funicular.** If you have extra time and enjoy city views, this can take you sweat-free up to the top of San Martino, the hill with a fortress and a monastery/museum looming over town. Across the street is the impressive Galleria Umberto I—but don't go in now, as you'll see it in a minute from the other side.*

For now, just keep heading down the main drag and through the smaller Piazza Trieste e Trento to the immense...

Piazza del Plebiscito: This square celebrates the 1861 vote (*plebiscito*, plebiscite) in which Naples chose to join Italy. Dominating the top of the square is the **Church of San Francesco di Paola,** with its Pantheon-inspired dome and broad, arc-

ing colonnades. If it's open, step inside to ogle the vast interior—a Neoclassical recreation of one of ancient Rome's finest buildings (free, daily 8:30-12:00 & 16:00-19:00).

• *Opposite is the...*

Royal Palace (Palazzo Reale): Having housed Spanish, French, and even Italian royalty, this building displays statues of all those who stayed here. Look for eight kings in the niches, each from a different dynasty (left to right): Norman, German, French, Spanish, Spanish, Spanish, French (Napoleon's brother-in-law), and, finally, Italian—Victor Emmanuel II, King of Savoy. The statues were done at the request of V. E. II's son, so his dad is the most dashing of the group.

• *Continue 50 yards past the Royal Palace (toward the trees) to enjoy a...*

Fine Harbor View: While boats busily serve Capri and Sorrento, Mount Vesuvius smolders ominously in the distance. Look back to see the vast "Bourbon red" palace—its color inspired by Pompeii. The hilltop above Piazza del Plebiscito is San Martino, with its Carthusian monastery-turned-museum and Castle of St. Elmo (remember, the Centrale funicular to the top is just across the square and up Via Toledo). This street continues to Naples' romantic harborfront—the fishermen's quarter (Borgo Marinaro)—a fortified island connected to the mainland by a stout causeway, with its fanciful, ancient Castel dell'Ovo (Egg Castle) and trendy harborside restaurants. Farther along the harborfront stretches the Lungomare promenade and Santa Lucia district. (The long harborfront promenade, Via Francesco Caracciolo, is a delightful people-watching scene on balmy nights.)

• *Head back through the piazza and pop into...*

Gran Caffè Gambrinus: This coffee house, facing the piazza, takes you back to the elegance of 1860. It's a classic place to sample a crispy *sfogliatella* pastry, or perhaps the mushroom-shaped, rum-soaked bread-like cakes called *babà*, which come in a huge variety. Stand at the bar *(banco)*, pay double to sit *(tavola)*, or just wander around as you imagine the café buzzing with the ritzy intellectuals, journalists, and artsy bohemian types who munched on *babà* here during Naples' 19th-century heyday (daily 7:00-24:00, Piazza del Plebiscito 1, tel. 081-417-582, http://grancaffegambrinus.com/en).

• *A block away, tucked behind the palace, you can peek inside the Neoclassical...*

Teatro di San Carlo: Built in 1737, 41 years before Milan's La Scala, this is Europe's oldest opera house and Italy's second-most-respected (after La Scala). The theater burned down in 1816, and was rebuilt within the year.

Beyond Teatro di San Carlo and the Royal Palace is the huge, harborfront **Castel Nuovo,** which houses government bureaucrats and the **Civic Museum.** It feels like a mostly empty shell, with a couple of dusty halls of Neapolitan art, but the views over the bay from the upper terraces are impressive (€6, Mon-Sat 9:00-19:00, closed Sun, last entry one hour before closing, tel. 081-795-7722, www.comune.napoli.it).

Cross the street from Teatro di San Carlo and go through the tall yellow arch into the Victorian iron and glass of the 100-year-

old shopping mall, **Galleria Umberto I.** It was built in 1892 to reinvigorate the district after a devastating cholera epidemic occurred here. Gawk up, then walk left to bring you back out on Via Toledo.

• For Part 3 of this walk, double back up Via Toledo to Piazza Carità, veering right (just above the first big fascist-style building we saw earlier) on Via Morgantini through Piazza Monteoliveto. Cross the busy street, then angle up Calata Trinità Maggiore to the fancy column at the top of the hill. (To avoid the backtracking and uphill walk, catch a €10 taxi to the Church of Gesù Nuovo—JAY-zoo noo-OH-voh.)

Part 3: Spaccanapoli Back to the Station

You're back at the straight-as-a-Greek-arrow Spaccanapoli, formerly the main thoroughfare of the Greek city of Neapolis.
• Stop at...

Piazza Gesù Nuovo: This square is marked by a towering 18th-century Baroque monument to the Counter-Reformation.

Although the Jesuit order was powerful in Naples because of its Spanish heritage, locals never attacked Protestants here with the full fury of the Spanish Inquisition.

If you'd like, you can visit two bulky old churches, start-

ing with the dark, fortress-like, 17th-century **Church of Gesù Nuovo,** followed by the simpler **Church of Santa Chiara** (in the courtyard across the street). Both are described in more detail later, under "Sights in Naples."
• After touring the churches, continue along the main drag. Since this is a

*university district, you'll see lots of students and bookstores. This neigh-
borhood is also famously superstitious. Look for incense-burning women
with carts full of good-luck charms for sale.*

*Farther down Spaccanapoli—passing Palazzo Venezia, the em-
bassy of Venice to Naples when both were independent powers—you'll
see the next square...*

Piazza San Domenico Maggiore: This square is marked by
an ornate 17th-century monument built to thank God for ending
the plague. From this square, detour left along the right side of the
castle-like church, then follow yellow signs, taking the first right
and walking one block to the remarkable **Cappella Sansevero.**
This Baroque chapel is well worth visiting (described later, under
"Sights in Naples").

*• After touring the chapel, return to Via B. Croce (a.k.a. Spaccanapoli),
turn left, and continue your cultural scavenger hunt. At the intersection
of Via Nilo, find the...*

Statue of the Nile (on the left): A reminder of the multi-
ethnic make-up of Greek Neapolis, this statue is in what was the
Egyptian quarter. Locals like to call this statue *The Body of Naples*,
with the overflowing cornucopia symbolizing the abundance of
their fine city. (I once asked a Neapolitan man to describe the local
women, who are famous for their beauty, in one word. He replied
simply, "Abundant.") This intersection is considered the center of
old Naples.

• Directly opposite the statue, inside of Bar Nilo, is the...

"Chapel of Maradona": The small "chapel" on the wall is dedicated to Diego Maradona, a soccer star who played for Naples in

the 1980s. Locals consider soccer almost
a religion, and this guy was practically a
deity. You can even see a "hair of Diego"
and a teardrop from the city when he
went to another team for more money.
Unfortunately, his reputation has since
been sullied by problems he's had with
organized crime, drugs, and police. Perhaps inspired by Maradona's example,
the coffee bar has posted a quadrilingual
sign (though, strangely, not in English)
threatening that those who take a picture without buying a cup of coffee may
find their camera damaged...*Capisce?*

• As you continue, you'll begin to see shops selling...

Presepi (Nativity Scenes): Just as many Americans keep an
eye out year-round for Christmas-tree ornaments, Italians regular-
ly add pieces to the family *presepe*, the centerpiece of their holiday
decorations. Stop after a few blocks at the tiny square, where Via

San Gregorio Armeno leads left into a colorful district with the highest concentration of shops selling fantastic *presepi* and their tiny components, including figurines caricaturing local politicians and celebrities.

• *Back on Spaccanapoli, as Via B. Croce becomes Via S. Biagio dei Librai, notice the...*

Gold and Silver Shops: Some say stolen jewelry ends up here, is melted down immediately, and gets resold in some other form as soon as it cools. At #95, find the Compro Oro ("I Buy Gold") shop. This is one of many pawn shops that have appeared in concert with Italy's economic tough times. At #81, the Ospedale delle Bambole (Doll Hospital) heals dolls that have been loved to pieces, and also sells restored classics.

• *Cross busy Via Duomo. If you have time and aren't already churched out, consider detouring five minutes north (left) up Via Duomo to visit Naples'* **Duomo;** *just around the corner is the* **Pio Monte della Misericordia Church,** *with a fine Caravaggio painting (both described later, under "Sights in Naples"). You're also close to the Via Tribunali and several recommended* pizzerie *(see "Eating in Naples," later). Afterward, continue straight along Via Vicaria Vecchia. As you stroll, ponder Naples' vibrant...*

Street Life, Past and Present: Here along Via Vicaria Vecchia, the street and side-street scenes intensify. The area is said to be a center of the Camorra (organized crime), but as a tourist, you won't notice. Paint a picture with these thoughts: Naples has the most intact street plan of any ancient Greek or Roman city. Imagine this city during those times (and retain these images as you visit Pompeii), with streetside shop fronts that close up after dark, and private homes on upper floors. What you see today is just one more page in a 2,000-year-old story of a city: all kinds of meetings, beatings, and cheatings; kisses, near misses, and little-boy pisses.

You name it, it occurs right on the streets today, as it has since ancient times. People ooze from crusty corners. Black-and-white death announcements add to the clutter on the walls. Widows sell cigarettes from buckets. For a peek behind the scenes in the shade of wet laundry, venture down a few side streets. Buy two carrots as a gift for the woman on the fifth

floor, if she'll lower her bucket to pick them up. The neighborhood action seems best at about 18:00.

A few blocks on, at the tiny fenced-in triangle of greenery, hang out for a few minutes to just observe the crazy motorbike action and teen scene.

• *From here, veer right onto Via Forcella (which leads to the busy boulevard that takes you to Centrale Station). A block down, a tiny, fenced-in traffic island protects a chunk of the ancient Greek wall of Neapolis. Turn right here on Via Pietro Colletta, walk 40 yards, and step into the North Pole, at the...*

Polo Nord Gelateria: The oldest *gelateria* in Naples has had four generations of family working here since 1931. Before you order, sample a few flavors, including their *bacio* or "kiss" flavor (chocolate and hazelnut)—all are made fresh daily. Low-sugar and soy ice cream are also available (Via Pietro Colletta 41). Via Pietro Colletta leads past two of Napoli's most competitive **pizzerias** (see "Eating in Naples," later) to Corso Umberto I.

• *Turn left on the grand boulevard-like Corso Umberto I. From here to Centrale Station, it's at least a 10-minute walk (if you're tired, hop on a bus; they all go to the station). To finish the walk, continue on Corso Umberto I—past a gauntlet of purse/CD/sunglasses salesmen and shady characters hawking stolen mobile phones—to the vast, ugly Piazza Garibaldi. On the far side is the station. You made it.*

NAPLES

Sights in Naples

The churches listed here are linked—in this order—on Part 3 of my self-guided walk, earlier. The fish market is near the end of the walk.

▲Church of Gesù Nuovo

This church's unique pyramid-grill facade survives from a fortified 15th-century noble palace. Step inside for a brilliant Neapolitan Baroque interior. The second chapel on the right features a much-adored **statue of St. Giuseppe Moscati** (1880-1927), a Christian doctor famous for helping the poor. In 1987, Moscati became the first modern doctor to be canonized. Sit and watch a steady stream of Neapolitans taking turns to kiss and touch the altar, then hold the good doctor's highly polished hand.

Continue on to the third chapel and enter the **Sale Moscati.** Look high on the walls of this long room to see hundreds of "Ex Votos"—tiny red-and-silver plaques of thanksgiving for prayers answered with the help of St. Moscati (each has a symbol of the ailment cured). Naples' practice of using Ex

Votos, while incorporated into its Catholic rituals, goes back to its pagan Greek roots. Rooms from Moscati's nearby apartment are on display, and a glass case shows possessions and photos of the great doctor. As you leave the Sale Moscati, notice the big bomb casing that hangs in the left corner. It fell through the church's dome in 1943, but caused almost no damage...yet another miracle.

Cost and Hours: Free, daily 7:30-13:00 & 16:00-19:00, Piazza del Gesù Nuovo, www.gesunuovo.it.

Church of Santa Chiara

Dating from the 14th century, this church is from a period of French royal rule under the Angevin dynasty. Consider the stark contrast between this church (Gothic) and the Gesù Nuovo (Baroque), across the street. Inside, notice the huge inlaid-marble Angevin coat of arms on the floor. The faded Trinity on the back wall (on the right as you face the door), shows a dove representing the Holy Spirit between the heads of God the Father and Christ (c. 1414). This is an example of the fine frescoes that once covered the walls. Most were stuccoed over during Baroque times or destroyed in 1943 by Allied bombs. The altar is adorned with four finely carved Gothic tombs of Angevin kings. A chapel stacked with Bourbon royalty is just to the right.

Cost and Hours: Free, daily 7:30-13:00 & 16:30-20:00, Piazza del Gesù Nuovo. Its tranquil cloistered courtyard, around back, is not worth its €6 entry fee.

▲▲Cappella Sansevero

This small chapel is a Baroque explosion mourning the body of Christ, who lies on a soft pillow under an incredibly realistic veil. It's

also the personal chapel of Raimondo de Sangro, an eccentric Freemason, containing his tomb and the tombs of his family. Like other 18th-century Enlightenment figures, Raimondo was a wealthy man of letters, scientist and inventor, and patron of the arts—and he was also a grand master of the Freemasons of the Kingdom of Naples. His chapel—filled with Freemason symbolism—is a complex ensemble, with statues representing virtues such as self-control, religious zeal, and the Freemason philosophy of freedom through enlightenment. Though it's a pricey private enterprise, the chapel is worth a visit.

Cost and Hours: €7, buy tickets at office at the corner, Mon and Wed-Sat 9:30-18:30, Sun 9:30-14:00, closed Tue, last entry 20 minutes before closing, no photos, Via de Sanctis 19, tel. 081-551-8470, www.museosansevero.it. Good English explanations are posted throughout; when you buy your ticket, pick up the free floor plan, which identifies each of the statues lining the nave.

Visiting the Chapel: Study the incredible *Veiled Christ* in the center. Carved out of marble, it's like no other statue I've seen (by Giuseppe "Howdeedoodat" Sammartino, 1753). The Christian message (Jesus died for our salvation) is accompanied by a Freemason message (the veil represents how the body and ego are obstacles to real spiritual freedom). As you walk from Christ's feet to his head, notice how the expression on Jesus' face goes from suffering to peace.

Raimondo's mom and dad are buried on either side of the **main altar.** To the right of the altar, marking his father's tomb, a statue representing *Despair* or *Disillusion* struggles with a marble rope net (carved out of a single piece of stone), symbolic of a troubled mind. The flames on the head of the winged boy represent human intellect—more Freemason symbolism, showing how knowledge frees the human mind. To the left of the main altar is a statue of *Modesty,* marking the tomb of Raimondo's mother (who died after his birth, and was only 20). The veiled woman fingers a broken tablet, symbolizing an interrupted life.

Raimondo de Sangro himself lies buried in a side altar (on the right). Among his inventions was the deep-green pigment used on the ceiling fresco. The inlaid M. C. Escher-esque maze on the floor around de Sangro's tomb is another Freemason reminder of how the quest for knowledge gets you out of the maze of life. This tilework once covered the floor of the entire chapel.

Your Sansevero finale is downstairs: two mysterious...**skeletons.** Perhaps another of the mad inventor's fancies: Inject a corpse with a fluid to fossilize the veins so that they'll survive the body's decomposition. While that's the legend, investigations have shown that the veins were artificial, and the models were created to illustrate how the circulatory system works.

▲Duomo

Naples' historic cathedral, built by imported French Anjou kings in the 14th century, boasts a breathtaking Neo-Gothic facade. Step

into the vast interior to see the mix of styles along the side chapels—from pointy Gothic arches to rounded Renaissance ones to gilded Baroque decor. Explore the two largest side-chapels—each practically a church in its own right. On the left, the Chapel of St. Restituta stands on the site of the original, early-Christian church that predated the cathedral. On the right is the Chapel of San Gennaro—dedicated to the beloved patron saint of Naples—decorated with silver busts of centuries of bishops, and seven paintings done on bronze. The stairs beneath the altar take you to a crypt with the relics of St. Gennaro and (across the room) a statue of the bishop who rescued the relics from a rival town and returned them to Naples.

Cost and Hours: Free, Mon-Sat 8:30-13:30 & 14:30-20:00, Sun 8:30-13:30 & 16:30-19:30, Via Duomo.

Pio Ponte della Misericordia

Art lovers come to this small church (near the Duomo, and run by a charitable foundation) to appreciate one of the best works by Caravaggio, *The Seven Works of Mercy,* which hangs over the main altar. In one crowded canvas, the great early-Baroque artist illustrates seven virtues: burying the dead (the man carrying a corpse by the ankles), visiting the imprisoned, feeding the hungry (Pero breastfeeding her starving father—a scene from a famous Roman story), sheltering the homeless (a pilgrim on the Camino de Santiago, with his floppy hat, negotiates with an innkeeper), caring for the sick, clothing the naked (St. Martin offers part of his cloak to the injured man in the foreground), and giving drink to the thirsty (Samson chugs from a jawbone in the background)—all of them set in a dark Neapolitan alley and watched over by Mary, Jesus, and a pair of angels.

Cost and Hours: €7, includes audioguide, Thu-Tue 9:00-14:30, closed Wed, last entry 30 minutes before closing, Via dei Tribunali 253, tel. 081-446-944, www.piomontedellamisericordia.it.

Porta Nolana Open-Air Fish Market

Naples' fish market squirts and stinks as it has for centuries under the Porta Nolana (gate in the city wall), immediately in front of the Napoli Porta Nolana Circumvesuviana station and four long blocks from Centrale Station. Of the town's many boisterous outdoor markets, this will net you the most photos and memories. From Piazza Nolana, wander under the medieval gate and take your first left down Vico Sopramuro, enjoying this wild and entirely edible cultural scavenger hunt (Tue-Sun 8:00-14:00, closed Mon).

Eating in Naples

CHEAP AND FAMOUS PIZZA

Naples is the birthplace of pizza. Its pizzerias bake just the right combination of fresh dough (soft and chewy, as opposed to Roman-style, which is thin and crispy), moz-

zarella, and tomatoes in traditional wood-burning ovens. You can head for the famous, venerable places (I've listed five below), but these can have a long line stretching out the door, and a half-hour wait for a table. If you want to skip the hassle, just ask a local for directions to the neighborhood pizzeria. An average one-person pie (usually the only size available) costs €4-8; most places offer both take-out and eat-in, and pizza is often the only thing on the menu.

Near the Station

These two pizzerias—the most famous—are both a few long blocks from the train station, and at the end of my "Slice of Neapolitan Life" self-guided walk.

Antica Pizzeria da Michele is for pizza purists. Filled with locals (and tourists), it serves just two varieties: *margherita* (tomato sauce and mozzarella) and *marinara* (tomato sauce, oregano, and garlic, no cheese). Come early to sit and watch the pizza artists in action. A pizza with beer costs €6-7. As this place is often jammed with a long line, arrive early or late to get a seat. If there's a mob, head inside to get a number. If it's just too crowded to wait, the less-exceptional Pizzeria Trianon (described next) generally has room (Mon-Sat 10:30-24:00, closed Sun; look for the vertical red *Antica Pizzeria* sign at the intersection of Via Pietro Colletta and Via Cesare Sersale at #1; tel. 081-553-9204).

Pizzeria Trianon, across the street and left a few doors, has been da Michele's archrival since 1923. It offers more choices, higher prices (€5-8, plus a 15 percent service charge), air-conditioning, and a cozier atmosphere. For less chaos, head upstairs. While waiting for your meal, you can survey the transformation of a humble wad of dough into a smoldering bubbly feast in their entryway pizza kitchen (daily 11:00-15:30 & 19:00-23:00, Via Pietro Colletta 42, tel. 081-553-9426).

On Via dei Tribunali

This street, which runs a couple of blocks north of Spaccanapoli, is home to several pizzerias that are more convenient to sightseeing. Three in particular are on all the "best pizza in Naples" lists...as you'll learn the hard way if you show up at peak mealtimes, when huge mobs crowd outside the front door waiting for a table. **Gino Sorbillo** is a local favorite (closed Sun, Via dei Tribunali 32—don't confuse this with his relatives' similarly named places on the same street, tel. 081-446-643). At **Pizzeria di Matteo,** people waiting out front snack on €0.50 croquettes *(crocché)*, sold at the little window (sometimes closed Sun, Via dei Tribunali 94, tel. 081-455-262). **Pizzeria I Decumani** has a bit nicer seating and is perhaps less chaotic (closed Mon, facing Piazza San Gaetano at Via dei Tribunali 58, tel. 081-557-1309).

EATING NEAR THE ARCHAEOLOGICAL MUSEUM

La Stanza del Gusto, two blocks downhill from the museum, tackles food creatively and injects crusty Naples with a little modern color and irreverence. The downstairs is casual, trendy, and playful, while the upstairs is more refined yet still polka-dotted (€5-8 *panini,* €10-15 *secondi;* fixed-price meals: €35 five-course vegetarian, €65 seven-course meat; Tue-Sat 12:00-15:30 & 19:30-23:30, closed Sun-Mon, Via Santa Maria di Constantinopoli 100, tel. 081-401-578).

Caffetteria Angela is a fun little eating complex: coffee bar; *tavola calda* with hot ready-to-eat dishes (€3-4); and a tiny meat, cheese, and bread shop with all you need for a cheap meal to go. It offers honest pricing and simple, peaceful, air-conditioned indoor seating (no cover, open Mon-Sat 7:00-21:00, Sun 9:00-14:00, 3 blocks below museum at Via Conte di Ruvo 21, between Via Pessina and Via Bellini, tel. 081-033-2928).

Pompeii

Stopped in its tracks by the eruption of Mount Vesuvius in A.D. 79, Pompeii offers the best look anywhere at what life in Rome must

have been like around 2,000 years ago.

A once-thriving commercial port of 20,000, Pompeii (worth ▲▲▲) grew from Greek and Etruscan roots to become an important Roman city. Then, on August 24, A.D. 79, everything changed. Vesuvius erupted and began to bury the city under 30 feet of hot volcanic ash. For the archaeologists who excavated it centuries later, this was a shake-and-bake windfall, teaching them

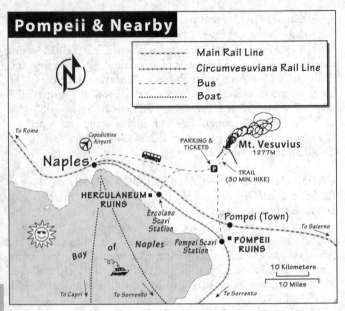

Pompeii & Nearby

‑ ‑ ‑ ‑ ‑ ‑ ‑	Main Rail Line
+++++++++	Circumvesuviana Rail Line
– – – – –	Bus
··············	Boat

To Rome

Capodichino Airport

PARKING & TICKETS

Mt. Vesuvius
1277M

Naples

TRAIL
(30 MIN. HIKE)

HERCULANEUM
RUINS

Ercolano
Scavi
Station

Pompei (Town)

To Salerno

Bay of Naples

Pompei Scavi
Station

POMPEII
RUINS

10 Kilometers

10 Miles

To Capri

To Sorrento

To Sorrento

NAPLES

volumes about daily Roman life. Pompeii was accidentally rediscovered in 1599; excavations began in 1748.

Orientation

Cost: €11.

Hours: Daily April-Oct 8:30-19:30, Nov-March 8:30-17:00, last entry 1.5 hours before closing.

Closures: Be warned that some buildings and streets are bound to be closed for restoration when you visit. If you get totally derailed, just use the map and numbers to find your way.

Crowd-Beating Tips: On busy days, there can be a wait of up to 30 minutes to buy a ticket. If you anticipate lines, buy your ticket at the "info point" kiosk at the train station (same price as at the site).

Getting There: Pompeii is roughly midway between Naples and Sorrento on the Circumvesuviana train line (2/hour, €2.90 and 40 minutes from Naples, €2.20 and 30 minutes from Sorrento, one-way, not covered by rail passes). Get off at the Pompei Scavi-Villa dei Misteri stop; from Naples, it's the stop after Torre Annunziata. From the Pompei Scavi train station, it's just a two-minute walk to the Porta Marina entrance: Turn right and walk down the road about a block to the entrance (on your left).

Pompei vs. Pompei Scavi: Remember, Pompei is the name of a separate train station on the national rail network that's a long, dull walk from the ruins. Make sure you're taking the Circumvesuviana commuter train to Pompei Scavi (*scavi* means "excavations").

Parking: Parking is available at Camping Zeus, next to the Pompei Scavi train station (€2.50/hour, €10/12 hours, 10 percent discount with this book); several other campgrounds/parking lots are nearby.

Information: The "info point" kiosk at the station is a private agency selling tours (not a real TI; see "Tours," later), but they can provide some information and also sell tickets for the site.

Be sure to pick up the free, helpful map at the entrance (ask for it when you buy your ticket, or check at the info window to the left of the WCs—the maps aren't available within the walls of Pompeii). Tel. 081-857-5347, www.pompeiisites. org.

The bookshop sells the small Pompeii and Herculaneum *Past and Present* book. Its plastic overlays allow you to re-create the ruins (€12; if you buy from a street vendor, pay no more than that).

Tours: My **self-guided tour** in this chapter covers the basics and provides a good framework for exploring the site on your own. You can download my Pompeii coverage as a free Rick Steves **audio tour;** see page 8.

Guided tours leave every hour from the "info point" kiosk near the train station (€12). You can also sign up for a guided tour of Pompeii offered to Rick Steves readers through Naples-based Mondo Tours (€15, entry fee extra, Mon-Fri at 10:30, meet at Ristorante Suisse, on Piazza Esedra, down the hill from the Porta Marina entrance; see page 475).

Private guides (around €110/2 hours) of varying quality—there really is no guarantee of what you're getting—cluster near the ticket booth at the site and may try to herd you into a group with other travelers, which makes the price more reasonable for you. For a private two-hour tour, consider **Gaetano Manfredi,** who is pricey but brings energy and theatricality to his tours (€120 for up to 4 people, reserve in advance by email and mention this book, www.pompeiitourguide.com, gaetanoguide@hotmail.it). **Antonio Somma** mainly specializes in Pompeii (from €120—varies with season and number of people, book in advance, evening tel. 081-850-1992, daytime mobile 393-406-3824 or 339-891-9489, www.pompeitour. com, info@pompeitour.com). Antonio can organize transport for visitors who want to fill up the rest of the day with a trip to the Amalfi Coast. The Naples-based guides recommended on page 474 can also guide you at Pompeii. Parents, note that the

Pompeii

See Pompeii Tour map

VESUVIUS (IN DISTANCE)

VILLA DEI MISTERI

PORTA DEL VESUVIO

CITY

To Naples

PATH

VIA SEPOLCRI

PORTA DI ERCOLANO

HOUSE OF THE VETTII

HOUSE OF THE FAUN

VIA FORTUNA

BATHS OF THE FORUM

To Naples

A-3

CAFETERIA & WC

AUTOSTRADA

CAMPING ZEUS OFFICE

CIRCUMVESUVIANA TRAIN STATION (WC & BAG STORAGE)

Bus to Vesuvius

PORTA MARINA MAIN ENTRANCE

FORUM

To Naples

SS-18

TICKETS

EXIT

TICKETS

Piazza Esedra

200 Meters

200 Yards

A-3

RISTORANTE SUISSE

HOTEL VITTORIA

VIA M.S.S.

To Salerno

To Sorrento

NAPLES

ancient brothel and its sexually explicit frescoes are included on tours; let your guide know if you'd rather skip that stop.

Audioguides are available from a kiosk near the ticket booth at the Porta Marina entrance (€6.50, €10/2 people, ID required), but they offer basically the same info as your free booklet.

Length of This Tour: Allow two hours, or three if you visit the theater and amphitheater. With less time, focus on the Forum, Baths of the Forum, House of the Faun, and brothel.

Baggage Check: The train station offers luggage storage for €3/ bag (downstairs, by the WC). Or use the free baggage check near the turnstiles at the site entrance.

Services: A WC is at the train station (€0.50). The site has two WCs—one near the entrance and another in the cafeteria.

Eating: The Ciao cafeteria within the site serves good sandwiches, pizza, and pasta at a reasonable price. A few mediocre restaurants cluster between the entrance and the train station. Your cheapest bet may be to bring your own food for a discreet picnic.

Starring: Roofless (collapsed) but otherwise intact Roman buildings, plaster casts of hapless victims, a few erotic frescoes, and the dawning realization that these ancient people were not that different from us.

BACKGROUND

Pompeii, founded in 600 B.C., eventually became a booming Roman trading city. Not rich, not poor, it was middle class—a perfect example of typical Roman life. Most streets would have been lined with stalls and jammed with customers from sunup to sundown.

Chariots vied with shoppers for street space. Two thousand years ago, Rome controlled the entire Mediterranean—making it a kind of free-trade zone—and Pompeii was a central and bustling port.

There were no posh neighborhoods in Pompeii. Rich and poor mixed it up as elegant houses existed side by side with simple homes. While nearby Herculaneum would have been a classier place to live (traffic-free streets, fancier houses, far better drainage), Pompeii was the place for action and shopping. It served an estimated 20,000 residents with more than 40 bakeries, 30 brothels, and 130 bars, restaurants, and hotels. With most of its buildings covered by brilliant white ground-marble stucco, Pompeii in A.D. 79 was an impressive town.

As you tour Pompeii, remember that its best art is in the Archaeological Museum in Naples (described earlier in this chapter).

The Tour Begins

• *Just past the ticket-taker, start your approach up to the...*

❶ Porta Marina

The city of Pompeii was born on the hill ahead of you. This was the original town gate. Before Vesuvius blew and filled in the harbor, the sea came nearly to here. Notice the two openings in the

gate (ahead, up the ramp). Both were left open by day to admit major traffic. At night, the larger one was closed for better security.

• *Pass through the Porta Marina and continue up to the top of the street, pausing at the three large stepping-stones in the middle.*

❷ Pompeii's Streets

Every day, Pompeiians flooded the streets with gushing water to clean them. These stepping-stones let pedestrians cross without getting their sandals wet. Chari-

ots traveling in either direction could straddle the stones (all had standard-size axles). A single stepping-stone in a road means it was a one-way street, a pair indicates an ordinary two-way, and three (like this) signifies a major thoroughfare. The basalt stones are the original Roman pavement. The sidewalks (elevated to hide the plumbing) were paved with bits of broken pots (an ancient form of recycling) and studded with reflective bits of white marble. These "cats' eyes" helped people get around after dark, either by moonlight or with the help of lamps.

Pompeii Tour

VESUVIUS
(IN DISTANCE)

PATH

CITY WALLS

PORTA DEL
VESUVIO

UNEXCAVATED AREA

VIA VETTII

VIA VESUVIO

VIA NOLA

HOUSE OF
THE VETTII
(MAY BE
CLOSED)

HOUSE
OF THE
FAUN

PORTA DI
ERCOLANO

VIA MERCURIO

VIA CONSULARE

VIA FORTUNA

TABERNA
HEDONES

VIA STABIANA

VIA

VIA AUGUSTALI

VIA ABBONDANZA

CAFETERIA
& WC

VIA TEATRI

CITY WALLS

TEMPLE
OF JUPITER

FORUM

Bus to
B Vesuvius

To 18

NAPLES

PORTA
MARINA
ENTRANCE

TICKETS

TEATRO
PICCOLO

THEATER

CIRCUM-
VESUVIANA
TRAIN
STATION

WALK BEGINS

WALK ENDS

EXIT

CITY WALLS

VIA DEI TEATRI

PIAZZA
ESEDRA
ENTRANCE

Piazza
Esedra

TICKETS

RISTORANTE
SUISSE

HOTEL
VITTORIA

SS-18

To →
Pompei
(Town)

VIA PLINIO

To
Sorrento

200 Meters

200 Yards

① Porta Marina
② Pompeii's Streets
③ Forum
④ Basilica
⑤ Via Abbondanza
⑥ Fish & Produce Market;
   Plaster Casts of Victims
⑦ Baths of the Forum
⑧ Fast-Food Joint
⑨ House of the Tragic Poet

⑩ Aqueduct Arch
⑪ House of the Faun
⑫ Original Lead Pipes
⑬ House of the Vettii
⑭ Bakery & Mill
⑮ Brothel
⑯ Temple of Isis
⑰ Theater &
   Piccolo Theater
⑱ To Amphitheater

• *Continue straight ahead, don your mental toga, and enter the city as the Romans once did. The road opens up into the spacious main square: the Forum. Stand at the near end of this rectangular space and look toward Mount Vesuvius.*

❸ The Forum (Foro)

Pompeii's commercial, religious, and political center stands at the intersection of the city's two main streets. While it's the most ruined part of Pompeii, it's grand nonetheless. Picture the piazza surrounded by two-story buildings on all sides. The pedestals that line the square once held statues (now safely displayed in the museum in Naples). In its heyday, Pompeii's citizens gathered here in the main square to shop, talk politics, and socialize. Business took place in the important buildings that lined the piazza.

The Forum was dominated by the **Temple of Jupiter,** at the far end (marked by a half-dozen ruined columns atop a stair-step base). Jupiter was the supreme god of the Roman pantheon—you might be able to make out his little white marble head at the center-rear of the temple.

At the near end of the Forum (behind where you're standing) is the **curia,** or city hall. Like many Roman buildings, it was built with brick and mortar, then covered with marble walls and floors. To your left (as you face Vesuvius and the Temple of Jupiter) is the **basilica,** or courthouse.

Since Pompeii was a pretty typical Roman town, it has the same layout and components that you'll find in any Roman city—main square, curia, basilica, temples, axis of roads, and so on. All power converged at the Forum: religious (the temple), political (the curia), judicial (the basilica), and commercial (this piazza was the main marketplace). Even the power of the people was expressed here, since this is where they gathered to vote. Imagine the hubbub of this town square in its heyday.

Look beyond the Temple of Jupiter. Five miles to the north looms the ominous backstory to this site: **Mount Vesuvius.** Mentally draw a triangle up from the two remaining peaks to reconstruct the mountain before the eruption. When it blew, Pompeians had no idea that they were living under a volcano, as Vesuvius hadn't erupted for 1,200 years. Imagine the wonder—then the horror—as a column of pulverized rock roared upward, and then ash began to fall. The weight of the ash and small rocks collapsed

Pompeii's roofs later that day, crushing people who had taken refuge inside buildings instead of fleeing the city.

• *As you face Vesuvius, the basilica is to your left, lined with stumps of columns. Step inside and see the layout.*

❹ Basilica

Pompeii's basilica was a first-century palace of justice. This ancient law court has the same floor plan later adopted by many Christian churches (which are also called basilicas). The big central hall (or nave) is flanked by rows of columns marking off narrower side aisles. Along the side walls are traces of the original marble.

The columns—now stumps all about the same height—were not ruined by the volcano. Rather, they were left unfinished when

Vesuvius blew. Pompeii had been devastated by an earthquake in A.D. 62, and was just in the process of rebuilding the basilica when Vesuvius erupted, 17 years later. The half-built columns show off the technology of the day. Uniform bricks were stacked around a cylindrical core. Once finished, they would have been coated with marble-dust stucco to simulate marble columns—an economical construction method found throughout Pompeii (and the Roman Empire).

Besides the earthquake and the eruption, Pompeii's buildings have suffered other ravages over the years, including Spanish plunderers (c. 1800), 19th-century souvenir hunters, WWII bombs, wild vegetation, another earthquake in 1980, and modern neglect. The fact that the entire city was covered by the eruption of A.D. 79 actually helped preserve it, saving it from the sixth-century barbarians who plundered many other towns into oblivion.

• *Exit the basilica and cross the short side of the square, where the city's main street hits the Forum.*

❺ Via Abbondanza

Glance down Via Abbondanza, Pompeii's main street. Lined with shops, bars, and restaurants, it was a lively, pedestrian-only zone.

The three "beaver-teeth" stones are traffic barriers that kept chariots out. On the corner (just to the left), take a close look at the dark travertine column standing next to the white one. Notice that the marble drums of the white column are not chiseled entirely round—another construction project left unfinished when Vesuvius erupted.

• *Head toward Vesuvius, walking along the right side of the Forum. Immediately to the right of the Temple of Jupiter (just before the four round arches), a door leads into the market hall, where you'll find two glass cases.*

❻ Fish and Produce Market—Plaster Casts of Victims

As the frescoes on the wall (just inside on the left) indicate, this is where Pompeiians came to buy their food—fish, bread, chickens, and so on. These fine examples of Roman art—with their glimpses of everyday life and their mastery of depth and illusion—would not be matched until the Renaissance, a thousand years after the fall of Rome.

The glass cases hold casts of Pompeiians, eerily captured in their last moments. They were quickly suffocated by a superheated avalanche of gas and ash, and their bodies were encased in volcanic debris. While excavating, modern archaeologists detected hollow spaces underfoot, created when the victims' bodies decomposed. By gently filling the holes with plaster, the archaeologists were able to create molds of the Pompeiians who were caught in the disaster.

• *Continue on, leaving the Forum through an arch behind the Temple of Jupiter. Here you'll find a pedestrian-only road sign (ahead on the right corner, above the* REG VII INS IV *sign) and more "beaver-teeth" traffic blocks. The modern cafeteria is the only eatery inside the archaeological site (with a coffee bar and WC upstairs). Twenty yards past the cafeteria, on the left-hand side at #24, is the entrance to the...*

❼ Baths of the Forum (Terme del Foro)

Pompeii had six public baths, each with a men's and a women's section. You're in the men's zone. The leafy courtyard at the entrance was the gymnasium. After working out, clients could relax with a hot bath *(caldarium)*, warm bath *(tepidarium)*, or cold plunge *(frigidarium)*.

The first big, plain room you enter served as the **dressing room.** Holes on the walls were for pegs to hang clothing. High up, the window (with a faded Neptune underneath) was originally covered with a less-translucent Roman glass. Walk over the non-slip mosaics into the next room.

The *tepidarium* is ringed by mini-statues or *telamones* (male caryatids, figures used as supporting pillars), which divided the

The Eruption of Vesuvius

At about 1:00 in the afternoon on August 24, A.D. 79, Mount Vesuvius erupted, sending a mushroom cloud of ash, dust, and rocks 12 miles into the air. It spewed for 18 hours straight, as winds blew the cloud southward. The white-gray ash settled like a heavy snow on Pompeii, its weight eventually collapsing roofs and floors, but leaving the walls intact. And though most of Pompeii's 20,000 residents fled that day, about 2,000 stayed behind. Then, at around 7:30 in the morning, another pyroclastic flow headed south and struck Pompeii, dealing a fatal blow to those who'd remained behind.

lockers. Clients would undress and warm up here, perhaps stretching out on one of the bronze benches near the bronze heater for a massage. Look at the ceiling—half crushed by the eruption and half intact, with its fine blue-and-white stucco work.

Next, admire the engineering in the steam-bath room, or *caldarium*. The double floor was heated from below—so nice with

bare feet (look into the grate to see the brick support towers). The double walls with brown terra-cotta tiles held the heat. Romans soaked in the big tub, which was filled with hot water. Opposite the big tub is a fountain, which spouted water onto the hot floor, creating steam. The lettering on the fountain reminded those enjoying the room which two

politicians paid for it...and how much it cost them (5,250 *sestertii*). To keep condensation from dripping annoyingly from the ceiling, fluting (ribbing) was added to carry water down the walls.

• *Today's visitors exit the baths through the original entry. If you're a bit hungry, immediately across the street is an ancient...*

❽ Fast-Food Joint

After a bath, it was only natural to want a little snack. So, just across the street is a fast-food joint, marked by a series of rectangular marble counters. Most ancient Romans didn't cook for themselves in their tiny apartments, so to-go places like this were commonplace. The holes

in the counters held the pots for food. Each container was like a thermos, with a wooden lid to keep the soup hot, the wine cool, and so on. Notice the groove in the front doorstep and the holes out on the curb. The holes likely accommodated cords for stretching awnings over the sidewalk to shield the clientele from the hot sun, while the grooves were for the shop's folding accordion doors. Look at the wheel grooves in the pavement, worn down through centuries of use. Nearby are more stepping-stones for pedestrians to cross the flooded streets.

• *Just a few steps uphill from the fast-food joint, at #5 (with a locked gate), is the...*

❾ House of the Tragic Poet (Casa del Poeta Tragico)

This house is typical Roman style. The entry is flanked by two family-owned shops (each with a track for a collapsing accordion door). The home is like a train running straight away from the street: atrium (with skylight and pool to catch the rain), den (where deals were made by the shopkeeper), and garden (with rooms facing it and a shrine to remember both the gods and family ancestors). In the entryway is the famous "Beware of Dog" *(Cave Canem)* mosaic.

Today's visitors enter the home by the back door (circle around to the left). On your way there, look for the modern exposed pipe on the left side of the lane; this is the same as ones used in the ancient plumbing system, hidden beneath the raised sidewalk. Inside the house, the grooves on the marble well-head in the entry hall (possibly closed) were formed by generations of inhabitants dragging the bucket up by rope. The richly frescoed dining room is off the garden. Diners lounged on their couches (the Roman custom) and enjoyed frescoes with fake "windows," giving the illusion of a bigger and airier room. Next to the dining room is a humble BBQ-style kitchen with a little closet for the toilet (the kitchen and bathroom shared the same plumbing).

• *Return to the fast-food place and continue about 10 yards downhill to the big intersection. From the center of the intersection, look left to see a giant arch, framing a nice view of Mount Vesuvius.*

❿ Aqueduct Arch—Running Water

Water was critical for this city of 20,000 people, and this arch was part of Pompeii's water-delivery system. A 100-mile-long aqueduct carried fresh water down from the hillsides to a big reservoir perched at the highest point of the city wall. Since overall water pressure was disappointing, Pompeians built arches like the brick one you see here (originally covered in marble) with hidden water tanks at the top. Located just below the altitude of the main tank, these smaller tanks were filled by gravity and provided each neighborhood with reliable pressure.

• *If you're thirsty, fill your water bottle from the modern fountain. Then continue straight downhill one block (50 yards) to #2 on the left.*

⓫ House of the Faun (Casa del Fauno)

Stand across the street and marvel at the grand entry with *"HAVE"* (hail to you) as a welcome mat. Go in. Notice the two shrines above

the entryway—one dedicated to the gods, the other to this wealthy family's ancestors.

You are standing in Pompeii's largest home, where you're greeted by the delightful small bronze statue of the *Dancing Faun,* famed for its realistic movement and fine proportion. (The original, described on page 479, is in Naples' Archaeological Museum.) With 40 rooms and 27,000 square feet, the House of the Faun covers an entire city block. The next floor mosaic, with an intricate diamond-like design, decorates the homeowner's office. Beyond that is the famous floor mosaic of the *Battle of Alexander.* (The original is also at the museum in Naples.) In 333 B.C., Alexander the Great beat Darius and the Persians. Romans had great respect for Alexander, the first great emperor before Rome's. While most of Pompeii's nouveau riche had notoriously bad taste and stuffed their palaces with over-the-top, mismatched decor, this guy had class. Both the faun (an ancient copy of a famous Greek statue) and the Alexander mosaic show an appreciation for history.

The house's back courtyard leads to the exit in the far-right corner. It's lined with pillars rebuilt after the A.D. 62 earthquake. Take a close look at the brick, mortar, and fake marble stucco veneer.

• *Sneak out of the House of the Faun through its back door and turn right. (If this exit is closed, return to the entrance and make a U-turn left, around to the back of the house.) Thirty yards down, along the right-hand side of the street are metal cages protecting...*

⓬ Original Lead Pipes

These 2,000-year-old pipes (made of lead imported from Britannia) were part of the city's elaborate water system. From the aqueduct-fed water tank at the high end of town, three independent pipe systems supplied water to the city: one for baths, one for private

NAPLES

homes, and one for public water fountains. If there was a water shortage, democratic priorities prevailed: First the baths were cut off, then the private homes. The last water supply to go was the public fountains, where all citizens could get drinking and cooking water.

• *If the street's not closed off, take your first left (on Vicolo dei Vettii), walk about 20 yards, and find the entrance (on the left) to the next stop. (If the street is closed, turn right down the street marked* REG VI INS XIV *and skip down to the next set of directions.)*

⓭ House of the Vettii (Casa dei Vettii)

Pompeii's best-preserved home has been completely blocked off for years; unfortunately, it's unlikely to reopen in time for your visit. The House of the Vettii was the bachelor pad of two wealthy merchant brothers. If you can see the entryway, you may spot the huge erection. This is not pornography. There's a meaning here: The penis and the sack of money balance each other on the goldsmith scale above a fine bowl of fruit. Translation: Only with a balance of fertility and money can you have abundance.

If it's open, step into the atrium with its ceiling open to the sky to collect light and rainwater. The pool, while decorative, was a functional water-supply tank. It's flanked by large money boxes anchored to the floor. The brothers were certainly successful merchants, and possibly moneylenders, too.

Exit on the right, passing the tight servant quarters, and go into the kitchen, with its bronze cooking pots (and an exposed lead pipe on the back wall). The passage dead-ends in the little Venus Room, which features erotic frescoes behind glass.

Return to the atrium and pass into the big colonnaded garden. It was replanted according to the plan indicated by the traces of roots that were excavated from the volcanic ash. Richly frescoed entertainment rooms ring this courtyard. Circle counterclockwise. The dining room is finely decorated in black and "Pompeiian red" (from iron rust). Study the detail. Notice the lead humidity seal between the wall and the floor, designed to keep the moisture-sensitive frescoes dry. (Had Leonardo da Vinci taken this clever step, his *Last Supper* in Milan might be in better shape today.) Continuing around, you'll see more of the square white stones inlaid in the floor. Imagine them reflecting like cats' eyes as the brothers and their friends wandered around by oil lamp late at night. Frescoes in the Yellow Room (near the exit) show off the ancient mastery of perspective, which would not be matched elsewhere in Europe for nearly 1,500 years.

• *Facing the entrance to the House of the Vettii, turn left and walk downhill one long block (along Vicolo dei Vettii) to a T-intersection (Via della Fortuna), marked by a stone fountain with a bull's head for a spout. Intersections like this were busy neighborhood centers, where the rent was highest and people gathered. With the fountain at your back, turn left, then immediately right, walking along a gently curving road (Vicolo Storto). On the left side of the street, at #22, find four big stone cylinders.*

NAPLES

⑭ Bakery and Mill (Forno e Mulini)

The brick oven looks like a modern-day pizza oven. The stubby stone towers are flour grinders. Grain was poured into the top, and

donkeys or slaves pushed wooden bars that turned the stones. The powdered grain dropped out of the bottom as flour—flavored with tiny bits of rock. Each neighborhood had a bakery like this.

Continue to the next intersection (Via degli Augustali, marked *REG VII*

INS XII, where there's another fast-food joint, at #33) and turn left. As you walk, look at the destructive power of all the vines, and notice how deeply the chariot grooves have worn into the pavement. Deep grooves could break wagon wheels. The suddenly ungroovy stretch indicates that this road was in the process of being repaved when the eruption shut everything down.

• *Head about 50 yards down this (obviously one-way) street to #44 (on the left). Here you'll find the Taberna Hedones (with a small atrium, den, and garden). This bar still has its original floor and, deeper in, the mosaic arch of a grotto fountain. Just past the tavern, turn right and walk downhill to #18, on the right.*

Possible detour: If the road past the tavern is blocked off, here's another way to reach the next stop: First, backtrack to the Forum—go back the way you came, turn left at the bull's-head fountain, then turn left again at the aqueduct arch. Back in the Forum, head down to the far end and turn left onto the main street, Via dell'Abbondanza (which we looked down earlier—remember the beaver teeth?). Follow this, turning left up the street after the second fountain (marked REG VII INS I, with a small Vicolo del Lupanare sign). This leads to the entrance of the...

⑮ Brothel (Lupanare)

You'll find the biggest crowds in Pompeii at a place that was likely popular 2,000 ago, too—the brothel. Prostitutes were nicknamed *lupe* (she-wolves), alluding to the call they made when trying to attract business. The brothel was a simple place, with beds and pillows made of stone. The ancient graffiti includes tallies and exotic names of the women, indicating the prostitutes came from all corners of the Mediterranean (it also served as feedback from satisfied customers). The faded frescoes above the cells may have been a kind of menu for services offered. Note the idealized women (white, which was considered beautiful; one wears an early bra) and the rougher men (dark, considered horny). The bed legs came with little disk-like barriers to keep critters from crawling up.

• *Leaving the brothel, go right, then take the first left, and continue going downhill two blocks to the intersection with Pompeii's main drag, Via dell'Abbondanza. The Forum—and exit—are to the right, for those who may wish to opt out from here.*

The huge amphitheater—which is certainly skippable—is 10 minutes to your left. But for now, go left for 60 yards, then turn right just beyond the fountain, and walk down Via dei Teatri (labeled REG VIII INS IV). Turn left before the columns, and head downhill another 60 yards to #28, which marks the...

⑯ Temple of Isis

This Egyptian temple served Pompeii's Egyptian community. The little white stucco shrine with the modern plastic roof housed holy water from the Nile. Isis, from Egyptian myth, was one of many foreign gods adopted by the eclectic Romans. Pompeii must have had a synagogue, too, but it has yet to be excavated.

• *Exit the temple where you entered, and go right. At the next intersection, turn right again, and head downhill to the adjacent theaters. Your goal is the large theater down the corridor at #20, but if it's closed, look at the smaller but similar theater (Teatro Piccolo) just beyond at #19.*

⑰ Theater

Originally a Greek theater (Greeks built theirs with the help of a hillside), this was the birthplace of the Greek port here in 470 B.C. During Roman times, the theater sat 5,000 people in three sets of seats, all with different prices: the five marble terraces up close (filled with romantic wooden seats for two), the main section, and

the cheap nosebleed sec-
tion (surviving only on the
high end, near the trees).
The square stones above
the cheap seats once sup-
ported a canvas rooftop.
Take note of the high-
profile boxes, flanking the
stage, for guests of honor.
From this perch, you can
see the gladiator bar-

racks—the colonnaded courtyard beyond the theater. They lived
in tiny rooms, trained in the courtyard, and fought in the nearby
amphitheater.

• *You've seen Pompeii's highlights. When you're ready to leave, backtrack
to the main road and turn left, going uphill to the Forum, where you'll
find the main exit. For a shortcut back to the entrance area (with the
bookstore, luggage storage, and quickest access to the train station), when
you are halfway down the exit ramp, take the eight steps on the right
and follow the signs. Otherwise, you'll end up on the main road—where
you'll head right and loop around.*

*However, there's much more to see—three-quarters of Pom-
peii's 164 acres have been excavated, but this tour has covered only
a third of the site. After the theater—if you still have energy to see
more—go back to the main road and take a right toward the eastern
part of the site, where the crowds thin out. Go straight for about 10
minutes, likely jogging right after a bit (just follow the posted maps).
You'll wind up passing through a pretty, forested area. At the far end
is the...*

⑱ Amphitheater

If you can, climb to the upper level of
the amphitheater (though the stairs are
often blocked). With Vesuvius looming
in the background, mentally replace
the tourists below with gladiators and
wild animals locked in combat. Walk
along the top of the amphitheater and
look down into the grassy rectangular
area surrounded by columns. This is the
Palaestra, an area once used for athletic
training. (If you can't get to the top of the
amphitheater, you can see the Palaestra
from outside—in fact, you can't miss it,
as it's right next door.) Facing the other way, look for the bell tower
that tops the roofline of the modern city of Pompei, where locals

go about their daily lives in the shadow of the volcano, just as their ancestors did 2,000 years ago.

• *If it's too crowded to bear hiking back along uneven lanes to the entrance, you can slip out the site's "back door," which is next to the amphitheater. Exiting, turn right and follow the site's wall all the way back to the entrance.*

ROMAN HISTORY

Three Millennia in Seven Pages

HISTORY IN A HURRY

Ancient Rome lasted a thousand years (500 B.C.-A.D. 500), half as an expanding republic, half as a dominating empire. When Rome fell to invaders, all of Europe suffered a thousand years of poverty and ignorance (A.D. 500-1500), though Rome's influence could still be felt in the Catholic Church. Popes rebuilt Rome for pilgrims—in Renaissance, then Baroque and Neoclassical styles (1500-1800). As capital of a newly united Italy, Rome followed fascist Mussolini into World War II (and lost), but rebounded in Italy's postwar economic boom.

Want more?

LEGENDARY BIRTH (1200-500 B.C.)

Aeneas flees burning Troy (1200 B.C.), wanders like Odysseus, and finally finds a home along the Tiber. His descendants, Romulus and Remus—orphaned at birth, suckled by a she-wolf, and raised by shepherds—grow up to steal wives and build a wall, thus founding Rome (753 B.C.).

Closer to fact, the local agrarian tribes were dominated by more sophisticated neighbors to the north (Etruscans) and south (Greek colonists). Their convenient location on the Tiber was perfect for a future power.

Sights
- Romulus' "huts" and wall (Palatine Hill)
- She-Wolf statue (Capitoline Museums)
- Frescoes of Aeneas and Romulus (National Museum of Rome)
- Bernini's Aeneas statue (Borghese Gallery)
- Etruscan wing (Vatican Museum)
- Etruscan Museum (in Villa Borghese Gardens)
- Etruscan legacy (the original Circus Maximus, the drained Forum)

THE REPUBLIC (509-27 B.C.)

The city expands throughout the Italian peninsula (500-300 B.C.), then defeats Hannibal's North African Carthaginians (the Punic Wars, 264-146 B.C.) and Greece (168 B.C.). Rome is master of the Mediterranean, and booty and captured slaves pour in. Romans bicker among themselves over their slice of the pie, pitting the wealthy landowners (the ruling Senate) against the working class (plebs) and the rebellious slaves (Spartacus' revolt, 73 B.C.). In the chaos, charismatic generals like Julius Caesar, who can provide wealth and security, become dictators. Change is necessary...and coming.

Sights
- Forum's Curia, Temple of Saturn, Temple of Castor and Pollux, Rostrum, Basilica Aemilia, Temple of Julius Caesar, and Basilica Julia (all rebuilt later)
- Appian Way built, lined with tombs
- Aqueducts, which carry water to a growing city
- Portrait busts of citizens (National Museum of Rome)

- The republic's "S.P.Q.R." monogram and motto, seen today on statues, buildings, and even manhole covers: *Senatus Populusque Romanus,* or the "Senate and People of Rome." (Some northern Italians, who feel the South is dragging them down, translate S.P.Q.R. as *Sono Porci Questi Romani*—"These Romans Are Pigs.")

THE EMPIRE—THE "ROMAN PEACE," OR PAX ROMANA (A.D. 1-200)

After Julius Caesar is killed by disgruntled republicans, his adopted son Augustus takes undisputed control, ends the civil wars, declares himself emperor, and adopts a family member to succeed him, setting the pattern of rule for the next 500 years.

Rome rules an empire of 54 million people, stretching from England to Africa, from Spain to Turkey. The city, with more than a million inhabitants, is decorated with Greek-style statues and monumental structures faced with marble...it is the marvel of the known world. The empire prospers on a (false) economy of booty, slaves, and trade, surviving the often turbulent and naughty behavior of emperors such as Caligula and Nero. You can see Roman history in the faces of the emperors by reading the ✪ National Museum of Rome Tour chapter.

Sights

- Colosseum
- Forum
- Palatine Hill palaces
- Ara Pacis ("Altar of Peace")
- Augustus' house (House of Livia and Augustus) on Palatine Hill
- Pantheon
- Trajan's Column and Forum
- Greek and Greek-style statues and emperors' busts (National Museum of Rome, Vatican Museum, Capitoline Museums)
- Piazza Navona (former stadium)
- Hadrian's Villa (Tivoli) and tomb (now Castel Sant'Angelo)

ROME FALLS (200-476)

Corruption, disease, and the constant pressure of barbarians pecking away at the borders slowly drain the unwieldy empire. Despite

Diocletian's division of the empire and Constantine's legalization of Christianity (313), the city is sacked (410), and the last emperor checks out (476). Rome falls like a huge column, kicking up dust that will plunge Europe into a thousand years of darkness.

Sights
- Arch of Constantine
- The Forum's Basilica of Constantine
- Baths of Diocletian
- Old Roman Wall (gates at Via Veneto or Piramide)

MEDIEVAL ROME (500-1500)

The once-great city of a million people dwindles to a rough village of 20,000, with a corrupt pope, forgotten ruins, and malaria-carrying mosquitoes. Cows graze in the ruined Forum, and wolves prowl the Vatican at night. During the 1300s, even the popes leave Rome to live in France. What little glory Rome retains is in the pomp, knowledge, and wealth of the Catholic Church.

Sights
- The damage done to ancient Roman monuments, caused by disuse, barbarian looting, and pillaging for pre-cut stones
- Early Christian churches built before Rome fell (Santa Maria Maggiore, San Giovanni in Laterano, and San Clemente)
- Churches of Santa Maria sopra Minerva and Santa Maria in Trastevere
- Castel Sant'Angelo

RENAISSANCE AND BAROQUE ROME (1500-1800)

As Europe's economy recovers, energetic popes rebuild Rome to attract pilgrims. The best artists decorate palaces and churches, carve statues, and build fountains. The city is not a great political force, but as the center of Catholicism during the struggle against Protestants (c. 1520-1648), it is an influential religious and cultural capital.

Renaissance Sights

- Michelangelo's Sistine Chapel (Vatican Museum), dome of St. Peter's, *Pietà* (St. Peter's), *Moses* (St. Peter-in-Chains Church), Christ statue (Santa Maria sopra Minerva), Piazza del Campidoglio (Capitoline Hill Square), Santa Maria degli Angeli church (in former Baths of Diocletian)

Church Architecture

History comes to life when you visit a centuries-old church. Even if you wouldn't know your apse from a hole in the ground, learning a few simple terms will enrich your experience. Note that not every church has every feature, and that a "cathedral" isn't a type of church architecture, but rather a designation for a church that's a governing center for a local bishop.

Aisles: The long, generally low-ceilinged arcades that flank the nave.

Altar: The raised area with a ceremonial table (often adorned with candles or a crucifix), where the priest prepares and serves the bread and wine for Communion.

Apse: The space beyond the altar, generally bordered with small chapels.

Barrel Vault: A continuous round-arched ceiling that resembles an extended upside-down U.

Choir: A cozy area, often screened off, located within the church nave and near the high altar, where services are sung in a more intimate setting.

Cloister: A square-shaped series of hallways surrounding an open-air courtyard, traditionally where monks and nuns got fresh air.

Facade: The outer wall of the church's main (west) entrance, viewable from outside and generally highly decorated.

Groin Vault: An arched ceiling formed where two equal barrel vaults meet at right angles. Less common usage: term for a medieval jock strap.

Narthex: The area (portico or foyer) between the main entry and the nave.

Nave: The long, central section of the church (running west to east, from the entrance to the altar) where the congregation stood through the service.

Transept: The north-south part of the church, which crosses (perpendicularly) the east-west nave. In a traditional Latin cross-shaped floor plan, the transept forms the "arms" of the cross.

West Portal: The main entry to the church (on the west end, opposite the main altar).

- Raphael's School of Athens and Transfiguration (Vatican Museum)
- Paintings by Raphael, Titian, and others (Borghese Gallery)

Baroque Sights
- St. Peter's Square and interior (largely by Bernini)
- Bernini statues (at Borghese Gallery; also *St. Teresa in Ecstasy* at Santa Maria della Vittoria church) and fountains (Piazza Navona, Piazza Barberini)
- Ancient obelisks erected in squares (Piazza del Popolo, Piazza Navona)
- Trevi Fountain and Spanish Steps
- Gesù and San Ignazio churches
- Caravaggio's *Calling of St. Matthew* (San Luigi dei Francesi Church) and other paintings (Borghese Gallery and Vatican Museum)
- Baroque paintings (Borghese Gallery)
- Borromini's facade of Santa Agnese Church (Piazza Navona)

MODERN ROME (1800-PRESENT)

Rome becomes the capital of a newly reunited Italy (1871) under King Victor Emmanuel II, is modernized by fascist Mussolini, and survives the destruction of World War II to become a republic. Italy's postwar "economic miracle" makes Rome a world-class city of cinema, banking, and tourism.

Sights
- Victor Emmanuel II Monument, which honors modern Italy's first (democratic) king
- Mussolini: the balcony he spoke from (at Palazzo Venezia, on Piazza Venezia), his planned city (E.U.R.), grand boulevards (Via dei Fori Imperiali, Via della Conciliazione), his home (Villa Torlonia), and Olympic Stadium
- Cinecittà film studios and Via Veneto nightlife, which have faint echoes of Fellini's *La Dolce Vita*
- Subway system, broad boulevards, smog

ROME TODAY

After surviving the government-a-year turbulence and Mafia-tainted corruption of the postwar years, Rome is stabilizing. Today, the average Roman makes more money than the average English-

Rome in World War II

By 1943, as bombs began falling just outside the walls of Rome, it was clear to all that Italy's alliance with Nazi Germa- ny was a huge mistake, leading the country to ruin. The fascist Grand Council dismissed Mussolini, and the king ordered his arrest. The ex-dictator fled north, and fascism collapsed without violence. Rome was declared an "open city" (meaning a city with no military bases). Italy surrendered to the Allies. The king fled to Allied-occupied southern Italy, abandoning Rome to Nazi forces, which occupied it for nine terrible months. The Roman people and the Vatican joined forces to save some citizens from the Nazis.

The Gestapo demanded 50 kilos of gold from the Roman Jews, who, with great difficulty and help from non-Jews, succeeded in providing it. Regardless, more than 2,000 Jews were deported to concentration camps. After Italian partisans planted a bomb near the Trevi Fountain, killing 32 Germans, more than 300 people randomly chosen from Rome's prison were executed in retaliation. This tragic event—called the Fosse Ardeatine massacre, for the caves near the Appian Way where it took place—remains an important landmark in the Italian consciousness (for details on visiting the memorial, see page 333). As the Allies marched closer, they bombed Rome and its surroundings, but avoided striking the center.

Thankfully, Hitler granted the occupying Nazi troops permission to leave the city, which he declared a "place of culture" that should not be "the scene of combat operations." Pope Pius XII agreed, declaring, "Whoever raises a hand against Rome will be guilty of matricide to the whole civilized world and in the eternal judgment of God." Finally, the Germans marched out, the Americans marched in (through the gate of San Giovanni) on June 4, 1944, and the exhausted city welcomed them with joy and relief.

man. The city is less polluted and more organized. In celebration of the millennium, the Eternal City gave its monuments a facelift. In 2010, Rome opened MAXXI, its new state-of-the-architecture museum of modern art. In 2013, the Vatican elected the first Jesuit pope, Francis I. And in 2014, Pope John Paul II was made a saint. Today's Rome is ready for pilgrims, travelers, and you to come and make more history.

For more on Roman history, consider *Europe 101: History and Art for the Traveler*, written by Rick Steves and Gene Openshaw (available at www.ricksteves.com).

PRACTICALITIES

Contents

This chapter covers the practical skills of European travel: how to get tourist information, pay for purchases, sightsee efficiently, use technology wisely, and get between destinations smoothly. To study ahead and round out your knowledge, check out "Resources" for a summary of recommended books and films.

Tourist Information

The Italian national tourist offices **in the US** are a wealth of information. Before your trip, scan their website (www.italia.it) or contact the nearest branch to briefly describe your trip and request information. You can download many brochures free of charge or call to order a free, general Italy guide. If you have a specific problem, they're a good source of sympathy. (**In New York:** Tel. 212/245-5618, newyork@enit.it; **In Chicago:** Tel. 312/644-0996, chicago@enit.it; **In Los Angeles:** Tel. 310/820-1898, losangeles@enit.it)

In Rome, a good first stop is generally the tourist information office (abbreviated **TI** in this book). TIs are good places to get a city map, advice on public transportation (including bus and train schedules), walking tours, special events, and nightlife. The TI's **call center** has English speakers and can answer most questions over the phone. Dial 06-0608 (answered daily 9:00-21:00, press 2 for English, www.060608.it). While Italian TIs are about half as helpful as those in other countries, their information is twice as important. Prepare a list of questions and a proposed plan to double-check.

Many TI offices and kiosks are scattered throughout Rome (listed on page 16; www.turismoroma.it). Other websites include www.vatican.va (St. Peter's Basilica) and http://mv.vatican.va (Vatican Museum).

Travel Tips

Emergency and Medical Help: In Italy, dial 113 for English-speaking police help. To summon an ambulance, call 118. If you get sick, do as the Romans do and go to a pharmacist for advice. Or ask at your hotel for help—they'll know the nearest medical and emergency services.

Theft or Loss: To replace a passport, you'll need to go in person to an embassy (see page 565). If your credit and debit cards disappear, cancel and replace them (see "Damage Control for Lost Cards" on page 527). File a police report, either on the spot or within a day or two; you'll need it to submit an insurance claim for lost or stolen rail passes or travel gear, and it can help with replacing your passport or credit and debit cards. For more information, see www.ricksteves.com/help. Precautionary measures can minimize the effects of loss—back up your digital photos and other files frequently.

Time Zones: Italy, like most of continental Europe, is generally six/nine hours ahead of the East/West Coasts of the US. The exceptions are the beginning and end of Daylight Saving Time: Europe "springs forward" the last Sunday in March (two weeks after most of North America), and "falls back" the last Sunday in October (one week before North America). For a handy online time converter, see www.timeanddate.com/worldclock.

Business Hours: Traditionally, Italy uses the siesta plan. People generally work from 9:00 to 13:00 and from 15:30 to 19:00, Monday through Saturday, although in tourist areas, shops are open longer. Many businesses have adopted the government's recommended 8:00 to 14:00 workday. Stores are usually closed on Sunday, and often on Monday. Banking hours are generally Monday through Friday 8:30 to 13:30 and 15:30 to 16:30, but can vary wildly.

Saturdays are virtually weekdays, with earlier closing hours. Sundays have the same pros and cons as they do in the US: Sightseeing attractions are generally open, while shops and banks are closed, public transportation options are fewer (for example, no bus service to or from the smaller towns), and there's no rush hour. Rowdy evenings are rare on Sundays.

Watt's Up? Europe's electrical system is 220 volts, instead of North America's 110 volts. Most newer electronics (such as laptops, battery chargers, and hair dryers) convert automatically, so you won't need a converter, but you will need an adapter plug with two round prongs, sold inexpensively at travel stores in the US. Avoid bringing older appliances that don't automatically convert voltage; instead, buy a cheap replacement in Europe.

Discounts: Discounts are not listed in this book. However, many sights offer discounts for youths (up to age 18), students (with proper identification cards, www.isic.org), families, seniors (loosely defined as retirees or those willing to call themselves a senior), and groups of 10 or more. Always ask. Italy's national museums generally offer free admission to children under 18, but some discounts are available only for citizens of the European Union (EU).

Online Translation Tip: You can use Google's Chrome browser (available free at www.google.com/chrome) to instantly translate websites. With one click, the page appears in (very rough) English translation. You can also paste the URL of the site into the translation window at www.google.com/translate.

Money

This section offers advice on how to pay for purchases on your trip (including getting cash from ATMs and paying with plastic), dealing with lost or stolen cards, VAT (sales tax) refunds, and tipping.

WHAT TO BRING

Bring both a credit card and a debit card. You'll use the debit card at cash machines (ATMs) to withdraw local cash for most purchases, and the credit card to pay for larger items. Some travelers carry a third card, in case one gets demagnetized or eaten by a temperamental machine.

For an emergency stash, bring several hundred dollars in hard cash in $20 bills. If you have to exchange the bills, go to a bank; avoid using currency-exchange booths because of their lousy rates and/or outrageous fees.

CASH

Cash is just as desirable in Europe as it is at home. Small businesses (mom-and-pop cafés, shops, etc.) prefer that you pay your bills with cash. Some vendors will charge you extra for using a credit

---

Exchange Rate

1 euro (€) = about $1.40

To convert prices in euros to dollars, add about 40 percent: €20 = about $28, €50 = about $70. (Check www.oanda.com for the latest exchange rates.) Just like the dollar, one euro is broken down into 100 cents. Coins range from €0.01 to €2, and bills ranging from €5 to €500.

---

card, and some won't take credit cards at all. Cash is the best—and sometimes only—way to pay for cheap food, bus fare, taxis, and local guides.

Throughout Italy, ATMs are the standard way for travelers to get cash. To withdraw money from an ATM (known as a *bancomat*), you'll need a debit card (ideally with a Visa or MasterCard logo for maximum usability), plus a PIN code. Know your PIN code in numbers; there are only numbers—no letters—on European keypads. For increased security, shield the keypad when entering your PIN code, and don't use an ATM if anything on the front of the machine looks loose or damaged (a sign that someone may have attached a "skimming" device to capture account information). Try to withdraw large sums of money to reduce the number of per-transaction bank fees you'll pay.

Whenever possible, use ATMs located outside banks—a thief is less likely to target a cash machine near surveillance cameras, and if your card is munched by a machine, you can go inside for help. Stay away from "independent" ATMs such as Travelex, Euronet, Moneybox, Cardpoint, and Cashzone, which charge huge commissions, have terrible exchange rates, and may try to trick users with "dynamic currency conversion" (described at the end of "Credit and Debit Cards," next).

Although you can use a credit card for an ATM transaction, it only makes sense in an emergency, because it's considered a cash advance (borrowed at a high interest rate) rather than a withdrawal.

While traveling, if you want to monitor your accounts online to detect any unauthorized transactions, be sure to use a secure connection (see page 541).

Pickpockets target tourists. To safeguard your cash, wear a money belt—a pouch with a strap that you buckle around your waist like a belt and tuck under your clothes. Keep your cash, credit cards, and passport secure in your money belt, and carry only a day's spending money in your front pocket.

CREDIT AND DEBIT CARDS

For purchases, Visa and MasterCard are more commonly accepted than American Express. Just like at home, credit or debit cards work easily at larger hotels, restaurants, and shops. I typically use my debit card to withdraw cash to pay for most purchases. I use my credit card only in a few specific situations: to book hotel reservations by phone, to cover major expenses (such as car rentals, plane tickets, and long hotel stays), and to pay for things near the end of my trip (to avoid another visit to the ATM). While you could use a debit card to make most large purchases, using a credit card offers a greater degree of fraud protection (because debit cards draw funds directly from your account).

Ask Your Credit- or Debit-Card Company: Before your trip, contact the company that issued your debit or credit cards.

• Confirm your **card will work overseas,** and alert them that you'll be using it in Europe; otherwise, they may deny transactions if they perceive unusual spending patterns.

• Ask for the specifics on transaction **fees.** When you use your credit or debit card—either for purchases or ATM withdrawals—you'll typically be charged additional "international transaction" fees of up to 3 percent (1 percent is normal) plus $5 per transaction. If your card's fees seem high, consider getting a card just for your trip: Capital One (credit cards only, www.capitalone.com) and most credit unions have low-to-no international fees.

• If you plan to withdraw cash from ATMs, confirm your daily **withdrawal limit,** and if necessary, ask your bank to adjust it. Some travelers prefer a high limit that allows them to take out more cash at each ATM stop (saving on bank fees), while others prefer to set a lower limit in case their card is stolen. Note that foreign banks also set maximum withdrawal amounts for their ATMs. Also, remember that you're withdrawing euros, not dollars—so if your daily limit is $300, withdraw just €200. Many frustrated travelers walk away from ATMs thinking their cards have been rejected, when actually they were asking for more cash in euros than their daily limit allowed.

• Get your bank's **emergency phone number** in the US (but not its 800 number, which isn't accessible from overseas) to call collect if you have a problem.

• Ask for your credit card's **PIN** in case you need to make an emergency cash withdrawal or encounter Europe's "chip-and-PIN" system; the bank won't tell you your PIN over the phone, so allow time for it to be mailed to you.

Chip and PIN: Europeans are increasingly using chip-and-PIN cards, which are embedded with an electronic security chip (in addition to the magnetic stripe found on American-style cards). To make a purchase with a chip-and-PIN card, the cardholder inserts the card into a slot in the payment machine, then enters a PIN (like using a debit card in the US) while the card stays in the slot. The chip inside the card authorizes the transaction; the cardholder doesn't sign a receipt. Your American-style card might not work at payment machines using this system, such as those at train and subway stations, toll roads, parking garages, luggage lockers, bike-rental kiosks, and self-serve gas pumps.

If you have problems using your American card in a chip-and-PIN machine, here are some suggestions: For either a debit card or a credit card, try entering that card's PIN when prompted. (Note that your credit-card PIN may not be the same as your debit-card PIN; you'll need to ask your bank for your credit-card PIN.) If your cards still don't work, look for a machine that takes cash, seek out a clerk who might be able to process the transaction manually, or ask a local if you can pay them cash to run the transaction on their card.

And don't panic. Many travelers who use only magnetic-stripe cards don't run into problems. Still, it pays to carry plenty of euros; remember, you can always use an ATM to withdraw cash with your magnetic-stripe debit card.

If you're still concerned, you can apply for a chip card in the US (though I think it's overkill). One option is the no-annual-fee GlobeTrek Visa, offered by Andrews Federal Credit Union in Maryland (open to all US residents; see www.andrewsfcu.org). In the future, chip cards should become standard issue in the US: Visa and MasterCard have asked US banks and merchants to use chip-based cards by late 2015.

Dynamic Currency Conversion: If merchants offer to convert your purchase price into dollars (called dynamic currency conversion, or DCC), refuse this "service." You'll pay even more in fees for the expensive convenience of seeing your charge in dollars. "Independent" ATMs (such as Travelex and Moneybox) may try to confuse customers by presenting DCC in misleading terms. If an ATM offers to "lock in" or "guarantee" your conversion rate, choose "proceed without conversion." Other prompts might state, "You can be charged in dollars: Press YES for dollars, NO for euros." Always choose the local currency in these situations.

Damage Control for Lost Cards

If you lose your credit, debit, or ATM card, you can stop people from using your card by reporting the loss immediately to the respective global customer-assistance centers. Call these 24-hour US numbers collect: Visa (tel. 303/967-1096), MasterCard (tel. 636/722-7111), and American Express (tel. 336/393-1111). In Italy, to make a collect call to the US, dial 800-172-444 (press zero or stay on the line for an English-speaking operator). European toll-free numbers (listed by country) can also be found at the websites for Visa and MasterCard.

PRACTICALITIES

Providing the following information allows for a quicker cancellation of your missing card: full card number, whether you are the primary or secondary cardholder, the cardholder's name exactly as printed on the card, billing address, home phone number, circumstances of the loss or theft, and identification verification (your birth date, your mother's maiden name, or your Social Security number—memorize this, don't carry a copy). If you are the secondary cardholder, you'll also need to provide the primary cardholder's identification-verification details. You can generally receive a temporary card within two or three business days in Europe (see www.ricksteves.com/help for more).

If you report your loss within two days, you typically won't be responsible for any unauthorized transactions on your account, although many banks charge a liability fee of $50.

TIPPING

Tipping in Italy isn't as automatic and generous as it is in the US. For special service, tips are appreciated, but not expected. As in the US, the proper amount depends on your resources, tipping philosophy, and the circumstances, but some general guidelines apply.

Restaurants: In Italy, a service charge *(servizio)* is usually built into your bill, so the total you pay already includes a basic tip. You can add on an additional tip, if you choose, by including a euro or two for each person in your party. For details on restaurant tipping, see page 368.

Taxis: To tip the cabbie, round up. For a typical ride, round up your fare a bit (for instance, if the fare is €4.50 fare, pay €5). If the cabbie hauls your bags and zips you to the airport to help you catch your flight, you might want to toss in a little more. But if you feel like you're being driven in circles or otherwise ripped off, skip the tip.

Services: In general, if someone in the service industry does a super job for you, a small tip of a euro or two is appropriate...but not required. If you're not sure whether (or how much) to tip for a service, ask your hotelier or the TI.

GETTING A VAT REFUND

Wrapped into the purchase price of your Italian souvenirs is a Value-Added Tax (VAT) of about 22 percent. You're entitled to get most of that tax back if you purchase more than €155 (about $200) worth of goods at a store that participates in the VAT-refund scheme. Typically, you must ring up the minimum at a single retailer—you can't add up your purchases from various shops to reach the required amount.

Getting your refund is usually straightforward and, if you buy a substantial amount of souvenirs, well worth the hassle. If you're lucky, the merchant will subtract the tax when you make your purchase. (This is more likely to occur if the store ships the goods to your home.) Otherwise, you'll need to:

Get the paperwork. Have the merchant completely fill out the necessary refund document. You'll have to present your passport. Get the paperwork done before you leave the store to ensure you'll have everything you need (including your original sales receipt).

Get your stamp at the border or airport. Process your VAT document at your last stop in the European Union (such as at the airport) with the customs agent who deals with VAT refunds. Arrive an additional hour early before you need to check in for your flight, to give you time to find the local customs office—and to stand in line. It's best to keep your purchases in your carry-on. If they're too large or dangerous to carry on (such as knives), pack them in your checked bags and alert the check-in agent. You'll be sent (with your tagged bag) to a customs desk outside security, which will examine your bag, stamp your paperwork, and put your bag on the belt. You're not supposed to use your purchased goods before you leave. If you show up at customs wearing your new leather shoes, officials might look the other way—or deny you a refund.

Collect your refund. You'll need to return your stamped document to the retailer or its representative. Many merchants work with a service, such as Global Blue or Premier Tax Free, that has offices at major airports, ports, or border crossings (either before or after security, probably strategically located near a duty-free shop). These services, which extract a 4 percent fee, can refund your money immediately in cash or credit your card (within two billing cycles). If the retailer handles VAT refunds directly, it's up to you to contact the merchant for your refund. You can mail the documents from home, or more quickly, from your point of departure (using an envelope you've prepared in advance or one that's been provided by the merchant). You'll then have to wait—it can take months.

CUSTOMS FOR AMERICAN SHOPPERS

You are allowed to take home $800 worth of items per person duty-free, once every 30 days. You can also bring in a liter of alcohol duty-free. As for food, you can take home many processed and packaged foods: vacuum-packed cheeses, dried herbs, jams, baked goods, candy, chocolate, oil, vinegar, mustard, and honey. Fresh fruits and vegetables and most meats are not allowed. However, canned meat is allowed if it doesn't contain any beef, veal, lamb, or mutton. Any liquid-containing foods must be packed in checked luggage, a potential recipe for disaster. To check customs rules and duty rates, visit www.cbp.gov.

PRACTICALITIES

Sightseeing

Sightseeing can be hard work. Use these tips to make your visits to Rome's finest sights meaningful, fun, efficient, and painless.

PLAN AHEAD

Set up an itinerary that allows you to fit in all your must-see sights. For a one-stop look at opening hours, see "Rome at a Glance" (page 46; also see "Daily Reminder" on page 17). Most sights keep stable hours, but you can easily confirm the latest by checking with the TI or visiting museum websites.

For Rome, if you want to see the Borghese Gallery, make reservations in advance (see page 265). It's smart to reserve for the Vatican Museum (see page 229) as well. And you can buy tickets in advance for the Colosseum, Forum, and Palatine Hill (see page 139)—although there are also other ways to skip the line at those ancient sites.

Don't put off visiting a must-see sight—you never know when a place will close unexpectedly for a holiday, strike, or restoration. Many museums are closed or have reduced hours at least a few days a year, especially on holidays such as Christmas, New Year's, and Labor Day (May 1). A list of holidays is on page 566; check museum websites for possible closures during your trip. In summer, some sights may stay open late. Off-season, many museums have shorter hours.

Going at the right time helps avoid crowds. This book offers tips on specific sights. Try visiting popular sights very early or very late. Evening visits are usually peaceful, with fewer crowds.

Study up. To get the most out of the self-guided tours and sight descriptions in this book, read them before you visit.

AT SIGHTS

Here's what you can typically expect:

Entering: Be warned that you may not be allowed to enter if you arrive 30 to 60 minutes before closing time. And guards start ushering people out well before the actual closing time, so don't save the best for last.

Some important sights have a security check, where you must open your bag or send it through a metal detector. Some sights require you to check daypacks and coats. (If you'd rather not check your daypack, try carrying it tucked under your arm like a purse as you enter.)

Photography: If the museum's photo policy isn't clearly posted, ask a guard. Generally, taking photos without a flash or tripod is allowed. Some sights ban photos altogether.

Temporary Exhibits: Museums may show special exhibits in addition to their permanent collection. Sometimes these exhibits are included in the entry price, while others come at an extra cost (which you may have to pay even if you don't want to see the exhibit).

Expect Changes: Artwork can be on tour, on loan, out sick, or shifted at the whim of the curator. To adapt, pick up a floor plan as you enter, and ask the museum staff if you can't find a particular item. Say the title or artist's name, or point to the photograph in this book and ask, *"Dov'è?"* (doh-VEH, meaning "Where is?").

Audioguides: Many sights rent audioguides, which generally offer excellent recorded descriptions in English (about $5). If you bring your own earbuds, you can enjoy better sound and avoid holding the device to your ear. To save money, bring a Y-jack and share one audioguide with your travel partner. Increasingly, sights are offering apps (often free) that you can download to your mobile device. And I've produced free downloadable audio tours of the major sights in Rome (see page 8).

Dates for Artwork: In museums, art is dated with *sec* (for *secolo*—century, often indicated with Roman numerals), A.C. (for *Avanti Cristo,* i.e., before Christ) and D.C. (for *Dopo Cristo,* a.k.a. A.D.). OK?

Services: Important sights may have an on-site café or cafeteria (usually a handy place to rejuvenate during a long visit). The WCs at sights are free and generally clean.

Before Leaving: At the gift shop, scan the postcard rack or thumb through a guidebook to be sure you haven't overlooked something that you'd like to see.

Every sight or museum offers more than what is covered in this book. Use the information in this book as an introduction—not the final word.

FIND RELIGION

Churches offer some amazing art (usually free), a cool respite from heat, and a welcome seat.

A modest dress code—no bare shoulders or shorts for anyone, even kids—is enforced at the Vatican City (St. Peter's Basilica and Vatican Museum) and at Rome's major churches, such as St. Paul's Outside the Walls, but is often overlooked elsewhere. If you're caught by surprise, you can improvise, using maps to cover your shoulders and a jacket for your knees. (I wear a super-lightweight pair of long pants rather than shorts for my hot and muggy big-city Italian sightseeing.)

Some churches have coin-operated audioboxes that describe the art and history; just set the dial on English, put in your coins, and listen. Coin boxes near a piece of art illuminate the art (and present a better photo opportunity). I pop in a coin whenever I can. It improves my experience, is a favor to other visitors trying to appreciate a great piece of art in the dark, and is a little contribution to that church and its work. Whenever possible, let there be light.

Communicating

"How can I stay connected in Europe?"—by phone and Internet—may be the most common question I hear from travelers. You have three basic options:

1. "Roam" with your US smartphone. This is the easiest option, but likely the most expensive. It works best for people who won't be making very many calls, and who value the convenience of sticking with what's familiar (and their own phone number). In recent years, as data roaming fees have dropped and free Wi-Fi has become easier to find, the majority of travelers are finding this to be the best all-around option.

2. Use an unlocked mobile phone with European SIM cards. This is a much more affordable option if you'll be making lots of calls, since it gives you 24/7 access to cheap European rates. Although remarkably cheap, this option does require a willingness to grapple with the technology and do a bit of shopping around for the right phone and card. Savvy travelers who routinely use SIM cards swear by them.

3. Use public phones and get online at your hotel or at Internet cafés. These options can work in a pinch, particularly for travelers who simply don't want to hassle with the technology, or want to be (mostly) untethered from their home life while on the road.

Each of these options is explained in greater detail in the following pages. Mixing and matching works well. For example, I routinely bring along my smartphone for Internet chores and Skyping on Wi-Fi, but also carry an unlocked phone and buy cheap SIM cards for affordable calls on the go.

For an even more in-depth explanation of this complicated topic, see www.ricksteves.com/phoning.

HOW TO DIAL

Many Americans are intimidated by dialing European phone numbers. You needn't be. It's simple, once you break the code.

Dialing Domestically Within Italy

The following instructions apply whether you're dialing from an Italian mobile phone or a landline (such as a pay phone or your

Hurdling the Language Barrier

Many Italians—especially those in the tourist trade and in big cities such as Rome—speak English. Still, you'll get better treatment if you learn and use Italian pleasantries. In smaller, non-touristy towns, Italian is the norm. For a list of survival phrases, see page 571.

Note that Italian is pronounced much like English, with a few exceptions, such as: c followed by e or i is pronounced ch (to ask, *"Per centro?"*—To the center?—you say, pehr CHEHN-troh). In Italian, ch is pronounced like the hard c in Chianti (*chiesa*—church—is pronounced kee-AY-zah). Give it your best shot. Italians appreciate your efforts.

hotel-room phone). If you're roaming with a US phone number, follow the "Dialing Internationally" directions described later.

Italy has a direct-dial phone system (no area codes). To call anywhere within Italy, just dial the number. For example, the number of one of my recommended Rome hotels is 06-482-4696. That's the number you dial whether you're calling it from Rome's main train station or from Milan.

Italy's land lines start with 0 and mobile lines start with 3. The country's toll-free lines begin with 80. These 80 numbers—called *freephone* or *numero verde* (green number)—can be dialed free from any phone without using a phone card. Note that you can't call Italy's toll-free numbers from the US, nor can you count on reaching American toll-free numbers from Italy. Any Italian phone number that starts with 8 but isn't followed by a 0 is a toll call, generally costing €0.10-0.50 per minute.

Dialing Internationally to or from Italy

Always start with the **international access code**—011 if you're calling from the US or Canada, 00 from anywhere in Europe. If you're dialing from a mobile phone, simply insert a + instead (by holding the 0 key).

• Then dial the country code of the country you're calling (39 for Italy, or 1 for the US or Canada).

• Dial the local number. Note that in most European countries, you have to drop the zero at the beginning of the local number—but in Italy, you dial it. (For specifics per country, see the European calling chart on the next page.)

Calling from the US to Italy: To call the recommended hotel in Rome from the US, dial 011 (US access code), 39 (Italy's country code), then 06-482-4696.

Calling from any European country to the US: To call my office in Edmonds, Washington, from anywhere in Europe, I dial

00 (Europe's access code), 1 (US country code), 425 (Edmonds' area code), and 771-8303.

More Dialing Tips

The chart on the next page shows how to dial per country. For online instructions, see www.countrycallingcodes.com or www.howtocallabroad.com.

Remember, if you're using a mobile phone, dial as if you're in that phone's country of origin. So, when roaming with your US phone number in Italy, dial as if you're calling from the US. But if you're using a European SIM card, dial as you would from that European country.

Note that calls to a European mobile phone are substantially more expensive than calls to a fixed line. Off-hour calls are generally cheaper.

Italian phone numbers vary in length; a hotel can have, say, an eight-digit phone number and a nine-digit fax number.

USING YOUR AMERICAN SMARTPHONE IN EUROPE

Even in this age of email, texting, and near-universal Internet access, smart travelers still use the telephone. I call TIs to smooth out sightseeing plans, hotels to get driving directions, museums to confirm tour schedules, restaurants to check open hours or to book a table, and so on.

Most people enjoy the convenience of bringing their own smartphone. Horror stories about sky-high roaming fees are dated and exaggerated, and major service providers work hard to avoid surprising you with an exorbitant bill. With a little planning, you can use your phone—for voice calls, messaging, and Internet access—without breaking the bank.

Start by figuring out whether your phone works in Europe. Most phones purchased through AT&T and T-Mobile (which use the same technology as Europe) work abroad, while only some phones from Verizon or Sprint do—check your operating manual (look for "tri-band," "quad-band," or "GSM"). If you're not sure, ask your service provider.

Types of Roaming

"Roaming" with your phone—that is, using it outside of its home region, such as in Europe—generally comes with extra charges, whether you are making voice calls, sending texts, or reading your email. The fees listed here are for the three major American providers—Verizon, AT&T, and T-Mobile; Sprint's roaming rates tend to be much higher. But policies change fast, so get the latest details before your trip. For example, as of mid-2014, T-Mobile waived voice and data roaming fees for some plans.

Voice calls are the most expensive. Most providers charge from $1.29 to $1.99 per minute to make or receive calls in Europe. (As you cross each border, you'll typically get a text message explaining the rates in the new country.) If you plan to make multiple calls, look into a global calling plan to lower the per-minute cost, or buy a package of minutes at a discounted price (such as 30 minutes for $30). Note that you'll be charged for incoming calls whether or not you answer them; to save money ask your friends to stay in contact by texting, and to call you only in case of an emergency.

Text messaging costs 20 to 50 cents per text. To cut that cost, you could sign up for an international messaging plan (for example, $10 for 100 texts). Or consider apps that let you text for free (iMessage for Apple, Google Talk for Android, or WhatsApp for any device); however, these require you to use Wi-Fi or data roaming. Be aware that Europeans use the term "SMS" ("short message service") to describe text messaging.

Data roaming means accessing an Internet signal that's carried over the cellular telephone network. Prices have dropped dramatically in recent years, making this an affordable way to bridge gaps between Wi-Fi hotspots. You'll pay far less if you set up an international data roaming plan. Most providers charge $25-30 for 100-120 megabytes of data. That's plenty for basic Internet tasks—100 megabytes lets you view 100 websites or send/receive 1,000 text-based emails, but you'll burn through that amount quickly by streaming videos or music. If your data use exceeds your plan amount, most providers will automatically kick in an additional 100- or 120-megabyte block for the same price. (For more on Wi-Fi versus data roaming—including strategies for conserving your data—see "Using Wi-Fi and Data Roaming," later.)

Setting Up (or Disabling) International Service

With most service providers, international roaming (voice, text, and data) is disabled on your account unless you call to activate it. Before your trip, call your provider (or navigate their website), and cover the following topics:

- Confirm that your phone will work in Europe.
- Verify global roaming rates for voice calls, text messaging, and data roaming.
- Tell them which of those services you'd like to activate.
- Consider any add-on plans to bring down the cost of international calls, texts, or data roaming.

When you get home from Europe, be sure to cancel any add-on plans that you activated for your trip.

Some people would rather use their smartphone exclusively on Wi-Fi, and not worry about either voice or data charges. If that's you, call your provider to be sure that international roaming op-

European Calling Chart

Just smile and dial, using this key:
AC = Area Code, LN = Local Number.

European Country	Calling long distance within ...	Calling from the US or Canada to ...	Calling from a European country to ...
Austria	AC + LN	011 + 43 + AC (without initial zero) + LN	00 + 43 + AC (without initial zero) + LN
Belgium	LN	011 + 32 + LN (without initial zero)	00 + 32 + LN (without initial zero)
Bosnia-Herzegovina	AC + LN	011 + 387 + AC (without initial zero) + LN	00 + 387 + AC (without initial zero) + LN
Britain	AC + LN	011 + 44 + AC (without initial zero) + LN	00 + 44 + AC (without initial zero) + LN
Croatia	AC + LN	011 + 385 + AC (without initial zero) + LN	00 + 385 + AC (without initial zero) + LN
Czech Republic	LN	011 + 420 + LN	00 + 420 + LN
Denmark	LN	011 + 45 + LN	00 + 45 + LN
Estonia	LN	011 + 372 + LN	00 + 372 + LN
Finland	AC + LN	011 + 358 + AC (without initial zero) + LN	999 (or other 900 number) + 358 + AC (without initial zero) + LN
France	LN	011 + 33 + LN (without initial zero)	00 + 33 + LN (without initial zero)
Germany	AC + LN	011 + 49 + AC (without initial zero) + LN	00 + 49 + AC (without initial zero) + LN
Gibraltar	LN	011 + 350 + LN	00 + 350 + LN
Greece	LN	011 + 30 + LN	00 + 30 + LN
Hungary	06 + AC + LN	011 + 36 + AC + LN	00 + 36 + AC + LN
Ireland	AC + LN	011 + 353 + AC (without initial zero) + LN	00 + 353 + AC (without initial zero) + LN
Italy	LN	011 + 39 + LN	00 + 39 + LN

European Country	Calling long distance within ...	Calling from the US or Canada to ...	Calling from a European country to ...
Latvia	LN	011 + 371 + LN	00 + 371 + LN
Montenegro	AC + LN	011 + 382 + AC (without initial zero) + LN	00 + 382 + AC (without initial zero) + LN
Morocco	LN	011 + 212 + LN (without initial zero)	00 + 212 + LN (without initial zero)
Netherlands	AC + LN	011 + 31 + AC (without initial zero) + LN	00 + 31 + AC (without initial zero) + LN
Norway	LN	011 + 47 + LN	00 + 47 + LN
Poland	LN	011 + 48 + LN	00 + 48 + LN
Portugal	LN	011 + 351 + LN	00 + 351 + LN
Russia	8 + AC + LN	011 + 7 + AC + LN	00 + 7 + AC + LN
Slovakia	AC + LN	011 + 421 + AC (without initial zero) + LN	00 + 421 + AC (without initial zero) + LN
Slovenia	AC + LN	011 + 386 + AC (without initial zero) + LN	00 + 386 + AC (without initial zero) + LN
Spain	LN	011 + 34 + LN	00 + 34 + LN
Sweden	AC + LN	011 + 46 + AC (without initial zero) + LN	00 + 46 + AC (without initial zero) + LN
Switzerland	LN	011 + 41 + LN (without initial zero)	00 + 41 + LN (without initial zero)
Turkey	AC (if there's no initial zero, add one) + LN	011 + 90 + AC (without initial zero) + LN	00 + 90 + AC (without initial zero) + LN

- The instructions above apply whether you're calling to or from a European landline or mobile phone.
- If calling from any mobile phone, you can replace the international access code with "+" (press and hold 0 to insert it).
- The international access code is 011 if you're calling from the US or Canada.
- To call the US or Canada from Europe, dial 00, then 1 (country code for US and Canada), then the area code and number. In short, 00 + 1 + AC + LN = Hi, Mom!

PRACTICALITIES

tions are deactivated on your account. To be double-sure, put your phone in "airplane mode," then turn your Wi-Fi back on.

Using Wi-Fi and Data Roaming

A good approach is to use free Wi-Fi wherever possible, and fill in the gaps with data roaming.

Wi-Fi (sometimes called "WLAN")—Internet access through a wireless router—is readily available throughout Europe. But just like at home, the quality of the signal may vary. Be patient, and don't get your hopes up. At accommodations, access is often free, but you may have to pay a fee, especially at expensive hotels. At hotels with thick stone walls, the Wi-Fi router in the lobby may not reach every room. If Wi-Fi is important to you, ask about it when you book—and be specific ("in the rooms?"). Get the password and network name at the front desk when you check in.

When you're out and about, your best bet for finding free Wi-Fi is often at a café. They'll usually tell you the password if you buy something. Or you can stroll down a café-lined street, smartphone in hand, checking for unsecured networks every few steps until you find one that works. Some towns have free public Wi-Fi in highly trafficked parks or piazzas. You may have to register before using it, or get a password at the TI.

Data roaming—that is, accessing the Internet through the cellular network—is handy when you can't find useable Wi-Fi. Because you'll pay by the megabyte (explained earlier), it's best to limit how much data you use. Save bandwidth-gobbling tasks like Skyping, watching videos, or downloading apps or emails with large attachments until you're on Wi-Fi. Switch your phone's email settings from "push" to "fetch." This means that you can choose to "fetch" (download) your messages when you're on Wi-Fi rather than having them continuously "pushed" to your device. And be aware of apps—such as news, weather, and sports tickers—that automatically update. Check your phone's settings to be sure that none of your apps are set to "use cellular data."

I like the safeguard of manually turning off data roaming on my phone whenever I'm not actively using it. To turn off data and voice roaming, look in your phone's menu—try checking under "cellular" or "network," or ask your service provider how to do it. If you need to get online but can't find Wi-Fi, simply turn on data roaming long enough for the task at hand, then turn it off again.

Figure out how to keep track of how much data you've used (in your phone's menu, look for "cellular data usage"; you may have to reset the counter at the start of your trip). Some companies automatically send you a text-message warning if you approach or exceed your limit.

There's yet another option: If you're traveling with an unlocked

---

Internet Calling

To make totally free voice and video calls over the Internet, all you need are a smartphone, tablet, or laptop; a strong Wi-Fi signal; and an account with one of the major Internet calling providers: Skype (www.skype.com), FaceTime (preloaded on most Apple devices), or Google+ Hangouts (www.google. com/hangouts). If the Wi-Fi signal isn't strong enough for video, try sticking with an audio-only call. Or...wait for your next hotel. Many Internet calling programs also work for making calls from your computer to telephones worldwide for a very reasonable fee—generally just a few cents per minute (you'll have to buy some credit before you make your first call).

---

smartphone (explained later), you can buy a SIM card that also includes data; this can be far, far cheaper than data roaming through your home provider.

USING EUROPEAN SIM CARDS

Using your American phone in Europe is easy, but it's not always cheap. And unreliable Wi-Fi can make keeping in touch frustrating. If you're reasonably technology-savvy, and would like to have the option of making lots of affordable calls, it's worth getting comfortable with European SIM cards.

Here's the basic idea: First you need an unlocked phone that works in Europe. Then, in Europe, shop around for a SIM card— the little data chip that inserts into your phone—to equip it with a European number. Turn on the phone, and bingo! You've got a European phone number (and access to cheaper European rates).

Getting an Unlocked Phone

Your basic options are getting your existing phone unlocked, or buying a phone (either at home or in Europe).

Some phones are electronically "locked" so that you can't switch SIM cards (keeping you tied to your original service provider). But it's possible to "unlock" your phone—allowing you to replace the original SIM card. An unlocked phone is versatile; not only does it work with any European provider, but many US providers now offer no-contract, prepaid (or "pay-as-you-go") alternatives that work with SIM technology.

You may already have an old, unused mobile phone in a drawer somewhere. Call your service provider and ask if they'll send you the unlock code. Otherwise, you can buy one: Search an online shopping site for an "unlocked quad-band phone," or buy one at a mobile-phone shop in Europe. Either way, a basic model typically costs $40 or less.

Buying and Using SIM Cards

Once you have an unlocked phone, you'll need to buy a SIM card—a small, fingernail-size chip that stores your phone number and other information. (A smaller variation called "micro-SIM" or "nano-SIM" cards—used in most iPhones—are less widely available.)

SIM cards are sold at mobile-phone shops, department-store electronics counters, and newsstands for $5–10, and usually include about that much prepaid calling credit (making the card itself virtually free). Because SIM cards are prepaid, there's no contract and no commitment; I routinely buy one even if I'm in a country for only a few days.

In about half of the European countries, buying a SIM card is as easy as buying a pack of gum. However, an increasing number of countries—including Italy—require you to register the SIM card with your passport (an antiterrorism measure). In Italy, the major mobile phone providers are Wind, TIM, Vodafone, and 3 ("Tre"). The vendor will make a copy of your passport to register the SIM card with the service provider. You'll receive a *Benvenuti!* text message once your service is activated (it can take a few hours).

When using a SIM card in its home country, it's free to receive calls and texts, and it's cheap to make calls—domestic calls average 20 cents per minute. You can also use SIM cards to call the US—sometimes very affordably (Lebara and Lycamobile, which operate in multiple European countries, let you call a US number for less than 10 cents a minute). Rates are higher if you're roaming in another country. But if you bought the SIM card within the European Union, roaming fees are capped no matter where you travel throughout the EU (about 25 cents/minute to make calls, 7 cents/minute to receive calls, and 8 cents for a text message).

While you can buy SIM cards just about anywhere, I like to seek out a mobile-phone shop, where an English-speaking clerk can help explain my options, get my SIM card inserted and set up, and show me how to use it. When you buy your SIM card, ask about rates for domestic and international calls and texting, and about roaming fees. Also find out how to check your credit balance (usually you'll key in a few digits and hit "Send"). You can top up your credit at any newsstand, tobacco shop, mobile-phone shop, or many other businesses (look for the SIM card's logo in the window).

To insert your SIM card into the phone, locate the slot, which is usually on the side of the phone or behind the battery. Turning on the phone, you'll be prompted to enter the "SIM PIN" (a code number that came with your card).

If you have an unlocked smartphone, look for a European SIM card that covers both voice and data. This is often much cheaper than paying for data roaming through your home provider.

LANDLINE TELEPHONES AND INTERNET CAFÉS

If you prefer to travel without a smartphone or tablet, you can still stay in touch using landline telephones, hotel guest computers, and Internet cafés.

Landline Telephones

Phones in your **hotel room** can be great for local calls and for calls using cheap international phone cards (described in the sidebar). Many hotels charge a fee for local and "toll-free" as well as long-distance or international calls—always ask for the rates before you dial. Since you'll never be charged for receiving calls, it can be more affordable to have someone from the US call you in your room.

While **public pay phones** are on the endangered species list, you'll still see them in post offices and train stations. Pay phones generally come with multilingual instructions. Most public phones work with insertable phone cards (described in the sidebar).

You'll see many cheap **call shops** that advertise low rates to faraway lands, often in train-station neighborhoods. While these target immigrants who want to call home cheaply, tourists can use them, too. Before making your call, be completely clear on the rates.

Internet Cafés and Public Internet Terminals

Finding public Internet terminals in Europe is no problem. Many hotels have a computer in the lobby for guests to use. Otherwise, head for an Internet café, or ask the TI or your hotelier for the nearest place to access the Internet.

European computers typically use non-American keyboards. A few letters are switched around, and command keys are labeled in the local language. Many European keyboards have an "Alt Gr" key (for "Alternate Graphics") to the right of the space bar; press this to insert the extra symbol that appears on some keys. When using an Italian keyboard, to type an @ symbol, press the "Alt Gr" key and the key that shows the @ symbol. If you can't locate a special character (such as the @ symbol), simply copy it (Ctrl-C) from a Web page and paste it (Ctrl-V) into your email message.

SECURITY OVER THE INTERNET

Whether you're accessing the Internet with your own device or at a public terminal, using a shared network or computer comes with

PRACTICALITIES

Types of Telephone Cards

Europe uses two different types of telephone cards. Both types are sold at post offices, newsstands, street kiosks, tobacco shops, and train stations.

Insertable Phone Cards: These cards can only be used at pay phones: Simply take the phone off the hook, insert the card, wait for a dial tone, and dial away. The phone displays your credit ticking down as you talk. These cards are sold by Italy's largest phone company, Telecom Italia. You can buy them in €5 or €10 denominations (many phone booths have signs indicating where the nearest phone-card sales outlet is located).

Rip off the perforated corner to "activate" the card, and then physically insert it into a slot in the pay phone. It displays how much money you have remaining on the card. Then just dial away. The price of the call is automatically deducted while you talk. Each European country has its own insertable phone card—so your Italian card won't work in a French phone.

International Phone Cards: These prepaid cards can be used to make inexpensive calls—within Europe, or to the US, for pennies a minute—from nearly any phone, including the one in your hotel room. The cards come with a toll-free number and a scratch-to-reveal PIN code. If the voice prompts aren't in English, experiment: Dial your code, followed by the pound sign (#), then the phone number, then pound again, and so on, until it works.

Buy a lower denomination in case the card is a dud. Because there are so many brand names, ask for an international phone card (*carta telefonica prepagata internazionale*, KAR-tah teh-leh-FOHN-ee-kah pray-pah-GAH-tah in-ter-naht-zee-oh-NAH-lay). Tell the vendor where you'll be making most calls (*"per Stati Uniti"*—to America), and he'll select the brand with the best deal.

the potential for increased security risks. Ask the hotel or café for the specific name of their Wi-Fi network, and make sure you log on to that exact one; hackers sometimes create a bogus hotspot with a similar or vague name (such as "Hotel Europa Free Wi-Fi"). It's better if a network uses a password (especially a hard-to-guess one) rather than being open to the world.

While traveling, you may want to check your online banking or credit-card statements, or to take care of other personal-finance chores, but Internet security experts advise against accessing these sites over Wi-Fi. If you need to log on to a banking website, try to do so on a secure hard-wired connection or by using your bank's app over a mobile telephone network, which is harder to hack.

If using a credit card online, make sure that the site is secure. Most browsers display a little padlock icon, and the URL begins with *https* instead of *http*. Never send a credit-card number over a website that doesn't begin with *https*.

If you're not convinced a connection is secure, avoid accessing any sites (such as your bank's) that could be vulnerable to fraud.

MAIL

You can mail one package per day to yourself worth up to $200 duty-free from Europe to the US (mark it "personal purchases"). If you're sending a gift to someone, mark it "unsolicited gift." For details, visit www.cbp.gov and search for "Know Before You Go."

The Italian postal service works fine, but for quick transatlantic delivery (in either direction), consider services such as DHL (www.dhl.com).

Transportation

If your trip will cover more of Italy than just Rome, you'll need to decide whether to rent a car or take public transportation. Cars are best for three or more traveling together (especially families with small kids), those packing heavy, and those scouring the countryside. Trains and buses are best for solo travelers, blitz tourists, and city-to-city travelers. While a car gives you more freedom, trains and buses zip you effortlessly and scenically from city to city, usually dropping you in the center, often near the TI.

TRAINS

To travel by train affordably in Italy, you can simply buy tickets as you go. Ticket machines are easy to use (see "Buying Tickets," later), so you can usually avoid long lines at ticket windows. Pay all ticket costs in the station before you board, or you'll pay a penalty on the train. For travelers ready to lock in dates and times weeks or months in advance, buying nonrefundable tickets online can cut costs in half.

Types of Trains: Most trains in Italy are operated by the state-run **Trenitalia** company (a.k.a. Ferrovie dello Stato Italiane, abbreviated FS or FSI). Since ticket prices depend on the speed of the train, it pays to know the different types of trains: pokey R or REG *(regionali)*, medium-speed RV *(regionali veloce)*, IR (InterRegio),

Italy's Public Transportation

D *(diretto)*, and E *(espresso)*; fast IC (InterCity) and EC (EuroCity); and super-fast Frecce trains: Frecciabianca ("White Arrow"), faster Frecciargento ("Silver Arrow"), and Frecciarossa ("Red Arrow"). (You may also see the Frecce trains marked on schedules as ES, AV, or EAV.) If you're traveling with a rail pass, note that reservations are required for EC and international trains (€5) and for Frecce trains (€10). Reservations are optional for IC trains, and you can't make reservations for regional trains, such as most Rome-Civitavecchia connections.

A new, private train company called **Italo** now runs fast trains on major routes in Italy (challenging Trenitalia's monopoly). Italo is focused on two high-speed corridors: Venice-Padua-Bologna-Florence-Rome and Turin-Milan-Bologna-Florence-Rome-Naples. Italo's trains run at more or less the same speed as Trenitalia's high-speed trains, but with fewer departures. Italo also offers discounts for tickets booked well in advance. In some cities, its trains use secondary stations—if taking Italo, pay attention to which station you need (this is most notable in Milan and Rome—though Italo trains will likely start using Rome's main Termini Station in the near future). Italo does not currently accept rail passes, but its affordable fares make it worth considering for point-to-point tickets. You can book in person (look for Italo ticket offices or machines—tickets not sold through Trenitalia), by phone (tel. 06-0708), or on their user-friendly website (www.italotreno.it).

Schedules: At the train station, the easiest way to check schedules is at a handy ticket machine (described later, under "Buying Tickets"). Enter the desired date, time, and destination to see all your options. Printed schedules are also posted at the station (departure—*partenzi*—posters are always yellow).

Newsstands sell up-to-date regional and all-Italy timetables (€5, ask for the *orario ferroviario*). Online, check www.trenitalia.it and www.italotreno.it (domestic journeys only); for international trips, use www.bahn.com (Germany's excellent all-Europe schedule website). Trenitalia offers a single all-Italy telephone number for train information (24 hours daily, toll tel. 892-021, in Italian only, consider having your hotelier call for you). For Italo trains, call tel. 06-0708.

Deciphering Italian Train Schedules

At the station, look for the big yellow posters labeled *Parten-ze*—Departures (ignore the white posters, which show arrivals). In stations with Italo service, the posted schedules also include the FS or Italo logos.

Schedules are listed chronologically, hour by hour, showing the trains leaving the station throughout the day. Each schedule has columns:

- The first column *(Ora)* lists the time of departure.
- The next column *(Treno)* shows the type of train.
- The third column *(Classi Servizi)* lists the services available (first- and second-class cars, dining car, *cuccetta* berths, etc.) and, more importantly, whether you need reservations (usually denoted by an R in a box). All Frecce trains, many EuroCity (EC) trains, and most international trains require reservations.
- The next column lists the destination of the train *(Principali Fermate Destinazioni)*, often showing intermediate stops, followed by the final destination, with arrival times listed throughout in parentheses. Note that your final destination may be listed in fine print as an intermediate destination. For example, if you're going from Rome to Orvieto, scan the schedule and you'll notice that regional trains that go to Florence usually stop in Orvieto en route. Travelers who read the fine print end up with a far greater choice of trains.
- The next column *(Servizi Diretti e Annotazioni)* has pertinent notes about the train, such as "also stops in..." *(ferma anche a...)*, "doesn't stop in..." *(non ferma a...)*, "stops in every station" *(ferma in tutte le stazioni)*, "delayed..." *(ritardo...)*, and so on.
- The last column lists the track *(Binario)* the train departs from. Confirm the *binario* with an additional source: a ticket-seller, the electronic board that lists immediate departures, TV monitors on the platform, or the railway officials who are usually standing by the train unless you really need them.

For any odd symbols on the poster, look at the key at the end. Some of the phrasing can be deciphered easily, such as *servizio periodico* (periodic service—doesn't always run). For the trickier ones, ask a local or railway official, try your *Rick Steves Italian Phrase Book & Dictionary,* or simply take a different train.

You can also check schedules—for trains anywhere in Italy, not just from the station you're currently in—at the handy ticket machines. Enter the date and time of your departure (to or from any Italian station), and you can view all your options.

Be aware that Trenitalia and Italo don't cooperate at all. If you buy a ticket for one train line, it's not valid on the other. Even if you just ask for information from one company, they will most likely ignore the other's options.

Point-to-Point Tickets

Train tickets are a good value in Italy. Fares are shown on the map on page 551, though fares can vary for the same journey, mainly depending on the time of day, the speed of the train, and more. **First-class** tickets cost from 30 to 50 percent more than **second-class.** Frecce and Italo trains each offer several classes of service where all seats are reserved: Standard, Premium, Business, or Executive on Frecciarossa; Smart, Prima, or Club on Italo; and standard first and second class on other trains. Buying up gives you a little more elbow room, or perhaps a better chance at seating a group together, if you're buying on short notice. Ticket price levels for both companies are Base (full fare, easily changeable or partly refundable before scheduled departure), Economy (one schedule change allowed before departure), and Super Economy or Low Cost (sells out quickly, no refund or exchange). Fares labeled *servizi abbonati* are available only for locals with monthly passes—not tourists.

Speed vs. Savings: For point-to-point tickets, you'll pay more the faster you go. Spending a modest amount of extra time in transit can save money. For example, a round-trip ticket between Rome and Civitavecchia costs €15 on a Frecce train (45 minutes each way), but €5 on a regional train (1.25 hours each way). On longer, mainline routes, fast trains save more time and provide most of the service. For example, super-fast Rome-Venice trains run hourly, cost €76 in second class, and make the trip in 3.75 hours, while infrequent InterCity trains (only 1-2/day) cost €50 and take 6 hours.

Discounts: Families with young children can get price breaks—kids ages 4 and under travel free; ages 4-11 at half-price. Ask for the "Offerta Familia" deal when buying tickets at a counter (or, at a ticket machine, choose "Yes" at the "Do you want ticket issue?" prompt, then choose "Familia"). With the discount, families of three to five people with at least one kid (under 12) get 50 percent off the child fare and 20 percent off the adult fare. The deal doesn't apply to all trains at all times, but it's worth checking out.

Discounts for youths and seniors require purchase of a separate card (Carta Verde for ages 12-26 costs €40; Carta Argento for ages 60 and over is €30), but the discount on tickets is so minor (10-15 percent respectively for domestic travel), it's not worth it for most.

Buying Tickets: Avoid train station ticket lines whenever possible by using the ticket machines in station halls. You'll be able to easily purchase tickets for travel within Italy (not international trains), make seat reservations, and even book a *cuccetta* (koo-

PRACTICALITIES

Open or Non-Reserved Ticket—Need to Validate

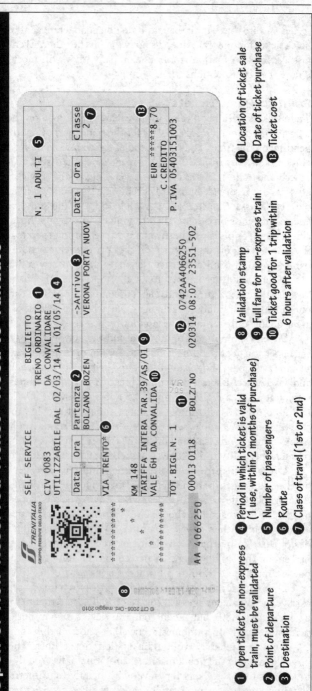

SELF SERVICE
BIGLIETTO
TRENO ORDINARIO ❶
DA CONVALIDARE
CIV 0083
UTILIZZABILE DAL 02/03/14 AL 01/05/14 ❹

| Data | Ora | Partenza ❷ | →Arrivo ❸ | Data | Ora | Classe ❼ |
| | | BOLZANO BOZEN | VERONA PORTA NUOV | | | 2 |

VIA TRENTO* ❻

KM 148
TARIFFA INTERA TAR. 39/AS/01 ❾
VALE 6H DA CONVALIDA ❿

TOT. BIGL.N. 1

00013 0118   BOLZ: NO ⓫

AA 4066250

0742AA4066250
020314 08:07 23551-502 ⓬

EUR ******8,70 ⓭
C. CREDITO
P.IVA 05403151003

N. 1 ADULTI ❺

❶ Open ticket for non-express train, must be validated
❷ Point of departure
❸ Destination
❹ Period in which ticket is valid (1 use, within 2 months of purchase)
❺ Number of passengers
❻ Route
❼ Class of travel (1st or 2nd)
❽ Validation stamp
❾ Full fare for non-express train
❿ Ticket good for 1 trip within 6 hours after validation
⓫ Location of ticket sale
⓬ Date of ticket purchase
⓭ Ticket cost

Reserved Ticket (Fast Train)—Need Not Validate

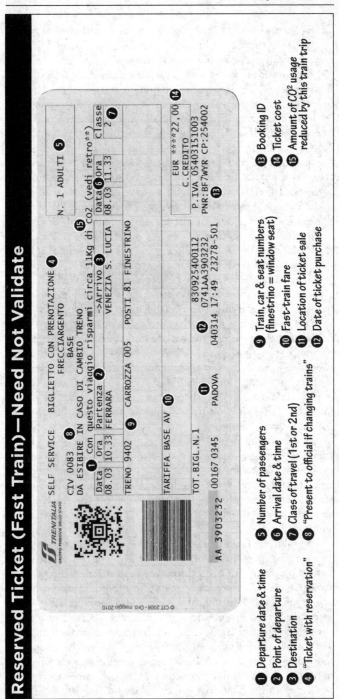

1. Departure date & time
2. Point of departure
3. Destination
4. "Ticket with reservation"
5. Number of passengers
6. Arrival date & time
7. Class of travel (1st or 2nd)
8. "Present to official if changing trains"
9. Train, car & seat numbers (finestrino = window seat)
10. Fast-train fare
11. Location of ticket sale
12. Date of ticket purchase
13. Booking ID
14. Ticket cost
15. Amount of CO2 usage reduced by this train trip

CHEH-tah; overnight berth). If you do use the ticket windows, be sure you're in the correct line. Key terms: *biglietti* (general tickets), *prenotazioni* (reservations), *nazionali* (domestic), and *internazionali*.

Trenitalia's ticket machines (usually green and white, marked *Biglietto Veloce/Fast Ticket*) are user-friendly and found in all but the tiniest stations in Italy. You can pay by cash (they give change) or by debit or credit card (even for small amounts, but you may need to enter your PIN). Select English, then your destination. If you don't immediately see the city you're traveling to, keep keying in the spelling until it's listed. You can choose from first- and second-class seats, request tickets for more than one traveler, and (on the high-speed Frecce trains) choose an aisle or window seat. Don't select a discount rate without being sure that you meet the criteria (for example, Americans are not eligible for certain EU or resident discounts). Rail pass holders can use the machines to make seat reservations. If you need to validate your ticket, you can do it in the same machine if you're boarding your train right away.

It's cheaper, but generally unnecessary, to buy Trenitalia tickets in advance online at www.trenitalia.it. Because most Italian trains run frequently and there's no deadline to buy tickets, you can keep your travel plans flexible by purchasing tickets as you go. (You can buy tickets for several trips at one station when you are ready to commit.) For busy weekend or holiday travel, however, it can be a good idea to buy tickets in advance, whether online or at a station.

To buy tickets for **Italo** trains, look for a dedicated service counter (in most major rail stations) or a red ticket machine labeled *Italo*. You can also book Italo tickets by phone (tel. 06-0708) or online (www.italotreno.it).

You can't buy international tickets from machines; for this and anything else that requires a real person, you must go to a ticket window at the station. A good alternative, though, is to drop by a local travel agency. Agencies sell domestic and international tickets and make reservations. They charge a small fee, the language barrier (and the lines) can be smaller than at the station's ticket windows.

Validating Tickets: If your ticket includes a seat reservation on a specific train *(biglietto con prenotazione)*, you're all set and can just get on board. An open ticket with no seat reservation (it may say *da convalidare* or *convalida*) must always be validated—stamp it before you board in the machine near the platform (usually marked *convalida biglietti* or *vidimazione*). Once you validate a ticket, you must complete your trip within the timeframe shown on the ticket (within 6 hours for medium-distance trips; within 1.25 hours for short rides under 6 miles). If you forget to validate your ticket, go right away to the train conductor—before he comes to you—or you'll pay a fine. Note that you don't need to validate a rail pass

Train Costs in Italy

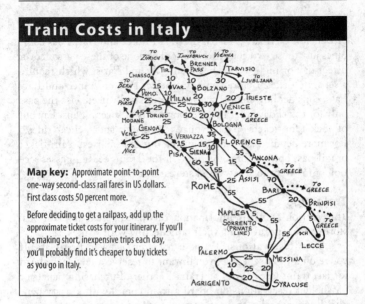

Map key: Approximate point-to-point one-way second-class rail fares in US dollars. First class costs 50 percent more.

Before deciding to get a railpass, add up the approximate ticket costs for your itinerary. If you'll be making short, inexpensive trips each day, you'll probably find it's cheaper to buy tickets as you go in Italy.

each time you board (just make sure you've validated it before its first use).

Rail Passes

The **Italy Pass** for Italian State Railways is generally no cheaper or easier than just buying point-to-point tickets. The pass may save you money if you're taking three long train rides or prefer first-class travel, but don't count on it for hop-on convenience on every train. Use the price map opposite to add up your ticket costs (ticket prices on the map are for the fastest trains on a given route, many of which have reservation costs built in). Note that rail passes are not valid on Italo trains.

Rail pass holders must make separate seat reservations for the fastest trains between major Italian cities (€10 each). Rail-pass travelers can just hop on InterCity trains (optional €5 reservation) and regional trains (no reservations possible). Making a reservation at a train station or travel agency is the same as the process to buy a ticket, so you may need to stand in line either way. Reservations for berths on overnight trains cost extra, aren't covered by rail passes, and aren't reflected on the ticket cost map.

A **Global Pass** can work well throughout most of Europe, but it's a bad value for travel exclusively in Italy. A cheaper version, the **Select Pass,** allows you to tailor a pass to your trip, provided you're traveling in four adjacent countries directly connected by rail or ferry. For instance, with a three-country pass allowing 10 days of train travel within a two-month period (about $850 for a single adult in 2014), you could choose France-Switzerland-Italy-Greece or Benelux-Germany-Austria-Italy. A **France and Italy Pass** combines just those two countries. Note that none of these passes cover direct day or night trains between Italy and Paris, which require a separate ticket. Before you buy a Select Pass or France and Italy Pass, consider how many travel days you'll really need. Use the pass only for travel days that involve long hauls or several trips. Pay out of pocket for tickets on days you're taking only short, cheap rides. For more detailed advice on figuring out the smartest train-ticket or rail-pass options for your trip, visit the Trains & Rail Passes section of my website at www.ricksteves.com/rail.

Train Tips

This section contains information on making seat reservations, storing baggage, avoiding theft, and dealing with strikes.

Seat Reservations: Trains can fill up, even in first class. If you're on a tight schedule, you'll want to reserve a few days ahead for fast trains (see "Types of Trains," earlier). Purchasing tickets or passholder reservations on board a train comes with a nasty penalty. Buying them at the station can be a time-waster unless you use the ticket machines.

If you don't need a reservation, and if your train originates at your departure point (e.g., you're catching the Rome-Assisi train in Rome), arriving at least 15 minutes before the departure time will help you snare a seat.

On the platforms of some major stations, posters showing the train composition *(composizione principali treni)* indicate where first- and second-class cars will line up when the trains arrive (letters on the poster are supposed to correspond to letters posted over the platform—but they don't always). Other stations may post the order of the cars on video screens along the track shortly before the train arrives. Since most trains now allow you to make reservations up to the time of departure, conductors post a list of the reservable and non-reservable seat rows (sometimes in English) in each train car's vestibule. This means that if you board a crowded train and get one of the last seats, you may be ousted when the reservation-holder comes along.

Baggage Storage: Many stations have *deposito bagagli* where you can safely leave your bag for about €8 per 12-hour period (payable when you pick up the bag, double-check closing hours). Due to security concerns, no Italian stations have lockers.

Theft Concerns: Italian trains are famous for their thieves. Never leave a bag unattended. Police do ride the trains, cutting down on theft. Still, for an overnight trip, I'd feel safe only in a *cuccetta* (a bunk in a special sleeping car with an attendant who keeps track of who comes and goes while you sleep—approximately €21

Railpasses

Prices listed are for 2014 and are subject to change. For the latest prices, details, and train schedules (and easy online ordering), see www.ricksteves.com/rail.

"Saver" prices are per person for two or more people traveling together. "Youth" means under age 26. The fare for children 4–11 is half the adult individual fare or Saver fare. Kids under age 4 travel free.

ITALY PASS

	Individual 1st Class	Individual 2nd Class	Saver 1st Class	Saver 2nd Class	Youth 2nd Class
3 days in 2 months	$307	$250	$262	$213	$204
Extra rail days (max 7)	32-37	26-30	26-30	22-26	22-25

FRANCE–ITALY PASS

	Individual 1st Class	Individual 2nd Class	Saver 1st Class	Saver 2nd Class	Youth 2nd Class
4 days in 2 months	$428	$364	$364	$310	$280
Extra rail days (max 6)	45-51	38-44	38-44	33-37	29-33

Be aware of your route. Direct Paris–Italy trains (day and overnight) and trains via Switzerland aren't covered by this pass. Connections through Nice are ok.

GREECE–ITALY PASS

	Individual 1st Class	Individual 2nd Class	Saver 1st Class	Saver 2nd Class	Youth 2nd Class
4 days in 2 months	$407	$327	$347	$279	$266
Extra rail days (max 6)	37-40	30-32	32-34	26-27	25-27

Covers deck passage on overnight Superfast Ferries between Patras, Greece and Bari or Ancona, Italy (starts use of one travel day). Does not cover travel to or on Greek islands. Very few trains run in Greece.

SPAIN–ITALY PASS

	Individual 1st Class	Individual 2nd Class	Saver 1st Class	Saver 2nd Class	Youth 2nd Class
4 days in 2 months	$428	$364	$364	$310	$280
Extra rail days (max 6)	45-51	38-44	38-44	33-37	29-33

Note: Pass does not cover trains in France.

SELECTPASS

This pass covers travel in four adjacent countries.

	Individual 1st Class	Saver 1st Class	Youth 2nd Class
5 days in 2 months	$582	$495	$379
6 days in 2 months	635	540	414
8 days in 2 months	739	629	482
10 days in 2 months	845	719	551

in a six-bed compartment, €26 in a less-cramped four-bed compartment, €50 in a more private, double compartment).

Strikes: Strikes, which are common, generally last a day (often a Friday). Train employees will simply explain, *"Sciopero"* (strike). But in actuality, sporadic trains, following no particular schedule, lumber down the tracks during most strikes. When a strike is pending, travel agencies (and hoteliers) can check the Web for you to see when the strike goes into effect and which trains will continue to run. Revised schedules may be posted in Italian at stations, and station personnel still working can often tell you what trains are expected to run. If I need to get somewhere and know a strike is imminent, I leave early (heading off the strike, which often begins at 9:00), or I just go to the station with extra patience in tow and hop on anything rolling in the direction I want to go.

BUSES

You can usually get anywhere you want to in Italy by bus, as long as you're not in a hurry and you plan ahead using bus schedules (pick up at local TIs). For reaching small towns, buses are sometimes the only option if you don't have a car. In many hill towns, trains leave you at a station in the valley far below, while buses bring you right into the thick of things.

Larger towns have a long-distance bus station *(stazione degli autobus)*, with ticket windows and several stalls (usually labeled *corsia*, *stallo*, or *binario*). Smaller towns—where buses are more useful—just have a central bus stop *(fermata)*, likely along the main road or on the main square, and maybe several more scattered around town. In small towns, buy bus tickets at newsstands or tobacco shops (with the big *T* signs). When buying your ticket, confirm the departure point *("Dov'è la fermata?")*, and once there, double-check that the posted schedule lists your destination and departure time. In general, orange buses are local city buses, and blue buses are for long distances.

Once the bus arrives, confirm the destination with the driver. You are expected to stow big backpacks underneath the bus (open the luggage compartment yourself if it's closed).

Sundays and holidays are problematic; even from large cities schedules are sparse, departing buses are jam-packed, and ticket offices are often closed. Plan ahead and buy your ticket in advance. Most travel agencies book bus (and train) tickets for just a small fee.

RENTING A CAR

If you're renting a car in Italy, bring your driver's license. You're also required to have an International Driving Permit—an official translation of your driver's license (sold at your local AAA office for $15 plus the cost of two passport-type photos; see www.aaa.com).

While that's the letter of the law, I've often rented cars without having this permit. If all goes well, you'll likely never be asked to show the permit—but it's a must if you end up dealing with the police.

Rental companies require you to be at least 21 years old and to have held your license for one year. Drivers under the age of 25 may incur a young-driver surcharge, and some rental companies do not rent to anyone 75 or older. If you're considered too young or old, look into leasing (described later), which has less-stringent age restrictions.

Research car rentals before you go. It's cheaper to arrange most car rentals from the US. Call several companies or look online to compare rates.

Most of the major US rental agencies (including Avis, Budget, Enterprise, Hertz, and Thrifty) have offices throughout Europe. Also consider the two major Europe-based agencies, Europcar and Sixt. It can be cheaper to use a consolidator, such as Auto Europe/Kemwel (www.autoeurope.com) or Europe by Car (www.europebycar.com), which compares rates at several companies to get you the best deal. Because you're working with a middleman, it's especially important to ask in advance about add-on fees and restrictions.

Regardless of the car-rental company you choose, always read the fine print carefully for add-on charges—such as one-way drop-off fees, airport surcharges, or mandatory insurance policies—that aren't included in the "total price." You may need to query rental agents pointedly to find out your actual cost.

For the best deal, rent by the week with unlimited mileage. To save money on gas, ask for a diesel car. I normally rent the smallest, least-expensive model with a stick shift (generally much cheaper than an automatic). Almost all rentals are manual by default, so if you need an automatic, request one in advance; be aware that these cars are usually larger models (not as maneuverable on narrow, winding roads). Roads and parking spaces are narrow in Italy, so you'll do yourself a favor by renting the smallest car that meets your needs.

Figure on paying roughly $200 for a one-week rental. Allow extra for insurance, fuel, tolls, and parking. For trips of three weeks or more, look into leasing (see page 558); you'll save money on insurance and taxes.

Big companies have offices in most cities; ask whether they can pick you up at your hotel. Small local rental companies can be cheaper but aren't as flexible.

Compare pickup costs (downtown can be less expensive than the airport) and explore drop-off options. Always check the hours of the location you choose: Many rental offices close from midday

PRACTICALITIES

Driving in Italy

AUSTRIA

SWITZERLAND

Brenner Pass

Villach

Mt. Blanc Tunnel

Lake Como (Varenna)

Dolomites (Bolzano)

SLOVENIA

70m-2h

260m-5h

Trieste

145m-2.5h

30m-.75h

110m-2.5h

100m-1.5h

160m-4.5h (via Cortina)

155m-2.5h

95m-1.75h

Milan

Verona

200m-4h

100m-1.75h

80m-1.5h

Venice

85m-2.5h

185m-3.25h

175m-2.75h

135m-2.5h

225m-4h

155m-3h

Ravenna

CROATIA

160m-2.75h

155m-2.25h

Cinque Terre (La Spezia)

90m-1.75h

115m-2h

50m-1h

70m-1.5h

Florence

Ventimiglia

Pisa

45m-1h

100m-2h

125m-2.25h

Siena

100m-1.75h

80m-2h

Assisi

Orvieto

55m-1.5h

115m-2.25h

75m-1.75h

210m-4h

75m-1.5h

Note: Your times may vary based on traffic, construction and road conditions.

Rome

155m-2.5h

35m-1h

Naples

Salerno

30m-.75h

Sorrento

30m-1h

30m-1.5h

Paestum

m = miles
h = hours

Saturday until Monday morning and, in smaller towns, at lunchtime.

When selecting a location, don't trust the agency's description of "downtown" or "city center." In some cases, a "downtown" branch can be on the outskirts of the city—a long, costly taxi ride from the center. Before choosing, plug the address into a mapping website to compare locations. You may find that the "train station" location is handier. But returning a car at a big-city train station or downtown agency can be tricky; get precise details on the car drop-off location and hours, and allow ample time to find it.

When you pick up the rental car, check it thoroughly and make sure any damage is noted on your rental agreement. Find out how your car's lights, turn signals, wipers, radio, and fuel cap function, and know what kind of fuel the car takes (diesel vs. unleaded). When you return the car, make sure the agent verifies its condition with you. Some drivers take pictures of the returned vehicle as proof of its condition.

Navigation Options

When renting a car in Europe, you have several alternatives for your digital navigator: Use your smartphone's online mapping app, download an offline map app, or rent a GPS device with your rental car (or bring your own GPS device from home).

Online mapping apps used to be prohibitively expensive for overseas travelers—but that was before most carriers started offering affordable international data plans. If you're already getting a data plan for your trip, this is probably the way to go (see "Using Your American Smartphone in Europe," earlier).

A number of well-designed apps allow you much of the convenience of online maps without any costly demands on your data plan. City Maps 2Go is one of the most popular of these; OffMaps, Google Maps, and Navfree also all offer good, zoomable offline maps for much of Europe (some are better for driving, while others are better for navigating cities).

Some drivers prefer using a dedicated GPS unit—not only to avoid the data-roaming fees, but because a stand-alone GPS can be easier to operate (important if you're driving solo). The major downside: It's expensive—around $10-30 per day. Also, your car's GPS unit may only come loaded with maps for its home country—if you need additional maps, ask. Make sure your device's language is set to English before you drive off. If you have a portable GPS device at home, you can take that instead. Many American GPS devices come loaded with US maps only—you'll need to buy and download European maps before your trip. This option is far less expensive than renting.

Car Insurance Options

Accidents can happen anywhere, but when you're on vacation, the last thing you need is stress over car insurance. When you rent a car, you're liable for a very high deductible, sometimes equal to the entire value of the car. Limit your financial risk in case of an accident by choosing one of these two options: Buy Collision Damage Waiver (CDW) coverage from the car-rental company (figure roughly 30 percent extra), or get coverage through your credit card (free, but more complicated).

In Italy, most car-rental companies' rates automatically include CDW coverage. Even if you try to decline CDW when you reserve your Italian car, you may find when you show up at the counter that you must buy it after all.

While each rental company has its own variation, basic CDW costs $10-30 a day and reduces your liability, but does not eliminate it. When you pick up the car, you'll be offered the chance to "buy down" the deductible to zero (for an additional $10-30/day; this is sometimes called "super CDW" or "zero-deductible coverage").

If you opt for credit-card coverage, there's a catch. You'll technically have to decline all coverage offered by the car-rental company, which means they can place a hold on your card for up to the full value of the car. In case of damage, it can be time-consuming to resolve the charges with your credit-card company. Before you decide on this option, quiz your credit-card company about how it works.

For more on car-rental insurance, see www.ricksteves.com/cdw.

Theft Insurance: Note that theft insurance (separate from CDW insurance) is mandatory in Italy. The insurance usually costs about $15-20 a day, payable when you pick up the car.

Leasing

For trips of three weeks or more, consider leasing (which automatically includes zero-deductible collision and theft insurance). By technically buying and then selling back the car, you save lots of money on tax and insurance. Leasing provides you a brand-new car with unlimited mileage and a 24-hour emergency assistance program. You can lease for as little as 21 days to as long as five and a half months. Car leases must be arranged from the US. One of many companies offering affordable lease packages is Europe by Car (www.europebycar.com/lease).

DRIVING

Driving in Italy can be scary—a video game for keeps, and you only get one quarter. Italian drivers can be aggressive. They drive fast and tailgate as if it were required. They pass where Americans are taught not to—on blind corners and just before tunnels. Roads have narrow shoulders or none at all. Driving in the countryside is less stressful than driving through urban areas, but stay alert. On one-lane roads, larger vehicles have the right-of-way. If you're on a truckers' route, stifle your Good Samaritan impulse when you see provocatively dressed women standing by camper-vans at the side of the road; they're not having car trouble.

Road Rules: Stay out of restricted traffic zones, or you'll risk huge fines. Car traffic is restricted in many city centers, including Rome. Don't drive or park anywhere with signs reading *Zona Traffico Limitato* (ZTL, often shown above a red circle; see image). If you do, your license plate will likely be photographed and a hefty (€100-plus) ticket charged to your credit card without your ever having met a cop. Bumbling in and out of these zones can net you multiple fines. If your hotel is within a restricted area, it's best to ask your hotelier where to park outside the zone. (Although your hotelier can register your car as an authorized vehicle permitted to enter the zone, this usually isn't worth the hassle.) If you get a ticket, it could take months to show up (see www.bella-toscana.com/traffic_violations_italy.htm for details).

Be aware of typical European road rules; for example, many countries require headlights to be turned on at all times, and it's generally illegal to drive while using your mobile phone without a hands-free headset. Seatbelts are mandatory and children under 12 must use child seats. In Europe, you're not allowed to turn right on a red light, unless there is a sign or signal specifically authorizing it, and on expressways it's illegal to pass drivers on the right. Ask your car-rental company about these rules, or check the US State Department website (www.travel.state.gov, search for your country in the "Learn about your destination" box, then click on "Travel and Transportation").

Tolls: Italy's freeway system, the autostrada, is as good as our interstate system, but you'll pay about a dollar for every 10 minutes of use. While I favor freeways because I feel they're safer, cheaper (saving time and gas), and less nerve-racking than smaller roads, savvy local drivers know which toll-free *superstradas* are actually faster and more direct than the autostrada. For more information, visit www.autostrade.it.

Fuel: Gas is expensive—often about €2/liter ($10 per gallon). Diesel cars are more common in Europe than back home, so be sure you know what type of gas your car takes before you fill up. Gas pumps are color-coded for unleaded *(senza piombo)* or diesel *(gasolio).* Autostrada rest stops are self-service stations open daily without a siesta break. Many 24-hour-a-day stations are entirely automated. Small-town stations are usually cheaper and offer full service but shorter hours.

Maps and Signage: A good map is essential. Learn the universal road signs (explained in charts in most road atlases and at service stations). Although roads are numbered on maps, actual road signs

AND LEARN THESE ROAD SIGNS

Speed Limit (km/hr)	Yield	No Passing	End of No Passing Zone
One Way	Intersection	Main Road	Expressway
Danger	No Entry	Cars Prohibited	All Vehicles Prohibited
No Through Road	Restrictions No Longer Apply	Yield to Oncoming Traffic	No Stopping
Parking	No Parking	Customs	Peace

PRACTICALITIES

don't list route numbers. Instead, roads are indicated by blue signs with a city name on them (for example, if you were heading east out of Rome, the map would be marked "route S-5"—but you'd follow signs to Tivoli, the next town along this road). The signs are inconsistent: They may direct you to the nearest big city or simply the next town along the route.

Theft: Cars are routinely vandalized and stolen. Thieves easily recognize rental cars and assume they are filled with a tourist's gear. Try to make your car look locally owned by hiding the "tourist-owned" rental-company decals and putting an Italian newspaper in your back window. Be sure all of your valuables are out of sight and locked in the trunk, or even better, with you or in your room.

Parking: White lines generally mean parking is free. Yellow lines mean that parking is reserved for residents only (who have permits). Blue lines mean you'll have to pay—usually €1.50 per hour (use machine, leave time-stamped receipt on dashboard). If there's no meter, there's probably a roving attendant who will take your money. Study the signs. Often the free zones have a 30- or 60-minute time limit. Signs showing a street cleaner and a day of the week indicate which day the street is cleaned; there's a €100 tow-fee incentive to learn the days of the week in Italian.

Zona disco has nothing to do with dancing. Italian cars come equipped with a time disk (a cardboard clock), which you set at your arrival time and lay on the dashboard so the attendant knows how long you've been parked. This is a fine system that all drivers should take advantage of. (If your rental car doesn't come with a *zona disco*, pick one up at a tobacco shop or just write your arrival time on a piece of paper and place it on the dashboard.)

Garages are safe, save time, and help you avoid the stress of parking tickets. Take the parking voucher with you to pay the cashier before you leave.

FLIGHTS

The best comparison search engine for both international and intra-European flights is www.kayak.com. For inexpensive flights within Europe, try www.skyscanner.com or www.hipmunk.com; for inexpensive international flights, try www.vayama.com. If you're not sure who flies to your destination, check its airport's website for a list of carriers.

Flying to Europe: Start looking for international flights four to five months before your trip, especially for peak-season travel. Off-season tickets can be purchased a month or so in advance. Depending on your itinerary, it can be efficient to fly into one city and out of another. If your flight requires a connection in Europe, see our hints on navigating Europe's top hub airports at www.ricksteves.com/hub-airports.

Flying within Europe: If you're considering a train ride that's more than five hours long, a flight may save you both time and money. When comparing your options, factor in the time it takes to get to the airport and how early you'll need to arrive to check in.

Well-known cheapo airlines include easyJet (www.easyjet.com) and Ryanair (www.ryanair.com), which both serve Rome.

Be aware of the potential drawbacks of flying on the cheap: nonrefundable and nonchangeable tickets, minimal or nonexistent customer service, treks to airports far outside town, and stingy baggage allowances with steep overage fees. If you're traveling with lots of luggage, a cheap flight can quickly become a bad deal. To avoid unpleasant surprises, read the small print before you book.

Resources

RESOURCES FROM RICK STEVES

Rick Steves Rome 2015 is one of many books in my series on European travel, which includes country guidebooks, city guidebooks (Venice, Florence, Paris, London, etc.), Snapshot guides (excerpted chapters from my country guides), Pocket Guides (full-color little

books on big cities, including Rome), and my budget-travel skills handbook, *Rick Steves Europe Through the Back Door*. Most of my titles are available as ebooks. My phrase books—for Italian, French, German, Spanish, and Portuguese—are practical and budget-oriented. My other books include *Europe 101* (a crash course on art and history designed for travelers); *Mediterranean Cruise Ports* and *Northern European Cruise Ports* (how to make the most of your time in port); and *Travel as a Political Act* (a travelogue sprinkled with tips for bringing home a global perspective). A more complete list of my titles appears near the end of this book.

Video: My public television series, *Rick Steves' Europe*, covers European destinations in 100 shows, with 17 episodes on Italy, including four on Rome. To watch full episodes online for free, visit www.ricksteves.com/tv. Or to raise your travel I.Q. with video versions of our popular classes, such as Italy Travel Skills and Michelangelo's Italy, see www.ricksteves.com/travel-talks.

Audio: My weekly public radio show, *Travel with Rick Steves*, features interviews with travel experts from around the world. I've also produced free, self-guided **audio tours** of the top sights in Rome. All of this audio content is available for free at Rick Steves Audio Europe, an extensive online library organized by

PRACTICALITIES

destination. Choose whatever interests you, and download it for free via the Rick Steves Audio Europe app, www.ricksteves.com/audioeurope, iTunes, or Google Play.

MAPS
The black-and-white maps in this book are concise and simple, designed to help you locate recommended places and get to local TIs, where you can pick up more in-depth maps of cities and regions (usually free). Better maps are sold at newsstands and bookstores. Before you buy a map, look at it to be sure it has the level of detail you want. Drivers will want to pick up a good, detailed map in Europe.

RECOMMENDED BOOKS AND MOVIES
To learn more about Rome past and present, check out a few of these books or films.

Nonfiction
Written in the 18th century, Edward Gibbon's *Decline and Fall of the Roman Empire* is considered *the* classic history of ancient Rome from its peak to its downfall.

Originally published as a series of *New Yorker* articles in the 1950s, *Rome and a Villa* reads as if it's Eleanor Clark's journal. Of Paul Hofmann's multiple books about Italy, *The Seasons of Rome* is the favorite among readers. Another good Americans-in-the-Eternal-City memoir is *As the Romans Do* (Epstein). A third of Elizabeth Gilbert's spiritual memoir/travelogue *Eat, Pray, Love* takes place in Rome.

The holy center of Christendom has plenty of worthwhile books documenting its history. *Saints & Sinners* (Duffy) is a warts-and-all illustrated guide to the popes. *Absolute Monarchs* (Norwich) covers similar territory. In *When in Rome*, Robert Hutchinson writes as a lapsed (sometimes irreverent) Catholic discovering the roots of Christianity in Vatican City. *Michelangelo and the Pope's Ceiling* (King) describes the drama behind the masterpiece. *The Pope's Elephant* (Bedini), written by a historian from the Smithsonian, tells the story of Pope Leo X's favorite pet.

Simon Schama's excellent *The Power of Art* includes biographies on two of Rome's most notable artists—Caravaggio and Bernini (the companion BBC series is good, too). *A Literary Companion to Rome* (Varriano) also includes 10 self-guided walking tours. Kids (and adults who like cool pictures) enjoy David Macaulay's two books about Rome: *Rome Antics* and *City: A Story of Roman Planning and Construction* (both for ages nine and up).

PRACTICALITIES

Begin Your Trip at www.RickSteves.com

My **website** is *the* place to explore Europe. You'll find thousands of fun articles, videos, photos, and radio interviews on European destinations; money-saving tips for planning your dream trip; monthly travel news; my travel talks and travel blog; my latest guidebook updates (www.ricksteves.com/update); and my free Rick Steves Audio Europe app. You can also find links to follow me on Facebook and Twitter.

Our **Travel Forum** is an immense, yet well-groomed collection of message boards, where our travel-savvy community answers questions and shares their personal travel experiences (www.ricksteves.com/forums).

Our **online Travel Store** offers travel bags and accessories that I've designed specifically to help you travel smarter and lighter. These include my popular bags (rolling carry-on and backpack versions), money belts, totes, toiletries kits, adapters, other accessories, and a wide selection of guidebooks, planning maps, and DVDs.

Choosing the right **rail pass** for your trip—amid hundreds of options—can drive you nutty. Our website will help you find the perfect fit for your itinerary and your budget: We offer easy, one-stop shopping for rail passes, seat reservations, and point-to-point tickets.

Want to travel with greater efficiency and less stress? We organize **tours** with more than three dozen itineraries and more than 700 departures reaching the best destinations in this book...and beyond. Our Italy tours include "the best of" in 17 days, Village Italy in 14 days, South Italy in 13 days, Sicily in 11 days, Venice-Florence-Rome in 10 days, the Heart of Italy in 9 days, a My Way: Italy "unguided" tour in 13 days, and a week-long Rome tour. You'll enjoy great guides, a fun bunch of travel partners (with small groups of 24 to 28 travelers), and plenty of room to spread out in a big, comfy bus. You'll find European adventures to fit every vacation length. For all the details, and to get our Tour Catalog and a free Rick Steves Tour Experience DVD (filmed on location during an actual tour), visit www.ricksteves.com or call us at 425/608-4217.

PRACTICALITIES

Fiction

No modern crime drama or soap opera can top the world of ancient Roman politics. Colleen McCullough describes the early days of the Roman Republic in her work of historical fiction, *The First Man in Rome*. Robert Graves wanders from Caesar Augustus to Caligula and beyond in *I, Claudius*.

Ancient Rome makes a great backdrop for mysteries, as shown in *Roman Blood* (Saylor) and *The Silver Pigs* (Davis), both the first in a series. *Cabal*, by Michael Dibdin, takes place in modern Rome.

The Dogs of Rome (Fitzgerald) is another mystery set in the modern city. In the blockbuster book *Angels and Demons,* written by *The Da Vinci Code* author Dan Brown, murders are linked by Rome's Bernini statues.

For a literary take on Rome, try *Open City: Seven Writers in Postwar Rome* (edited by William Weaver).

Films

Two masterpieces of Italian Neorealism—set in the bleak, post-WWII years—take place in Rome: Roberto Rossellini's *Open City* (1945) and Vittorio De Sica's touching, heartbreaking film *Bicycle Thieves* (1949).

A feel-good love story, *Roman Holiday* (1953) made a star out of Audrey Hepburn. *Three Coins in the Fountain* (1954) is another romantic crowd-pleaser.

During the era of epics, Hollywood couldn't get enough of ancient Rome. *Quo Vadis* (1951) contains three hours of religious-historic drama. *Ben-Hur* (1959) is a campy mash-up of Christianity, Charlton Heston, and chariot races. *Spartacus* (1960) casts Kirk Douglas as a rebel fighting Rome. In 2000, *Gladiator* turned Hollywood's attention back to ancient Rome, winning five Academy Awards for its portrayal of life in the bloody arena.

La Dolce Vita (1961) is Federico Fellini's seductive masterpiece. (His 1972 film *Roma* seems tacky in comparison.)

The warm-hearted Italian epic *Best of Youth* (2003) takes place in several Italian locations, including Rome; this story of two brothers gives you a good sense of the last several decades of Italian history.

Originally a BBC miniseries, *I, Claudius* (1976) puts Derek Jacobi and John Hurt at the center of a pulpy classic. The BBC/HBO miniseries *Rome* (2005-2007) gives an *Upstairs-Downstairs* look at the lives and loves of Julius Caesar and Augustus.

The 2009 film *Angels and Demons,* based on the book by *The Da Vinci Code* author Dan Brown, is set in Rome. Banned from filming in Vatican City, cameramen disguised themselves as tourists to gather some of the shots. The 2010 film version of *Eat, Pray, Love,* starring Julia Roberts, was filmed partly in Rome and Naples.

APPENDIX

Contents

Useful Contacts

Emergency Needs
English-Speaking Police Help: 113
Ambulance: 118
Road Service: 116

Embassies
US Embassy: 24-hour emergency line—tel. 06-46741, non-emergency—tel. 06-4674-2420 answered Mon-Fri 15:00-17:00 (passport services Mon-Fri 8:30-12:00, Via Vittorio Veneto 121, www.usembassy.it)
Canadian Embassy: Tel. 06-854-441 (Via Zara 30, www.italy.gc.ca)

Directory Assistance
Telephone Help (in English; free directory assistance): 170
Directory Assistance (for €0.50, an Italian-speaking robot gives the number twice, very clearly): 12

Holidays and Festivals

In Italy, holidays seem to strike without warning. For instance, every town has a festival honoring its patron saint. The Vatican Museum closes for a multitude of Catholic holidays; check its schedule at http://mv.vatican.va.

This list for 2015 includes selected festivals in Rome, plus national holidays observed throughout Italy. Many sights and banks close on national holidays—keep this in mind when planning your itinerary. Before planning a trip around a festival, verify its dates by checking the festival's website or TI sites (www.italia.it and www.turismoroma.it).

In Rome, hotels get booked up on Easter weekend (from Good Friday through Monday), April 25 (Liberation Day), May 1 (Labor Day), June 29 (Sts. Peter and Paul), November 1 (All Saints' Day), and on Fridays and Saturdays year-round. Some hotels require you to book the full three-day weekend around a holiday.

Jan 1	New Year's Day
Jan 6	Epiphany
March 22	Rome Marathon (www.maratonadiroma.it)
April 5	Easter Sunday
April 6	Easter Monday
April 21	City Birthday
April 25	Italian Liberation Day
May 1	Labor Day
June 2	Anniversary of the Republic
June 4	Feast Day of Corpus Christi
June 24	St. John the Baptist Day
June 29	Sts. Peter and Paul Day
Mid-July	Trastevere's Noantri Festival
Aug 10	St. Lawrence's Day
Aug 15	Feast of the Assumption (Ferragosto)
Nov 1	All Saints' Day
Dec 8	Feast of the Immaculate Conception
Dec 25	Christmas
Dec 26	St. Stephen's Day

2 0 1 5

JANUARY						
S	M	T	W	T	F	S
				1	2	3
4	5	6	7	8	9	10
11	12	13	14	15	16	17
18	19	20	21	22	23	24
25	26	27	28	29	30	31

FEBRUARY						
S	M	T	W	T	F	S
1	2	3	4	5	6	7
8	9	10	11	12	13	14
15	16	17	18	19	20	21
22	23	24	25	26	27	28

MARCH						
S	M	T	W	T	F	S
1	2	3	4	5	6	7
8	9	10	11	12	13	14
15	16	17	18	19	20	21
22	23	24	25	26	27	28
29	30	31				

APRIL						
S	M	T	W	T	F	S
			1	2	3	4
5	6	7	8	9	10	11
12	13	14	15	16	17	18
19	20	21	22	23	24	25
26	27	28	29	30		

MAY						
S	M	T	W	T	F	S
					1	2
3	4	5	6	7	8	9
10	11	12	13	14	15	16
17	18	19	20	21	22	23
24/31	25	26	27	28	29	30

JUNE						
S	M	T	W	T	F	S
	1	2	3	4	5	6
7	8	9	10	11	12	13
14	15	16	17	18	19	20
21	22	23	24	25	26	27
28	29	30				

JULY						
S	M	T	W	T	F	S
			1	2	3	4
5	6	7	8	9	10	11
12	13	14	15	16	17	18
19	20	21	22	23	24	25
26	27	28	29	30	31	

AUGUST						
S	M	T	W	T	F	S
						1
2	3	4	5	6	7	8
9	10	11	12	13	14	15
16	17	18	19	20	21	22
23/30	24/31	25	26	27	28	29

SEPTEMBER						
S	M	T	W	T	F	S
		1	2	3	4	5
6	7	8	9	10	11	12
13	14	15	16	17	18	19
20	21	22	23	24	25	26
27	28	29	30			

OCTOBER						
S	M	T	W	T	F	S
				1	2	3
4	5	6	7	8	9	10
11	12	13	14	15	16	17
18	19	20	21	22	23	24
25	26	27	28	29	30	31

NOVEMBER						
S	M	T	W	T	F	S
1	2	3	4	5	6	7
8	9	10	11	12	13	14
15	16	17	18	19	20	21
22	23	24	25	26	27	28
29	30					

DECEMBER						
S	M	T	W	T	F	S
		1	2	3	4	5
6	7	8	9	10	11	12
13	14	15	16	17	18	19
20	21	22	23	24	25	26
27	28	29	30	31		

Conversions and Climate

NUMBERS AND STUMBLERS

- Europeans write a few of their numbers differently than we do. 1 = 1, 4 = 4, 7 = 7.
- In Europe, dates appear as day/month/year, so Christmas 2015 is 25/12/15.
- Commas are decimal points and decimals are commas. A dollar and a half is $1,50, one thousand is 1.000, and there are 5.280 feet in a mile.
- When counting with fingers, start with your thumb. If you hold up your first finger to request one item, you'll probably get two.
- What Americans call the second floor of a building is the first floor in Europe.
- On escalators and moving sidewalks, Europeans keep the left "lane" open for passing. Keep to the right.

METRIC CONVERSIONS

A kilogram is 2.2 pounds, and one liter is about a quart, or almost four to a gallon. A kilometer is six-tenths of a mile. I figure kilometers to miles by cutting them in half and adding back 10 percent of the original (120 km: 60 + 12 = 72 miles, 300 km: 150 + 30 = 180 miles).

1 foot = 0.3 meter	1 square yard = 0.8 square meter
1 yard = 0.9 meter	1 square mile = 2.6 square kilometers
1 mile = 1.6 kilometers	1 ounce = 28 grams
1 centimeter = 0.4 inch	1 quart = 0.95 liter
1 meter = 39.4 inches	1 kilogram = 2.2 pounds
1 kilometer = 0.62 mile	32°F = 0°C

ROMAN NUMERALS

In the US, you'll see Roman numerals—which originated in ancient Rome—used for copyright dates, clocks, and the Super Bowl. In Italy, you're likely to observe these numbers chiseled on statues and buildings. If you want to do some numeric detective work, here's how: In Roman numerals, as in ours, the highest numbers (thousands, hundreds) come first, followed by smaller numbers. Many numbers are made by combining numerals into sets: V = 5, so VIII = 8 (5 plus 3). Roman numerals follow a subtraction principle for multiples of fours (4, 40, 400, etc.) and nines (9, 90, 900, etc.). The number four, for example, is written as IV (1 subtracted from 5), rather than IIII. The number nine is IX (1 subtracted from 10).

Rick Steves Rome 2015 would translate as *Rick Steves Rome MMXV.* Big numbers such as dates can look daunting at first. The easiest way to handle them is to read the numbers in discrete chunks. For example, Michelangelo was born in MCDLXXV. Break it down: M (1,000) + CD (100 subtracted from 500, or 400) + LXX (50 + 10 + 10, or 70) + V (5) = 1475. It was a very good year.

M = 1000	XL = 40
CM = 900	X = 10
D = 500	IX = 9
CD = 400	V = 5
C = 100	IV = 4
XC = 90	I = duh
L = 50	

CLOTHING SIZES

When shopping for clothing, use these US-to-European comparisons as general guidelines (but note that no conversion is perfect).

- Women's dresses and blouses: Add 30
  (US size 10 = European size 40)
- Men's suits and jackets: Add 10
  (US size 40 regular = European size 50)

- Men's shirts: Multiply by 2 and add about 8
  (US size 15 collar = European size 38)
- Women's shoes: Add about 30
  (US size 8 = European size 38-39)
- Men's shoes: Add 32-34
  (US size 9 = European size 41; US size 11 = European size 45)

ROME'S CLIMATE

First line—average daily high; second line—average daily low; third line—average days without rain. For more detailed weather statistics for Rome (as well as the rest of the world), check www.wunderground.com.

J	F	M	A	M	J	J	A	S	O	N	D
52°	55°	59°	66°	74°	82°	87°	86°	79°	71°	61°	55°
40°	42°	45°	50°	56°	63°	67°	67°	62°	55°	49°	44°
13	19	23	24	26	26	30	29	25	23	19	21

TEMPERATURE CONVERSION: FAHRENHEIT AND CELSIUS

For Weather   For Health

Europe takes its temperature using the Celsius scale, while we opt for Fahrenheit. For a rough conversion from Celsius to Fahrenheit, double the number and add 30. For weather, remember that 28°C is 82°F—perfect. For health, 37°C is just right. At a launderette, 30°C is cold, 40°C is warm (usually the default setting), 60°C is hot, and 95°C is boiling.

Packing Checklist

Whether you're traveling for five days or five weeks, you won't need more than this. Pack light to enjoy the sweet freedom of true mobility.

Clothing

- ❏ 5 shirts: long- & short-sleeve
- ❏ 2 pairs pants or skirt
- ❏ 1 pair shorts or capris
- ❏ 5 pairs underwear & socks
- ❏ 1 pair walking shoes
- ❏ Sweater or fleece top
- ❏ Rainproof jacket with hood
- ❏ Tie or scarf
- ❏ Swimsuit
- ❏ Sleepwear

Money

- ❏ Debit card
- ❏ Credit card(s)
- ❏ Hard cash ($20 bills)
- ❏ Money belt or neck wallet

Documents & Travel Info

- ❏ Passport
- ❏ Airline reservations
- ❏ Rail pass/train reservations
- ❏ Car-rental voucher
- ❏ Driver's license
- ❏ Student ID, hostel card, etc.
- ❏ Photocopies of all the above
- ❏ Hotel confirmations
- ❏ Insurance details
- ❏ Guidebooks & maps
- ❏ Notepad & pen
- ❏ Journal

Toiletries Kit

- ❏ Toiletries
- ❏ Medicines & vitamins
- ❏ First-aid kit
- ❏ Glasses/contacts/sunglasses (with prescriptions)
- ❏ Earplugs
- ❏ Packet of tissues (for WC)

Miscellaneous

- ❏ Daypack
- ❏ Sealable plastic baggies
- ❏ Laundry soap
- ❏ Spot remover
- ❏ Clothesline
- ❏ Sewing kit
- ❏ Travel alarm/watch

Electronics

- ❏ Smartphone or mobile phone
- ❏ Camera & related gear
- ❏ Tablet/ereader/media player
- ❏ Laptop & flash drive
- ❏ Earbuds or headphones
- ❏ Chargers
- ❏ Plug adapters

Optional Extras

- ❏ Flipflops or slippers
- ❏ Mini-umbrella or poncho
- ❏ Travel hairdryer
- ❏ Belt
- ❏ Hat (for sun or cold)
- ❏ Picnic supplies
- ❏ Water bottle
- ❏ Fold-up tote bag
- ❏ Small flashlight
- ❏ Small binoculars
- ❏ Insect repellent
- ❏ Small towel or washcloth
- ❏ Inflatable pillow
- ❏ Some duct tape (for repairs)
- ❏ Tiny lock
- ❏ Address list (to mail postcards)
- ❏ Postcards/photos from home
- ❏ Extra passport photos
- ❏ Good book

Italian Survival Phrases

English	Italian	Pronunciation
Good day.	Buon giorno.	bwohn **jor**-noh
Do you speak English?	Parla inglese?	**par**-lah een-**glay**-zay
Yes. / No.	Sì. / No.	see / noh
I (don't) understand.	(Non) capisco.	(nohn) kah-**pees**-koh
Please.	Per favore.	pehr fah-**voh**-ray
Thank you.	Grazie.	**graht**-seeay
You're welcome.	Prego.	**pray**-go
I'm sorry.	Mi dispiace.	mee dee-spee**ah**-chay
Excuse me.	Mi scusi.	mee **skoo**-zee
(No) problem.	(Non) c'è un problema.	(nohn) cheh oon proh-**blay**-mah
Good.	Va bene.	vah **behn**-ay
Goodbye.	Arrivederci.	ah-ree-vay-**dehr**-chee
one / two	uno / due	**oo**-noh / **doo**-ay
three / four	tre / quattro	tray / **kwah**-troh
five / six	cinque / sei	**cheeng**-kway / **sehee**
seven / eight	sette / otto	**seht**-tay / **ot**-toh
nine / ten	nove / dieci	**nov**-ay / dee**eay**-chee
How much is it?	Quanto costa?	**kwahn**-toh **kos**-tah
Write it?	Me lo scrive?	may loh **skree**-vay
Is it free?	È gratis?	eh **grah**-tees
Is it included?	È incluso?	eh een-**kloo**-zoh
Where can I buy / find...?	Dove posso comprare / trovare...?	**doh**-vay **pos**-soh kohm-**prah**-ray / troh-**vah**-ray
I'd like / We'd like...	Vorrei / Vorremmo...	vor-**rehee** / vor-**ray**-moh
...a room.	...una camera.	**oo**-nah **kah**-meh-rah
...a ticket to ____.	...un biglietto per ____.	oon beel-**yeht**-toh pehr
Is it possible?	È possibile?	eh poh-**see**-bee-lay
Where is...?	Dov'è...?	**doh**-veh
...the train station	...la stazione	lah staht-see**oh**-nay
...the bus station	...la stazione degli autobus	lah staht-see**oh**-nay **dayl**-yee **ow**-toh-boos
...tourist information	...informazioni per turisti	een-for-maht-see**oh**-nee pehr too-**ree**-stee
...the toilet	...la toilette	lah twah-**leht**-tay
men	uomini, signori	**woh**-mee-nee, seen-**yoh**-ree
women	donne, signore	**don**-nay, seen-**yoh**-ray
left / right	sinistra / destra	see-**nee**-strah / **dehs**-trah
straight	sempre diritto	**sehm**-pray dee-**ree**-toh
When do you open / close?	A che ora aprite / chiudete?	ah kay **oh**-rah ah-**pree**-tay / keeoo-**day**-tay
At what time?	A che ora?	ah kay **oh**-rah
Just a moment.	Un momento.	oon moh-**mayn**-toh
now / soon / later	adesso / presto / tardi	ah-**dehs**-soh / **prehs**-toh / **tar**-dee
today / tomorrow	oggi / domani	**oh**-jee / doh-**mah**-nee

In an Italian-speaking Restaurant

English	Italian	Pronunciation
I'd like...	Vorrei...	vor-**rehee**
We'd like...	Vorremmo...	vor-**ray**-moh
...to reserve...	...prenotare...	pray-noh-**tah**-ray
...a table for one / two.	...un tavolo per uno / due.	oon **tah**-voh-loh pehr **oo**-noh / **doo**-ay
Non-smoking.	Non fumare.	nohn foo-**mah**-ray
Is this seat free?	È libero questo posto?	eh **lee**-bay-roh **kwehs**-toh **poh**-stoh
The menu (in English), please.	Il menù (in inglese), per favore.	eel may-**noo** (een een-**glay**-zay) pehr fah-**voh**-ray
service (not) included	servizio (non) incluso	sehr-**veet**-seeoh (nohn) een-**kloo**-zoh
cover charge	pane e coperto	**pah**-nay ay koh-**pehr**-toh
to go	da portar via	dah **por**-tar **vee**-ah
with / without	con / senza	kohn / **sehn**-sah
and / or	e / o	ay / oh
menu (of the day)	menù (del giorno)	may-**noo** (dayl **jor**-noh)
specialty of the house	specialità della casa	spay-chah-lee-**tah dehl**-lah **kah**-zah
first course (pasta, soup)	primo piatto	**pree**-moh pee**ah**-toh
main course (meat, fish)	secondo piatto	say-**kohn**-doh pee**ah**-toh
side dishes	contorni	kohn-**tor**-nee
bread	pane	**pah**-nay
cheese	formaggio	for-**mah**-joh
sandwich	panino	pah-**nee**-noh
soup	minestra, zuppa	mee-**nehs**-trah, **tsoo**-pah
salad	insalata	een-sah-**lah**-tah
meat	carne	**kar**-nay
chicken	pollo	**poh**-loh
fish	pesce	**peh**-shay
seafood	frutti di mare	**froo**-tee dee **mah**-ray
fruit / vegetables	frutta / legumi	**froo**-tah / lay-**goo**-mee
dessert	dolci	**dohl**-chee
tap water	acqua del rubinetto	**ah**-kwah dayl roo-bee-**nay**-toh
mineral water	acqua minerale	**ah**-kwah mee-nay-**rah**-lay
milk	latte	**lah**-tay
(orange) juice	succo (d'arancia)	**soo**-koh (dah-**rahn**-chah)
coffee / tea	caffè / tè	kah-**feh** / teh
wine	vino	**vee**-noh
red / white	rosso / bianco	**roh**-soh / bee**ahn**-koh
glass / bottle	bicchiere / bottiglia	bee-kee**ay**-ray / boh-**teel**-yah
beer	birra	**bee**-rah
Cheers!	Cin cin!	cheen cheen
More. / Another.	Ancora un po.' / Un altro.	ahn-**koh**-rah oon poh / oon **ahl**-troh
The same.	Lo stesso.	loh **stehs**-soh
The bill, please.	Il conto, per favore.	eel **kohn**-toh pehr fah-**voh**-ray
tip	mancia	**mahn**-chah
Delicious!	Delizioso!	day-leet-see**oh**-zoh

For more user-friendly Italian phrases, check out *Rick Steves' Italian Phrase Book & Dictionary* or *Rick Steves' French, Italian, and German Phrase Book*.

INDEX

A

Accommodations: *See* Sleeping

Aeneas, Anchises, and Ascanius (Bernini): 272–273

Air-conditioning, in hotels: 340

Airports: 440–442; customs regulations, 529–530; souvenir shopping, 428

Air travel: budgeting, 5; carry-on restrictions, 8–9; cheap flights, 560–561

Alexander the Great: 285–286, 311, 509

Almanac, Rome: 6

Altar of Peace: *See* Ara Pacis

Ambulance: 19, 523, 565

American Catholic Church: 20, 85, 86

American Express: 526, 527

Americans, as "temporary locals": 9

Amphitheaters: Ostia Antica, 454; Pompeii, 513–514. *See also* Colosseum

Ancient Appian Way: *See* Appian Way

Ancient Rome: 11, 35–59; books about, 562–3; with children, 412; eating, 146, 400–404; guided tours, 29–33; history of, 156–157, 163, 166, 515–518; maps, 39, 147, 354–355; modern amenities, 146; religion in, 163; sights, 35–59; sleeping near, 353–356; tourist information, 146; walking tours, 121–189. *See also* Appian Way; Capitoline Hill; Colosseum; Palatine Hill; Pantheon; Roman Forum

Anthony, Saint: 322

Antinous: 290

Antipasti (appetizers): 369, 383–384. *See also* Eating

Antiques, shopping for: 418, 419, 421, 426, 427

Antoninus Pius, Temple of Faustina and: 158–159

Apartment rentals: 344–345

Aperitivo: 375–376, 380, 385

Aphrodite Crouching: 290

Apollo and Daphne (Bernini): 270–271

Apollo Belvedere: 237–238

Apollo del Tevere: 291

Appian Way: 107–109, 325–336; eating, 329; map, 331; walking tour, 329–336

Aquapiper: 416

Aqueduct Park: 335–336

Aqueduct (Pompeii): 508–509

Aracoeli Church: 44–45

Ara di Cesare: 162

Ara Pacis (Altar of Peace): 47, 75–77, 435; eating near, 398–400

Archaeological museums: Etruscan Museum, 68–70; Museum of Roman Civilization, 106–107, 414; Museum of the Walls, 336; Naples Archaeological Museum, 475–481; Ostia Museum, 458–459; Palazzo Nuovo, 181, 188–189. *See also* Art museums; Capitoline Museums; National Museum of Rome; Vatican Museum

Archeobus: 32–33, 327

Architecture, church: 519

Arch of Constantine: 35, 38, 47, 148–149

Arch of Septimius Severus: 165

Arch of Titus (Arco di Tito): 155–157

Art: books about, 562. *See also* Archaeological museums; Art museums; Churches and cathedrals; Mosaics; *and specific artists and artworks*

Art museums: daily reminder, 17; Etruscan Museum, 68–70; Galleria d'Italia Palazzo Zevallos Stigliano (Naples), 486–487; Galleria Doria Pamphilj, 61; general tips and hours, 42–43, 530–531; MAXXI, 70, 429–430; Montemartini Museum, 101, 414; Museo dell'Ara Pacis, 47, 75–77; Museo della Via Ostiense, 98; Museo Palatino (Imperial Palace), 174–175; Museum of the Imperial

INDEX

INDEX

MAP INDEX

MAP INDEX

Start your trip at

Our website enhances this book and turns

Explore Europe

At ricksteves.com you can browse through thousands of articles, videos, photos and radio interviews, plus find a wealth of money-saving travel tips for planning your dream trip. And with our mobile-friendly website, you can easily access all this great travel information anywhere you go.

TV Shows

Preview the places you'll visit by watching entire half-hour episodes of Rick Steves' Europe (choose from all 100 shows) on-demand, for free.

ricksteves.com

your travel dreams into affordable reality

Radio Interviews

Enjoy ready access to Rick's vast library of radio interviews covering travel

tips and cultural insights that relate specifically to your Europe travel plans.

Travel Forums

Learn, ask, share! Our online community of savvy travelers is a great resource for first-time travelers to Europe, as well as seasoned pros. You'll find forums on each country, plus travel tips and restaurant/hotel reviews. You can even ask one of our well-traveled staff to chime in with an opinion.

Travel News

Subscribe to our free Travel News e-newsletter, and get monthly updates from Rick on what's happening in Europe.

Audio Europe™

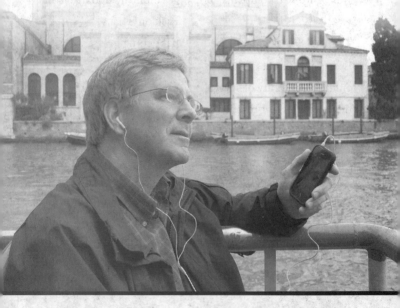

Pack Light and Right

Gear up for your next adventure at ricksteves.com

Light Luggage

Pack light and right with Rick Steves' affordable, custom-designed rolling carry-on bags, backpacks, day packs and shoulder bags.

Accessories

From packing cubes to moneybelts and beyond, Rick has personally selected the travel goodies that will help your trip go smoother.

Shop at ricksteves.com

Rick Steves has

Experience maximum Europe

Save time and energy

This guidebook is your independent-travel toolkit. But for all it delivers, it's still up to you to devote the time and energy it takes to manage the preparation and logistics that are essential for a happy trip. If that's a hassle, there's a solution.

Rick Steves Tours

A Rick Steves tour takes you to Europe's most interesting places with great

great tours, too!

with minimum stress

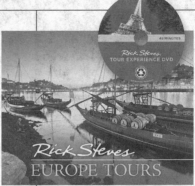

guides and small groups of 28 or less. We follow Rick's favorite itineraries, ride in comfy buses, stay in family-run hotels, and bring you intimately close to the Europe you've traveled so far to see. Most importantly, we take away the logistical headaches so you can focus on the fun.

Join the fun

This year we'll take 18,000 free-spirited travelers— nearly half of them repeat

customers—along with us on 40 different itineraries, from Ireland to Italy to Istanbul. Is a Rick Steves tour the right fit for your travel dreams? Find out at ricksteves.com, where you can also get Rick's latest tour catalog and free Tour Experience DVD.

Europe is best experienced with happy travel partners. We hope you can join us.

See our itineraries at ricksteves.com

Rick Steves guidebooks are published by Avalon Travel,
a member of the Perseus Books Group.

NOW AVAILABLE:
eBOOKS, DVD & BLU-RAY

TRAVEL CULTURE

Europe 101
European Christmas
Postcards from Europe
Travel as a Political Act

eBOOKS

Nearly all Rick Steves guides are available as eBooks. Check with your favorite bookseller.

RICK STEVES' EUROPE DVDs

11 New Shows 2013–2014
Austria & the Alps
Eastern Europe
England & Wales
European Christmas
European Travel Skills & Specials
France
Germany, BeNeLux & More
Greece, Turkey & Portugal
Iran
Ireland & Scotland
Italy's Cities
Italy's Countryside
Scandinavia
Spain
Travel Extras

BLU-RAY

Celtic Charms
Eastern Europe Favorites
European Christmas
Italy Through the Back Door
Mediterranean Mosaic
Surprising Cities of Europe

PHRASE BOOKS & DICTIONARIES

French
French, Italian & German
German
Italian
Portuguese
Spanish

JOURNALS

Rick Steves Pocket Travel Journal
Rick Steves Travel Journal

PLANNING MAPS

Britain, Ireland & London
Europe
France & Paris
Germany, Austria & Switzerland
Ireland
Italy
Spain & Portugal

RickSteves.com 📘📱 **@RickSteves**

Rick Steves books and DVDs are available at bookstores and through online booksellers.

Photo © Patricia Feaster.

Credits

RESEARCHERS
To update this book, Rick relied on principal research by Cameron Hewitt, with help from Ben Cameron and Patricia Feaster.

BEN CAMERON

Ben experienced his first taste of European travel when he was three, exploring medieval castles with his parents. Returning after graduation, he was hooked and has spent much of his time since exploring Europe independently and leading tours for Rick Steves. When not living out of his backpack, Ben splits his time between Rome and Seattle.

PATRICIA FEASTER

As a high-school Spanish teacher, Trish enjoyed taking her students on summer trips to Europe, sharing her passion for language, history, culture, and cuisine. She later earned a degree in French and now uses her language and teaching skills as a travel blogger, tour guide, and guidebook researcher. She and her partner enjoy traveling together, barbecuing on their deck, and playing *pétanque* in their hometown of Edmonds.

CAMERON HEWITT

Cameron writes and edits guidebooks for Rick Steves, specializing in Eastern Europe. To update this book, he toured dozens of churches and ancient ruins, dodged Vespas on "pedestrianized" lanes, downed more than a few *caffè macchiati,* and scoured Rome's characteristic back streets for hidden-gem shops and restaurants. When he's not traveling, Cameron lives in Seattle with his wife, Shawna.

Avalon Travel
a member of the Perseus Books Group
1700 Fourth Street
Berkeley, CA 94710, U.S.A.

Printed in Canada by Friesens
First printing August 2014

ISBN 978-1-61238-958-5

For the latest on Rick's lectures, guidebooks, tours, public radio show, and public television series, contact Rick Steves' Europe, Inc., 130 Fourth Avenue North, Edmonds, WA 98020, 425/771-8303, www.ricksteves.com, rick@ricksteves.com.

Rick Steves' Europe
Managing Editor: Risa Laib
Editorial & Production Manager: Jennifer Madison Davis
Editors: Glenn Eriksen, Tom Griffin, Cameron Hewitt, Suzanne Kotz, Cathy Lu, Carrie Shepherd
Editorial Intern: Julia Alforde
Researchers: Ben Cameron, Cameron Hewitt
Maps & Graphics: David C. Hoerlein, Sandra Hundacker, Lauren Mills, Mary Rostad

Avalon Travel
Senior Editor and Series Manager: Madhu Prasher
Editor: Jamie Andrade
Assistant Editor: Maggie Ryan
Copy Editor: Patrick Collins
Proofreader: Kelly Lydick
Indexer: Beatrice Wikander
Production & Typesetting: Tabitha Lahr
Cover Design: Kimberly Glyder Design
Maps & Graphics: Lohnes and Wright, Kat Bennett, Mike Morgenfeld

Front Cover Photo: St. Peter's Basilica, Rome © Getty Images
Front Matter Color Photos: Title page, Victor Emmanuel Monument © Michael Potter, XII Montage, © Dominic Bonuccelli, Ben Cameron
Additional Photography: Dominic Bonuccelli, Ben Cameron, Robyn Stencil, Cameron Hewitt, David C. Hoerlein, Gene Openshaw, Michael Potter, Amanda Scotese, Rick Steves, Bruce VanDeventer, Laura VanDeventer, Wikimedia Commons (Agência Brasil), Wikimedia Commons (LACMA.org)
Sistine Chapel photo, page 255, © Erich Lessing / Art Resource, NY

More for your trip!
Maximize the experience with Rick Steves as your guide

Guidebooks
Florence, Venice and Italy guides make side-trips smooth and affordable

Phrase Books
Rely on Rick's Italian Phrase Book & Dictionary

Rick's TV Shows
Preview where you're going with 18 shows on Italy

Free! Rick's Audio Europe™ App
Get free audio tours for Rome's top sights

Small Group Tours
Rick offers several great itineraries through Italy

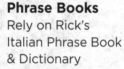

For all the details, visit ricksteves.com